READING MARX IN THE INFORMATION AGE

Renowned Marxist scholar and critical media theorist Christian Fuchs provides a thorough, chapter-by-chapter introduction to *Capital Volume 1* that assists readers in making sense of Karl Marx's most important and groundbreaking work in the information age, exploring Marx's key concepts through the lens of media and communication studies via contemporary phenomena like the Internet, digital labour, social media, the media industries, and digital class struggles. Through a range of international, current-day examples, Fuchs emphasises the continued importance of Marx and his work in a time when transnational media companies such as Amazon, Google, and Facebook play an increasingly important role in global capitalism. Discussion questions and exercises at the end of each chapter help readers to further apply Marx's work to a modern-day context.

Christian Fuchs is Professor at and Director of the University of Westminster's Communication and Media Research Institute. He is author of *Culture and Economy in the Age of Social Media* (Routledge, 2015), *Social Media: A Critical Introduction* (Sage, 2014), *OccupyMedia! The Occupy Movement and Social Media in Crisis Capitalism* (Zero Books, 2014), *Digital Labour and Karl Marx* (Routledge, 2014), *Foundations of Critical Media and Information Studies* (Routledge, 2011), and *Internet and Society: Social Theory in the Information Age* (Routledge, 2008). He edits the open access journal *tripleC: Communication, Capitalism & Critique.*

READING MARX IN THE INFORMATION AGE

A Media and Communication Studies Perspective on *Capital Volume 1*

Christian Fuchs

Routledge
Taylor & Francis Group

NEW YORK AND LONDON

First published 2016
by Routledge
711 Third Avenue, New York, NY 10017

and by Routledge
2 Park Square, Milton Park, Abingdon, Oxon OX14 4RN

Routledge is an imprint of the Taylor & Francis Group, an informa business

Library of Congress Cataloging-in-Publication Data
Fuchs, Christian, 1976– author.
  Reading Marx in the information age : a media and communication studies perspective on Capital, volume 1 / Christian Fuchs.
     pages cm
Includes bibliographical references and index.
  1. Marx, Karl, 1818–1883.   Kapital.   2. Communism and mass media.   I. Title.
  HB501.M37.F83 2016
  335.4'1—dc23
  2015019639

ISBN: 978-1-138-94855-6 (hbk)
ISBN: 978-1-138-94856-3 (pbk)
ISBN: 978-1-315-66956-4 (ebk)

Typeset in Bembo
by Apex CoVantage, LLC

Printed and bound in the United States of America
By Edwards Brothers Malloy on sustainably sourced paper.

CONTENTS

FIGURES

TABLES

ACKNOWLEDGEMENT

This book is a companion for reading Marx's *Capital Volume 1* from a media and communication studies perspective:

Marx, Karl. 1867. *Capital: A Critique of Political Economy*, Volume 1. Trans. by Ben Fowkes. London: Penguin.

All quotes from *Capital Volume 1* are taken from the English Penguin edition and are reproduced with permission of *New Left Review.*

Introduction

READING MARX IN THE INFORMATION AGE: A MEDIA AND COMMUNICATION STUDIES PERSPECTIVE ON *CAPITAL VOLUME 1*

1 Why Should I read Marx? I'd Rather Go on Facebook and Have Some Fun There . . .

The reader of this book may ask: Why should I read *Capital Volume 1*? And what has it to do with communications? Marx obviously did not write it on a laptop; he did not have a blog and a Facebook profile and wasn't on Twitter. Such media have become ubiquitous in our lives; we use them for work, politics, and in everyday life. What many of them share is that they are organised by profit-oriented businesses. They are a manifestation of what Marx termed the "accumulation of capital". At the same time they enable us to inform ourselves, communicate, and maintain social relations. Information, communication, and sociality is their "use-value", which is a term that Marx uses for describing how goods satisfy human needs.

Communications companies do not always foreground that they are profit-oriented, but rather often only stress their use-value: Facebook, for example, says that it "helps you connect and share with the people in your life". Twitter argues it allows you to "connect with your friends—and other fascinating people". These claims are not untrue, but only one side of the story. Marx would say that they are ideologies that overstate or, as he says, "fetishise" use-value in order to distract attention from exchange-value, from the fact that communications companies are out to make lots of money. Marx still matters because we live in a capitalist communications world and many forms of communications spread ideologies and are organised as for-profit businesses. Capitalism is a somewhat different capitalism today than at the time Marx lived in the 19th century—it is global; finance, technology, transport, consumer culture and advertising plays a larger role, etc. Yet Marx already saw the foundations of all these phenomena and anticipated their future relevance. And he stressed that society is historical: Capitalism develops and obtains new qualities and discontinuities in order to reproduce its underlying foundational structures, the structures of capital accumulation. And Marx cared about ethics and politics: He was convinced that we need alternatives to capitalism because we do not live in the best possible world. So Marx would welcome the social side of contemporary capitalist media, but argue that they should be changed so that we can overcome their capitalist design and usage. And he would have supported struggles for such a different world.

So Marx has a lot of relevance to tell us about contemporary communications. In order to understand laptops, mobile phones, Twitter, Facebook, etc. we need to engage with Marx. He is an essential thinker for understanding the information and Internet age critically. So Marx and Facebook are not opposites. You cannot understand the second without the first and the first gives us a critical perspective on the second. This book is a companion for obtaining such an understanding. It is a step-by-step guide on how to read *Capital Volume 1* from a media and communication studies perspective.

Why Read *Capital* from a Media and Communications Perspective?

Many introductory books to Marx's *Das Kapital, Band 1* (*Capital Volume 1*) have been written since the first edition was published in 1867. It is up to everyone's own judgment how feasible and helpful s/he finds a particular introduction to Marx's most widely read work. The book at hand has a somewhat different purpose. It is not another general introduction or accompanying guide. Its task is to provide assistance to the reader of Marx's *Capital Volume 1* for asking questions about the role of media, information, communication, the computer, and the Internet in capitalism. It provides an introduction and is an accompanying guide for reading *Capital Volume 1* for people interested in media and communication studies. It is a contribution to the foundations of the critique of the political economy of media, information, and communication.

Why is such a book needed? Why should one read Marx's *Capital* from the perspective of and with a focus on media and communication? Claims that we live in the information, knowledge, or network economy and society are often overdrawn and advance the view that we live in an economy/society that is completely new and has nothing in common with the 19th-century capitalism that Marx analysed. Such assertions often serve the purpose of communicating that new technologies have in capitalism created great economic opportunities for everyone and that the capitalist mode of production has inherent potentials for democracy, wealth, freedom, and stability. The history of capitalism is, however, a history of war, inequality, control, and crisis. Capitalism's reality undermines and puts into questions liberal ideology. Information society euphoria is one-dimensional and uncritical. One should be sceptical of it.

It is a wrong reaction to information society euphoria to belittle and ignore the role of information, the media, and communication in capitalism. If one looks at statistics that display the profits, revenues, capital assets, and stock market values of the largest transnational corporations in the world, then one sees that quite a few of them are located in economic sectors and branches such as advertising, broadcasting and cable, communications equipment, computer hardware; culture, entertainment, and leisure; computer services, computer storage devices, electronics, Internet platforms, printing and publishing, semiconductors, software, and telecommunications. The information economy may not be the dominant sector of capitalism; it is, however, just like other capitalist industries, of significance for understanding capitalism. Contemporary capitalism is an informational capitalism just like it is finance capitalism, imperialist capitalism, crisis capitalism, hyper-industrial capitalism (the importance of fossil fuels and the mobility industries), etc. Capitalism is a multidimensional economic and societal formation. Information is one of these dimensions. To study the role and contradictions of information in capitalism is an important undertaking and dimension of a critical theory of society.

Critique of the Political Economy of the Media and Communication

The critique of the political economy of the media and communication is one of the subfields of media and communication studies. It has resulted in a significant academic infrastructure that includes, *for example*, the following:

- introductory text books (Mosco 2009; Hardy 2014);
- an academic network of scholars (the International Association of Media and Communication Research's Political Economy Section);
- handbooks (Wasko, Murdock, and Sousa 2011);

- journals (*tripleC: Communication, Capitalism & Critique*—http://www.triple-c.at; *The Political Economy of Communication*—http://www.polecom.org);
- introductory readers (Mattelart and Siegelaub 1979, 1983; Golding and Murdock 1997); and
- most importantly, an active community of scholars who have a political interest in a better world and an academic interest in understanding capitalism and communication. I have been fortunate to enjoy the company of and discussions with scholars in this community, from which I have learned a lot and for which I am very grateful. This community's continuous effort to maintain and develop the field of the critique of the political economy of media and communication is important and inspiring.

Graham Murdock and Peter Golding (1973) argued in their seminal article "For A Political Economy of Mass Communications" that critique of the political economy of communications means to critically study capitalism and communication: "The obvious starting point for a political economy of mass communications is the recognition that the mass media are first and foremost industrial and commercial organizations which produce and distribute commodities" (Murdock and Golding 1973, 205–206). "In addition to producing and distributing commodities, however, the mass media also disseminate ideas about economic and political structures. It is this second and ideological dimension of mass media production which gives it its importance and centrality and which requires an approach in terms of not only economics but also politics" (Murdock and Golding 1973, 206–207).

For Murdock and Golding, media in capitalism have a double role as fostering (a) commodification and (b) ideologies. This analysis corresponds to two important aspects that Marx points out as important for the critique of capitalism's political economy in *Capital Volume 1*:

(a) *The logic of commodities*: "The wealth of societies in which the capitalist mode of production prevails appears as an 'immense collection of commodities'; the individual commodity appears as its elementary form. Our investigation therefore begins with the analysis of the commodity" (125). The critique of the political economy of communication asks questions about how the commodity form shapes communications and the contradictions and struggles connected to it.

(b) *Commodity fetishism*: Ideologies present phenomena such as commodities as endlessly existing and absolutely necessary for human existence. They discard that social phenomena are made by humans in social relations and can therefore be changed. Capitalist media are important spaces, where ideologies are constructed, disseminated, reproduced, contradicted, and contested.

It is nothing but the definite social relation between men themselves which assumes here, for them, the fantastic form of a relation between things. In order, therefore, to find an analogy we must take flight into the misty realm of religion. There the products of the human brain appear as autonomous figures endowed with a life of their own, which enter into relations both with each other and with the human race. So it is in the world of commodities with the products of men's hands. I call this the fetishism which attaches itself to the products of labour as soon as they are produced as commodities, and is therefore inseparable from the production of commodities. (Marx 1867, 165)

Vincent Mosco in his seminal introductory book *The Political Economy of Communication* defines this field as "the study of the social relations, particularly the power relations, that mutually constitute the production, distribution, and consumption of resources, including communication resources" (Mosco 2009, 2). Janet Wasko (2014, 260) stresses that the critical political economy of the media and communication is concerned with the "allocation of resources within capitalist societies" in the context of media and communication and gives special focus to ownership, control, power, class, structural inequalities, contradictions, resistance, and intervention. Murdock and Golding argue that the approach of the critical political economy of communications analyses "the wider structures that envelop and shape everyday action, looking at how the economic organization of media industries impinges on the production and circulation of meaning and the ways in which people's opinions for consumption and use are structured by their position within the general economic formation" (Murdock and Golding 2005, 61). It "starts with sets of social relations and the play of power. It is interested in seeing how the making and taking of meaning is shaped at every level by the structured asymmetries in social relations" (62). "What marks critical political economy out as distinctive is that it always goes beyond situated action to show how particular micro contexts are shaped by general economic dynamics and the wider formations they sustain" (62).

Mosco (2009) argues that the critique of the political economy of communication gives especially attention to three aspects of research:

1. Commodification: "the process of transforming things valued for their use into marketable produces that are valued for what they can bring in exchange" (Mosco 2009, 2). In the realm of the media, there is, for example, the commodification of content, audiences, labour, users, access, and technologies.
2. Spatialisation: "the process of overcoming the constraints of geographical space with, among other things, mass media and communication technologies" (Mosco 2009, 2). This dimension is linked to the media's commercialisation, privatisation, liberalisation, and internationalisation (Mosco 2009, 15).
3. Structuration: "the process of creating social relations, mainly those organized around social class, gender, and race" (Mosco 2009, 2). Media in modernity matter in the context of class, gender, race, and their intersections.

Mosco (2009, 2–4, 26–36) and Murdock and Golding (2005) stress that the critique of the political economy especially focuses on four methodological principles:

1. History: It is interested in the historical development of the economy and society, the dynamics and changes of capitalism, the history of the media, civil society, commodification, and the state, and how these dimensions interconnect.
2. Social totality: "Political economy has always believed that there is a big picture of society. [. . .] The political economist asks: How are power and wealth related and how are these in turn connected to cultural and social life? The political economist of communication wants to know how all of these influence and are influenced by our systems of mass media, information, and entertainment" (Mosco 2009, 4).
3. Moral philosophy: Political economy tends to argue for "extending democracy to all aspects of social life" (Mosco 2009, 4): politics, economy, workplace culture, everyday life, and the media. It asks "basic moral questions of justice, equity and the public good" (Murdock and Golding 2005, 61). Today's "leading mainstream economists are less averse to using moral language in their economic discourse. [. . .] it is chiefly the heterodox schools of thought, rooted in political economy, that take up the moral concern. [. . .] The Marxian and institutional traditions are steeped in debates over the place of moral philosophy" (Mosco 2009, 34).
4. Social praxis: The field is interested in studying and informing struggles that aim to change the world in order to create a better society.

The critique of the political economy of media and communication is a "Marxist theory of communication" (Smythe 1994, 258) and "broadly marxisant" in character (Murdock and Golding 2005, 61). Janet Wasko (2014, 260) writes that political economy of the media and communication most often uses a "Marxist/neo-Marxist theoretical framework". She concludes a review of the field in the 21st century: "As Jean Paul Sartre once said, 'Marxism remains the philosophy of our time because we have not gone beyond the circumstances which engendered it'. A similar argument could be made for the study of political economy of the media" (Wasko 2014, 268).

Graham Murdock (2006, 3) argues that Marx is our contemporary and that a "properly critical analysis of the cultural landscapes of present-day capitalism must begin by engaging with three central themes in Marx's writing—commodification, contradiction, and globalisation". Murdock (2014b, 125) adds that such an analysis should "begin by engaging with Marx across the whole range of his writings".

Vincent Mosco (2012) says that Marx's writings are in a manifold way relevant for a critical understanding of communication. There is the

> importance of [. . .] the Marx of *Capital* and political economy, for understanding global communication. Yet there is another Marx not unrelated to the first whose writing about culture and ideology featured in *The German Ideology*, *The Economic and Philosophical Manuscripts*, and other works of the younger Marx have inspired analysis and critique in cultural studies. It is not an exaggeration to conclude that the Marx of political economy and of cultural studies form pillars of critical communication study. [. . .] In addition to the Marx of political economy and the Marx of cultural studies, there is the Marx of his famous, and also infamous, notebooks *The Grundrisse* and the work of Marx the professional journalist. Indeed although Marx practiced journalism throughout his life, both *The Grundrisse* and the best of Marx's journalism bridged the critical period between the earlier and later years of his career. (Mosco 2012, 571)

The critique of the political economy of media and communication has played a significant role in the field of media and communication studies and has helped to illuminate the role of the media and communication in capitalism. Marx's works have had a major influence on it. This book is indebted to this tradition and understands itself as part of it.

Communications: Marxism's Blind Spot

Aspects having to do with the role and contradictions of culture, information, communication, the media, and the Internet have been critically analysed by the field of the critique of the political economy of media and communication. They have, however, often not been taken seriously or seriously enough in Marxist theory. They have been considered as being superstructural, secondary, unproductive, mere aspects of circulation and consumption, determined or overdetermined by the base, immaterial, mere ideas, dependent, a support structure of exploitation, etc. This relegation and degradation of the realm of information was one of the reasons why the Canadian political economist of the media Dallas W. Smythe argued in 1977 that communications is the blind spot of Western Marxism. "The mass media of communications and related institutions concerned with advertising, market research, public relations and product and package design represent a blindspot in Marxist theory in the European and Atlantic basin cultures" (Smythe 1977, 1). This absence is also one of the reasons why the British Marxist cultural theorist Raymond Williams, in the same year as Smythe published his "Communications: Blindspot of Western Marxism" article, coined the notion of "Cultural Materialism" in the book *Marxism and Literature* for stressing that "[c]ultural work and activity are not [. . .] a superstructure" (Williams 1977, 111). The significance of the cultural industry, the information economy, and information work have made evident that culture and communication matter, are material, and are part of capitalism's productive economy (Fuchs 2015).

I have in my life attended too many Marxist and critical studies conferences and talks where media and communication either played no or a subordinated role. One example suffices for illustration.

On May 31, 2013, David Harvey gave the lecture "From Rebel Cities to Urban Revolution" at the "Dangerous Ideas for Dangerous Times" Festival in London. The rather small room was jam-packed with hundreds of interested listeners. In the discussion section, I asked why it is that communication is a blind spot of Harvey's Marxist theory of space and of much other Marxist theory although social spaces can only exist in and through human communication that is conditioned by and produces and reproduces social space. Harvey in his answer did not consider the relationship of space and communication, but rather said that the whole realm of media and communication is overstressed, that the Arab Spring was no Facebook revolution, but took place in the streets and on the squares. Harvey makes exactly the often-repeated Marxist mistake to dismiss the analysis of communication in capitalism because non-Marxists overestimate its role.

I have in my life also read too many Marxist books and articles in which media and communication play no or only a subordinated role. This is one of the reasons why as editors of the journal *tripleC: Communication, Capitalism & Critique* (http://www.triple-c.at), Marisol Sandoval and I have tried to provide a space for the publication and discussion of critical analyses of communication in capitalism that make use of or are inspired by Marx's works. *tripleC* is neither a general Media and Communication Studies journal nor a general journal in Marxist theory. It is, rather, interested in the intersection of Marxist/critical theory and the study of media, communication, and the Internet.

What Are Information, Media, and Communication?

The terms "information", "media", and "communication" are not self-explanatory. There is a tendency that they are separated, which has resulted in specialist fields such as information science, media studies, and communication studies. In my view, the study of these phenomena cannot and should not be separated. Any attempt at separation is artificial and tears apart phenomena that inherently belong, exist, and appear together. Matter is the process-substance of the world. It is a *causa sui*, a cause of itself: Matter produces and organises itself and has the capacity to create new levels of existence in the world. Given this assumption, it is not necessary to revert to religious, spiritualistic, or esoteric explanations of the existence of the world that assume an existence or creator of the world outside of matter. To assume that information is immaterial or exists outside of matter violates the philosophical law of ground that every phenomenon must have an adequate cause and foundation. If the world has two substances—matter and information/spirit—then there are two phenomena that are ungrounded, which violates the law of ground. If one assumes that a spiritual force—God—created matter, then this means that an external spiritual force is taken to be the ground of the world and that it created something out of nothing. No rational answers can, however, be provided to the question of who created God. Therefore also idealism and spiritualism are ungrounded and violate the law of ground. Information is part of the material world. It is matter in movement, the process-relationship and interaction of at least two material systems. Such interactions are productive in that they help re-creating the material systems, create new internal qualities of these systems, and they pose potentials for the emergence of new material systems in the world that emerge from the interactions of existing material systems.

Humans exist in society and society is re-created and sustained by humans. Society is a level of the organisation of matter. Information in society is the social interaction process of human beings. Humans are working and thinking beings who anticipate, make ethical judgments, create and re-create society. The human brain is a storage mechanism of cognitive information that in complex manners reflects the state of the world and the human interpretation and political and moral assessment of the world. In communication processes, parts of a human's cognitive information are in symbolic form made available to at least one other human being. If there is reciprocity, then these other humans make parts of their interpretations of the world available to the human being who communicated in the first instance.

Communication creates changes of cognitive information of others once it is recognised—that is, new meanings, interpretations, and judgements emerge through communication. Cognitive information and communication are material: they change the status and activation patterns of the brain's neural network. We cannot touch and feel information because it is intangible and nonphysical. This does, however, not make it immaterial. We can observe the consequences of informational processes, how it brings about changes of meanings and interpretations of the world. Communication takes place with the help of media such as the air, which transmits sound; the Internet, television, and radio; books and other printed materials; electronic books, posters, stickers, paintings, artworks, etc. Wherever there is communication, there is a medium.

Media are structures that organise and enable communication. They mediate between humans and enable them to communicate. Human communication can take place in a rather ephemeral or in a more regularised manner. All communication produces changes of thought patterns. Sustained communication in addition has the potential to create new social systems and new emergent qualities of existing social systems. In such cases, humans don't just cognise and communicate, but they also cooperate: they collaboratively produce new social systems or new structural qualities of social system. Information is therefore a threefold nested process of cognition, communication, and cooperation (Hofkirchner 2013).

Reading Marx's *Capital*

A Marxist theory and analysis of information, media, and communication is interested in these phenomena's contradictory roles in capitalism. Reading Marx's *Capital* can help us to understand these roles and to make sense of informational contradictions today. Marx wrote in German. For the non-German speaker, which is the majority of the world population, the question arises about which translation one should choose. *Capital* is without a doubt a difficult book. When you read this book as accompanying guide to an exploration of media and communication in Marx's *Capital Volume 1*, I recommend that you use Marx's original work in English, but also have a translation of it in your mother tongue at hand, which can help. My own mother tongue is German. I have read Marx both in German and English. I do, however, not write about Marx in German because this would relegate the availability of my guide to the small number of German-speaking critical scholars interested in media and communication. Native German speakers are unfortunately often not willing to read English because they expect in a cultural imperialist manner that everything should be translated into German. Sometimes this attitude hides the fact that many of them simply have problems speaking and reading English because the school system does not support good practice of foreign languages enough and there is a lack of practical engagement with non-German speakers. With some effort even the German speaker will, however, be able to follow the book at hand.

This companion uses the Penguin edition of *Capital I* as reference, which is in my view the best available translation, although it has imperfections. It also follows the structure of this edition. I cover the book chapter by chapter (except for part VIII, which consists of several short chapters that in the German edition form one single chapter). I have also included one additional chapter for Marx's appendix ("Results of the Immediate Process of Production") as well as two appendixes, which discuss communication aspects of Thomas Piketty's (2014) much discussed book *Capital in the Twenty-First Century* (appendix 1) and the role of knowledge and technology in the *Grundrisse*, the first draft of *Capital* (appendix 2). When I have read introductions and accompanying guides to Marx's *Capital*, I have always disliked the books that do not follow Marx's chapter structure. They make it difficult to follow the structure and sequence of Marx's thoughts. Most of the readers will read Marx's book chapter by chapter from the beginning to the end. Therefore a chapter-wise guide is most appropriate.

This is a book about Marx and not about Marxism. It is complex enough to come to grips with Marx's theory, which is why I tend to focus on explaining his arguments and do not extensively go into explaining the history of the reception of specific concepts in Marxist theory. The latter is the task of books that focus on the history of Marxist theory, such as the *Historical-Critical Dictionary of Marxism* (*Historisch-Kritisches Wörterbuch des Marxismus*). I explain the connections of Marx's arguments to the realm of the media, technology, culture, and communications and for this purpose also make cross-references to thinkers who engage with these realms of study. The task of this book, however, is to focus closely on Marx's text and provide interpretative explanations that link the text to communication and the media. It does not provide an in-depth discussion of the history of the field of the political economy of media and communication, in which Marx plays a significant role. This book does not allow space for a closer engagement with the important history of and current developments in this field. I, however, strongly recommend to the reader interested in the issues addressed in this book, to participate and engage in discussions in the International Association of Media and Communication Research's (IMACR) Political Economy Section and to consult and contribute to current debates (for example, in the journals *tripleC: Communication, Capitalism & Critique*—http://www.triple-c.at—and *The Political Economy of Communication*—http://www.polecom.org).

Communications phenomena develop quickly. Communicative capitalism stays the same at the most basic level in and through dynamic change and the dialectic of continuity and discontinuity. This book therefore cannot and does not want to give a full account of current developments in communications. As I write this book, some of the significant communications developments taking place are as follows: big data, cloud computing, large-scale government surveillance revealed by Edward Snowden, maker culture, mobile advertising, social media, targeted online advertising, the quantified self movement, and the sharing economy. Such phenomena can come and go, whereas capitalism, communications and its contradictions have had a longer history. This book's aims to give a longer-term perspective so that it can still be read in 30 or 50 years from now. It draws on examples that are thousands of years old just like it gives examples from 19th-, 20th-, and 21st-century society.

The chapters in this book also provide exercises that help readers to further engage with Marx's ideas. They are provided at the end of each chapter. There are two kinds of exercises:

- Group exercises (G) are suited for supporting the discussions of a group engaging in reading Marx's *Capital Volume 1*. They are not time-consuming.
- Project exercises (P) are more time-consuming and allow the reader or a group of readers to conduct in-depth analyses of communications phenomena based on Marx's ideas.

The English Edition of Marx's *Capital*

One must note that the English translation of *Capital Volume 1* has 33 chapters, whereas the most commonly read German edition (MEW 23: Marx-Engels-Werke Volume 23) has only 25 chapters. Therefore also the numbering of chapters differs in the English and the German editions. The original 1867 German edition consisted of just six chapters. For the second, the 1872 edition, Marx introduced the structure consisting of 25 chapters. Moore, Aveling, and Engels changed this structure for the first, published in 1887, English edition. The Penguin edition has maintained this revised structure. The table below (Table 0.1) shows how the chapters in the English edition correspond to the ones in the German MEW edition.

The History of How Marx Wrote *Capital Volume 1*

One of the reasons why Marx set out to write up a systematic critique of the political economy of capitalism may have been the financial panic and economic crisis of 1857 (Wheen 2006, 27). He indeed sat down in 1857/1858 and wrote the political-economic *Manuscripts*, which were later published as the *Grundrisse* and form a kind of early draft of *Capital*. The *Grundrisse* were first published

TABLE 0.1 A mapping of chapters in the English and German editions of Marx's *Capital*

Chapters in Capital Volume 1 *(Penguin)*	*Chapters in Marx's* Das Kapital *(MEW)*
Part One: Commodities and Money	*Erster Abschnitt: Ware und Geld*
Chapter 1: Commodities	1: Die Ware
Chapter 2: The Process of Exchange	2: Der Tauschprozess
Chapter 3: Money, or the Circulation of Commodities	3: Das Geld oder die Warenzirkulation
Part Two: The Transformation of Money into Capital	*Zweiter Abschnitt: Die Verwandlung von Geld in Kapital*
	4: Die Verwandlung von Geld in Kapital
Chapter 4: The General Formula for Capital	4.1: Die allgemeine Formel des Kapitals
Chapter 5: Contradictions in the General Formula	4.2: Widersprüche der allgemeinen Formel
Chapter 6: The Sale and Purchase of Labour-Power	4.3: Kauf und Verkauf der Arbeitskraft
Part Three: The Production of Absolute Surplus-Value	*Dritter Abschnitt: Die Produktion des absoluten Mehrwerts*
Chapter 7: The Labour Process and the Valorization Process	5: Arbeitsprozeß und Verwertungsprozeß
Chapter 8: Constant Capital and Variable Capital	6: Konstantes Kapital und variables Kapital
Chapter 9: The Rate of Surplus-Value	7: Die Rate des Mehrwerts
Chapter 10: The Working-Day	8: Der Arbeitstag
Chapter 11: The Rate and Mass of Surplus-Value	9: Rate und Masse des Mehrwerts
Part Four: The Production of Relative Surplus-Value	*Vierter Abschnitt: Die Produktion des relativen Mehrwerts*
Chapter 12: The Concept of Relative Surplus-Value	10: Begriff des relativen Mehrwerts
Chapter 13: Co-Operation	11: Kooperation
Chapter 14: The Division of Labour and Manufacture	12: Teilung der Arbeit und Manufaktur
Chapter 15: Machinery and Large-Scale Industry	13: Machinerie und große Industrie
Part Five: The Production of Absolute and Relative Surplus-Value	*Fünfter Abschnitt: Die Produktion des absoluten und relativen Mehrwerts*
Chapter 16: Absolute and Relative Surplus-Value	14: Absoluter und relative Mehrwert
Chapter 17: Changes of Magnitude in the Price of Labour-Power and in Surplus-Value	15: Größenwechsel von Preis der Arbeitskraft und Mehrwert
Chapter 18: Different Formulae for the Rate of Surplus-Value	16: Verschiedene Formeln für die Rate des Mehrwerts
Part Six: Wages	*Sechster Abschnitt: Der Arbeitslohn*
Chapter 19: The Transformation of the Value (and Respectively the Price) of Labour-Power into Wages	17: Die Verwandlung von Wert resp. Preis der Arbeitskraft in Arbeitslohn
Chapter 20: Time-Wages	18: Der Zeitlohn
Chapter 21: Piece-Wages	19: Der Stücklohn
Chapter 22: National Differences in Wage	20: Nationale Verschiedenheiten der Arbeitslöhne
Part Seven: The Process of Accumulation of Capital	*Siebenter Abschnitt: Der Akkumulationsprozeß des Kapitals*
Chapter 23: Simple Reproduction	21: Einfache Reproduktion
Chapter 24: The Transformation of Surplus-Value into Capital	22: Verwandlung von Mehrwert in Kapital
Chapter 25: The General Law of Capitalist Accumulation	23: Das allgemeine Gesetz der kapitalistischen Akkumulation
Part Eight: So-Called Primitive Accumulation	24: Die sogenannte ursprüngliche Akkumulation
Chapter 26: The Secret of Primitive Accumulation	24.1: Das Geheimnis der ursprünglichen Akkumulation
Chapter 27: The Expropriation of the Agricultural Population from the Land	24.2: Expropriation des Landvolks von Grund und Boden
Chapter 28: Bloody Legislation against the Expropriated since the End of the Fifteenth Century. The Forcing Down of Wages by Act of Parliament	24.3: Blutgesetzgebung gegen die Expropriierrten seit Ende des 15. Jahrhunderts. Gesetze zur Herabdrückung des Arbeitslohns

(Continued)

TABLE 0.1 Continued

Chapters in Capital Volume 1 *(Penguin)*	Chapters in Marx's *Das Kapital (MEW)*
Chapter 29: The Genesis of the Capitalist Farmer	24.4: Genesis der kapitalistischen Pächter
Chapter 30: Impact of the Agricultural Revolution on Industry. The Creation of a Home Market for Industrial Capital	24.5: Rückwirkung der agrikolen Revolution auf die Industrie, Herstellung des inneren Marktes für das industrielle Kapital
Chapter 31: The Genesis of the Industrial Capitalist	24.6: Genesis des industriellen Kapitalisten
Chapter 32: The Historical Tendency of Capitalist Accumulation	24.7: Geschichtliche Tendenzen der kapitalistischen Akkumulation
Chapter 33: The Modern Theory of Colonization	25: Die moderne Kolonisationstheorie
Appendix: Results of the Immediate Process of Production	

in German in 1939–1941 and did not become more widely known before a more popular version was put out in 1953.

In 1858, Ferdinand Lassalle arranged the contact between Marx and the Berlin-based publishing house Duncker, and Marx planned a six-book edition of the critique of the political economy of capitalism (Wheen 2006, 29). Poverty as well as Marx's and his family members' illnesses delayed the delivery of the first planned manuscript from autumn 1858 until 1859 (Wheen 2006, 29–31), when Duncker published the German version of *A Contribution to the Critique of Political Economy* (*Zur Kritik der politischen Ökonomie*). Marx's work on the sequel to *A Contribution to the Critique of Political Economy* that became *Capital Volume 1* was interrupted by an intellectual feud with Karl Vogt, unsuccessful plans to return to Germany, poverty, visitors, and illness, as well as the formation of Marx's engagement in the International Working Men's Association (Wheen 2006, 31–35).

So Marx wrote *Capital Volume 1* in the midst of poverty and illness (such as liver troubles, boils, and carbuncles, which made it difficult for him to sit and write; see Wheen 1999, 294; 2006, 35). Some of the boils that covered Marx's body had to be removed by a surgeon and he even removed some of them himself with a razor (McLellan 2006, 311). He wrote about this fact to Engels on February 20, 1866:

> As regards the carbuncles, the position is: Concerning the upper one, from my long practical experience I was able to tell you that it really needed lancing. Today (Tuesday), after receiving your letter, I took a sharp razor, a RELICT OF DEAR LUPUS, and lanced the cur myself. (I cannot abide doctors meddling with my private parts or in their vicinity. Furthermore, I have Allen's testimony THAT I AM ONE OF THE BEST SUBJECTS TO BE OPERATED UPON. I always recognise what has to be done.) The sang brûlé, AS MRS LORMIER SAYS, spurted, or rather leapt, right up into the air, and I now consider this carbuncle buried, although IT STILL WANTS SOME NURSING. (MECW 42, 231)

This paragraph is not just one of the more obscure passages in Marx and Engels's collected works, but also shows that Marx wrote *Capital Volume 1* at a time when he had severe health problems.

Sam Shuster (2008), who was professor of dermatology at Newcastle University, analysed the passages in Marx's correspondences where health issues are discussed. The common assumption is that Marx had a liver disease and boils, and that his death was caused by tuberculosis. Shuster concludes that it is likely that Marx suffered from hidradenitis suppurativa. He says that when Marx wrote *Capital*, "his hidradenitis was at its worst" (Shuster 2008, 3).

Hidradenitis suppurativa (sometimes known as acne inversa) is a painful long-term skin disease that causes abscesses and scarring on the skin—usually around the groin, buttocks, breasts and armpits. [. . .] It causes a mixture of red boil-like lumps, blackheads, cysts, scarring and channels in the skin that leak pus. [. . .] Some of the lumps may become infected with bacteria, causing a secondary infection that will require antibiotics to treat. HS is very painful.[1]

The disease causes heavy pain and open wounds that do not or only badly heal, and it can lead to death. If Shuster's interpretation is right, then this means that Karl Marx wrote *Capital* under heavy pain stemming from a rare disease. It is therefore even more impressive that he managed to write such a masterpiece with high analytical and literary quality.

Marx often was not pleased with what he had written and therefore reworked it (McLellan 2006, 308). He delivered *Capital Volume 1*'s manuscript in person to the Hamburg-based publisher Meissner in April 1867 (Wheen 1999, 295). Marx had signed the contract with Meissner in March 1865 (McLellan 2006, 311). In September 1867, Meissner published 1,000 copies of *Capital Volume 1* as the first edition (McLellan 2006, 316).

Capital and Hegel's Dialectical Philosophy

In presenting Marx's categories, I in this book frequently refer to Hegel's dialectical philosophy in order to show how it shaped Marx's thought. Representatives of a systematic dialectic, such as Christopher Arthur (2004), Tony Smith (1990), and Kozo Uno and his followers (Sekine 1998), have attempted to parallelise Hegel's *Logic* and Marx's *Capital* (see Table 0.2).

Given that Arthur and Uno have come up with fairly different interpretations of the Hegel–*Capital* parallelisation, one can have doubts that Marx sat down with the idea in mind to construct *Capital Volume 1* in exact correspondence to Hegel's *Logic*. But he certainly had Hegel in mind, used specific Hegelian dialectical categories for explaining particular aspects of capitalism, and developed his categories that analyse capitalism based on Hegel's dialectic as a method for analysing capitalism's ontology. Alex Callinicos (2014, 129) argues that Marx "extracted categories from the Logic to set them

TABLE 0.2 Attempts to logically map Hegel's *Logic* and Marx's *Capital* (based on Sekine 1998; Arthur 2004, 108–109; Bidet 2005, 122)

Hegel's Logic	*Arthur: Marx's* Capital	*Sekine/Uno: Marx's* Capital
I. BEING	COMMODITY	CIRCULATION
a. Quality	Exchangeability of commodities	Commodity
b. Quantity	Quantity of commodities exchanged	Money
c. Measure	Exchange-value of commodities	Capital
II. ESSENCE	MONEY	PRODUCTION
a. Ground	Value in itself	Production of capital
b. Appearance	Forms of value	Circulation of capital
c. Actuality	Money	Reproduction
III: CONCEPT	CAPITAL	DISTRIBUTION
a. Subjective concept	Price list	Price, profit
b. Objective concept	Metamorphoses of money and commodities	Rent
c. Idea	Self-valorisation	Interest

to work, but in a fairly pragmatic way". Marx thereby did, however, not progressively move away from Hegel, as Callinicos (2014, 157) says. He rather stayed throughout his whole life influenced by Hegel's dialectical philosophy and so in *Capital* dialectically related categories that constitute capitalism's ontology so that they do not independently stand on their own, but are connected to each other in a dialectical manner. Tony Smith (1990) in his book *The Logic of Marx's Capital* presents an interpretation that uses interconnected Hegelian triangles for showing how Marx analysed capitalism's dialectical ontology, but he does not attempt to exactly map *Capital's* structure to the structure of Hegel's *Logic*. Marx "nowhere even hinted that he derived the specific content of his theory through taking a category from the Logic and directly translating it into an economic category. If anything remotely like this had been his procedure, somewhere or other he most likely would have mentioned it" (Smith 1990, 44). Smith like Callinicos (2014, 115) holds the view that Marx took from Hegel the dialectical method of developing categories in a systematic and connected manner:

> Reading Capital as a dialectical theory is a matter of grasping this specificity of categories and their connections. The logic of the content must be allowed to develop within the theory. [. . .] *Capital* is also a systematic theory of categories. Despite all the profound differences that separate Marx and Hegel, *Capital* nonetheless can be termed a 'Hegelian' theory from this perspective. (Smith 1990, 45)
>
> Hegel and Marx both insisted that a systematic dialectical theory must be governed by the 'inner nature' of what is being examined, the 'soul of the object'. It would be an amazing coincidence if there were a one-to-one mapping of each step in the two systematic progressions unless Hegel's and Marx's projects were in some crucial respect the same project. Defenders of this view disagree among themselves about what this 'crucial respect' might be. (Smith 2014a, 36)

Marx Is Alive as Long as Capitalism Is Alive . . .

Capital Volume 1 is one of the books that has been most discussed, most declared dead, and most revived. There have again and again been claims about what is wrong in Marx's analysis. Continued interest and surges of waves of reading initiatives have, however, shown the continued relevance of Marx's book. Crisis, exploitation, and inequality have remained continuous features of modern society. As long as they persist, there will be interest in Marx's analysis of capitalism because people are looking for explanations and ways to overcome the problems they are confronted with. Media, information, and communication matter in this context because they form a particular industry of capitalism and culture is a means for the public communication of ideologies that justify exploitation and domination as well as for the critique of capitalism. Reading Marx's *Capital* from a media and communication studies perspective can help us to understand and criticise capitalist media and can inform struggles for an alternative, democratic communication system that is not controlled by capitalist companies, but the people themselves.

Note

1 NHS: Hidradenitis suppurativa. http://www.nhs.uk/conditions/hidradenitis-suppurativa/Pages/Introduction. aspx (accessed on July 7, 2014).

PART I

COMMODITIES AND MONEY

1

PREFACES, POSTFACES, AND CHAPTER 1: THE COMMODITY

What Is *Capital* about?

The Marxist theorist Ernest Mandel (1923–1995) opens the Penguin edition of *Capital Volume 1* with a long introduction that focuses on the book's purpose, methods, the plans for the structure of *Capital*, the plan of volume 1, Marx's labour theory of value, his theory of surplus-value, capital, capital accumulation, wages, money, and the destiny of capital.

The introduction is followed by prefaces and postfaces written by Marx and Engels: Marx's preface to the first edition, his postface to the second edition, his preface and postface to the first French edition, Engels's preface to the third and fourth edition, and Marx's preface to the first English edition.

Marx defines *Capital*'s purpose as follows: "What I have to examine in this work is the capitalist mode of production, and the relations of production and forms of intercourse [*Verkehrverhältnisse*] that correspond to it" (90). A mode of production is for Marx a dialectical unity of productive forces and relations of production. The relations of production are the social relations that organise the economy. The productive forces are specific modes for the organisation of labour-power and the means of production (natural forces, technologies, infrastructures, resources). Labour-power is itself the most important means of production, so Marx tends to treat it in a special way. The social relations that Marx looks at in *Capital* are those between workers and capitalists—class relations. Class relations also govern other class societies, such as feudalism and slavery. So the question for Marx is what the specific characteristic of class relations and the productive forces are in capitalism. The term "forms of intercourse" (Verkehrsverhältnisse) points to different means that organise social relations. Means of communication such as the Internet, telephone, telegraph, book, television, radio, and postal mail organise the symbolic interaction of humans. They are forms of symbolic intercourse that establish the social relations of information. One can therefore say that the study of the means of information and communication under capitalism is one of the tasks of *Capital*.

Dialectical Analysis

Marx's postface to the second edition makes clear that he employs a materialist interpretation of Hegel's dialectical method in *Capital* for the analysis of capitalism. Dialectical analysis identifies and studies how contradictions between two dimensions of reality work, how two phenomena are identical and different at the same time, how they exclude and require each other mutually, how such contradictions result in crisis and struggles, and how contradictions are sublated ("aufgehoben" in German: eliminated, preserved, and uplifted at the same time; the corresponding noun is "Aufhebung": sublation), and so give rise to new systems. The dialectic includes in its positive understanding of what exists a simultaneous recognition of its negation, its inevitable destruction; because it regards every historically developed form as being in a fluid state, in motion, and therefore grasps its transient aspects as well; and because it does not let itself be impressed by anything, being in its very essence critical and revolutionary. (103)

The dialectic has for Marx an objective-structural dimension and an aspect of subjective agency/class struggle. Marx identifies structural contradictions of capitalism, capitalism's objectivity, that result in crisis. "The fact that the movement of capitalist society is full of contradictions impresses itself most strikingly on the practical bourgeois in the changes of the periodic cycle through which modern industry passes, the summit of which is the general crisis" (103).

The dialectic's subjective side has for Marx to do with class struggles that question capitalist interests. He points out in the postface to the second edition that *Capital* is not just an analysis of how capitalism works and of its objective contradictions, but also a revolutionary theory that sides with the interests of the working class and wants to provide intellectual means of class struggle against capitalism: "In so far a such a critique represents a class, it can only represent the class whose historical task is the overthrow of the capitalist mode of production and the final abolition of all classes—the proletariat" (98).

Materialism

Marx considered Hegel's dialectic as idealist, as a fetishisation of what Hegel termed the "idea" or the "spirit". For Hegel, the world is an unfolding of a spiritual force, an organisation of spirit that culminates in the Absolute Spirit, the unity of art, religion, and philosophy (Hegel 1830b, §§553–577). For Hegel, Christianity is the revelation of the spirit. He argues that mind or spirit is founded on religion because "the spirituality of God is the lesson of Christianity" (Hegel 1830b, §384). Marx questions this focus of the dialectic on God, religion, art, and philosophy—the world of the idea:

> For Hegel, the process of thinking, which he even transforms into an independent subject, under the name of 'the Idea', is the creator of the real world, and the real world is only the external appearance of the idea. With me the reverse is true: the ideal is nothing but the material world reflected in the mind of man, and translated into forms of thought. (102)

Marx was impressed by Hegel's dialectical method and at the same time sceptical of its focus on the spirit and religion. For him, the economy, in which human beings produce their livelihood, is a crucial dimension of society. Marx starts from matter, Hegel from the spirit. That Marx says that ideas are "the material world reflected in the mind" does not mean that he sees the mind and ideas as "immaterial" or outside of matter. He expresses that the mind and ideas are forms of matter: The human being is part of the material world, in which s/he interacts with other humans and nature. As a result, the world outside of the human is in a complex way perceived and mapped onto thought patters. Given that humans are themselves material and part of the material world, also thoughts and the mind are therefore forms of matter.

1.1. The Two Factors of the Commodity: Use-Value and Value (Substance of Value, Magnitude of Value)

Capital's Famous Opening Sentence

"The wealth of societies in which the capitalist mode of production prevails appears as an 'immense collection of commodities'; the individual commodity appears as its elementary form" (125).

Marx begins *Capital Volume 1* with this famous sentence. Also in the preface to the first edition, Marx argues that "for bourgeois society, the commodity-form of the product of labour, or the value-form of the commodity, is the economic cell-form" (90).

The Origin of Money: Lydia in the 5th Century BC

The commodity is a crucial foundation of capitalism. But capitalism is not the only commodity-producing society: Lydia was a region in Anatolia (Turkey) that existed from the second millennium BC until 546 BC when Cyrus the Great, the ruler of the Achaemenid Empire (the First Persian Empire), conquered the Lydian Empire. The first historian Herodotus described the Lydians the following way:

> The customs of the Lydians are like those of the Greeks, save that they make prostitutes of their female children. They were the first men (known to us) who coined and used gold and silver currency; and they were the first to sell by retail. And, according to what they themselves say, the pastimes now in use among them and the Greeks were invented by the Lydians: these, they say, were invented among them at the time when they colonised Tyrrhenia. (Herodotus 1920, 123)

The Lydians used minted gold coins and traded goods. So they already used money and commodities long before Christ. What is the specific feature of capitalism? It does not seem to be the commodity, the market, or money because all these phenomena had already existed long before capitalism.

What Is Capitalism?

Capitalism is a form of generalised commodity production: The commodity is the main form of the organisation of property. Labour is compelled to produce commodities that are sold in order that capitalists can accumulate ever more capital—that is, money that is intended to increase itself. Capitalism is a unity of many elements—money, the commodity, the exploitation of labour-power, the means of production, commodity production, and capital. This functional unity has emergent qualities so that the sum of these elements is more than the combination of the elements. Capital accumulation is enabled by all of these elements, but is itself a new quality of capitalist society in comparison to other economic formations. Commodities are one of the cells of capitalism. The accumulation of capital is the whole body. Capital is a body that tries to increase its size by letting labour produce commodities that are sold on markets so that capital grows.

How (not) to define capitalism

Marx argues in Capital Volume 3 that the general definition of capitalism, i.e. its basic quality, is the combination of generalised commodity production and the exploitation of surplus-value generating labour so that capital is accumulated:

> Two characteristic traits mark the capitalist mode of production right from the start.
> *Firstly.* It produces its products as commodities. The fact that it produces commodities does not in itself distinguish it from other modes of production; but that the dominant and determining character of its product is that it is a commodity certainly does so! This means, first of all, that the worker himself appears only as: a seller of commodities, and hence as a free wage-labourer – i.e. labour generally appears as wage-labour. [...] The character (1) of the product as a commodity, and (2) of the commodity as the product of capital, already involves all the relations of circulation [...]

But even leaving this aside, the two above characters of the product as commodity and the commodity as capitalistically produced commodity give rise to the entire determination of value and the regulation of the total production by value. In this quite specific form of value, labour is valid only as social labour; on the other hand the division of this social labour and the reciprocal complementarity or metabolism of its products, subjugation to and insertion into the social mechanism, is left to the accidental and reciprocally countervailing motives of the individual capitalist producers. Since these confront one another only as commodity owners, each trying to sell his commodity as dear as possible (and seeming to be governed only by caprice even in the regulation of production), the inner law operates only by way of their competition, their reciprocal pressure on one another, which is how divergences are mutually counterbalanced. [...]

The *second* thing that particularly marks the capitalist mode of production is the production of surplus-value as the direct object and decisive motive of production. Capital essentially produces capital, and it does this only as long as it produces surplus-value. In dealing with relative surplus-value and then with the transformation of surplus-value into profit, we have seen how a mode of production peculiar to the capitalist period is based on this – a particular form of development of the social productive powers of labour, but as powers of capital that have asserted their autonomy vis-à-vis the worker, thus directly opposing his own development. Production for value and surplus-value involves a constantly operating tendency, as we went on to show, to reduce the labourtime needed to produce a commodity, i.e. to reduce the commodity's value, below the existing social average at any given time. The pressure to reduce the cost price to its minimum becomes the strongest lever for raising the social productivity of labour, though this appears here simply as a constant increase in the productivity of capital. [...]

It is only because labour is presupposed in the form of wage-labour, and the means of production in the form of capital (i.e. only as a result of this specific form of these two essential agents of production), that one part of the value (product) presents itself as surplus-value and this surplus-value presents itself as profit (rent), the gains of the capitalist, as additional available wealth belonging to him. And it is only because it presents itself as his profit that the new additional – means of production, designed for the expansion of reproduction and forming a portion of the product, present themselves as new additional capital, and the expansion of the reproduction process in general presents itself as a process of capitalist accumulation. (Marx 1885, 1019–1021)

The institutional economist Joseph A. Schumpeter gave explicitly in opposition to Marx a different definition of capitalism, defining it as "that form of private property economy in which innovations are carried out by means of borrowed money, which in general, though not by logical necessity, implies credit creation" (Schumpeter 1939, 216). Schumpeter's definition of capitalism is that it is a system in which "[c]reative destruction is the essential fact" (Schumpeter 1943/2003, 83). So he sees it as a system, in which entrepreneurs based on credit bring innovations to the market so that the economy grows after situations of crisis. This definition is theoretically devoid of the notions of labour, class, and surplus-value so that in a methodological-individualist manner capitalism is reduced to individual entrepreneurialism that is fetishished as the source of innovation and value.

For Marx, capitalism is the system of expanded capital reproduction in the form $M - C .. P .. C' - M'$, in which capitalist buy with money M the commodities C (labour-power, means of production) so that labour creates in the production process a new commodity C' that contains a surplus value that upon sale on the market realises a profit p that increases the invested capital M by a surplus and allows capital to be accumulated and new investments to be made. For Marx, capitalism turns labour-power and means of production into instruments for the production of the end of accumulating capital, i.e. "money breeding money, value breeding value" (Marx 1885, 160).

Use-Value

Chapter 1.1 in Marx's *Capital Volume 1* analyses the commodity's dimensions: A commodity has a qualitative aspect (use-value) and a quantitative one (exchange-value). "The commodity is, first of all, an external object, a thing which through its qualities satisfies human needs of whatever kind. The nature of these needs, whether they arise, for example, from the stomach, or the imagination, makes no difference" (125). "The usefulness of a thing makes it a use-value" (126). Use-values "constitute the material content of wealth" (126).

For Marx, a use-value is something that satisfies human needs. Marx says that these needs can arise from the stomach or from imagination. With this formulation he indicates that use-values are not just physical things that we can touch and feel, such as food that satisfies the need of nourishment, and intangible products of the human mind—information that satisfies the need of humans to understand the world and each other. The use-values that Marx mentions in chapter 1.1 are as follows: iron, corn, diamonds, watches, linen, wheat, boot-polish, silk, gold, lead, silver, tables, houses, yarn, fabric, sugar, coffee, carbon, bricks, air, soil, meadows, forests. Except for air these are all things you can touch. This focus reflects the circumstance that physical commodities dominated production at the time when Marx wrote *Capital*. One can add informational use-values such as books, computer games, concerts, educational courses, Internet websites, newspapers, magazines, mobile phone applications, movies, online communities, operating systems, phone calls, radio programmes, software, songs, television programmes, theatre plays, etc. For Marx, use-values constitute the material content of wealth. Information is material and constitutes parts of the material content of human wealth.

William Morris: The Destructive Character of Some "Use-Values"

The term use-value has the connotation of being "useful". There are, however, use-values that satisfy particular needs, but are destructive in nature, such as energy supply in the case of the nuclear power plant or killing enemies in the case of nuclear and biological weapons or a gas chamber for exterminating Jews and communists during the time of Nazi Germany. It is evident that there are use-values that have the capacity to destroy, eradicate, and extinguish humans, society, and nature. Such use-values are not useful, but harmful.

The British socialist and artist William Morris (1834–1896) questioned whether "all work is useful" (Morris 1884, 98). It is a conservative ideology to assume that "all labour is good in itself" (Morris 1884, 98). There is work that is a curse and should be refused (Morris 1884, 98) and abolished. Morris distinguished between unnecessary/useless labour, harmful labour, useful labour, and pleasurable labour. Correspondingly, there are also unnecessary, harmful, and useful use-values or goods.

There is *unnecessary, useless labour* (a waste of human energy) and labour that can be automated. Unnecessary labour is work that is not needed for the survival of humankind and that creates unnecessary goods and services. It includes, for example, labour that controls the work force and private property, such as that of managers, directors, chief executives, protective and security workers, employment agents; labour that secures the state's monopoly of violence, such as that of lawyers, judges, police inspectors, police officers, prison guards, soldiers; labour that organises the monetary economy, such as that of accountants, brokers, securities and finance dealers, insurance representatives, bank personnel, debt collectors, estate agents, cashiers, sales personnel, and vendors. A society that abolishes money and the private property of the means of production can abolish or drastically reduce a lot of these occupations because money then no longer mediates the economy; there are no longer any wage earners who need to be controlled and monitored, private property no longer needs to be secured and guarded, and property-related conflicts and crimes are likely to be reduced.

Useless labour is today accompanied by some useless forms of entertainment that should no longer exist in a free society, especially those that are directly about winning money, such as gambling and the lottery. Also other stupefying activities, such as reading tabloids and horoscopes, are likely to vanish because tabloids are an expression of a highly commercialised press and horoscopes just like any religion a form of organised irrationality. This does not mean that useful forms of playful entertainment, such as music, films, noncompetitive sports, etc. should no longer exist in a free society, but that money-mediated and ideological culture is likely to cease to exist. Many forms of organised and administered sports reflect the ideologies of nationalism, patriarchy, racism, individualism, and competition, as well as the fascist idealisation of bodily strength, which implies an implicit disregard of the weak. The liberal standard argument against these thoughts is as follows: Wait a minute, there are also female soccer teams, antinationalist and antiracist soccer fan clubs, the Paralympic Games, etc. These phenomena are like light beer: They are created for consoling the critics, but those who take joy in ideological sports that they consider as the "real thing" covertly or overtly laugh about and make fun of those who watch female soccer or the Paralympic Games, which even more asserts the ideologies that the liberal phenomena are supposed to dampen. But what if administered competitive sports are inherently racist, fascist, patriarchal, and nationalist? We will have to reinvent sports in a new society.

Harmful labour is labour that harms the survival-capacities of humans and either destroys humans, nature, and society or creates destructive use-values. It includes, for example, the killing conducted by soldiers, the operation of nuclear power plants and fossil-fuel power stations, all forms of work that involve health risks (such as coal mining, which increases lung cancer risks; labour conducted at toxic workplaces; etc.), the production of cars powered by fossil fuels, job-centre staff responsible for sanctioning unemployed people, etc.

There is also *repetitive, hard, and physically exhausting labour* that can be reduced and minimised by labour-saving technologies. Examples are the labour conducted by cleaners, waste workers, machine operators, assemblers, metal workers, builders, miners and quarry workers, agricultural workers, forestry workers, waiters and waitresses, housekeepers, mail carriers, warehouse workers, transport workers, secretaries, data entry operators, call centre agents. Robots and automation can reduce the amount of repetitive, hard, and exhausting work in society. It may, however, not be possible to entire abolish such activities. The question of how well work in a free society functions can be envisioned by imagining how the most degrading and disgusting work would be organised.

William Morris (1884, 87) stresses the importance that work is pleasurable and that workers enjoy "hope of rest, hope of product, hope of pleasure in the work itself; and hope of these also in some abundance and of good quality". The precondition for these hopes to become reality is that "class robbery is abolished" (Morris 1884, 99) and that a "Society of Equality" (Morris 1893, 265) is established. Morris imagined a postcapitalist condition, in which labour-saving technology reduces hard labour and humans are enabled to engage in creative and artistic work, by which they create "ornaments of life" (Morris 1884, 116) as popular art (Morris 1884, 113) and "a beautiful world to live in" (Morris 1885, 25).

Uses and Gratification Theory: A Theory of Media's Use-Values with Limits

The uses and gratification theory is a media theory that deals with the media's use-values for audiences and users. Katz, Blumler, and Gurevitch (1973, 517) argue that media can allow individuals to ease tensions and conflicts, to give attention to social situations and problems, to complement, supplement or substite "impoverished real-life opportunities", to affirm or reinforce moral values, and to support group membership and familiarity. Katz, Gurevitch, and Haas (1973) identify five groups of needs that audiences can seek in media use and that media can gratify: cognitive needs (information, knowledge, understanding), affective needs (aesthetics, pleasure, emotions), integrative needs (credibility, confidence, stability, status), social needs (contact with family, friends, the world), escape or tension-release (in order to weaken the contact with oneself and the social roles one acts in). Denis McQuail (2010, 427) lists the following 16 possible gratifications that users and audiences can seek in and obtain from the media: information, education, guidance, advice, diversion, relaxation, social contact, value reinforcement, cultural satisfaction, emotional release, identity formation, identity conformation, lifestyle expression, security, sexual arousal, filling time.

The identification of the media's use-values is important, but in a capitalist society use-value is often only obtainable through exchange-value. Uses and gratification theory leaves out aspects of exchange-value—that is, the question of how political economy shapes, limits, and constrains the media's use-values. In a highly commercialised media system, it is, for example, likely that entertainment programmes dominate over educational programmes (Smythe 1954; Williams 1974/1990, 78–86), which makes it easier for audiences to satisfy the first need and may expose them less to the second type of programme, so that capitalism gives preference to one type of need and need satisfaction over another one. The theory also does not much discuss the role of ideology and power in the satisfaction of informational and social needs—that is, the question of to what extent powerful groups, everyday citizens, and minorities are in control of defining and shaping information that can satisfy human needs and if the information provided for needs satisfaction provides an adequate or rather distorted picture of reality. Even though users and audiences are active in the sense that they actively seek out information that fits the purposes they are looking to satisfy, power asymmetries and the capitalist control of media tend to make ideological content more prevalent than critical content, so that informational need satisfaction is confronted with asymmetries.

Various cultural studies approaches have stressed that media texts are open for different interpretations, appropriations, and forms of decoding. The problem of this approach is, however, its relativism, which tends to neglect that not all forms of decoding and interpretation are equally likely to occur if the media landscape is dominated by particular kinds of texts, such as highly commercial ones focusing on entertainment and the logic of commodity consumption. If the only relevant power is the one of the audience then there is no longer any need to challenge the capitalist ownership of media because even if there is distortion one can in such a theory be assured that audiences can engage in some subversive reading. Celebratory versions of cultural studies thereby underestimate the power of owners and producers. A newer version is the argument that social media turns us all into producers, but the reality shows that some of these prosumers' products gain much more attention and visibility than others and the most popular social media content is produced by celebrities and large companies.

As long as we live in capitalism and class societies, a theory of the media's use-values must be combined with a theory of the media's exchange-value as systems that sell content, access, audiences, technologies and users as commodities in order to satisfy capital's need to accumulate profits and advertisers' needs to market commodities.

A theory that is centrally focused on informational and other use-values within a society dominated by class, exploitation, and domination risks not grasping how use-values' potentials are limited by the actuality of heteronomy. A positive theory without negativity within a negative society tends to affirm that which is. We must therefore see that in capitalism, use-values stand in an inherently dialectical and antagonistic relationship to exchange-value.

Exchange-Value

"Exchange-value appears first of all as the quantitative relation, the proportion, in which use-values of one kind exchange for use-values of another kind" (126). If something is a commodity, then one can only get hold of it if one exchanges something else for it. A quantitative exchange relationship mediates how people obtain use-values: x commodity A = y commodity B. In the commodity form, use-value is subordinated to exchange-value. You cannot obtain a commodified use-value without entering a quantitative exchange relationship. Exchange-value is the quantitative side of the commodity.

Marx asks himself what all commodities have in common. What do songs and a pint of beer that are both sold as commodities have in common? The song and the beer are fairly different use-values—the song is predominantly a product of the human mind, the beer predominantly a product of the brewing process. For writing a song, one, however, not just uses the mind, but the whole body for writing it down, playing instruments, etc. And conceiving a new beer is also a creative process of the human mind. So physical work always presupposes and is mediated by information work, and information work presupposes and is mediated by physical work. Both the song and the beer can make humans happy or sad. But a song cannot make you drunk, whereas beer can. You cannot hum a beer in your mind, but you can hum a song.

Given these differences, what do the beer and the song have in common? Marx's answer is that they are both products of human work. "If then we disregards the use-value of commodities, only one property remains, that of being products of labour" (128). Commodities have the "same phantom-like objectivity"; "human labour is accumulated in them" (128). Here Marx introduces a third term that characterises the "common factor in the exchange relation" (128): "value". "A use-value, or useful article, therefore, has value only because abstract human labour is objectified or materialized in it" (129). Exchange-value is the form of appearance of value (128). Labour is the substance of value (129). Value's measure or magnitude is labour-time: "How, then, is the magnitude of this value to be measured? By means of the quantity of the 'value-forming substance', the labour, contained in the article. This quantity is measured by its duration, and the labour-time is itself measured on the particular scale of hours, days etc." (129).

Value

A commodity has an individual value, a specific number of minutes it takes to produce it. To tap a pint of beer sometimes takes a minute, sometimes just half a minute. Writing a new song takes an artist sometimes an hour, sometimes a month. Marx says that the average production time is a decisive economic phenomenon that shapes how well a company can survive in the economy. Marx speaks in this context of socially necessary labour-time, the average time it takes to produce a specific commodity: "Socially necessary labour-time is the labour-time required to produce any use-value under the conditions of production normal for a given society and with the average degree of skill and intensity of labour prevalent in that society" (129). So value has an individual and a social dimension. What is decisive is the average kind of commodity—"the average sample of its kind" (130)—that is produced in the typically average amount of minutes.

As different as a song and a beer may be as use-values, if on average it takes two minutes to write a song and two minutes to tap a pint of beer, then the song and the pint "have therefore the same value" because they "contain equal quantities of labour" (130). In reality we know that on average it takes longer to write a song than to tap a pint of beer.

Knowledge and technology have an important influence on a commodity's value: Commodity value "is determined amongst other things by the workers' average degree of skill, the level of development of science and its technological application, the social organization of the process of production, the extent and effectiveness of the means of production, and the conditions found in the natural environment" (130). A person tapping a pint of beer for the first time will on average be much slower than a bartender who has practiced this skill over 20 years. A machine designed to tap as much beer as possible in as little time as possible for mega events is in contrast likely to be faster than a good bartender. What Marx wants to tell us with this specific passage is that scientific progress and education can reduce the average value of commodities. Given that there is a tendency for a historical increase of productivity due to scientific progress, many commodities have experienced a historical fall of their average value.

Marx discusses that there are use-values that do not have value: air, soil, meadows, or forests have been produced by nature (131). If somebody, however, monopolises the meadow by putting a fence around it and protects access with security guards, s/he can charge access fees so that the meadow has an exchange-value: You suddenly have to pay a £5 fee for enjoying the meadow's flowers, rivulet, and butterflies together with your kids or others.

Information as a Peculiar Use-Value

Information is a use-value with peculiar characteristics: It is not used up in consumption; it is not scarce; it can be easily, cheaply, and endlessly shared and copied; and it can be used simultaneously by many people. Drinking a pint of beer uses up the beer so another person cannot drink it. Listening to a song does not use up the music. Others can still consume it without the artist having to rerecord it. Creating the prototype, first edition, or first exemplar of a piece of information is labour-intensive and often expensive. The "sunk cost rule" says that the initial production costs and labour-times of information are high: Large costs are sunk into information. At the same time it is uncertain if there is a big demand for a specific kind of information and if people will be interested in it. Information commodities are therefore a high-risk good. This is the "nobody knows anything" rule of information. Cultural corporations try to offset this risk by creating large varieties of cultural commodities. A record label or publishing house may, for example, produce 1,000 new albums or publish 1,000 new books a year. Only five of them may become "hits", which may suffice for making the company profitable. This is the "hit rule" of information. Another strategy is that media companies provide their products to different channels (this process is also called "windowing"): There is a different price for seeing a movie in a movie theatre, downloading it on iTunes, buying it on DVD, or watching it on TV.

The theory of public goods considers information a public good because of its non-rival and non-excludable consumption: The song is not used up in consumption like the beer. Humans are not rivals in its consumption. If there is just one bottle of beer in the world, then the owner of this bottle can easily exclude others from drinking beer. Given that songs can easily be copied and shared, it is much more difficult to exclude others from listening to the song. Even if there are just 2 copies of one song, the owner of 1 of these copies may make 100 copies and distribute them to 10 friends, who again distribute copies to 10 friends, etc. The second person wanting to keep the song limited in reach will therefore not be able to exclude others from consumption.

Information as Commodity and Exchange-Value

It is, however, wrong to assume that physical goods have to be or should always be commodities and that information cannot be a commodity. Both beer and songs can be sold, although it is easier to turn the song into a public good available to everyone than the beer. But any good, including beer, can be turned into a public good if it is not traded, but given to people without payment. The theory of public goods poses the danger that it tends to naturalise physical goods as commodities. In what Marx terms a communist society, most goods are available to all. They are common goods. There are no commodities in communism.

Information is more difficult to subsume under the commodity form. Special strategies for accumulating capital in the realm of information are therefore needed. These include creating monopolies that control the distribution of information, engaging legal mechanisms such as copyrights and intellectual property rights, using advertising that sells audiences to advertisers and provides information without payment to audiences, reformatting of information onto new channels or into new media formats that allow reselling, charging for access to distribution channels, the constant updating of information so that reconsumption is required to stay up-to-date (e.g., news change constantly; you are not pleased to just watch the 1962 James Bond movie *Dr. No*—you also want to see the latest one), making media products obsolete (you do not and probably cannot use MS Word 1.0 because you do not have a computer and operating system that supports it, but rather you use a newer version).

"A thing can be useful, and a product of human labour, without being a commodity" (131). Marx here reminds us that not everything is a commodity and that there are non-commodities. Capitalism has a tendency that it tries to turn ever more aspects of human life into the commodity form. There are, however, also things that are non-commodified and aspects of life where we consider the commodity form totally inappropriate. Imagine a couple that has been together for a while. They spend a romantic evening together at home, cook and eat together, talk about their joint future, drink a good bottle of wine together, and have sex. After the sexual intercourse, one of the two stands up, puts a £50 note on the bedside table, and says, "This was really great. I pay you £50 for it". The other partner starts screaming, "Are you crazy? I am not a prostitute! And I thought we are in love and will have a future together". The example shows that there are situations and social phenomena where we consider the logic of commodities inappropriate and want to stay away from it. If society is a generalised form of mutual care and cooperation, then the commodity logic that makes people compete and excludes, divides, and separates and individualises them may not just be inappropriate for love relationships, but for society as well. The commodity form alienates people and benefits some at the expense of others. A true and fully social society can only be based on something different to the commodity.

Three Political Economies of Information and the Media

Graham Murdock (2011, 18) argues that the three possibilities for the political economy of the media are ownership by capital (the commodity form of communications), the state (public service form of communications), and civil society (communications as gifts/commons). Culture and communication for him have a triple relationship to commodity culture (Murdock 2011, 20):

1. Media products as commodities
2. Media as platforms for advertising
3. Media transport ideologies that celebrate commodity culture

The commodity form of information—the selling of content, technologies, the labour-power of information workers, and audiences/users as commodities—is important in the capitalist world. It is, however, not the only possible form of organising information. Public service media such as the BBC tend to reject the logic of the commodity. They make use of state power for collecting licence fees or parts of taxes in order to fund their operations. Alternative, citizen, and community media such as open channels, free radio stations, the alternative press, or alternative Internet platforms are run by civil society groups. They do not embrace, but reject the commodity logic. They tend to not want to sell content, technologies, and audiences. Given that they reject exchange-value, they have to look for other sources of funding if they want to exist within capitalism. Such sources are, for example, voluntary unpaid labour, state funding, donations, endowments from foundations, etc. Table 1.1 presents a distinction between (a) capitalist, (b) public service media, and (c) civil society media.

TABLE 1.1 Two levels and three political economies of information

	Capitalist media	*Public service media*	*Civil society media*
Economy (ownership)	Corporations	State-related institutions	Citizen-control
Culture (public circulation of ideas)	Content that addresses humans in various social roles and results in meaning-making	Content that addresses humans in various social roles and results in meaning-making	Content that addresses humans in various social roles and results in meaning-making

These media are respectively based on (a) information commodities, (b) information commons, and (c) information as public good. Information is owned in specific ways and has a specific cultural role in which it allows humans to inform themselves, communicate, and organise social systems.

There is a tension and contradiction between public service and alternative media on the one hand and capitalist media on the other hand. Capitalism is expansive, imperialist, and colonising—it tries to subsume everything under the commodity form and to destroy realms of life that do not adhere to the commodity logic. It can therefore be difficult for public and civil society media to exist in capitalism. At the same time, media, information, and other goods and services can also be de-commodified by social struggles and thereby turned into public or common goods. The more the logic of the commodity asserts itself, the more difficult the existence of public service and civil society media. The more this logic is constricted, the more these alternative forms of organisation can flourish. In a communist society, there are no capitalist media and information has no commodity form.

The Relationship of Use-Value, Value, and Exchange-Value

Figure 1.1. summarises the three dimensions of the commodity that Marx outlines in chapter 1.1: A commodity has a *qualitative side*, its use-value. It takes a specific average time to produce a commodity, which is its *quantitative* value-side. In capitalism, a lot of use-values (but not all use-values because there are also common and public goods) are mediated by exchange-value. There is a contradiction between use-value and exchange-value in capitalism: We can only obtain use-values organised as commodities through exchanges on markets. If we do not have what is demanded in return for obtaining access (normally money), then we are excluded. Commodities are related to each other in and through exchange. In such exchanges, an equalisation of values takes place. We say that one amount of a commodity equals a specific amount of another commodity: x commodity A = y commodity B, for example; 1 song on iTunes = £0.99; 1 chocolate bar = £0.99. A common characteristic of commodities is that they are the result and crystallisation of specific average amounts of labour. The commodity value equalises the different qualities of commodities by indicating that they contain equal, comparable, or different amounts of labour. Labour-time is an abstract measure that allows and enables quantifying, comparing, and exchanging commodities that have different qualities. Exchange-value is an organisational principle of commodity exchange in capitalism. It allows the opportunity to equalise qualitatively different commodities A and B in a quantitative manner by setting specific amounts of them and the labour congealed in these amounts equal: x commodity A = y commodity B. Exchange-value is the commodity's *quantitative quality*. It combines the commodity's quantitative and the qualitative side.

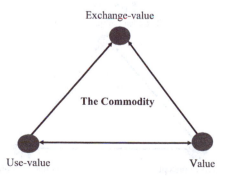

FIGURE 1.1   The commodity's dialectical unity of use-value, exchange-value, and value

1.2. The Dual Character of the Labour Embodied in Commodities

In chapter 1.2, Marx switches the presentation of his analysis of capitalism from the level of the commodity to labour. Whereas chapter 1.1 views capitalism from an output perspective, chapter 1.2 sees it from a process perspective. Labour is an activity, whereas commodities are outputs of labour.

Georg Wilhelm Friedrich Hegel: The Dialectic of Subject and Object

Hegel (1830a) has spoken of a dialectical relation of subject and object: The existence of a producing subject is based on an external objective environment that enables and constrains—that is, conditions the subject's existence. The subject's activities can transform the external environment. As a result of the interaction of subject and object, a new reality is created—Hegel terms the result of this interaction "subject-object". Figure 1.2 shows that Hegel's notions of subject, object, and subject-object form a dialectical triangle.

Hegel (1991) characterises the "subjective concept" as formal (§162), finite, determinations of the understanding, general notions (§162), "altogether concrete" (§164). He defines "the subject" (§164) as "the posited unseparatedness of the moments in their distinction" (§164). Objectivity is totality (§193), "external objectivity" (§208), "external to an other" (§193), "the objective world in general" (§193) that "falls apart inwardly into [an] undetermined manifoldness" (§193), "immediate being" (§194), "indifference vis-à-vis the distinction" (§194), "realisation of purpose" (§194), "purposive activity" (§206), "the means" (§206). The Idea is "the Subject-Object" (§162), absolute Truth (§162), the unity of the subjective and the objective (§212), "the absolute unity of Concept and objectivity" (§213), "the Subject-Object" understood as "the unity of the ideal and the real, of the finite and the infinite, of the soul and the body" (§214). Hegel also says that the "Idea is essentially process" (§215).

These definitions may sound very complex. But what Hegel wants to express is that the subject is a concrete phenomenon, whereas the object is external to the subject. The subject and the object mutually condition each other. The subject-object is the unity of the subject and the object, which results from the productive dialectical process between the two.

The World Is A Dialectical Totality

The world can, based on dialectical philosophy, be explained as a dialectic of subject and object. In any system, there is a subject that interacts with another subject that is an object for it. For the object, the subject is an object. This dialectic constitutes a contradiction between subject and object from

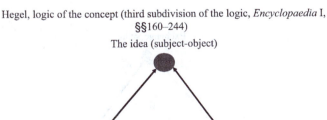

Hegel, logic of the concept (third subdivision of the logic, *Encyclopaedia* I, §§160–244)

The idea (subject-object)

Subjective concept
(Subject)

Objective concept
(Object)

FIGURE 1.2 The dialectical triangle of subject-object-subject/object

which new qualities (a subject–object) or new systems can emerge when the contradiction is sublated. Take the example of human communication: A human subject S_1 communicates information to another human being S_2. S_2 is S_1's object because the symbols communicated by S_1 result in some interpretation of it by S_2. S_2 gives meaning to it, which means that the cognitive patterns in his/her brain change. S_1's information has been objectified in S_2. If S_2 responds to S_1, then S_2 is the subject and S_1 the object who interprets the communicated information. The subject is at the same time an object and the object a subject. New qualities and systems can emerge from this contradictory relation. If two people communicate long enough, they may find out that they have joint interests and so a new social system such as a friendship or a hobby group or a professional organisation may emerge. Conversely they may find out they really hate each other, that they compete and want to harm each other. Such a competitive relationship is also an emergent quality, albeit a negative one, in which that which emerges may be the destruction of existing qualities. If two nations go to war, they interact as subjects and objects. Their bombings result in the emergence of something—this something is, however, a destruction of what exists. The emergence then is an immergence, a disappearance of that which exists. The Austrian philosopher of information Wolfgang Hofkirchner (2013) has interpreted the dialectic of subject and object in the world of information as a threefold process of cognition, communication, and cooperation. He applies this dialectic not just to the human world, but to the universe at large.

What Is Work?

In chapter 1.2, Marx explains that just like the commodity has aspects of use-value and exchange-value/value, the labour that creates the commodity has a corresponding dialectical character: It has a concrete use-value–creating dimension and an abstract value-generating aspect. He discusses capitalism from the perspective of the subject, whereas he in chapter 1.1 explained the dimension of the object. To be more precise, we can say that the logic of the commodity is focused on the object and the object-subject of the capitalist production process: Labour-power becomes an object itself in the form of wage-labour. Commodities are being produced along with capital as subject-object. Capitalists purchase not just labour-power, but also other means of production such as resources and technologies as commodities that function as objects of work in the production process.

Marx uses in German the term "Arbeit" that in the Penguin edition of *Capital* has mostly been translated as "labour". In English there are, however, two terms: "labour" and "work". They have different etymological roots. Marx in German sometimes also uses the term "Werktätigkeit" instead of "Arbeit". "Werktätigkeit" is a term that is focused on creating a work. In German a *Werk* is an output of the work process, a work. The German language also knows the term "werken", which is the process of work.

In the *Economic and Philosophic Manuscripts*, Marx (1844) also employs the term "Werktätigkeit" for describing the human species being, which expresses that humans in their practices create works (Werk = a work, Tätigkeit = practice, Werktätigkeit = practices that create works): "Eben in der Bearbeitung der gegenständlichen Welt bewährt sich der Mensch daher erst wirklich als ein *Gattungswesen*. Diese Produktion ist *sein* werktätiges Gattungsleben. Durch sie erscheint die Natur als sein Werk und seine Wirklichkeit. Der Gegenstand der Arbeit ist daher die *Vergegenständlichung des Gattungslebens des Menschen*: indem er sich nicht nur eine im Bewußtsein intellektuell, sondern werktätig, wirklich verdoppelt und sich selbst daher in einer von ihm geschaffnen Welt anschaut" (Marx 1844 [German], MEW 40, 517).

This passage has been translated into English the following way: "It is just in the working-up of the objective world, therefore, that man first really proves himself to be a species being. This production is his active species life. Through and because of this production, nature appears as his work and his reality. The object of labour is, therefore, the *objectification of man's species life*: for he duplicates himself not only, as in consciousness, intellectually, but also actively, in reality, and therefore he contemplates himself in a world that he has created" (Marx 1844 [English], 77). The adjective "werktätig" has here been twice translated as active, which is not a very suitable translation and can easily mislead English-speaking readers: "Active species life" could literally be better translated as "working species-being". Marx also writes that by this kind of species-being, nature appears as man's "Werk and Wirklichkeit", which is translated as "work and reality", a translation that does not capture the full meaning: Marx has here deliberately chosen the two words "Werk" and "Wirklichkeit" because they are connected: "Wirklichkeit" comes from the German term "wirken", which could be translated as "creative work that transforms and has transformative effects on reality" (*Wirklichkeit*). "Wirken" and "werken" are connected: in their work humans transform reality—*das menschliche Werken wirkt in der Wirklichkeit* (human work works on reality).

The Difference between Work and Labour

There is an etymological difference between "work" (*Werktätigkeit*) and "labour" (*Arbeit*): The German media and cultural scholar Brigitte Weingart (1997) describes the origins of the terms "work" in English and "Arbeit" and "Werk" in German: In German, the word "Arbeit" comes from the Germanic term "arba", which meant "slave". The English term "work" comes from the Middle English term "weorc". It was a fusion of the Old English terms "wyrcan" (creating) and "wircan" (to affect something). So "to work" means to create something that brings about some changes in society. "Weorc" is related to the German terms "Werk" and "werken". Both "work" in English and "Werk" in German were derived from the Indo-European term "uerg" (doing, acting). "Werken" in German is a term still used today for creating something. Its origins are quite opposed to the origins of the term "Arbeit". The result of the process of *werken* is called *Werk*. Both "werken" and "Werk" have the connotative meaning of being creative. Both terms have an inherent connotation of artistic creation. The philosopher Hannah Arendt (1906–1945) (1958, 80–81) confirms the etymological distinction between a) "ergazesthai" (Greek)/"facere", "fabricari" (Latin)/"work" (English)/"werken" (German)/"ouvrer" (French), and b) "ponein" (Greek)/"laborare" (Latin)/"labour" (English)/"arbeiten" (German)/"travailler" (French).

The Marxist cultural theorist Raymond Williams (1921–1988) (1983, 176–179) argues that the word "labour" comes from the French word "labor" and the Latin term "laborem" and appeared in the English language first around 1300. It was associated with hard work, pain, and trouble. In the 18th century, it would have attained the meaning of labour under capitalist conditions that stands in a class relationship with capital. The term "work" comes from the Old English word "weorc" and is the "most general word for doing something" (Williams 1983, 334). In capitalism the term on the one hand has, according to Williams (1983, 334–337), acquired the same meaning as "labour"—a paid job—but would have in contrast also kept its original broader meaning. In order to be able to differentiate the dual historical and essential character of work, it is feasible to make a semantic differentiation between "labour" and "work".

Given the etymological difference between "work" and "labour" as general creative practice and hard and alienated toil, it is in my view best to translate Marx's usage of the term "Arbeit" for the concrete creation of use-values as "work" and the abstract production of value as "labour". This is, however, not the case in the Penguin edition of *Capital*, where the terms "concrete labour" and "abstract labour" are used. Whereas the term "abstract labour" is precise, the term "concrete work" is more appropriate than "concrete labour". Whenever I quote the term "concrete labour" from the Penguin edition, I will therefore substitute it with "[concrete work] ['concrete labour' in the original translation]".

Marx uses the term "['useful work'] ['useful labour' in the original translation] for [work] [labour in the original translation] whose utility is represented by the use-value of its product, or by the fact that its product is a use-value. In this connection we consider only its useful effect" (132). He argues that the existence of qualitatively different forms of work and labour that result in qualitatively different commodities has as its precondition the social division of labour (132). Concrete work is "productive activity of a definite kind, carried on with a definite aim" (133).

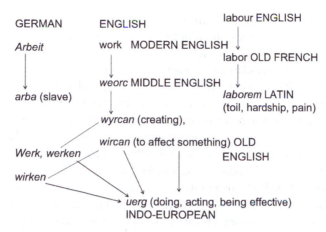

FIGURE 1.3 The etymology of the terms "work", "labour", and "Arbeit"

> [Work] ["labour" in the original translation] then, as the creator of use-values, as useful [work] ["labour" in the original translation], is a condition of human existence which is independent of all forms of society: it is an external natural necessity which mediates the metabolism between man and nature, and therefore human life itself. Use-values like coats, linen, etc., in short, the physical bodies of commodities, are combinations of two elements, the material provided by nature, and [work] ["labour" in the original translation]. (133)

In this passage it becomes evident that for Marx use-value–generating work is not just an aspect of capitalism and class societies, but is a quality of all societies. He writes that work mediates the metabolism of humans and nature and that it transforms material provided by nature. If we think of a carpenter producing tables, this definition becomes clear: the carpenter takes wood—a material supplied and produced by nature—works on it, and as a result creates a table. S/he thereby transforms the raw material into a new physical use-value. But think in comparison of an academic writer: s/he takes ideas and research results of other writers, conducts analyses of some part of the world, and writes down the results with reference to previous ideas and analyses. S/he creates new systematic ideas that analyse the status of parts of the world. The main input are ideas; the main output are ideas. These ideas refer to and are representations of nature and society. If you think of a writer of fiction, then his/her ideas refer to nature and society, but mainly not as it is, but as it could be or as we can imagine them to be in a fictive world.

The Work of Producing Ideas: A Metabolism between Man and Nature and/or an Activity of Humans in Culture?

So are ideas as resources a "material provided by nature" and ideas as output part of the "metabolism between man and nature"? Human beings and society have aspects of nature in themselves, such as the fact that humans are living systems that share drives such as sexuality, care, and aggression with animals. Humans are, however, also different from animals—they can make ethical judgements about what is right and wrong, can with the power of envisioning and imagination anticipate the future state of society and nature and possible impacts of their actions, and can therefore also plan which actions and work they undertake and which ones not. Humans are working and cultural beings. Culture is a specific human and societal organisation of matter that has to do with the creation of social meanings and judgements about the world. Some scholars say that culture is the human's second nature. If culture is not immaterial, as assumed by cultural materialists, then it is a specific form of the organisation of matter. Nature is the dynamic self-organisation and self-production of forms of matter. Culture and society are therefore specific forms of the organisation of matter that have emergent qualities that make these systems different from the nonhuman world of animals, plants, cells, molecules, genes, planets, rocks, particles, etc.

We saw earlier that Marx considers all use-values, including information, as constituting "the material content of wealth" (126). Information work mediates the social relations between humans, which could be said to be a social metabolism between humans. So the "metabolism between man and nature" is in culture a symbolic interaction between a human being and other human beings. Ideas used as input for information work are a material provided by culture. Given that culture is a specific form of the organisation of matter and nature, it is a "material provided by nature". Because of the importance of information work today, one can make Marx's definitions more concrete by arguing that work uses resources provided by nature and culture in order to create use-values that satisfy human needs and thereby mediate the metabolism between man and nature and the social relations between humans. This addition does not separate nature and culture; it just stresses the importance of culture as one specific form of the organisation of matter and nature in society. When Marx writes that work is the "father of material wealth, the earth is its mother" (134), then he refers to both human activities and nature. Also ideas are a material wealth and culture is a specific form of the organisation of nature.

Work's Dialectic of Brain and Body

> Tailoring and weaving, although they are qualitatively different productive activities, are both a productive expenditure of human brains, muscles, nerves, hands etc., and I this sense both human [work] ["labour" in the original translation]. (134)

Also in chapter 1.3, Marx writes that work that creates use-values "is essentially the expenditure of human brain, nerves, muscles and sense organs" (164).

Marx in this passage makes clear that all work necessarily is a dialectical combination of the brain and the rest of the human body, especially the muscles and hands. A tailor or carpenter not just uses his/her hands for creating a dress or a table, s/he also has to imagine how the thing s/he creates will look and has to constantly use his/her imagination to envision if what s/he produces corresponds to how s/he imagines the final product to look. A writer not only uses his/her brain, but also uses his/her fingers for writing and typing, the mouth for discussing the ideas of his/her books with others, etc. The output is in the case of the tailor and the carpenter a tangible thing and in the case of the writer intangible information. In order to disseminate information it is stored physically on computer storage devices, web servers, paper, electronic book readers, etc. To distinguish physical and information work has mainly to do with the quality of the final product. Both forms of work require, however, as Marx points out, the human brain and the rest of the body.

Marx distinguishes between simple average work and complex work. "[E]very ordinary man" (135) with average skills can conduct simple work. Complex work is "intensified, or rather multiplied simple [work] [labour in the original translation], so that a smaller quantity of complex [work] [labour in the original translation] is considered equal to a larger quantity of simple [work] [labour in the original translation]" (135). Complex work is more productive: It creates more commodities in less time than simple work. This can, for example, be the case if work becomes more skilful or more educated, or if new scientific methods or technologies are used. A single commodity created by complex work therefore also has a smaller value than the same commodity produced by simple work.

Labour

Discussing the level of value-generating labour, Marx says that all labour, no matter if it creates tables, clothes, ideas, or something else, objectifies "congealed quantities of homogenous labour"

(135–136). Labour is organised in space-time and therefore extended over a specific time period. Labour as the substance of value has to do with the time it takes to produce a commodity on average. Value is an *abstraction* from the specific contents of work and use-values. Therefore Marx terms value-generating activity as "abstract labour". Whereas concrete work is "a matter of the 'how' and the 'what'" (qualities of work), abstract labour is a matter "of the 'how much', of the temporal duration of labour. Since the magnitude of the value of a commodity represents nothing but the quantity of labour embodied in it, it follows that all commodities, when taken in certain proportions, must be equal in value" (136). The values of specific quantities of specific qualitatively different kinds of labour equal each other. If it takes on average six hours to produce a table and three hours to write a poem, then 1 table = 2 poems or the abstract labour of a carpenter required for producing 1 table = the abstract labour of 2 poets each writing 1 poem or 1 poet writing 2 poems.

An "increase in the amount of material wealth may correspond to a simultaneous fall in the magnitude of its value. This contradictory movement arises out of the twofold character of labour" (137). There is a contradiction of wealth and value: The more productive society, the more wealth can be created per hour. But each unit of wealth, such as a table, then has less value than before. With increasing wealth, the average value of goods declines. The same work "provides different quantities of use-values during equal periods of time; more, if productivity rises; fewer, if it falls. For this reason, the same change in productivity which increases the fruitfulness of labour, and therefore the amount of use-values produced by it, also brings about a reduction in the value of this increased total amount, if it cuts down the total amount of labour-time necessary to produce the use-values" (137).

The contradiction between value and use-value of a commodity (the double character of a commodity as use-value and value that is created by concrete labour and abstract labour) is sublated in the form of the exchange-value—that is, by the fact that the value of the commodity is expressed in the use-value of another commodity via the exchange relationship. Value has at the same time an objective and a social form.

Hegel's Distinction among Quality, Quantity, Quantum

For Hegel (1830a, §90), quality means "[b]eing with a *determinacy* [. . .] As reflected *into itself* in this its determinacy, being-there is *that which is there, something*". Quantity measures how "the many ones are the same, unity" (Hegel 1830a, §100). "Quantity, posited essentially with the excluding determinacy that it contains, is quantum or limited quantity. [. . .] And in this way quantum is determined as number" (Hegel 1830, §101). Quantum is about the question, "How much?" The dialectical unity of quantity and quality is called the measure. "Measure is qualitative quantum; at first, as immediate [measure], it is a quantum, with which a being-there or a quality is bound up" (Hegel 1830a, § 107). "For instance, we measure the length of various strings that have been made to vibrate, with an eye to the corresponding distinction between the sounds that are brought about by the vibration. Likewise, in chemistry, we calculate the quantity of the substances that have been brought into combination, so as to be cognizant of the measure by which these combinations are conditioned-in other words, to discover the quantities that underlie determinate qualities. And in statistics, too, the numbers with which we are occupied have an interest only on account of the qualitative results which are conditioned by them" (Hegel 1830a, §106). Measure is the dialectic of quantity and quality. Figure 1.4 visualises the dialectic of quality, quantity, and measure.

The Dialectic of Concrete Work and Abstract Labour

We have already seen in the discussion of the commodity in chapter 1.1 how Marx uses the dialectic of quality and quantity: He characterises the commodity's qualities (use-value), quantities

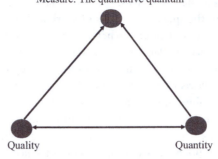

FIGURE 1.4 The dialectic of quality, quantity, and measure

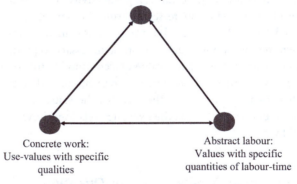

FIGURE 1.5 Work's dialectic of quantity and quality

(values), and measure (exchange-value that equalises units of qualitatively different commodities in the exchange x commodity A = y commodity B).

Also in chapter 1.2, this dialectic is important in respect to work and labour: Concrete work produces use-values that have different qualities. Abstract labour produces commodities that are expressions of abstract quanta of homogenous human labour measured. A commodity's value is therefore measured in average labour-time. The productivity of labour is its measure; it combines the quantitative and the qualitative side: Higher productivity means that the measure of value changes: More goods that have a specific quality are produced in a specific time period. Figure 1.5 visualises the work and labour process' dialectic of quantity and quality.

The Dialectic of Labour and Time

The Marxist theorist Moishe Postone (1995, 193) observes that "[c]hanges in average productivity do not change the total value created in equal periods of time": If in 1970 100,000 people worked 4 million hours a week and produced 4 million commodities in this period and the productivity doubled in 1990 and the number of workers remained constant, then the number of hours worked per week was still 4 million. Some companies acquired the new level of productivity in 1990, whereas others still worked based on the old level of productivity. The first produced x commodities per hour, the second just half: x / 2. Both, however, had to pay the same number of workers.

The first company produced in line with the new socially necessary labour-time needed for the production of a commodity, the second at a level of labour time higher than this. The first company at first has extra profits. The second company has to sell its commodities at the same price as the first company, which means that it makes less profit. It will either have to adopt the new level of higher productivity or is facing the threat of bankruptcy. The new level of productivity will assert itself as a new norm and change the standards of temporality of capitalism: Abstract time changes in the sense that the amount of units produced per hour changes. One hour of labour produces more units than previously.

> Increased productivity increases the amount of value produced per unit of time—until this productivity becomes generalized; at that point the magnitude of value yielded in that time period, because of its abstract and general temporal determination, falls back to its previous level. This results in a new determination of the social labor hour and a new base level of productivity. What emerges, then, is a dialectic of transformation and reconstitution: the socially general levels of productivity and the quantitative determinations of socially necessary labour-time change, yet these changes reconstitute the point of departure, that is, the social labour hour and the base level of productivity. (Postone 1993, 289–290)

The dialectic of labour and time in capitalism is a dialectic of the transformation of labour-time standards and a reconstitution of the new standards as norm of production. There is a dialectic of abstract and concrete time in capitalism: 1 hour of labour is always a constant expenditure of human energy during 60 minutes. But the amount of units produced during these 60 minutes varies depending on the level of productivity and the speed of work. Concrete time is historical and variable, whereas abstract time is invariable. Concrete time is associated with concrete work, abstract time with abstract labour. Abstract labour creates value: 1 hour of labour is always 60 minutes long and an expenditure of the combination of human physical and mental energy for 60 minutes. Concrete work produces use-values in their physical and symbolic dimension of existence. Given the dialectic of labour and time, abstract labour of one hour tends historically to be associated with an increase of the amount of use-values generated by concrete labour during this time period, whereas the value of these products tends to decrease. The consequences of the dialectic of labour and time are the increased technification of production and a progressively increasing importance of knowledge work in production.

Marx's Short Summary of Chapter 1.2

Marx summarises chapter 1.2's main result in the following words:

> On the one hand, all labour is an expenditure of human labour-power, in the physiological sense, and it is in this quality of being equal, or abstract, human labour that it forms the value of commodities. On the other hand, all work ["labour" in the original translation] is an expenditure of human labour-power in a particular form and with a definite aim, and it is in this quality of being concrete useful labour that it produces use-values. (137)

1.3. The Value-Form or Exchange-Value

All production in general has an object and a subject side. Marx studies in chapters 1.1 and 1.2 capitalism from the object side (1.1, the commodity) and the subject side (1.2, labour and work). He identifies a dialectic of quantity and quality of both the object and the subject that produces the object: concrete work creates use-values, abstract labour value. In chapter 1.3, Marx turns to the side of the measure that unites and thereby sublates the dialectic of the commodity's use-values and value. The value-form analysis is an exposition of the logic of the exchange-value as social relation. Some argue that it is also a historical exposition, whereas others hold the opinion that it is mainly a logical presentation. In chapter 1.1, Marx says that the social form "which stamps value as exchange-value, remains to be analysed" (131). He presents this analysis of the social form of value as various organisational forms of exchange-value in chapter 1.3. So Marx goes back to the objective side of capitalism and here analyses the dialectical unity of use-value and value in the social form that brings together and sublates the contradiction between the two: exchange-value. This means that in capitalism, a lot of use-values can only be obtained through exchange and the quantities of labour that enter a commodity are set equal in market exchanges. Exchange-value is a social form of organisation in capitalism. In modern society, we do not simply produce use-values for ourselves, but for others: relations of exchange govern the way we produce. In chapter 1.3 Marx switches from the level of the relations and organisation of the production of commodities to the exchange relations, in which commodities are traded on markets.

The Forms of Value

Exchange-value and the forms of value are qualities that "the commodity never has [. . .] when looked at in isolation, but only when it is in a value-relation or an exchange relation with a second commodity of a different kind" (152). Exchange-value is a social relation that relates commodities and the labour objectified in them to each other. It is furthermore the dominant way of organising the distribution of goods and services in capitalism.

In modern society, we do not trade tables for books, but rather we trade both tables and books for money. The value-form analysis explains also the emergence of a general equivalent that organises exchange. Exchange-value is a measure that organises a relationship that determines which specific quantities of qualitatively different commodities are exchanged with each other. In the equation 1 computer = 500 €, we have qualities of the economy (computer, money) that are present in certain quantities (1 computer, 500 units of money). In their exchange, we measure a relationship between the two commodities, a certain quantity (value) of one commodity is expressed in the use-value of the other. Measure is the dialectic of quantity and quality. Figure 1.6 shows Hegel's dialectic of quality, quantity, and measure in relationship to the commodity, where it appears as use-value, value,

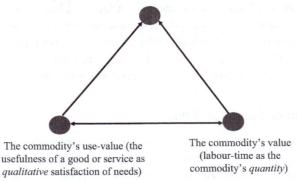

Chapter 1.3.: The value-form or exchange-value: The exchange of qualitative different commodities that are objetifications of abstract quanta of human labour (the commodity's *measure*)

The commodity's use-value (the usefulness of a good or service as *qualitative* satisfaction of needs)

The commodity's value (labour-time as the commodity's *quantity*)

FIGURE 1.6 The commodity's dialectic of quality and quantity as dialectic sublation of use-value and value in the value-form

and exchange-value. We here again see the relevance of Hegel's notion of the measure as dialectic of quality and quantity: The exchange-value form x commodity A = y commodity B measures in which quantity qualitatively different use-values are exchanged.

The four forms of value

Marx distinguishes in chapter 1.3 four forms of value:

A. The simple/isolated/accidental form of value (pp. 139–154):

   x commodity A = y commodity B

B. The total/expanded form of value (pp. 154–157):

   z commodity A = u commodity B = v commodity C = w commodity D = x commodity E = . . . etc.

C. The general form of value (pp. 157–162):

   u commodity B = z commodity A, v commodity C = z commodity A, w commodity D = z commodity A, x commodity E = z commodity A, etc.

D. The money form (pp. 162–163):

   a ounces of gold = z commodity A, a ounces of gold = u commodity B, a ounces of gold = v commodity C, a ounces of gold = w commodity D, a ounces of gold = x commodity E, etc.

x commodity A = y commodity B—An Important Formula

In exchange, concrete use-values that satisfy human needs are set as equals. They are all different in that they satisfy different human needs, but setting them as equals (x commodity A = y commodity B; or: x commodity A = a units of money; y commodity B = a units of money) abstracts from this difference. It constructs an equality by establishing an exchange relationship between two quantities of different commodities. The equalised commodities are considered to represent the same amount of value. The exchange relationship that in capitalism is organised with the help of money, which acts as general equivalent of exchange, constructs a unity in diversity, a unity of the different use-values of commodities. In the exchange process, commodities are reduced to that which they have in common—value. Value is the common moment of commodities. One amount of a commodity is equalised with another one in and through exchange: x commodity A = y commodity B. Exchange is therefore a social relationship in which specific quantities of labour objectified in commodities are considered to have equal value. It is a peculiarity of this equalisation of commodities that "private labour takes the form of its opposite, namely labour in its directly social form" (151).

Value has an objective form in the sense that certain quanta of abstract human labour are objectified in it on average. This objectivity is social and societal because all commodities are products of human labour that is organised in society, and the production process is itself a social process. But value is not only objective and in this objectivity societal, but also social as an exchange relationship itself: In the exchange relationship x commodity A = y commodity B, the value of commodity A is expressed in the use-value of commodity B, and the value of commodity B in the use-value of commodity A.

The contradiction between value and use-value of a commodity (the double character of a commodity as use-value and value that is created by concrete labour and abstract labour) is sublated in the form of the exchange-value—that is, by the fact that the value of the commodity is expressed in the use-value of another commodity via the exchange relationship. Value has at the same time an objective and social form.

The Commodity Body as Reflection of the Commodity Value

Marx describes the value form as a dialectic of use-value, value, and exchange-value. In the equation 1 laptop computer = 2 mobile phones, the value of the computer is expressed in the use-value of the mobile phone. If we reverse the equation, 2 mobile phones = 1 laptop computer, then the value of two mobile phones is expressed in the use-value of the laptop. "The value of" commodity A "is therefore expressed by the physical body of" commodity B, "the value of one by the use-value of the other" (143).

> By means of the value-relation, therefore, the natural form of commodity B becomes the value-form of commodity A, in other words the physical body of commodity B becomes a mirror for the value of commodity A. Commodity A, then, in entering into a relation with commodity B as an object of value [*Wertkörper*], as a materialization of human labour, makes the use-value B into the material through which its own value is expressed. The value of commodity A, thus expressed in the use-value of commodity B, has the form of relative value. (144)
>
> The internal opposition between use-value and value, hidden within the commodity, is therefore represented on the surface by an external opposition, i.e. by a relation between two commodities such that the one commodity, whose own value is supposed to be expressed, counts directly only as a use-value, whereas the other commodity, in which that value is to be expressed, counts directly only as exchange-value. Hence, the simple form of value of a commodity is the simple form of appearance of the opposition between use-value and value which is contained within the commodity. (153)

Marx here expresses the dialectic of use-value and exchange-value with the metaphor of the mirror: The value of one commodity A is in the exchange x commodity A = y commodity B mirrored or reflected in the use-value of the other commodity B. One should, however, bear in mind that a mirror's image can be blurred and distorted. If two commodities are traded as equals because they cost the same amount of money, then there is an assumption that they have equal value. The actual average amount of labour-time represented in the commodities can, however, differ because the equalisation is first and foremost a social relation and therefore a cultural convention that is variable within certain limits. A computer is likely to be always more expensive than a toothbrush because more labour and components go into it than into a toothbrush. The computer has on average a much higher value than the toothbrush. If we know the labour-time it takes on average to produce a specific computer, then we can, however, not automatically calculate its price. We can say that it will be higher than the price of a lot of other commodities, but it can certainly be the case that the production of an Apple and an Asus laptop take the same time, but the Apple costs £840.00 and the Asus £289.99 because Apple is making use of its accumulated reputation for selling its laptop at a higher price than Asus. Asus in contrast does not have as good of a reputation as Apple and has to sell its laptop at cheaper prices in order to sell enough to be profitable. The production costs and labour-time may be equal, but Asus has to sell more pieces in order to achieve the same profitability that Apple achieves by the sale of fewer laptops. One in principle can calculate the average production time and price of a laptop in an industry. Doing so allows one to find out if Apple and Asus produce their laptops above or below or at the average production time—that is, if their commodities have individual values that are equal, lower, or higher than the average social value, and if they sell their commodities at prices equal to, lower, or higher than the average price. Prices reflect labour-times, but they do so not in a linear but in a complex manner. The question of how commodities' labour-times and their prices are related is a complex issue that has in Marxist theory been termed the "transformation problem".

Communication as Reflection

When introducing the metaphor of the commodity body mirroring the commodity value, Marx mentions in a footnote a parallel to humans' social relations:

> In a certain sense, a man is in the same situation as a commodity. As he neither enters into the world in possession of a mirror, nor as a Fichtean philosopher who can say 'I am I', a man first

sees and recognizes himself in another man. Peter only relates to himself as a man through his relation to another man, Paul, in whom he recognizes his likeness. With this, however, Paul also becomes from head to toe, in his physical form as Paul, the form of appearance of the species man or Peter. (144)

Communication is the way that humans relate to each other in a symbolic way in order to interpret the social world, make sense of each other, construct joint meaning, and transform social reality. Communication is a complex, nonlinear process of reflection. This does not mean that A's thoughts are copied into B's brain. Rather A communicates something to B. B then interprets A's communicated ideas in a specific way that is not predetermined and depends on B's experiences and norms and the qualities of the social relationship between A and B. In any case there will be a change of B's thought patterns: S/he interprets what A says. This structural cognitive change encompasses the possibility for understandings, misunderstandings, agreement, partial agreement, disagreement, etc. So A's ideas will have some reflection in B's mind, but to which extent there is identity, variation, distortion, blurring, etc. depends on many factors.

The World's Dialectic as a Process of Reflection

The translator of Hegel's *Encyclopaedic Logic* (1830a, xxv–xxvi) argues that for Hegel the German terms "Schein" and "erscheinen" have three meanings: (1) "Erscheinung" (appearance) as a "higher development" (xxv), (2) "the physical analogy" (xxvi) to the shining of a light or the reflection in a mirror, (3) "Schein" as deceptive—"it is what seems to be, but is not really so" (xxvi). Reflection is one of the meanings that Hegel associates with appearance (Schein) and the process of appearing (erscheinen). The words "reflection" in English and "Reflexion" in German have the double-meaning of (a) the repulsion of light (e.g., in the mirror), sound, or heat and (b) deep contemplation.

Hegel makes clear that all these meanings of reflection have in common that there is mediation, a relationship between two systems or phenomena. So the most general meaning of "reflection" is that things are related and that there is a mutual subject-object relationship that creates a difference:

> The term "reflection" is primarily used of light, when, propagated rectilinearly, it strikes a mirrored surface and is thrown back by it. So we have here something twofold: first, something immediate, something that is, and second, the same as mediated or posited. And this is just the case when we reflect on an object or 'think it over' (as we also say very often). For here we are not concerned with the object in its immediate form, but want to know it as mediated. And our usual view of the task or purpose of philosophy is that it consists in the cognition of the essence of things. By this we understand no more than that things are not to be left in their immediate state, but are rather to be exhibited as mediated or grounded by something else. (Hegel 1830a, addition to §112)

Hegel characterises his philosophy as speculative philosophy. The translators explain how he uses the concept of speculation and that this use is connected to the idea of reflective or mirroring thought:

> The 'mirroring' (speculum = "mirror") is for Hegel not that of reality or nature in the mind. It takes place in the thinking-together of thought determinations that for the understanding are radically opposed, and even contradict each other. In speculative thought they 'mirror' each other and only in this way can they be genuine comprehension. (Hegel 1830a, 352)

Mirroring, speculation, and reflection do not just have etymological connections, but are for Hegel aspects of the dialectic. He does not use the terms "speculation" and "speculative" in the everyday meaning of ungrounded hypothetical thought, but uses them in the sense of the comprehension of dialectical relations:

> The speculative or positively rational apprehends the unity of the determinations in their opposition, the affirmative that is contained in their dissolution and in their transition. (Hegel 1830a, §82)
>
> The term 'speculation' tends to be used in ordinary life in a very vague, and at the same time, secondary sense—as, for instance, when people talk about a matrimonial or commercial speculation. All that it is taken to mean here is that, on the one hand, what is immediately present must be transcended, and, on the other, that whatever the content of these speculations may be, although it is initially only something subjective, it ought not to remain so, but is to be realised or translated into objectivity. (Hegel 1830a, addition to §82)

Speculative thought tries to understand how in a dialectical relationship one thing encroaches on or overgrasps (*übergreifen*) another. "Hegel uses übergreifen to express the positive aspect of the process of Aufhebung. The concept that results from speculative 'comprehension' (begreifen) reaches back and 'overgrasps' the opposition of the moments produced by thought in its dialectical stage" (Hegel 1830a, xxvi). Hegel (1830a, §20), for example, says that "thought is itself and its other, that it overgrasps its other and that nothing escapes it".

When Hegel and Marx use formulations such as that commodities, humans, thoughts, or concepts reflect or mirror each other, then they express that there is a dialectic relationship between two moments in which the two are identical and different from each other, overgrasp into each other, so that their contradictory relationship creates some form of change of the one in the other and of the other in the one. They do not mean that one moment mechanically determines changes in the other or the other way around. Reflection is a basic interactive process that connects units of matter in a dialectical manner.

Labour as the Commodity's and Value's Soul

Marx argues that value and exchange-value are not visible: "No atom of matter enters into the objectivity of commodities as values; in this it is the direct opposite of the coarsely sensuous objectivity of commodities as physical objects. We may twist and turn a single commodity as we wish; it remains impossible to grasp it as a thing possessing value" (138). If you look at a commodity that you bought, such as an iPhone, then you cannot see the labour that went into it and the class relations that underpin it. If the phone was produced by Chinese assembly labourers who work long hours, earn little money for it, and are controlled and disciplined by a security force in a military manner, then you cannot see these social relations by just looking at the phone. You will have to conduct a search for information or a detailed analysis in order to find out more about the social relations that underpin the commodity. The human labour that is the substance of value and the class relations organising labour make value "purely social" (139, 149). The commodity's sociality is, however, not immediately apparent to the consumers and producers. That labour underpins a commodity only becomes apparent to the consumers and producers because they have to pay a specific sum of money for it. Exchange-value is therefore the form of the appearance of value. The commodity is a "bearer of value" (143). In exchange, the accumulated human labour stored in commodities is set as something equal. Labour is the "splendid kindred soul, the soul of value" (143). Labour as the commodity's soul is something that is not visible in the commodity, but forms its substance.

The Equivalent and Relative Form of Value

In the equation 1 laptop computer = 2 mobile phones, two phones' value is the equivalent of the computer's value. The phones stand, as Marx says, in the equivalent form of value ("two phones' worth is the equivalent of one laptop's value"). The laptop's value has a relation to the phone's value; it has, as Marx says, a relative form of value ("one laptop is worth two phones"). "The relative form of value and the equivalent form are two inseparable moments, which belong to and mutually condition each other; but, at the same time, they are mutually exclusive or opposed extremes, i.e. poles of the expression of value" (140).

Given that the relative and the equivalent forms of value condition each other, but are also different, the relative form is at the same time an equivalent form and the equivalent form a relative form of value. This becomes apparent in the fact that the relationship can be reversed: 2 mobile phones = 1 laptop computer. The value of two mobile phones now stands in the relative form of value ("two mobile phones are worth one laptop's value") and the value of the laptop computer in the equivalent form ("one laptop's worth is the equivalent of two phones' value). "I must reverse the equation, in order to express the value of the coat relatively; and, if I do that, the linen becomes the equivalent instead of the coat. The same commodity cannot, therefore appear in both form in the same expression of value. These forms rather exclude each other as polar opposites" (140). The relative and the equivalent form are at the same time "polar opposites"/"mutually exclusive"/"opposed extremes" as well as "inseparable moments" that "mutually condition each other" (140).

Hegel's Dialectic of the One and the Many: Attraction and Repulsion

Marx's value-form analysis can be interpreted with the help of Hegel's dialectic of the One and the Many and of Attraction and Repulsion (see Figures 1.7 and 1.8). Repulsion means the "distinguishing of the One from itself, the *repulsion* of the One", the "positing of *many Ones*" (Hegel 1830a, §97). The One "expels itself out of itself, and what it posits itself as is what is many" (Hegel 1830a, §97). Repulsion turns into attraction: The One "excludes itself from itself and posits itself as what is many; each of the many, however, is itself One, and because it behaves as such, this all-round repulsion turns over forthwith into its opposite—*attraction*" (Hegel 1830a, §97). "But the *many* are each one what the other is, each of them is one or also one of the many; they are therefore one and the same. Or, when the repulsion is considered in itself then, as the negative *behaviour* of the many ones against

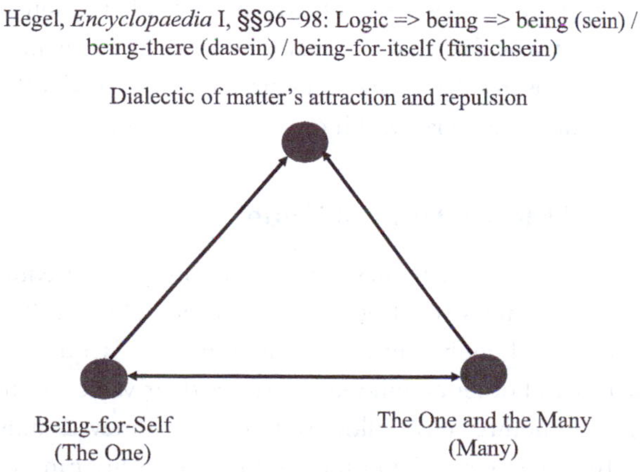

Hegel, *Encyclopaedia* I, §§96–98: Logic => being => being (sein) /
being-there (dasein) / being-for-itself (fürsichsein)

Dialectic of matter's attraction and repulsion

Being-for-Self
(The One)

The One and the Many
(Many)

FIGURE 1.7 The dialectic of the One and the Many, Repulsion, and Attraction

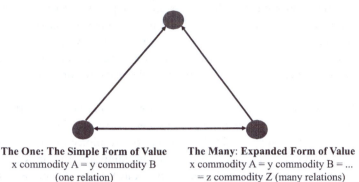

General Form of Value, Money Form: Unity in diversity of commodities:
x commodity A = a units of money M,
y commodity B = b units of money M , ... z commodity Z = c units of money M

The One: The Simple Form of Value
x commodity A = y commodity B
(one relation)

The Many: Expanded Form of Value
x commodity A = y commodity B = ...
= z commodity Z (many relations)

FIGURE 1.8   The dialectic of the value-forms as the dialectic of the One and the Many

each other, it is just as essentially their *relation* to each other; and since those to which the One relates itself in its repelling are ones, in relating to them it relates itself to itself. Thus, repulsion is just as essentially *attraction*; and the excluding One or being-for-itself sublates itself" (Hegel 1830a, §98).

The Attraction and Repulsion of Commodities

Marx shows in the value form analysis that commodities attract and repulse each other. They repulse each other because they have different natural forms, qualities, materials, and use-values. There are many different commodities. But abstract labour equalises them in the production process, and money (or another general equivalent) equalises them in the exchange process: They all contain quanta of human labour and are therefore objectifications of value that are in the exchange process assessed as representations of equal human labour. Qualitatively different commodities that repulse each other attract each other via a general equivalent in the exchange process. The general form of value constructs a unity of the diversity of commodities. Marx describes the general form of value as "simple and common to all, hence general" because there is "a single commodity" that functions as general equivalent of exchange so that there is a "unified form" that uses "the same commodity each time" (157).

In chapter 3, Marx comes back to the question of the attraction of commodities and says that the commodity's measurement function has a role of attraction to other commodities: "The commodity, as a use-value, satisfies a particular need and forms a particular element of material wealth. But the value of a commodity measures the degree of its attractiveness for all other elements of material wealth, and therefore measures the social wealth of its owner" (230).

The General Form and Money Form of Value

In the general form of value and the money form, there are general equivalents of exchange—commodities that express the values of all other commodities. Historically gold and money have taken on the role of the general equivalents. "A commodity only acquires a general expression of its value if, at the same time, all other commodities express their values in the same equivalent; and every newly emergent commodity must follow suit" (159). Money as universal equivalent has a monopoly status (162–163). The general and money forms of value can be traced back to simple forms of exchange x commodity A = y commodity B so that the "simple commodity form is [. . .] the germ of the money form" (163).

In the period 9000 to 6000 BC, cattle and grain were used as general equivalents of exchange in many societies.[1] Around 1200 BC cowries were used as money in China. In the period 1000 to 500 BC, tools such as spades, hoes, and knives became the general equivalents in China. Around 640 BC the Lydians made the first coins out of electrum. Base metal coins originated around 600 to 300 BC in China. The Lydians were the first to produce gold and silver coins, around 550 BC. The Romans adopted coins relatively late; around 269 BC silver coins replaced bronze bars as currency. Around 118 BC, the Chinese used leather money. They issued paper money around 960 AD. Europeans learned of the existence of paper money in China around 1275 to 1292 as a result of Marco Polo's travels to China, but it took until the 17th century for banknotes to be introduced. In 1690, a 200-year history of using tobacco as currency started in Virginia. In modern society, banks have become crucial mechanisms that with the help of credits enable the operation of capital. The gold standard, in which banknotes can be converted into gold, became important in modern society. After World War II, the Bretton Woods agreement introduced fixed exchange rates of currencies. It collapsed in 1973 and the USA abolished the gold standard.

The above discussion shows that money has historically not been the only general equivalent of exchange—cattle, grain, cowries, tools, leather, and tobacco have been used. The virtualisation of money has included developments such as credits, loans, mortgages, stocks, bonds, derivatives, debit and credit cards, electronic banking, centralised electronic payment systems such as PayPal, and decentralised electronic/virtual/digital/crypto-currencies like Bitcoin, Ripple, Litecoin, and Dogecoin.

When Marx discusses the exchange of commodities in chapter 1.3, he mentions physical goods: iron, linen, corn, coats, coffee, sugar, beds, houses, tea, and gold. He uses the example 20 yards of linen = 1 coat to explain the forms of value. One can, however, also exchange informational goods. In modern society, this is predominantly done with the help of money. For example, 1 song on iTunes = £0.99, 1 CD = £14.99, 1 book = £12.91, 1 operating system = £69.99, 1 software application = £70.18. Producing one BMW takes a specific number of hours. Producing a second BMW takes on average the same number of hours. Producing the master or initial version of one song, album, book, operating system, or software application can take many hours. Producing one or more copies does in contrast to the BMW take little time. Information is a peculiar good, for which Marx's labour theory of value has to take on a specific form. The first version has high value, whereas copies have low value. Information commodities tend to be sold at prices that do not reflect the amount of hours necessary for the reproduction of copies, but the higher amount needed for the initial production as well as the time needed for creating updates, new versions, and customer support. The small value of the copy-time is not the determining feature of information goods' prices. Rather the price of such goods tends to stand above the monetary equivalent of the average copying/reproduction time. The high risks that information commodities face (nobody knows if a specific information good will be a "hit" or a "flop", the risk of "pirating", the outdating risk, etc.) is partly offset by selling information commodities at prices that stand above the monetary equivalents of their average reproduction/copying time. Discussions of Marx's labour theory of value in relation to information commodities have especially since the end of the 20th century and in the 21st century become important because one started to talk about the existence of an information economy. So the reason is the emergence of what some term the "information age", in which the production of information accounts for significant shares of the work force, value-added, and economic growth.

1.4. The Fetishism of the Commodity and Its Secret

Commodity Fetishism

Marx argues that a commodity is a peculiar thing that is "strange" (163), "metaphysical" (163), "mystical" (164), and "mysterious" (164) because its value "transcends sensuousness" (163) so that the commodity "stands on its head" and "grotesque ideas" (163) about the nature of the commodity can emerge.

Commodity producers do not relate to each other directly, but only in exchange in the form x commodity A = a money M, y commodity B = b money M. Therefore "the relationship between the producers [. . .] take on the form of a social relation between the products of labour" (164). The "definite social relation between men themselves" assumes "the fantastic form of a relation between things" (165). Marx stresses explicitly the important role that money plays in the commodity fetish: "It is however precisely this finished form of the world of commodities—the money form—which conceals the social character of private labour and the social relations between the individual workers, by making those relations appear as relations between material objects, instead of revealing them plainly" (169).

The money fetishism is a particular form of commodity fetishism. The social relations between workers' labour appear not "as direct social relations between persons in their work, but rather as material relations between persons and social relations between things" (166). Marx calls this phenomenon "the fetishism which attaches itself to the products of labour as soon as they are produced as commodities" (165). He summarises the causes of the commodity's fetish character in the following words:

> Objects of utility become commodities only because they are the products of the labour of private individuals who work independently of each other. [. . .] Since the producers do not come into social contact until they exchange the products of their labour, the specific social characteristics of their private labours appear only within this exchange. (165)

The Contradiction of the Commodity's Use-Value and Value

The contradiction of the commodity's use-value and value is at the heart of commodity fetishism.

Fetishism is an objective quality of commodities that stems from the fact that commodities are the output of labour that becomes invisible in exchange. In fetishism, the social reality and essence of the commodity appears as a thing, impersonal, and unsocial. But fetishism stands in a relation to the human subjects on whom the appearance of the commodity—its fetish character—has certain effects. Commodity exchange means that people are equating their labour values—labour values they are not automatically aware of because the labour-time and class relations are invisible when one exchanges money for a commodity. Therefore they "do this [setting labour-times equal] without being aware of it" so that value "does not have its description branded on its forehead" and a commodity is "a social hieroglyphic" (167). Given that commodities are difficult phenomena that are not self-explanatory, humans try to make sense of them in different ways. The commodity's complexity that appears in its fetish character makes such interpretations prone to ideology. This does not mean that every explanation of capitalism, money, and commodities is necessarily false. But Marx documents examples of ideological interpretations of these phenomena.

What Is Ideology?

The Marxist critique and theory of ideology are complex subfields of Marxist analysis. There is no overall agreement on how to define ideology. The Marxist theorist Terry Eagleton (1991, 28–31) has noted six core understandings of the concept of ideology:

(a) The "general material process of production of ideas, beliefs and values in social life" (28)
(b) Ideas that coherently "symbolize the conditions and life-experiences of a specific group or class" (29)
(c) The "promotion and legitimatization of the interests of a group or class in the face of opposing interests" (29)
(d) The "promotion and legitimatization" (29) of the interests of a dominant social group in order to "unify a social formation" (30)

(e) Ideas and beliefs that "help to legitimate the interests of a ruling group or class by distortion and dissimulation" (30)

(f) "False or deceptive beliefs" arising from the "material structure of society as a whole" (30)

All of these definitions of ideology have to do with social ideas diffused in society. Only from definition (c) on is the definition of ideology specific for class societies. Marx understands the term "ideology" mostly as a legitimatisation strategy of class and domination. Commodity fetishism is a deceptive appearance of the commodity. The question is if the commodity fetishism is itself already an ideology emerging from capitalism's social form or if it becomes an ideology by creating fetishist ideas in human subjects. Eagleton's definition (a) contains the material process that creates ideologies, whereas definitions (c) through (f) focus on ideology's potential effects on human subjectivity. Ideology has social foundations, such as the commodity form or suffering, that are part of ideology itself as well as specific effects on human subjectivity.

Ideology as a Critical Concept

A critical concept of ideology requires a normative distinction between true and false beliefs and practices. It understands ideology as thoughts, practices, ideas, words, concepts, phrases, sentences, texts, belief systems, meanings, representations, artefacts, institutions, systems, or combinations thereof that represent and justify one group's or individual's power, domination, or exploitation of other groups or individuals by misrepresenting, one-dimensionally presenting, or distorting reality in symbolic representations. Ideologies are practices and modes of thought that make claims that do not accord to reality or present aspects of human existence that are historical and changeable as eternal and unchangeable. Domination means in this context that there is a system that enables one human side to gain advantages at the expense of others and to sustain this condition. It is a routinised and institutionalised form of asymmetric power in which one side has the opportunity to shape and control societal structures (such as the production and control of wealth, political decision-making, public discussions, collective ideas, norms, rules, values), whereas others do not have these opportunities and are facing disadvantages or exclusion from the opportunities of others. Exploitation is a specific form of domination in which an exploiting class derives wealth advantages at the expense of an exploited class by controlling economic resources and means of coercion in such a way that the exploited class is forced to produce new use-values that the exploiting class controls. Ideology presupposes "societal structures, in which different groups and conflicting interests act and strive to impose their interest onto the total of society as its general interest. To put it shortly: The emergence and diffusion of ideologies appears as the general characteristic of class societies" (Lukács 1986, 405, translation from German).

Classical Political Economy as Ideology that Postulates Commodity Fetishism

One realm of thought, where fetishist thought has played a role in the interpretation of the commodity and capitalism, is "classical political economy", a term by which Marx means "all the economist who, since the time of W. [William] Petty, have investigated the real internal framework of bourgeois relations of production" (174–175, footnote 33). He explicitly mentions the approaches of David Ricardo, Destutt de Tracy, Jean-Baptiste Say, Adam Smith, Claude Frédéric Bastiat, and Samuel Bailey, for whom commodities, money, and capitalism appear to be "a self-evident and nature-imposed necessity" (175).

Marx admired the works of Adam Smith and David Ricardo and learned a lot from reading them. He, for example, took the distinction between use-value and value (Smith speaks of exchange-value) as the two dimensions of the commodity from Adam Smith's (1776, 32) *An Inquiry into the Nature and Causes of the Wealth of Nations*. Marx's labour theory of value and especially the insight that labour is the substance of value was inspired by David Ricardo's (1819) *On the Principles of Political Economy and Taxation*: "The value of a commodity, or the quantity of any other commodity for which it will exchange, depends on the relative quantity of labour which is necessary for its production" (Ricardo 1819, 11).

But Marx was also very critical of these two liberal economists' attempts to justify capitalism as the best possible order and a natural order of humans. Adam Smith, for example, writes that exchange is a natural aspect of humanity. He speaks of "a certain propensity on human nature [. . .] to truck, barter, and exchange one thing for another. [. . .] It is common to all men, and to be found in no other race of animals, which seem to know neither this nor any other species of contracts" (Smith 1776, 18). Ricardo sees both capital and money as naturally appropriate means of the human economy. He generalises the concept of capital and speaks, for example, of "the hunter's capital, the weapon" (Ricardo 1819, 23) and sees money as "the general medium of exchange between all civilized countries" (Ricardo 1819, 48). Given the naturalisation of capital and money, Ricardo generalises that striving for profitability is also a natural human property: "Whilst every man is free to employ his capital where he pleases, he will naturally seek for it that employment which is most advantageous; he will naturally be dissatisfied with a profit of 10 per cent, if by removing his capital he can obtain a profit of 15 per cent" (Ricardo 1819, 88–89).

Smith naturalises exchange-value, Ricardo capital, money, and the accumulation of capital and profit. Smith's argument is that exchange lies in the nature of humans. Ricardo first defines money and capital in a very general sense for all societies and, having done so, then naturalises striving for profit. For both thinkers a communist society in which there is no exchange, capital, and money, is not imaginable and is not part of their conceptual universe. They neglect the class relations that underpin exchange, capital, and money, which means that the commodity fetishism, in which exchange relations appear natural, shaped the thoughts of both Smith and Riccardo in an ideological way so that they tried to justify capitalism as a natural and civilised order.

Marx argues about Ricardo's political economy that "his analysis is by far the best" (*Capital Volume 1*, 173, footnote 33) and criticises him at the same time for not seeing through commodity fetishism: "Ricardo, ultimately (and consciously) made the antagonism of class interests, of wages and profits, of profits and rent, the starting-point of his investigations, naively taking this antagonism for a social law of nature" (96).

Religion as Fetishism and Ideology

Marx says that the commodity and money fetishism are a kind of capitalist religion by pointing out parallels of them to religious ideology. He compares the commodity fetishism to "theological niceties" (163) and uses religion as an analogy:

> In order, therefore, to find an analogy we must take flight into the misty realm of religion. There the products of the human brain appear as autonomous figures endowed with a life of their own, which enter into relations both with each other and with the human race. So it is in the world of commodities with the products of men's hands. (165)

The commodity fetishism and religion have in common that they naturalise, mystify, and distort reality by creating the appearance that one specific imaginary or real phenomenon such as God or the commodity is naturally given and exists endlessly. Money and the commodity are forms of the secularised God of capitalism.

In his early works, the young Marx (1843b, 250) characterised religion in the famous passage of the *Introduction to the Critique of Hegel's Philosophy of Law*:

> This state and this society produce religion, which is an *inverted consciousness of the world* because they are an *inverted world*. [. . .] *Religious* suffering is the *expression* of real suffering and at the same time the *protest* against real suffering. Religion is the sigh of the oppressed creature, the heart of a heartless world, as it is the spirit of spiritless conditions. It is the *opium* of the people. (Marx 1843b, 250)

Marx here uses the notion of ideology as inversion: Religion just like the commodity fetishism makes the world "stand[s] on its head" (*Capital Volume 1*, 163). Religion explains the world as being created and governed by God. It sets the idea of God as absolute and sees it as something endless. Commodity fetishism makes the commodity appear as absolute and endless. Religion and the commodity fetishism have in common that they mystify the social relations that underpin society.

Commodity Fetishism Does Not Exist in All Types of Society

Marx argues that commodity fetishism does not exist in societies with individual (the example of Robinson Crusoe alone on an island) or family subsistence production, slave-holding societies, feudal societies, and communism (170–174) because commodity trade is, in such economies, not the general social form. All class societies are, however, likely to be shaped by religion or other ideologies so that the

> religious [and other ideological] reflections of the real world can, in any case, vanish only when the practical relations of everyday life between man and man, and man and nature, generally present themselves to him in a transparent and rational form. The veil is not removed from the countenance of the social life-process, i.e. the process of material production, until it becomes production by freely associated men, and stands under their conscious and planned control. (173)

Ideology as a general form of fetishist relations and thoughts can only stop to have a material foundation in "an association of free men, working with the means of production held in common, and expending their many different forms of labour-power in full self-awareness as one single social labour force" (171). Marx and others term such a society "communism" because the means of production and other power structures are owned and controlled in common by those affected by them.

Hegel: The Dialectic of Essence and Existence

Hegel draws a distinction between the essence and the existence of the world. His *Logic* is divided into three parts: being, essence, and concept. The second part is again divided into three parts: A. Essence, B. Appearance, C. Actuality.

> The immediate being of things is here represented as a sort of rind or curtain behind which the essence is concealed. Now, when we say further that all things have an essence, what we mean is that they are not truly what they immediately show themselves to be. A mere rushing about from one quality to another, and a mere advance from the qualitative to the quantitative and back again, is not the last word; on the contrary, there is something that abides in things, and this is, in the first instance, their essence. (Hegel 1830a, §112)

"The truth of being is essence"; it is a "background" that "constitutes the truth of being" (Hegel 1812/1833, 337). Essence externalises itself in specific forms. The essence must appear; it is shining forth into something. Essence as something's internal dimension appears in an outer dimension:

Hegel: The Doctrine of Essence, *Encyclopaedia* I: §§112–159

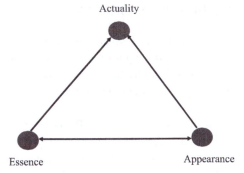

FIGURE 1.9   Hegel's dialectic of essence, appearance, and actuality

> Shining is the determination, in virtue of which essence is not being, but essence, and the developed shining is [shining-forth or] appearance. Essence therefore is not behind or beyond appearance, but since the essence is what exists, existence is appearance. (Hegel 1830a, §131)

Existence, posited in its contradiction, is appearance (Hegel 1830a, Addition to §131).

For Hegel, not everything that exists is actual. Actuality is rather an existence that corresponds to its essence, the truth of a phenomenon: "Actuality is the unity, become immediate, of essence and existence, or of what is inner and what is outer" (Hegel 1830a, §142).

The essence is the grounding and hidden reality of a phenomenon. It appears in specific forms that are to a specific extent corresponding to or diverging from the essence. Existence that is brought into correspondence with essence is a true existence, an actuality. Figure 1.9 visualises the dialectic of essence, appearance, and actuality.

The Dialectical Logic of Essence, Appearance, and Actuality in Marx's Fetishism Chapter

Figure 1.10 shows the relevance of Hegel's dialectic of essence, appearance, and actuality for *Capital Volume 1*'s chapter 1.3

The true essence of the human economy is concrete work that creates use-values in societal relations. In capitalism, the economy takes on a specific appearance: the commodity, exchange-value, and abstract labour. As a result, the social relations of the producers appear as relations between things, concrete labour appears as abstract labour, and use-value as exchange-value. Establishing a communist society means the sublation of the antagonism between the essence and ideological appearance of the economy.

The media and culture, such as live entertainment, television, film, radio, newspapers, magazines, the telephone, Internet platforms and applications, social media, etc., have a double character:

(a) They are owned and operated in specific economic ways (commodity, public funding, civil society voluntarism and donations, etc.).
(b) They communicate information in public.

In class societies, media are means of communicating ideologies and deconstructions of ideologies, as well as hybrids of the two. They can present parts of the world in an ideological manner so that its essence and its mass-mediated appearance diverge; in an identical manner, where appearance and essence coincide; in a deconstructive manner, where either true or false representations are challenged; or in hybrid forms.

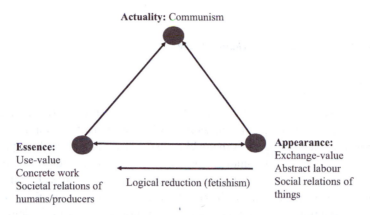

FIGURE 1.10 The dialectical logic of essence, appearance, and actuality in Marx's fetishism chapter

Advertising is one of the means of accumulation in the capitalist media world. It is a particularly good example for how the fetish of commodity relates to the media. The commodity fetish empties out meaning of commodities. Commodities are produced in social labour relations, but in the exchange relationship their social origin in human labour is hidden and so commodities appear as the natural results of the relationship between things. Consumers cannot make true sense and meaning of commodities because they are not able to meet those who produced these goods. Producers mostly also do not know the other producers who as part of the societal division of labour participate in the production of the same goods. The result is an informational vacuum, the commodity's emptiness. Advertising has, however, discovered this emptiness. It tries to fill the symbolic meaninglessness and emptiness created by commodity fetishism. It creates illusionary meanings and bestows them upon commodities in order to try to make them more sellable. Advertising is pure ideology because it tries, often with sophisticated and unconscious means, to convince audiences and users to purchase and consume specific commodities. For doing so, it makes use of specific advertising strategies.

Advertising strategies are fetishist themselves: They try to create the impression that a specific commodity is absolutely needed, that the commodity only has positive qualities, that life without commodities is impossible, or that life with commodities will become much better. Advertising neglects possible negative impacts or dimensions of the presented commodities. It does not provide information about the working conditions of those producing the displayed commodities and possible negative impacts these commodities may have on human health, the environment, society, etc. A truly communist society abolishes money, the commodity, labour, and exchange, and thereby also exploitation. It therefore also gets rid of all capitalist media. Communism has no need for commodity fetishism and ideology. It liberates humanity from capital, fetishism, and ideology and therefore also from capitalist media and commodity fetishism.

Marx discusses specific examples of how bourgeois economists reflect commodity fetishism in their works in the "Results of the Immediate Production Process", which is included as an appendix to the Penguin edition of *Capital Volume 1*. The fetishism section in chapter 1 is, for those reading it the first time, often difficult to understand. For illustrative examples, I therefore refer the reader to the *Results* and the discussion in section 27.1 in this book.

Exercises for Chapter 1

Group exercise (G)
Project exercise (P)

Chapter 1.1

Key Categories: Use-Value, Value, Exchange-Value

Exercise 1.1 (G)

Work in groups: Make a list of different information goods and services. Try to give precise definitions of the use-values of all the goods and services. Work out what these informational use-values have in common and what distinguishes them. Use the distinction between the capitalist, public, and civil organisation of the media and information for classifying all of your identified informational use-values. Ask yourself what the role of the commodity and money is in each of these use-values: Is there a commodity or not? If so, what is the commodity and how is it traded? Is money involved in the organisation of the production of these use-values or not? If so, what role does it play?

Chapter 1.2

Key Categories: Work, Labour, Concrete Work, Abstract Labour, the Measure

Exercise 1.2 (G)

Work in groups: Make a list of typical forms of work that can be found in the field of information, media, the digital, culture, and the arts. Ask yourself the following: What exactly is it that distinguishes these forms of work from other forms? What is it that makes such work attractive and interesting for many?

Exercise 1.3 (P)

Work in groups: Marx's chapter 1.2 shows that abstract labour creates the commodity's value and that it has to do with labour-time. Search in databases such as the Social Sciences Citations Index, Communication and Mass Media Complete, Scopus, Google Scholar, and Directory of Open Access Journals for an article that analyses working conditions and labour-times in one specific kind of job in the media/cultural/information/digital industries. Try to find out what typical labour-times per week are in this job and how high the productivity is—that is, how many informational goods or services are typically created per week or month or year. You can also consider consulting platforms such as glassdoor.com or interviewing some information professionals in order to gather this information. Try to calculate the average value of a typical commodity (measured in labour hours) created by the abstract labour performed in the job you analyse.

Chapter 1.3

Key Categories: Forms of Value, Simple/Isolated/Accidental Form of Value, the Total/Expanded Form of Value, the General Form of Value, the Money Form, Dialectic, Attraction, Repulsion

Exercise 1.4 (P)

Work in groups: Marx gives examples for the value form that mainly focus on physical commodities. The task of this exercise is to create a general form of value of a series of information goods. Make a list of information goods that could have roughly the same price. Look into the offers of an online retailer in order to identify at least five exemplars of different information goods in your list that have the same price. This allows you to formulate a general and money form of value in the following format: a commodity A = b commodity B = c commodity C = d commodity D = e commodity E =…. = x £. Try to find information or make estimations about how long it typically takes on average to produce new versions of these information goods and how long it takes to copy or reproduce them.

The Monetary Expression of Labour-Time (MELT) is a measure that allows one to transform labour-times into monetary units and monetary units into labour-times. The MELT is the ratio of money to labour-time in the whole economy. It is an average measure that tells us how much monetary value is produced on average during one working hour. It is measured as money unit per hour (e.g., £/hour). A commodity's value can be measured both in units of labour-time (hours) or money (monetary units).

MELT = gross domestic product of an economy / total number of hours worked in the economy

Try to find data for the country you live in on the size of the gross domestic product (in the national currency) and the total number of hours worked in the economy. You can consult national statistic offices and/or databases such as the International Labour Organization's ILOSTAT, the EU's Annual Macro-Economic Database, OECD Statistics (OECD.Stat), the International Monetary Funds' statistics, the World Bank's statistics, etc. If you cannot find data for the country you live in, then switch to another country and adapt the price data for information goods to this country by looking for data on what these goods cost in the selected country.

Based on all obtained data, calculate the MELT. Based on the MELT, calculate how many hours of average labour (value) your information commodities represent by multiplying the price with the MELT: average working-hours = price ★ MELT

Compare the average working hours with the information that you obtained about how much labour-time it takes to create the initial version of the information goods and to copy it. Do the average individual labour-times for producing the initial versions and for copying them correspond to, stand above, or stand below the socially necessary labour-times that the prices of the information goods represent and that you have obtained with the help of the MELT? Try to interpret the results.

Reflect also on the peculiarities of information and discuss how they influence the relationship of labour-times (labour values) and prices (monetary values) of information commodities.

Chapter 1.4

Key Categories: Fetishism, Ideology

Exercise 1.5 (G or P)

Work in groups: Search for and read articles, op-ed pieces, and comments about capitalism in general and the role of the Internet and computer in capitalism in the business press (for example, *Financial Times, The Economist, Wall Street Journal, International Business Times, Bloomberg*, etc.). Analyse the way capitalism and corporations are presented in these texts and try to identify passages where commodity fetishism results in ideology.

Exercise 1.6 (P)

Work in groups: Each group chooses one specific information goods, entertainment, or other media company and looks for and collects advertisements provided by this corporation in magazines, online, and on television. Discuss the questions below. Afterwards, each group presents its analysis.

- To whom does the ad appeal/speak? To whom not?
- What meanings does it communicate? What does it want the viewer to think and do?
- How does it communicate these meanings?

- Which moral values does it consciously or unconsciously address and appeal to? Which moral values does it exclude?
- In which respect is the advertisement related to commodity fetishism?

Detailed Guidelines for This Exercise

Try to find more information about the company whose ads you analyse: Which other media does it own? Who are the owners of the company? In which countries does the company operate? Is it a rather small or large company (employees, profits, etc.)? Which company runs the ad that you analysed? What kind of products does your chosen company sell (make a list by looking at its website)? Is it only active in one industry or in multiple ones? In which one(s) is it active? How large are the annual profits of the company and how large is its advertising budget (see company website, company annual report, SEC-filings form 10-K, forms 10-Q, media reports)?

Which group does the ad you analysed address? Which groups does it not address/exclude? What are the typical sociodemographic characteristics of the group that the ad appeals to (gender, class, income, age, education, jobs, location, place of living (home owner, etc.), origin/ethnicity, lifestyle, consumer behaviour, and mobility, as well as typical goods that this group possesses and is interested in, etc.)?

Which product or service is advertised? What is the role of this product or service in society?

What is the main message of the ad? Which visual and textual elements and strategies does it use for communicating this message? Does the ad use metaphors, symbols, and hidden meanings that are represented in specific forms? If so, which ones? How are they expressed in visual and textual form?

Information: Typical elements in ads that have a specific meaning can include the following: characteristics of the persons shown (hair colour, hairstyle, hair length, eye colour, facial expressions, body type, age, gender, origin, race, body language, makeup, clothes, eyeglasses, earrings, body adornments), settings, social relationships shown or implied, power relationships among the persons or groups shown, spatiality, signs of education level, signs of occupations, shown objects, activities, background, lightning, sound, music, colours, typeface in text, design, words used, questions asked, textual metaphors, associations, use of negations in texts, use of affirmations in texts, arguments, appeals, slogans, headlines, paradoxes, tone and style of the text, the way the reader/viewer/listener is addressed, angle of photographs and videos, etc.

Make a list of five moral values that you consider important for life and society. Are there any specific values expressed in the advertisement (e.g., individualism, individuality, sexual desire, jealousy, hard work, patriotism, nationalism, success, power, good taste, etc.)? How are these values expressed? Why are they expressed and what picture of society do they communicate? Compare the values in the ad to your values listed previously. Are there commonalities/differences? Are there any myths, biases, ideologies, or stereotypes present in the ad? If so, which ones?

What image of society does the company express in this ad? How does it present society in the ad? Do you agree or disagree with this presentation of reality? Is it a realistic picture of society as it is or not? Are there important dimensions of society that are left out? If so, which ones?

Does the ad appeal to any specific conscious or subliminal human wishes, desires, or fantasies? If so, how?

Try to find out negative impacts of the company you analyse on society, humans, or the environment. You can for this purpose consult news media and websites of corporate watchdog websites. Do the ads you saw address any of these concerns? If not, why do you think this is the case? What role does commodity fetishism play in this context?

Examples of Watchdogs

CorpWatch Reporting: http://www.corpwatch.org
Transnationale Ethical Rating: http://www.transnationale.org

The Corporate Watch Project: http://www.corporatewatch.org
Multinational Monitor: http://www.multinationalmonitor.org
Responsible Shopper: http://www.greenamerica.org/programs/responsibleshopper/
Endgame Database of Corporate Fines: http://www.endgame.org/corpfines.html,
Corporate Crime Reporter: http://www.corporatecrimereporter.com,
Corporate Europe Observatory: http://www.corporateeurope.org
Corporate Critic Database: http://www.corporatecritic.org
Labourleaks: https://www.labourleaks.org/
Wikileaks: https://wikileaks.org/
Students and Scholars against Corporate Misbehaviour: http://sacom.hk
China Labour Watch: http://www.chinalaborwatch.org
Center for Media and Democracy's PR Watch: http://www.prwatch.org

Exercise 1.7 (G)

Watch Naomi Klein's movie *No Logo: Brands. Globalization. Resistance* (2003). Discuss the following questions in groups:

- What is it that makes brand-name products appealing to some people? Do you buy specific brands? Why? Are there brands that you would never buy? If so, why?
- What exactly is lifestyle branding? Try to compile a list of examples of lifestyle branding and describe what lifestyle is presented and in which way?
- What are branding's actual or possibly negative effects? Search for news stories and information on watchdog platforms (see the list provided in exercise 1.6) that present negative consequences of specific brand products for humans, society, or the environment.
- How is branding related to commodity fetishism?

Exercise 1.8 (G)

Discuss in groups:

- How is advertising related to commodity fetishism?
- How does commodity fetishism work in advertisements?
- Discuss an example.

Note

1 The short overview of some events in the history of money is based on the following source: A Comparative History of Money: Monetary History from Ancient Times to the Present Day: http://projects. exeter.ac.uk/RDavies/arian/amser/chrono1.html, http://projects.exeter.ac.uk/RDavies/arian/amser/ chrono2.html, http://projects.exeter.ac.uk/RDavies/arian/amser/chrono3.html, http://projects.exeter. ac.uk/RDavies/arian/amser/chrono4.html, http://projects.exeter.ac.uk/RDavies/arian/amser/chrono5. html, http://projects.exeter.ac.uk/RDavies/arian/amser/chrono6.html, http://projects.exeter.ac.uk/ RDavies/arian/amser/chrono7.html, http://projects.exeter.ac.uk/RDavies/arian/amser/chrono8.html, http://projects.exeter.ac.uk/RDavies/arian/amser/chrono9.html, http://projects.exeter.ac.uk/RDavies/ arian/amser/chrono10.html, http://projects.exeter.ac.uk/RDavies/arian/amser/chrono11.html, http:// projects.exeter.ac.uk/RDavies/arian/amser/chrono12.html, http://projects.exeter.ac.uk/RDavies/arian/ amser/chrono13.html, http://projects.exeter.ac.uk/RDavies/arian/amser/chrono14.html, http://projects. exeter.ac.uk/RDavies/arian/amser/chrono15.html, http://projects.exeter.ac.uk/RDavies/arian/amser/ chrono16.html, http://projects.exeter.ac.uk/RDavies/arian/amser/chrono17.html, http://projects.exeter. ac.uk/RDavies/arian/amser/chrono18.html

2

THE PROCESS OF EXCHANGE

Marx writes in the preface to *Capital Volume 1*'s first edition: "Beginnings are always difficult in all sciences. The understanding of the first chapter, especially the section that contains the analysis of commodities, will therefore present the greatest difficulty" (89). Chapter 1 is long and challenging. If you have come so far and have read and basically understood chapter 1, then you have already acquired an excellent foundation and are unlikely to find the chapters that follow difficult.

Chapter 2 is in comparison to chapter 1 relatively short. Marx extends the analysis of exchange and money made in chapter 1 with some comments. The chapter leads over from the analysis of the commodity in chapter 1 to the detailed analysis of money in chapter 3.

Agency and Capitalism's Structures

Marx points out that commodities are things that "cannot themselves go to market and perform exchanges" (178). A sale is a process that humans organise in social relations. For organising exchange of commodities owned by private property holders, humans must "recognize each other as owners of private property," which requires a "juridical relation, whose form is the contract" (178). A society in which generalised commodity production and exchange are the economy's basic social form of organisation therefore requires state institutions and laws that regulate, protect, and defend private property and markets.

A societal system such as capitalism limits human action. It is difficult to survive without money and exchange in a capitalist society. The structures of capital, markets, and commodities compel humans to position themselves on the inside of capitalism and to act within capitalist social relations. Marx therefore says that humans in capitalism are "on the economic stage [. . .] merely personifications of economic relations" and "the bearers of these economic relations" (179). This does not mean that economic structures mechanically determine human action and thoughts, but that they condition, exercise pressure, and limit the possibilities of human action. Most of us have relative freedom to decide if we want to be wageworkers (including freelancers) or strive to set up a business or become managers (who are in most cases also share-owners and share the norms of the capitalist class). It is, however, difficult to refuse to become neither of these because capitalism forces us to position ourselves and act within class relations. We can, however, not so easily bring about that we are monetarily rich so that we don't have to work because richness often has to do with inheritance, family relations, and mere luck. Capitalist structures allow relative freedom of action within given structures and at the same time limit the ways that are available for organising human survival.

The structures of capitalism compel commodity owners to exchange their commodities because "commodities are non-use-values for their owners, and use-values for their non-owners" (179). In an exchange relationship x commodity A = y commodity B, owner A, who sells a commodity, exchanges something that has no use-value for him and that s/he treats from the perspective of exchange in order to get hold of a use-value (money or another commodity). Owner B, who owns another commodity or money, and purchases A's commodity, views the thing s/he wants to obtain from the use-value perspective and treats his/her commodity (money, another use-value) as a non-use-value. In the exchange process, A's non-use value turns into a use-value for B, and B's exchange-value turns into a use-value for A. Historically gold and silver have become through "the action of society [. . .] the universal equivalent" (180)—money.

Entäußerung and Äußerung

Marx argues that goods are in principle exchangeable because they exist outside of human beings; they are "external to man" (182). The German terms "veräußerlicht" and "Veräußerung" (MEW 23, 102) have in chapter 2 been translated as "alienable" and "alienation" (182). A related German term is "Entäußerung." These terms cannot be properly translated. Alienation is not a good choice because it is also the translation of Marx's term "Entfremdung", which he uses for characterising class relations in which humans do not own the means of production and their products of labour. In "Entäußerung", an inner becomes an outer; it is turned outwards in a productive manner. Labour-power externalises the inner potentials of humans and is an expenditure of energy so that a good emerges. "Entäußerung" may therefore best be translated as "externalisation", not "alienation". "Äußerung" also means "utterance" in German, which is a symbolic externalisation of information. The inner is symbolically externalised by language in the communication process.

In the *Economic and Philosophic Manuscripts*, Marx speaks of "Arbeit" as "Ausdruck der menschlichen Tätigkeit innerhalb der Entäußerung, der Lebensäußerung als Lebensentäußerung" (MEW 40, 557). This passage was translated the following way: "[L]abor is only an expression of human activity within alienation, of the living of life as the alienating of life" (Marx 1844 [English], 128). Here again, "Äußerung" and "Entäußerung" were translated as "alienation", which creates the impression that a historical feature of society is an eternal and essential feature of all societies. So this particular translation is itself a form of fetishism. A more appropriate translation is that "work is only an expression of human activity within externalisation, the utterance of life as the externalisation of life". This complex-sounding passage actually means that Marx sees work as a form of externalisation so that life reproduces itself by externalising itself through human work in goods and services that satisfy human needs. Marx here speaks at an anthropological level valid for all societies, not at the level of specific historical class societies. There is an interesting implication of conceiving work as an utterance of life, in which life externalises itself. Externalisation takes on both physical and symbolic forms.

Utterance: Communication as Symbolic Äußerung

Humans' main form of symbolic utterance is communication through language. The implication of Marx's formulation is that also human communication as symbolic utterance (*symbolische Lebensäußerung*) is work—an externalisation of human thoughts that serves the need of social meaning making and the creation of understanding. In class societies, physical and symbolic externalisation (Entäußerung) turn into alienation and work into labour: we are not in control and do not own the means and products of our labour. In capitalism, these externalised products become a private property sold and acquired as commodities. This is true for both physical (e.g., tables) and informational (e.g., software) goods that are sold as commodities. Turning to the realm of ideology, we can say that in class societies, in which dominant groups succeed in ideologically distorting and manipulating representations of reality, subordinated humans taking up these ideologies positively are no longer themselves when they speak, but their utterances (Äußerungen) are alienated utterances and externalisations that are alienated from their true interests.

One of Money's Roles: It Is a Symbol of a Commodity's Price

Money as universal commodity serves "as the form of appearance of the value of commodities" (184). It is "a material embodiment of abstract and therefore equal human labour" (184). "The fact that money can, in certain functions, be replaced by mere symbols of itself, gave rise to another mistaken notion, that it is itself a mere symbol" (185) that is "the arbitrary product of human reflection" (186). A specific amount of gold or other material minted into a coin or a certain banknote symbolically represent a certain value of goods (e.g., £10). Marx stresses that a monetary exchange relation such as 1 computer = £500 is not an arbitrary idea, but reflects the amount of labour and material that humans think a computer is worth. Monetary price is information about what it costs to acquire a specific commodity on the market. This information is, however, also a symbol for the underlying labour that forms the substance of value. Just like any information, price information is not immaterial and arbitrary, but part of material reality itself and a specific complex symbolic representation of matter and material relations.

Marx generalises the role of symbols in exchange economies: Not only money is a symbol, but each commodity is a symbol too: "In this sense every commodity is a symbol, since, as value, it is only the material shell of the human labour expended on it" (185). Commodities are not just use-values that you can sensually experience, but also extra-sensual social values. "Custom fixes their values at definite magnitude" (182). Every commodity symbolises a specific average amount of labour. This symbolisation is translated into complex, nonlinear ways into yet another symbol: the commodity's price.

Exercises for Chapter 2

Group exercise (G)
Project exercise (P)

Key Categories: Exchange, Money, Externalisation, Symbol

Exercise 2.1 (P)

Work in groups: Conduct a search for historical and contemporary academic publications that document the history of exchange and money. Each group can focus on a specific time period (e.g., the history of exchange and money BC, 0–1000, 1000–1700, 1700–1900, 1900–2000, developments since 2000). Present the results. Reflect on the relationship among exchange, money, and symbols that Marx points out.

Exercise 2.2 (G)

Exchange-value in the form x commodity A = y commodity B or x commodity A = m units of Money M is not a universal economic condition, but rather a specific historical feature of particular societies. Societies tend to have aspects of altruism, mutual aid, and gifts, for which humans do not expect anything in return.

Work in groups: Conduct a search and document historical and contemporary examples, where information is treated not as exchange-value, but as gift without the expectation for returns. Reflect about why these forms of information are gifts and not commodities. What are the peculiarities of information that support that it is being turned into a gift? How exactly do capitalist companies manage to turn information into commodities?

3

MONEY, OR THE CIRCULATION OF COMMODITIES

Chapter 3 focuses on money. Money is the dialectical other of commodities: money cannot be discussed without its relation to commodities, and commodities have an inherent relation to money. So what Marx actually describes in chapter 3 is the relationship of money and commodities (figure 3.1).

Money's First Characteristic: Money as a Measure of Commodities' Economic Value

Marx points out three characteristics of money. Money's *first characteristic is that it is the measure of commodities' economic value*: "The first main function of gold is to supply commodities with the material for the expression of their values, or to represent their values as magnitudes of the same denomination" (188). Money allows to express the value of a commodity in monetary units: x commodity A = y money commodity.

Money is not just the measure of value, but also "the standard of price as a quantity of metal with a fixed weight" (192). Each commodity that has a price is expressed as a specific amount of money that in turn represents a specific quantity of gold. "For the standard of price, a certain weight of gold must be fixed as the unit of measurement" (192). Marx assumes a system in which 100% of the circulating money is backed by gold reserves.

Currencies' relation to gold today looks different than at the time when Marx wrote *Capital*. Around 1880, most countries in the world had started using such a gold standard and had ceased to back their currencies by silver. During World War I, the gold standard collapsed. From 1925 to 1931, there was the Gold Exchange Standard, in which only the USA and the UK backed their currencies in gold, whereas other countries used gold, dollars, or pounds as reserves. Under the Bretton Woods agreement (1944–1971), only the US dollar was backed to a large degree by gold, and other currencies had a fixed exchange rate with it. In the Bretton Woods system, 35US$ represented 1 troy ounce (0.0311034768 kg) of gold. Trade deficits, public debt caused by military investments in the Vietnam War, and inflation made it more and more difficult to back the dollar by gold. In 1971, the US cancelled the convertibility of the dollar into gold. The US dollar became a Fiat money that derives its value from regulations issued by governments or Central Banks. The end of the Bretton Woods system was also the end of the gold standard. It was substituted by a system with fiat monies that have floating exchange rates. All major currencies used today, including the US dollar, the Euro, the British pound, and the Japanese yen, are fiat monies. Only a small share of these currencies can be backed by gold reserves.

Commodity C   Money M

FIGURE 3.1   The subject-matter of *Capital Volume 1*'s chapter 3: the relationship of money and the commodity

Without money or another general equivalent of exchange there can be no prices. Money enables the existence of commodity prices. "Price is the money name of the labour objectified in a commodity" (195–196, see also 202). Marx points out that prices and labour-values stand in "a necessary relation" (196), but that this relation is not fixed, calculable, and determined. Prices can stand at, above, or below average commodity values. There is the possibility for "a quantitative incongruity between price and magnitude of value, i.e. the possibility that the price may diverge from the magnitude of value, is inherent in the price-form itself" (196). Marx argues that there are things "such as conscience, honour, etc." or "uncultivated land" (197) that can be sold for a price, but such prices do not have labour values because no human labour is objectified in them. "The expression of price is in this case imaginary" (197).

Money's Second Characteristic: Money as a Means of Circulation

A *second characteristic of money is that it is a means of circulation.* In the relationship C-M (commodity – money), "commodities as use-values confront money as exchange-value" (199). Both the good that is sold and the money that is paid for it have a use-value and an exchange-value. The commodity is made for the purpose of being used but must take on the exchange-form in order to be a use-value that is consumed. Money is made for the purpose of exchange but takes on the form of a general equivalent that organises exchange, which is a use-value of the circulation process. Marx describes this dialectic of the commodity and money:

> Exchange, however, produces a differentiation of the commodity into two elements, commodity and money, an external opposition which expresses the opposition between use-value and value which is inherent in it. In this opposition, commodities as use-values confront money as exchange-value. On the other hand, both sides of this opposition are commodities, hence themselves unities of use-value and value. But this unity of differences is expressed at two opposite poles, and at each pole in an opposite way. This is the alternating relation between the two poles: the commodity is in reality a use-value; its existence as a value appears only ideally, in its price, through which it is related to the real embodiment of its value, the gold which confronts it as its opposite. Inversely, the material of gold ranks only as the materialization of value, as money. It is therefore in reality exchange-value. Its use-value appears only ideally in the series of expressions of relative value within which it confronts all the other commodities as the totality of real embodiments of its utility. These antagonistic forms of the commodities are the real forms of motion of the process of exchange. (199).

Money enables the process of commodity circulation in which one commodity owner sells his good and thereby obtains money that he then uses for buying another commodity: C-M-C, Commodity-Money-Commodity (200)—"selling in order to buy" (200). This process consists of two parts: (a) C-M—the sale of a commodity or the first metamorphosis of the commodity

(200–205), and (b) M–C—the purchase of another commodity or the second/concluding metamorphosis of the commodity (205–209).

Marx points out that the process of selling in order to buy exists because of a social division of labour, in which not everyone is able to produce the commodities s/he needs to survive, but only specific commodities, which necessitates economic relations. The division of labour is "a web which has been, and continues to be, woven behind the backs of the producers of commodities" (201).

The Dialectic of the Commodity and Money

The dialectic of the commodity and money entails the sale of the commodity C–M and is at the same time a purchase M–C:

> The realization of a commodity's price, or of its merely ideal value-form, is therefore at the same time, and inversely, the realization of the merely ideal use-value of money; the conversion of a commodity into money is the conversion of money into a commodity. This single process is two-sided: from one pole, that of the commodity-owner, it is a sale, from the other pole, that of the money-owner, it is a purchase. In other words, a sale is a purchase, C–M is also M–C. (203)

The commodity's two forms, "the commodity-form and the money-form, exist simultaneously but at opposite poles, so every seller is confronted with a buyer, every buyer with a seller" (206).

In the process C–M–C, "[n]o one can sell unless someone else purchases. But no one directly needs to purchase because he has just sold. Circulation bursts through all the temporal, spatial and personal barriers imposed by the direct exchange of products" (209). C–M does not automatically result in M–C. The uncertainty if commodities can be sold respectively if people are willing to buy specific commodities with the money they have can result in an "external independence" of the two processes C–M and M–C that can make itself "violently [...] felt by producing—a crisis" (209). Such crises are called overproduction (commodities are produced that cannot be sold) or underconsumption (people do not buy commodities that are available on the market) crises.

In the process C–M–C–M–C–..., not just commodities circulate, but also money. "Money [...] haunts the sphere of circulation and constantly moves around within it" (213). Marx assumes a specific chain of sales as an example: "1 quarter of wheat—£2; 20 yards of linen—£2; 1 Bible—£2; 4 gallons of brandy—£2" (215). The sum of prices in this example is £8. There are four processes of sale and purchase: wheat, linen, a Bible, and brandy are sold for £2. Furthermore, each seller is a buyer and throws all of this money acquired by a previous sale into circulation by buying for the full amount of his own sales. The exception is the distiller, who sells brandy and acquires £2, but does not conduct a further purchase.

The Quantity of Circulating Money

Marx provides based on this example the following formula:

$$Quantity\ of\ circulating\ money = \frac{Sum\ of\ the\ prices\ of\ sold\ commodities}{Number\ of\ turnovers\ of\ money}$$

In the example, the quantity of circulating money = 8 / 4 = £2, which means that the total money circulating in exchange is £2.

The total sum of circulating money depends on the sum of commodity prices, the constancy or change of prices, and the speed of sales and purchases (217–218). As these three factors are variable, the total amount of money that is put to use in a specific period of time varies depending on the size of these influencing factors.

Coins, Paper Money, and the Role of the State

Marx discusses two specific forms of money that symbolise the value of commodities: the coin and paper money. Also, state power plays a role in this context because it can define how much gold or silver is represented by one coin or banknote so that it defines "a standard measure of prices" (222). State power is also needed for "replacing metallic money with tokens made of some other material, i.e. symbols which would perform the function of coins" (223). Historically paper money has taken on this role. "Relatively valueless objects, therefore, such as paper notes, can serve as coins in place of gold. [...] Pieces of paper on which money-names are printed, such as £1, £5, etc., are thrown into the circulation process from outside by the state" (223–224). It is possible to replace gold as money by "valueless symbols" (226).

Marx discusses with coins and paper money two important historical forms of money that continue to exist until today. The history of money is also a history of dephysicalisation: Whereas first coins were made out of silver or gold, the next steps in this process were the reduction of the amount of gold and silver in coins, the use of other materials such as copper or paper that represent specific amounts of gold, the use of future-oriented forms of money (credits, loans, mortgages, stocks, bonds, derivatives), the cancellation of the gold standard in 1971, plastic money (debit, cash and credit cards), electronic banking, and electronic currencies.

The state also decides which units and sub-units the money it issues has. Take, for example, the British pound sterling:[1] Before 1971, 1 pound had 20 shillings and 1 shilling 12 pence. In 1971, a new system was introduced, in which 1 pound consists of 100 pence. The old system goes back to a time when the weight of coins determined their value: 240 pence made of 1 pound weighed 1 pound of silver. So the term "pound" originally was a measure for the weight of money. Over the centuries the amount of real silver in the coins was gradually reduced and replaced by copper. In the 14th century, gold coins were introduced, but silver coins remained important. The Bank of England introduced paper money at the end of the 17th century.

Money's Third Characteristics: Money as a Means of Hoarding, Credit, and World Trade

The *third characteristic of money* is that, besides organising the circulation of commodities, it also takes on *additional roles*, such as the *enablement of hoarding, credit, and world trade*.

Hoarding means that "sales are not supplemented by subsequent purchases, money is immobilized" (227). The hoarding drive has to do with the fact that money "is the universal representative of material wealth because it is directly convertible into any other commodity" (230–231). Money plays a special role in modern societies because of its universal character. It is therefore unconvincing if somebody argues that the labour performed by users on corporate social media platforms such as Facebook, by which data emerges that is sold as commodity to advertisers that in return can target ads to users, is not unremunerated because users enjoy as "payment" the possibility to use social and communicative services. You cannot buy food or any other commodities by this social "payment", whereas you can buy all other commodities by money, which shows that this "payment" in comparison to money does not have the same universal features and can therefore not be considered as constituting a currency.

Money also enables the existence of credit, a system in which "the seller sells an existing commodity" and the buyer is "the representative of future money" so that "the buyer becomes a debtor" (233) who owes money to the creditor. There is a "promise of the buyer to pay" (234). In modern society's relationships between creditors and debtors, the state enforces this promise by law and dispossesses the debtor if s/he becomes unable to pay his/her debt back to the creditor at a specific point of time at which parts of the debt are due.

The globalisation of the economy evokes the phenomenon of trade in the world market so that money and commodities leave domestic and national spheres of circulation. For this purpose, a form of "world money" (240–244) is needed that helps organising world trade. "In world trade, commodities develop their value universally. Their independent value-form thus confronts them here too as world money" (240). Marx points out the important role that gold and silver have historically played in world trade as "money of the world" (243). "World money serves as the universal means of payment, as the universal means of purchase, and as the absolute social materialization of wealth as such (universal wealth)" (242).

The Spanish Silver Dollar, the US Dollar, and the Euro as Forms of World Money

The Spanish silver dollar was widely used as world money in world trade in the 18th and 19th centuries. With the rise of the gold standard, the possibility emerged that world trade could be organised in different currencies that were all in specific quantities related to gold. During the Bretton Woods system, the US dollar had the role of world money. Under the system of floating exchange rates, world trade is dependent on the fluctuations of currency exchange rates. Take a historical example: The Euro was introduced as coin and paper notes on January 1, 2002. Its aim has been to challenge the US dollar's role as world money. The exchange rate to the US dollar and the British pound sterling amounted on that day in 2002 to the following values: 1 Euro = 0.8863217652 US\$ = 0.6093652563 £. More than 12 years later, the exchange rates had substantially changed: 1 Euro = US\$1.3607386089 = £0.7948007412 £ (July 13, 2014).

Assume that a person had €10,000 on January 1, 2002. Back then s/he could have obtained around US\$8,863 or £6,094 for this money and could have bought 8,952 songs on iTunes USA for a price of US\$0.99 per song or 6,155 songs for a price of £0.99 on iTunes UK. If s/he, however, had waited for 12 years, until 2014, before converting the money, s/he would have obtained around US\$13,607 or £7,948. If the price of a song on iTunes remained constant at US\$0.99 and £0.99, she could now have obtained 13,744 songs on iTunes US and 8,028 songs on iTunes UK, which corresponds to 4,792 songs more in the USA and 1,873 more in the UK than in 2002. The example shows that a system of floating exchange rates confronts world trade with uncertainties.

Commodities produced under different conditions compete with each other on the world market. Countries and companies that have highly productive technologies can produce one piece of a certain commodity relatively quickly, whereas the production of a similar commodity in countries and companies with low productivity will be more labour-intensive. So the first commodity will have lower value than the second one. Developed countries tend to have higher levels of productivity because science and technology are more developed there. They are able to set the average values and prices on the world market. Companies and producers in developing countries with low productivity can, however, realistically only compete with Western countries if they sell at average prices set on the world market, which requires them to sell commodities below their individual values and to pay low wages in order to be competitive. They face fundamentally unequal conditions on the world market, which is why representatives of world systems theory have spoken of a transfer of value from the periphery to the centres of the capitalist world system in the form of unequal trade (Amin 1974, 13).

Tony Smith's Dialectical Interpretation of Chapter 3

The Hegelian-Marxist philosopher Tony Smith (1990, 83–97) has provided a dialectical interpretation of *Capital Volume 1*'s chapter 3: "The systematic ordering proposed by Marx first moves from 'money as measure of value' to 'money as means of circulation' (C-M-C), and then culminates with 'money as end of exchange' (M-C-M)" (Smith 1990, 85). The three steps in this dialectic are logically connected: first, each commodity needs to have a price assigned to it in order to be able to be exchanged. So the first step in the dialectic is the assignment of prices to commodities: x commodity A = y money M, w commodity B = z money M, etc. In a second step, money acts as means that organises the circulation of commodities so that commodities are sold in order to buy other commodities: C-M-C. But Marx shows that the two moments C-M and M-C are not automatically connected because one can sell and then decide not to buy, which is one of the sources of overproduction and underconsumption crises. Therefore in the third logical step, money "becomes the end of exchange itself" (Smith 1990, 89): Sellers of commodities view money as an end-in-itself in order to hoard/accumulate it, save it in order to later make payments of bills to debtors, to keep it in order to speculate, or to derive benefits from investments on global markets. Money as an end-in-itself is the cycle M-C-M.

Money's Dialectic

Figure 3.2 summarises the dialectic of money. Money in the first logical step is an identity—the price: it sets the price for commodities that in this logic step have a separate existence in themselves. In the second logical step, commodities can be exchanged in the social form C-M-C. Money organises another social purpose outside of and mediated by the price form—the exchange of commodities. It is money-for-another. The connection of C-M and M-C in the cycle C-M-C is artificial because nobody can be forced to buy commodities after s/he has sold her/his commodity and acquired money. This dialectical tension between buying and selling is sublated to a new logical level by money becoming an end in and of itself in the social form M-C-M, which brings together the monetary identity of the price form and the monetary difference of the exchange and circulation of different commodities as dialectical unity in diversity of money's roles: money sets prices of commodities and enables the circulation of commodities, which are necessary preconditions for money-in-and-for-itself that is an identity and difference at the same time, a unity-of-diversity of money's roles.

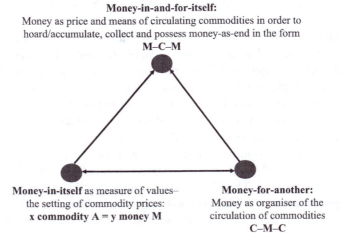

Money-in-and-for-itself:
Money as price and means of circulating commodities in order to
hoard/accumulate, collect and possess money-as-end in the form
M–C–M

Money-in-itself as measure of values–
the setting of commodity prices:
x commodity A = y money M

Money-for-another:
Money as organiser of the
circulation of commodities
C–M–C

FIGURE 3.2 The dialectic of money in *Capital Volume 1*'s chapter 3

Ferruccio Rossi-Landi's Analogy between Communication and Exchange-Value/Money

The Italian Marxist semiotician Ferruccio Rossi-Landi (1921-1985) thought about the connection of language and the economy. His achievement is that he interpreted communication as a work process and thereby questioned the separation of work and communication as well as the economy and culture. For Rossi-Landi, language and communication are work that produce words, sentences, interconnected sentences, arguments, speeches, essays, lectures, books, codes, artworks, literature, science, groups, civilisation, and the linguistic world as totality (Rossi-Landi 1983, 133–136). As "words and messages do not exist in nature" (Rossi-Landi 1983, 36), they must be the products of human work that generates use-values. They are use-values because they satisfy the human needs of expression, communication, and social relations (Rossi-Landi 1983, 37). "Like the other products of human work, words, expressions and messages have a use-value or utility insofar as they satisfy needs, in this case, the basic needs for expression and communication with all the changing stratifications that have historically grown up around them" (Rossi-Landi 1983, 50).

Rossi-Landi goes, however, one step too far in trying to apply Marx's critique of the political economy of capitalism and so tries to find a homology between language and the specifics of capitalism such as value, exchange-value, capital, the commodity, and money. He draws homologies between human language and capitalism. For example, he argues that x commodity A = y commodity B corresponds to a linguistic statement such as "God is the omnipotent being", in which "God" is "measured" by setting it "in relationship with the use value of 'omnipresent being'" (Rossi-Landi 1983, 60). He also introduces the concept of linguistic money, by which he means that language is "a means of universal exchange. He who speaks can address anyone, he can say anything—similarly a person who has money in his pocket can go into any store and buy any commodity" (Rossi-Landi 1983, 162). "Linguistic money is that aspect of the language which permits and indeed promotes communication with anyone whomsoever in addition to and beyond the needs which emerge in the division of labor" (Rossi-Landi 1983, 164).

Marx shows in chapter 3 that money is a measure of commodity-values, that it is a means for organising the circulation of commodities through exchanges in the form x commodity A = y money M, and that it enables hoarding, credit, and world trade. Rossi-Landi's homology between capitalism and language is problematic because the first is a historic feature and the second an anthropological quality of society. Setting historical and anthropological qualities as homologous can create the impression that capitalism is, like language, an eternal feature of society. So the problem of Rossi-Landi's argument is that his homology fetishises capitalism. When we form sentences or speak with others, we do not perform measurements and weigh one word or sentence against another word or sentence in a quantitative manner. Money has the role of expressing and representing the amount of average labour objectified in commodities so that they can be exchanged. It quantifies the value of commodities. Human language is fundamentally different from money. It is first and foremost qualitative in character; it has certain general rules agreed upon by custom over hundreds of years (syntax), operates with meanings of combinations of symbols (semantics), and is used in specific contexts that interact with meanings (pragmatics). It is a combination of linguistic form and structure, social interpretation, and societal effects. The German Marxist information scientist and philosopher of science Klaus Fuchs-Kittowski argues in this context: "Information is relational: information appears as a triple of form (syntax), content (semantic) and effect (pragmatic) generated and used in a multistage process of (in)forming, meaning and evaluation" (Fuchs-Kittowski 2014, 53–54).

Why Humans Are Not Computers

Computers can imitate the pure syntactical dimension of human language; that is, the combination of symbols to words and words to sentences (e.g., in translation software such as Google Translate).

They are, however, incapable of understanding the semantics and pragmatics of information, which feeds back to errors on the syntactic level (e.g., a computer translation of sentences from one language into another often has mistakes because the computer cannot understand the context and meanings of words and sentences). When we think or speak, we do not make measurements such as "1 word A = 2 words B". When we communicate with others, we do not quantify sentences in the form "1 sentence of person A = 2 sentences of person B". We can organise society without measuring letters, words, sentences, and interactions. Humans are not computers and computers can never substitute human intelligence. Human language and thought is far more complex than computing.

Hegel was critical of the mathematical logic of pure quantitative computation. He expressed his doubts when discussing the relationship of philosophy and mathematics. It would be wrong that "quantity is elevated to the rank of an absolute category", as mathematics does, because metaphysical ideas that concern human thought, such as "freedom, law, ethical life, and even God himself [. . .] cannot be measured and computed" (Hegel 1830a, Note to §99). "In mathematics, numbers have no conceptual content, no meaning outside equality or inequality, that is, outside relations which are entirely external; neither in themselves nor in connection are they a thought" (Hegel 1812/1833, 32). Computing does not know good and bad, metaphysics, political norms. It is a pure quantification and combination of quantifying operations. Not just philosophy, but human language and communication in general concern themselves with such questions of meaning, ethics, and politics that a computer can never address. The calculation x commodity A = y commodity B = m money M is in contrast a quantitative calculation that computers can perform. Humans' qualitative judgments do not work based on this logic.

Take, for example, a family and their baby: They speak to the baby by making use of language, but the baby for a long time does not speak any words and so cannot answer in this specific language. The family, however, does not measure how much time they have invested in order to take care of the baby and how much time it took until the baby started speaking. They do not expect a specific quantity of a good in return for the time they invest in speaking to the baby. Only this altruistic logic, which transcends measurement, can make language happen and results in the phenomenon that parents pass on language to their children.

If two friends speak to each other and one is sad and they talk about it, then A may talk for two hours about why s/he is sad and B only talks for five minutes. A, however, does not expect from B to then talk another hour and 55 minutes because their friendship transcends standards of measurement. B can expect that A listens to him/her when s/he is sad, but if they are true friends then talking to and helping each other is not a game of measurements, but a form of voluntary altruism brought about by feelings of empathy and belonging together.

Linguistic Products as Commodities

Language does not function based on the logic x commodity A = y money M. Its essence is that it is qualitative and transcends the logic of measurement. This does, however, not mean that the products of language and communication cannot be turned into commodities. In commodity-producing societies, the access to linguistic products can certainly be commodified, which then results in exchange-relationships and measurements such as the following:

- one hour of psychological consultation = £60
- one hour of financial advice = £100
- one hour of nutritional consulting = £40
- one hour of private tutoring for a pupil = £30

- one hour of private child care = £20
- entry to one theatre performance = £12.50
- translation of a text from German to English, one word = £0.1
- proofreading of a book or article, one word = £0.05
- ghost-writing of a fiction book, 80,000 words = £10,000

Rossi-Landi misses the difference between the foundational qualities of human language and the capitalist organisation of language and communication. Communication as such is alien to the commodity form; it can in a capitalist society however be force-fit into measurements such as 1 linguistic unit = £y. Language and communication are qualities of society that all humans need in order to survive just like food, water, shelter, love, access to nature, education, rest, etc. Such foundational qualities of human life are also termed commons: they are common features of all societies and common necessities for the existence of all humans. Communication is symbolic commoning, the making-common and sharing of information, the social co-construction of meaning. In communication, we refer to a common pool of language and linguistic skills in order to try to create common understandings of society.

Because the social (= welfare), natural (= access to nature), and communication commons (= access to means of communication) are so crucial for humans to exist, it is feasible to argue that from a normative perspective they should never be treated as a commodity.

If commons are turned into commodities, basic features of human life become exclusive for those who can afford them, which is likely to result in inequalities. Consider a society in which you have to pay for surgeries and seeing a doctor. The rich will be able to afford health care, whereas many poor will die from curable diseases because they do not have the money for getting treatment. If communication costs money, then comparable inequalities will emerge. If you, for example, have to pay for the education of your children, then those having more money tend to be able to get access to higher quality education for their children.

Exercises for Chapter 3

Group exercise (G)
Project exercise (P)

Key Categories: Money, Price, Commons, Communication Commons

Exercise 3.1 (P)

Language and communication are in essence different from money and capital. They can, however, in capitalism be turned into commodities.

Make a list of communication services and linguistic products that are sold as commodities (comparable to the list of examples that I provided at the end of the chapter).

Work in groups: Each group focuses on one communication service or linguistic product and tries to find price information for it (within the country you live). Search on the Internet, visit or phone local providers, and ask about prices saying that you work on an exercise, etc. Each group should try to find prices from about 10 providers and then calculate the average price.

Report your results in class. Compare the average prices: What are the most expensive and what the cheapest services? How can the price differences be explained?

Exercise 3.2 (G or P)

Work in groups: Conduct a search for books, book chapters, and academic articles for the term "commons". Read and compare the literature in order to come up with your own synthetic definition of what commons are. Discuss and give reasons for why communication is a commons. Discuss what the differences are between communication as commons and communication as commodity.

Note

1   For a detailed history, see the Wikipedia entry on the pound sterling. http://en.wikipedia.org/wiki/Pound_sterling (accessed on July 28, 2015).

PART II
THE TRANSFORMATION OF MONEY INTO CAPITAL

4

THE GENERAL FORMULA FOR CAPITAL

Chapter 4 is a short but nonetheless fairly important chapter because in it Marx introduces the notions of capital and surplus-value. After all, his book is called *Capital: A Critique of Political Economy*, which shows that capital must be an important theoretical concept for Marx. Chapter 4 allows us to find out what he exactly means by capital.

Did Marx Use the Term "Capitalism"?

Given that capital is a key category for Marx, one wonders if he also used the now fairly common term "capitalism" for characterising a society or economy in which the capitalist mode of production prevails. Looking at the English translation of *Capital Volume 1*, it appears like he frequently used this word. He speaks of "the application of machinery under capitalism" (492) [in the German version: "kapitalistischen Anwendung der Maschinerie" (Marks and Engels, *Marx Engels Werke*, hereafter MEW 23, 416)], the "moral degradation which arises out of the exploitation by capitalism of the labour of women and children" (522) ["kapitalistischen Exploitation der Weiber- und Kinderarbeit" (MEW 23, 421)], "the apologists for capitalism" (566) ["jene Apologeten" (MEW 23, 462)], "the transition to capitalism" (645) ["Übergang" zur "kapitalistische[n] Produktionsweise" (MEW 23, 533)], "capitalism's illusions about freedom" (680) ["Mystifikationen der kapitalistischen Produktionsweise, alle ihre Freiheitsillusionen" (MEW 23, 562)], "money will therefore be less in the nation with a more developed capitalist mode of production than in the nation with a less developed capitalism" (702) ["relative Wert des Geldes wird also kleiner sein bei der Nation mit entwickelterer kapitalistischer Produktionsweise als bei der mit wenig entwickelter" (MEW 23, 584)], "in the period of capitalism" (733) ["in der kapitalistischen Periode" (MEW 23, 613)], "the basis of capitalism, a system in which the worker does not employ the means of production, but the means of production employ the worker" (798) ["auf kapitalistischer Grundlage, wo nicht der Arbeiter die Arbeitsmittel, sondern die Arbeitsmittel den Arbeiter anwenden" (MEW 23, 674)], "under capitalism" (798) ["kapitalistisch" (MEW 23, 798)], "a feature of every process of production and not merely that of capitalism" (986) ["jedem Produktionsprozess, nicht nur dem des Kapitals, eigen ist" (Marx 1863/1864, 80)], "enslaved by the relationships of capitalism" (990) ["unter der Knechtschaft des Kapitalverhältnisses" (Marx 1863/1864, 86)], "the life-blood of capitalism" (1007) ["Lebensblut des Kapitals" (Marx 1863/1864, 106)], "the soil from which modern capitalism has grown" (1023) ["Form, woraus sich zum Teil das moderne Kapitalverhältnis entwickelt hat" (Marx 1863/1864, 124)], "the transition to capitalism proper" (1023) ["den Übergang zum eigentlichen

Kapitalverhältnis" (Marx 1863/1864, 124)], "the standpoint of capitalism" (1039) ["Standpunkt des Kapitals" (Marx 1863/1864, 146)], "subjugated by capitalism" (1042) ["von ihr (der herrschenden Produktionsweise) noch nicht subsumierten" (Marx 1863/1864, 150)], "the standpoint of capitalism itself" (1045) ["Standpunkt der kapitalistischen Produktion" (Marx 1863/1864, 154)], "the number of people profitable to capitalism" (1049) ["nur die für das Kapital profitable Menschenzahl" (Marx 1863/1864, 158)], "the standpoint of capitalism" (1051) ["vom kapitalistischen Standpunkt" (Marx 1863/1864, 160)], "the relations of capitalism" (1052) ["Kapitalverhältnis" (Marx 1863/1864, 162)], "in capitalism" (1054) ["die kapitalistische Produktionsweise" (Marx 1863/1864, 164)], "the productive forces of capitalism" (1054) ["Produktivkräfte des Kapitals" (Marx 1863/1864, 165)], "the framework of capitalism" (1055) ["kapitalistischen Zusammenhang" (Marx 1863/1864, 166)], "this development first occurs in capitalism" (1058) ["zuerst (. . .) in der kapitalistischen Produktionsweise diese Entwicklung stattfindet" (Marx 1863/1864, 170)], "the mode of production specific to capitalism," (1062) ["der spezifisch kapitalistischen Produktionsweise" (Marx 1863/1864, 173)], "the contradictory form of capitalism" (1065) ["die gegensätzliche Form der kapitalistischen Produktionsweise" (Marx 1863/1864, 177)].

The original German formulations provided in square brackets show that the translations are rather sloppy and that Marx used terms such as "kapitalistisch" (capitalist), "kapitalistische Produktionsweise" (capitalist mode of production), "kapitalistische Periode" (capitalist period), "Kapital" (capital), "Kapitalverhältnis" (capital relation, relation of capital), "herrschende Produktionsweise" (dominant mode of production), "kapitalistischer Zusammenhang" (capitalist context). In fact Marx did not use the term "Kapitalismus" (capitalism) in *Capital Volume 1*. The circumstance that the term, however, appears fairly often in the English translation and also in Ernest Mandel's introduction shows that people convinced by Marx's analysis seem to be keen to use it. Given that Marx uses the adjectives "kapitalistisch" and "kapitalistische" (capitalist) more than 330 times in *Capital Volume 1* for characterising the system and mode of production he analyses, one can speculate that he would not mind usage of the terms "Kapitalismus" and "capitalism" as characterisations homologous to the terms he uses because these are the nouns corresponding to the adjective "kapitalistisch" and "capitalist".

There is of course a certain interpretable difference between "capitalist mode of production" and "capitalism". The first term is mainly focused on the economy, whereas capitalism can signify both a mode of the organisation of the economy and society. One can argue that the capitalist mode of economic production shapes modern society at large: Modern society is a form of society dominated by the accumulation of money capital in the economy, power in politics, and reputation/distinction in culture. These forms of accumulation are all interlinked. The economy shapes modern society and its subsystems in the form of the logic of accumulation that takes on specific forms with relative autonomy in each of these subsystems that mutually shape each other. Society's subsystems are therefore identical and different at the same time.

The Difficulty of Translating Marx

When starting to write this book I had to make a choice regarding to which English translation of Marx's *Capital* I will refer. The two most commonly read English versions are the Penguin edition, which was translated by Ben Fowkes and introduced by Ernest Mandel, and the first English translation, which was published in 1887, translated by Samuel Moore and Edward Aveling, and edited by Friedrich Engels. The Moore/Aveling edition has been published as Volume 35 of the Marx Engels Collected Works (MECW). I have no doubt that the Fowkes translation is the better one and have therefore used the Penguin edition of *Capital* as foundation for this book. Fowkes points out in the translator's preface that the English language has changed since the 19th century and that Engels tried to make the translation of Marx's book as popular and easily readable as possible, which resulted in simplifications. According to Fowkes, it is no longer necessary to water down *Capital* in order to spare the reader (who was, in any case, generally put off by the bulk of the book rather than its difficulty). Hence whole sentences omitted by Engels can be restored, and theoretical difficulties, instead of being swept under the carpet, can be exposed to the daylight, in so far as the English language is capable of this. This comment relates above all to German philosophical terms, used repeatedly by Marx in *Capital*, as indeed elsewhere. In translating these, I have tried not to prejudge the philosophical questions, the question of Marx's relation to Hegel and that of the relation between his philosophy and his political economy, but rather to present a text which would permit the reader to form his own view. (87–88)

An Example Translation and Its Problems

Let us consider two examples. Here is a passage from the most widely read German edition (Marx Engels Werke [MEW] Band 23).

MEW 23, 558 + Urfassung[1] von 1867, 521: "Von diesen Widersprüchen abgesehn, würde ein direkter Austausch von Geld, d.h. vergegenständlichter Arbeit, mit lebendiger Arbeit entweder das Wertgesetz aufheben, welches sich grade erst auf Grundlage der kapitalistischen Produktion frei entwickelt, oder die kapitalistische Produktion selbst aufheben, welche grade auf der Lohnarbeit beruht".

MECW 35, 536: "Apart from these contradictions, a direct exchange of money, i.e., of realised labour, with living labour would either do away with the law of value which only begins to develop itself freely on the basis of capitalist production, or do away with capitalist production itself, which rests directly on wage labour".

Penguin, 676: "Apart from these contradictions, a direct exchange of money, i.e., of objectified labour, with living labour would either supersede the law of value, which only begins to develop freely on the basis of capitalist production, or supersede capitalist production itself, which rests directly on wage labour".

In my view, a better translation is as follows:

> Apart from these antagonisms, a direct exchange of money—that is, objectified labour—with living labour would either sublate the law of value that just now develops itself freely on the basis of capitalist production, or sublate capitalist production itself that precisely rests on wage-labour.

The Hegelian term "Aufhebung" has three meanings in German: to eliminate, to preserve, and to lift up/transcend. Doing away is not a good translation. Supersession is somewhat better. The most common translation, however, is "sublation".

Another Example Translation

MEW, 791:"Die aus der kapitalistischen Produktionsweise hervorgehende kapitalistische Aneignungsweise, daher das kapitalistische Privateigentum, ist die erste Negation des individuellen, auf eigne Arbeit gegründeten Privateigentums. Aber die kapitalistische Produktion erzeugt mit der Notwendigkeit eines Naturprozesses ihre eigne Negation. Es ist Negation der Negation. Diese stellt nicht das Privateigentum wieder her, wohl aber das individuelle Eigentum auf Grundlage der Errungenschaft der kapitalistischen Ära: der Kooperation und des Gemeinbesitzes der Erde und der durch die Arbeit selbst produzierten Produktionsmittel".

Kapital, Urfassung [original edition, 1st German edition], 1867, 744–745: "Die kapitalistische Produktions- und Aneignungsweise, daher das kapitalistische Privateigenthum, ist die erste Negation des individuellen, auf eigene Arbeit gegründeten Privateigenthums. Die Negation der kapitalistischen Produktion wird durch sie selbst, mit der Nothwendigkeit eines Naturprozesses, producirt. Es ist Negation der Negation. Diese stellt das individuelle Eigentum wieder her, aber auf Grundlage der Errungenschaft der kapitalistischen Aera, der Cooperation freier Arbeiter und ihrem Gemeineigenthum an der Erde und den durch die Arbeit selbst producirten Produktionsmitteln".

MECW, 751: "The capitalist mode of appropriation, the result of the capitalist mode of production, produces capitalist private property. This is the first negation of individual private property, as founded on the labour of the proprietor. But capitalist production begets, with the inexorability of a law of Nature, its own negation. It is the negation of negation. This does not re-establish private property for the producer, but gives him individual property based on the acquisition of the capitalist era: *i.e.*, on cooperation and the possession in common of the land and of the means of production".

Penguin, 929: "The capitalist mode of appropriation, which springs from the capitalist mode of production, produces capitalist private property. This is the first negation of individual private property, as founded on the labour of its proprietor. But capitalist production begets, with the inexorability of a natural process, its own negation. This is the negation of the negation. It does not re-establish private property, but it does indeed establish individual property on the basis of the achievements of the capitalist era: namely co-operation and the possession in common of the land and the means of production produced by labour itself".

Taking into account both the formulation in the MEW and the Urfassung, in my view a better English translation is as follows:

> The capitalist mode of appropriation emerging from the capitalist mode of production, hence capitalist private property, is the first negation of private property founded on an individual's own labour. But capitalist production produces with the necessity of a natural process its own negation. It is the negation of the negation. This does not reestablish private property, but indeed individual property on the basis of the capitalist era's attainments: the cooperation of free labourers, their common possession of the Earth, and the means of production produced by labour itself.

There is a difference between "a law of Nature" and "a natural process". The second translation is closer to Marx's original formulation. The Fowkes translation published by Penguin has its own imprecisions. It is, however, in my view the best available English translation and will provide a good foundation for everyone undertaking the project of reading *Capital Volume 1*. There is, however, no doubt that even Fowkes's translation could be much improved and that a new translation is due.

Capital's Preconditions

Marx describes capital as emerging from two logical preconditions: the processes C − M − C— "selling in order to buy" (247)—and M − C − M—"buying in order to sell" (248). He characterises the two processes' commonalities and differences.

> What however first and foremost distinguishes the two paths C − M − C and M − C − M from each other is the inverted order of succession of the two opposed phases of circulation. The simple circulation of commodities begins with a sale and ends with a purchase, while the circulation of money as capital begins with a purchase and ends with a sale. In the one case both the starting-point and the terminating-point of the movement are commodities, in the other they are money. The whole process is mediated in the first form by money, and in the second, inversely, by a commodity. (249)

C − M − C consists of C − M and M − C, M − C − M of M − C and C − M. So the two circuits have identical components, but are nonetheless at the same time polar opposites because they have different starting points and end-points. C − M − C starts with a commodity and ends with the consumption of a use-value, whereas M − C − M starts with money and ends with money and so is all about exchange-value (250). There are two logical possibilities for C − M − C and M − C − M: In the circuit C − M − C, the seller of the commodity C who obtains money M can buy another commodity C_2 or the same commodity C. In the circuit M − C − M, the buyer of the commodity C can sell it for the same amount M or a different amount M_2. The option that in buying to sell (M − C − M) one sells the commodity for the purchase price, is rather "purposeless" and "absurd" (251) because the fetish character of money advances individualism, hoarding, and egoism.

The Circuit of Capital: The Dialectic of the Circulation of Commodities, Money, and Capital

The two interconnected processes C − M − C and M − C − M give rise to a circuit that is the dialectical unity of the two: M − C − M′.

> The cotton originally bought for £100 is for example re-sold at £100 + £10, i.e. £110. The complete form of this process is therefore M − C − M′, where M′ = M + ΔM, i.e. the original sum advanced plus an increment. This increment or excess over the original value I call "surplus-value". The value originally advanced, therefore, not only remains intact while in circulation, but increases its magnitude, adds to itself a surplus-value, or is valorized. And this movement converts it into capital. (251)

M − C − M′ means buying in order to sell at a higher price. Money becomes capital if in the commodity circuit M − C − M′ the commodity C is sold at a price that is larger than M and the resulting surplus is reinvested for again buying in order to sell. Capital is money aimed at increasing itself, buying in order to sell so that more money is the result, and selling in order to again buy commodities that are again sold in order to accumulate more money. The two processes M − C and C − M that make up the simple circulation of commodities C − M − C and of money M − C − M are in the circulation of capital M − C − M′ fused in such a way that there is a dynamic accumulation of capital:

$$M − C − M′ = M + ΔM − C′ − M″ = M′ + ΔM′ − C″ − M‴ = M″$$
$$+ ΔM″ − C‴ − M⁗ = M‴ + ΔM‴ − \ldots.$$

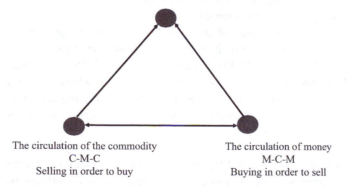

The circulation of capital, M-C-M': Buying in order to sell at a higher price = the general formula of capital
M-C-M′ = M+ΔM-C′-M″ = M′+ΔM′-C″-M‴ = M″+ΔM″-C‴-M⁗ = M‴+ΔM‴- ....

The circulation of the commodity
C-M-C
Selling in order to buy

The circulation of money
M-C-M
Buying in order to sell

FIGURE 4.1 The dialectic of the circulation of commodities, money, and capital in *Capital Volume 1's* chapter 4

What Is Capital? What Is a Capitalist?

Marx characterises capital as "valorization of value" (253), "an end in itself" (253), "limitless" (253), "ceaseless augmentation of value [. . .] achieved by the [. . .] capitalist by [. . .] throwing his money again and again into circulation" (254–255), "self-valorization" (255), value that as "subject [. . .] lays golden eggs" and adds "value to itself" (255), the process of "making still more money out of money" (256), "value [. . .] as a self-moving substance" (256), "value in process, money in process" that "preserves and multiplies itself within circulation, emerges from it with an increased size, and starts the same cycle again and again" (256), "money which begets money" (256), the process of "buying in order to sell dearer" (256), "money which is worth more money, value which is greater than itself" (257). The point is that the capitalist's aim is to constantly increase capital by investing and reinvesting money and buying and selling commodities at prices that are higher than the investment costs.

Marx in chapter 4 also introduces the notion of the capitalist—"the conscious bearer of this movement" $M - C - M'$ who "as the possessor of money becomes a capitalist. His person, or rather his pocket, is the point from which the money starts, and to which it returns" (254). The "appropriation of ever more wealth in the abstract is the sole driving force behind his operations that he functions as a capitalist, i.e. as capital personified and endowed with consciousness and a will. [. . .] the capitalist is a rational miser" (254).

Capitalists are confronted with the structures of capital, accumulation, and competition. They certainly can choose not to be capitalists and to rather earn a living as wageworkers, but are because of commodity fetishism's ideological effects rather unlikely to do so. As capitalists they cannot refuse to accumulate because of the pressures exerted by competition on them. They have to try to increase their capital, exploit workers by letting them produce ever more commodities that are sold at prices higher than the investment costs, etc. Otherwise their businesses will collapse, which may mean an end of their personal wealth and survival. Capital is a structure that compels capitalists to act within class relations and competitive relations.

Surplus-Value: A Key Category

Marx uses the notion of surplus-value in chapter 4 as a monetary increment/surplus ΔM over the invested sum of money M: $M' = M + \Delta M$. It should be noted that he later in the course of his exposition of capital introduces the term "profit" for monetary surplus-value. Surplus-value also plays a role at the level of labour-time. A commodity has certain investment costs and yields a monetary profit. It is produced during a certain average production time. This production time can be divided into one part that represents the investment costs and another part that represents profit. The labour time that represents profit is unpaid labour time or surplus labour time. Marx also uses the notion of surplus-value for this part of the working day.

The Argentinian-Mexican Marxist philosopher Enrique Dussel argues that in his work on the *Grundrisse*, Marx had "for the first time in his work [. . .] discovered the category of surplus value" (Dussel 2008, 77) in December 1857. The *Grundrisse* (Marx 1857/1858) was Marx's first rough draft of *Das Kapital*. Marx makes clear in the passages in the *Grundrisse*, where he introduces surplus-value, that by this concept he not just means monetary profit, but also the unpaid labour-time that capitalists appropriate from workers, that objectifies itself in the commodity, and that is the foundation of profit when the commodity is sold:

> The surplus value which capital has at the end of the production process—a surplus value which, as a higher price of the product, is realized only in circulation, but, like all prices, is realized in it by already being ideally presupposed to it, determined before they enter into

it—signifies, expressed in accord with the general concept of exchange value, that the labour time objectified in the product—or amount of labour (expressed passively, the magnitude of labour appears as an amount of space ; but expressed in motion, it is measurable only in time)—is greater than that which was present in the original components of capital. This in turn is possible only if the labour objectified in the price of labour is smaller than the living labour time purchased with it. (Marx 1857/1858, 321)

The matter can also be expressed in this way: if the worker needs only half a working day in order to live a whole day, then, in order to keep alive as a worker, he needs to work only half a day. The second half of the day is forced labour; surplus labour. What appears as surplus value on capital's side appears identically on the worker's side as surplus labour in excess of his requirements as worker, hence in excess of his immediate requirements for keeping himself alive. (Marx 1857/1858, 324–325)

It also becomes apparent that given the transformation problem of how to transform working hours into monetary prices, there is no simple way of calculating actual profits from surplus-labour and the other way around. Not all commodities may be sold and therefore not all of them may yield a profit. Surplus-labour as the substance of surplus-value becomes however already crystallised and objectified in commodities during their production.

Capital as a Dialectic of Money and Commodities

Capital as the self-increasing circulation of money in the form $M - C - M' - C'' - M'' - C''' - M''' - \ldots$ is a dialectic of money and commodities: Money is invested for buying commodities and producing new commodities; these are sold at a higher price so that more money is achieved, which is invested for again buying commodities and producing new commodities; these are again turned into a larger sum of money, etc. This dialectic of capital as the dialectical unity of money and commodities is visualised in figure 4.2. The figure also shows how Marx logically unfolds this dialectic in *Capital Volume 1*: He first discusses the commodity in chapter 1, then turns to money in chapter 3, and introduces the notion of capital as dialectic of the commodity and money in chapter 4.

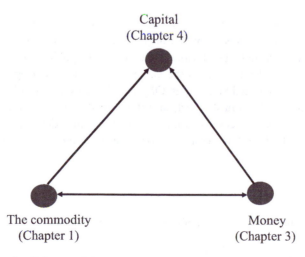

FIGURE 4.2 Capital as the dialectic of the commodity and money and the logical unfolding of this dialectic in *Capital Volume 1*

Exercise for Chapter 4

Group exercise (G)
Project exercise (P)

Key Categories: Capital, Surplus-Value

Exercise 4.1 (G or P)

Forbes 2000 is an annually published list of the world's largest transnational corporations.

Work in groups: Have a look at the current Forbes 2000 list. Each group selects one corporation active in the realm of information—that is, a company belonging to one of the following realms of production: advertising, broadcasting, communications equipment, computer hardware, computer services, computer storage devices, consumer electronics, Internet services, printing and publishing, semiconductors, software and programming, telecommunications.

Look at the annual financial reports of your selected company and the figures published by Forbes 2000 for the current and previous years in order identify for this specific corporation the following data *for the past 10 years (P)/for the past year (G)*:

1. How large is the total capital (capital assets) of the corporation, and how has it developed over the past 10 years (P)/in the past year (G)?
2. How large are the monetary profits of the corporation and how have they developed over the past 10 years (P)/over the past year (G)?
3. How large is the wage sum the corporation paid in the last year (G)/in each of the past 10 years (P) to its employees? How have the wages developed in comparison to the growth of capital assets and profits?
4. Who are the main shareholders of the corporation and which percentage of shares and voting power do they hold? How have the company's main shareholders and their percentage of shares and voting power looked over the past year (G)/developed over the past 10 years (P)?
5. Who are the members of the corporation's board of directors (G)? How large is their compensation? How has membership of the board developed over the past 10 years (P)? How has the compensation of individual board members developed over the past 10 years (P)?

Visualise and summarise the results with the help of graphs and tables.

Note: In financial reports, profits are often called net revenue(s) or net profit(s). In most countries, corporations—that is, stock trading companies—are obliged to publish annual financial reports. For the USA, these data are available online in the U.S. Securities and Exchange Commission's (SEC's) EDGAR database. They are called SEC filings. Of particular relevance for obtaining the data for this exercise are SEC filing 10-K (annual report) and the annual Proxy Statement. For non-US companies, I recommend that you check the companies' websites in order to look for financial reports. Such reports can often be found in website sections that have titles such as "Investor Relations" or "Finances".

Note

1   The *Urfassung* is the first German edition of *Capital*. It was republished in 1980 by Gerstenberg Verlag.

5

CONTRADICTIONS IN THE GENERAL FORMULA

Simple Commodity Production

Marx distinguishes the general formula of capital from the simple circulation of commodities C-M-C, in which "two owners of commodities buy from each other, and on the date of settlement the amounts they owe to each other balance out equally" (259). This means that in simple commodity production, no monetary profits are being made. The formula of capital M-C-M′ distinguishes itself from simple commodity production by "the inverted order of succession of the two antithetical processes, sale and purchase" (258): first there is a purchase M-C and then a sale C-M′. "As a capitalist, I buy commodities from A and sell them again to B, but as a simple owner of commodities I sell them to B and then purchase further commodities from A" (258). Marx points out that simple commodity production is an "exchange of equivalents" with no "formation of surplus-value" (262).

Production and Exchange

Marx criticises the assumption of classical political economists such as Étienne Bonnot de Condillac (1714–1780), Samuel Phillips Newman (1797–1842), and Robert Torrens (1780–1864) that "the circulation of commodities" and commerce are a "source of surplus-value" (261). In such attempts "lurks an inadvertent substitution, a confusion of use-value and exchange-value" (261). Marx points out that the "formation of surplus-value, and therefore the transformation of money into capital, can consequently be explained neither by assuming that commodities are sold above their value, nor by assuming they are bought at less than their value" (263). The decisive factor that brings about profits and surplus-value is for Marx not money, but something different.

   The point that Marx wants to make is that the "exchange of commodities [. . .] creates no value" (266). The form M-C-M′ would in its pure version be the form of merchants' capital that assumes that the commodity has already been produced. One would, however, also have to take into account that labour produces the commodity so that there is not just the circulation, but also the production of commodities. Something "must take place in the background which is not visible in the circulation itself" (268). For Marx, it is not money that brings about the existence of surplus-value and profit, but labour. The point Marx wants to make is that capitalists buy commodities (labour power, resources) not in order to resell them, but to let labour produce new commodities that contain surplus-value and a surplus-product: The commodity-owner can increase the value of his commodity by adding fresh labour, and therefore more value, to the value in hand, by making leather into boots, for instance. The same material now has more value, because it contains a greater quantity of labour. The boots have therefore more value than the leather, but the value of the leather remains what it was. It has not valorized itself, it has not annexed surplus-value during the making of the boots. It is therefore impossible that, outside the sphere of circulation, a producer of commodities can, without coming into contact with other commodity-owners, valorize value, and consequently transform money or commodities into capital. (268)

A boots-making company such as Doc Martens, the Frye Company, Red Wing, or Timberland does not buy and sell leather. It rather buys leather and sells boots. Boots emerge from leather not by magic, but because workers invest a specific amount of time during which they employ their labour-power in order to transform the leather into boots. The boot therefore contains leather and a specific amount of average labour time. Marx hints in chapter 5 towards the fact that most commodity production is more complex than M-C-M′ and that M-C-M′ is just an abbreviation for M-C.. P.. C′-M′: A capitalist buys labour power, technologies, and resources as commodities. Workers take the resources and by expending energy for a specific amount of time create a new commodity C′. The new commodity C′ has new qualities and more value than the commodities C that function as inputs for the production of C′: C′ = C + ΔC. The profit ΔM that the boots-making company realises by selling boots does not stem from the fact that leather is sold above or below its value, but that labour has created a new commodity C′ that is sold at a price M′; that price is higher than the purchase price M of input commodities. The profit ΔM is the monetary expression of the surplus-value and surplus-product ΔC contained in the commodity C′ = C + ΔC. The commodity C′ is both an experienceable product or service that you can consume so that some need you have is satisfied and an economic value that objectifies a specific amount of human labour. C′ contains in comparison to C both a surplus-product and surplus-labour. M′ and ΔM emerge from surplus-labour, not from sale. For Marx, sale transforms surplus-labour and surplus-value into monetary profit. He says that sale "realises" the surplus-value contained in the commodity C′. Surplus-value does not arise from money, but from labour.

Circulation Labour

Specific forms of labour are also needed for the organisation of the circulation process C′-M′: Boots are marketed and advertised in order to have a specific brand image; they are transported from factories to retailers and sold by shop assistants in shoe shops. The total labour required for the accumulation of the capital of a pair of boots is the labour of shoemakers; marketing, advertising and public relations workers; transport workers, and salesclerks. Marx does not discuss the role of circulation workers in chapter 5, but rather in *Capital Volume 2*'s chapter 6: The Costs of Circulation (Marx 1885, 207–299) and *Capital Volume 3*'s part 4: The Transformation of Commodity Capital and Money Capital into Commercial Capital and Money-Dealing Capital (Merchant's Capital) (chapters 16–20; Marx 1894, 379–455).

A question related to the discussion of circulation labour is, what kind of labour is productive—that is, creates surplus-value? And, is advertising, transport, and sales labour a form of productive labour or not? I discuss these questions and Marx's views on it in detail in chapter 5: Social Media and Productive Labour of my book *Culture and Economy in the Age of Social Media* (Fuchs 2015). Marxist theorists have interpreted what Marx wrote on this issue in different ways, so there is not just one view of it.

Baran and Sweezy on Advertising

Paul A. Baran (1909–1964) and Paul M. Sweezy (1910–2004) were two American Marxist economists. They were involved in setting up and editing the socialist journal *Monthly Review* and developed a theory of monopoly capitalism. Their most well-known book is *Monopoly Capital: An Essay on the American Economic and Social Order* (Baran and Sweezy 1966). They explain the formation of monopolies in capitalism and show that capitalism is not a competitive economy, but one where competition tends to turn into monopolies.

Baran and Sweezy argue that monopoly capitalism has a tendency to increase surplus that is absorbed by luxury goods, advertising and sales promotion, increased military spending, and the expansion of finance. All of this spending would be unproductive and therefore further stagnation and capitalism's crisis tendencies. Baran and Sweezy position advertising as a form of manipulation in the sales efforts. Advertising and advertising labour would be an unproductive attribute of monopoly, "the very offspring of monopoly capitalism" (Baran and Sweezy 1966, 122), one form of "surplus eaters" (Baran and Sweezy 1966, 127), and "merely a form of surplus absorption" (Baran and Sweezy, 1966, 141).

Ernest Mandel on Advertising

Ernest Mandel (1923–1995) was a Marxist theorist and one of the leaders of the Fourth International, an international communist organisation that has gathered followers of Leon Trotsky. His most well-known book is *Late Capitalism* (Mandel 1978), his dissertation with which he obtained the PhD at the Free University of Berlin in 1972. Mandel combined Marxist crisis theory and the theory of long economic waves. Late capitalism was for him one specific phase of capitalist development characterised by the third industrial revolution that enabled large-scale automation, transnational capital, neocolonialism, a permanent arms economy, the expansion of the service sector, and mass consumption (the "consumer society"). Mandel praised Baran and Sweezy's analysis of sales, distribution, and administration as "excellent" (Mandel 1978, 399, footnote 48). The tendency of the rate of profit to fall would have resulted in "non-invested surplus capitals" (Mandel 1978, 387) that capitalists would have tried to offset by penetration "into areas which are non-productive" (Mandel 1978, 388).

Advertising, market research, and consumer credit would be the "unmistakable expression of the growing difficulties of realization in late capitalism" (Mandel 1978, 399) and the attempts to sell more commodities more quickly—that is, to reduce the turnover-time of capital. At the same time services such as transport, theatre, and film would be replaced by commodities such as cars, TV sets, and videotapes (Mandel 1978, 406). "The logic of late capitalism is therefore necessarily to convert idle capital into service capital and simultaneously to replace service capital with productive capital, in other words, services with commodities" (Mandel 1978, 406). The service sector would be unproductive: "The capitalist services sector is a deduction from, rather than an addition to, the surplus-value created by productive capital" (Mandel 1978, 407).

Dallas W. Smythe on Advertising

Dallas W. Smythe (1907–1992) was a Canadian political economist who had major influence on the development of the field of the critical political economy of information, media, and communication (Mosco 2009). He felt that many Marxists do not take the realm of communication serious, reduce it to a superstructure, and do not want to see the importance of the commercial mass media as not just a realm of the manipulation of needs, but also a realm of labour of audiences and advertising workers. He argues in his famous article "Communications: Blindspot of Western Marxism"

(Smythe 1977) that Baran and Sweezy in an idealist manner reduce advertising to a form of manipulation. He criticises them for "rejecting expenses of circulation as unproductive of surplus" (Smythe 1977, 14) and concludes that the "denial of the productivity of advertising is unnecessary and diversionary: a cul de sac derived from the pre-monopoly-capitalist stage of development, a dutiful but unsuccessful and inappropriate attempt at reconciliation with Capital" (Smythe 1977, 16).

Ernest Mandel gives a hint at the real difference underlying the two positions. He says that humans "first have to eat, drink, clothe themselves, obtain homes and guarantee their sources of energy before they could go to the doctor, have their shoes mended, or take a holiday trip" (Mandel 1978, 407). Thinkers such as Baran, Sweezy, and Mandel hold that eating, drinking, clothing, shelter, and energy are at the heart of the economy, whereas culture and communication are secondary and superstructural. This assumption is expressed by Mandel's formulation "first . . . before". Baran and Sweezy (1966, 8) argue that "modes of utilization of surplus constitute the indispensable mechanism linking the economic foundation of society with what Marxists call its political, cultural, and ideological superstructure". This formulation implies that culture is non-economic, which disregards the fact that music, film, games, entertainment, software, advertising, public relations, art, literature, science, sports, Internet communication, etc. do in informational capitalism not stand outside the economy and the commodity form, but have to specific degrees become part of a capitalist culture industry, in which information workers produce cultural commodities that are sold in order for capitalists to accumulate profit.

Cultural-materialist Marxist thinkers such as Dallas Smythe and Raymond Williams stress in contrast that communication and culture are not secondary or a superstructure, but are foundational for human existence and have become a capitalist industry, in which labour power is expended, capital exploits workers, and capital is accumulated. The question about productive and unproductive labour is one about primary and secondary realms of production and one about which workers have the power to bring down capitalist production by going on strike or refusing to work.

Raymond Williams's Cultural Materialism

Raymond Williams (1921–1988), who was a Welsh Marxist cultural theorists, novelist, and literary critic, responded in an interview with *New Left Review* to a question about the importance of culture in capitalism in the following way:

> NLR: *Even a bourgeois liberal will admit, on reflection, that if all novelists stopped writing for a year in England, the results would scarcely be of the same order as if all car workers halted their labour. To take a more relevant example for your argument, a complete cessation of the main communications industries—television, radio and press—would serious effect [sic] the life of any modern capitalist society: but its effects would not be comparable to major strikes in the docks, mines or power stations. The workers in these industries have the capacity to disrupt the whole fabric of social life, so decisive is the importance of their productive activity.* (Williams 1979, 354)
>
> Raymond Williams: [. . .] I would not be willing to say that at the top of the hierarchy is productive industry, then come political institutions or means of mass communication, and then below them the cultural activities of philosophers or novelists. Not that there wouldn't be a certain scale of that kind, but it is increasingly in the nature of modern capitalist economy that there is a slide in the first bracket from indispensable needs to the dispensable conditions of reproduction of this order or of the ability to maintain life within it, for we can imagine certain breakdowns to which human beings could make adaptations of a very difficult kind by living in different ways. The hierarchies, while in general following a line from activities which answer to basic physical needs down through to those of which you at least can state negatively that if they were not performed, human life would not be immediately threatened,

are not immutable. After all, stoppages of electrical power or oil would now make life impossible in the very short terms yet it is obvious enough historically that our society didn't possess them until recently, yet life could be sustained by other methods. To take another example: there have been some estimates that over half the employed population of the United States, the most advanced capitalist country, is now involved in various kinds of information handling and parcelling. If that were so, an information strike would call the maintenance of human life *in that social order* very quickly into question. (Williams 1979, 355)

Williams stresses that cultural work, such as work in advertising, is not superstructural or unproductive, but has become an important realm of capitalism.

Marx sees a contradiction between production and exchange at the heart of the general formula of capital M-C-M' or M-C.. P.. C'-M'. Capital cannot exist in exchange only, but also not independent of exchange: "Capital cannot therefore arise from circulation, and it is equally impossible for it to arise apart from circulation. It must have its origin both in circulation and not in circulation" (268).

Exercise for Chapter 5

Group exercise (G)
Project exercise (P)

Key Categories: Capital, Circulation, Exchange, Surplus–Value

Exercise 5.1 (P)

Read the following four texts:

1.   Baran, Paul A. and Paul M. Sweezy. 1966. *Monopoly capital. An essay on the American economic and social order*. New York: Monthly Review Press. Chapter 5: The Absorption of Surplus: The Sales Effort.
2.   Mandel, Ernest. 1978. *Late capitalism*. London: Verso. Chapter 12: The Expansion of the Services Sector, the "Consumer Society", and the Realization of Surplus-Value.
3.   Smythe, Dallas W. 1977. Communications: Blindspot of Western Marxism. *Canadian Journal of Political and Social Theory* 1 (3): 1–27.
4.   Williams, Raymond. 1979. *Politics and letters: Interviews with* New Left Review. London: Verso. Part IV: Chapter 5: Marxism and Literature.

Discuss in groups and present the results: What are the commonalities of Baran and Sweezy's and Mandel's way of understanding culture, advertising, sales, and circulation? What are the commonalities of Smythe's and Williams's understanding of these phenomena? And what are the major differences between Baran, Sweezy, and Mandel on the one hand and Smythe and Williams on the other hand? How do you position yourself on the question of what role culture and communication play in society in general and in contemporary capitalism in particular?

6

THE SALE AND PURCHASE OF LABOUR-POWER

At the start of chapter 6, Marx summarises the main insight of chapter 5—namely, that not money creates value and profit, but labour does:

> The change in value of the money which has to be transformed into capital cannot take place in the money itself, since in its function as means of purchase and payment it does no more than realize the price of the commodity it buys or pays for, while, when it sticks to its own peculiar form, it petrifies into a mass of value of constant magnitude. [. . .] In order to extract value out of the consumption of a commodity, our friend the money-owner must be lucky enough within the sphere of circulation, on the market, a commodity whose use-value possesses the peculiar property of being a source of value, whose actual consumption is therefore itself an objectification of labour, hence a creation of value. The possessor of money does find such a special commodity on the market: the capacity for labour, in other words labour-power. (270)

Labour-Power, Work Capacity

Chapter 6 deals with the concept of labour-power. Marx defines labour-power, or work capacity, as "the aggregate of those mental and physical capabilities existing in the physical form, the living personality, of a human being, capabilities which he sets in motion whenever he produces a use-value of any kind" (270).

This definition shows that no strict separation can be made between physical and information work: All work requires and makes use of the human's mental and physical capabilities, the brain and the limbs. A human is only human in and through the combination of the brain and the rest of the body. Information work makes use of the human mental and physical capabilities in order to create an information product, whereas physical work makes use of these capabilities in order to create a physical product. Both information and physical products are manifestations of matter in society. When writing this sentence, I simultaneously use my brain and my fingers. My brain creates thoughts about Marx's book that I write down while my brain coordinates my fingers in such a way that they press specific keys on my laptop so that sentences are created in the word processor that runs on my laptop. In the work process, "a definite quantity of human muscle, nerve, brain, etc. is expended" (274).

Wageworkers and Slaves

Marx argues that capitalism requires two dimensions of labour: (1) that labourers are the possessors of their own labour-power, and (2) that they are compelled to work for others in order to survive.

When discussing the first condition, Marx draws a distinction between slaves and wage-labour. The wageworker is "the free proprietor of his own labour-capacity, hence of his person" (271). The body and mind of the wageworker, which make up his or her person, are not the property of the capitalist, whereas the slave's full human person is property of the slaveholder. The slaveholder can choose to kill the slave without having to fear legal consequences because the slave is the slaveholder's property. In this respect the slave is more like a thing that somebody possesses—s/he is unfree. In modern society, the law and human rights guarantee the freedom of the person. The Universal Declaration of Human Rights' articles 3 and 4 therefore specify the following: "Article 3: Everyone has the right to life, liberty and security of person. Article 4: No one shall be held in slavery or servitude; slavery and the slave trade shall be prohibited in all their forms".

Private Property as Unfreedom in Capitalism

Marx argues, however, that this freedom of the person has turned into another form of unfreedom in capitalism. Given that not everyone owns means of production, most humans are in modern society compelled to work for others in order to earn a living. The legal structure of private property and commodity production compels humans to enter class relationships, in which their labour is exploited and creates goods owned by others. Marx therefore speaks of the double freedom of labour in modern society:

> For the transformation of money into capital, therefore, the owner of money must find the free worker available on the commodity-market; and this worker must be free in the double sense that as a free individual he can dispose of his labour-power as his own commodity, and that, on the other hand, he has no other commodity for sale, i.e. he is rid of them, he is free of all the objects needed for the realization of his labour-power. (272–273)

The Universal Declaration of Human Rights defines a right to private property in article 17: "(1) Everyone has the right to own property alone as well as in association with others". It also defines wage-labour as a human right: "Article 23: (1) Everyone has the right to work, to free choice of employment, to just and favourable conditions of work and to protection against unemployment. (2) Everyone, without any discrimination, has the right to equal pay for equal work". The Declaration does not exclude the possibility that the means of production are collectively owned ("in association with others"). It, however, equally defines a right to individual property of the means of production and a right to work in the form of wage-labour. It therefore at the same time reifies and slightly questions capitalism.

Private Property in Liberal Ideology

Classical liberal thinkers have interpreted the freedom of private property as a right of capitalists to own as much as they want to. So, for example, the British political economist John Stuart Mill (1806–1873) propagated an individualism that gives humans the right to pursue their own good in their own way:

> No society in which these liberties are not, on the whole, respected, is free, whatever may be its form of government; and none is completely free in which they do not exist absolute and

unqualified. The only freedom which deserves the name, is that of pursuing our own good in our own way, so long as we do not attempt to deprive others of theirs, or impede their efforts to obtain it. (Mill 1859, 17)

Liberal ideology assumes that individual civil liberties are connected to an individual right to private property that stands above considerations of socioeconomic equality. Marx formulated in this context the critique that the individualism advanced by classical liberalism results in egoism that harms the public good. The rights to private property of the means of production and to accumulate as much capital as one pleases would harm the community and the social welfare of others who are by this process deprived of wealth. The young Marx formulated this criticism in his essay "On the Jewish Question" in the following way: "The right of property is thus the right to enjoy and dispose one's possessions as one wills, without regard for other men and independently of society. It is the right of self-interest" (Marx 1843a, 236). "Thus none of the so-called rights of men goes beyond the egoistic man, the man withdrawn into himself, his private interest and his private choice, and separated from the community as a member of civil society" (Marx 1843a, 236–237).

Freedom, Equality, Property, and Bentham

Marx was convinced that capitalism is founded on an antagonism between the freedom of private property and social justice (social freedom) that renders capitalism an unjust and unfree society. In *Capital Volume 1*'s chapter 6 he formulates the unfreedom of modern freedom as the double freedom of labour: Modern labour is free because it is better off than slaves (although slavery has continued to exist in global capitalism), but it is also unfree because it is compelled to be exploited by capital and has to enter class relations in order to be able to survive.

Marx formulates capitalism's (un)freedom as the unity of "Freedom, Equality, Property, and Bentham" (280). In capitalism, freedom reduces itself to the freedom to buy and sell, equality to contracts that regulate exchange, property to private property. Jeremy Bentham (1748–1832) was a British philosopher who argued in his utilitarian philosophy that a "thing is said to promote the interest, or to be for the interest, of an individual, when it tends to add to the sum total of his pleasures: or, what comes to the same thing, to diminish the sum total of his pains" and an "action [. . .] may be said to be conformable to the principle of utility, or, for shortness sake, to utility, (meaning with respect to the community at large) when the tendency it has to augment the happiness of the community is greater than any it has to diminish it" (Bentham 1781, 15).

For Marx, utilitarianism is a principle that in modern society underpins capital accumulation. This becomes evident in Adam Smith's principle of the invisible hand, according to which each capitalist pursues his/her own interest and the result is the best possible form of general wealth. He argued that the rich, whom he considered to be naturally selfish, "are led by an invisible hand to [. . .] advance the interest of the society" (Smith 1790, 215). He considered private property as fundamental human right and that one of the "most sacred laws of justice" (Smith 1790, 101) is to "guard his property and possessions" (Smith 1790, 102).

Marx formulates his criticism of liberal freedom at the end of chapter 6 by adding "Bentham" to "Freedom, Equality, Property": "And Bentham, because each looks only to his own advantage. The only force bringing them together, and putting them into relation with each other, is the selfishness, the gain and the private interest of each. Each pays heed to himself only, and no one worries about the others" (280). Capitalist unfreedom would result in the class relation between the capitalist and the worker.

Marx on Freedom

Marx had a different concept of freedom. He saw communism as a realm of freedom, "where labour determined by necessity and external expediency ends" (Marx 1894, 959), for which the "reduction of the working day is the basic prerequisite" (Marx 1894, 959). This is a realm, where there is "the all-round development of the individual" enabled by high productivity so that "all the springs of common wealth flow more abundantly", and society inscribes on its banners the following principle: "From each according to his abilities, to each according to his needs!" (Marx 1875, 87). Communism is for Marx true freedom, a society, in which toil has come to an end, people are not compelled to work for others, everyone does the things voluntarily the s/he wants to do, and everyone gets what s/he requires to survive without having to pay for it or having to exchange anything for it. A high level of productivity would be a precondition for this freedom.

In chapter 24, Marx formulated in a footnote an explicit criticism of Bentham's utilitarian theory: "With the dryest naiveté, he assumes that the modern petty bourgeois, especially the English petty bourgeois, is the normal man. Whatever is useful to this peculiar kind of normal man, and to his world, is useful in and for itself. He applies this yardstick to the past, the present and the future" (759, footnote 51).

Marx writes that Bentham has "piled up mountains of books" with such "kind of rubbish" and that he is "a genius in the way of bourgeois stupidity" (759, footnote 51).

The Value of Labour-Power

Every commodity has a specific value, the average time it takes to produce it. Given that labour-power is sold as commodity, it must also have value. Marx asks in chapter 6 what the value of labour-power is.

> The value of labour-power is determined, as in the case of every other commodity, by the labor-time necessary for the production, and consequently also the reproduction, of this specific article. [. . .] Given the existence of the individual, the production of labour-power consists in his reproduction of himself or his maintenance. For his maintenance he requires a certain quantity of the means of subsistence. Therefore the labour-time necessary for the production of labour-power is the same as that necessary for the production of those means of subsistence; in other words, the value of labour-power is the value of the means of subsistence necessary for the maintenance of its owner. However, labour-power becomes a reality only by being expressed; it is activated only through labour. [. . .] If the owner of labour-power works today, tomorrow he must again be able to repeat the same process in the same conditions as regards health and strength. His means of subsistence must therefore be sufficient to maintain him in his normal state as a working individual. (274–275)

Marx mentions in chapter 6 parts of the means of subsistence that reproduce labour-power: food, clothing, housing, procreation; survival of the family, including the children; education and training. The means of reproduction of a worker include his/her own subsistence costs, the ones of her/his family, taking care of children, education for obtaining skills, and health care for maintaining labour-power in a physical and mental status that allows the continuance of work. Historically, predominantly women in households have conducted the organisation and production of the means of subsistence. Marxist feminists have therefore introduced the concept of reproductive labour in order to stress that the value of labour-power is created by another form of labour that operates in the household economy and has predominantly been conducted by women. This labour would be unwaged and therefore a gratis resource for the capitalist, who does not have to pay for the reproduction of labour-power and can put to use reproduced, recreated, and refreshed labour-power day in and day out thanks to the unremunerated activities of house-workers.

Marx points out that the means of subsistence are not immutably fixed, but vary historically and depend "to a great extent on the level of civilization attained by a country" (275). "The value of labour-power can be resolved into the value of a definite quantity of the means of subsistence. It therefore varies with the value of the means of subsistence, i.e. with the quantity of labour-time required to produce them" (276). Labour-power has a value that "is already determined before it enters into circulation, for a definite quantity of social labour has been spent on the production of labour-power" (277). The use-value of labour-power consists in the subsequent exercise of labour-power that creates use-values that satisfy human needs and value that satisfies the need of capital to be accumulated.

Housework and Reproductive Work

Marxist feminists have stressed that housework is not a peripheral, secondary, or unproductive form of activity, but is central, primary, and productive for the existence of capitalism. Marx says in chapter 1 that the commodity is the cell-form of capitalism. All those who produce commodities are therefore performing crucial labour for the existence of capitalism. House-workers and reproductive workers produce and reproduce the commodity labour-power. They are commodity producers and important for capitalism's survival. Capital exploits not just wageworkers, but also house-workers and reproductive workers.

The Marxist feminists Mariarosa Dalla Costa and Selma James were involved in the International Wages for Housework Campaign and wrote the feminist classic *The Power of Women and the Subversion of the Community* (Dalla Costa and James 1972), in which they argue that reproductive work in capitalism is productive labour. They say that "domestic work produces not merely use values, but is essential to the production of surplus value" and that the "productivity of wage slavery" is "based on unwaged slavery" (Dalla Costa and James 1972, 31).

The feminist political theorist Zillah Eisenstein edited a classical collection of Marxist feminist essays titled *Capitalist Patriarchy and the Case for Socialist Feminism*. In this anthology, she argues that the gender division of labour guarantees "a free labor pool" and "a cheap labor pool" (Eisenstein 1979, 31).

The German Marxist-feminist sociologist Maria Mies (1986) wrote an analysis of capitalist patriarchy titled *Patriarchy and Accumulation on a World Scale*, in which she argues that women are exploited in a triple sense: "They are exploited [...] by men and they are exploited as housewives by capital. If they are wage-workers they are also exploited as wage-workers" (Mies 1986, 37). Capitalist production would be based on the

> *superexploitation* of non-wage labourers (women, colonies, peasants) upon which wage labour exploitation then is possible. I define their exploitation as super-exploitation because it is not based on the appropriation (by the capitalist) of the time and labour over and above the 'necessary' labour time, the *surplus* labour, but of the time and labour *necessary* for people's own survival or subsistence production. It is not compensated for by a wage. (Mies 1986, 48)

The Italian feminist Leopoldina Fortunati (1995) argues in her book *The Arcane of Reproduction. Housework, Prostitution, Labor and Capital* that reproductive labour is productive because "it produces and reproduces the individual as a commodity" (70) by "producing and reproducing labor-power" (70) and "the use-value of labor-power" (69).

These Marxist-feminist approaches have in common that they stress that capitalism requires for its existence unpaid and low-paid spheres that are highly exploited. The Marxist theorist Rosa Luxemburg (1871–1919), who together with Karl Liebknecht founded the Spartakusbund (Spartacus League), which in 1919 became the Kommunistische Partei Deutschlands (KPD, Communist Party of Germany), argued in this context that capitalism requires the exploitation of noncapitalist milieus: "Capital feeds on the ruins of such organisations, and, although this non-capitalist milieu is indispensable for accumulation, the latter proceeds, at the cost of this medium nevertheless, by eating it up" (Luxemburg 1913/2003, 363).

Slavery in Capitalism

Class societies have in common that one class controls economic systems in which another class is forced to work and create a surplus-product that is controlled by the dominant class. The dominant class exploits the subordinate class and thereby appropriates that latter's surplus labour and surplus product. Marx starts chapter 6 by describing the difference between the modern "double free" worker and the unfree slave who is a property of a slaveholder. Slavery has not come to an end with the rise of capitalism, but rather continues to exist within it. The Global Slavery Index report has estimated that in 2014 there were 30 million slaves in the world.[1] Well known has become the example of so-called conflict minerals such as tin, tungsten, and tantalum, which have been sourced by slaves in Africa and have been used for the production of electronics such as laptops, mobile phones, and MP3 players.[2]

So slavery is a class relation that is older than capitalism, but continues to exist within capitalism. Also patriarchy is older than capitalism, but is as capitalist patriarchy subsumed under and sustaining capitalism. Women have historically conducted the vast majority of low-paid, precarious, and unpaid labour. Where slavery and patriarchy coincide, women are the victims of sexual slavery, forced marriage, rape, genital mutilation, etc. Marx points out in chapter 6 that labour power needs to be reproduced by the production and consumption of means of subsistence. Marxist feminism has in this context extended Marx's analysis and argued that capitalist patriarchy is a mode of production within capitalism that is organised in the household, where reproductive workers recreate and reproduce labour-power so that it can over and over be exploited by capital. The capitalist therefore does not just exploit wageworkers, but also the reproductive labour that sustains wage-work.

Capitalism is a mode of production, in which capitalists accumulate capital by selling commodities and exploiting labour that creates these commodities. Capitalists cannot stop exploiting labour because in order for their businesses to survive, they have to grow their capital, make profits, and try to outcompete other capitals. The capitalist dream is therefore that companies have to pay no wages at all, which would allow them to maximise profits. In a fascist form of capitalism, in which basic civil liberties are abolished, it becomes possible that capitalists let labourers work themselves to death and that they substitute dead workers with those who are still alive. Such a system is based on military violence that represses the working class, trade unions, and socialist movements, and enforces a system of slavery as the core of capitalist class relations.

Wages: The Price of Labour-Power

The price of labour-power (wages) depends on the politically set working conditions, which are the actual, temporal, and dynamically changing result of the class struggle between capital and labour. Working class struggles, strikes, and trade union activities aim at increasing wages, which always means a decrease of profits and an increase of capital's crisis-proneness. Capital has an inherent fascist tendency that tries to suppress worker rights and reduce wages to an absolute minimum, even below the subsistence level of wage labour—that is, below the value of labour power.

The working class in contrast has an inherent interest for its own empowerment and for an increase of wages to a maximum. The absolute maximum is the abolition of capital and the overtaking of the economy by the workers so that self-managed companies emerge that are operated within a communist economy. The dialectic of capital and labour is in the very last instance a struggle between fascist and communist interests. Successful class struggle on the side of the proletariat empowers workers and allows them to raise the price of labour power. Workers have an objective interest that the price of labour power is set as far as possible above its value, for which the maximum is that the wage-sum permanently includes all profits, which means that workers own the companies they work in. Capitalists in contrast have an objective interest to reduce the wage sum as far as possible in order to maximise profits. The price of labour-power fluctuates around its value and is the outcome of class struggles between capital and labour.

Wage Struggles and Unpaid Audience Labour

Given the capitalist drive to maximise profits, capital seeks opportunities to decrease wage-costs. One method for doing this is to create colonies of unpaid, precarious, and low-paid labour. The political economist of media and communication Dallas Smythe (1977, 1981) has stressed that in commercial, advertising-funded media, capital exploits unremunerated audience labour that creates an audience commodity that media companies sell to advertisers. Smythe described yet another form of unpaid labour within capitalism. The notion of the audience commodity has gained new relevance with the emergence of so-called "social media" platforms such as Facebook, Twitter, Google, or Weibo on the World Wide Web in the 2000s (Fuchs 2014a, 2014c). These media use a capital accumulation model in which the users' personal data (profile data, browsing and interest data, communication content, social network data) is turned into a data commodity that is sold to advertising clients that in return can present individually targeted ads on users' profiles.

Whereas the audience commodity on mass media depends on audience statistics for estimating what kind of social groups make up the audiences of particular media or of specific media contents, the knowledge social media platforms have about their users is relatively total and complete because there is real-time surveillance of all of their social media activities. Targeted advertising–based social media exploit users' unpaid digital labour. They are an expression of a specific form of unpaid labour organised within capitalism.

Outsourcing and Transnational Corporations

One way of reducing labour-costs that especially transnational companies use is the outsourcing of labour to parts of the world where low wages can be paid and labour protections are weak. This allows these companies to let their commodities be produced under low-wage conditions and to maximise profits. Especially in the 1990s there was a lot of talk about the emergence of globalisation. As Marx knew, globalisation is nothing particularly new, because capitalism has long been based on colonies as sources of cheap raw materials and labour, and as destinations for selling commodities and dumping waste. In chapter 4, Marx stresses that "[w]orld trade and the world market date from the sixteenth century, and from then on the modern history of capital starts to unfold" (247).

Globalisation is a harmless-sounding category that conceals the circumstance that in the last quarter of the 20th century a new form of imperialism emerged, in which transnational companies make use of a new international division of labour in order to exploit labour in developing countries to a high degree, which allows them to maximise their profits.

Crowdsourcing as Online Outsourcing

In the Internet economy, a specific form of outsourcing has emerged: crowdsourcing. Crowdsourcing is the outsourcing of labour to the Internet: The search for it takes place online, it is often conducted in a distributed or collaborative way, and given the global nature of the Internet, it is mostly unregulated (there is no global minimum wage for crowdsourced labour), unpaid, or low paid.

Crowdsourcing is an inner colony of capitalism by which capital tries to minimise labour costs in order to maximise profits.

Colonies of capitalism have in common that they are spaces for the conduct of low-paid, precarious, or unpaid labour that is exploited by capital in order to maximise profits. The forms of repression and violence that control these colonies vary: The repression of slaves operates with direct violence. The control of house-workers is a complex combination of labour with positive emotions such as love, feelings of togetherness, and responsibility; and physical and sexual family violence. The control of audience labour and digital labour on social media operates more ideologically and socially so that labour and exploitation appear as fun, socialising, and entertainment. Crowdsourcing operates with the commitment of fans to celebrities and brands, by presenting itself ideologically as a democratisation of capitalism ("participatory culture"), and by the dull compulsion exercised by the precarious lives of knowledge workers who struggle as freelancers or in other forms of precarious labour to make ends meet and therefore have to take on crowdsourced jobs.

The Hidden Abode of Production

The exchange of money against commodities—that is, the realm of circulation—is something that is visible to all of us. The realm of production is in contrast because of commodity fetishism hidden from the consumers and workers who are not directly active in it. It is what Marx terms "the hidden abode of production" (279). We have seen in this chapter that capitalist abodes are not just offices and factories, but also realms such as patriarchal households, developing countries, slavery, commercial media, and the capitalist Internet that are quite different class relations that, however, have in common high levels of exploitation that sustain capitalism.

Chapter 1 shows that Marx identifies quality, quantity, and the measure (qualitative quantum) as three aspects of a commodity: use-value, value, and exchange-value. In chapter 6, Marx argues that labour-power in capitalism is a commodity that as commodity has these three characteristics. Figure 6.1 shows the dialectic of labour-power's use-value, value, and exchange-value. Labour-power's exchange-value is its sale as commodity and its character as double-"freedom" that is not slavery and at the same time a form of coercion and unfreedom exercised by the dull compulsion of capitalism that forces workers to enter class relations in order to survive within a society governed by markets, the commodity form, and private property. So it is a new form of slavery that is qualitatively different from ancient and feudal slavery. In order to be sold as commodity (the exchange-value of

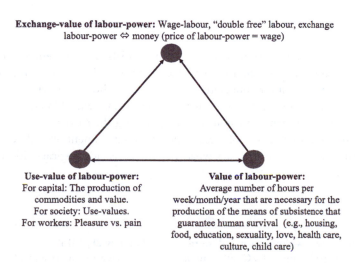

Exchange-value of labour-power: Wage-labour, "double free" labour, exchange
labour-power ⇔ money (price of labour-power = wage)

Use-value of labour-power:
For capital: The production of
commodities and value.
For society: Use-values.
For workers: Pleasure vs. pain

Value of labour-power:
Average number of hours per
week/month/year that are necessary for the
production of the means of subsistence that
guarantee human survival (e.g., housing,
food, education, sexuality, love, health care,
culture, child care)

FIGURE 6.1   The dialectic of labour-power's use-value, value, and exchange-value

labour-power) labour power needs to be reproduced by reproductive labour that creates and recreates labour-power's value. Here capitalist patriarchy and the exploitation of women's housework have historically played an important role. Labour-power also has specific use-values for capital (the production of value), for society (the production of use-values), and for the workers themselves (a continuum ranging from absolute pain derived from heteronomous labour and absolute pleasure derived from self-determined, enjoyable work).

Exercises for Chapter 6

Group exercise (G)
Project exercise (P)

Key Categories: Labour-Power, Work Capacity, Double Free Labour, Slavery, Reproduction, Value of Labour-Power, Means of Subsistence

Exercise 6.1 (P)

Work in groups: Each group reads one part in one of the Global Slavery Index Reports, which document the existence of slavery in the contemporary world. Conduct an additional search on the Internet and in newspapers in order to find out if the products of slave labour in the countries that you read about play a role in the creation of media, entertainment, cultural, or information goods or services within the international division of labour. Document your results.

Exercise 6.2 (P)

Marx points with his notion of the reproduction and the value of labour-power and the category of the means of subsistence towards the importance of capitalist patriarchy in capitalism. Women continue to conduct a large share of reproductive, low-paid, and unpaid labour in contemporary capitalism.

Work in groups: Conduct a search for reports, statistics, analyses, academic articles, books, and book chapters that study the working conditions of women in the information, media, and cultural industries. Discuss, document, and present how the working conditions of women look in the specific cases you analyse. How can these working conditions be analysed with the help of the notion of capitalist patriarchy?

Exercise 6.3 (G)

Work in groups: Try to find an example of crowdsourced labour or unremunerated digital labour that is organised with the help of the Internet. Document how this labour comes about, what kind of commodity it produces, if it is remunerated or not (and if so, how large typical levels of remuneration are), what rules (terms of use, privacy policies) govern it, and what kind of ideologies the online platforms organising these forms of labour use for justifying their existence. Search for interviews with the CEOs, managers, or owners of these platforms and document what they say the advantages of their platforms are. Try to deconstruct what they say by an ideological-critical analysis (critical discourse analysis).

Notes

1 Data source: http://www.globalslaveryindex.org (accessed on July 28, 2015).
2 See http://en.wikipedia.org/wiki/Conflict_resource, https://www.freetheslaves.net/ (accessed on July 28, 2015).

PART III

THE PRODUCTION OF ABSOLUTE SURPLUS-VALUE

7

THE LABOUR PROCESS AND THE VALORISATION PROCESS

In chapter 7, Marx takes up the theoretical discussion of work and labour that he started in chapter 1, section 1.2, "The Dual Character of the Labour Embodied in Commodities", where he distinguished between concrete work and abstract labour as the two forms of human activity embodied in the commodity. In chapter 7, he outlines the components of these two forms in a more systematic manner. The chapter is divided into two sections, one focusing on the work process, the other on the valorisation process (in German, *Verwertungsprozess*).

7.1. The Work Process (in the English Original: The Labour Process)

What Is Work?

I have shown in the discussion in chapter 1, section 1.2, that Hegel conceives the world as dialectical relations between subject and object and that this distinction matters for understanding the work process.

In section 7.1, Marx discusses the work process "independently of any specific social formation" (283) and defines it as

> a process between man and nature, a process by which man, through his own actions, mediates, regulates and controls the metabolism between himself and nature. [. . .] He sets in motion the natural forces which belong to his own body, his arms, legs, head and hands, in order to appropriate the materials of nature in a form adapted to his own needs. Through this movement he acts upon external nature and changes it, and in this way he simultaneously changes his own nature. He develops the potentialities slumbering within nature, and subjects the play of forces to his sovereign power. (283)

The Role of the Body and the Mind in Work

The human body and the human mind as part of the body are material systems. Through their dialectical interplay the human being emerges, constitutes, and reconstitutes itself. The human is a sublation of the interplay of the mind and the rest of the body. Marx by the definition just provided therefore not just describes agricultural work, but also industrial and information work. In all human work, humans use their brains and extremities. This is true for both writing a book and working in a coal mine. In writing, brain activity is mostly amplified through the fingers.

An exception from the use of the fingers or other limbs for typing is the use of speech recognition software that, however, has faults because computers do not have semantics—that is, they cannot understand the meaning of words. Another exception would be the capacity to directly tap into human brains with a chip and to transform thought patterns into digital text. If this capacity becomes technologically feasible, then the implications within a capitalist society are highly dangerous. Powerful groups, companies, or the state could try to analyse all human thought. Typical ideological legitimations could be that this could help humans to better find information on the Internet that may be interesting for them or that thought patterns can reveal who is an actual or a potential terrorist. The privacy and freedom of thought would thereby be compromised and a totalitarian society would emerge.

Writing and Mining: The Role of the Brain and the Body

In coal mining, the workers not just use their arms, legs, and bodies, but have to coordinate their movements with their brains and have to constantly monitor what they do because it is rather dark and their work is highly dangerous. The difference between writing and mining is that the second is physically much more exhausting and requires much more physical energy. It is rather unlikely that you sweat a lot while you write (except if you write in the sun on a beach, in a sauna, or in a solarium), whereas it is very likely that you sweat when mining coal. So there are differences in the degree to which bodily energy is exercised in the work process.

Nature and Culture

Marx writes that the human appropriates the materials of nature, acts upon external nature, and changes nature in the work process. Humans are material systems that form social systems through their communication. Humanity and society are material systems with specific qualities. Humans create a kind of second nature through social relations and communication—culture and society. In specific forms of information and communication work such as teaching or acting, humans also act on an external object, but in this case these objects are other humans. They change a specific form of matter—culture and society—in these work processes. Use-values that satisfy specific human needs emerge from human work. These use-values can have different qualities: They can be part of nature, such as a park that is kept by gardeners; they can be industrial products, such as petrol that is refined from oil; or they can be cultural goods, such as a rock concert, a speech, a play, a book, software code, or a movie.

For Marx, work "is the universal condition for the metabolic interaction between man and nature, the everlasting nature-imposed condition of human existence, and it is therefore independent of every form of that existence, or rather it is common to all forms of society in which human beings live" (290). This general character of work is also relevant for information and communication work that organises the "symbolic metabolism" between humans—that is, social reproduction through communication. Communication is a form of symbolic and cultural work that is common to all societies. Without communication we cannot be truly human.

Marx says that through work the human being changes its own nature. For any work, humans need to acquire specific skills. Although anybody is in principle capable of doing many forms of work, s/he practically cannot pursue all of them because there is not enough time in life for acquiring all the necessary skills. In modern society, it has become a habit that one person learns and practices one job. It is extremely difficult to practice several completely different forms of labour in order to earn a living. In a communist society, where necessary work is automated to a large degree, humans have freedom from toil and more time for (if they want to and have interest in it) learning, practicing, and conducting several forms of work. The division of labour, in which one person practices one job, can then come to an end. That humans acquire skills means that they realise and develop their own human capacities in specific ways. Work has effects on the mind and the body. These can be positive or negative ones. Coal miners are, for example, highly likely to later in life develop respiratory diseases. If somebody experiences bad working conditions and bad treatment by management, s/he may react in specific ways to it—for example, by gaining the political insight that capitalism is a form of exploitation that should be abolished. When Marx says that the human being changes its own nature in the work process, then he means that work has effects on the human mind and the rest of the body.

Human Creativity: Why Human Work Is Different from Spiders' and Bees' Activities

In a famous passage in chapter 7, Marx points out a difference between humans and animals:

> A spider conducts operations which resemble those of the weaver, and a bee would put many a human architect to shame by the construction of its honeycomb cells. But what distinguishes the worst architect from the best of bees is that the architect builds the cell in his mind before he constructs it in wax. At the end of every labour process, a result emerges which had already been conceived by the worker at the beginning, hence already existed ideally. Man not only effects a change of form in the materials of nature; he also realizes [*verwirklicht*] his own purpose in those materials. And this is a purpose he is conscious of, it determines the mode of his activity with the rigidity of a law, and he must subordinate his will to it. (284)

Humans can anticipate in their mind how the future can look like when they change society and nature in specific ways. They are not just anticipatory, but also moral beings that are capable of drawing a distinction between what they find desirable and undesirable, good and bad. The architect has a specific taste and there are particular requirements for the building s/he designs, which are considerations that let him/her make specific choices and construct models before the actual construction begins. A writer anticipates what s/he wants to write about before starting; s/he, for example, decides if it is a novel, an art book, or a social science book, where the novel is set, what kind of art the book covers, or what part of society the social science study shall cover. A bee in contrast acts much more driven by instincts and immediate needs. Creativity, self-consciousness, empathy, and morality are crucial forms of the human constitution that also shape the work process.

The Work Process' Dialectic of Subject and Object

Marx systematically develops and describes moments of the work process: "The simple elements of the work ['labour' in the original English translation] process are (1) purposeful activity, that is work itself, (2) the object on which that work is performed, and (3) the instruments of that work" (284). In any work process, we find one or more human subjects who change an object by using other objects on them so that a new subject-object, a product of work that is a use-value that satisfies specific human needs, emerges. Figure 7.1 visualises the work process' dialectic of subject and object.

The Productive Forces

The work process, in which humans use technologies in order to create new use-values from nature or culture, is also what Marx terms the "productive forces". In work processes, humans stand in specific social relations to others because they under normal circumstances are not alone as Robinson was on his island. Marx terms the social relations, in which the economy takes place, the "relations of

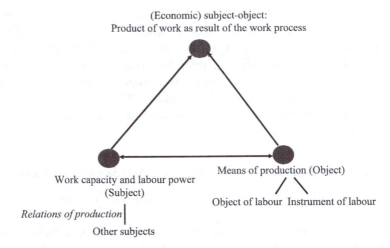

FIGURE 7.1   The work process' dialectic of subject and object

production". Class relations are specific relations of production organised within class societies: one class owns the means of production and the created products, whereas another one is property-less and is forced to work for the propertied class in order to survive.

Marx distinguishes between objects of work that are (a) "spontaneously provided by nature" (284) such as fish, water, timber, and ores; and (b) raw materials that have "been filtered through previous labour" (284) such as extracted minerals that are used in industrial production. Marx here has specifically goods in mind that stem from nature. The same distinction between spontaneous and raw material can also be found in the realm of cultural work: A writer creating a novel creates his/her novel based on his/her own life experiences and spontaneous thoughts. If s/he writes a novel in several parts, then starting with the second part the previous books are raw materials. They define a storyline on which the novelist builds further stories.

Marx defines an instrument of work as "a thing, or a complex of things, which the worker interposes between himself and the object of his work ['labour' in the original translation] and which serves as a conductor, directing his activity onto that object" (285). Marx supports Benjamin Franklin's assumption that man is a "tool-making animal" (286). He argues that different economic epochs distinguish each other not by what is made, but how and with the help of which instruments it is made (286). An expression of this circumstance is the distinction among the Stone Age (approx. 3.4 million BC–2000 BC),[1] the Bronze Age (approx. 4000 BC–1000 BC),[2] and the Iron Age (approx. 1000 BC– 400 AD).[3] These different materials were used for making tools.

Three Modes of Organisation of the Productive Forces

The instruments of work can be the human brain and body, mechanical tools, and complex machine systems. They also include specific organisations of space-time—that is, locations of production that are operated at specific time periods. The most important aspect of time's role in capitalism is the necessary work time that depends on the level of productivity. At the level of society, it is the work time that is needed per year for guaranteeing the survival of a society. The objects and products of work can be natural, industrial, or informational resources or a combination thereof.

The productive forces are a system of production that creates use-values. There are different modes of organisation of the productive forces, such as agricultural productive forces, industrial productive forces, and informational productive forces. Table 7.1 gives an overview.

TABLE 7.1 Three modes of organisation of the productive forces

Mode of the organisation of the productive forces	Instruments of work	Objects of work	Products of work
Agricultural productive forces	Body, brain, tools, machines	Nature	Basic products
Industrial productive forces	Body, brain, tools, machines	Basic products, industrial products	Industrial products
Informational productive forces	Body, brain, tools, machines	Experiences, ideas	Informational products

TABLE 7.2 The subject, object, and subject-object of cognitive, communicative, and cooperative information work

	Subject	Object of work	Instruments of work	Product of work
Cognition = human brain work	Human being	Experiences	Brain	Thoughts, cognitive patterns, ideas
Communication = human group work	Group of humans	Thoughts	Brain, mouth, ears	Meaning
Cooperation = collaborative human group work	Group of humans	Meaning	Brain, mouth, ears, body	Information product with shared and cocreated meaning

Information as Production Process

The production of information content can be conceptualised with the help of the subject-object dialectic that Marx introduces in section 7.1: Information is threefold process of cognition, communication, and cooperation (Hofkirchner 2003). Table 7.2 gives an overview of the cognitive, communicative and cooperative dimensions of information work (Fuchs 2014a, 2015).

Figure 7.2 shows that these three processes are connected dialectically and form together the process of information work. Each of the three behaviours—cognition, communication, and cooperation—is a work process: cognition is work of the human brain; communication and cooperation work of human groups. Communication is based on cognition and uses the products of cognition—ideas—as its object of work. Cooperation is based on communication and uses the products of communication—meanings—as object of work. Information is a work process in which cognitive work creates ideas, communicative work creates meanings, and cooperative work cocreates information products that have shared and cocreated meaning. Information is a dialectical process of human work in which cognition, communication, and cooperation are dialectically connected. Each of these three processes forms a work process that has its own subject-object dialectic in itself.

Using the Hegelian-Marxist triangle model of the work process, one can argue that the development that Marx points out can be formalised as follows: S-O>SO ... S-SO>SSO ... S-SSO>SSSO, and so forth. The object position of a dialectical work triangle starts with the result, the subject-object of a previous triangle, and so on. The advantage of this kind of thinking is that the reference to an object and ultimately nature never gets completely lost in the theory. Hence a dualism between subject and object—for example, communication and work—is prevented. Dialectical thinking is capable of providing an integrative theory of human activity.

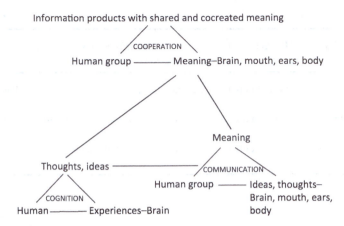

FIGURE 7.2 The information process as work process

An example: A person likes reading books about gardening and builds up a sophisticated knowledge of how to create and maintain a good-looking public guerrilla garden by reading more and more books and applying this knowledge in the garden. The created knowledge is a use-value in the sense that it helps him/her organise the public garden in a nice-looking manner. S/he meets another person who has comparable knowledge. They start exchanging ideas on gardening. In this communication process, the shared knowledge of one person forms an object that is interpreted by the other person so that meaning—that is, an interpretation of parts of the world—is formed. The process also works vice versa. As a result, meanings are created as use-values on both sides; each person understands something about the other. After continuous conversations and mutual learning, the two hobby gardeners decide to write an open access book about gardening. They develop new ideas by discussing and bringing their experiences together, whereby synergies, new experiences, and new gardening methods emerge. In the book, they describe these new methods that they have tried in practice in the guerrilla garden. The representations of the joint experiences and of the cocreated methods in the form of a book are a use-value not just for the two, but for others as well.

Productive Consumption and the Media

Marx argues that all work is productive because there is a "result, the product" (287). All work is creative and productive because it is based on human anticipatory and self-conscious thinking that creates a product. Marx points out in a footnote (287, footnote 8) that for the understanding of the capitalist economy further specifications of what is productive labour need to be made. He provides such an analysis in chapter 15, "Absolute and Relative Surplus-Value", where he refers back to chapter 7 (643).

In chapter 7, Marx also introduces the notion of "productive consumption", by which he means that work consumes "its objects and its instruments" in the work process so that they are "elements in the formation of new use-values, new products" (290). The notion of productive consumption has since the late 20th century also taken on another meaning—namely, that the production and consumption of goods or services coincides so that consumption is production: The American futurist Alvin Toffler (1980) introduced in this context the notion of the prosumer in his book *The Third Wave*:

> Above all, as we shall see, Third Wave civilization begins to heal the historic breach between producer and consumer, giving rise to the 'prosumer' economics of tomorrow. For this reason,

among many, it could with some intelligent help from us—turn out to be the first truly humane civilization in recorded history. (Toffler 1980, 11)

As this practice becomes widespread, the customer will become so integrated into the production process that we will find it more and more difficult to tell just who is actually the consumer and who the producer. (Toffler 1980, 185)

We see a progressive blurring of the line that separates producer from consumer. We see the rising significance of the prosumer. (Toffler 1980, 267)

Toffler points out that the capitalist use of consumers as value-producing prosumers is not entirely new: "Getting the customer to do part of the job—known to economists as 'externalizing labor cost'—is scarcely new. That's what self-service supermarkets are all about" (Toffler 1980, 270). Other examples are Ikea furniture, self-service gas stations, and fast food restaurants.

Toffler stresses that prosumption has become of particular importance in what he terms the "third wave"—the information society (that in his approach followed the first wave of agricultural societies and the second wave of industrial societies). He also holds the opinion that prosumption democratises the economy and that therefore prosumption information technologies and media ("third wave media") democratise culture:

The German poet and social critic Hans Magnus Enzensberger has noted that in yesterday's mass media the 'technical distinction between receivers and transmitters reflects the social division of labor into producers and consumers'. Throughout the Second Wave era this meant that professional communicators produced the messages for the audience. The audience remained powerless to respond directly to, or to interact with, the message senders.

By contrast, the most revolutionary feature of the new means of communication is that many of them are interactive—permitting each individual user to make or send images as well as merely to receive them from the outside. Two-way cable, video cassette, cheap copiers and tape recorders, all place the means of communication into the hands of the individual. (Toffler 1980, 390)

On YouTube, Facebook, Twitter, Pinterest, and similar Internet platforms, users are not just audiences, but can be prosumers—they can consume, create, and cocreate digital content. These capitalist Internet platforms have, however, in contrast to the claims made by some cultural theorists, not brought about a "participatory culture" because participation implies among other dimensions also an ownership democracy, whereas these capitalist Internet platforms are privately owned and accumulate capital by exploiting users' digital labour (Fuchs 2014c).

Toffler describes the age of prosumption as the arrival of a new form of economic and political democracy, self-determined work, labour autonomy, local production, and autonomous self-production. But he overlooks that prosumption is in capitalism used for outsourcing work to users and consumers who work without or for low payment. Thereby corporations reduce their investment costs and labour costs, jobs are destroyed, and consumers who work for free are extremely exploited. They produce surplus-value that is appropriated and turned into profit by corporations without paying wages.

The Implications of Alvin Toffler's Conservative Notion of Prosumption

In 1996, Esther Dyson, George Gilder, George Keyworth, and Alvin Toffler (1996/2004) published a *Magna Carta for the Knowledge Age*. They argue for the commercialisation, deregulation, and commodification of cyberspace and telecommunications. Their *Magna Carta* reveals that the new form of "freedom" that Toffler pointed out in *The Third Wave* is all about the "freedom" of private property to accumulate as much capital as possible. As a result, the World Wide Web has predominantly become a giant shopping mall and capital accumulation machine.

> Unlike the mass knowledge of the Second Wave—'public good' knowledge that was useful to everyone because most people's information needs were standardized—Third Wave customized knowledge is by nature a private good. If this analysis is correct, copyright and patent protection of knowledge (or at least many forms of it) may no longer be unnecessary. (Dyson, Gilder, Keyworth, and Toffler 1996/2004, 34)
>
> Defining property rights in cyberspace is perhaps the single most urgent and important task for government information policy. Doing so will be a complex task, and each key area—the electromagnetic spectrum, intellectual property, cyberspace itself (including the right to privacy)—involves unique challenges. (Dyson, Gilder, Keyworth, and Toffler 1996/2004, 39)

The implication of these passages is that Toffler and his colleagues favour the criminalisation of people who foster file sharing because peer-to-peer platforms in their opinion threaten property rights in cyberspace. An argument against intellectual property rights on knowledge in cyberspace is that knowledge is a foundation of human cognition, communication, and flourishing and that making it available to all for free will foster development of humans and society. If knowledge and communication are basic resources needed for human existence, then in the knowledge age access to cyberspace and knowledge should be free in order to advance human development. Knowledge is always produced based on already existing knowledge, and it is produced in social interaction with others. Therefore it is difficult to argue that there is one originator of knowledge who should hold a property right in owning and selling this knowledge. In most cases, where a piece of knowledge, as, for example, a book or a song, is distributed to a mass audience, it is not the cultural producers who primarily benefit, but large media corporations that sell knowledge as commodities.

Workers' Alienation

At the end of section 7.1 (291–292), Marx argues that labour in capitalism has two characteristics: (1) Labour belongs to the capitalist who controls and monitors the workers (291), and (2) the product belongs to the capitalist and not the worker (292). "The labour process is a process between things the capitalist has purchased, things which belong to him. Thus the product of this process belongs to him just as much as the wine which is the product of the process of fermentation going on in his cellar" (292).

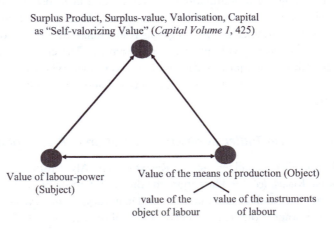

FIGURE 7.3 The alienation of labour

For Marx, the workers' non-ownership of the means of production (the instruments and objects of labour) and the labour product are important characteristics of capitalism. Marx also says that the workers are alienated from the means of production and their products of labour. Workers also face the compulsion to let capitalists exploit them in order to survive, which means that they cannot fully control their lives and are facing alien forces that compel them to do something—to work for a capitalist—that they may otherwise not freely do. In chapter 28, Marx describes the violence of the market and capitalism as the "silent compulsion of economic relations" that "sets the seal on the domination of the capitalist over the worker" (899). "Direct extra-economic force is still of course used, but only in exceptional cases" (899).

Figure 7.3 visualises the multidimensional alienation of the worker in capitalism.

Alienation in the 1844 Economic-Philosophic Manuscripts

Marx (1844, 69–84) has the first time used the notion of alienation in a detailed manner in the *Economic-Philosophic Manuscripts'* section "On Estranged Labour". He there identifies four forms of alienation:

1. The alienation of humans from the product
2. The alienation of humans from the labour process in the form of forced labour (Marx 1844, 74)
3. The alienation of humans from themselves ("Estranged labour turns thus: (3) Man's species being, both nature and his spiritual species property, into a being alien to him, into a means to his individual existence. It estranges man's own body from him, as it does external nature and his spiritual essence, his human being" [Marx 1844, 77–78])
4. The alienation from other humans and society.

On the one hand, the exposition of alienation in the *Economic-Philosophic Manuscripts* is not as systematic as in the *Grundrisse* and *Capital*. On the other hand, Marx in his early work focuses more on the anthropological consequences of alienation for the human being and thereby employs the notion of the species-being. He formulated the foundations of the concept of alienation in the *Economic-Philosophic Manuscripts* and elaborated later systematically and in more detail the economic foundations of alienation.

Slavery and Alienation: The Movie Django Unchained

Alienation is not just a feature of capitalism, but of all class societies. The defining feature of class societies is that the dominated class does not own the means of production and the products of labour and is forced to enter class relations, in which the dominant class exploits it. In slave economies, the slave does not own the objects and products of his/her work. One difference to capitalism is that the slave is, like a machine, the physical property of the slave master. The coercion the slave is confronted with is not a dull compulsion of the market, but the physical violence of the whip and the gun as movies such as Steve McQueen's *12 Years a Slave* or Quentin Tarantino's *Django Unchained* show.

In *Django Unchained*, the former slave Django and the bounty hunter King Schultz fight against the plantation owner Calvin Candie. Django's wife, Broomhilda, works on Candie's Candyland plantation as a house servant. In one scene, Calvin Candie says: "You see, under the laws of Chickasaw County, Broomhilda here is my property. And I can choose to do with my property, whatever I so desire". He threatens to kill Broomhilda by smashing a hammer on her head and shouts: "What I'm gonna desire to do is . . . take this goddamn hammer here and beat her ass to death with it! Right in front of both y'all! Then we can examine the three dimples inside Broomhilda's skull".

This scene in its brutal faithfulness to slaves' reality makes clear that slaves are unfree because they are the property of slave masters, who can choose to kill them if they please without having to fear any legal consequences. Marx writes in chapter 7 of *Capital Volume 1* that in slavery, "the worker is distinguishable only as *instrumentum vocale* [vocal instrument] from an animal, which is *instrumentum semi-vocale* [semi-vocal instrument], and from a lifeless implement, which is *instrumentum mutum* [silent instrument]" (303, footnote 18). The slave is for the slave owner a thing, an instrument that can be treated and mistreated as the owner pleases.

Louis Althusser's Opposition to Marx's Concept of Alienation

Louis Althusser (1918–1990) was a French structuralist philosopher. He argued that Marx's notion of alienation is an "ideological concept" used in "his Early Works" (Althusser 1969, 249). "In his later works, however, the term appears very rarely" (Althusser 1969, 249). Althusser speaks of an "epistemological break" that "divides Marx's thought into two long essential periods: the 'ideological' period before, and the scientific period after, the break in 1845" (Althusser 1969, 34). This means that Althusser considers the notion of alienation and works such as the *Economic-Philosophic Manuscripts* as esoteric. My own view is that Marx did not give up the notion of alienation, but that it is rather a concept that he first created in his early works and that is present also in his major writings. The final passages in *Capital Volume 1*'s section 7.1 are a good example, showing that Marx saw the concept of alienation as crucial throughout his life.

Marx on Alienation in Chapter 23

In chapter 23 ("Simple Reproduction"), there is another passage that shows the importance of the notion of alienation understood as non-ownership and dispossession in *Capital*:

> On the one hand, the production process incessantly converts material wealth into capital, into the capitalist's means of enjoyment and his means of valorization. On the other hand, the worker always leaves the process in the same state as he entered it—a personal source of wealth, but deprived of any means of making that wealth a reality for himself. Since, before he enters the process, his own labour has already been alienated [*entfremdet*] from him, appropriated by the capitalist, and incorporated with capital, it now, in the course of the process, constantly objectifies itself so that it becomes a product alien to him [*fremdes Produkt*]. Since the process of production is also the process of the consumption of labour-power by the capitalist, the worker's product is not only constantly converted into commodities, but also into capital, i.e. into value that sucks up the worker's value-creating power, means of subsistence that actually purchase human beings, and means of production that employ the people who are doing the producing. Therefore the worker himself constantly produces objective wealth, in the form of capital, an alien power that dominates and exploits him; and the capitalist just as constantly produces labour-power, in the form of a subjective source of wealth which is abstract, exists merely in the physical body of the worker, and is separated from its own means of objectification and realization; in short, the capitalist produces the worker as a wage-labourer. This incessant reproduction, this perpetuation of the worker, is the absolutely necessary condition for capitalist production. (716)

Marx argues here that labour-power is in capitalism alienated labour-power because workers must sell this capacity as a commodity in order to survive and as a result of capitalism do not own the products their labour creates and are facing capital in a class relation, in which workers are dominated and exploited by an alien power.

The Althusserian Way of Playing Tricks on Marx

When reading such passages in *Capital*, one wonders how Althusser could claim that alienation was an esoteric concept that Marx stopped using in his later "scientific" works. Althusser wrote in his autobiography that he only knew "a few passages of Marx" (Althusser 1993, 165) and that his method of getting to know philosophy was "all done by hearsay": "I learnt from Jacques Martin, who was cleverer than me, by gleaning certain phrases in passing from my friends, and lastly seminar papers and essays of my own students. In the end, I naturally made it a point of honour and boasted that 'I learnt by hearsay'. This distinguished me quite markedly from all my university friends who were much better informed than me" (Althusser 1993, 166). He described himself as "a trickster and deceiver and nothing more, a philosopher who knew almost nothing about the history of philosophy or about Marx" (Althusser 1993, 148). One wonders how a person who hardly read Marx could become one of the most highly regarded French "Marxist" theorists. Althusser's claims about Marx's usage of the term "alienation" show that he indeed did not understand and had not read Marx.

Alienation and Advertising

People who work for a wage in companies belonging to the culture industry, such as publishing houses, record labels, movie production companies, software and Internet firms, and computer hardware producers, experience the same form of alienation that is typical for all capitalist industries and that is displayed in figure 7.3.

The situation is somewhat different for advertising-funded media, where not just the paid employees but also audiences are workers who create value. They create value by watching, listening, or reading—that is, by paying attention to the content—which allows commercial media to sell audience attention as a commodity to advertisers. Audiences of advertising-funded media are alienated because they do not own the media themselves—that is, the means of production and the capital derived from sales. Humans have the desire to be informed about what is happening in society. In modern society, media are crucial sources of information. Nobody is compelled to read one particular newspaper, such as Murdoch's *The Sun*. One can also choose to pick a left-wing news blog as the main source of information and ignore *The Sun*. The media consumer is, however, not a sovereign consumer because markets tend to become centralised and as an effect specific media tend to dominate the market, which makes it more likely that a lot of people will buy and read *The Sun* and more unlikely that they will discover and read a left-wing news website such as AlterNet.org.

So market concentration and the market power of large media companies alienate audiences as human subjects by marginalising alternative sources of information and making it more unlikely that audience members will choose to give attention to alternative information sources. Especially tabloid media are likely to present news in a biased, one-dimensional, and simplistic form that distorts the complexity of reality and is an attempt to ideologically manipulate audience members. In such cases, audiences are also alienated by ideological and distorted content: They are alienated from a true picture of reality, reality as it truly is. Alienation means in this context that media present an alien world, a media world that is alien to the real world. That ideological content alienates humans does not mean that they are necessarily manipulated by this content. They may be smart enough to see through and deconstruct ideology. What matters is, however, the objective attempt to spread ideological and distorted content.

Alienation and Social Media

The question arises about how alienation looks in the case of capitalist Internet platforms such as YouTube or Facebook, where users can create content themselves. The users do not own the Internet platforms and the monetary profit that such companies make. They are alienated from the ownership of objects and products. They are not compelled by markets or physical violence to use these platforms, but by the dominant position these platforms have and the social disadvantages they can suffer if they do not sign up to Facebook or do not watch videos on YouTube. If you are not on Facebook, then you may not be invited to a party of your friends. If you do not watch clips on YouTube, you may have no idea what videos your friends talk about, which may let them see you as an uncool, uninformed outsider. Not using such platforms threatens humans to be treated as outsiders and to thereby suffer social disadvantages. The compulsion that alienates humans and tries to compel them to use capitalist Internet platforms is social in nature. Capitalist Internet companies threaten to alienate human beings from their own social nature by giving them the feeling that they will miss out on social opportunities and by the circumstance that they may be treated as outsiders if they do not use specific platforms.

The slave cannot stop working because otherwise the slave master might kill him/her. The wage-worker cannot easily refuse to work for a wage because otherwise s/he might die, become homeless, etc. The reader of *The Sun* is coerced by the Murdoch corporation's market power, which does not allow him/her to get information about the existence of alternative sources of information. *The Sun's* biased reporting alienates the reader from access to complex and true information about the world. The Facebook user cannot simply reject using the platform if many of his/her friends are on it because this may render him/her an outsider. There are different forms of violence—physical, structural, ideological, and social—that compel people to work for and be exploited by capital. They cannot really escape exploitation individually, but only collectively as a united class that organises strikes, protests, campaigns, and alternatives.

7.2. The Valorisation Process

Marx turns his attention in section 2 to the capitalist production process of commodities, which is "a unity, composed of the labour process and the process of creating value" (293). The capitalist's aim is "to produce a use-value which has exchange-value", "a commodity greater in value than the sum of the values of the commodities used to produce it" (293). Marx here analyses labour from the perspective of value: the goal for the capitalist is not predominantly to let workers produce use-values, but to produce value and surplus-value (293).

Marx's Examples for the Valorisation Process

Marx uses the example of a cotton manufactory, in which workers use spindles and looms in order to spin cotton into yarn. Other examples he uses in this section are cannon-drilling, coal-mining, oil production, jewel-making, fustian-cutting, prick-laying, and damask-weaving. These are all examples typical for the industrial age Marx lived in. One can today add information labour such as journalism, software engineering, acting, singing, dancing, writing, work as secretary, receptionist, call-centre agent, etc. conducted under capitalist relations of production. The point is that on the level of value that Marx analyses in chapter 7.2 all these forms of labour that create commodities that capitalists sell in order to accumulate capital are equal forms of abstract labour that create value, surplus-value, and exchange-value that enable monetary profits.

Surplus-Value: A Key Category

Marx shows that during one part of the working day, the workers, who create commodities that objectify the value of parts of the means of production (objects of labour, instruments of labour), create the equivalent of their wage (the necessary working time) and that they create unremunerated surplus-value during the other part of the working day. In this unpaid form of labour lies the riddle of capitalism, the reason for the accumulation of capital: Capitalists exploit workers, who do not own the use-value and surplus-value and monetary profit they create. No matter if capitalists let workers create software, books, movies, yarn, cannons, or notes, they always exploit labour that creates surplus-value that is realised in the form of monetary profits. Marx provides a specific example, where half of the working day amounts to the production of the wage-equivalent and the other half is unpaid surplus-labour:

> On the one hand the daily sustenance of labour-power costs only half a day's labour, while on the other hand the very same labour-power can remain effective, can work, during a whole day, and consequently the value which its use during one day creates is double what the capitalist pays for that use. (301)

Marx argues that valorisation takes place in the production process, but that the transformation of money into capital requires both commodity circulation (the buying of labour power and the means of production, the sale of the new commodity) and the valorisation process in production (302).

Valorisation is a regular work process that creates value objectified in the product. It is, however, taken beyond the point, where labour reproduces the wage equivalent and the value of labour-power, so that surplus-labour and surplus-value emerge:

> If we now compare the process of creating value with the process of valorization, we see that the latter is nothing but the continuation of the former beyond a definite point. If the process is not carried beyond the point where the value paid by the capitalist for the labour-power is replaced by an exact equivalent, it is simply a process of creating value; but if it is continued beyond that point, it becomes a process of valorization. (302)
>
> The production process, considered as the unity of the labour process and the process of creating value, is the process of production of commodities; considered as the unity of the labour process and the process of valorization, it is the capitalist process of production, or the capitalist form of the production of commodities. (304)

Aspects of the Valorisation Process

Work is a concrete process that creates qualitative use-values, whereas valorisation is labour that creates a specific quantity of value and surplus-value (302). Surplus-value "results only from a quantitative excess of labour, from a lengthening of one and the same labour-process" (305), no matter if this labour at the concrete level creates "jewels" (305), "yarn" (305), software, emotions, music, or education.

Figure 7.4 visualises the dimensions of valorisation that Marx discusses in section 7.2.

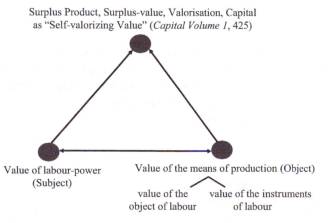

FIGURE 7.4   Aspects of the valorisation process

Marx analyses the subjective side of valorisation, the value of labour-power, in detail in chapter 6. He shows that the value of labour-power is the average time needed for the production of the means of subsistence necessary for humans to survive. Aspects of reproductive labour and housework are of particular importance in this context (see the discussion in chapter 6 of this book). Also the instruments and the objects of labour—the objective side of valorisation—have value. By making use of their labour-power, workers in the labour process transfer parts of the value of the means of production to a new product and create not just a new use-value, but also new value, surplus-value, that is turned into monetary profits in the sales process. Surplus-value is also the foundation for further processes of production and accumulation.

Exercises for Chapter 7

Group exercise (G)
Project exercise (P)

Key Categories: Work Process, Object of Work, Instruments of Work, Products of Work, Productive Consumption, Valorisation, Surplus-Value

Exercise 7.1 (G)

Work in groups: Identify a capitalist media company that is important in the country you live in. Discuss what the subject of work, the objects of work, the instruments of work, and the products of work are and how they are organised.

Present the results of the group work.

Exercise 7.2 (G)

Work in groups: Each group chooses one specific capitalist media company. Discuss how alienation of the human subject's labour, the alienation from the objects of labour, the instruments of labour, and the products of labour exactly look in your case. Try to find out if there are different forms of alienation. Reflect on the differences between wage-labour in media companies and the labour of watching, reading, listening, and creating content and how their alienation differs. Discuss the following question: How would a nonalienated media world look? How can it be achieved? What can you do in order to help overcoming alienation?

Present the results of the group work.

Exercise 7.3 (G)

Work in groups: Each group chooses a specific capitalist media company. Discuss how this company's valorisation process works. Reflect on how the company lets workers create surplus-value, what the commodity is that contains surplus-value, who the workers are who create surplus-value, and how they create the commodity and its surplus-value.

Present the results of the group work.

Notes

1   See http://en.wikipedia.org/wiki/Stone_Age.
2   See http://en.wikipedia.org/wiki/Bronze_Age.
3   See http://en.wikipedia.org/wiki/Iron_Age.

8

CONSTANT CAPITAL AND VARIABLE CAPITAL

In chapter 8, Marx further discusses aspects of the value of labour-power and the means of production. The basic point is that the "value of the means of production is [. . .] transferred to the product" and the "worker adds fresh value to the material of his labour" (307).

The Preservation and Creation of Value

In the production process, the "old form of the use-value" (308), the object of labour, "disappears, but it is taken up again in a new form of use-value" (308), a new emergent product. Concrete work creates this new use-value. It is at the same time abstract labour by which new value is created and objectified in the product (308).

> On the one hand, it is by virtue of its general character as expenditure of human labour-power in the abstract that spinning adds new value to the values of the cotton and the spindle; and on the other hand, it is by virtue of its special character as a concrete, useful process that the same labour of spinning both transfers the values of the means of production to the product and preserves them in the product. Hence a twofold result emerges within the same period of time. (308–309)

Labour at the same time creates and preserves value. There can be no creation of new value without value preservation: "The workers is unable to add new labour, to create new value, without at the same time preserving old values" because "he cannot do work of a useful kind without employing products as the means of production of a new product, and thereby transferring their value to the new product" (315). "While labour, because it is directed to a specific purpose, preserves and transfers to the product the value of the means of production, at the same time, throughout every instant it is in motion, it is creating an additional value, a new value" (316).

Marx and the Materiality of Information

Marx mentions in a parenthesised comment that man "himself, viewed merely as the physical existence of labour-power, is a natural object, a thing, although a living, conscious thing, and labour is the physical manifestation of that power" (301). From an information perspective it is important to note that Marx sees the human as a special form of the organisation of matter. He stresses consciousness as a particularly important aspect of this human form of matter. The original German formulation is as follows: "Der Mensch selbst, als bloßes Dasein von Arbeitskraft betrachtet, ist ein Naturgegenstand, ein Ding, wenn auch lebendiges, selbstbewußtes Ding, und die Arbeit selbst ist eine dingliche Äußerung jener Kraft" (MEW 23, 217). The German passage shows that Marx speaks of a "self-conscious thing" (*selbstbewußtes Ding*), not just of a conscious thing. Humans do not just think, they think and reflect about themselves and their role in the world and define their identities.

The translation that "labour is the physical manifestation of that power" is also not correct because Marx speaks of "dingliche Äußerung", which was translated as "physical manifestation". What Marx wants to stress is that labour creates a product in which it is objectified. By using the translation "physical" for "dinglich", the translators imply that work cannot create something nonphysical—that is, information. In Hegelian philosophy, also everything that exists is often termed a "thing". Therefore in Hegelian theory also information is a thing. So Marx does not want to express that work only creates things we can touch and feel, but that it creates all kind of physical and nonphysical products. A better translation is "material externalisation/utterance". In a materialist philosophy, both information and physical things are material.

The German term "Äußerung" has two meanings: (a) that an inner is turned outwards (externalised) and (b) that something is uttered. It therefore has both a general meaning and one related to information and communication. "Dingliche Äußerung" can both mean that speaking/uttering results in a change of the social world—that is, has positive results—and that an activity has external results.

Information: A Peculiar Good

Marx argues that means of production in the labour process lose their original use-value and form part of a new use-value (310). They also lose their exchange-value because once objectified in a new product, they cannot be exchanged any longer, only as part of the new use-value (311). Marx writes that "raw material and auxiliary substances" such as coal or oil "lose the independent form with which they entered into the labour process" (311). The situation is different if information enters as a resource into a production process because it is a peculiar good that is not used up in consumption, does not wear out in use, and can be endlessly copied without having to reconstruct all components. For copying the file named "8_Chapter8" that I am currently writing onto a flash drive, I do not have to rewrite all characters, words, and sentences that constitute the file's text. For getting another piece of coal if I have burned one, someone in contrast has to mine coal. Once created, information can enter into numerous production processes without having to be newly created. If I write a book, then a chapter from it can be reused in another book by reprinting it without me having to rewrite the chapter. In contrast, if the car body of one specific old-timer shall be reproduced so that a replica is created, one cannot use the original car's carriage without destroying the original car; additional metal sheets need to be put into the production process. One and the same idea can exist in multiple books, but one and the same metal plate cannot exist in two different products.

There are means of production that have no value—that is, have not been created by human work. Marx mentions, for example, land, wind, and water (312). A windmill transforms wind into energy. Wind is the object of work. Nature supplies and produces it. Wind created by nature does not have any value. It enters the energy production process as a gratis resource.

Marx argues that parts of the means of production can as waste "enter as a whole in the valorization process, although it enters only piece by piece into the labour process" (313). An example is that a special pair of trousers is tailored out of fabric. The fabric is cut to the right proportion and parts of it remain as waste. It is not enough fabric for making another pair of trousers and is therefore useless to the tailor, who throws it away. The tailor, however, has to pay for the full fabric, not just the part s/he uses for the trousers.

The Definition of Constant and Variable Capital

Labour does not transfer the full value of the instruments of labour to one product because such tools persist in the production period for a longer time and are used for creating a larger number of products: "Suppose its use-value in the labour process lasts only six days. It then loses on average one-sixth of its use-value every day, and therefore parts with one-sixth of its value to each day's product" (312). A tool or machine enters and reenters with its whole use-value into the production process, "while it only enters in parts into the valorization process" (312).

Labour-power has a specific value that is accounted for by paying a wage. Labour is "labour-power in action" (315) that as part of this action transfers value to a new use-value, but also creates new value, surplus-value. The means of production in contrast do not create value, but labour transfers only part of their value to the product. Based on this analysis, Marx introduces the concepts of constant and variable capital for the monetary expression of the value of the objective and the subjective side of the capitalist production process:

> That part of capital, therefore, which is turned into means of production, i.e. the raw material, the auxiliary material and the instruments of labour, does not undergo any quantitative alteration of value in the process of production. For this reason, I call it the constant part of capital, or more briefly, constant capital. On the other hand, that part of capital which is turned into labour-power does undergo an alteration of value in the process of production. It both reproduces the equivalent of its own value and produces an excess, a surplus-value, which may itself vary, and be more or less according to circumstances. This part of capital is continually being transformed from a constant into a variable magnitude. I therefore call it the variable part of capital, or more briefly, variable capital. The same elements of capital which, from the point of view of the labour process, can be distinguished respectively as the objective and subjective factors, as means of production and labour-power, can be distinguished, from the point of view of the valorization process, as constant and variable capital. (317)

The value of the means of production can change if there is technical or scientific progress and they can be produced quicker and cheaper (318–319). In such cases, an old machine "undergoes a certain amount of depreciation, and therefore transfers proportionately less value to the product" (318).

The Dialectic of Constant and Variable Capital

Figure 8.1 visualises the dialectic of variable and constant capital.

Valorisation = Value-transfer and creation of new value: Monetary value of the new product $V = c + v + s$ (Subject-Object)

Variable capital v: Monetary expression of the value of labour-power: Variable capital (Subject)

Constant capital c: Monetary expression of the value of the means of production (raw materials, auxiliary materials, instruments of labour) (Object)

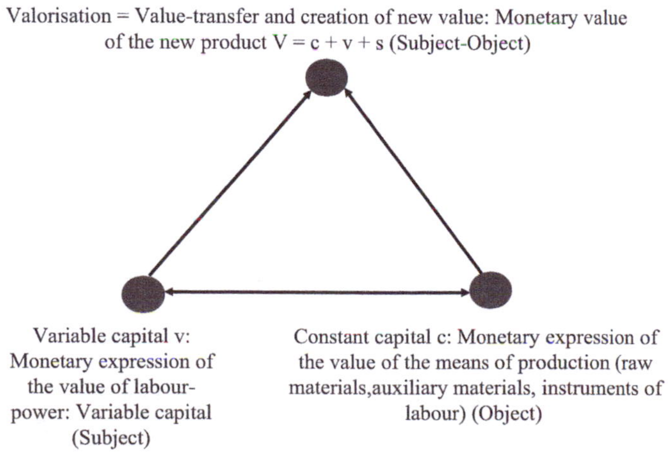

FIGURE 8.1 The dialectic of variable and constant capital

In the capitalist production process, the capitalist purchases labour-power and means of production. Humans in the actual labour process transfer the value of the means of production and of labour-power to a new product. Labour creates, however, also new value so that a surplus-value and a surplus product emerge. The value of the new product is $V = c + v + s$ (constant capital + variable capital + surplus-value). Only labour creates new value, which is why Marx terms the monetary expression of the labour-power's value "variable capital".

Exercise for Chapter 8

Group exercise (G)
Project exercise (P)

Key Categories: Preservation of Value, Transfer of Value, Constant Capital, Variable Capital

Exercise 8.1 (G)

Work in groups: Each group chooses one capitalist media product that it is familiar with. Discuss what aspects of constant and variable capital can be found. Reflect if information plays a specific role as object or instrument of labour and how it differs from noninformational means of production.

Search for information sources that specify the wage level (variable capital) and costs of the components of constant capital for your chosen media product.

Present and compare the results of the group work.

9

THE RATE OF SURPLUS-VALUE

9.1 The Degree of Exploitation of Labour-Power

Profit as the Monetary Expression of Surplus-Value

Marx explains in section 9.1 how the value of capital changes in the capitalist production process. The invested capital has the monetary value $C = c + v$ (constant capital + variable capital). In the capitalist production process, a new commodity C' emerges that has an emergent use-value and emergent value that did not exist before and that labour creates. The new commodity's value is $C' = c + v + s$ (constant capital + variable capital + profit).

Marx in this and other chapters speaks of surplus-value in monetary terms—for example, a "surplus-value of £90" (320). One should note that when he initially introduces the notion of value in chapter 1, Marx makes clear that labour is the substance of value and labour-time its measure. Value can be measured in average labour hours and monetary units. Marx assumes in *Capital Volume 1* that "prices = values" (329, footnote 9), but points out that the situation is more complex, which is the topic of the transformation problem (the transformation of labour values into prices) that is covered in *Capital Volume 3* (see 329, footnote 9). Profit is the monetary expression of surplus-value. Surplus-value also takes on the form of a specific number of unpaid average working hours. s in the formula $C' = c + v + s$ stands for surplus-value, but one should bear in mind that Marx speaks about monetary expressions, which is why this formula could also be written as $C' = c + v + p$, where p stands for profit.

It is important for Marx's theory that the "new value actually created in the process, the 'value-product', is [...] not the same as the value of the product" (321). The monetary value of the means of production that is expressed in constant capital is not new value, but value that labour already created in the past. Its value is transferred to the new commodity C', but not newly created. Constant capital is dead value objectified in means of production. Labour-power is living value that as labour in action transfers the value c to the new product C'. It also creates the value of its own labour-power that monetarily is expressed as a wage and produces the surplus-value that in monetary terms is expressed as profit. It "is v alone that varies" (322). Constant capital is solid, whereas labour is "fluid, value-creating" (323).

Necessary Labour-Time, Necessary Labour, Surplus Labour, Surplus Labour-Time

Based on these assumptions, Marx introduces the notions of necessary labour-time, necessary labour, surplus labour, and surplus labour-time:

> We have seen that the worker, during one part of the labour process, produces only the value of his labour-power, i.e. the value of his means of subsistence. [. . .] I call the portion of the working day during which this reproduction takes place necessary labour-time, and the labour expended during that time necessary labour; necessary for the worker, because independent of the particular social form of his labour; necessary for capital and the capitalist world, because the continued existence of the worker is the basis of that world.
>
> During the second period of the labour process, that in which his labour is no longer necessary labour, the worker does indeed expend labour-power, he does work, but his labour is no longer necessary labour, and he creates no value for himself. He creates surplus-value which, for the capitalist, has all the charms of something created out of nothing. This part of the working day I call surplus labour-time, and to the labour expended during that time I give the name of surplus labour. (324–325)

Marx writes that "economic formations of society" distinguish themselves from each other "in the form in which this surplus labour is in each case extorted from the immediate producer, the worker" (325). Surplus-labour is not specific for capitalism, but exists in all class societies, such as slavery, feudalism, and capitalism. The dominant class organises the exploitation of the dominated class' labour in different manners. Marx comes back to this issue in chapter 10's section 2, "The Voracious Appetite for Surplus Labour. Manufacturer and Boyar."

The Rate of Surplus-Value: The Degree of Exploitation

Marx defines the rate of surplus-value that he also calls the degree of exploitation as follows:

$$rate\ of\ surplus\ value\ rs = \frac{s}{v} = \frac{surplus\ labour}{necessary\ labour} \quad (326)$$

He gives two examples, one calculated in labour hours (326, footnote 7), the other in British pounds (£) (327), which shows that for him value has both a labour-time and a monetary dimension:

1) necessary labour = 5 hours, surplus labour = 5 hours; => working day = 10 hours; rs = 5 / 5 = 100%
2) c = £410, v = £90, p = £90, C = c + v + p = 590; rs = 90 / 90 = 100%

That Marx uses the term "degree of exploitation" shows that his theory is not just a new analytical political economy that goes beyond classical political economy, but that it is a highly political theory that takes the standpoint and interest of the working class and opposes the capitalist class and capitalism. It is a critique of the political economy of capitalism. The term "exploitation" is a moral and political term. It can never have a positive meaning, but implies that something is wrong, a scandal, unjust, and should be abolished. Marx shows with analytical means that the capitalist class makes the working class work beyond necessary labour-time so that a surplus emerges that the capitalists own. The rate of surplus-value is an important dimension of capitalism because it determines how much profit can be achieved per unit of time. By calling the rate of surplus-value also degree of exploitation, Marx brings the dimension of political struggle and ethics into the analysis. His theory is therefore not just scientific and analytical, but also ethical.

What Is Exploitation, and What's Wrong with It? Is Marx an Ethical Thinker or Is Ethics Always a Form of Class Morality?

Here is an example of how Marx uses the term "exploitation" in chapter 13: "The driving motive and determining purpose of capitalist production is the self-valorization of capital to the greatest possible extent, i.e. the greatest possible production of surplus-value, hence the greatest possible exploitation of labour-power by the capitalist" (449). Marx here points out that exploitation of labour-power is an absolute need for capital to exist. At the same time, he chooses the term "exploitation" deliberately in order to note that capitalism is morally unacceptable, should be abolished, and needs to be abolished in order to enable a truly human life for all.

Ethics and morality are often viewed as idealistic, a realm of pure ideas as represented most prominently by religious ideology. Friedrich Engels argues in his work *Anti-Dühring: Herr Eugen Dühring's Revolution in Science* that morality in class society is class morality that justifies the interests of the ruling class:

> From the moment when private ownership of movable property developed, all societies in which this private ownership existed had to have this moral injunction in common: Thou shalt not steal. [. . .] We maintain on the contrary that all moral theories have been hitherto the product, in the last analysis, of the economic conditions of society obtaining at the time. And as society has hitherto moved in class antagonisms, morality has always been class morality; it has either justified the domination and the interests of the ruling class, or ever since the oppressed class became powerful enough, it has represented its indignation against this domination and the future interests of the oppressed. That in this process there has on the whole been progress in morality, as in all other branches of human knowledge, no one will doubt. But we have not yet passed beyond class morality. (Engels 1878, 87–88)

Marxists sometimes argue that Marx's approach was not ethical, but scientific. Such an opposition, however, implies that morals, which are parts of culture, play no particular role for the economy and are determined or overdetermined by economic development. Capitalism moves in and through contradictions, but economic contradictions alone do not result in revolutions. Revolutions often take place in situations of objective crisis, but such crises alone do not result in the breakdown of societies. Revolutions require a collective subjective factor, the collective insight that a specific rule shall be abolished. If a person joins revolutionary forces or opposes them is not simply determined by his or her class position, but by the sum total of experiences he or she has made throughout his or her life in all social relations s/he has entered, including the economy, politics, family, personal relations, etc. Political and moral beliefs are material and come about through experiences in such social relations and the various group memberships and relations, including class relations, that humans enter. Humans who have comparable group memberships are more likely to share political and moral worldviews, but they do not necessarily do so because experiences are complex and multidimensional. Culture, morals, and ideology are therefore not simple superstructures, but important material dimensions of society. A revolutionary socialist theory is necessarily analytical and ethical: It analyses the constitution and contradictions of class societies and provides foundations for making grounded judgements as to why class societies are false forms of human existence that should be abolished.

Engels, however, also speaks of a true human morality in communism: "A really human morality which stands above class antagonisms and above any recollection of them becomes possible only at a stage of society which has not only overcome class antagonisms but has even forgotten them in practical life" (Engels 1878, 88). Moral values do not die out in a communist society, but take on specific forms that differ from class morality.

Marx's Critique of Kantian Ethics

Ethics is a theory of morality, a theory of principles that can be used for discerning what one can consider as good and evil. The German philosopher Immanuel Kant (1724–1804) is considered to be an important representative of so-called deontological ethics, which judge each single action according to specific rules. The autonomy of the will is for Kant (1785, 109) "the supreme principle of morality". The consequence of his principle of autonomy is the Golden Role as categorical imperative: "Act only according to that maxim by which you can at the same time will that it should become a universal law. [. . .] Act as though the maxim of your action were by your will to become a universal law of nature. [. . .] So act that you use humanity, in your own person as well as in the person of any other, always at the same time as an end, never merely as a means" (Kant 1785, 71, 87). The German critical theorist Jürgen Habermas (2008, 140) argues that Kant's categorical imperative is reflected in the insight that freedoms are only limited by the freedom of others. Habermas (2011, 14) says that Kant's principle of autonomy and his categorical imperative is present in the *Universal Declaration of Human Rights'* §1: "All human beings are born free and equal in dignity and rights".

Marx criticised that liberalism is highly individualistic and that liberal freedoms justify the freedom of private property that comes in contradiction with social freedom—that is, equality—and the right of everyone to lead a good life. He writes in this context that Kant stresses autonomy and the human will as individual principles and thereby sees emancipation attainable by individual reason, not by the social emancipation from class: "Kant was satisfied with 'good Will' alone, even if it remained entirely without result, and he transferred the realisation of this good will, the harmony between it and the needs and impulses of individuals, to the world beyond. Kant's good will fully corresponds to the impotence, depression and wretchedness of the German burghers, whose petty interests were never capable of developing into the common, national interests of a class and who were, therefore, constantly exploited by the bourgeois of all other nations" (Marx and Engels 1845, 208).

Marx's Categorical Imperative: Ethics as the Politics of Class Struggles against Class Society

Marx, however, formulated his own ethical principle in the introduction to the *Contribution to the Critique of Hegel's Philosophy of Law*, a categorical imperative that is an alternative to the one by Kant. It is based on the principle that "man is the highest being for man", from which Marx derives "the categorical imperative to overthrow all relations in which man is a debased, enslaved, forsaken, despicable being" (MECW 3, 182). Marx deeply opposed all class societies because he thought that class is deeply unjust and does not correspond to what humans can and should be. At the same time he thought that as foundation for a free society highly productive technology is needed in order to free humans from toil. The concept of the rate of exploitation is an important tool for the analysis of capitalism and at the same time an expression of Marx's critical categorical imperative and therefore the expression of the ethical judgment that capitalism and class are wrong and should be abolished.

9.2. The Representation of the Value of the Product by Corresponding Proportional Parts of the Product

The Measurement of Weight and Money in 19th-Century Britain

The one or the other reader may find some of Marx's example calculations difficult to follow. One factor contributing to this circumstance is that not everyone is familiar with the measurements of weight, length, area, capacity, and money he uses. In section 9.2 he speaks, for example, of pounds (lb) of cotton and yarn and shillings (s). These measurements of weight and money were commonly used in 19th-century Britain, which formed the historical context of *Capital*. The pound is today still the common measure of mass in the USA. The Commonwealth countries use both the kilogramme and the pound, whereas most other countries in the world have adopted the kilogramme, which, in contrast to the pound, is based on the metric system as measure of weight. Today one pound equals 0.45359237 kg. At the time of Marx, a different definition of the pound was used, the troy pound. One troy pound is 0.372242 kg.

From 1707 until 1971, the UK used a measurement of money, in which one British pound sterling (£) consisted of 20 shillings (s) and 1 shilling of 12 pence. So 1 £ consisted of 240 pence so that the measurement of the pound was not a decimal. In addition, also the sixpence (d) (also called a half-shilling or tanner) was used. It equalled six pence. One pence (also called one "penny") was subdivided into four farthings.

For the contemporary reader, it is easier to consider Marx's examples by converting troy pounds (lb) into kilogrammes (kg) and shillings (s) into pence (p). Converting the measures, Marx speaks in his example used in section 9.2 of the production of 7.4 kg of yarn with a total monetary value of £1.5. The total value is made up of the following: c = £1.2, v = £0.15, p = £0.15. Marx points out that of the 7.4 kg of yarn, the constant capital of £1.2 represents 80% of the weight (5.92 kg), variable capital 10% (0.74 kg), and profit also 10% (0.74 kg). Marx assumes that it takes on average 12 hours to spin 7.4 kg of yarn. Variable capital equals profit in the example. Therefore the rate of surplus-value rs = £0.15 / £0.15 = 100%. This also means that the necessary labour-time is six hours and the surplus labour-time is equally six hours so that rs = 6 / 6 = 100%.

An Example: The US Information Economy

In order to illustrate the rate of surplus-value, let us discuss an example from the world of the media and information. Table 9.1 shows some macroeconomic data for the US information economy in the year 2010.

The OECD uses a classification of industries (International Standard Industrial Classification Revision 4.0) in the database from which the data was derived that sees publishing, audiovisuals and broadcasting, telecommunications, IT, and other information services as the industries forming the information sector. This can certainly be debated because one could argue that also hardware, electronics equipment, semiconductors, arts, entertainment, science, education, and advertising belong

TABLE 9.1 Macroeconomic data about the US information economy, year 2010 (data source: OECD STAN database), FTE = full time equivalents

	Value added (million US$)	FTE total employees (in 1,000s)	Compensation of employees (million US$)	Gross operating surplus (million US$)	Rate of surplus-value
Information and communication	807,753 (5.6%)	3,904 (3.2%)	404,712 (5.1%)	361,087 (6.5%)	89.2%
Publishing	143,519 (1.0%)	1,063 (0.9%)	81,783 (1.0%)	59,607 (1.1%)	72.9%
Audiovisuals, broadcasting	58,445 (0.4%)	753 (0.6%)	27,811 (0.3%)	27,597 (0.5%)	99.2%
Tele-communications	347,282 (2.4%)	1,168 (1.0%)	107,202 (1.3%)	208,430 (3.8%)	194. 4%
IT and other information services	258,027 258,507 (1.8%)	1,673 1,673 (1.4%)	187,916 (2.4%)	65,453 (1.2%)	34.8%
Total	14,526 547	120,921	7,980,612	5,549,257	69.5%

to this industry. For statistical purposes that allow us to calculate the monetary rate of surplus-value, we stick with the database's assumptions. The table also shows the percentage shares the information sector and its industries have in the total US economy. The entire information economy accounted in 2010 for 5.6% of the US value added, 3.2% of the employees, 5.1% of employee compensation, and 6.5% of pretax profits.

Calculating the relationship of pretax profits to employee compensation allows approximating the rate of surplus-value in these industries for the year 2010. Whereas the rate of surplus-value was around 70% in the total US economy in 2010, it was around 90% in the information economy as a whole. It is in all information industries, except IT and other information services, significantly higher than in the total US economy. IT workers, such as software engineers, tend to have relatively high salaries, which explains the circumstance that the rate of surplus-value is in this industry with 35% significantly lower than in the total US economy.

Data about the number of full-time equivalent employees in the industry allows us to calculate necessary and surplus labour-time. So, for example, according to the data in the table, profit-to-compensation stood in a relationship of 47.2% to 52.8% in the US information economy in the year 2010. Therefore we can assume that out of the 3,904,000 full-time equivalents, 2,064,624 represent necessary labour-time and 1,840,801 unremunerated surplus labour-time. If one calculates the relationship of surplus labour-time to necessary labour-time for the US information economy in 2010 as 1,840,801 / 2,064 624, then the rate of surplus-value is again 89.2%, which is the same rate as in the calculation based on monetary units for profits and employee compensation.

Marx's Critique of Bourgeois Economists' Concepts of Value

Marx argues that bourgeois economists often confuse the fact that new value is not the same as the value of the product. They assume that also constant capital is new value. But human labour has already been produced in the past both as value and use-value. Such confusion therefore double-counts something that already exists. Marx argues that such economists conduct such double-counting deliberately for ideological reasons because they are "as much interested, practically, in the valorization process, as they are, theoretically, in misunderstanding it" (332).

Marx discusses one such ideological interpretation of new value in section 9.3: "Nassau William Senior's 'Last Hour'".

9.3. Senior's "Last Hour"

Who Was Nassau William Senior?

Nassau William Senior (1790–1864) was a British economist who held the Drummond Professorship of Political Economy at the University of Oxford. Marx explains that Senior was asked by Manchester manufacturers to help them to publicly argue against the political demand that the working day should be limited to 10 hours a day. The Factory Act of 1833 had limited the number of hours the 14- to 18-year-olds were allowed to work in textile mills per day to 12 hours. In the 1830s, the Ten Hours Movement emerged, which demanded that adolescents' working time should be restricted to 10 hours per day. Senior tried to develop a rationale called the "last hour" argument, which could be used for opposing such a reduction. He published this idea in the work *Letters on the Factory Act, as It Affects the Cotton Manufacture*, which came out in 1837. Marx shows that bourgeois polemics against the 10-hour day again and again took up Senior's argument.

Senior's "Last Hour" Argument

Marx quotes a full page from Senior's book (333–334) in order to explain the "last hour" argument. The mathematics in this passage is difficult to understand because, as Marx says, "Senior's presentation is confused" (334, footnote 10). Marx explains the argument in easier terms in footnote 10 on page 334. It goes as follows:

A manufacturer invests £80,000 in machines and £20 000 in wages and raw materials. The invested capital is £100,000. The profit rate is 15% per year so that the profit p = £15,000 per year. Senior argues that the total value of £115,000 is created in the following way:

- The invested capital of £100,000 represents 100/115 = 20/23 (87.0%) of the value and therefore 10 hours of work per day (20/23 of 11.5 hours) throughout the year.
- The technology would deteriorate by £5,000 per year, which would represent 5/115 = 1/23 (4.3%) of the value and therefore half an hour of work per day (1/23 of 11.5 hours) throughout the year.
- profit of £15,000 per year would be reduced by technology's depreciation so that a net profit of £10,000 remains that represents 10/115 = 2/23 of the value and therefore 1 hour of work per day (2/23 of 11.5 hours) throughout the year. The profit would therefore be produced within the last hour of the working day.
- Reducing the working day from 11.5 to 10 hours per day would therefore reduce the profit to zero and destroy the textile industry.
- Increasing the working day from 11.5 to 13 hours would in contrast more than double the profit.

The Problems of Senior's Approach

An error in Senior's assumptions is that he considers all commodity value, also the value of constant capital, as new. This circumstance derives from his assumption that capital is productive—that is, that capital and not labour is the decisive factor that creates wealth. This assumption is ludicrous because nobody can survive in an economy that exists only of money and no goods. Everyone can, in contrast, survive in an economy that does not know money, but that is constituted by work that creates goods that are distributed to all. An economy that consists purely of money cannot survive. An economy that exists purely of the production of goods and has no money and no exchange can survive. This thought experiment shows that work is more fundamental than money and exchange. Work creates wealth. One cannot eat, sleep in, and communicate with money, but one can eat the food, sleep in the houses, and communicate with the help of the media that human work creates.

Senior also makes the mistake to assume that the machine's full value is accounted for by the labour conducted in one year. The spinning machines that the manufacturers buy are, however, in contrast to the annual cotton supply not just used during one year, but for several years. The value that is transferred from machines to the commodities is in the example therefore not £80,000, but rather the deterioration of £5,000. Senior double-counts the full value of machines over several years, which is a fundamental error of calculation.

Marx's Criticism of Senior's "Last Hour" Argument

Marx criticises Senior's "last hour" argument. He says Senior lumps together raw materials and wages into a capital of £20,000. For a more thorough accounting, it would make sense to keep them separate—for example, raw materials = £10,000 and wages v = £10,000. Given this assumption, profits p and wages v have the same size of £10,000. If wages and profits are equal, then the rate of surplus-value must be 100%, which means that half of the working day is necessary labour-time and the other half surplus-labour time. Therefore 5¾ hours per day are necessary labour-time, during which the workers produce the monetary wage-equivalent of the value of their labour power, and 5¾ hours are unremunerated surplus labour-time. If the working time is increased to 13 hours a day and wages remain unchanged, as Senior and his bourgeois friends would like to have it, then necessary labour-time is still 5¾ hours and surplus labour-time increases to 7¼ hours so that the rate of surplus-value is 7¼ / 5¾ = 126.1%. One can in this example therefore not expect, as Senior did, that profits double, but that they rather rise by about 11.1%. If in contrast, the working day is reduced to 10 hours and wages remain constant, as trade unions and the workers want to have it, then the necessary labour-time is 5¾ hours and the surplus labour-time 4¼ hours. The rate of surplus-value is therefore 4¼ / 5¾ = 73.9%. Profits therefore are not reduced to 0%, as Senior assumes, but can be expected to somewhat fall because the rate of exploitation decreases from 100% to around 73.9%.

9.4. The Surplus Product

The Surplus Product

A commodity has a use-value and a value. Surplus-value or profit p constitutes one part of the commodity's total value $C' = c + v + p$. Given the dual character of the commodity, profit represents a specific share of the use-value. If the total use-value is, for example, 7.4 kg yarn, as in the example Marx uses in section 9.2, profit is p = £0.15, and the total commodity value $C' = 1.5$, then the profit accounts for 10% of the monetary value, which corresponds to 0.74 kg of the yarn at the level of use-value.

Marx ends chapter 9 with a passage that leads over to chapter 10, in which he focuses on the working day:

> The sum of the necessary labour and the surplus labour, i.e. the sum of the periods of time during which the worker respectively replaces the value of his labour-power and produces the surplus- value, constitutes the absolute extent of his labour-time, i.e. the working day. (339)

The Three Dimensions of Surplus

Marx argues in *Capital Volume 1*'s chapter 1 that a commodity has use-value, value, and exchange-value. Use-value can be measured in units of a specific good (e.g., 1 sofa), value in the average amount of hours it takes to produce the commodity (e.g., 1 hour), and exchange-value as money (e.g., £500). Surplus is organised on all three levels: It takes the form of use-value, value, and exchange-value—surplus product, surplus-labour time, and monetary surplus-value (profit). Figure 9.1 visualises this connection.

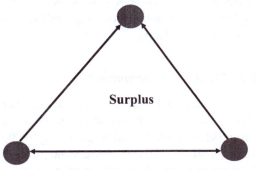

FIGURE 9.1   The three dimensions of surplus

The Process of Capital Accumulation

Given that Marx makes clear in chapters 8 and 9 that the value of a newly produced commodity is $C' = c + v + p$, one can, based on these insights, describe the capitalist economic process as visualised in figure 9.2.

Marx does not introduce the formula M–C (Mp, L).. P.. C'–M' that describes the accumulation of capital in *Capital Volume 1*, but rather in *Volume 2*, where it appears at the start of chapter 1, "The Circuit of Money Capital" (Marx 1885, 109). The logical foundations for this formula are, however, already laid out in *Volume 1*. Capitalists invest money capital M (which they often obtain from banks, to which they pay interest for loans) for buying labour power L and means of production Mp. The monetary value of labour-power is called variable capital, the monetary value of the means of production is termed constant capital. Marx distinguishes in *Volume 2* between two forms of constant capital: circulating constant capital and fixed constant capital. Circulating constant capital refers to resources that lose their value through full productive consumption in the production process. It includes raw- and auxiliary-materials, operating supply items, and semifinished products. Fixed constant capital in contrast stays in the production process for a longer time and only gradually loses and transfers value to the commodity. One can count machines, buildings, and equipment to this form of capital. Marx introduces the terms "fixed capital" and "circulating capital" in *Volume 2*'s chapter 8, "Fixed Capital and Circulating Capital", where he, however, refers back to *Volume 1*'s chapter 8, where the distinction has already been established logically, but not with detailed terminology.

In the production process P, workers conduct labour in order to transfer the value of parts of the means of production to a new commodity and create the value of their labour-power, as well as new surplus-value. The new commodity's value C' is $c + v + s$; it is larger than the value of the initial commodities. The commodity value has been increased by a surplus-value (measured in hours of labour) and surplus product Δc. The new commodity C' is sold at a price M', which is larger than the initial capital M so that a monetary profit p emerges and $M' = M + p = M + \Delta m$. Part of the profit is reinvested for expanding economic operations; other parts are used for other purposes such as paying interest to banks and dividends to shareholders. The main goal and purpose of capitalism is that capital increases—that is, is accumulated—by exploiting human labour.

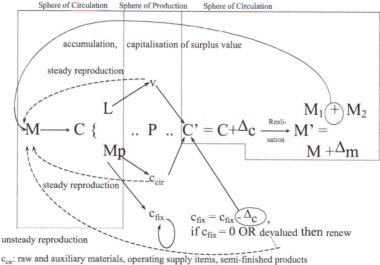

FIGURE 9.2   The accumulation of capital

Exercises for Chapter 9

Group exercise (G)
Project exercise (P)

Key Categories: Necessary Labour, Necessary Labour-Time, Surplus Labour, Surplus Labour-Time, Rate of Surplus-Value, Degree of Exploitation, Exploitation, Surplus Product

Exercise 9.1 (P)

Work in groups: Inform yourself where you can obtain macroeconomic statistics about the economy you live in. Each group selects one specific media, cultural, or information industry. For specific years or a series of specific years, look for data about the total profits and the total wages in this industry. Calculate the rate of exploitation. If groups focus on different industries for the same years, then the rates of exploitation can be compared to each other. Which media/cultural/information industry has the highest rate of exploitation? Why?

Exercise 9.2 (G)

"Exploitation" is for Marx both an *analytical* term that describes the rate of surplus-value as an important factor that has influence on the profits that companies can make and as an *ethical* term for criticising capitalism as an unjust system that should be abolished and substituted by a democratic–communist society.

Discuss in groups and compare your results: What is ethics? What is the role of ethics and morality in capitalism? Why exactly is exploitation in Marx's opinion bad? How could a nonexploitative economy look? How does exploitation work in the capitalist information economy? How could a nonexploitative information economy look?

10

THE WORKING DAY

10.1 The Limits of the Working Day

The Lengthening of the Working Day: An Example

Marx gives an example for the lengthening of the working day by considering three different working conditions (340):

Working day I: A - - - - - - B - C	necessary labour-time: 6 hours, surplus labour-time: 1 hour
Working day II: A - - - - - - B - - - C	necessary labour-time: 6 hours, surplus labour-time: 3 hours
Working day III: A - - - - - - B - - - - - - C	necessary labour-time: 6 hours, surplus labour-time: 6 hours

The corresponding rates of surplus-value rs = surplus labour-time / necessary labour-time are therefore as follows:

rs I:	16.67%
rs II:	50%
rs III:	100%

Absolute Surplus-Value Production

The example shows that lengthening the working-day absolutely is a method for increasing labour's degree of exploitation. Marx calls this method the method of absolute surplus-value production: The working-day's length is increased. Part III's (chapters 7–11) title is "The Production of Absolute Surplus-Value", and it becomes apparent in chapter 10 why Marx has chosen it. Having introduced the notions of constant capital, variable capital, and surplus-value/profit, he in chapter 9 defines the rate of surplus-value and makes clear that the capitalist is structurally compelled to try to ever more increase this rate and to thereby extend or intensify the exploitation of labour. Given the notion of the exploitation of labour, Marx turns in chapter 10 to the method of absolute surplus-value production as one way of increasing the exploitation of labour.

Marx argues that the working day is "variable" and "fluid"; it can vary (341). It has a maximum that is set by the fact that the worker needs time for sleeping, resting, social and intellectual life, etc. (341).

The "soul of capital" is that it has "one sole driving force, the drive to valorize itself, to create surplus-value" (342). "Capital is dead labour which, vampire-like, lives only by sucking living labour, and lives the more, the more labour it sucks" (342). The capitalist has the interest to make the worker work as much and as fast as possible for the same wage. The worker in contrast has the interest to get as much of a wage as possible for the performed work in order to live a better life. Wage and profit, the respective interest of the worker and the capitalist, are polar opposites that are inversely proportional. The result of this class contradiction is "a struggle between collective capital, i.e. the class of capitalists, and collective labour, i.e. the working class" about the "norm for the working day" (344).

10.2. The Voracious Appetite for Surplus Labour. Manufacturer and Boyar

Historical Forms of the Appropriation of Surplus Labour

Marx points out in section 9.1 that "economic formations of society" distinguish themselves from each other "in the form in which this surplus labour is in each case extorted from the immediate producer, the worker" (325). He discusses this topic in more detail in section 10.2:

> Capital did not invent surplus labour. Wherever a part of society possesses the monopoly of the means of production, the worker, free or unfree, must add to the labour-time necessary for his own maintenance an extra quantity of labour-time in order to produce the means of subsistence for the owner of the means of production, whether this proprietor be an Athenian *kaloz k'agadoz* [aristocrat], an Etruscan theocrat, a *civis romanus*, a Norman baron, an American slave-owner, a Wallachian boyar, a modern landlord or a capitalist. (344–345)

Marx describes that in ancient societies the production of surplus labour often took on the form of forced overwork or even forced labour until death. In US slavery, forced overwork would have been an important principle. He also describes the system of corvée labour, in which the days worked for the lord create surplus labour and the other days form necessary labour time. Marx argues that as a pure form of production, corvée labour existed in Moldavia and Wallachia, which later became part of Romania. He describes that in Wallachia the days of the corvée were 56 out of a total of 140 working days per year. The rate of surplus-value was therefore according to Marx sv = 56/84 = 66.67%.

Marx quotes from factory inspectors' public reports to show that mill-owners let employees work for and after the formal start, and cut short the breakfast and dinner breaks. Both the capitalist who exploits labour and the boyar who exploits slaves share the "appetite for surplus labour" (346).

Modes of Production: The Grundrisse and the German Ideology

In the *Grundrisse*'s section "Forms which Precede Capitalist Production" (Marx 1857/1858) as well as in the *German Ideology*'s section "Feuerbach: Opposition of the Materialist and Idealist Outlooks" (Marx and Engels 1845), Marx discusses the following historical sequence of modes of production that are class societies:

1. The tribal community based on the patriarchal family
2. Ancient communal property in cities (Rome, Greece)
3. Feudal production in the countryside
4. Capitalism

A Typology of Modes of Production

Table 10.1 provides a classification of modes of production based on the dominant forms of ownership (self-control, partly self-control and partly alien control, full alien control)

A mode of production is a unity of productive forces and relations of production (Marx and Engels 1845, 91). If these modes are based on classes as their relations of production, then they have specific contradictions that result in the sublation (*Aufhebung*) of one mode of production and the emergence of a new one. The emergence of a new mode of production does not necessarily abolish but rather sublates (*aufheben*) older modes of production. This means that history is for Marx a dialectical process precisely in Hegel's threefold meaning of the term "Aufhebung" (sublation): (1) uplifting, (2) elimination, (3) preservation: (1) There are new qualities of the economy, (2) the dominance of an older mode of production vanishes, (3) but this older mode continues to exist in the new mode in a specific form and relation. The rise of, for example, capitalism did not bring an end to patriarchy and slavery, but the latter two continued to exist in such a way that a specific household economy emerged that fulfils the role of the reproduction of modern labour power. A sublation can be more or less fundamental. A transition from capitalism to communism requires a fundamental elimination of capitalism. Elimination and preservation can take place to differing degrees. A sublation is also no linear progression. It is always possible that relations that resemble earlier modes of organisation are created.

Slavery as Mode of Production in the Media and Culture Industry

In 2014, American companies such as Alcatel–Lucent and Google acknowledged that their hardware products are likely to contain minerals such as tin, gold, tungsten, or tantalum from war-torn regions in the Congo. Many other companies, including Walt Disney, reported that they do not know if their products contain such "conflict minerals".[1]

> People in the DRC are at risk of forced labour in the mining and agriculture industry, sexual exploitation and domestic servitude. The reasons for this are complex. Decades of political instability and a violent civil war, which erupted in 1997, have left the DRC as one of the countries with the highest number of displaced people in the world. [. . .] Despite being a mineral rich nation, the DRC is one of the poorest countries in the world. [. . .] Often called 'Conflict Minerals', tin, tungsten, gold and tantalum, or coltan, originating from the DRC are used by manufacturers in portable consumer electronics, medical devices and advanced aeronautics. [. . .] The vast majority, as many as 90%, of the men working in the mines of eastern DRC are trapped in a system of debt bondage. New workers borrow money from their employers to buy the necessary tools to carry out the work, as well as food, basic supplies and accommodation. The minimal payment they receive for their work is designed not to cover their expenses, and the interest rates for loans are unfairly high, with employers capitalising on workers' illiteracy and lack of knowledge surrounding debt repayment schemes. Though

TABLE 10.1 The main forms of ownership in various modes of production

	Owner of labour power	Owner of the means of production	Owner of the products of work
Patriarchy	Patriarch	Patriarch	Family
Slavery	Slave master	Slave master	Slave master
Feudalism	Partly self-control, partly lord	Partly self-control, partly lord	Partly self-control, partly lord
Capitalism	Worker	Capitalist	Capitalist
Communism	Self	All	Partly all, partly individual

most workers realise that the debt is impossible to pay off, they are locked into the system, where any objection could lead to severe penalties, violence or arrest by the implicated authorities. [. . .] Women and children are often abducted by armed rebel groups, often in village raids, and forced to work in the mines, as well as performing other tasks around the mining camps. With a high level of sexual violence in the DRC, women and girls are often forced to labour in the mines during the day, and are sexually exploited at night.[2]

Slavery has stayed a reality within the capitalist world society. The production of electronics, computers, phones, and other hardware is to a specific degree based on slavery. Slavery allows high rates of exploitation. That within a global division of labour, the production of some commodities, including media commodities, is connected to slavery, shows that this class relation benefits corporations in maximising their profits by reducing wage costs.

Factory Inspectors' Reports as Empirical Data

Marx in section 10.2 introduces the method of citing from the reports of factory inspectors that he uses in many of the chapters that follow. He notes that Britain is a very good case study because it is "the classic representative of capitalist production, and is the only country to possess a continuous set of official statistics" about working conditions (349, footnote 15). The factory inspectors observed the working conditions in English factories and wrote about them in reports published every six months. Marx's method in *Capital* is not just theoretical and logical, but also historical and empirical. He uses many examples that he takes from systematic observations and then interprets them theoretically. The inspectors used the qualitative social science method that is today called structured observation in order to create data about the social conditions in Britain. Marx had access to these data and made heavy use of them in *Capital* in order to underpin his theory empirically.

Corporate Watchdogs: Contemporary Factory Inspectors

Corporate watchdogs are noncommercial, nongovernment organisations that document corporate crimes and how capitalist companies exploit workers. They predominantly make use of the Internet for publishing the reports of their studies and leaking documents. Here are some examples:

CorpWatch Reporting (http://www.corpwatch.org)
Transnationale Ethical Rating (http://www.transnationale.org)
The Corporate Watch Project (http://www.corporatewatch.org)
Multinational Monitor (http://www.multinationalmonitor.org)
Responsible Shopper (http://www.greenamerica.org/programs/responsibleshopper/)
Endgame Database of Corporate Fines (http://www.endgame.org/corpfines.html)
Corporate Crime Reporter (http://www.corporatecrimereporter.com)
Corporate Europe Observatory (http://www.corporateeurope.org)
Corporate Critic Database (http://www.corporatecritic.org)
Students and Scholars against Corporate Misbehaviour (http://sacom.hk)
China Labour Watch (http://www.chinalaborwatch.org)
Center for Media and Democracy's PR Watch (www.prwatch.org)
Labour Leaks (https://www.labourleaks.org/)

The Corporate Watch Project describes itself the following way:

We investigate the social and environmental impacts of corporations and corporate power. [. . .]
Our research is a vital resource for campaigns looking to target particular companies and we are

a reliable source of original and cutting-edge knowledge about the latest forms and manifestations of corporate power. We believe our focus on the structural features of corporations and the social context in which they operate is fundamental to tackling the root causes of corporate power. Corporate Watch is a small workers' co-operative, we work non-hierarchically and share responsibility for the collective running of the organisation. Legally, Corporate Watch is registered as a not-for-profit company limited by guarantee, which gives us the freedom to express our political opinions. Our work includes investigative journalism, analysis and publishing. Corporate Watch strives for a society that is truly democratic, equitable, non-exploitative and ecologically sustainable.[3]

Students & Scholars against Corporate Misbehaviour describes its work in the following way:

Students and Scholars Against Corporate Misbehavior (SACOM) is a new nonprofit organization founded in Hong Kong in June 2005. SACOM originated from a students' movement devoted to improving the labor conditions of cleaning workers and security guards under the outsourcing policy. The movement attained relative success and created an opportunity for students to engage in local and global labor issues. SACOM aims at bringing concerned students, scholars, labor activists, and consumers together to monitor corporate behavior and to advocate for workers' rights. We believe that the most effective means of monitoring is to collaborate closely with workers at the workplace level. We team up with labor NGOs to provide in-factory training to workers in South China. Through democratic elections, we support worker-based committees that can represent the voices of the majority of workers.[4]

Such organisations are the 21st century's factory inspectors. They can, however, only document what is happening, which is sometimes dangerous and difficult for the researchers, and do not have legal power to enforce working standards. They make heavy use of the Internet for disseminating information and reports about bad working conditions.

Leaking information on the Internet that documents the behaviour of powerful organisations has in the 21st century especially become popular with the emergence of WikiLeaks, which defines itself as "a not-for-profit media organization", whose "goal is to bring important news and information to the public. We provide an innovative, secure and anonymous way for sources to leak information to our journalists (our electronic drop box)".[5]

10.3. Branches of English Industry without Legal Limits to Exploitation

Exploitation without Limits

Marx points out that capital has a "werewolf-like hunger for surplus labour" (353). He also characterises capital as "vampire-like"; it "lives only by sucking living labour, and lives the more, the more labour it sucks" (342). Capital has a "vampire thirst for the living blood of labour" (367). Marx uses the metaphor of the vampire and the werewolf in order to point out that capitalism as system of exploitation is morally detestable, a scandal that confronts the working class and that should be abolished.

Marx presents examples from the factory inspectors' reports that show that in the 1860s there were industries without a legal limit to the working day: the lace trade in Nottingham, potteries in Staffordshire, the manufacture of matches and wallpapers, bakeries, the railways, dressmaking, blacksmiths' workshops. The documented working conditions include child labour, work-related illnesses, overwork; the regular contamination of bread dough with abscesses, cobwebs, putrid, alum, yeast, or cockroaches in order to save costs; work on Sundays, and death from overwork and badly ventilated rooms.

Unregulated Labour in the Internet Economy

Labour in early the 19th century was highly unregulated in British industry and therefore completely subject to capital's despotic rule. Unregulated capitalist rule is not a phenomenon of the past. Global systems such as the Internet require global regulation. The legal system operates, however, predominantly at the nation state level. Globally organised forms of online labour are therefore difficult to regulate. Crowdsourcing is a form of online labour in which knowledge work tasks are outsourced to users over the Internet. A well-known crowdsourcing platform is the Amazon Mechanical Turk that describes itself as an online platform that enables "access to a global, on-demand, 24 × 7 workforce", where employers "[p]ay only when you're satisfied with the results", and where turk workers ("turkers") "[g]et paid for doing good work".[6] If one looks at the rewards paid for specific tasks, then it becomes evident that hourly wages tend to be very low. Crowdsourcing is a method that capitalists use for minimising work costs. They make use of unregulated forms of labour to achieve this aim. At the time of writing this book (2014), there was no global minimum and living wage for crowdsourced labour and no union of crowdsourced labour and online labour. A decrease of wages results in an increase of surplus labour-time. Decreasing wages is a method of absolute surplus-value production.

Child Labour

Marx analyses child labour in 19th-century British industry. Child labour is not a phenomenon of the past: In 2014, 11% of the world's children (5–17 years) were engaged in child labour. 5.4% of the world's children conducted hazardous labour (ILO 2013). The largest number of child workers could be found in Asia and Africa (ILO 2013). Poverty is a factor that favours child labour and makes children vulnerable to exploitation. 58.8% of child labour took place in agriculture, 7.2% in industry, and 32.2% in the service sector (ILO 2013). A political question is if child labour should be completely outlawed or if poor families would thereby just get poorer so that demanding regulation of child labour is a better demand. The problem is that the drive to exploit labour to the highest degree leads certain capitalists to exploit child labour. Labour regulation can try to reduce child labour; it is, however, likely that as long as capitalism exists, such forms of labour will exist.

The International Labour Organization's (ILO) Convention Number 182 (Worst Forms of Child Labour Convention) prohibits the worst forms of child labour—namely, slavery, prostitution, drug trafficking, and hazardous labour. Around 180 countries had ratified this convention by 2014. ILO Convention Number 138 (Minimum Age Convention) defines the allowable minimum age for conducting employment as 15 and regulates that nobody shall be in employment who has not finished compulsory schooling. Hazardous labour shall only be conducted by people aged 18 or over. By 2014, around 170 countries had ratified this convention.

Walt Disney and Child Labour: Toy Labour Stories of Horror

Walt Disney is known for making kids happy with cartoons about Donald Duck, Mickey Mouse, and Goofy; Disneyland theme parks; and movies such as *The Lion King, Toy Story, The Jungle Book, Alice in Wonderland,* and *Pocahontas.*

The Hong Kong–based corporate watchdog organisation Students and Scholars against Corporate Misbehaviour (SACOM) has since 2005 monitored working conditions at factories that produce toys for Walt Disney. One of them is Dongguan Tianyu Toys Co. Ltd. in the Chinese province Guangdong. It produces electronic plush toys for Disney. The workers, including children aged 12 to 17, in this factory are unlike the kids consuming Disney products; they are not happy at all. The SACOM report describes its findings:

The toy brands like Disney and Mattel are only concerned [about] the quality and unit price of their products when they place orders at the suppliers. [. . .] Toy stories in the factories are not fairy tales. Excessive overtime, low wages, delayed payment, hazardous working environment, denial of pension and so on are the realities in the toy factories. [. . .] In the peak season, the work shift begins at 8am and ends at 10pm. Dispatched workers are found underpaid. Paint-spraying workers are exposed to chemicals without adequate protection. Production line workers are often hurt by unsafe devices. Worker needs to acquire an 'off-duty permit' if he or she has to be excused for a toilet break. (SACOM 2013)

The report also shows that in the peak season, Tianyu hires junior secondary school (aged 12–14) or high school pupils (aged 15–17), who work the same hours as other workers but only receive CNY 6.0 (US$0.96) per hour instead of the CNY 6.32 per hour that the other workers earn. They also do not receive overtime payment.

Highly exploitative and unregulated working conditions are not a phenomenon of the 19th century. They have not been superseded and are likely to continue to exist as long as capitalism exists because capital has an inherent drive to increase profits and minimise investment costs. Also the 21st-century information economy is affected by such conditions.

Precarious Labour under Neoliberalism

The 2008 economic crisis and the embracing of neoliberalism, an ideology and mode of regulation of capitalism that uses state power and laws for supporting the class struggle of capital against labour in order to maximise profits by decreasing wages, privatising and commodifying public services, deteriorating working conditions, weakening workers' rights, etc., have resulted in worsening living conditions for labour, especially for young workers. Global unemployment has increased from around 170 million in 2007 to 202 million in 2014 (source for all data in this and the next paragraph: ILO 2014). The projection for 2018 is a further increase to 215 million. The global unemployment rate of young people aged 15 to 24 increased from 11.6% in 2007 to 13.1% in 2013. The number and share of young people aged 15 to 29 who are not in employment, training, or school have increased in most countries over the world in the same time period.

Informal employment defined as self-employment in precarious conditions or employment on a casual basis without a contract and access to social security was in 2014 very high in Africa, Asia, Latin America, and the Caribbean with a cross-country average of 40% to 50%. Young people and women are particularly affected. The average youth unemployment rate in developed countries increased from 17.4% in 2009 to 18.0% in 2014. The ILO defines vulnerable employees as contributing family workers and own-account workers.[7] They are likely to have low incomes and face precarious labour conditions. They lack social security and trade union representation, and experience discrimination. According to projections, 46.8% of the world's workers will be vulnerable workers in 2018. This amount to around 1.57 billion people.

More and more companies have become unwilling to fully hire young employees with the argument that they are not experienced enough. This has led to a culture of young people having to perform unpaid or low-paid internships over long time periods in order to increase their chances for finding employment.

Internships as Exploitation

A 2013 survey conducted among young people who completed internships in the UK (N = 200) showed that 27% only received coverage of expenses such as commuting and 14% received no payment; 4 out of 10 were not paid the minimum wage.[8] A study conducted in 2011 (N = 22,000) showed that half of the UK interns who responded to the survey were not paid.[9]

The 2012 National Internship and Co-Op Study conducted by Intern Bridge (N = 11,000) in the USA showed that 33.9% of students completing internships in the arts and entertainment industry and 42.6% of those in information services (publishing, broadcasting, telecommunications) received compensation.[10] Among those students who received compensation, the average hourly rate was, at US$9.82, lowest in the arts and entertainment industry. The data show that the media industry is a realm of high exploitation of interns.

Unpaid and low-paid internships are a way for companies to reduce wage costs and maximise profits. Unpaid internship also destroy paid employment and put young people under pressure to work precariously over a long time. If no wage is paid at all to interns, then surplus labour time is 100% of the total labour time and the rate of exploitation calculated as surplus labour-time divided by necessary labour-time or profits divided by wages converges towards infinity. Capitalists can maximise their profits and interns get the lowest possible wage—namely, nothing. The only imaginable situation that could be worse would be that students have to pay for conducting internships.

10.4. Day-Work and Night-Work: The Shift-System

Shift-Work

Marx argues that capital wants to make workers labour for as many hours and as little wage as possible. There are, however, physical, psychological, social, and legal limits to extending the working day beyond certain hours per day. This has historically led to the emergence of shift-work, an alteration "between the labour-powers used up by day and those used up by night" (367). Marx mentions that at the time he wrote, shift-work existed in Britain in "blast-furnaces, forges, rolling mills and other metallurgic establishments" (367). Night-work tends to have harmful effects on the body because it tends to lead to the workforce's lack of exposure to sunlight and to irregular sleeping times.

Shift-Work in the Global Software Industry: The Case of India

US software companies have found a way of keeping software development going 24 hours a day: They outsource parts of the coding to India. When it is 8:00 p.m. in California, where many software companies are located, it is 8:30 a.m. in the morning in India. "The concept of virtual migration underscores that a programmer sitting in India and working for a local firm can directly provide services in the United States" (Aneesh 2006, 2). "It may range from the real-time work performed on mainframe computers and servers in the United States by a worker based in India to a distributed work design, allowing a firm to be geographically dispersed, without a central work station, among several sites throughout the world" (Aneesh 2006, 69). Different time zones become integrated in such a way that information and communication technology (ICT) companies become globally dispersed entities in which labour operates 24 hours a day. One Indian programmer explains: "Basically [when] it's night in the U.S., it's early morning here. [. . .] At the end of their day [the Americans] just have to [compile] their problems and the changes they want us to do, and we can fix them in our normal working hours, fix them just in time, and it will be there next morning when they come to their office" (Aneesh 2006, 84).

In virtual migration, spatial flexibility means that the company extends its operations into India. The Indian workers do not physically migrate to a host country, but remain in India and perform tasks for Western ICT capitalists from there. Space is organised in such a way that ICT-mediated communication and data transmission enables a specific form of work collaboration so that Indian software engineers provide parts of the code that are needed for software projects. Virtual migration reduces wage costs by paying lower wages to Indian workers than to workers under regular conditions. Being an Indian worker then means being highly exploited. Origin is transformed into a higher level of exploitation and a more insecure employment strategy. While it is night in the USA, software companies keep producing value in India with rates of exploitation much higher than in the USA. There is a globally organised shift-work in the software industry that makes use of the global division of labour.

10.5. The Struggle for a Normal Working Day: Laws for the Compulsory Extension of the Working Day, from the Middle of the 14th to the End of the 17th Century

Marx argues that capital has a "blind and measureless drive", an "insatiable appetite for surplus labour" (375). This drive is not a moral failure of individual capitalists, but stems from the fact that competition and other capitalist principles "confront the individual capitalist as a coercive force external to him" (381). "Capital asks no questions about the length of life of labour-power. What interests it is purely and simply the maximum of labour-power that can be set in motion in a working day" (376). Marx points out that the death of workers and overwork can also cause a problem for capital if labour supply thereby decreases and new workers, who have to be trained and work less efficiently than skilled ones, have to be constantly sought.

Flight from the Land

Historically, the demand for highly exploitable labour has been satisfied by flight from the land because capitalist cities and metropolises tend to attract not just companies and to foster the building and supply of infrastructures, but also promise better living conditions for members of the rural populations, who tend to face higher levels of toil, poverty, a precarious life, and lack of infrastructures. Marx speaks in this context of the "surplus population" (378) that is migrating from agricultural regions to the cities.

Flight from rural areas and urbanisation processes connected to it were not limited to the 19th century, but have continued to shape global capitalism. China's urbanisation has taken place in the context of neoliberal politics that favour private capital interests over workers' interests and public services. The results have been large inequality and income and wealth gaps within cities and between urban and rural areas, air pollution, shortages and pollution of water, urban poverty, housing and transport problems, challenges for the supply of energy/water/land, restrictions that migrants are facing concerning social security and housing, lack of public funding, unsafe food, and urban pollution.

Flight from the Land in Chinese Capitalism

The example of 21st-century China shows that flight from the land was not just a 19th-century phenomenon, but continues to be part of capitalist development. The formation of capitalist industries comes along with the need for labour. Capitalism promises better living conditions for poor rural populations. Often urbanisation is, however, accompanied by societal problems and inequality because capital mainly cares about cheap labour forces and not about the conditions in which workers live.

China's economic growth and industrialisation since the late 1970s have resulted in massive migration from rural provinces into the large urban metropolises that form the centres of China's manufacturing and service industries. In 2011, for the first time more Chinese lived in cities than in the countryside. The urbanisation rate (the share of the population living in urban areas) increased from 17.9% in 1978 to 52.6% in 2012 (UNDP 2013). "China's urbanisation process is of particular importance for two main reasons: speed and scale. It took 6 decades for China's urbanisation to expand from 10 to 50 percent. This same transition took 150 years to occur in Europe and 210 years in Latin America and Caribbean" (UNCDP 2013, i). China's share of the world's urban population increased from 10% in 1980 to 19% in 2010 (UNDP 2013). According to the National Bureau of Statistics of China,[11] the number of migrant workers, defined as people who during a year worked for more than six months outside of their villages and towns, was 268.94 million in 2013.

Struggles about the Length of the Working Day

Capital "takes no account of the health and the length of life of the worker, unless society forces it to do so" (381). Capitalists think: "Should that pain [of the working class] trouble us, since it increases our pleasure (profit)?" (381). Marx argues that capital has no interest to reduce the working day voluntarily and that therefore only state power can force it to do so by law. The length of the working day is subject to class struggle. "The establishment of a normal working day is the result of centuries of struggle between the capitalist and the worker" (382).

Marx points out that the law was used from the 14th to the end of the 17th century to forcefully extend the working day. In Britain, the 1349 and the 1496 Statutes of Labourers regulated the working day in such a way that its length was 14 to 15 hours, including 3 hours for meals (383).

The Nazis' Labour and Extermination Camps: Capitalism's Negative Factories

Capitalism has an inherent structural fascist tendency that makes capital not care about workers and see them only as an exploitable resource. If capital could do as it wants to, it would work as many labourers to death as long as there would be labour supply. The victories of the working-class movement have installed basic labour protections in many countries so that laws can contain capital's fascist tendencies.

National Socialism was the ultimate realisation of capitalism's fascist tendencies. It was a political project that tried to destroy the Jews as well as the working class and its political representatives with utmost violence, including forced labour and extermination camps. It was not simply an extension or the highest form of capitalism, of Fordism or the capitalist factory system, but rather a negative factory for the extermination of Jews, political opponents, and others whom the Nazis considered as enemies. The Marxist historian and political economist Moishe Postone describes this system the following way:

> A capitalist factory is a place where value is produced, which "unfortunately" has to take the form of the production of goods, of use-values. The concrete is produced as the necessary carrier of the abstract. The extermination camps were not a terrible version of such a factory but, rather, should be seen as its grotesque, Aryan, "anticapitalist" negation. Auschwitz was a factory to "destroy value", that is, to destroy the personifications of the abstract. Its organization was that of a fiendish industrial process, the aim of which was to "liberate" the concrete from the abstract. The first step was to dehumanize, that is, to rip away the "mask" of humanity, of qualitative specificity, and reveal the Jews for what "they really are"—shadows, ciphers, numbered abstractions. The second step was to then eradicate that abstractness, to transform it into smoke, trying in the process to wrest away the last remnants of the concrete material "use-value": clothes, gold, hair, soap. (Postone 1980, 114)

The Nazis fully turned labour into a killing and extermination device. Forced labour forces had to work in the arms industry and other industries that were privately run and required workforces. Auschwitz and other extermination camps were to large degrees negative factories—factories that aimed at the killing of Jews and other minorities.

Capitalist Companies' Exploitation of Forced Labour in Nazi Germany: The Example of the Communications Company Telefunken

A list of 2,500 German companies that used forced labour during National Socialism was published on the Internet.[12] These companies include, for example, the following (the information in parentheses indicates the economic activities of these companies during the time of National Socialism): Adam Opel AG (automobiles, trucks for the Germany army, engines for rockets and fighter planes), IG Farben (chemical industry, including the production of Zyklon B, the gas that was used in German extermination camps such as Auschwitz for killing Jews and others), BMW (automobiles, engines for fighter planes, motorbikes and cars for the German army), Continental (automotive parts), Daimler Benz (tanks, military vehicles, engines for war planes and war ships), Lufthansa (repair of the German army's war planes), Messerschmitt AG (fighter planes), Telefunken (telegraphy, radio communication, television sets, direction finders, television sets, radio networks, loudspeakers), Volkswagen (cars, cruise missiles).

Telefunken[13] was a German company that built and sold communication technologies, including telegraphy, amplification, and radio. In 1941, Telefunken became a subsidiary of AEG. After the war, it again became a separate company. It was merged with AEG in 1967 so that AEG–Telefunken emerged. Telefunken supplied loudspeakers for the Nazis' assemblies and marches, and the 1936 Berlin Olympics. All German transport and communications companies were integrated into the arms industry during World War II. Telefunken supplied the Nazi army with radar equipment, logistical technology, tracking devices, airborne radar systems, radio communication units, radio transmission paths, and tubes used in radio systems. After World War II, Telefunken specialised in producing tube radios and tube television sets for private use. Transistors replaced tubes in radios and TV sets, a development with which Telefunken did not keep up with so that the company was sold in 1979.

"We Were Forced Labourers. We Were Slave Labourers and We Became the Assembly Workers."

The Polish forced labourer Melania Czeranowicz remembers how it was working for AEG–Telefunken during the Nazi time: "Very little bread, no eggs, no milk, no fruits, and no onions. [. . .] We built small parts for airplanes' radio equipment for ten hours during the winter and twelve hours during the summer. [. . .] Today, only very few of us are still alive. [. . .] We will die before we get any compensation payments".[14]

Penina Piroska Bowman was born in 1927 in Cluj in Romania. The Nazis killed 42 members of her Jewish family. She was a forced labourer for Telefunken in the Nazi labour camp Mährisch Weißwasser in today's Czech Republic. In an interview, she reports how it was to be a forced labourer for Telefunken:

> Penina Piroska Bowman: We were forced labourers. We were slave labourers [. . .] And we became the assembly workers. So they, they supervised us, and they had, like, um, half a dozen Frenchmen, and they had four or five SS women who guarded us, and we had to go, you know, every morning, and work in the factory and we soldered wires and to telephone, and I thought it was walkie-talkie radios and, and telephones. So we learned how to use the lead and solder the wires in them and we were under, you know, strict German supervision, and we weren't allowed to talk to each other. [. . .]
>
> We would hear this gong go off I think probably early in the morning, like six o'clock, and we get dressed, and then line up [. . .] we lined up, and we walked to the factory, which was, I don't know, it was pretty far. It wasn't just around the corner. We walked there, and the SS women were guarding us, and we were not allowed to talk to each other and just, you

know, be real quiet and walk. And then we got there, and then we were all assigned to the different jobs.

[. . .] I learned the actual soldering the wires. And you know, it was the lead that you had to, you know, this tool that you had to melt the lead and then connect the wires. I was able to do that. And I even, later, when I made this little diary, I made the button from lead, and I put holes in it, and I attached it to my diary. [. . .] We weren't allowed to communicate with each other. [. . .] we [. . .] worked and I don't remember how long, but it was quite a few hours, and then we were walked, marched back to the uh, barracks, and we went back to the barracks. [. . .]

But basically it was a, you know, monotonous. I mean, every day we did pretty much the same thing. We just marched to work, we worked and we were marched back. [. . .]

Interviewer. You said one of the guards was especially mean. [. . .]

Penina Piroska Bowman: She always, if you didn't walk straight, she would hit you with her, . . . she had this, you know, cord, this, this wood thing that she walked with. She would hit you with that if you didn't walk fast enough, or, or also if she caught you talking or something. And she, she would . . . As soon as you did something, you wouldn't work fast enough, she, she would, uh, used the cane all the time. [. . .]

Her biggest joy was to shave the hair again, because she knew that women um, treasured, you know, their hair was growing back. And this, this is six months later, and the hair was growing. We were so proud of that. The punishment was to shave the person's hair again, so she did that. And she just was very sadistic, and she enjoyed hitting people, and just, just beating them for the smallest thing, or take away the food, if, if you did something wrong [. . .]

[After most Nazis had fled the camp at the time of liberation:] they dragged her out, and they were, you know, kicking her. We all shouted that we're going to kill her because she was the meanest to us. [. . .] They killed her with their bare hands, this one SS woman that was left behind, because the others escaped.[15]

"Once They Also Wanted to Shoot Me, because of Nothing" . . .

Issoif Awsejewitsch Graifer was born in 1926 in Minsk (Belorussia). He was a forced worker in the Minsk Ghetto's Telefunken factory, where he and others repaired radio sets and wireless equipment for the Nazis. He reports about life in the ghetto and the slave-work for Telefunken:

> Once they also wanted to shoot me, because of nothing. But I survived. They shot, all fell and for some reason I also fell, I lost consciousness, and then all were dead and I was alive. [. . .]
>
> Again and again there were shootings. Besides these pogroms that were mass pogroms, every day someone was killed, day in and day out, always. There was almost no hope. [. . .] And my cousins were buried near alive near the wallpaper factory [. . .] But the punishments, when one was hung on a pillar, was undertaken formally with the commander's permission. That was hard: to hang there for two to three hours. Afterwards the people passed out unconscious.[16]

Telefunken just like thousands of other German companies played an integral role in the Nazi economy. The company used forced workers like slaves in order to produce for the German arms industry and the civilian economy. The workers were not paid, but seen as resources that could be killed if they no longer worked efficiently and effectively enough. The necessary labour time of these slave workers was zero hours because they earned no wage and hardly received any or only rotten food for their survival, whereas the surplus-labour time was maximised. The labourers in the Nazi's forced slave labour system were exploited to the highest possible degree. The rate of exploitation/rate of surplus-value sv is calculated as sv = surplus labour-time / necessary labour-time. The surplus-labour time at AEG-Telefunken of slave labourer was 10 to 12 hours per day, and the necessary labour-time was zero hours. If in a mathematical fraction the denominator is zero, then the entire fraction converges towards infinity. The exploitation of slave-workers in Nazi Germany was an infinite form of exploitation—it was the realisation of the dream of all capitalists to not have to pay workers anything. Such a terror labour system that operates with death by labour was an important element of Nazi Germany's economic and political system.

The New Categorical Imperative

A foundation of the German government tried in the first decade of the 2000s to make German companies that had employed forced labour during National Socialism pay specific sums of money to the survivors or deceased victims' families. Between 2001 and 2007 the foundation paid a total of 4.5 billion Euros to around 1.6 million survivors and the families of forced labourers.[17] Telefunken existed no longer at this time and its successor companies denied responsibility and so rejected to make any payments.[18]

Such payments cannot be seen as compensation because there can never be a monetary compensation for fascism, slave labour, and extermination. The payments were modest and ranged between €2,500 and €7,670 per victim. They can be considered as a very late attempt to provide a small token that says, "We are sorry for what our German fathers, grandfathers, mothers, and grandmothers who supported the Nazis and made up the Nazi system did to you". There can and should never be any forgiveness or forgetting for Nazi Germany's crimes. One can also not "work through" these crimes because this formulation implies that one does some penitence and after it everything is forgiven and forgotten. There can only be remembrance and attempts to implement and live what the Marxist philosopher Theodor W. Adorno (1903–1969), who being a Marxist and coming from a Jewish family had himself to flee from Nazi Germany, called the "new categorical imperative", the need that humans "arrange their thoughts and actions so that Auschwitz will not repeat itself, so that nothing similar will happen" (Adorno 1973, 365).

10.6. The Struggle for a Normal Working Day: Laws for the Compulsory Limitation of Working Hours—the English Factory Legislation of 1833–1864

Marx points out that industrialisation led to large actual increases of labour times in British manufacturing beyond every "boundary set by morality and nature, age and sex, day and night" (390). Labour would have resisted these developments by demands for a normal working day.

The British Factory Acts

Marx says that the five Labour Laws passed in Britain between 1802 and 1833 were not enforced. Therefore they "remained a dead letter" (390). The Factory Act of 1833 applied to the cotton, wool, flax, and silk industries and limited the daily maximum working time of young people aged between 13 and 18 years of age to 12 hours. Labour for children under 9 was forbidden, the maximum working hours for children between 9 and 13 was set with 8 hours a day, and night-labour was prohibited for all young people below the age of 18. Factory inspectors had problems enforcing the factory regulations because breaches were ubiquitous.

Marx discusses that British industrialists started a political campaign against the 1833 Factory Act. They suggested lowering the childhood age. The 1833 Act regulated that 13 to 18 year olds should work a maximum of 12 hours between 5:30 a.m. and 8:30 p.m. Capitalists developed a relay system, in which young workers were sent around from one factory or one part of the factory to another to conduct different forms of labour, which allowed capitalists to keep the machines running for all

15 hours between 5:30 a.m. and 8:30 p.m. Marx writes that this practice "annulled the whole Factory Act" (393).

The 1844 Factory Act limited the daily working hours for women to a maximum of 12 and forbade night-labour for women. Furthermore children under 13 were not allowed to work more than 6.5 hours a day, a reduction by 1.5 hours. The 1844 Act also regulated that the 12 hours of labour for young people had to be normalised to specific labour hours measured by a public clock. One practical result of the 1844 Act was that also the working hours of adult men were reduced to 12 hours per day.

Factory workers, "especially since 1838, had made the Ten Hours Bill their economic, as they had made the Charter their political, election cry" (393). The Factory Act of 1847 introduced the 10-hour working day. It was therefore also called the Ten Hours Bill. Capitalists as a result reduced wages on average by 25% and petitioned against the law. Many of them argued that they would ignore the new regulations, which, as one of the goals, wanted to abolish the relay system. They did everything possible to keep their machines going for 12 to 15 hours a day without interruption. Many workers because of the relay system, idle time, and the time it took to go from one factory shop to the next, spent 15 hours a day in the factory. The working class felt that capitalist practices turned the Ten Hours Bill into a fraud; this resulted in protests and an intensification of class struggle.

The 1850 Factory Act constituted a compromise between capitalist and working-class interests. Young peoples' and women's working days were lengthened from 10 to 10.5 hours from Monday to Friday and shortened to 7.5 hours on Saturday. The labour had to be performed between 6 a.m. and 6 p.m. with at least 1.5 hours for meals, which needed to be taken by all workers at the same time. "By this the relay system was ended once and for all" (405). The 10-hour working day was finally fully established after a long time of working-class struggle.

Robert Owen and the Struggle for the Eight-Hour Working Day

Robert Owen (1771–1858) was a Welsh socialist. He played an important role in the cooperative movement and instituted social reforms, such as the 10- and 8-hour working day, in his mills. Owen was an early proponent of the eight-hour working day. The International Working Men's Association (IWA, 1864–1876) was the first international association of socialists, communists, and anarchists. The Geneva Congress of the International Working Men's Association in 1866 proposed to formulate a demand for "eight hours work as the legal limit of the working day" (International Working Men's Association 1868, 5). Karl Marx was a member of the IWA's council.

In 1919, the International Labour Organization passed the Hours of Work (Industry) Convention, which regulates in article 2 that "working hours of persons employed in any public or private industrial undertaking or in any branch thereof, other than an undertaking in which only members of the same family are employed, shall not exceed eight in the day and forty-eight in the week".[19] In 1930, the Hours of Work (Commerce and Offices) Convention followed. It says in article 3 that the "hours of work of persons to whom this Convention applies shall not exceed forty-eight hours in the week and eight hours in the day".[20] An international convention for the introduction of the eight-hour day was thereby introduced. Fifty-two countries had ratified the 1919 Convention in 2014, 30 the 1930 Convention.

Average Working Hours

The length of the standard working week varies today: In 2014 it was 40 hours, for example, in Austria, China, Finland, Germany, Italy, Japan, Spain, Sweden, the USA; 48 hours, for example, in India and Thailand; 45 hours in Turkey; 44 hours in Israel; 35 to 40 hours in the UK; 38 hours in Belgium; 37 hours in Denmark; and 35 hours in France.[21] France introduced the 35-hour workweek in 2000 under a socialist government. The EU's 2003 Working Time Directive regulates that the average workweek must not exceed 48 hours (including overtime) in EU member states.

The actual hours worked vary from country to country because of overtime, the amount of public holidays, individual holiday entitlement, and the degree of part-time labour. Table 10.2 gives an overview of average weekly working hours in the OECD countries.

The lowest number of average working hours per week is in the Netherlands, where there is a high level of part-time labour. In the year 2012, people worked very high average hours—namely, more than 50 per week—in Turkey and Qatar. The average weekly hours worked in all 63 countries that can be found in the ILO statistics is 41.2. So on average there is roughly a correspondence to the eight-hour day, which is what the ILO's conventions recommend.

Labour time has always been a highly antagonistic aspect of capitalism. Capitalism advances automation in order to increase productivity, but thereby creates the problem that people are put out of work, which has negative effects on consumption and therefore on demand. There is a tendency that the costs for maintaining technology increase. Capitalism in the 21st century is being shaped by a contradiction between overtime and precarious labour: On the one hand there are professions such as software engineering, where people work very long hours, whereas on the other hand there are people who work precariously, hardly find employment, have low incomes, or are unemployed. Labour is asymmetrically distributed. The only real solution is to reduce labour time from the average standard of 40 hours to 30 hours or less with full wage compensation. Capital, however, does not welcome such reforms because paying more workers a living wage for fewer standard hours is less profitable than paying fewer workers who work overtime. A 20-, 25- or 30-hour workweek for

TABLE 10.2 Average number of hours worked per week in specific countries, 2012 (data source: ILO Statistics)

Country	Average working hours per week
Austria	35.7
Belgium	34.7
Denmark	34.3
Egypt	46.4
Finland	35.6
France	35.5
Germany	34.8
Greece	38.6
Hong Kong, China	45.0
Ireland	33.8
Italy	35.1
Japan	40.3
Korea, Republic of	43.8
Malaysia	48.0
Netherlands	30.8
Norway	34.4
Panama	42.9
Poland	39.9
Portugal	38.8
Qatar	50.0
Spain	36.1
Sweden	35.4
Switzerland	36.6
Turkey	50.3
United Kingdom	35.5

the wage of 40 hours is urgently needed in order to mitigate the antagonism between profit maximisation and labour time.

The history of the working day is a history of class struggle and the fundamental antagonisms of capitalism.

10.7. The Struggle for a Normal Working Day: Impact of the English Factory Legislation on Other Countries

In British capitalism, the struggles about the length of the working day "first gave rise to outrages without measure, and then called forth, in opposition to this, social control, which legally limits, regulates and makes uniform the working day and its pauses" (411–412).

> The establishment of a normal working day is therefore the product of a protracted and more or less concealed civil war between the capitalist class and the working class. Since the contest takes place in the arena of modern industry, it is fought out first of all in the homeland of that industry—England. The English factory workers were the champions, not only of the English working class, but of the modern working class in general. (412–413)

In France, the 12-hour working day was introduced after the 1848 Revolution. The difference to the UK was that the working day was at once limited in all industries, whereas the legislation process in the UK was longsome and piecemeal, and did not affect all industries at once.

In chapter 10, Marx discusses a fundamental capitalist contradiction between necessary and surplus labour-time that results in class struggles about the length of the working day. Capitalists try to ever more increase surplus-labour time—that is, the unpaid part of the working day—whereas workers have a natural interest to increase their wages. Marx in chapter 10 discusses methods that capital uses for lengthening the working day and necessary labour-time. They include the following:

- the legal lengthening of the working day
- shortening of breaks
- using child labour
- using shift-work: labour all day and night long
- working labourers to death
- insisting on constant labour without breaks
- employing workhouses that organise compulsory labour

Exercises for Chapter 10

Group exercise (G)
Project exercise (P)

Key Categories: Working Day, Lengthening of the Working Day, Struggles Over the Length of the Working Day

Exercise 10.1 (P)

Watchdog organisations are the 21st century's factory inspectors. Work in groups: Select a media, cultural, or information technology company and search for online information that shows if it has conducted corporate misbehaviour or corporate crimes. Look for information on the online watchdog platforms listed in section 10.2 and conduct also a search in alternative news media. Document and present the results.

Ask yourself and discuss the following questions: What are the potentials of corporate watchdogs? What difficulties that limit their work may they face in capitalism? Are there ways you can think of that allow mitigating these problems?

Exercise 10.2 (P)

Crowdsourcing is a method of absolute surplus value production in which users perform labour online for rather low wages.

Work in groups: Analyse a set of 50 work tasks in a job that you are interested in and could perform or have performed yourself. Search for wage data on platforms that crowdsource labour or where freelancers offer their services. Note the hourly wage levels in a spreadsheet and calculate the average wage level.

What would you expect to earn if you conducted this work? Go to websites of professionals who conduct the same work to find out how high their average hourly rates are for the same labour that is also offered on crowdsourcing platforms. Compare and present the results.

Exercise 10.3 (G)

Work in groups: Each group searches in newspaper online archives for an example of child labour conducted in a media or cultural industry. Present your example to the other groups. Ask yourself and discuss the following questions: Why does child labour exist? What political measures can be taken against child labour? How can child labour be stopped? What are the problems of stopping child labour without abolishing capitalism? How can one react to them?

Exercise 10.4 (G)

Discuss in groups and present your results to the following questions:

- Have you worked as an intern? If yes, what were your experiences (working conditions, etc.)? Do you plan to work as an intern? Did you have other jobs? If yes, what were your experiences (salary, working conditions, etc.)?
- What constitutes a good internship? What qualities does a good internship have?
- Should internships be paid? Why/why not? If yes, what should be the level of remuneration?
- What measures can be taken in order to ensure that companies treat interns fairly?
- Why have internships become such a big thing? What are the structural reasons underlying this development?

Exercise 10.5 (G)

Work in groups: Search for announcements of internships in media and cultural industries. Which ones are paid? Which ones unpaid? Which ones have no specification? Which information should a job announcement for an internship specify?

Exercise 10.6 (P)

The Nazis used forced labour for supporting the arms industry and as method for exterminating Jews and others. A list of 2,500 German companies that used forced labour during National Socialism was published on the Internet.[22]

Work in groups: Each group selects one of these German companies and conducts a search on the Internet and in academic databases and books in order to find out what exactly this company's role was in National Socialism. Try also to find out what role forced labour played in this context and how the company positions itself towards its own history and if and how it describes its involvement in the Nazi system in its own historical accounts.

Each group presents its results.

Notes

1 Companies detail use of "conflict" metals. *Wall Street Journal Online*. June 2, 2014. http://online.wsj.com/articles/companies-detail-use-of-conflict-metals-1401751678 (accessed on July 28, 2015).

2 Global Slavery Index 2013: Democratic Republic of Congo. http://www.globalslaveryindex.org/country/democratic-republic-of-the-congo/ (accessed on July 30, 2014).

3 http://www.corporatewatch.org/pages/about-corporate-watch (accessed on July 28, 2015).

4 http://sacom.hk/about-us/ (accessed on July 28, 2015).

5 https://wikileaks.org/About.html (accessed on August 1, 2014).

6 https://www.mturk.com/mturk/welcome (accessed on August 1, 2014).

7 http://www.ilo.org/global/about-the-ilo/newsroom/features/WCMS_120470/lang—de/index.htm (accessed on April 21, 2014).

8 http://info.monster.co.uk/UK-interns-still-being-exploited/article.aspx (accessed on July 28, 2015).

9 http://www.theguardian.com/money/2011/sep/05/half-student-internships-unpaid (accessed on July 28, 2015).

10 Intern Bridge. 2013. *Intern Bridge 2012 internship salary report*. Austin, TX: Intern Bridge (accessed on July 28, 2015).

11 Statistical Communiqué of the People's Republic of China on the 2013 National Economic and Social Development. http://www.stats.gov.cn/english/PressRelease/201402/t20140224_515103.html (accessed on September 6, 2014).

12 http://www.schoah.org/shoah/zwangsarbeit/firmen.htm (accessed on August 2, 2014).

13 See http://de.wikipedia.org/wiki/Telefunken and http://www.heise.de/ct/artikel/Synergien-zerbroeselt-289306.html (accessed on July 28, 2015).

14 Translation from German, original: „Sehr wenig Brot, keine Eier, keine Milch, kein Obst und keine Zwiebeln. [. . .] Im Winter haben wir zehn, und im Sommer zwölf Stunden Kleinteile für Radioanlagen von Flugzeugen gebaut. [. . .] Heute leben von uns nur noch ganz wenige. [. . .] Wir werden sterben, ehe wir eine Entschädigung bekommen. Source: Nach 55 Jahren besuchen ehemalige NS-Zwangsarbeiter erstmals Berlin: „Wir werden sterben, ehe wir eine Entschädigung bekommen". *Berliner Zeitung Online*. May 18, 2000. http://www.berliner-zeitung.de/archiv/nach-55-jahren-besuchen-ehemalige-ns-zwangsarbeiter-erstmals-berlin—wir-werden-sterben—ehe-wir-eine-entschaedigung-bekommen-,10810590,9800252.html (accessed on July 28, 2015).

15 Data source: Zwangsarbeit 1939–1945: Erinnerungen und Geschichte. Ein digitales Archiv für Bildung und Wissenschaft. Archive-ID: ZA563.

16 Data source: Zwangsarbeit 1939–1945: Erinnerungen und Geschichte. Ein digitales Archiv für Bildung und Wissenschaft. Archive-ID: ZA032. Translation into English. German version: „Einmal wollten sie mich auch erschießen, bei mir war auch so was, wegen nichts. Aber ich bin am Leben geblieben. Man schoss, alle fielen um und aus irgendeinem Grund fiel ich auch, oder ich verlor das Bewusstsein, und dann waren alle tot und ich lebendig. [. . .] Immer wieder Erschießungen, außer diesen Pogromen, die Massenpogrome waren, wurde jeden Tag irgend jemand ermordet, am Tag und in der Nacht, immer. Das heißt, es gab fast keine Hoffnung. [. . .] Und meine Vettern wurden unweit der Tapetenfabrik lebendig begraben [. . .] Aber die Bestrafung, wenn man an eine Säule gehängt wurde, unternahmen sie offiziell, mit seiner Erlaubnis. Ich wurde nicht bestraft, aber das war sehr [. . .] schwer, zwei bis drei Stunden zu hängen, das war sehr schwer. Die Menschen fielen danach ohnmächtig um".

17 http://de.wikipedia.org/wiki/Stiftung_%E2%80%9EErinnerung,_Verantwortung_und_Zukunft%E2%80%9C (accessed on July 28, 2015).

18 Zuwenig Milliarden für Zwangsarbeiter—Neue Ausreden der deutschen Industrie. *ARD Online*. June 8, 2000. http://www.rbb-online.de/kontraste/ueber_den_tag_hinaus/diktaturen/zuwenig_milliarden.html (accessed on July 28, 2015).

19 http://www.ilo.org/dyn/normlex/en/f?p=NORMLEXPUB:12100:0::NO:12100:P12100_ILO_CODE:C001 (accessed on August 1, 2014).
20 http://www.ilo.org/dyn/normlex/en/f?p=NORMLEXPUB:12100:0::NO::P12100_INSTRUMENT_ID:312175 (accessed on August 1, 2014).
21 http://en.wikipedia.org/wiki/Workweek_and_weekend (accessed on August 1, 2014).
22 http://www.schoah.org/shoah/zwangsarbeit/firmen.htm (accessed on August 2, 2014).

11

THE RATE AND MASS OF SURPLUS-VALUE

The Mass of Surplus-Value

In chapter 11 Marx discusses the relationship of the rate and mass of surplus-value. The mass of surplus-value S can in labour terms be measured in hours and in monetary terms as a specific amount of a particular currency. There are three specific laws that govern the relationship of the rate and mass of surplus-value.

The First Law

The *first law* says that "the mass of surplus-value produced is equal to the amount of the variable capital advanced multiplied by the rate of surplus-value" (418). The mass of surplus-value S is directly proportional to both the amount of variable capital and the rate of surplus-value. This can mathematically be expressed by the following notation (418):

$$S = \frac{s}{v} * V = P * \frac{a'}{a} * n \text{ , where}$$

S = mass of surplus-value
s = average surplus-value produced by one worker per day
v = daily value of labour-power of one worker
V = total sum of variable capital, total value of the used labour-power
P = average value of the used labour-power
a' / a = average rate of surplus-value
n = number of workers

The first equation expresses that the mass of surplus-value S is determined by the average rate of surplus-value and the total variable capital. The second equation says that the mass of surplus-value S is determined by the average rate of surplus-value, the average value of the used labour-power, and the total number of workers.

Here is an example: v = £30, V = £300, s/v = 100%
=> S = 100% * 300£ = £300.
The mass of surplus-value is £300. This result can also be calculated in the following form:

$a'/a = 100\%, n = 10, P = \pounds30;$
$S = \pounds30 \star 100\% \star 10 = \pounds300.$

The Second Law

The *second law* is that the "absolute limit of the average working day—this being by nature always less than 24 hours—sets an absolute limit to the compensation for a reduction of variable capital by a higher rate of surplus-value, or for the decrease of the number of workers exploited by a higher degree of exploitation of labour-power" (419–420).

Let us assume a production process corresponding to the one described in the example with the difference being that the number of workers is reduced from $n = 10$ to $n = 1$ in order to save costs. The working day was in the situation before eight hours, which means that both surplus-labour s and necessary labour v were each four hours long. The capitalist wants to compensate the reduction of the number of employed workers by increasing length of the working day, which means that s/he increases the rate of surplus-value. The absolute maximum is 24 hours, which is unrealistic, because the one employed worker would then no longer sleep and soon die. If we assume extreme working conditions, then the working time may be 20 hours, an increase by 12 hours. The wage remains constant at £30. Necessary labour-time is still 4 hours, so surplus labour-time is 16 hours, and the rate of surplus-value = 16 / 4 = 400%.

The daily mass of surplus-value is then $S = (s/v) \star V = 400\% \star \pounds30 = \pounds120$. The total mass of surplus-value is £120, whereas it was £300 under the old working conditions. In the example, no matter how much the capitalist increases working time, the temporal limit of the working day does not allow to create the same mass of surplus-value as before.

The Third Law

The *third law* says that the mass of surplus-value produced is not affected by variations of what Marx terms in chapter 25 the "organic composition of capital"—that is, the relationship between constant and variable capital (c / v)—if the rate of surplus-value remains unchanged. Here is an example:

$v = \pounds30, n = 10, V = \pounds300, s/v = 100\%, c_1 = \pounds600;$
$S = (s/v) \star V = 100\% \star \pounds300 = \pounds300.$

Let as assume new buildings are rented, but the number of workers remains the same, so that $c_2 = \pounds900$. At the first point of time, the organic composition $o = c_1/v = \pounds600/\pounds300 = 200\%$. At the second point of time, $o = c_2/v = \pounds900/\pounds300 = 300\%$. The organic composition of capital has increased from 200% to 300%, but given that the rate of surplus-value and the mass of variable capital remain constant, the mass of surplus-value is still $S = (s/v) \star V = 100\% \star \pounds300 = \pounds300$. Marx assumes in this example constancy of the rate of surplus-value. If constant capital increases, for example, by investments in machines, then it is likely that this has impacts on the mass of variable capital and/or the rate of surplus-value: Capital may lay off some workers and productivity may change.

Freelancers

Marx points out that the population size and the maximum possible length of the working day form limits to the mass of surplus-value that can be produced (422). He furthermore points out that if a capitalist participates "directly in the process of production, [...] he is only a hybrid, a man between capitalist and worker, a 'small master'" (423). In the 21st century, the phenomenon of freelancing has become prevalent. Freelancers are single-person companies. In many countries, freelancing is particularly prevalent in the media, cultural, and digital industries. A freelancer is at the same time the only capitalist and the only worker in the company. S/he owns all capital and exploits himself/herself. S/he is a hybrid worker-capitalist.

Many companies outsource parts of their labour in such a way that they tell all people working for them that they have to become freelancers. So, for example, a capitalist fitness centre that owns a sports hall then may no longer employ tennis coaches, but demand payment from them for each hour they want to occupy a tennis court in order to give lessons. The tennis coach then has to become a freelancer who works for 60 hours a week in the fitness centre in order to earn enough money to survive. S/he is a worker-capitalist and exploits herself/himself, but at the same time the situation is not so different from the fitness centre employing him/her full-time, so one can also say that the fitness centre exploits the tennis coach.

Marx argues that capitalists participating in labour tend to strive for increasing their capital to such a degree that they are "able to devote the whole of the time during which he functions as a capitalist, i.e. as capital personified, to the appropriation and therefore the control of the labour of others, and to the sale of the products of that labour" (423). A certain amount of capital is required for being able to employ and exploit others. Marx says that there is a certain sum of capital that poses a point at which "merely quantitative differences pass over by a dialectical inversion into qualitative distinctions" (423) so that the capitalist can become a pure capitalist, not a worker-capitalist, and can devote himself/herself to management and control purposes. "The capitalist, who is capital personified, now takes care that the worker does his work regularly and with the proper degree of intensity" (424). The capitalist is an "extractor of surplus labour and an exploiter of surplus-labour" (425).

The Dialectical Transition from Quantity to Quality

Marx in the above mentioned quote from page 423 uses Hegel's concept of the transition from quantity to quality: Capital must be large enough so that the capitalist no longer has to be part of the work force, but can employ workers who produce commodities for him/her. If this capital is too small, then such a division of functions is not possible. If it passes a certain threshold, then the division becomes possible. Hegel introduces the dialectical notion of the transition from quantity into quality as part of the discussion of what he terms the "measure", which is the unity of quantity and quality.

> But now, when the quantity that is present in measure exceeds a certain limit, the corresponding quality is thereby sublated, too. What is negated in this way, however, is not quality in general, but only this determinate quality, whose place is immediately taken again by another one. This process of measure, which proves to be alternately a mere alteration of quantity and an overturning of quantity into quality, can be visualised in the image of a knotted line. We find these knotted lines first in nature, in a variety of forms. We have already given the example of water's qualitatively various states of aggregation, conditioned by increase and decrease [of temperature]. The various stages of oxidation of metals are a similar case. The distinctions of musical notes can also be regarded as an example of the overturning of what is initially a merely quantitative into a qualitative alteration that takes place in the process of measure. (Hegel 1830a, §109)

The Transition from Quantity to Quality in Society

Hegel here employs examples from nature for explaining the transition from quantity to quality. It should of course be stressed that the dialectic of nature is different from the dialectic of society. In nature, we find specific natural laws that determine, for example, that water at zero degrees Celsius becomes ice. Society is also dialectical, but the societal dialectic's degree of freedom is much higher than and qualitatively different from the dialectic of nature. Humans shape society. There is no law that determines that at a specific intensity of repression or manipulation humans start to revolt.

Crises, domination, and exploitation are objective preconditions of collective action; there is, however, no determined law of nature that dictates when or even if revolt, protest, or revolution will occur because human subjectivity and group action is very complex and involves a capacity of making conscious choices that natural systems do not have. We know for sure that if the outside temperature in winter increases and reaches above zero degrees Celsius, the snow melts. We do not know for sure that if a fascist regime imprisons or kills a specific number of communists, that at a specific killing rate a revolution will emerge because the noncommunist population may be convinced it is good to kill communists.

What Is a Manager?

In 20th-century capitalism, the social role of the manager emerged in factories and offices. Not all capitalists take care of the control of workers and the organisation of the labour process themselves, but rather have with the growth and complexity of companies, division of labour, and productivity created special positions for these tasks. Managers also receive a wage that normally is much higher than an average worker's salary.

Often managers also own parts of the company. If it is a stock trading company, then they typically own a specific amount of share options. Although managers receive a wage, they cannot be seen as being part of the working class because they play an important part in organising the exploitation of workers. Managers in capitalist companies should therefore be seen as belonging to the capitalist class.

The Capitalist Contradiction between Technology and Labour

Marx argues that technology takes on a special role in capitalist production. It is a means of production, but a means for the domination and exploitation of the working class. There is therefore a capitalist contradiction between technology and labour. Marx expresses this antagonism the following way:

> It is no longer the worker who employs the means of production, but the means of production which employ the worker. Instead of being consumed by him as material elements of his productive activity, they consume him as the ferment necessary to their own life-process, and the life-process of capital consists solely in its own motion as self-valorizing value. (425)

Technology is in capitalist production a form of capital. It thereby is a means that capitalists control, own, and use in order to organise the exploitation of workers. Technology thereby becomes alienated technology, a technology that is not owned and controlled by the workers, but merely operated by them in order to produce capital and commodities owned by the capitalists. All modern technology, no matter if it is a computer or a shovel, is the result of and objectification of scientific knowledge. So there is an aspect of knowledge to all technologies. All technologies used in production therefore incorporate knowledge. The difference between the computer and the shovel is certainly that the first processes information, whereas the second does not. So the computer is an information technology, whereas the shovel is not.

Stalinist Dialectics: The Ideological Misuse of Dialectical Philosophy in the Soviet Union

In the Soviet Union, the dialectic of nature was used for arguing that society develops based on a law of nature and that therefore bourgeois society must by necessity be superseded by socialism. The argument was that the Soviet Union superseded by natural law bourgeois society and that therefore everyone criticising Stalin was a bourgeois counterrevolutionary who needed to be killed. The point is that the societal dialectic operates differently than the dialectic of nature. Reducing the dialectic of society to the dialectic of nature is a dangerous ideology. In class societies, the dialectic of society is a dialectic of class antagonism that pits one class against the other. Whether class struggle emerges and what its results are depends on many complex factors, such as the objective structural conditions of society, ideology, the distribution of power, etc.

Chapter 11's Main Result

It is not an accident that Marx mentions the role of technology in capitalism at the end of chapter 11, which is also the end of part III: "The Production of Absolute Surplus-Value". He wants to point out that the lengthening of the working day, the method of absolute surplus-value production, is not sufficient for capital's increase of surplus-value. Technology plays an important role in a strategy that Marx calls relative surplus-value production, on which he focuses his analysis in part IV.

Figure 11.1 visualises chapter 11's main result: The mass of surplus-value depends on the total mass of labour (the mass of variable capital) and the degree to which this labour is exploited. The more labour is exploited, the larger the produced mass of surplus-value. The higher the amount of labour active in production, the more surplus-value is created.

Exercises for Chapter 11

Group exercise (G)
Project exercise (P)

Key Categories: Mass of Surplus-Value, Rate of Surplus-Value

Exercise 11.1 (G)

Work in groups: Each group chooses one media corporation. Search for information for one specific year or a series of years about the company's profits (monetary surplus-value) and its labour costs.

Calculate the rate of surplus-value and compare the total value of labour-power, the rate of surplus-value, and the mass of surplus-value. Calculate how the mass of surplus-value would change

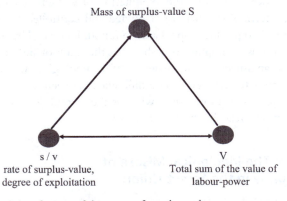

The mass of surplus-value is determined by the number of workers and the degree of their exploitation

Mass of surplus-value S

s / v
rate of surplus-value,
degree of exploitation

V
Total sum of the value of
labour-power

FIGURE 11.1 The determining factors of the mass of surplus-value

if you (a) increased or decreased the rate of surplus-value by 10%, 20%, or 60%, and (b) if total variable capital increased or decreased by 10%, 20%, 60%.

Present your results.

Exercise 11.2 (P)

In chapter 11, Marx points out that there are hybrids that are both capitalists and workers. Freelancers are particularly prevalent in media, cultural, and digital industries. Try to find statistical data about the share of freelancers in the media/cultural/digital/information industries in one country. Compare the share to other sectors in the same economy.

Create a questionnaire that focuses on the analysis of various aspects of freelancers' working dimensions in the media/cultural/digital/information industries.

Conduct one interview per person with a freelancer in these industries. Present the results and compare them to each other.

Reflecting on their class status, how would you classify the freelancers in your interviews? Are they part of the working class? Or do they belong to the capitalist class? Or both? Or are they something different? Try to find reasons for your answers.

Exercise 11.3 (G)

A manager has a specific control function in companies: S/he controls and organises workers' labour.

Work in groups: The International Standard Classification of Occupations (ISCO) classifies all occupations. The International Labour Organization's statistical databases provide economy-wide data for many countries that are using this classification. Have a look at which version of ISCO (e.g., ISCO-88) the ILO currently uses in its databases. Identify management occupations in the classification. Each group looks up for one country the latest average wages of managers. Compare these wages to the salaries of specific information/media/cultural occupations. What is the difference?

Present the results.

Finally, discuss and reflect on the class status of managers.

PART IV

THE PRODUCTION OF RELATIVE SURPLUS-VALUE

12

THE CONCEPT OF RELATIVE SURPLUS-VALUE

Relative Surplus-Value

In part III, Marx discusses absolute surplus-value production as one method capitalists use for increasing the rate of surplus-value. In part IV, he introduces another method: relative surplus-value production.

> I call that surplus-value which is produced by the lengthening of the working day, *absolute surplus-value*. In contrast to this, I call that surplus-value which arises from the curtailment of the necessary labour-time, and from the corresponding alteration in the respective lengths of the two components of the working day, *relative surplus-value*. (432)

The method Marx describes is called relative surplus-value because the working day is not absolutely prolonged, but rather the relationship between necessary labour and surplus-labour is transformed in such a way that the first decreases and the second increases. Marx visualises this change the following way (429):

| Working day I: A - - - - - - - - - B - - C | necessary labour-time: 10 hours, surplus labour-time: 2 hours |
| Working day II: A - - - - - - - - B - - - C | necessary labour-time: 9 hours, surplus labour-time: 3 hours |

The Increase of Labour Productivity

The main form of relative surplus-value production is the increase of the productivity of labour, by which Marx means "an alteration in the labour process of such a kind as to shorten the labour-time socially necessary for the production of a commodity, and to endow a given quantity of labour with the power of producing a greater quantity of use-value" (431).

In order for necessary labour to decrease, the increase in productivity must affect those industries that produce means of subsistence whose value determines the average value of labour-power (432). An "increase in the productivity of labour in those branches of industry which supply neither the necessary means of subsistence nor the means by which they are produced leaves the value of labour-power undisturbed" (432). The means of subsistence consist of many different commodity-types. The combined decrease of necessary labour-time is a combination of the decrease of the reduction of the labour-times of those commodities that make up the means of subsistence (433).

Marx provides some mathematical examples in chapter 12. These may be a bit difficult to understand for the contemporary reader because he uses units of British currency that are no longer in use today: 1 pound sterling at the time of Marx consisted of 20 shillings (sh) and 1 shilling of 12 pence (d). In order to simplify, I have transformed the units of currency that Marx uses in the example calculations that he provides on pages 433–436 into modern equivalents.

The Relation of Value and Productivity: Extra Surplus-Value, Extra-Profit

"Each article has now embodied in it 1/24th of this value instead of 1/12th, [. . .] only half an hour of labour-time, instead of a whole hour, is now added to the means of production while they are being transformed into each article" (434). If the average productivity is at such a level that on average the production of one exemplar of the commodity takes one hour, then the individual commodity value in the example stands, because of a higher productivity level, below the commodity's social value (434). "The real value of a commodity, however, is not its individual, by its social value; that is to say, its value is not measured by the labour-time that the article costs the producer in each individual case, but by the labour-time socially required for its productions" (434). If the capitalist who enjoys higher productivity sells the commodity at its value, then s/he can make an "extra surplus-value" (434) and extra-profit.

More productive labour "acts as intensified labour; it creates in equal periods of time greater values than average social labour of the same kind" (435). If the higher standard of productivity has been generalised and so becomes the standard throughout the entire economy or industry, then the surplus-value of the individual capitalist who previously produced more productively vanishes because "the difference between the individual value of the cheapened commodity and its social value vanishes" (436).

"The value of commodities stands in inverse ratio to the productivity of labour" (436). This means that the higher the productivity, the lower the value of the individual commodity—that is, the time it takes to produce it. If productivity increases, then more commodities of the same type can be produced per hour or day than before. Capital has "an immanent drive, and a constant tendency, towards increasing the productivity of labour, in order to cheapen commodities and, by cheapening commodities, to cheapen the worker himself" (437). "The objective of the development of the productivity of labour within the context of capitalist production is the shortening of that part of the working day in which the worker must work for himself, and the lengthening, thereby, of the other part of the day, in which he is free to work for nothing for the capitalist" (438).

An Example for the Effects of Higher Productivity in One Company than in Others

Let us discuss an example in which one company has productivity advantages:

Average price of a laptop: $V_1 = £400$
Production time of an average laptop: 1 hour
Average wage costs of a laptop production worker per hour: $v_1 = £10$
Average constant capital costs per laptop: $c_1 = £290$
Average profit: $p_1 = £100$
Rate of surplus-value: $rs_1 = p_1/v_1 = 100/10 = 10$

More productive labour in one specific company:

Production time of one laptop: ½ hour
Hourly wage costs are kept the same as the average wage: => wage costs per laptop $v_2 = £5$
The constant capital costs are also $c_2 = £290$
The laptop is sold at the average market price of £400, therefore this value is made up as follows:
$$V_2 = £400 = c_2 + v_2 + p_2 = 290 + 5 + 105 = £400$$
The prices V_1 and V_2 are equal, but the relationship of necessary labour and surplus-labour is different:

$$rs_1 = p_1/v_1 = £100/£10 = 10$$
$$rs_2 = p_2/v_2 = £105/£5 = 21$$

The capital that controls labour that produces the laptop more productively makes an extra surplus-value of £5 per laptop. The wage costs for the production of one laptop because of the higher productivity are just half the average wage costs. The rate of surplus-value of the more productive company is 2.1 times higher than the average rate. Rising productivity intensifies exploitation: More surplus-value can be produced in the same or less time than before.

World Systems Theory: Uneven Development in Global Capitalism

World systems theory is an approach that conceives of capitalism as an inherently global system in which there is a differentiation between (a) developed, rich core countries and regions, (b) underdeveloped and poor periphery regions and countries. The (c) semi-periphery is a buffer zone between the core and the periphery. World systems theory has identified productivity differences as an important source of global inequality in capitalism. The US sociologist and historian Immanuel Wallerstein was one of the founders of world systems theory. He argues that the centres are economically stronger than the periphery, which leads to a flow of value from the periphery to the centres. This flow arises through uneven trade and/or the exploitation of the workforce in the periphery. "A capitalist world-economy was said to be marked by an axial division of labour between core-like production processes and peripheral production processes, which resulted in an unequal exchange favouring those involved in core-like production processes" (Wallerstein 2004, 17).

The Egyptian economist Samir Amin (1974, 1976, 1997, 2010) has especially worked on characterising the periphery. The main insight is that the development of the core and the periphery are not independent, but connected to each other: The periphery is poor because the core is rich and the other way around. There is development on the one side because there is underdevelopment on the other side. Amin describes the capitalist world system as a relationship between the centres (the core) and the periphery that is shaped by elements like a global class structure, low wages and dependent production in the periphery, an international division of labour, unequal trade, unequal economic structures, differences in productivity, and global monopolistic structures.

Amin (2010) identifies a law of worldwide value from which a transfer of value from the periphery to the core results. Productivity differences and unequal competition, the topics Marx focuses on in chapter 12, play an important role in Amin's law of worldwide value. Amin identifies an inherent connection between productivity differences, unequal economic structures, and unequal exchange.

Global Productivity Differences and Unequal Development

There are often big *differences in productivity*, and therefore in wages, in the various economic sectors of peripheral regions (Amin 1976, 215–218). There are also quite often great disparities in wages between urban and rural as well as better- and lesser-trained labour forces (Amin 1976, 221). There are also differences in productivity between the core and the periphery to the disadvantage of the periphery.

Connected to the differences in productivity is an *unequal economic structure*: The economies of the peripheral regions often have a high proportion of agriculture and the service sector in their value and employment structures, while the newest economic developments take place in the centres (Amin 1976, 239–246). The industries in peripheral regions often have difficulty competing with companies in the centres. The services resulting from this phenomenon often have low productivity. There has been more industrialisation in the periphery since 1945, but it is nevertheless an unequal industrialisation relative to the core (Amin 1997, 2).

The unequal economic structures between core and periphery feature *unequal trade*: In reaction to their status in the capitalist world system, peripheral countries and regions often have industries that are strongly export-oriented (Amin 1974; 1976, 203, 206). The trade of the periphery takes place primarily with the core, while the core countries trade largely internally and with each other (Amin 1976, 247). Given the higher levels of productivity in the core, the products exported from the periphery contain more hours of labour than the products of the core, which are produced with higher productivity and therefore with less labour. However, the products are paid for at global prices, which are set in the higher productivity environments of the core, creating a transfer of value from the periphery to the core in the form of unequal trade (Amin 1974, 13).

An Example for Unequal Development

Here is an example of unequal development: Let us assume that the average production of a car takes 20 hours, the average time at Ford in Europe 16 hours, and at JMC in China 100 hours. If Ford pays an average wage of €15 per hour, then the average wage costs per car are as follows: 16 * €15 = €240. If JMC has the same wage level, then its wage costs per car are as follows: 100 * 15 = €1,500. In the chosen example, JMC's productivity is lower. In order to compete with Ford on the world market, JMC has to reduce the total wage costs per car to €240 or less. The average hourly wage is thereby reduced to a maximum of 240 / 100 = €2.4. This means that in the example labour power is sold at a much lower value in China than in the West. Global capitalist structures impose a low-wage structure on peripheral regions.

Marx argues in chapter 12 that the importance of productivity increases in capitalism. Technology plays an important role in this context as a means for increasing productivity. Marx described the capitalism of the time he lived in, when especially the steam engine impacted the economy. In economic theory, particularly Schumpeter and neo-Schumpeterian approaches have given attention to the history of technological innovations and revolutions.

Kondratieff Cycles: Long Wave Theory

The Russian economist Nikolai Kondratieff (1892–1938) published his book (Kondratieff 1925) about the long waves of the business cycle in 1925 and a major article on the same issue in 1926 (Kondratieff 1926), which led the Austrian-American economist Joseph A. Schumpeter (1883–1950) to later celebrate Kondratieff's discovery and introduce the notion of the Kondratieff cycle as long wave. Schumpeter (1939) describes the history of capitalism as a succession of long Kondratieff waves: 1787–1842, 1843–1897, 1897–. Each long wave would contain smaller cycles: "We now go on to postulate that each Kondratieff should contain an integral number of Juglars and each Juglar an integral number of Kitchins" (Schumpeter 1939, 180). He writes that his "schema" involves "speaking of a Long Wave" (Schumpeter 1939, 292) and even claims that the analysis of "long waves in economic activity [. . .] reveals the nature and mechanism of the capitalist process better than anything else" (Schumpeter 1943, 67). Esben Sloth Andersen (2009, 193) in his study of Schumpeter as an evolutionary economist argues that Schumpeter "had a certain preference for the long waves".

Joseph Schumpeter's Crisis Theory

Schumpeter says that there are "three classes of cycles, to which we shall refer simply as Kondratieffs, Juglars and Kitchins, because the average spans by which we choose to identify the individuals belonging to each of our three classes approximately correspond to the spans of the cycles 'discovered' by those three investigators, respectively" (Schumpeter 1939, 176). He also parallelises long waves with technological innovations/revolutions: "Historically, the first Kondratieff covered by our material means the industrial revolution, including the protracted process of its absorption. We date it from the eighties of the eighteenth century to 1842. The second stretches over what has been called the age of steam and steel. It runs its course between 1842 and 1897. And the third, the Kondratieff of electricity, chemistry, and motors, we date from 1898 on" (Schumpeter 1939, 178). "Each of them [the long waves, CF] consists of an 'industrial revolution' and the absorption of its effects" (Schumpeter 1943, 67). "These revolutions periodically reshape the existing structure of industry by introducing new methods of production—the mechanized factory, the electrified factory, chemical synthesis and the like; new commodities, such as railroad service, motorcars, electrical appliances; new forms of organization—the merger movement; new sources of supply—La Plata wool, American cotton, Katanga copper; new trade routes and markets to sell in and so on" (Schumpeter 1943, 68).

Neo-Schumpeterian Crisis Theory

Carolta Perez is one of the major representatives of neo-Schumpeterianism. She identifies five successive long waves of economic development that were initiated by technological revolutions that led to techno-economic paradigms. Technological revolutions and associated techno-economic paradigms result for Perez (2010, 189) in "a vast reorganisation and a widespread rise in productivity across pre-existing industries". The result is economic growth: "The processes of diffusion of each technological revolution and its techno-economic paradigm [. . .] constitute successive *great surges of development*" (Perez 2010, 190).

TABLE 12.1 Waves of economic development and corresponding technological innovations and revolutions according to Joseph Schumpeter (1939), Carolta Perez (2010), and Ernest Mandel (1978)

Joseph Schumpeter	Carolta Perez	Ernest Mandel
1st wave (1780–1842): water-power, turnpikes, shipbuilding	1st wave: the industrial revolution (key innovation 1771: Arkwright's mill)	1st wave (1793–1847): handicraft-made or manufacture-made steam engine
2nd wave (1842–1897): steam, steel, railroad	2nd wave: age of steam and railways (1829: rocket steam engine)	2nd wave (1848–1893): first technological revolution: machine-made steam engine and machines, railways
3rd wave (1898–): electricity, chemistry, and motors	3rd wave: age of steel, electricity and heavy engineering (1875: steel plant)	3rd wave (1894–1939): second technological revolution: electric and combustion engines
	4th wave: age of oil, the automobile, and mass production (1908: Ford Model-T)	4th wave (1940/1945–): third technological revolution: electronic apparatuses, nuclear energy
	5th wave: age of information and telecommunications (1971: Intel microprocessor)	

In Marxist theory, the Belgian economist Ernest Mandel (1978, chapter 4) combined Marx's theory of the falling rate of profit with Kondratieff and Schumpeter's long wave theory in order to argue that technological innovations result in the start of a new long wave and at the same time advance the contradictions of capitalism so that after a specific time the profit rate tends to fall and capitalism enters crisis, which requires a new technological revolution for a new wave of economic development to start.

"The characteristic element in the capitalist mode of production, however, is the fact that each new cycle of extended reproduction begins with different machines than the previous one. In capitalism, under the whip of competition and the constant quest for surplusprofits, efforts are continually made to lower the costs of production and cheapen the value of commodities by means of technical improvements" (Mandel 1978, 110–111). Factors contributing to a rise of the rate of profit could in the first phase of a new wave be the fall of the organic composition of capital (because capital penetrates into new spheres that are not yet heavily technologised), an increase of the rate of surplus-value (because of a defeat of the working class in class struggles), the cheapening of constant capital, and the acceleration of the turnover-time of circulating capital (due to new systems of communication and transport and new methods of distribution) (Mandel 1978, 115).

In the medium-term, technological revolutions according to Mandel result in an increase of the organic composition of capital and therefore in the tendency of profit-rates to fall and for economic crisis: "A general transformation of productive technology also generates a significant rise in the organic composition of capital and, depending on concrete conditions, this will lead sooner or later to a fall in the average rate of profit. [. . .] The increasing difficulties of valorization in the second phase of the introduction of any new basic technology lead to growing under-investment and increasing creation of idle capital" (Mandel 1978, 115).

For Mandel, technological innovations in energy supply are connected to changes of production technologies and communication as well as transport technologies:

> It is not difficult to provide evidence to show that each of the three fundamental revolutions in the machine production of energy sources and motive machines progressively transformed the whole productive technology of the entire economy, including the technology of the communications and transport systems. Think, for example, of the ocean steamers and diesel locomotives, automobiles and radio communications in the epoch of the electric and combustion engines; and the jet transport planes, television, telex, radar and satellite communication networks, and atom-powered container freighters of the electronic and nuclear age. The technological transformation arising from the revolution of the basic productive technology of motive machines and sources of energy thus leads to a new valorization of the excess capitals which have gradually been piling up from cycle to cycle within the capitalist mode of production. By exactly the same process, however, the gradual generalization of the new sources of energy and new motive machines must lead, after a longish phase of accelerated accumulation, to a longish phase of decelerating accumulation, i.e., renewed under-investment and reappearance of idle capital. (Mandel 1978, 119)

Global Economic Crises

Important global economic crisis years acknowledged in economic history are, e.g. 1873 (start of the Long Depression), 1929 (start of the Great Depression), 1973 (oil price shock, banking crisis), and 2008/2009 (Global Financial Crisis). Figures 12.1 and 12.2 show historical data for the annual growth rates of the Gross Domestic Products (GDPs) of the USA and the UK.

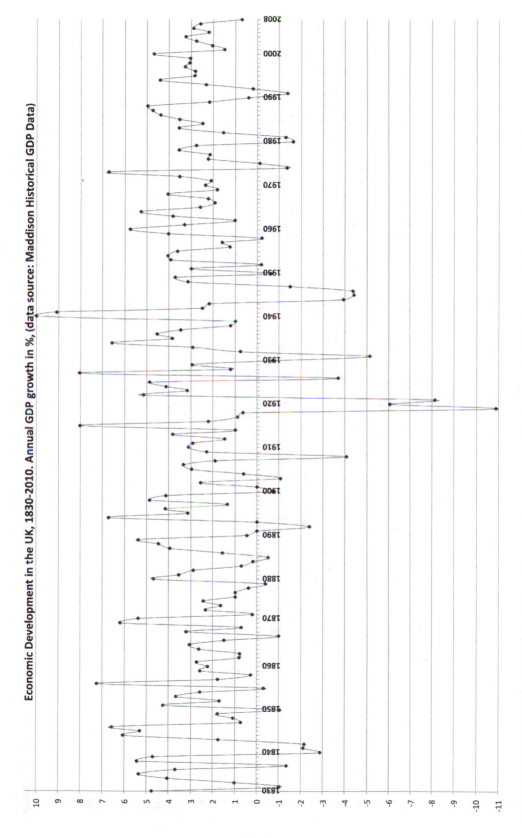

FIGURE 12.1   The UK's historical economic development

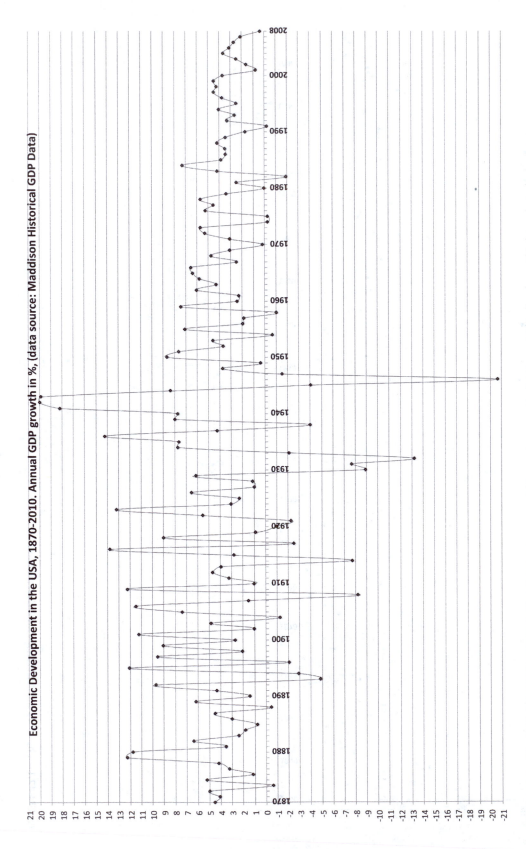

FIGURE 12.2 The US's historical economic development

The data show overall large growth rates in the 1880s, 1890s, and the first decade of the 1900s; economic instability in the 1930s and 1940s at the time of World War II; and again large growth rates in the 1950s and 1960s. Some representatives of neo-Schumpeterian theory such as Carolta Perez assume that the microelectronic revolution that brought about advances in automation, the rise of the computer, the Internet, and the mobile phone started a new long wave in the middle of the 1970s. Others, such as Ernest Mandel, however, assume that a new wave started around 1945, which means that the crisis of the mid 1970s is for them the start of a 25-year long downswing.

The Instability of Neoliberal Capitalism

The economic data for both the UK and the USA show constant fluctuations of growth, including negative growth, which are indications that capitalist economies have since the 1970s become very instable, been prone to constant crisis, and not been able to set off a new economic growth miracle that one would have to expect in the upward phase of a Kondratieff cycle. Carolta Perez's assumption that a new long wave started in the early 1970s is falsified by the fact that the years 1970 to 2010 were economically very instable in both the UK and the USA. Mandel's assumption would be more in line with the fluctuations experienced in the period 1975 to 2000. The dot.com crisis 2000 would then, however, have had to be the start of a new long wave instigated by the Internet. This is definitely not the case because the 2008 crisis and the recession that followed in many countries was the deepest crisis since the Great Depression, which started in 1929. According to Mandel's assumptions, we would have had to see a long upswing after 2000, which did not taken place.

The capitalist world economy was continuously struck by crises in the 1980s, 1990s, and 2000s: the financial crisis in 1987, the financial crisis in Finland and Sweden in the early 1990s, the 1994 currency crisis in Mexico, the 1997 Asian financial crisis, the 2000 Internet stock market bubble crisis, the financial crisis of 2008, and the subsequent new world economic crisis.

The Failures of Long Wave Theory

After the crisis of 1973 to 1975, according to the assumptions of long wave theory, economic prosperity would have had to follow for the next 25 years, until 2000. Many national economies and the world economy were, however, ridden by economic fluctuations, crises, and instability in these 25 years. A big crisis followed in the years after 2008, which was 35 years and not 50 years after the onset of the second world economic crisis. Whereas the time between the economic crises of 1873 and 1929 was 56 years and the time between the crises of 1929 and 1973 was 44 years, which given some deviations can still be interpreted based on long wave theory's assumption that there is a big crisis all 50 years, followed by 25 years of economic upswing and 25 years of downturn, 35 years is a much shorter time. Long wave theory has been historically falsified and cannot adequately explain economic development since the 1970s. Given the problems of instability, vulnerability, and fluctuations since the 1970s, a new long wave based on the information technology paradigm simply did not emerge. Long wave theory is plainly wrong. It is not just a bourgeois theory. It is not just a techno-deterministic theory. It is a wrong theory.

For figure 12.3, I have reorganised the data used for figures 12.1 and 12.2 in such a way that I calculated five-year growth rates of the GDP. The figure shows the historical development of GDP growth in the UK and the USA in five-year periods. One can clearly see a slump in the mid-1970s. In the period 1975 to 2008, economic development measured in five-year intervals fluctuated in both the UK and the USA. The microelectronic revolution—the rise of the computer in the economy and society—did not, as predicted by long wave theory, result in sustained economic growth.

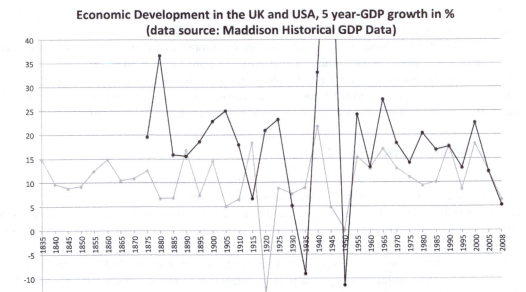

FIGURE 12.3 Historical data for five-year GDP growth in the UK and the USA

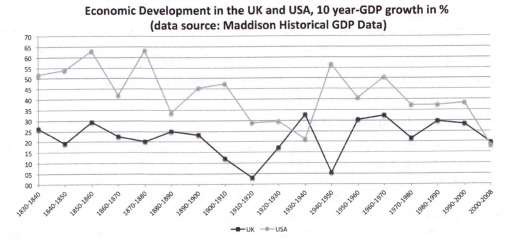

FIGURE 12.4 Historical data for 10-year GDP growth in the UK and the USA

Figure 12.4 shows a reorganisation of the data in 10-year long periods for both the USA and the UK.

In macroeconomic theory, Kondratieff cycles are around 50 years long, Kuznet cycles around 15 to 25 years, Juglar cycles around 10 years, and Kitchin cycles 4 to 5 years. Figure 12.4 visualises that, measured in periods of 10 years, economic growth in the UK and the USA has historically in the 19th and 20th centuries displayed cycle-like development. The length of these cycles, however, varies and has, based on the assumptions in Figure 12.4, taken on periods of 20, 30, 40, and 60 years. There is no clear pattern in terms of Kondratieff or Kuznet cycles, but rather an oscillation between cycles that are Kuznet cycles or somewhat longer and cycles that are either somewhat shorter than Kondratieff cycles or somewhat longer. Marx observed in chapter 25 that "a general crisis [. . .] is the end of one cycle and the starting-point of another" and that "[u]ntil now the duration of these cycles has been ten or eleven years, but there is no reason to consider this duration as constant" (786). So other than long wave theories Marx did not assume a deterministic economic cycle- or wave-length, but thought that it is rather variable and historically varying. Marx's crisis theory is dialectical and historical materialist. Long wave theories are in contrast deterministic and metaphysical. It almost seems like they assume that a cosmic or unexplainable force determines wavelengths and cycle lengths. It is inexplicable why a complex human system should display the same patterns over history and longer time periods.

The Marxist theorist Tony Smith compares neo-Schumpeterian theories of technology to Marx's concept of technology in *Capital Volume 1*. He concludes that neo-Schumpeterian theories lack of focus on how technology is shaped by and shapes capital, labour, class, global capitalism, and class struggles. He says that neo-Schumpeterian theories are addressed to "scientists, technologists, investors, managers, political elites, and so on" (Smith 2004, 237), whereas "Marx's theory, in contrast, is addressed to working men and women and their communities" (Smith 2004, 238). "The manner in which technological developments in capitalism necessarily tend to further the material preconditions for the formation of a world community of wage-labourers and their allies is thoroughly occluded. In contrast, this world historical possibility is a central theme of *Capital*" (Smith 2004, 238).

Technology in Regulation Theory

Long wave theory assumes that technology is a determining external factor of the economy. In contrast, Robert Boyer (1988), a representative of French regulation theory, sees technology as an endogenous factor of the economy. Regulation theory sees economic development as shaped by phases called capitalist modes of development. Each mode consists of an accumulation regime and a mode of regulation. The accumulation regime includes the way surplus and commodities are produced, including aspects of technology, class relationships, modes of consumption, market relations, division of labour, and international competition. The mode of regulation includes the political and institutional forms that regulate monetary and credit relations, as well as the wage-labour nexus, competition, international relations, and forms of state intervention.

In regulation theory, a capitalist mode of development does not last 50 years, as assumed by long wave theory. And other than in long wave theory, crises and growth are not technologically determined. A mode of development develops its own internal contradictions and technology is embedded into such contradictions. Boyer describes the contradictory role of technology in a capitalist mode of development the following way:

> [Technology] cannot be dealt with in isolation from the rest of *the economic and social system*. The major question is, then, the coherence and compatibility of a given technical system with a pattern of accumulation [. . .] Within each mode of development the very factors which account for a successful, long-lasting boom also explain the reversal of economic dynamics *from growth to crisis*. Once totally mature, a socio-technical system gives rise to new economic imbalances and social conflicts. Hence possible obstacles arise during the process of accumulation itself, leading to a major, i.e. a structural, crisis, characterized by quasi-stagnation and large instabilities. Therefore the same ongoing technical change—crudely measured by average productivity growth—might have negative effects upon employment, in complete opposition to the situation during periods of high and stable growth. (Boyer 1988, 68)
>
> Out leitmotiv is [. . .] the fate of any technological system cannot be disentangled from social (particularly the wage-labour nexus) and economic determinants (the evolution of the mode of development as a whole). (Boyer 1988, 89)

Other than long wave theory, regulation theory avoids technological determinism as well as fixed and determined lengths of cycles, waves, or modes of capitalist development. Its theoretical problem has, however, been the assumption that the crisis of a mode of development results in a new accumulation regime that is combined with new forms of regulation. Regulation theory defined regulation as active state-intervention into the economy and the creation and maintenance of a welfare state. It does not consider the neoliberal deregulation, liberalisation, and privatisation of the welfare state as a form of regulation itself (Fuchs 2002, 2004). Therefore regulation theory waited for a new mode of regulation to emerge that, however, never developed. If one in contrast also sees deregulation as a form of regulation, then one can avoid such theoretical problems (Fuchs 2002, 2004). Another problem of regulation theory is its relative neglect of the realm of culture and ideology, which can be resolved by assuming the existence of a disciplinary and ideological regime within a capitalist mode of development (Fuchs 2002, 2004) or the approach of a cultural political economy (Jessop and Sum 2006).

Technology in Capitalism

My own position on how to theorise the role of technology in capitalism is that technology has in capitalism antagonistic potentials, realities, and effects on the economy and society. Dialectical logic shapes the role of technology in capitalism. The rate of profit is indirectly proportional to the organic composition of capital c/v and directly proportional to the rate of surplus-value s/v. New technologies can both have effects on the organic composition and the rate of surplus-value. The question is if the rate of surplus-value due to technological development rises more than the organic composition or the other way round. Factors such as class struggle, state regulation, and other factors play an important role in this context. Marx (1894, chapter 14), in *Capital Volume 3*, identifies as such factors that influence the rate of profit: the lowering of wages, the usage of the methods of absolute and relative surplus value production, the cheapening of constant capital, foreign trade and the sale of commodities above their value, high exploitation rates of labour in colonies, the devaluation of fixed constant capital, increasing speed of the turnover of capital, and violent devaluation of capital by war or crises. Technology has in capitalism both crisis- and growth-fostering potentials. It can increase the rate of exploitation and/or the organic composition of capital, two factors that have inverse influences on the rate of profit.

The Role of Technology in the Rate of Profit

The rate of profit is the relationship of profit and investment or of the monetary expression of surplus-value and the value of the means of production (constant and variable capital).

$$ROP = \frac{s}{c + v}$$

If we divide the numerator and the denominator by v, then we get:

$$ROP = \frac{\frac{s}{v}}{\frac{c}{v} + 1}$$

This formula shows that the rate of profit depends (a) on the rate of surplus-value, which Marx also calls the rate of exploitation because it describes the relationship of unpaid and paid labour, and

(b) the organic composition of capital, which represents the relationship of dead and living labour, constant and variable capital, and the value of machinery/resources and labour-power. The rate of profit is directly proportional to the rate of surplus-value and indirectly proportional to the organic composition of capital.

Capitalists have to constantly strive for increasing productivity in order to produce more commodities in less time and to survive. So they want to invest in more efficient production technologies and to speed up production and circulation. The rise of computing in production or what some term the information economy and information society is grounded in the technification of production and the development of the productive forces. As a result, also knowledge in production and society has historically increased in importance. Technification for raising productivity means an increase of the organic composition of capital because more money tends to be spent on technology than before. It, however, also tends to increase the rate of surplus value because technology in production is according to Marx (1867) a means of relative surplus-value production resulting in the production of more value in less or the same time. So the same amount of labour measured in hours suddenly produces more surplus-value than before.

It is clear that if the rate of surplus-value remains constant, while the organic composition rises, the rate of profit decreases. There is a contradiction between the rate of surplus-value, which is directly proportional to the rate of profit, and the organic composition of capital, which is indirectly proportional to it. In a situation of technological innovation in which many companies adopt these technologies, which thereby widely diffuse into the economy, additional constant capital investments tend to be made. If technologies are not cheapened, then this will result in an increase of the organic composition. The question is, how do capitalists react to such downward pressure on their profits? It is likely that many of them attempt to mobilise countervailing tendencies, such as laying off labour, reducing wages, outsourcing labour, making employees work more for the same or less wages, etc. They aim to increase the rate of surplus-value by various methods of absolute and relative surplus-value production. Technification is a method of relative surplus-value production itself, so raising the organic composition can increase the rate of surplus-value. There is, however, no guarantee that this increase is larger than the increase of the organic composition and so capitalists will tend to try to reduce wage costs in order to increase profitability. Methods of absolute and relative surplus-value production are, however, contested, as Marx knew. Workers have the capacity to resist capitalists' attacks so that the rate of surplus-value is also shaped by the outcomes of class struggle. If workers' struggles are successful, the rate of surplus-value and therefore their exploitation decrease. If such struggles are unsuccessful, capitalists triumph and increase the rate of exploitation. The increase of the organic composition as structural tendency of capital stands in a contradiction with class struggles. The outcomes of this contradiction cannot be predicted in advance, but depend on historical circumstances. If the organic composition increases and there are no or unsuccessful workers' struggles so that the wage sum decreases, then the rate of profit can increase. If, however, workers' struggles are successful and they resist layoffs and achieve wage-increases, the profit rate is more likely to fall.

Capitalism displays upswings and downswings resulting from the dynamics of the interplay of class struggle and structural antagonisms. There is, however, no law that determines how long waves, upswings, and downswing lasts.

Absolute and Relative Surplus-Value Production

Figures 12.5 and 12.6 show the distinction between absolute and relative surplus-value production that Marx draws in chapter 12.

In absolute surplus value-production, at a new point of time t+1, surplus labour time is increased to a larger extent than necessary labour-time so that the working day is prolonged.

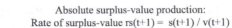
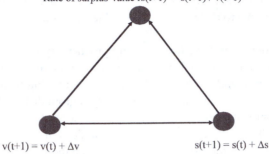

FIGURE 12.5 The method of absolute surplus-value production

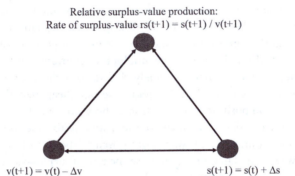

FIGURE 12.6 The method of relative surplus-value production

In relative surplus-value production, at a new point of time t+1 necessary labour-time is decreased and this decrease is larger than any increases in surplus labour-time so that the relative relationship between surplus labour-time and necessary labour-time changes in such a way that surplus labour-time increases relative to necessary labour-time.

Exercises for Chapter 12

Group exercise (G)
Project exercise (P)

Key Categories: Relative Surplus-Value Production, Productivity, Extra Surplus-Value, Extra-Profit

Exercise 12.1 (P)

Work in groups: Each group chooses one specific country. Search for data in economic databases (e.g., OECD Statistics, AMECO, World Bank, IMF, UN Statistics, national statistical offices, etc.) in order to determine the absolute GDP data or GDP growth data for this country from the 1960s until today. Copy or import the data to a spreadsheet application (such as Microsoft Excel, Libre Office Spreadsheet, Open Office Spreadsheet). Calculate the annual growth rates of the GDP (in %) in a separate column as follows: GDP growth(t + 1) = [GDP(t+1)/GDP(t) * 100]-100.

Plot a graph that shows the development of the GDP growth (similar to Figures 12.1 and 12.2). Analyse the economic development since the 1960s: Are there indications for the existence of a long wave? If so, which ones? If not, why not?

Present your results.

Discuss: What are the differences between a Marxist theory of economic development and the theory of long waves? What role does technology have in both approaches?

Exercise 12.2 (G)

Read the following:

Perez, Carolta. 2010. Technological revolutions and techno–economic paradigms. *Cambridge Journal of Economics* 34 (1): 185–202.

Mandel, Ernest. 1978. Chapter 4: "Long Waves" in the History of Capitalism. In *Late capitalism*, 108-146. London: Verso.

Boyer, Robert. 1988. Technical change and the theory of "regulation". In *Technical change and economic theory*, ed. Giovanni Dosi, Christopher Freeman, Richard Nelson, Gerald Silverberg, and Luc L. Soete, 67–94. London: Pinter.

Carolta Perez is a representative of neo-Schumpterianism. Ernest Mandel tried to combine Marx's theory of crisis and the theory of long waves. Robert Boyer is a representative of regulation theory who discusses aspects of technology in capitalism.

Discuss

- How does each of the three approaches conceptualise the history and development of capitalism?
- What is the role of technology in each of the three approaches?
- What are general commonalities and differences of the three approaches? What are the commonalities and differences in respect to the role that is assigned to technology in capitalism?
- What are core assumptions of the role of technology in a Marxist theory of economic development?

13

COOPERATION

In chapters 13 through 15, Marx discusses three forms of relative surplus-value production:

- Cooperation: Many workers in one space so that a more efficient collective worker emerges (chapter 13)
- Manufacture: Cooperation based on a low degree of technification and manual labour (chapter 14)
- Large-scale industry: Cooperation with a large degree of technification (chapter 15)

Cooperation

Marx argues that the logical and historical starting point for capitalism is that a "large number of workers" work "together, at the same time, in one place (or, if you like, in the same field of labour), in order to produce the same sort of commodity under the command of the same capitalist" (439).

The simplest form of cooperation is that in which workers' labour is not connected, but performed individually; they are, however, all located in the same workshop. This situation results in "a revolution in the objective conditions of the labour process" (441): They consume parts of the means of production together—for example, the raw materials, infrastructure, or tools—which cheapens the means of production (442): "But it costs less labour to build one workshop for twenty persons than to build ten to accommodate two weavers each" (442). When means of production are consumed in common, then the smaller parts of their value are objectified in the produced commodities (442). When constant capital is cheapened this way, the total commodity value decreases.

Marx defines the notion of cooperation: "When numerous workers work together side by side in accordance with a plan, whether in the same process, or in different but connected processes, this form of labour is called co-operation" (443).

Cooperation's Synergies

Synergies arise from cooperation: The result is emergent—that is, the sum of the cooperative work of x individuals is more and qualitatively different than x individual work processes carried out independently. Such an "effect of the combined labour could either not be produced at all by isolated individual labour, or it could be produced only by a great expenditure of time" (443).

The twelve masons, in their collective working day of 144 hours, make much more progress with the building than one mason could make working for 12 days, or 144 hours. The reason for this is that a body of men working together have hands and eyes both in front and behind, and can be said to be to a certain extent omnipresent. The various parts of the product come to fruition simultaneously. (445)

Cooperation allows changing the organisation of work's space-time: Work can be organised over a large space—for example, in the "building of canals, roads and railways" (446)—and a lot of labour-hours can be compressed in time by employing a large number of workers in parallel (446).

Cooperation and the Computer

Cooperation requires that workers are "brought together" so that there is an "assembly in one place" (447). Place on the one hand can mean that humans gather face-to-face in the same physical location. Networked computer technology allows also work-over-distance so that people work together although they are not in the same physical space. Computer-supported cooperative work (CSCW) means that "collaborative activities and their coordination" are "supported by means of computer systems" (Carstensen and Schmidt 1999) and the use of the "computer in group work" (Schmidt and Bannon 1992, 9). CSCW can either be performed at the same time or at different points of time. It can be the case that workers are supported by computers in the same physical space, but the more frequent case is that CSCW involves spatial distance between those engaged in the work process.

Editing a Wikipedia article is probably the most well-known form of CSCW today. Most Wikipedians working on an encyclopaedic entry have never met in person. Collaboration is coordinated by an article's talk page, in which contributing users discuss possible changes and additions, and by numerous rules that are often difficult to understand and apply for new Wikipedians because these writers contribute voluntarily and unpaid in their free time, which makes it difficult to find the time to work through hundreds of pages of rules. Wikipedia is an asynchronous over-distance CSCW system. Wikipedia work is spatially and temporally disembedded: Contributors do not have to work in the same physical space because Wikipedia is an online space; this enables collaboration over distance, and contributors do not have to work at the same time because the online space stores edits and communications.

Humans as Social Animals, Media as Social Media

Marx argues that the phenomenon of cooperation shows that the human is not just, as Aristotle assumed, a political animal, but a "social animal" (444). Cooperative workers form a collective productive power (443). "When the worker co-operates in a planned way with others, he strips off the fetters of his individuality, and develops the capabilities of his species-being" (447).

Some observers and scholars have characterised Internet platforms such as Facebook (social networking site) and Twitter (microblog), as well as Instagram, Pinterest, Flickr, and YouTube (user-generated visual content sharing sites) as "social media" because they enable communication, sharing, and community. Most of these platforms are, however, mainly focused on individuals who show off who they are and what they do. These are platforms for impressing others and performing identities and fostering individualism; this sets individuals against each other as competitors who accumulate friends, attention, and visibility. Such media could therefore better be called individualistic, neoliberal media, not social media. Wikipedia is in contrast not about individual show-off, but the collaborative editing of an encyclopaedia. It is a true social medium.

In chapter 13, Marx uses the notion of the "species-being", a term that he coined in his early philosophical works. This usage in chapter 13 shows that there is, other than claimed by Louis

Althusser (1969), not an epistemological break between the young and the old Marx: Philosophical notions such as species-being and alienation were important both for the young and the old Marx.

The Human Species-Being

Marx (1844) introduced the term "species-being" (Gattungswesen) in the *Economic and Philosophic Manuscripts*. By this notion, he means that humans are both natural in that they interact with nature and social in that they act together in society:

> The individual is the social being. His life, even if it may not appear in the direct form of a communal life carried out together with others—is therefore an expression and confirmation of social life. Man's individual and species life are not different, however much—and this is inevitable—the mode of existence of the individual is a more particular, or more general mode of the life of the species, or the life of the species is a more particular or more general individual life. (Marx 1844 [English], 105)

Cooperation as the essence of the social is for Marx and Engels a fundamental human capacity. They even define the social as cooperation: The social denotes "the co-operation of several individuals, no matter under what conditions, in what manner and to what end. It follows from this that a certain mode of production, or industrial stage, is always combined with a certain mode of cooperation, or social stage, and this mode of cooperation is itself a 'productive force'" (Marx and Engels 1845, 49).

Cooperation is an aspect of all societies and takes on specific historical forms. Marx discusses historical forms of cooperation, such as the building of pyramids and other "gigantic structures" (451) and hunting (452), as well as agricultural communities that owned the means of production in common (452). He shows in chapter 13 that in capitalism, cooperation serves the purpose of capital accumulation and private property and is therefore alienated cooperation—cooperation that does not serve all humans, but capital. Cooperation is in capitalism subsumed under the rule of capital. Workers form "as co-operators [. . .] merely [. . .] a particular mode of existence of capital. Hence the productive power developed by the worker socially is the productive power of capital. The socially productive power of labour develops as a free gift to capital" (451). Cooperation is a "productive power of capital" (453). Marx sees communism as a mode of production and society in which cooperation has been generalised so that the cooperative essence of humans and society can be fully and truly realised. He speaks of communism as "the co-operative society based on common ownership of the means of production" (Marx 1875) in which "the springs of co-operative wealth flow more abundantly" (Marx 1875).

Capitalist Supervision, Control, and Surveillance

Capitalism implies large-scale cooperation so that it enables "to liberate the employer himself from manual labour" (448). Cooperating workers are better equipped to form social bonds, organise politically as unions or parties, protest, refuse labour, or go on strike. In order to try to control these potentials and to compel workers to labour as much and as intensely as possible, capital has to organise the labour of supervision, surveillance, control, and management.

> That a capitalist should command in the field of production is now as indispensable as that a general should command on the field of battle. All directly social or communal labour on a large scale requires, to a greater or lesser degree, a directing authority, in order to secure the harmonious co-operation of the activities of individuals, and to perform the general functions that have their origin in the motion of the total productive organism, as distinguished from the motion of its separate organs. [. . .] The work of directing, superintending and adjusting

becomes one of the functions of capital, from the moment that the labour under capital's control becomes co-operative. As a specific function of capital, the directing function acquires its own special characteristics. (448–449)

Capitalist control makes capitalism "purely despotic" (450). The more cooperative capitalism becomes, the more the need for control and surveillance—"the labour of superintendence" (450)—of the workers. "An industrial army of workers under the command of a capitalist requires, like a real army, officers (managers) and N.C.O.s (foremen, overseers), who command during the labour process in the name of capital. The work of supervision becomes their established and exclusive function" (450).

Surveillance Studies

In late 20th century, an academic field called "surveillance studies", which analyses the role of surveillance practices, structures, ideologies, and technologies in society emerged (Fuchs 2011, 2012).

The Canadian sociologist David Lyon has through a vast number of publications on the topic become the guru of surveillance studies. Surveillance studies tends to roam around between a critique of surveillance and a general definition of surveillance as systematic information processing, which it needs in order to blow up the scope of its field far enough so that it can claim a discipline-like status. "New" inter- and trans-disciplines such as surveillance studies, Internet research, science and technology studies, etc. claim to transcend disciplinary boundaries, but at the same time pretty much behave like orthodox disciplines when it comes to institutionalising themselves. For Marxists, in contrast, it does not matter which academic discipline they belong to because they are Universalists and first and foremost critical theorists. To be a critical theorist is a more important than claiming belonging to any discipline or self-proclaimed inter-, anti-, or trans-discipline, and also is the most interdisciplinary task.

Lyon argues that surveillance is Janus-faced and says he regards "some form of surveillance as an inherent—and not necessarily evil—feature of all human societies" (Lyon 1994, 19). Foucault's negative notions of the panopticon and disciplinary power have much influenced the study of surveillance, but not so much surveillance studies: There have been strong tendencies within this field that have tried to get rid of the critical definition of surveillance. The Canadian sociologist Kevin Haggerty (2006) argues, for example, that surveillance scholars do not want to see positive aspects of surveillance such as infectious disease control or surveillance in parenting because they "are trained in a tradition of critique" (Haggerty 2006, 36).

David Lyon defines surveillance as "the focused, systematic and routine attention to personal details for purposes of influence, management, protection or direction. Surveillance directs its attention in the end to individuals" (Lyon 2007, 14). This definition leaves the boundary between surveillance on the one hand and personal data processing as well as information collection on the other open. It is so general that surveillance becomes the same as information processing and thereby loses its critical-theoretical potential. The Norwegian sociologist Thomas Mathiesen (2013, 17), a socialist who has been very active in the prison abolition movement, therefore draws in contrast to David Lyon a distinction between information systems and surveillance systems. The latter enable bringing information to the fore and against individuals and groups. Information systems can turn into surveillance system: An example is that the Norwegian Census Bureau's registration of Jews was first conducted only for statistical purposes, but was used by the Nazis to track "down and eventually" exterminate "Jews during the German occupation of Norway 1940–1945" (Mathiesen 2013, 18).

Michel Foucault on Surveillance

For the French philosopher Michel Foucault (1926–1984), surveillance is a form of disciplinary power. Disciplines are "general formulas of domination" (Foucault 1977, 137). Surveillance is for Foucault panoptic disciplinary power, a "system of permanent registration" (Foucault 1977, 196) in which "all events are recorded" (Foucault 1977, 197)—a "machine for dissociating the see/being seen dyad" (Foucault 1977, 202). In surveillance, "[o]ne is totally seen, without ever seeing" (Foucault 1977, 202). Foucault helped in grounding a critical theory of surveillance, but never gave a full definition of the term.

In the age of the Internet, an argument against a Foucauldian view is that surveillance has become decentralised, bottom-up, manifold, and networked. On the Internet, there are indeed forms of counter-power and counter-watching such as online watchdog and leaking platforms. Edward Snowden's 2013 revelations of a global Internet surveillance system operated by secret services in cooperation with corporate Internet platforms shows, however, that also decentralised surveillance is dominated by the state and capital. The NSA and Google can watch what you do online, whereas you cannot watch what exactly these watchers are watching.

Capitalist and Bureaucratic Surveillance

The Japanese economist Toshimaru Ogura (2006) and the American political economist of information Oscar Gandy (1993) argue therefore that a common characteristic of surveillance is the management of population based on capitalism and/or the nation state. Surveillance is a negative form of information collection and use that only exists in dominative societies. Surveillance can be defined as the collection and use of data on individuals or groups so that control and discipline of behaviour can be exercised by actual violence or the threat of being targeted by violence or by (for a more detailed discussion, see Fuchs 2011, 2012b). Surveillance is an expression of instrumental reason and competition because it is based on the idea that others are watched, and data on their behaviour, ideas, look, etc. are gathered so that they can be controlled and disciplined and choose certain actions and avoid others that are considered undesirable. Competitive interests and behaviours are involved. The controlling group, class, or individuals try to force the surveilled to avoid certain actions by conveying to the latter that information on them is available that could be used for actions that could have negative influences on their lives. Surveillance can, however, also operate fully covertly so that people are monitored, but do not at all know that this is the case. They may only find out at a later point of time or not at all. Surveillance often operates with threats and fear; it is a form of psychological and structural violence that can turn into physical violence.

Modern society is based on the nation state and capitalism. Surveillance conducted by nation states and corporations aims at controlling the behaviour of individuals and groups—that is, they should be forced to behave or not behave in certain ways because they know that their appearance, movements, location, or ideas are or could be watched by surveillance systems. Nation states require internal and external defence mechanisms—the police, secret services, and the army. Controlling the population, unrest, political uproar, intervening and defending itself militarily are therefore important tasks of the nation state. State surveillance of citizens and other countries is therefore a necessary task of any modern nation state. In political surveillance, individuals are threatened by the potential exercise of organised violence (of the law) if they behave in certain ways that are undesired. They are then watched by specific political insitutions (such as secret services or the police).

In the case of economic surveillance, individuals are threatened by the violence of the market, which wants to force them to buy or produce certain commodities and help reproduce capitalist relations by gathering and using information on their economic behaviour with the help of monitoring systems. Toshimaru Ogura (2006) argues that there are five roles of surveillance in capitalism: (1) workplace surveillance, (2) population management, (3) control of the human mind, (4) consumer surveillance, and (5) computerised surveillance.

TABLE 13.1 The role of surveillance in the cycle of capital accumulation

Sphere of the accumulation process	Surveillance target	Description	Methods (examples)
Circulation	Potential variable capital (v), M => C	*Applicant surveillance:* Surveillance of potential workers	Access to criminal records, health databases, bank data, employment histories, and other databases; talks with former employers and supervisors; information search on the Internet
Production	Variable capital (v)	*Workplace and workforce surveillance:* Surveillance of labour forces at the work place; surveillance of productivity	Managers; supervisors; work place surveillance technologies; databases; corporate identities; integrative management strategies; participatory management; identification systems; electronic work flow systems; e-mail surveillance; surveillance of employees' Internet activities; fixation of workers' knowledge, answers to problems, and best practices in databases; Taylorism, in order to increase productivity; data on the activities of workers are collected, recorded, measured, stored, and analysed
Production	Constant capital (c)	*Property surveillance:* Surveillance of private property (commodities, capital, means of production) in order to circumvent theft and sabotage	Security guards, alarm systems, CCTV, access control systems, invisible security labelling or electronic tagging of commodities
Circulation	C' => M'	*Consumer surveillance:* Consumption interests and processes are systematically observed and analysed in order to guarantee the selling of as much commodities as possible and the realisation of profit	Marketing research, consumer research, electronic consumer surveillance (especially on the Internet: cookies, targeted advertising mechanisms, spyware, profiling of Internet usage behaviour, data gathering by intelligent Internet spiders, spam mail databases, data mining, clickstream monitoring, collaborative filtering), loyalty cards, product testing
Circulation	C' => M'	*Surveillance of competitors:* Corporations have the interest to minimise competition by other firms in order to maximise market shares and profits, therefore they are interested in collecting and analysing data about the technologies, labour force, organisational structures, commodities, economic performance, etc. of their competitors	Marketing research, industrial espionage, information gathering on the Internet

Surveillance in the Labour Process and in Capitalist Accumulation

Harry Braverman (1920–1976) was an American political economist and the founder of the labour process theory. He studied forms of control and surveillance of labour. Braverman (1974/1998, 69) shows that the assembly line, management, Taylorism, mechanisation, automation, and computerisation have functioned as means for destroying workers' control in the production process and establishing capital's "control and dictation of each step of the process". Braverman operates with concepts such as control and deskilling, whereas he mentions the notion of surveillance explicitly only once in his book *Labor and Monopoly Capital*—namely in a quotation by Thorsten Veblen (see Braverman 1974/1998, 185).

Table 13.1 discusses the role of surveillance at the various points in the capital accumulation process M–C . . P . . C′–M′. It identifies five different forms of economic surveillance (see Fuchs 2012).

The table shows that surveillance is a central method that capital uses for the exertion of control and discipline in the accumulation process. Corporations conduct a systematic gathering of data about applicants, employees, the labour process, private property, consumers, and competitors in order to minimise economic risks, discipline workers, increase productivity; circumvent theft, sabotage, and protests; control consumers through advertising; and adapt to changing conditions of competition. The overall aim of the employment of multiple surveillance methods and technologies in the capital accumulation process is the maximisation of profit and the increased exploitation of surplus-value. Surveillance is a method that capital employs for controlling the production and circulation process and for controlling and disciplining the workforce. Economic surveillance is a way of minimising the risk of making losses and maximising the opportunities for making profits.

The Dialectic of the One and the Many as the Dialectic of the Single Worker and Many Workers in the Cooperation Process

In chapter 1, I pointed out that Hegel speaks of a dialectic of attraction and repulsion for characterising the relationship of the One and the Many. Each One is individual and therefore repulses the Others, but at the same time it is just One of Many and exists only in the attraction by and mutual constitution through Others. I used this dialectic in chapter 1 for characterising Marx's analysis of the value-forms. It can also be used for understanding the process of cooperation (see Figure 13.1): Each worker has an individual existence and unique experiences and skills. In the cooperation process, different workers and their unique histories and experiences meet and attract each other. They are different individuals, but work in common on a common goal and with common means of production during a common time and in a common space. Through the attraction of their combined works, synergies are created so that their relationship is sublated into a unity of diversity that constitutes a new quality of the production process: A new product emerges that has new qualities. It is more than the sum of individual works: A single individual could not at all or only with huge efforts create this product.

In capitalism, cooperation is a method of relative surplus-value production: By cooperating, workers create more products in less time and save constant capital so that the capitalist can accelerate production, the value of the commodities drops, and more surplus-labour is performed in the same amount of time as before. Cooperation has an antagonistic character in capitalism: It develops the productive forces and makes labour and the economy evermore social and productive, which is the precondition for a capitalist society. Social connection is also a precondition for labour's resistance against capital. But with increasing cooperation, capital comes up with ever newer means of control in order to subordinate workers and try to contain potential or actual resistance against capitalist rule so that cooperation is subsumed under surveillant power. There is an antagonism

Dialectic of attraction and repulsion, One of the Many:
Emergence of a new product from co-operative synergies

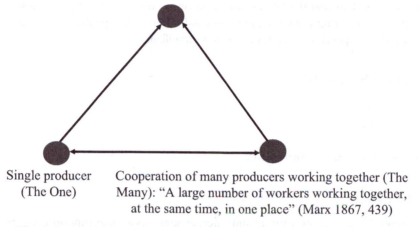

Single producer   Cooperation of many producers working together (The
(The One)   Many): "A large number of workers working together,
at the same time, in one place" (Marx 1867, 439)

FIGURE 13.1   The dialectic of the single worker and many workers in the cooperation process

Resistance, communist potentials vs. Surveillance and control as
"pure despotism" (Marx 1867, 452)

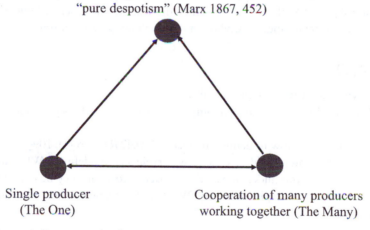

Single producer   Cooperation of many producers
(The One)   working together (The Many)

FIGURE 13.2   The capitalist antagonism between cooperation and surveillance

between surveillance and cooperation in capitalism that Marx describes in chapter 13. Cooperation has communist potentials that capitalism tries to contain so that cooperation is turned into a productive force for capital. Figure 13.2 visualises the capitalist antagonism between cooperation and surveillance.

Single producers, who have unique experiences that make them unique individuals different from others (repulsion), meet in the cooperation process as coworkers (attraction), where they constitute a productive power that creates use-values. Capital tries to control cooperation and to subsume it under its rule by putting workers under surveillance in order to produce relative and/or absolute surplus-value. At the same time, the cooperation process constitutes starting points, meeting and communication spaces that can be the source of resistance against capitalist rule and political organisation. Cooperation itself also fosters potentials for the societalisation (*Vergesellschaftung*) of the means of production so that the labour process becomes more social; this constitutes communist potentials that ripen within capitalism, point beyond it, but that capitalists try to control with the help of methods of supervision, management, and surveillance.

Exercises for Chapter 13

Group exercise (G)
Project exercise (P)

Key Categories: Cooperation, Surveillance

Exercise 13.1 (G)

Work in groups: Make a list of software and Internet applications that support cooperative work—that is, that are computer-supported cooperative work (CSCW) applications.

Reflect for each application on the questions of if it fosters communist potentials of ownership and work and/or if it is controlled by capital and/or used by capital for controlling and monitoring workers. If there are communist potentials, then reflect on how exactly they look and are organised, and what constrains them within capitalism. How would they be different in a communist society? If there are control potentials that capital uses, then think about and describe how exactly capital uses these technologies for repressing, controlling, and surveilling workers, consumers, or others.

Exercise 13.2 (G)

Read the following two articles about surveillance:

Fuchs, Christian. 2012. Political economy and surveillance theory. *Critical Sociology* 39 (5): 671–687.

Fuchs, Christian. 2011. How to define surveillance? *MATRIZes* 5 (1): 109–133.

Discuss in a group: How should in your view surveillance be defined? What are the commonalities and differences of Foucault's and Marx's approach? How can they be combined for studying and criticising surveillance in capitalist society? What are foundations of a critical theory and critical political economy of surveillance?

Exercise 13.3 (G)

Work in groups: Conduct a search in the news media for contemporary and historical forms of economic surveillance. Characterise these forms of surveillance with the help of the information presented in Table 13.1.

Present your results. Discuss: What are the purposes of the identified technologies? Which dangers do they entail? What changes need to happen in order to overcome these dangers? What can be done in order to advance such changes?

14

THE DIVISION OF LABOUR AND MANUFACTURE

The term "manufacture" comes from the Latin word "manufactura", which means making something by hand. Marx describes in chapter 14 factories, in which products were made by hand, so-called manufactures or manufactories. He speaks of a manufacturing period of capitalism that existed from the mid-16th century until the last third of the 18th century (455). Marx discusses origins of the manufacture (14.1), the role of the worker in it (14.2), two forms of the manufactory (14.3), the division of labour in the manufactory and society (14.4), and the manufactory's capitalist character (14.5).

14.1. The Division of Labour and Manufacture

Origins of the Manufacture

Marx says there were two origins of the manufacture:

1. One capitalist employed various workers whose different forms of labour were required for creating one commodity in one place.
2. One capitalist employed workers in one place. They all individually conducted one full manufacturing process side-by-side.

In general, if there is a need for a larger quantity of commodities, it is likely that labour is reorganised so that not each worker performs the whole manufacturing process individually, but each of them "performs one, and only one, of the constituent partial operations" (457) so that a "particular sort of co-operation" emerges, where the workers are a "life-long organ of this partial function" (458).

14.2. The Specialised Worker and His Tools

The Collective Worker (Gesamtarbeiter)

Marx introduces the notion of the collective or combined worker (*Gesamtarbeiter*). The collective worker is in the manufactory the form of cooperative labour in which each worker performs one specific operation:

> The collective worker, who constitutes the living mechanism of manufacture, is made up solely of such one-sidedly specialized workers. Hence, in comparison with the independent

handicraft, more is produced in less time, or in other words the productivity of labour is increased. (458)

The manufacture is a form of relative surplus-value production: Each worker conducting a single operation and amassing workers in one factory, where they use the same means of production, accelerates production by decreasing the time it takes for the product to pass from one production stage to the next, accelerating the access to raw materials, accelerating individual performance, and adapting tools to the special operations of individual workers. The "division of labour in manufacture is merely a particular method of creating relative surplus-value, or of augmenting the self-valorization of capital" (486).

14.3. The Two Fundamental Forms of Manufacture— Heterogeneous and Organic

The Heterogeneous and the Homogeneous Manufacture

Marx describes two forms of the manufacture that arise "from the nature of the article produced" (461):

1. In the heterogeneous manufacture, partial products made independently are assembled. In this form of manufacturing, the workers tend to work at home, not in the factory (462–463).
2. In the homogeneous manufacture, the products "go through connected phases of development, go step by step through a series or processes" performed by "different specialized workers" (463).

The Work of Independent Craftspersons

Figure 14.1 visualises the work of the individual independent craftsperson, whom Marx considers characteristic for the precapitalist form of production.

In independent craftspersonship, one worker owns tools and uses resources for creating one product. The work process shown in Figure 14.1 is based on the subject-object dialectic introduced in chapter 1 and especially chapter 7: A human subject uses means of production (objects, instruments) to transform nature and/or culture so that s/he creates a new subject-object, a new product.

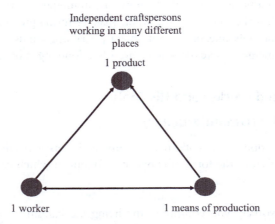

FIGURE 14.1 The work process of craftspersons

Labour in the Heterogeneous and the Organic Manufacture

Figures 14.2 and 14.3 visualise labour in the heterogeneous and the organic manufacture.

In the heterogeneous manufacture, independent producers create different partial products or conduct different steps in the labour process independently in separate spaces. In the manufacture, these separate products are assembled together. In the organic manufacture, all of the single production processes are spatially integrated into one workshop. The production process is divided into many small steps that are all performed by single workers. "The different stages of the process, previously successive in time, have become simultaneous in space" (464).

For Marx, the collective worker in the manufactory is like a machine body in which every limb represents one worker. "The habit of doing only one thing converts him into an organ which operates with the certainty of a force of nature, while his connection with the whole mechanism compels him to work with the regularity of a machine" (469).

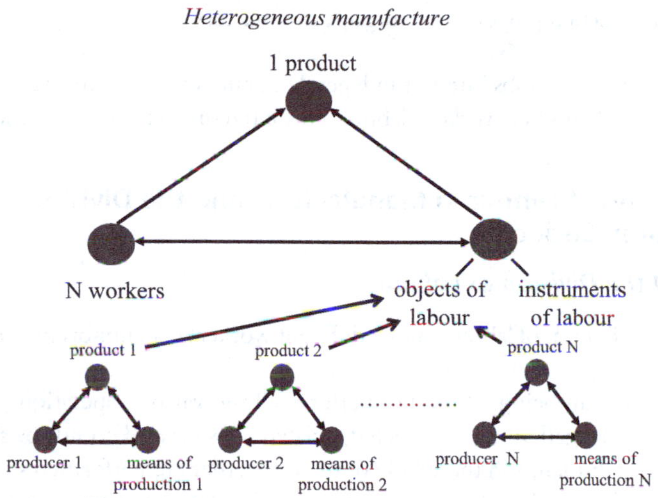

Heterogeneous manufacture

FIGURE 14.2 Labour in the heterogeneous manufacture

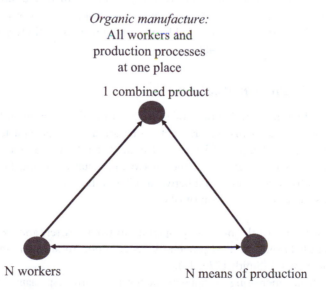

FIGURE 14.3 Labour in the organic manufacture

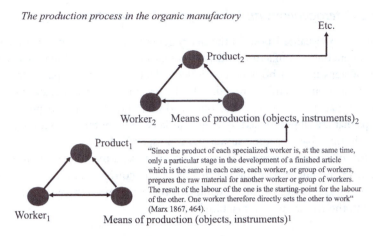

FIGURE 14.4 The production process in the organic manufactory

The collective workers' "limbs" are not independent, but connected to each other: One workers' product is the object of another workers' labour. This interconnection is visualised in Figure 14.4.

14.4. The Division of Labour in Manufacture, and the Division of Labour in Society

Capitalism and the Division of Labour

Marx argues that the division of labour among different workers is an important element of capitalism:

> Instead of each man being allowed to perform all the various operations in succession, these operations are changed into disconnected, isolated ones, carried on side by side; each is assigned to a different craftsman, and the whole of them together are performed simultaneously by the co-operators. This accidental division is repeated, develops advantages of its own and gradually ossifies into a systematic division of labour. (456)
>
> While the division of labour in society at large, whether mediated through the exchange of commodities or not, can exist in the most diverse economic formations of society, the division of labour in the workshop, as practised by manufacture, is an entirely specific creation of the capitalist mode of production. (480)

Adam Smith on the Division of Labour

Adam Smith gave the title "The Division of Labour" to the first chapter in his famous book *The Wealth of Nation*, which shows that he saw such a division as an important feature of the modern economy. He defined the division of labour as labour that is "divided among a great number of hands" (Smith 1776, 11). He forgot the division between mental and manual labour; labour can also be divided between hands and brains and between different brains.

Smith discusses causes of the division of labour:

- It is the consequence of the human "propensity to truck, barter, and exchange one thing for another" (Smith 1776, 18). This propensity "is common to all men, and to be found in no other race of animals" (Smith 1776, 18).
- It occurs with the increasing complexity of the economy, especially in the most advanced economies (Smith 1776, 9–11): "those great manufactures [. . .] which are destined to supply

the great wants of the great body of the people [. . .] employ[s] so great a number of workmen, that it is impossible to collect them all into the same workhouse [. . .] the work may really be divided into a much greater number of parts" (Smith 1776, 9).

He describes as effects of this division (Smith 1776, 12) the increase of the dexterity of labour, its abridgement, the saving of labour time, and that the development of productive technology results in "universal opulence which extends itself to the lowest ranks of the people" (Smith 1776, 15).

The Fetishism of Adam Smith's Concept of the Division of Labour

One can criticise this understanding of the division of labour in the following ways:

- Smith sees exchange as omnipresent in any society and as a fundamental human characteristic. There are surely situations without exchange, where voluntary altruism and solidarity substitute instrumental reason and exchange logic—for example, care for others in personal relations. Smith fetishises exchange and the division of labour as endless and necessary elements of all societies. His conceptualisation of the division of labour is a good example for what Marx in chapter 1.4 terms "fetishism".
- Smith neglects power structures: The division of labour is a means of the powerful to derive benefits at the expense of workers who are compelled to work for low wages.
- Smith overlooks that the division of labour between men and women, developed and developing countries, and manual and mental labour has not resulted in general wealth, but inequalities.

Marx remarks in chapter 3 that "Smith begins his work in the official manner with an apotheosis of the division of labour" (220, footnote 29) and thereby criticises Smith's fetishist understanding.

Marx on the Division of Labour in Earlier Works

Marx already in his early works characterised the division of labour as specific for class societies: "The *division of labor* is the expression in political economy of the *social character of labor* within the estrangement" (Marx 1844, 128). "Division of labour and private property are, moreover, identical expressions" (Marx and Engels 1845, 52). A division of labour presupposes the existence of a class society, in which one group or person derives advantages at the expense of others through the division of labour between or among men and women, town and country, regions, countries, mental and physical labour, politicians and citizens, legislative and executive power, agriculture and industry.

Marx and Engels (1845) in the *German Ideology* characterise the first division of labour as one that occurred in tribes and families: The gender division of labour, in which patriarchal family chieftains dominate over their family and slaves. In the family, "the wife and children are the slaves of the husband" (Marx and Engels 1845, 52). Marx in chapter 14 argues that in commodity-producing societies, the division of labour between town and country is foundational: "The foundation of every division of labour which has attained a certain degree of development, and has been brought about by the exchange of commodities, is the separation of town from country" (472).

Another division of labour is "the division of social production into is main *genera* such as agriculture, industry, etc. as division of labour in general" (471). Historically, there has been a shift away of the number of employees and the share of value-added from agriculture to industry and then from agriculture and industry to the service and information sector. An important aspect has in this respect been the technification, mechanisation, and digital automation of agriculture and manufacturing, which has resulted in an increased demand for science and knowledge production.

The Global Division of Labour

Marx also speaks of a colonial global division of labour: "The colonial system and the extension of the world market, both of which form part of the general conditions for the existence of the manufacturing period, furnish us with rich materials for displaying the division of labour in society" (474).

He here describes what in Marxist literature has been called the old or first international division of labour, in which colonies were markets for commodities and sources of slaves and raw materials that were plundered. In the new international division of labour that emerged in the second half of the 20th century, the periphery often provides the raw materials and manufacturing steps, while the knowledge, research, and technological innovations are situated in the capitalist centres. Transnational corporations have become important in the capitalist world economy and outsource labour in a flexible manner to countries and regions where they can minimise wages and other investment costs in order to maximise profits.

The New International Division of Labour

Fröbel, Heinrichs, and Kreye (1981) have defined the concept of the new international division of labour: "The development of the world economy has increasingly created conditions (forcing the development of the new international division of labour) in which the survival of more and more companies can only be assured through the relocation of production to new industrial sites, where labour-power is cheap to buy, abundant and well-disciplined; in short, through the transnational reorganization of production" (Fröbel, Heinrichs, and Kreye 1981, 15). A further development is that "commodity production is being increasingly subdivided into fragments which can be assigned to whichever part of the world can provide the most profitable combination of capital and labour" (Fröbel, Heinrichs, and Kreye 1981, 14). In critical media and cultural studies, Toby Miller et al. (2004) have used this concept for explaining the new international division of cultural labour (NICL). A typical example is that many Hollywood movies are not directed in Hollywood, but in China and other low-wage countries in order to save costs.

Quentin Tarantino's Movie Kill Bill and the International Division of Cultural Labour

Take, for example, Quentin Tarantino's movie *Kill Bill*, which features Uma Thurman as Beatrix Kiddo (also called "The Bride" or "Black Mamba") and David Carradine as Bill (also called the "Snake Charmer"), those being the lead roles:

> The lead character, called "The Bride", was a member of the Deadly Viper Assassination Squad, lead by her lover "Bill". Upon realizing she was pregnant with Bill's child, "The Bride" decided to escape her life as a killer. She fled to Texas, met a young man, who, on the day of their wedding rehearsal was gunned down by an angry and jealous Bill (with the assistance of the Deadly Viper Assassination Squad). Four years later, "The Bride" wakes from a coma, and discovers her baby is gone. She, then, decides to seek revenge upon the five people who destroyed her life and killed her baby.[1]

The shooting of *Kill Bill* was partly conducted in Chinese studios in Beijing in order to save costs. Tarantino made use of the international division of cultural labour:

> *Kill Bill*'s Asian scenes, including those set in Japan, were shot in Beijing in a studio that Mao Zedong built to produce propaganda pictures. [. . .] Tarantino's longtime collaborator, the producer Lawrence Bender, is tight-lipped about the budget for *Kill Bill* but allows that vastly

lower personnel costs and the absence of labor union restrictions mean a day of shooting in Beijing costs as little as half of what it would cost in Hollywood. (Blood Sport. *Time Magazine* September 30, 2002)

The International Division of Digital Labour

The production of computers, laptops, mobile phones, and computing periphery devices is based on an international division of digital labour (IDDL) (for details see Fuchs 2014a, 2015). In the IDDL different forms of alienation and exploitation can be encountered. Examples are slave workers in mineral extraction (e.g., so-called conflict mineral extraction in the Congo), Taylorist hardware assemblers (e.g., the highly exploited assemblage workers in Foxconn factories), software engineers, professional online content creators (e.g., online journalists), call centre agents, and social media prosumers. The IDDL shows that various forms of labour that are characteristic of various stages of capitalism and capitalist and precapitalist modes of production interact so that different forms of separated and highly exploited forms of double free wage labour, unpaid "free" labour, casualised labour, and slave labour form a global network of exploited labour that creates value and profits for companies involved in the capitalist information and communication technology (ICT) industry. The IDDL shows that stages of capitalist development and historical modes of production (such as patriarchal housework, classical slavery, feudalism, capitalism in general) and modes of organisation of the productive forces (such as agriculture, industrialism, informationalism) are not simply successive stages of economic development, where one form substitutes an older one, but that they are all dialectically mediated. Capitalism has not destroyed the possibility of slavery, but slavery on the one hand exists in a new form as wage slavery, and on the other hand possibilities for the existence of classical and feudal forms of slavery remain and, as the example of slavery in mining shows, exist today in a way that benefits Western ICT companies. Figure 14.5 visualises the IDDL.

"Digital labour" is not a term that only describes the production of digital content (Fuchs 2014a, 2015). It rather describes the entire interconnected international division of labour in the production of digital media technologies and content that involves various modes of production and

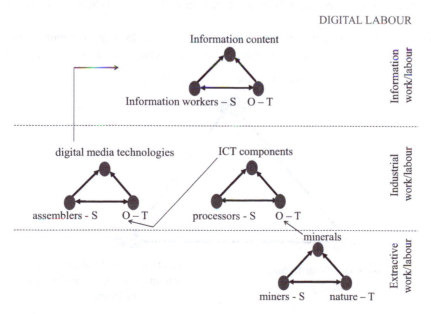

FIGURE 14.5   The international division of digital labour

different forms of the organisation of the productive forces (extractive/agricultural work, industrial work, information work). The IDDL contains a network of agricultural/extractive, industrial, and informational forms of work that enables the existence and usage of digital media. The subjects involved in the digital mode of production (S)—miners, processors, assemblers, information workers, and related workers—stand in specific relations to production that are either class related or nonclass related. So what I designate as S in figure 14.5 is actually a relationship S_1—S_2 between different subjects or subject groups. In contemporary capitalist society, most of these digital relations of production tend to be shaped by wage labour, slave labour, unpaid labour, precarious labour, and freelance labour. The political task is that people working under such class relations emancipate themselves so that a communist mode of production can emerge that contains a communist mode of digital production as well as nondigital communist modes of production.

The Division of Labour's Organisational Levels

The division of labour operates (a) at the level of factories and offices, (b) the family, (c) regionally between the town and the countryside, (d) at the level of the economy as division into economic sectors and industries, and (e) globally as a division into core, semiperiphery, and periphery. The divisions between the town and the countryside and the global division of labour are both an expression of the "territorial division of labour" (474).

Figure 14.6 visualises the organisational levels of the division of labour: It operates in single companies (the One), in entire branches and sector of the economy (from which the division into agriculture, manufacturing, finance, services, information, etc. results) (the Many), and at the level of entire society (the gender division of labour, the international division of labour, the spatial division between town and countryside, core/semiperiphery/periphery).

The Division of Labour in Companies and Society at Large

Marx describes a contradiction between the division of labour in the workshop and at the level of society: Capitalists celebrate centralised authority and control of ownership in the factory and the office, but call for competition and the "war of all against all" (477) in the market (476–477):

> The same bourgeois consciousness which celebrates the division of labour in the workshop, the lifelong annexation of the worker to a partial operation, and his complete subjection to

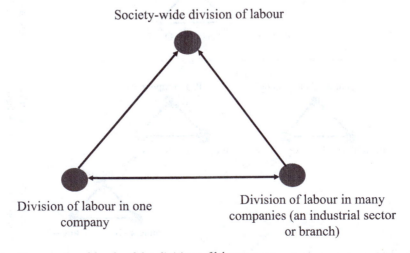

FIGURE 14.6 Organisational levels of the division of labour

capital, as an organization of labour that increases its productive power, denounces with equal vigour every conscious attempt to control and regulate the process of production socially, as an inroad upon such sacred things as the rights of property, freedom and the self-determining 'genius' of the individual capitalist. (477)

Mario Tronti: The Social Factory

Marx says that the capitalist would oppose to "turn the whole of society into a factory" (477), by which he means a communist society, in which society as a whole controls the economy. Autonomist Marxism is a form of Marxist theory and class struggle in which the goal is that class struggles widen the workers' and social movements' autonomy from capital and create spaces of relative autonomy from capitalism that if ever more enlarged turn into communism. This approach first developed in Italy. In Italian Autonomist Marxism, the notion of the social factory has been given a somewhat different meaning: Mario Tronti (1962) argues that the technical changes of capitalism—that is, the technical increase of productivity or what Marx termed "relative surplus-value production"—has resulted in the emergence of a social factory. The factory extends its boundaries into all areas of society:

> The more capitalist development proceeds, i.e. the more the production of relative surplus value asserts and extends itself, the more the cycle production—distribution—exchange—consumption closes itself inevitably, the societal relation between capitalist production and bourgeois society, between factory and society, between society and the state become more and more organic. At the highest level of capitalist development the societal relation becomes a moment of the relations of production, and the whole of society becomes cause and expression of production, i.e. the whole society lives as a function of the factory and the factory extends its exclusive domination to the whole of society. [. . .] When the factory raises itself to the master of the whole of society—the entire societal production becomes industrial production—, then the specific characteristics of the factory get lost inside of the general characteristics of society. (Tronti 1962, 30–31, translation from German)

Antonio Negri: The Social Worker

Antonio Negri has become the most well-known representative of Autonomist Marxism. He interpreted Tronti's notion of the social factory at the level of the labour process and first introduced the notion of the social worker, which he later, taking into account the rise and importance of the networked information economy, developed into the notion of the multitude. Negri uses the term "social worker" for arguing that there is a broadening of the proletariat—"a new working class" that is "now extended throughout the entire span of production and reproduction" (Negri 1982/1988, 209). He here takes up Marx's idea of the collective workers, who form an aggregated and combined workforce, are heterogeneous, and are organised as a whole of singularities that is necessary for creating profit. Negri (1971/1988) first developed this concept in a reading of Marx's "Fragment on Machines" in the *Grundrisse*. He argued that the main contradiction of capitalism is that money is the specific measure of value, while labour with the development of the productive forces acquires an increasingly social character and so questions value. The socialisation of labour would have resulted in the "emergence of a massified and socialised working class" (Negri 1971/1988, 104).

The notion of the socialised working class was later developed into the concept of the social worker (Negri 1982/1988), which emerged by a reorganisation of capitalism that dissolved the mass worker, who had been characterised by Taylorism, Fordism, Keynesianism, and the planner-state

(Negri 1982/1988, 205). The social worker signifies "a growing awareness of the interconnection between productive labour and the labour of reproduction" (Negri 1982/1988, 209), the emergence of "diffuse labour" (= outsourced labour, Negri 1982/1988, 214), and mobile labour (= labour flexibility, Negri 1982/1988, 218).

The advantage of the concept of the social worker, which is a reformulation of Marx's notion of the collective worker in the context of informational and post-Fordist capitalism, is that it allows us to consider also irregular and unpaid workers (house workers, slaves, precarious workers, migrant workers, education workers, public service workers, the unemployed, etc.) as productive labourers. Negri goes, however, so far as to say that "labour time" as a consequence of this tendency "becomes increasingly irrelevant in the context of a full socialisation of the productive machine" (Negri 1971/1988, 100). This is just another formulation for saying that the law of value ceases to exist—it is "in the process of extinction" (Negri 1971/1988, 148). As a consequence, Negri assumes that communism is near: "communism is the present-day tendency, an active force operating in the here and now" (Negri 1971/1988, 112).

The law of value, however, operates as long as capitalism exists: The emergence of social or knowledge work does not stop it from operating and has in fact not stopped operating this law in all the years that have passed since Negri first formulated this idea. The labour time of a specific part of the social worker can perfectly be measured: It is the average number of hours of unpaid work performed by a specific group or overall in a society that results in the production of commodities that contribute to the accumulation of capital. That the socialisation of work increases due to the rise of productivity means that the time needed for producing certain goods has historically decreased. High productivity is a precondition of communism, but it is not communism itself and does not automatically lead to communism. There are communist potentials within capitalism. Democratic communism can only be established by struggles.

Digital Labour and the Social Worker

Notwithstanding these limits of Negri's approach, the logical consequence of the concept of the social or collective worker is that one is exploited and productive if one is part of the collective workers who produce commodities. Digital labour on Facebook and other corporate digital media is enabled by and connected to an entire value chain and global sphere of exploitation that constitutes the ICT industry. The reality of ICTs today is enabled by the existence of a plenitude of exploited labour: The slave labour of people of colour in Africa who extract minerals, out of which ICT hardware is produced; the highly exploited labour of industrial workers in China and other countries who assemble hardware tools; the labour of low-paid software engineers and knowledge workers in developing countries; the activities of a labour-aristocracy of highly paid and highly stressed engineers in Western software companies; the labour of precarious service workers in the knowledge industry who process data (e.g. call-centre workers); and the digital labour of unpaid users. All of these varied forms of exploited labour depend on each other and are needed for creating profits in the ICT industry. Knowledge workers of the world are therefore connected by the circumstance that they are all exploited by capital. They form a combined labour force of social ICT and knowledge workers that constitutes a knowledge proletariat. The question that therefore arises is if the social knowledge proletariat of the world will organise itself politically and become a class-for-itself that struggles against capitalism.

The Division of Labour's Impact on Humans

Marx sees the division of labour as an impoverishment of human activities and capacities:

- The "social division of labour makes the nature of his labour as one-sided as his needs are many-sided" (201).

- The division of labour means the "development in a man of one single faculty at the expense of all others" (474).
- "But the division of labour is an organization of production which has grown up naturally, a web which has been, and continues to be, woven behind the backs of the producers of commodities" (201).
- "While the division of labor raises the productive power of labor and increases the wealth and refinement of society, it impoverishes the worker and reduces him to a machine" (Marx 1844, 26).
- The division of labour limits creativity: "as soon as the distribution of labour comes into being, each man has a particular, exclusive sphere of activity, which is forced upon him and from which he cannot escape. He is a hunter, a fisherman, a herdsman, or a critical critic, and must remain so if he does not want to lose his means of livelihood" (Marx and Engels 1845, 53).

The Dialectic of the Alienation of the Collective Worker and the Individual Worker in Capitalism

Figure 14.7 visualises the alienation that the division of labour poses for the worker in capitalism. Capital exploits the collective power of the workers, who act together as collective workers and thereby are more powerful, efficient, and effective than any single worker could ever be alone or all of them could be independently. The capitalist controls, owns, dominates, and exploits this collective labour-power and thereby also impoverishes the capacities of the single worker, who is reduced to the status of an individual cog in the capitalist machine, which accumulates ever more capital. The alienation of the collective worker and the alienation of the individual worker in capitalism presuppose and enable each other mutually.

The Abolishment of the Division of Labour in Communism: Well-Rounded Individuals

Marx puts against the alienating effects of the division of labour the idea and communist potential of the well-rounded individual in a communist society, where the abolishment of the division of labour enables everyone to become a creative worker. In communist society, "nobody has one exclusive sphere of activity but each can become accomplished in any branch he wishes, society regulates the general production and thus makes it possible for me to do one thing today and another tomorrow,

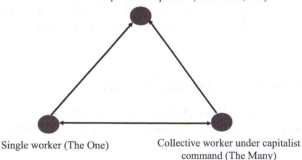

Alienation: "In manufacture, the social productive power of the collective worker, hence of capital, is enriched through the impoverishment of the worker in individual productive power" (Marx 1867, 483).

Single worker (The One)

Collective worker under capitalist command (The Many)

FIGURE 14.7 The dialectic of the alienation of the collective worker and the individual worker in capitalism

to hunt in the morning, fish in the afternoon, rear cattle in the evening, criticise after dinner" (Marx and Engels 1845, 53).

Engels points out that communism is a highly productive, post-scarcity society that enables the abolishment of the division into classes and the division of labour: "Thus society will produce enough products to be able so to arrange distribution that the needs of all its members will be satisfied. The division of society into various antagonistic classes will thereby become superfluous. Not only will it become superfluous, it is even incompatible with the new social order. Classes came into existence through the division of labour and the division of labour in its hitherto existing form will entirely disappear" (Engels 1847, 353).

A well-rounded development of individuals who are involved in, capable, educated, and skilful in manifold activities can emerge:

> Industry carried on in common and according to plan by the whole of society presupposes moreover people of all-round development, capable of surveying the entire system of production. Thus the division of labour making one man a peasant, another a shoemaker, a third a factory worker, a fourth a stockjobber, which has already been undermined by machines, will completely disappear. Education will enable young people quickly to go through the whole system of production, it will enable them to pass from one branch of industry to another according to the needs of society or their own inclinations. It will therefore free them from that one-sidedness which the present division of labour stamps on each one of them. Thus the communist organisation of society will give its members the chance of an all-round exercise of abilities that have received all-round development. With this, the various classes will necessarily disappear. Thus the communist organisation of society is, on the one hand, incompatible with the existence of classes and, on the other, the very establishment of this society furnishes the means to do away with these class differences. (Engels 1847, 353)

14.5. The Capitalist Character of Manufacture

The Capitalist Manufacture

The capitalist form of manufacture is a specific form of cooperation in which the capitalist controls a large number of workers and a large amount of constant capital (480). This form of exploitation limits the workers' capacities: It subjects them to "the discipline and command of capital", "converts the worker into a crippled monstrosity", and suppresses "a whole world of productive drives and inclinations" (481) so that the worker becomes an appendage of the workshop (482).

Marx argues that the capitalist division of labour and mode of production also cripples the workers' intellectual capacities: Capital controls "knowledge, judgement and will", "intelligent direction of production", and "the intellectual potentialities" (482). Capitalism results in some "crippling of body and mind" (484).

The Division between Manual and Mental Labour

The division between manual and mental labour and between labour and management has historically been capital's method for maintaining control over workers by limiting their power and influence within the organisation. The increasing importance of information work has not abolished the division between decision-making and management on the one side and labour's value-creation on the other side. Interpreting organisations as political systems shows that in the 21st century just like in the 19th century, capitalist companies are dictatorships of capital. It is peculiar and constitutive for capitalism that many modern societies understand themselves as democracies, but limit democracy to voting and the political realm. When entering the office or factory, the individual is no longer a sovereign citizen, but an exploited object in a totalitarian economic system. A change in the division of labour has occurred in late 20th and the 21st century so that more activities than before produce information. Information workers just like manual workers use both the brain and the rest of the body, but their work and products are predominantly informational in character. Information work is not automatically experienced as something creative, although it is just like all work creative in the sense that it produces a result. If we think of the repetitive labour in outbound call centres, then it becomes clear that information labour can be as monotonous, standardised, and meaningless as manual labour on a conveyor belt. Information work is also just like other work subject to automation. In a capitalist information company, there is a crucial separation between decision-making, which is also an informational activity, and value-creating labour, which includes both information and manual labour.

Michael Hardt and Antonio Negri on Information Work

The Autonomist Marxists Michael Hardt and Antonio Negri's (2000) book *Empire* has been the most widely read Marxist book of the 21st-century's first decade. It may be an overestimation that it is a rewriting of the "Communist Manifesto for the twenty-first century" (Žižek 2001), but it is undoubtedly an important book, especially also because Hardt and Negri have in it taken up the discussion of the role of the information economy in capitalism, which is, no matter if one agrees with their analysis or not, in itself an important task. In chapter 3.4 "Postmodernization, or The Informatization of Production" (Hardt and Negri 2000, 280–303), Hardt and Negri discuss the emergence of what they term the "multitude", a new informational collective worker and class of networked information workers that use computers, engage in cooperative work, and produce knowledge and other societal commons. They also speak of "immaterial labour". "Immaterial labor immediately involves social interaction and cooperation" (Hardt and Negri 2000, 294). Hardt and Negri see information work as an empowerment of workers so that it is a "potential for a kind of spontaneous and elementary communism" (Hardt and Negri 2000, 294).

"Immaterial" labour is a rather odd term because in a materialist theory, such as the one by Marx, the whole world, and also ideas, are considered as being material. Therefore "information work" as a specific form of the organisation and transformation of matter in the human economy is a more appropriate term. Information work and any kind of cooperative work are definitely expressions of the socialisation and high development of the productive forces, which are preconditions of communism. Information workers are, however, not automatically revolutionary and do not have more revolutionary capacities than other workers. If one thinks of freelance work, which is the prevalent form of economic activity among many information workers in the 21st century, then it becomes evident that many such workers are rather isolated, work alone, lack unions, and are a fragmented class faction. There have been initiatives to form coworking spaces, where freelance knowledge workers share an office in order to have more social contacts at work. Such spaces can also be starting points for unionisation, political organisation, and struggles, because people come together there, which allows them to overcome isolation and to communication, which is a first step towards and precondition of political organisation. Freelance knowledge workers are their own bosses. They are workers, managers, and owners at the same time so that the division among value-creators, owners, and managers is sublated. The problem is, however, that many of them own nothing or hardly anything so that they are working poor depending on contract labour for larger capitalist companies. They thereby become dependent on the capital of larger firms and are de facto wage workers who are just formally self-employed, which introduces a new division.

Marx argues that the manufactory was an "artificial economic construction" (490) that was not able to bring about massive increases in productivity. The technological limits came in contradiction with capitalism's economic requirements (490) so that a technification and the rise of what Marx terms "machinery" and "large-scale industry" was the result. Marx discusses this development in chapter 15.

Exercises for Chapter 14

Group exercise (G)
Project exercise (P)

Key Categories: *Manufacture/Manufactory, Heterogeneous Manufacture, Organic Manufacture, Division of Labour, International Division of Labour, Social Factory, Well-Rounded Individual*

Exercise 14.1 (P)

Read the following text:

Fuchs, Christian. 2013. Theorising and analysing digital labour: From global value chains to modes of production. *The Political Economy of Communication* 1 (2): 3–27.

Work in groups: Each group selects one type of digital medium (e.g., a particular mobile phone, laptop, computer, digital game, console, printer, etc.). Conduct a search for information using various sources (news media, alternative media, a corporate watchdogs platform, investigative journalists' reports, academic articles, interviews you conduct, etc.) in order to find out more about the international division of digital labour involved in the production of your chosen medium.

Discuss and present the results:
What kinds of labour are involved?
How do the working conditions look?

Why has the international division of digital labour developed and why does it exist in the case of the medium you are analysing?

Who benefits and how from the international division of digital labour? And who does not benefit, but rather suffers?

How would a communist alternative that involves the kind of well-rounded work that Marx and Engels talk about look in the case of the production of the medium you are analysing?

Exercise 14.2 (G)

Michael Hardt and Antonio Negri's book *Empire* is one of the most widely read and cited Marxist books published in the 21st century's first decade. It is of particular importance for the Marxist analysis of information work.

Read the following chapter:

Hardt, Michael and Antonio Negri. 2000. Postmodernization, or The Informatization of Production. In *Empire*, (280–303). Cambridge, MA: Harvard University Press.

Discuss the following questions:

What is "immaterial labour", and what is according to Hardt and Negri its role in 21st-century capitalism?

How do working conditions of "immaterial" workers look in 21st century? What problems do such workers face today? Discuss some examples.

What would be the role of information workers (who Hardt and Negri term "immaterial workers") in a communist society?

Are there communist potentials of information and information work? If so, which ones? What are the limits, contradictions, and problems of information work in capitalism?

Conduct a search for reviews and criticisms of Hardt and Negri's book *Empire* (entire books and collected volumes have been published about this book). Document the criticisms and position yourself towards them.

Exercise 14.3 (G)

Think of specific information work that you have experienced yourself or that friends or people you know conduct.

Discuss: What are the positive and negative aspects of this work? How could the negative aspects be overcome in a communist society? What could the role of information work be in a communist society? How would information work have to change in communism?

Work in groups for comparing your experiences.

Marx argues that capitalist cooperation in the manufactory alienates the human mind and body, including intellectual activity. Today information work is much more important than at the time of the manufactory.

To what degree are knowledge workers confronted with alienation, and how does their labour and alienation differ from that which Marx describes in chapter 14? What forms of alienation shape knowledge labour today? How are our brains' cognitive activities alienated in contemporary capitalism?

Note

1   http://www.imdb.com/title/tt0266697/plotsummary?ref_=tt_ql_6 (accessed on August 9, 2014).

15

MACHINERY AND LARGE-SCALE INDUSTRY

Chapter 15 is *Capital Volume 1*'s longest chapter. Marx analyses the role and stresses the importance of technology in capitalism. The chapter is made up of 10 sections. It shows that Marx's method is both logical and historical-empirical: He analyses the role of technology in capitalism in general (the logic of technology in capitalism) and underpins his analysis with historical examples, which he documents with the help of empirical data that derived from factory inspectors' reports, for whose work he had deep respect. Marx, for example, wrote that these reports "form a valuable contribution to the social anatomy of the United Kingdom" (Marx 1857, 21) and "prove beyond doubt that the infamies of the British factory system are growing with its growth" (Marx 1857, 253).

The Logical and the Historical Reading of *Capital*

The Marxist political economist David Harvey (2010, 86) argues that he has "preferred the logical reading to the historical one, even though there may be important historical insights to be gained in considering the circumstances necessary to facilitate the rise of a capitalist mode of production". The Marxist philosopher Wolfgang Fritz Haug (2013, 183–188, 223) argues that Harvey says that he gives a logical interpretation, although his approach is much more genetic-reconstructive and oriented on human praxis. Haug (2013, section 10.2) discusses how Harvey treats the question of the logical and the historical in *Capital*'s chapter 15. Haug (2013, section 10.2) criticises that Harvey (2010, 189) says on the one hand that the chapter's sections "are logically ordered" and stresses on the other hand that it is "a critical history of technology". He says that Harvey understands the logical simply as "everything not historical" and as "conceptual" (Haug 2013, 228). Haug (2013) himself does, however, also not provide an analysis of the longest chapter in *Capital Volume 1* that could clarify the relationship of the dialectical-logical and the historical. The English translation of chapter 15 is almost 150 pages long and is of particular interest for a critical sociology of technology and the media. It is also one of the chapters in *Volume 1* that contains the most historical elements.

Chapter 15 is a dialectical combination of historical and dialectical-logical elements: Marx describes the historical development from the predominance of physical labour towards machines and machine systems. At the same time this historical transition changes the logic of how the productive forces are organised, which Marx describes by making use of dialectical reasoning. The historical is itself dialectical because the machine system dialectically sublates (*aufheben*) physical labour and simple machines. In chapter 15, Marx describes in detail which effects technology has on society. He does so by logically and dialectically characterising phenomena such as the prolongation of the working day, the intensification of labour, the inversion of subject and object and of means and ends of production as a process of alienation, etc. Marx characterises and theorises these phenomena dialectically and shows based on reports of factory inspectors how these dimensions of capitalist industry shaped the life of workers in 19th-century Great Britain. The historical dimension is a detailed analysis of the bad working conditions wageworkers were facing. It is coupled to a dialectical analysis of technology in capitalism and its effects on everyday life. My own view is that *Capital* is a logically and a historically organised text, that these two dimensions are interconnected and strive towards being connected to political praxis.

15.1. The Development of Machinery

What Is Machinery?

Marx argues that John Wyatt's invention of the spinning machine in 1735 started the industrial revolution (493). At the same time he warns that the history of technology should not be written as a history of single great persons because the organisation of work is as important as the invention of technology (493, footnote 4).

For Marx, machinery consists of three parts (494):

1. the motor mechanism, which creates energy
2. the transmission mechanism, which transports energy to and distributes it among the working machines so that they can operate
3. the working machine, which "seizes on the object of labour and modifies it as desired" (494); the 18th century's industrial revolution would have been a revolution of working machines (494)

Marx argues that before James Watt invented the double-acting steam engine in 1784, factories had to be located on the countryside, where the motor mechanism was made up by waterwheels and mills located next to streams (499). Urban factories only became possible once energy supply could be decentralised, which was enabled by the steam engine. In the 19th-century British industry that Marx described, many factories had their own steam engines. It is therefore no surprise that Marx considers the motor and transmission mechanisms to be part of machinery, although he sees the working machine as the central part. Today, energy sources such as wind, water, sunlight, coal, oil, nuclear energy, gas, geothermal heat, tides, and biomass tend to be only partly decentralised in single households, companies, or organisations. There is certainly a new tendency towards renewable energies that are organised in a decentralised manner. Energy supplies have, however, become a capitalist industry that centrally supplies energy. Energy can be stored and transported with the help of pipelines, power lines, electricity grids, ships, railways, lorries, accumulators, batteries, dams, tanks, etc. In 2010, energy production accounted for 4.0% of value-added in the US economy (data source: OCED STAN Database). In comparison, the information and communication sector (defined as publishing, audio-visuals, broadcasting, telecommunications, IT, information services) made up 5.6% of value-added (data source: OECD STAN Database).

We saw in chapter 12 (Table 12.1) that, inspired by Joseph Schumpeter, Carolta Perez (2010) argues that the third long wave of capitalist development was based on electricity and the fourth on oil, whereas the fifth wave, which started in the 1970s, is according to her based on information and communication. The assumption is that the economy has become softer and dematerialised. Computers and media need, however, to be powered by electricity. The cited data shows that that electricity and the information sector are contributing almost equally large parts to the US economy's value-added. We can therefore not conclude that advanced economies have become information economies. Rather capitalist economies have multiple characteristics: They are information economies, financial economies, and hyper-industrial economies depending on energy sources, etc. Fossil fuels are crucial resources, over which imperialist wars have been fought. Given the existence and importance of the energy industry, one may therefore today speak of machinery just as a working machine and leave out the motor and transmission machine in the definition of machinery. Not every company needs to operate its own motor mechanism, but only connect itself to an energy supplier.

Two Types of Machines

Marx distinguishes between two types of machines. The first type integrates a whole production process in one mechanism. An example he mentions is an envelope machine that prints 3,000 envelopes per hour and successively performs all work processes such as cutting the paper, pasting, folding, and finishing. The "whole process, which under the manufacturing system was split up into a series of operations and carried out in that order, is completed by a single machine, operating a combination of different tools" (500). An envelope factory is then made up of many envelope machines working side-by-side and using the same motor and transmission mechanisms.

The second type is a "real machine system", in which "the object of labour goes through a connected series of graduated processes carried out by a chain of mutually complementary machines of various kinds" (501). There is a division of labour between different machines so that each machine has a special function it performs in the production process. Just like Marx describes the emergence of the collective worker in the manufacture, he speaks of a "collective working machine" that "constitutes itself a vast automaton" (502), a cooperation of machines that are all operated by individual workers or teams of workers. "Each particular machine supplies raw material to the machine next in line; and since they are all working at the same time, the product is always going through the various stages of its formation, and is also constantly in a state of transition from one phase of production to another" (502). Figure 15.1 visualises the integrated machine system.

For Marx, production means that a subject (labour-power) uses objects (means of production) to create a labour product (a subject-object). Each working machine is a dialectical system that creates a product. In a machine system, working machines are dialectically connected to each other so that the labour-product created in one stage enters as an object of labour into the labour process that is part of another working machine in the next stage. Figure 15.1 shows the dialectic of the machine system. It visualises the cooperation of three working machines WM1, WM2, WM3 at three temporal stages of production t1, t2, t3 so that changing products P1, P2, P3 that pass from one working machine to the next are created. Marx calls this system machine system "automatic system of machinery" (503) or "organized system of machines" (503).

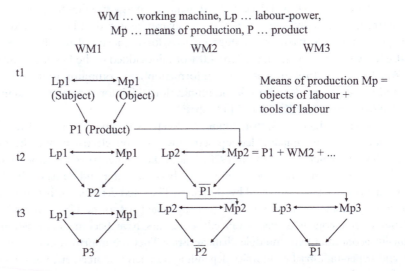

FIGURE 15.1 The machine system

The Impacts of the Machine System on the Economy and the Role of Communications

Marx argues that changes in the mode of production in one industry are likely to be connected to changes in other industries. The emergence of the machine system has therefore also brought about "a revolution in the general conditions of the social process of production—that is, in the means of communication and transport" (506). The "means of communication and transport gradually adapted themselves to the mode of production of large-scale industry by means of a system of river steamers, railways, ocean steamers and telegraphs" (506). Large-scale industry required the transport of commodities and machines from one place to another and the coordination of production across larger distances so that new means of communication and transport became necessary. Economic production requires to different degrees the transport of physical goods, persons, and information. In the 19th century, the railway and ships were the main means for transporting physical goods and persons, whereas the telegraph was the main means for transporting information. The postal system is a combination of both: It transports written information (and parcels) by land, air, and sea.

Means of Communication

Marx points out that means of transport and communication are part of fixed constant capital. They are means that help to organise the transport of commodities. However, computers and computer networks are not only organisers of the circulation of commodities, but also the means of production for the creation of information products. They are furthermore the platforms for companies' internal and external communication. While trains, buses, automobiles, ships, lorries, and airplanes transport people and physical goods, computer networks transport information, information products, and flows of communication. Physical and informational means of transport are similar in that they present a common infrastructure: "Regarded as a means of production, it distinguishes itself from machinery, etc., here in that it is used up by various capitals at the same time, as a common condition for their production and circulation" (Marx 1857/1858, 725).

In capitalism, means of transport and communication play an important role in the organisation of the exchange of physical and informational commodities and in the communicative organisation of production and circulation: "The more production comes to rest on exchange value, hence on exchange, the more important do the physical conditions of exchange—the means of communication and transport—become for the costs of circulation" (Marx 1857/1858, 524). The means of communication and transport determine "the sphere of those who are in exchange, in contact, but also the speed with which the raw material reaches the producer and the product the consumer" (Marx 1857/1858, 187). In capitalism, means of communication and transport have thus the primary role of accelerating production and exchange so that commodities can be produced and sold more quickly, which allows the production of more goods in the same or less time than before. Communication and transport technologies are means of acceleration: "Capital by its nature drives beyond every spatial barrier. Thus the creation of the physical conditions of exchange—of the means of communication and transport—the annihilation of space by time—becomes an extraordinary necessity for it" (Marx 1857/1858, 524).

The Computer: A Means for the Production, Circulation, and Consumption of Information

Other than smoke signals, the drum, mail, the semaphore (a visual telegraph), the electrical telegraph, radio, television, and the telephone, the computer and the networked computer (as in the case of many computers connected by local area networks, wide area networks, or the Internet) are not just means of communication, but at the same time means of production.

The computer is a universal machine that is simultaneously a means of production, circulation, and consumption. This feature of being a universal machine combined with networking has resulted in the emergence of the figure of the prosumer (the producing consumer), the consumer of information who has the potential to also produce and disseminate information. Whereas on radio and television, consumers are receivers of information, networked computing enables them to also produce information.

The networked computer is a universal machine: It is a combined production, storage, distribution, and consumption technology. In print, radio, and TV, separate technologies are needed for the production, distribution, and consumption of information.

Traditional media are systems of information and communication as well as tools of cognition and communication. Both are also true of the networked computer, which, however, adds production and cooperation as a third level so that it is a system of cognition, communication, and cooperation. The computer is both a means of production and communication. It is a means of information and communication that at the same time is a means of economic production and cooperation.

The computer can only take on all the roles it has by storing, processing, and transporting information in digital format—that is, as a combination of zeros and ones. Texts, speech, images, videos, animations, etc. can be turned into series of zeros and ones. The computer is a digital medium and digital production technology. One therefore also often speaks of computers and computing as "digital media".

Marx argues that the machine system "necessitates the replacement of human force by natural force" (508), the development of the sciences (508), and an industry that produces machines by machines (506). In the machine system, the collective machine system dictates the collective worker (508). The machine "is a mechanism that, after being set in motion, performs with its tools the same operations as the worker formerly did with similar tools" (495). The automatic machine system only needs "supplementary assistance from the worker" (503).

Communism and Technology

Marx remarks in a footnote that the "field of application for machinery would" be "entirely different in a communist society from what it is in bourgeois society" (515). Technology cannot be used in a communist society as it is because domination shapes also the design and not just the application of machines. Technology does, however, also not have to be completely reinvented. Destructive technologies should be abolished in a communist society. Other technologies that do not inherently harm humans, society, and nature can be redesigned and redeveloped. The Internet has to, for example, in a communist society lose its corporate character and therefore also the way capitalist culture is designed into platforms in the form of advertising, data surveillance (dataveillance), complex privacy policies, and terms of use, etc. It does, however, not have to be completely replaced or abolished because it contains many elements that enable communication commons, communication systems that are universally available to all without access restrictions, that can in a communist society lose their contradictory character and take on new emergent qualities. To transcend capitalist technologies requires a redesign of both technology and society.

15.2. The Value Transferred by the Machinery to the Product

Technology as Fixed Constant Capital

Marx argues that machinery, or generally technology in production, is a means used "to cheapen commodities" and for producing relative surplus-value (492). A journalist who uses a computer and a digital audio recorder as his/her means of production not just uses these technologies for writing one, but many articles. This example shows that machinery and technologies are fixed constant capital that stays fixed in the production process for a long time. Only parts of a machines' value are transferred to a single commodity. "Machinery, like every other component of constant capital, creates no new value, but yields up its own value to the product it serves to beget. [...] In the first place, it must be observed that machinery, while always entering as a whole into the labour process, enters only piece by piece into the process of valorization" (509). Machinery enters with its whole use–value into the production of every commodity, while "only piecemeal, in proportion to its average daily depreciation, into the process of valorization" (509). The fixed constant capital contained on average in a single commodity is the machine's "average daily wear and tear" (510). Machine systems tend to be used over an extended period of time so that only a small average value is added by it to a single commodity (511).

Machinery and the Transfer of Value

The less value a machine has, the less machine value labour transfers to the product (512). The more productive a machine, the less machine value labour transfers to the product (512). This means, for example, that if one machine takes one minute to burn a DVD and another one just takes 30 seconds, then the second machine transfers less value to the product than the first. Decisive in this respect are of course also the price of each machine and the average machine life. Let us assume that both DVD writers have an average machine life of two years and are used for 40 hours per week during 50 weeks a year. The price of the first machine is £30, the price of the second £40.

DVD writer 1: £30
usage time: 40 hours * 50 weeks * 2 years = 4,000 hours
burns 1 DVD per minute => 60 DVDs per hour, burns a total of 240,000 DVDs
the average value of this DVD writer that is transferred to the product is £30/240,000 = approx.
  £0.0001
DVD writer 2: £40
usage time: 40 hours * 50 weeks * 2 years = 4,000 hours
burns 2 DVDs per minute => 120 DVDs per hour, burns a total of 480,000 DVDs
the average value of this DVD writer that is transferred to the average product is £40/480
  000 = approx. £0.00008

So although the second DVD writer is more expensive, given its high productivity, the average value it transfers to a single DVD is smaller than in the case of the cheaper writer. If the capitalist therefore intends to use a DVD writer for two years, then s/he is better off buying the second one.

Technology and the Substitution of Human Labour

Machines are in capitalism developed and used as means for substituting human labour. A capitalist tends to be especially interested in using new technologies if they overall help to reduce the average labour-power required for the production of commodities.

> As long as the value added to the product remains smaller than the value added by the worker to the product with his tool, there is always a difference of labour saved in favour of the machine. The productivity of the machine is therefore measured by the human labour-power it replaces. (513)
>
> The use of machinery for the exclusive purpose of cheapening the product is limited by the requirement that less labour must be expended in producing the machinery than is displaced by the employment of that machinery. (515)

This means, for example, if a new machine costs £100,000, is used over a five-year period, and makes labour of £50,000 redundant during this time, then the capitalist can expect a total increase of the investment costs of £50,000. He/she will therefore tend to assess this technology as not very profitable and is likely not to invest in it. If in contrast investment of £100,000 in new technology saves labour costs of £200,000, then commodities can be cheapened by £100,000, which makes it a more attractive investment for a capitalist. At the same time, this technology will result in some workers losing their jobs. Marx mentions the example that a printing machine prints as much calico in one hour with the labour of 1 person as a block-printing machine did with the labour of 200 persons (514).

Scientific and Technological Progress

Capitalists pay for the machines they buy. All machines are, however, grounded in general technological and scientific progress that is only paid for once in the form of wages for scientists and engineers. Once established, scientific and technological progress is consumed by capital without payment as a gratis resource. "Once discovered, the law of the deflection of a magnetic needle in the field of an electric current, or the law of the magnetization of iron by electricity, cost absolutely nothing" (508). "Science, generally speaking, costs the capitalist nothing, a fact that by no means prevents him from exploiting it" (508, footnote 23).

Marx argues that science, technology and nature – general conditions of production – cost the capitalist nothing. Many large contemporary capitalist companies today have their own research and development departments, so they pay scientists for developing new scientific knowledge that can result in new technologies and production methods. In general, once some invention has been made or scientific knowledge has been published, also other scientists, individuals, and companies can benefit from it without paying the full costs of invention. New scientific knowledge is always based on knowledge that preceded it. New knowledge can only emerge out of and is based on already existing knowledge. In science, access to a lot of existing knowledge is gratis, so one does not have to pay for consuming it and basing one's own ideas on it. Knowledge has a social and historical character.

The Knowledge Commons

Marx formulated the same idea of scientific knowledge and progress as common good in *Capital Volumes 2* and *3*:

- "Apart from natural materials, natural forces that cost nothing may also be incorporated more or less effectively as agents in the production process. Their level of effectiveness depends on methods and scientific advances that cost the capitalist nothing" (Marx 1885, 431–432).
- "Natural elements which go into production as agents without costing anything, whatever role they might play in production, do not go in as components of capital, but rather as a free natural power of capital" (Marx 1894, 879).

Elinor Ostrom (1933–2012) was an American political economist, who in 2009 was awarded the Nobel Memorial Prize in Economic Sciences for her analysis of the commons. She started her analysis of the commons from the study of "shared natural resources, such as water resources, forests, fisheries, and wildlife" (Hess and Ostrom 2007, 4), but later generalised the commons concept so that it also includes the knowledge commons:

> *Commons* is a general term that refers to a resource shared by a group or people. In a commons, the resource can be small and serve a tiny group (the family refrigerator), it can be

community-level (sidewalks, playgrounds, libraries, and so on), or it can extend to international and global levels (deep seas, the atmosphere, the Internet, and scientific knowledge). The commons can be well bounded (a community park or library); transboundary (the Danube River, migrating wildlife, the Internet); or without clear boundaries (knowledge, the ozone layer). (Hess and Ostrom 2007, 4–5)

Common goods (or commons) are aspects of society that are produced by many or all humans and that are fundamental for the survival of society, groups, organisations, and the economy. We can distinguish between the natural commons (natural forces and goods such as sunlight, fresh air, water, land, etc.), social commons (education, health care, leisure and reproduction, other social services and benefits), and knowledge commons (scientific knowledge, communication, means of communication, technologies). Given their fundamental importance, one can argue that the commons should not be commodities that are bought or sold, but should be freely available to all and organised and controlled by society, not corporations.

Hess and Ostrom argue that knowledge is a common and public good because it is difficult "to exclude people from knowledge once someone had made a discovery. One person's use of knowledge (such as Einstein's theory of relativity)" furthermore does not "subtract from another person's capacity to use it" (Hess and Ostrom 2007, 9). Knowledge is a commons with particular characteristics: It is difficult to exclude others from it and its consumption is non-rivalrous; one person's use does not subtract from another person's capacity to use it.

The American sociologist Robert Merton (1910–2003) (1988, 620) stresses the importance of the common character of academia and academic knowledge: "Institutionalized arrangements have evolved to motivate scientists to contribute freely to the common wealth of knowledge according to their trained capacities, just as they can freely take from that common wealth what they need. [...] In the commons of science it is structurally the case that the give and the take both work to enlarge the common resource of accessible knowledge". He speaks therefore of science as a communist system.

Universal Work

In society, information can only be produced jointly in cooperative processes, not individually. It is a social good. "Universal work [labour in the original translation] is all scientific work, all discovery and invention. It is brought about partly by the cooperation of men now living, but partly also by building on earlier work" (Marx 1894, 199). Whenever new information emerges, it incorporates the whole societal history of information—that is, information has a historical character. Hence, it seems to be self-evident that information should be a public good, freely available to all. But in global informational capitalism, information has become an important productive force that favours new forms of capital accumulation. Information is today often not treated as a public good and common, but rather as a commodity. There is an antagonism between information as a public good and as a commodity.

Capitalism has, however, partly privatised the commons so that humans have to pay for access to it, which is a source of social inequality. The commons have become a commodity. Furthermore not just humans consume the commons for free, but also capital does, by which it increases its productivity and reduces its investment costs by not having to pay for the work that creates and re-creates the commons of society.

Left-wing experts and politicians have suggested that contributions of companies to social security payments of their employees should not be based on the wage sum, but on the company's value-added. The more technologies a company uses, the smaller its wage sum tends to be because labour can be automated. Capital consumes society's technological progress (the knowledge commons) without payment, but as an effect reduces its contributions to funding the social commons. It thereby tends to put people out of work and to reduce its tax payments, which is a fundamental mismatch and injustice. A value creation tax (also called "machine tax") taxes the total revenue of a company. If as a result of technological progress and investments in machines, a company reduces its wage sum, and thus increases its productivity and profits, then it is fair that it contributes more and not less to financing the social commons of society (e.g., the school and university system, health care, public transport infrastructures, etc.). The value-creation tax is a tax on the advantages that companies derive from the costless usage of society's commons such as scientific and technological progress, nature, reproductive labour, or the education system.

15.3. The Most Immediate Effects of Machine Production on the Worker

Marx describes three connected effects that the introduction of machine systems had on the working conditions in 19th-century Britain:

(a)   The employment of women and children
(b)   The prolongation of the working day
(c)   The intensification of labour

Child Labour

The rise of machinery in production has decoupled labour more and more from heavily exhaustive physical labour, which has made it an incentive for capitalists to employ women and children (517). Capitalists lowered wages so that entire families had to become wage-workers in order to be able to survive. Male workers became compelled to become "slave-dealer[s]" who sold their wives and children to capitalists (519). When the Factory Acts introduced that young workers had to attend school for a couple of hours per day, capitalists created pseudo-schools in their factories that were partly run by illiterates and where the pupils learned nothing (523–526).

It took until more than 10 years after Marx had published *Capital Volume 1* that compulsory full-time schooling was introduced in the UK. The Factory and Workshop Act 1878 and the Elementary Education Act 1880 introduced compulsory education for all children aged 5 to 10 years old and regulated that no children below 10 could be employed. In 1899, raising the school leaving age to 12 years extended compulsory school education. The Education Act 1918 raised it further to 14 years, and the Education Act 1944 (which came into effect in 1947) to 15 years. In 1973, the school-leaving age was set to 16 years. These developments certainly set important limits to capital's access to young people's labour capacities and helped to raise the general educational standards.

The Physical and Moral Deterioration of Machines

Machinery deteriorates by use and by lack of use. "Deterioration of the first kind is more or less directly proportional, and that of the second kind to a certain extent inversely proportional, to the use of the machine" (528). In addition there is what Marx calls "moral depreciation" (528): Machinery loses exchange-value "either because machines of the same sort are being produced more cheaply than it was, or because better machines are entering into competition with it" (528). Just like in all capitalist industries, there is also competition for producing more productive commodities in the machine-producing industry. Such progress is related to scientific-technological progress.

Symbolic Depreciation, Cultural Signification, and Distinction

A specific form of moral depreciation occurring in consumer societies is symbolic depreciation: New technologies are not only bought because they are more productive, but also because they have a higher symbolic status that is culturally created and enables reputation and distinction. The French sociologist Pierre Bourdieu (1930–2002) has in this context introduced the notions of symbolic capital and cultural distinction. Symbolic capital is a "capital of honour and prestige" (Bourdieu 1977, 179). Symbolic capital depends on publicity and appreciation. It has to do with prestige, reputation, honour, etc.

Symbolic class struggles are fights over symbolic capital and tastes that shall establish distinction between classes in order to ideologically secure the domination of certain groups (Bourdieu 1986a, 1986b). Symbolic struggles are cultural struggles in the sense that they make use of signification processes in order to produce signs that draw borders, erect a social hierarchy, and produce distinction. Cultural struggles are semiotic struggles because in them meaning is contested—that is, there are fights about who defines and controls values and knowledge in society. Modern society is according to Bourdieu characterised by competition—that is, struggles for the accumulation of not just economic (money), but also cultural (reputation) and political (social connections, political influence) capital (Bourdieu 1986b).

Cultural signification processes are of large importance in capitalism because they constitute a symbolic dimension of class struggle that is not just imaginative, but has real material results. Cultural forms like technologies, language, music, clothing, artworks, furniture, styling, food, drinks, toiletries, books, newspapers, magazines, sports, records, toys, body care, cosmetics, appearance, manners, etc. are symbols that signify class differences in modern society and are used as forms of class distinction.

Distinction is a principle that is at the heart of the antagonistic cultural development in modern society; it produces cultural classes and symbolic struggles.

Culture fulfils "a social function of legitimating social differences" (Bourdieu 1986a, 7).

Cultural, social/political, and symbolic capital are just like economic capital unequally distributed in modern society: Dominant classes derive profits from these forms of capital at the expense of others—profits in distinction and legitimacy as well as monetary profits (Bourdieu 1986a, 228). Think, for example, of Apple computing tools, such as the MacBook, the iPhone, or the iPad. These machines are today not just means of communication and entertainment, but also means of production in labour processes that create commodities. Apple has created a specific brand image so that many people associate it with being modern, young, future-oriented, urban, multicultural, and international. The successes of Apple and other producers of communications hardware are based on high levels of exploitation of Chinese workers in Foxconn and other factories (Sandoval and Arcskog Bjurling 2013; Sandoval 2013, 2014). Apple technologies have a high symbolic reputation and therefore a fast symbolic moral depreciation. If there is a new version of a specific machine available, then many want to buy it for symbolic reasons. The average life span of a laptop was around three years during the period 2012 to 2017.[1] Given the high symbolic status of Apple, we can assume that the life span of an Apple laptop is on average lower than three years.

The Prolongation of the Working Day

Marx argues that given pressures of moral (and in the age of consumer capitalism also symbolic) depreciation, capitalists have incentives to prolong the working day after introducing new machinery in order to put them to use as much as possible before moral depreciation sets in (528) and because in early stages of the use of new technologies they may yield higher profits due to above-average productivity levels (530):

> During this transitional period, while the use of machinery remains a sort of monopoly, profits are exceptional, and the capitalist endeavours to exploit thoroughly 'the sunny time of this his first love' by prolonging the working day as far as possible. The magnitude of the profit gives him an insatiable hunger for yet more profit.

As machinery comes into general use in a particular branch of production, the social value of the machine's product sinks down to its individual value, and the following law asserts itself: surplus-value does not arise from the labour-power that has been replaced by the machinery, but from the labour-power actually employed in working with the machinery. (530)

Technology in production is a means that replaces variable capital by constant capital, labour by technology. The rate of surplus-value is therefore shaped by a contradiction between constant and variable capital:

[There] is an immanent contradiction in the application of machinery to the production of surplus-value, since, of the two factors of the surplus-value created by a given amount of capital, one, the rate of surplus-value, cannot be increased except by diminishing the other, the number of workers. (531)

Marx analyses in chapter 10 how capitalists tried to evermore lengthen the working day, which resulted in class struggles that successfully set legal limits. I discussed in chapter 10 of this book that in the UK, the Factory Act 1844 introduced the 12-hour working day and the Factory Act 1847 the 10-hour working day. In chapter 15.3, Marx comes back to the issue of working time and argues that the legal limits have resulted in "the inversion of extensive magnitude into intensive magnitude" (533).

Capital had to switch from extending the working day to intensifying labour, from absolute to relative surplus-value production. Capital therefore on the one hand tried to increase the speed of machines and on the other hand tried to develop and use evermore productive machines in order to increase productivity. "Capital's tendency, as soon as a prolongation of the hours of labour is once for all forbidden, is to compensate for this by systematically raising the intensity of labour, and converting every improvement in machinery into a more perfect means for soaking up labour-power" (542).

Hegel's Dialectic of Quantity

When describing how absolute surplus-value production dialectically inverts itself into relative surplus-value production, Marx uses very Hegelian language and speaks of extensive magnitude, intensive magnitude, and degree (533–534). Marx here has Hegel's dialectic of quantity in mind,

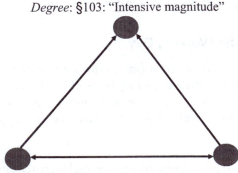

Hegel, *Encyclopaedia* I: Quantity

Degree: §103: "Intensive magnitude"

Pure quantity:
§99: A magnitude that "can be increased or decreased"

Quantum: §100: "Limited quantity", §103: "Extensive magnitude"

FIGURE 15.2 Hegel's dialectic of quantity

which he describes in his *Encyclopaedia Logic* (Hegel 1830a, §§99–106): Pure quantity is a variable magnitude that "can be increased or decreased" (§99). It stands in a dialectical relationship with what Hegel terms "quantum", by which he means "limited quantity" (§101) and "extensive magnitude" (§103). The dialectical relationship is sublated when the extensive magnitude by being limited turns into a degree, an "intensive magnitude" (§103). Figure 15.2 visualises this dialectical process.

The Dialectic of Absolute and Relative Surplus-Value Production

Marx describes the relationship of absolute and relative surplus-value production in 19th-century Britain with the help of Hegel's dialectic of quantity. Absolute surplus-value production aims to increase the working day as much as possible. It focuses on the pure quantity of the working day, a pure increase. Class struggles and the law set limits during the 19th century so that a limited quantity, a quantum, emerged. The working day can no longer be extended and must due to legal measures be shortened. As a result, capital strives to sublate the contradiction between pure quantity and limited quantity, which it does by introducing machinery as method of relative surplus-value production so that according to Marx "labour-time now acquires a measure of its intensity, or degree of density" (534). Figure 15.3 visualises the dialectic of absolute and relative surplus-value production.

15.4. The Factory

The Inversion of Means and Ends and of Subject and Object

An important theoretical aspect of chapter 15 is that Marx in section 15.4 argues that technology in capitalism does not serve human needs, but is a means of domination and relative surplus-value production that puts the logic of profit above human interests. Marx expresses this circumstance as inversion of means and ends and of subject and object—that is, an antagonism between worker and technology that is caused by class relations into which both are embedded:

> These two descriptions are far from being identical. In one, the combined collective worker appears as the dominant subject [*übergreifendes Subjekt*], and the mechanical automaton as the object; in the other, the automaton itself is the subject, and the workers are merely conscious organs, co-ordinated with the unconscious organs of the automaton, and together with the latter subordinated to the central moving force. The first description is applicable to every

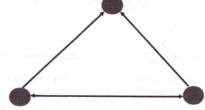

Degree: Intensification of labour, more value is produced in the same or less time as before by increasing the productivity of labour and introducing new machines, labour-hours become more intensive, more surplus-value and commodities are produced per unit of time = intensification of exploitation (relative surplus-value production)

Pure quantity:
Absolute increase of the working day
(absolute surplus-value production)

Quantum:
Class struggles and the law set limits to
the prolongation of the working day

FIGURE 15.3 The dialectic of absolute and relative surplus-value production

possible employment of machinery on a large scale, the second is characteristic of its use by capital, and therefore of the modern factory system. (Marx 1867, 544–545)

Factory work exhausts the nervous system to the uttermost; at the same time, it does away with the many-sided play of the muscles, and confiscates every atom of freedom, both in bodily and in intellectual activity. Even the lightening of the labour becomes an instrument of torture, since the machine does not free the worker from the work, but rather deprives the work itself of all content. Every kind of capitalist production, in so far as it is not only a labour process but also capital's process of valorization, has this in common, but it is not the worker who employs the conditions of his work, but rather the reverse, the conditions of work employ the worker. However, it is only with the coming of machinery that this inversion first acquires a technical and palpable reality. Owing to its conversion into an automaton, the instrument of labour confronts the worker during the labour process in the shape of capital, dead labour, which dominates and soaks up living labour-power. The separation of the intellectual faculties of the production process from manual labour, and the transformation of those faculties into powers exercised by capital over labour, is, as we have already shown, finally completed by large-scale industry erected on the foundation of machinery. (Marx 1867, 548–549)

Technology in the Context of Labour's Exploitation as Instrument for Accumulation

Technology as such is a means to an end: It is a tool that humans use for the creation of goods that serve human needs. In capitalism, technology as instrument of work becomes an instrument that capital uses for exploiting labour-power and compelling workers to produce surplus-value. Technology is no longer a means to an end, but rather it serves a specific instrumental aim—namely, capital accumulation—and as part of this end turns the worker into an object of exploitation. It is no longer the worker who uses technology as a means to satisfy human needs, but capital and the capitalist's use of machinery turn workers into a means for achieving the aim of capital accumulation. "Machinery is misused in order to transform the worker […] into a part of a specialized machine" (547). The "conditions of work employ the worker" so that workers become "living appendages" of the factory and the machine (548).

Figure 15.4 shows the inversion of subject and object typical for capitalism, which Marx theorises and analyses in section 15.4. It presents this process dialectically-logically. There is, however, also a historical dimension to it: Independent craftspeople in precapitalist economies controlled their

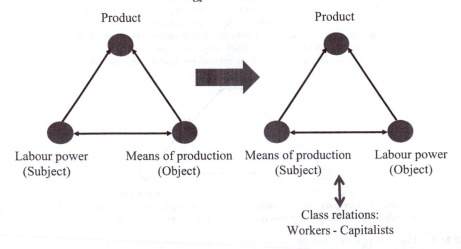

The inversion of subject and object and of means and ends in capitalism: Technology as a means of domination

FIGURE 15.4 The inversion of subject and object: Technology as capitalist means of domination

means of production and their labour-power; they were not alienated from both. In capitalism there is a tendency of the commodification of labour-power and the private ownership of the means of production by a dominant class that makes others work for a wage.

Factory and Office Labour

Marx describes the terrible working conditions associated with machinery use in 19th-century factories. In the 21st century, a specific share of labour has moved from the factory to the office and from industrial to information labour. Office work is on the one hand partly organised like factory labour. An example is low-skill information work such as, for example, in call centres or data centres, which can be described as factories of information workers who conduct telephone and data processing work like on an assembly line. Marx speaks of "barrack-like discipline" and a system of control that divides roles between "manual labour and overseers" in the factory (549). The computer enables new forms of worker control because it allows monitoring and measuring what exactly workers are doing at their workplace. The computerised workplace under capitalist control allows new forms of surveillance and control. Freelancers in the cultural and digital sector own their own means of production and capital. They are one-person companies, workers, and capitalists at the same time. The capital they own often reduces itself to a computer, so they are low- or no-capital companies. They are often precarious workers who are compelled to survive on contractual labour. In their case, control turns into self-control of the body and the mind so that they have to work long hours in order to make ends meet.

The classical factory labour Marx describes in chapter 15 has not ceased to exist and is unlikely to be abolished as long as capitalism exists. Information capitalism is in need of computers, laptops, mobile phones, consumer electronics, and hardware periphery that are all used as means of information, communication, collaboration, and production. The production and assemblage of such equipment is a profitable industry that has largely outsourced labour to low-wage countries, especially China. Assembly workers in this industry are confronted with the "systematic robbery of what is necessary for the life of the worker while he is at work, i.e. space, light, air and protection against the dangerous or the unhealthy concomitants of the production process, not to mention the theft of appliances for the comfort of the worker" (553). ICT manufacturing workers often face poor working conditions such as lack of protective equipment, health hazards, precarious short-term contracts, low wages, lack of unionisation, lack of support by unions, yellow unions, unsafe factory environments, crowded dormitories, forced labour, long working hours, repetitive and monotonous labour, military management styles, and insufficient legal protection. Information capitalism is based on the highly exploitative factory labour that is part of an international division of digital labour (Fuchs 2014a, 2015; see also chapter 14, on the division of labour in this book).

15.5. The Struggle between Worker and Machine

Machine Breaking

In section 15.5, Marx describes that the inversion of subject and object that turned capitalist technology into a subject that dominates and helps capitalists to exploit workers as objects constitutes an antagonism between workers and capitalist technology, to which the workers have historically answered with the destruction of machines. Marx argues that in capitalism there is a "complete and total antagonism" (558) between the worker and machinery. Figure 15.5 visualises this particular sublation of this antagonism.

Marx argues that workers tend to revolt against capitalist technology because "it is the material foundation of the capitalist mode of production" (554) that "becomes a competitor of the worker

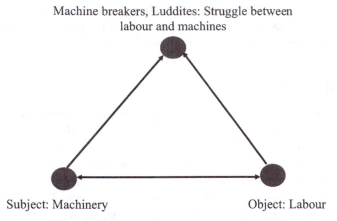

Machine breakers, Luddites: Struggle between
labour and machines

Subject: Machinery   Object: Labour

FIGURE 15.5   Machine breaking as sublation of the antagonism between labour and capitalist technology

himself" (557) and destroys workers' "conditions of existence" (557). Marx argues that technological automation and mechanisation substitutes labour by capital, which tends to result in layoffs and therefore in technologically induced unemployment. "The worker becomes unsaleable, like paper money thrown out of currency by legal enactment" (557). Furthermore machinery would also be "the most powerful weapon for suppressing strikes" (562) because technification would allow substituting workers by machinery and once unemployed, workers struggle for existential survival and only have a strongly reduced power to bring production to a standstill.

The Luddite Movement

Marx says that one of the historically most frightful examples of mechanisation was the substitution of the handloom by the power-loom in Britain in the first four decades of the 19th century (557–558), which made many workers unemployed. As a reaction, in the 1810s the Luddite movement emerged in the UK. It named itself after Ned Ludd, a weaver who was punished and as revenge destroyed his employer's knitting frames in 1770. The members of the movement destroyed power-looms that put workers who formerly had worked with handlooms out of work. Marx argues that the problem is not technology as such and that therefore it does not suffice to destroy technology, as the Luddites did, but protest must be an attack on and revolt against capital:

> The large-scale destruction of machinery which occurred in the English manufacturing districts during the first fifteen years of the nineteenth century, largely as a result of the employment of the power-loom, and known as the Luddite movement, gave the anti-Jacobin government, composed of such people as Sidmouth and Castlereagh, a pretext for the most violent and reactionary measures. It took both time and experience before the workers learnt to distinguish between machinery and its employment by capital, and therefore to transfer their attacks from the material instruments of production to the form of society which utilizes those instruments. (554–555)

Edward P. Thompson's Analysis of the Luddite Movement

Marx did not analyse the Luddite movement in detail. Consulting additional sources allows us to get a closer picture of it. Edward P. Thompson (1924–1993) was a British Marxist historian who became well known for the book *The Making of the English Working Class* (Thompson 1966), which tells the history of working-class struggles and working-class culture in the late 18th and early 19th century. Thompson studied the Luddite movement thoroughly and devoted a 130-page chapter to it (Thompson 1966, chapter 14). The movement existed in the years 1811 to 1817 and was centred in Lancashire (where destruction focused on power-looms), Yorkshire (destruction of shearing-frames), and the Midlands (knitting industry) (Thompson 1966, 484, 521–522).

Thompson argues that the context of this movement was formed by food shortages, riots, and high prices arising from Napoleon's embargo against and blockade of British trade as part of the British-French War (1803–1815); bad harvests that drove up the corn price; stagnation in the textile industry; laissez faire politics; and the economic crisis (Thompson 1966, 543). In this situation, many capitalists in the textile industry made use of the vulnerability of the workers in order to introduce mechanisation with the aim of "beating-down wages", "undercutting [. . .] rivals, and undermining standards of craftsmanship" (Thompson 1966, 549).

Thompson's Interpretation of Luddism as a Radical Working-Class Movement

Thompson argues that the Luddites were not primitives (Thompson 1966, 543) who blindly resisted machinery (552), but created a well-organised and articulate movement (543) that had a tendency to become a revolutionary movement (553) and thoroughly planned its attacks (554). It did not blindly attack machinery, but rather chose those capitalists who had reduced wages and had laid off workers with the help of new machinery (564). Thompson discusses that the movement was confronted with government spies and agent provocateurs, but understood well how to protect itself by organising in a conspirative manner and taking oaths from its members.

Thompsons cites an example warning letter that a manufacturer in Huddersfield (West Riding, Yorkshire) received:

> Information has just been given in that you are a holder of those detestable Shearing Frames, and I was desired by my Men to write to you and give you fair Warning to pull them down. [. . .] You will take Notice that if they are not taken down by the end of next week, I will detach one of my Lieutenants with at least 300 Men to destroy them and furthermore take Notice that if you give us the Trouble of coming so far we will increase your misfortune by burning your Buildings down to Ashes and if you have Impudence to fire upon any of my Men, they have orders to murder you, & burn all your Housing, you will have the Goodness to your Neighbours to inform them that the same fate awaits them if their Frames are not speedily taken down. (Thompson 1966, 558)

This example letter shows that the Luddite movement was quite militant. Thompson argues that it had both a revolutionary wing and one that argued for constitutional and parliamentary reforms (Thompson 1966, 594, 602). The Frame-Breaking Act 1812 made machine-breaking a capital felony so that the death penalty was introduced for it (Thompson 1966, 535). The movement was limited by this act, but its demands such as wage increases were also partly successful (Thompson 1966, 556). It had to face fierce repression (Thompson 1966, 556) and finally became part of the movement for constitutional reforms (556).

E.P. Thompson interprets Luddism as "a violent eruption of feeling against unrestrained industrial capitalism" (Thompson 1966, 550), the struggle for "a democratic community, in which industrial growth should be regulated according to ethical priorities and the pursuit of profit be subordinated to human needs" (552), and a transitory movement that temporally stood between the growing experiences of the illegal trade union movement, which influenced the Luddites, and the emergence of a full-fledged working-class movement (601). He sees it as the most advanced political movement in the early 19th century: "One can see Luddism as a manifestation of a working-class culture of greater independence and complexity than any known to the 18th century" (Thompson 1966, 601).

Peter Linebaugh and Eric Hobsbawm on the Luddite Movement

The Marxist historian Peter Linebaugh (2012, 13) argues that the Luddite movement emerged as a response to the fact that the "expropriation from the commons and the mechanization of labor worked upon each other as in a feedback loop" and that workers perceived machinery as "hurtful to Commonality" (16). He says that capitalist technology had destructive potentials in the 1810s and still has 200 years later. Is "Fukushima but a scaling up of the machine opposed by the Luddites? [...] The war machine and the machines of war, that military-industrial complex, arise from attempts to destroy the world's commons by X^2" (Linebaugh 2012, 45).

The Marxist historian Eric Hobsbawm (1917–2012), similarly to E.P. Thompson, describes the Luddites the following way:

> Nottinghamshire, Leicestershire and Derbyshire Luddites were using attacks upon machinery, whether new or old, as a means of coercing their employers into granting them concessions with regard to wages and other matters. [...] This sort of wrecking was a traditional and established part of industrial conflict in the period of the domestic and manufacturing system, and the early stages of factory and mine. It was directed not only against machines, but also against raw material, finished goods and even the private property of employers, depending on what sort of damage these were most sensitive to. (Hobsbawm 1952, 58–59)

For Hobsbawm (1952, 59), the Luddite movement is therefore "collective bargaining by riot". "In none of these cases—and others might be mentioned—was there any question of hostility to machines as such. Wrecking was simply a technique of trade unionism in the period before, and during the early phases of, the industrial revolution" (Hobsbawm 1952, 59).

The Age of the Internet: 21st Century Luddism?

In the 21st century, phenomena such as the Unabomber Theodore Kaczynski, deep ecologists, and primitivism (a movement that advocates life in self-sufficient villages without technology), have sometimes been interpreted as a form of 21st-century Luddism (see, for example, Jones 2006). They share the radical critique of modern society and modern technology, as well as the longing for rural communities and premodern forms of living, where according to these ideas humans live in balance with nature. The question is of course if these are true forms of Luddism.

Were the Luddites romantics who rejected technology in favour of craft and physical labour or revolutionaries who opposed capitalism? Probably they were a bit of both. According to Marxist historians such as E. P. Thompson and Eric Hobsbawm, who have spent a lot of time studying the Luddites, the Luddites were first and foremost a working-class movement. The critique of class and labour is, however, rather absent from the writings and practices of the Unabomber, deep ecologists, and anarcho-primitivists. According to the Marxist historians' analyses, the Luddites cared first and foremost about a good life, society's commons, and wages that allowed them to survive. Smashing machines was one of their means, but not an end in itself. Anti-civilisationists long for premodern life in agricultural communities. They romantically idealise manual and agricultural labour and oppose modern technologies and electricity. Such a life is, however, necessarily associated with hard work and therefore inherently unfree. A free society requires freedom from toil.

If Kaczynski, deep ecology, and primitivism are not forms of 21st-century Luddism, can there be a contemporary equivalent?

Modern technology is not an evil in itself, as the anti-civilisationists believe, but is rather, as Marx shows, embedded into capitalism's contradictions. It is, however, also not enough to get rid of the capitalist relations of production and to then apply the same kind of modern technologies within a socialist framework. A nuclear power plant is also in a socialist society still a threat to humans, society, and nature, although the workers in it may be treated fairly. A socialist nuclear power plant is not a good power plant. Domination can deeply penetrate into the design of technologies themselves. There are technologies and use-values that are harmful and destructive powers. They should be abolished and substituted by alternative technologies. So whereas energy supply is a crucial positive accomplishment of modern society that should not be undone, nuclear energy is certainly a danger that should be undone. Progressive technology politics are Luddite in the sense that they oppose destructive technologies. But at the same time such a politics is not antimodern, but rather wants to achieve an alternative modernity. Whereas antimodernity wants to, for example, abolish energy supply, alternative modernity wants to substitute nuclear and other harmful forms of energy supply by alternative energy forms such as wind power and solar energy. Twenty-first-century Luddism opposes destructive technologies and struggles for an alternative modernity in which exploitation is abolished and technologies serve the commons and human interests.

Why Not to Quit the Internet

What about the Internet? One can again and again hear "I quit" suggestions; for example, that people should quit using Facebook because it exploits users and fosters surveillance or that one should stop using mobile phones and wireless Internet because its health impacts are not entirely clear. An example for a method of how to quite social media is the "Web 2.0 Suicide Machine" that allows users to delete Facebook, MySpace, LinkedIn, and Twitter profiles. The makers of this software application describe its goal the following way:

> This machine lets you delete all your energy sucking social-networking profiles, kill your fake virtual friends, and completely do away with your Web2.0 alterego. [...] Everyone should have the right to disconnect. Seamless connectivity and rich social experience offered by web2.0 companies are the very antithesis of human freedom. Users are entraped in a high resolution panoptic prison without walls, accessible from anywhere in the world. We do have a healthy amount of paranoia to think that everyone should have the right to quit her 2.0-ified life by the help of automatized machines. [...] What shall I do after I've killed myself with the web2.0 suicide machine? Try calling some friends, take a walk in a park or buy a bottle of wine and start enjoying your real life again.[2]

It is not the capitalist application and design of social media that results in surveillance and the exploitation of digital labour that is seen as a problem here, but rather social media as such is seen as being unreal, isolating humans, and destroying social contacts, as well as alienating humans. Whereas this position is antimodern and directed against online communication as such, alternative modernity considers online communication as a possibility for enhancing our lives and social contacts, but criticises the capitalist design of social media, which is an attempt to turn the Internet and our lives into a shopping mall, to commodify personal data and social relations, and to make human communication an object of corporate and state surveillance.

The alternative is not to quit social media and the Internet, but to design alternative, noncommercial platforms and to struggle for reforms that drive back online surveillance and online exploitation and enable alternative media to gain power, support, visibility, and attention. The Internet should not be abolished, but transformed from a capitalist Internet into a socialist Internet in a socialist society, which requires qualitative changes of both society and the Internet. One should oppose the blind belief in technological determinism and that technology solves social problems, but at the same time bear in mind the importance to struggle for alternative technologies and an alternative society that enable a good life for all. The critical theorist and historian of technology David F. Noble (1945–2010) argues therefore that against the "hegemonic system of blind belief, rationality demands resistance—a struggle not for salvation but for survival" (Noble 1995, 142).

15.6. The Compensation Theory, with Regard to the Workers Displaced by Machinery

Say's Law

Jean-Baptiste Say (1767–1832) was a French classical political economist who formulated what is called Say's Law in his book *A Treatise on Political Economy*. The main point of Say's Law is that supply and demand for a commodity always equal each other. Say argues that production implies demand because producers would be keen to sell and to spend their profits on other products so that profits in one industry would benefit other industries and that growth in one industry would lead to growth in others and stagnation in one to stagnation in others:

> It is worthwhile to remark, that a product is no sooner created, than it, from that instant, affords a market for other products to the full extent of its own value. When the producer has put the finishing hand to his product, he is most anxious to sell it immediately, lest its value should diminish in his hands. Nor is he less anxious to dispose of the money he may get for it; for the value of money is also perishable. But the only way of getting rid of money is in the purchase of some product or other. Thus, the mere circumstance of the creation of one product immediately opens a vent for other products.
>
> For this reason, a good harvest is favourable, not only to the agriculturist, but likewise to the dealers in all commodities generally. The greater the crop, the larger are the purchases of the growers. A bad harvest, on the contrary, hurts the sale of commodities at large. And so it is also with the products of manufacture and commerce. The success of one branch of commerce supplies more ample means of purchase, and consequently opens a market for the products of all the other branches; on the other hand, the stagnation of one channel of manufacture, or of commerce, is felt in all the rest. (Say 1803, 134–135)

Say on Demand and Supply

According to Say, supply creates demand so that supply and demand for a commodity correspond to each other. Therefore there could also be no overproduction or underconsumption of goods. Say argues that if there is a "glut of commodities" in one sector, then this is because "the production of other commodities has fallen short" (Say 1803, 135). Therefore there would be a natural tendency that the capital that overproduces one commodity moves into another industry where higher profits can be achieved: "It is observable, moreover, that precisely at the same tie that one commodity makes a loss, another commodity is making excessive profit" (Say 1803, 135). If there is "scarcity on the one hand, and consequent glut on the other", then "the cause of this political disease" is removed because "the means of production feel a natural impulse towards the vacant channels, the replenishment of which restores activity to all the others" (Say 1803, 135).

Say argues that if one industry employs new machines that put people out of work, then this would at the level of the entire economy not result in a reduction of jobs because these workers could find jobs in other sectors with increasing demand that results from the new machinery: "[V]iewing human labour and machinery in the aggregate, in the supposition of the extreme case, viz. that machinery should be brought to supersede human labour altogether, yet the numbers of mankind- would not be thinned, for the sum total of products would be the same" (Say 1803, 88). Machinery would multiply products (Say 1803, 89).

Marx's Criticism of Say's Law

Marx questions Say's Law in section 15.6. A *first argument* in this context has to do with the *value of the involved labour-power*. He uses the example of the carpet and the machine industries (565–567). If labour that receives wages of £1,500 is replaced by machines that cost £1,500, then the machine industry has with this sales price to account for the employed mechanics' wages, the used means of production (raw materials, machines that produce machines), and profits. If new jobs for mechanics are therefore created in the machine-producing industry, then the total value of the employed labour-power is likely to be lower than the value of the labour-power set free in those industries that use the new machines so that a compensation of new labour and unemployed labour is not possible.

A *second* argument has to do with *negative rebound effects* of increased unemployment. Marx furthermore argues that workers tend to use their wages for buying consumer goods in order to survive and sustain their labour-power. If machines replace workers, then these workers are turned from "buyers into non-buyers" (567) of consumer goods. We can add that, even though there are nowadays unemployment benefits in many countries, these benefits are normally smaller than the wages the unemployed received before so that a reduction of the purchase of consumer goods is very likely. Unemployment benefits tend not to hinder the reduction of the demand for consumer goods. Reduced demand can in turn reduce the profits of and create unemployment in the consumer goods industry: "If this diminution of demand is not compensated for by an increase in demand from another direction, the market price of the commodities falls. If this state of things lasts for some time, and increases in extent, there follows the displacement of the workers employed in the production of those commodities [consumer goods]. [...] the workers employed in the production of the necessary means of subsistence are in turn 'set free' from a part of their wages" (567). Increasing unemployment in one industry can have negative impacts on other industries and cause unemployment there so that automation and mechanisation set off a spiral of unemployment that amplifies itself.

A *third argument* against Say's Law concerns the *skills gap*: Labour that is automated tends to be rather low skilled because such activities tend to be relatively standardised and are therefore the ones that machines can easiest replace. Labour created in the development and production of machines in contrast tends to demand special skills that unemployed workers do not readily possess. "Crippled as they [the unemployed workers] are by the division of labour, these poor devils are worth so little outside their old trade that they cannot find admission into any industries except a few interior and therefore over-supplied and under-paid branches" (568).

An example is that in many countries there have been reskilling programmes that have taught computing skills to unemployed manufacturing workers. The question in this respect is, however, if such workers, who have for their whole life conducted physical labour, have the interest and capacity to become information workers. It is unlikely that many of them will overnight become software engineers because such knowledge professions require special skills for which training is complex and time-intensive. Reskilling is a time-intensive process that is no rapid fix to technologically induced unemployment.

Technology's Dialectic of Essence and Existence

I have in chapter 1 explained Hegel's dialectic of essence and existence. Marx makes use of this logic in section 15.6 in order to explain the dialectic of technology in capitalism. He argues that technology has an antagonistic character in capitalism:

> machinery in itself shortens the hours of labour, but when employed by capital it lengthens them; [...] in itself it lightens labour, but when employed by capital it heightens its intensity; [...] in itself it is a victory of man over the forces of nature but in the hands of

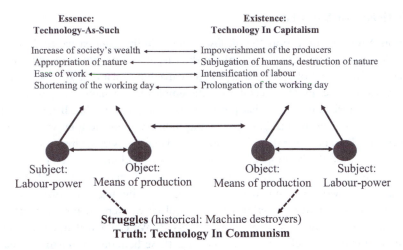

FIGURE 15.6 The dialectic of technology in capitalism

capital it makes man the slave of those forces; [. . .] in itself it increases the wealth of the producers, but in the hands of capital it makes them into paupers. (568–569)

Marx in chapter 15 also uses Hegel's dialectic of essence and existence for arguing that modern technology has a dialectical character. He does not oppose modern technology, but only class character and therefore argues that a lot of modern technologies have positive potentials, but under class relations turn into destructive forces so that a reconstruction of modern technology and modern society is together needed. Figure 15.6 visualises this dialectic of the essence and existence of modern technology. It lists the most important contradictions of modern technology that Marx mentions.

Marx argues that many modern technologies as such have the potential to improve human life, but that under capitalist relations they take on a form and designs that contribute to societal problems so that technology's essence and existence diverge. Technology's means–end relationship thereby gets inverted and technology acts as tool for exploitation and domination. Struggles around technology are a result of this antagonism. An example is the Luddite movement that Marx analyses in section 15.5. If class relations and along with them the class character of technology were sublated, then a qualitatively different form of modern technology could emerge so that technology's existence could correspond to its essence and positive potentials. Certain inherently destructive technologies would then cease to exist, whereas others could be redesigned, and also new ones would emerge.

Bourgeois Ideology: Technology as a Fetishism

Marx argues that bourgeois economists and thinkers treat technology as a fetishism: "Any other utilization of machinery than the capitalist one is to him impossible" (569). Technological fetishism sees technology either as a fix to societal problems (technological determinism) or as inherently good or as inherently bad or only from an instrumental perspective as a way of increasing monetary profits for businesses.

One of the most well-known and widely read digital media publications is *Wired* magazine. The September 2014 UK edition's main features focused on the following topics:

- "Fashion forward: Federico Marchetti's company, Yoox, has turned the luxury-goods industry digital" (86)

- "Destiny beckons: Bungie, the games studio behind Halo, has spent £300 million making Destiny. If it isn't the most successful game ever, it may well be considered a failure" (98)
- "A bigger boat: The Triple-E is Maersk's latest—and the world's largest—model of container ship" (114)
- "The inspiration factory: How Pinterest fosters creativity" (122)
- "The Craigslist killers: In 2011, three men were murdered in Ohio, lured to their deaths by a seemingly innocent Craigslist ad" (128)
- "Europe's 100 hottest start-ups" in the Internet industry located in Istanbul, Stockholm, Berlin, London, Amsterdam, Tel Aviv, Moscow, Helsinki, Barcelona, and Paris—a 34-page special

One of these features focuses on a classical tabloid press issue (the Craigslist killers), whereas the others exclusively express admiration for new technologies (a luxury clothing online retailer, a commercial computer game, a new ship model, the economic growth of Pinterest and its use by young professionals such as fashion designers and chefs, new Internet platforms and mobile apps) and capitalist companies producing and selling them (Yoox, Bungie, Maersk, Pinterest). The overall message is that capitalism is great because it brings about technical innovations in the digital media world and other sectors. Craigslist is a capitalist company, but says that it is little interested in profit and therefore has a "relatively non-commercial nature", a "public service mission, and non-corporate culture". It runs the Craigslist Charitable Fund, which gives grants to nonprofits, events, and organisations. It is telling that *Wired* reports something negative about Craigslist, an organisation that at least has some doubts about capitalism, whereas the rest of the stories in the same issue celebrate capitalist companies. The media sociologist Eran Fisher concludes in an in-depth study of *Wired* magazine's ideology and related phenomena that they are expressions of a digital discourse that "naturalizes, theologizes and teleologizes network technology" and informational capitalism (Fisher 2010, 185). *Wired*'s ideology and digital discourse in general are 21st-century expressions of the capitalist fetishism of technology that Marx criticised.

The Impacts of New Technologies: The Example of Digitisation

Marx argues that the growth and extension of the productive forces that brings about increased importance of knowledge and technology in production results in the emergence of new economic branches: "Entirely new branches of production, creating new fields of labour, are also formed as the direct result either of machinery or of the general industrial changes brought about by it. [. . .] The chief industries of this kind are, at the present [in the 1860s], gas-works, telegraphy, photography, steam navigation and railways" (573).

The British printing industry is a good example for the impacts of digitisation. In January 1986, London's printers went on strike because News International wanted to open a new printing plant in Wapping for producing *The Times*, *The Sun*, and the *News of the World*. It started to use offset printing with computer typesetting instead of Linotype printing, where the typesetting is nondigital and conducted with a linotype machine. The printers' unions—the National Graphical Association (NGA) and the Society of Graphical and Allied Trades (SOGAT)—feared that the newer method would put many printers out of work. Six thousand striking workers were laid off. The Thatcher government had put antiunion legislation (e.g., employers were allowed to sue unions for damages, introduction of secret ballots to hold industrial actions, restrictions on running closed shops, etc.) into action that enabled Murdoch to crush the print unions and to employ an alternative workforce of 600 represented by the renegade EETPU (Electrical, Electronic, Telecommunications and Plumbing Union—a yellow union welcoming neoliberal politics) in the new Wapping plant. The EETPU was a union of electricians, which means that the scab workers who replaced the printers were electricians.

Since the 1980s, the printing industry has experienced further vast changes, such as the impact of the personal computer, especially the Macintosh; desktop publishing; and layout software such as QuarkXPress, Adobe Illustrator, and Adobe InDesign; as well as the rise of the digital printing press, web publishing, print on demand, open access online publishing, e-books, e-readers, and tablets. Table 15.1 shows that the number of print workers in the UK almost halved in the period from 1981 until 1990. At the same time the number of computer professionals doubled, which shows that new industries create new employees, whereas the application of their products reduces employment in other sectors.

According to Say's theorem, one would have to assume that many printers have become software engineers if the one industry is in decline and the other is expanding. Tables 15.1 and 15.2 show, however, that not just the number of printers has drastically decreased, but also the number of jobs in occupations such as, for example, sewers, machine tool operators, packers, bottlers, canners, and miners has been vastly reduced. Table 15.2 shows that the number of British manufacturing workers fell from around 8.5 million in 1969 to 2.9 million in 2012, which means that employment in this sector was over a time period of 45 years reduced by two-thirds. During the same time period, manufacturing productivity more than tripled so that one-third of the workers produced a three times larger output. According to Marx's criticism of Say's theorem it is very unlikely that a large share of the workers set free have been upskilled and have found highly skilled employment.

TABLE 15.1 The development of number of employees in selected occupations in the UK (data sources: Household Survey 1981, 1990; Labour Force Survey 2000, 2014)

	1981	1990	2000	2014
Printing machine minders and assistants	64,918	42,893		
Compositors, typesetters, prepress workers	21,303	20,235		
Electro-typists and stereo-typists	10,086	8,861		
Screen and block printers	7,160	9,183		
Printers	39,212	16,059		
Print finishing and binding workers	14,989	9,073		
Total print workers	142,679	88,370		
Systems analysts and computer programmers	96,113	212,892		
Information technology professionals			451,000	847,000
Sewers, embroiderers / Sewing machinists	187,494	166,244	74,000	32,000
Machine tool operators	275,289	109,982	N/A	N/A
Packers, bottlers, canners, etc.	253,808	192,532	157,000	152,000
Coalmining workers	73,763	34,739	–	–
Miners (not coal), quarrymen, well drillers	13,236	15,518	15,000	9,000

TABLE 15.2 Development of the total employment and labour productivity in the UK manufacturing sector (data source: ILOSTAT [employment], UNCTAD STAN [productivity])

	1969	1971	1979	1988	1998	2008	2012
Manufacturing	8 477,000		7,318,000	5 437,000	4 534,000	3 326,500	2 886,800
Labour productivity index in manufacturing		42.1	49.8	70.9	90.3	133.6	

15.7. Repulsion and Attraction of Workers through the Development of Machine Production: Crises in the Cotton Industry

Technology and Un/Employment

In section 15.7, Marx further discusses the impact of new technologies on employment and unemployment. He argues that the introduction of machinery can in one stage extend ("attraction") and in another stage reduce ("repulse") employment. The employment of new machinery tends to increase the organic composition of capital in a factory—that is, constant capital rises in relation to variable capital, which falls. If the industry that adopts a new technology promises to be prosperous, then one, several, or many capitalists may seek to invest more capital than before in it; they may seek to get additional loans from banks for these investments, etc. Therefore the absolute amount of workers and variable capital employed may rise. At the same time, the constant capital share, however, rises in relation to the variable one in comparison to the previous conditions of production. When technification, mechanisation, and automation are introduced, there can be an absolute rise of variable capital that is accompanied by a relative decline of variable capital in relation to constant capital—that is, a rise of the organic composition of capital. In such a case, "a relative decrease in the number of workers employed is consistent with an actual increase in that number" (577).

There is, however, no guarantee that additional capital and workers are employed as a result of new technologies. Marx discusses the example of the introduction of the power-loom in Lancashire, Cheshire, and Yorkshire, which resulted in a reduction of workers from 94,119 in 1860 to 88,913 in 1865 (576).

As a result of the application of new technologies, the total number of workers can increase or decrease. In any case, there is a tendency that "the use of machinery entails an increase in the constant component of capital, that part which consists of machinery, raw material, etc., and a decrease in its variable component, the part laid out in labour-power" (578).

Imperialism and Communication Technologies

Marx argues that new machinery tends to increase the demand for raw material and therefore capital's imperialist global search for cheap sources of such material. Large-scale industry would therefore spur the "colonization of foreign lands" (579) and result in an "international division of labour" (579) that "converts one part of the globe" into a "field of production for supplying the other part" (580). Marx here again takes up the topic of the global division of labour, which he discusses in more detail in section 14.4. In chapter 14 of this book, I pointed out the difference between the old and the new international division of labour: Whereas in the first, colonies acted as cheap pools of raw materials and markets, in the latter, parts of the production process have since the 1970s been outsourced to developing countries in order to save labour costs. One can in this respect also speak of imperialism in the first case and a new imperialism in the second case, which is a more critical term than the positive-sounding concept of the globalisation of the economy that has become popular in the 1990s. Marx mentions that in the 19th century's division of labour, especially India was a colony for the production of "cotton, wool, hemp, jute and indigo for Great Britain" (579).

When discussing the 19th century's division of labour, Marx points out that transport and communication technologies are important tools for organising imperialism: The "cheapness of the articles produced by machinery and the revolution in the means of transport and communication provide the weapons for the conquest of foreign markets" (579). Communication technologies allow the global dissemination of information, which is a necessary means for organising imports and exports (the world market), transnational companies' production of commodities and the organisation of their labour in foreign countries, and the transport of commodities.

Technology and Economic Crises

Marx argues that technology plays a role both in the growth and contraction of an economic sector—that is, in boom and bust:

> The factory system's tremendous capacity for expanding with sudden immense leaps, and its dependence on the world market, necessarily give rise to the following cycle: feverish production; a consequent glut on the market, then a contraction of the market, which causes production to be crippled. The life of industry becomes a series of periods of moderate activity, prosperity, over-production, crisis and stagnation. The uncertainty and instability to which machinery subjects the employment, and consequently the living conditions, of the workers becomes a normal state of affairs, owing to these periodic turns of the industrial cycle. Except in the periods of prosperity, a most furious combat rages between the capitalists for their individual share in the market. This share is directly proportional to the cheapness of the product. Apart from the rivalry this struggle gives rise to in the use of improved machinery for replacing labour-power, and the introduction of new methods of production, there also comes a time in every industrial cycle when a forcible reduction of wages beneath the value of labour-power is attempted so as to cheapen commodities.
>
> A necessary condition for the growth of the number of factory workers is thus a proportionally much more rapid growth in the amount of capital invested in factories. But this process of growth takes place only within the ebbs and flows of the industrial cycle. It is, in addition, constantly interrupted by the technical progress that at one time virtually takes the place of additional workers, and at another time actually drives workers out of employment. This qualitative change in machine production continually removes workers from the factories, or closes their doors to the fresh stream of recruits, while the purely quantitative extension of the factories absorbs not only the men thrown out of work but also fresh contingents of workers. The latter are thus continually repelled and attracted, slung backwards and forwards, while, at the same time, constant changes take place in the sex, age and skill of the industrial conscripts. (580, 582–583)

Technology has uncertain effects on employment, both a tendency to attract and repulse labour. Capitalism has inherent crisis tendencies, which is an important factor that influences employment and the uptake of new technology. In general it can be said that capitalists have an inherent drive to increase profits by making use of more productive labour-saving technologies, reducing wages, lengthening the working day, and outsourcing labour to low-wage regions and countries. In light of capitalist technologies' contradictory potentials and capitalist waves of expansion and contraction, labour is confronted with conflicting tendencies of times when capital seeks additional labour, and times when it tries to lay off workers.

Marx discusses as an example the booms and busts of the English cotton industry in the years from 1770 until 1863 (583–588). Lancashire was the stronghold of the English cotton industry. It is good to know for the reader that the power-loom invented by Edmund Cartwright in 1784 and the Lancashire loom introduced in 1842 by James Bullough and William Kenworthy transformed the cotton industry during this time period. The Lancashire industry depended on cotton imported mainly from the USA, where slaves picked it on plantations. The finished cloth was to specific degrees exported to India, China, and Africa. The American Civil War (1861–1865) was a war about the expansion or abolishment of slavery. The Southern states had cotton-based industries founded on slave labour. During the war, British import came to a halt, which resulted in a cotton crisis.

Ernest Mandel on the Contradictory Role of New Technologies in Economic Growth and Crises

Ernest Mandel summarises the contradictory role of new technologies in economic growth and crises in the following way:

> [There is] an initial phase, in which the technology actually undergoes a revolution, and when such things as the production sites for the new means of production have first to be created. This phase is distinguished by an increased rate of profit, accelerated accumulation, accelerated growth, accelerated self-expansion of previously idle capital and the accelerated devalorization of capital previously invested in Department I [Department I is a term that Marx uses for the part of the economy that produces means of production] but now technically obsolescent. This first phase is followed by a second, in which the actual transformation in productive technology has already taken place, i.e., the new production sites for new means of production are for the most part already in existence and can only be further extended or improved in a quantitative sense. It is now a matter of getting the means of production made in these new production sites generally adopted in all branches of industry and economy. The force that determined the sudden extension by leaps and bounds of capital accumulation in Department I thus falls away, and accordingly this phase becomes one of retreating profits, gradually decelerating accumulation, decelerating economic growth, gradually increasing difficulties in the valorization of the total accumulated capital, and particularly of new additionally accumulated capital, and the gradual, self-reproducing increase in capital being laid idle. (Mandel 1978, 121)

Mandel, as a follower of long wave theory, thought that this contraction and expansion of the capitalist economy takes place in waves that last around 50 years. I have discussed long wave theory in more detail in chapter 12. It is not feasible that such waves should last 50 years. Making such an assumption is almost religious and esoteric because it creates the impression that a mystical force drives capitalism. Human behaviour and societal structures are complex and their development is therefore partly unpredictable. All we can say is that the history of capitalism is a history of economic crisis and that capitalism's antagonisms constitute inherent crisis tendencies. There can be no crisis-free capitalism, but it is not predetermined when crises emerge and how long a phase of expansion lasts. It is also not guaranteed that an upswing must occur. There are indications that capitalism can over a sustained period of time remain very prone to constant crisis and fluctuations.

Technology and the Rate of Profit

Marx argues in section 15.7 that technology has contradictory effects on the capitalist economy. It is therefore worthwhile to again mention a point made in chapter 12: The rate of profit is the relationship of profit and investment or of the monetary expression of surplus-value and the value of the means of production (constant and variable capital):

$$ROP = \frac{s}{c+v}.$$

If we divide the numerator and the denominator by v, then we get the following:

$$ROP = \frac{\frac{s}{v}}{\frac{c}{v}+1}.$$

This formula shows that the rate of profit depends (a) on the rate of surplus-value, which Marx also calls the rate of exploitation because it describes the relationship of unpaid and paid labour, and (b) the organic composition of capital, which represents the relationship of dead and living labour, constant and variable capital, and the value of machinery/resources and labour-power. The rate of profit is directly proportional to the rate of surplus-value and inversely proportional to the organic composition of capital.

New technology has the potential to both increase the rate of surplus-value and the organic composition of capital. The effects of new technology on the rate of profit depend on the relationship between the rate of surplus-value and the organic composition. If the organic composition increases more than the rate of surplus-value, then a fall of the rate of profit emerges, and, vice versa, if the rate of surplus-value increases more than the organic composition, then the rate of profit increases. An important factor in this respect is class struggle, which influences the absolute value of variable capital v. In any case, the formula for the profit-rate shows that technification has contradictory potentials: It can increase productivity and the exploitation of labour. Marx also points out in section 15.7 that there can be increased demand for labour in newly emerging or expanding economic sectors due to the effects of new technology, whereas technology can also be a factor for laying off workers in those industries that are automated and in the growing industries once the growth potential is saturated.

Capitalist Technologies' Potentials for the Attraction and Repulsion of Workers

Figure 15.7 summarises one of the main points Marx makes in section 15.7: Technology in production has antagonistic potentials in capitalism. It develops in relationship to the capitalist economy's booms and busts and has potentials to attract and repulse workers—that is, to create temporary demand for labour in new and expanding industries that attract investments in line with economic reorganisation and to shorten the demand in sectors that undergo technological rationalisation and in the formerly expanding sectors once technological innovations have diffused widely into the economy. Technology in capitalism transforms workers into nonworkers and nonworkers into workers; its antagonistic character means uncertainties for both workers and capitalist development.

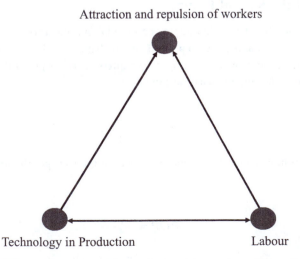

FIGURE 15.7 Capitalist technologies' potentials for the attraction and repulsion of workers

15.8. The Revolutionary Impact of Large-Scale Industry on Manufacture, Handicrafts, and the Domestic Industry

Marx in this section provides examples of how machinery has overthrown and changed handicraft labour, the manufactory, and homework in the domestic industry as well as examples of related working conditions. He points out issues such as the high exploitation of children and women, over-work, and long working hours; the lack of sanitation, space, light, and fresh air; occupational health hazards, night work, poor schooling, workers' death from starvation, the overinvestment of capital, and the overproduction of commodities.

One example concerns the bookbinding and printing industry: "Owing to the excessive labour performed by their workers, both adult and non-adult, certain London firms where newspapers and books are printed have gained for themselves the honourable name of 'slaughter-houses'. Similar excesses occur in book-binding, where the victims are chiefly women, girls and children" (592).

Means of Communication, the Annihilation of Space by Time, and the Acceleration of Capitalist Accumulation

Marx argues that the rise of the railway and the telegraph encouraged giving small or large orders with short notice that required immediate execution (608). There would have been an "absence of regularity in the expenditure of labour-power" and an "anarchy in production itself" (608). Ocean navigation and the means of communication would have "destroyed the actual technical foundation of seasonal labour" (610). Marx describes how communication and transportation technology have accelerated the production and circulation of commodities. In the *Grundrisse*, he describes the acceleration of capital accumulation as annihilation of space by time:

> The more production comes to rest on exchange value, hence on exchange, the more important do the physical conditions of exchange—the means of communication and transport—become for the costs of circulation. Capital by its nature drives beyond every spatial barrier. Thus the creation of the physical conditions of exchange—of the means of communication and transport—the annihilation of space by time—becomes an extraordinary necessity for it. (Marx 1857/1858, 524)

The Example of Amazon

Amazon has in the 21st century become the world's largest retailer and online shop. It sells among other commodities music, books, films, software, baby products, bags, beauty products, car and motorbike accessories, clothes, computers and laptops, peripheral computer equipment, tools, consumer electronics, garden and outdoor supply, gift cards, groceries, health and personal care products, jewellery, kitchen and home appliances, large electronic appliances, lamps and lights, musical instruments, office supplies, pet supplies, shoes, sports supplies, toys, travel accessories, watches.

Criticisms of Amazon have focused on issues such as the military surveillance and control of the workforce, zero-hour and temporary contracts, low-wage rates; price cutting that centralises the retail market and destroys small local stores, especially bookstores; tax avoidance, opposition to trade unions, Taylorist control, high work pressure with set performance targets that are electronically controlled and enforced by management with disciplinary actions, long shifts or heavy physical demands on warehouse workers, who have to walk many miles per shift.

BBC reporter Adam Littler worked undercover at the Amazon Swansea warehouse in South Wales. The result was the BBC Panorama-documentary *Amazon: The Truth behind the Click*.[3] He concluded: "I managed to walk 11 miles [17.7 kilometres] last night. [. . .] I have never done a job like this. The pressure is unbelievable. [. . .] For those ten hours, we are basically machines, we are robots. [. . .] We don't think for ourselves". Professor Michael Marmot, one of the UK's leading public health scholars, commented as part of the documentary on the secretly filmed footage: "The characteristics of this type of job, the evidence shows increased risk of mental illness and physical illness. [. . .] It is organisational injustice. [. . .] The way the organisation is structured is unjust and does injustice".

Marx describes in section 15.8 how transport and communication technologies accelerate capitalist production and circulation. Amazon is a good example of how ordering commodities has in the 21st century been sped up with the help of the Internet and how this increased speed of ordering has been accompanied by poor working conditions and intense work pressure on warehouse workers, as well as permanent control, threats, and health hazards these workers face. Furthermore the work is low-paid and insecure. Amazon combines absolute surplus-value production (working long hours for low wages) with relative surplus-value production (measuring and accelerating the delivery process by conducting permanent measurements in a Tayloristic manner and a repressive military management style that tries to ever more increase the speed of labour). Ordering a book or another commodity on Amazon makes the distribution process invisible. If you in contrast buy a book in a shop or groceries in a supermarket, you are experiencing parts of the distribution process yourself. You also do not experience how the commodities have come into the shelves, which is a result of the impact of transport technologies on the sales process. In the case of Amazon, the distribution process is almost completely invisible and anonymous to the consumer. The ordering process is experienced as something nonphysical, without human contact, but the actual labour underlying delivery is constituted by heavy sweat and intense human suffering. Once in a while, you may have to sign for the parcel you receive, but Amazon has already considered delivering all parcels by air with the help of drones, which is a further step in the automation of commodity circulation. The acceleration of commodity distribution that Amazon stands for comes at the price of high levels of exploitation.

15.9. The Health and Education Clauses of the Factory Acts: The General Extension of Factory Legislation in England

In section 15.9, Marx discusses basic aspects of education and health that the Factory Extension Act 1867 and the Workshops Regulation Act 1867 introduced. He argues that both the telegraph and factory legislation are the products of large-scale industry (620).

Capitalism and Education

Marx points out that capitalism has undermined educational opportunities for children and that both capitalists and bourgeois intellectuals have seen education as harmful for business. Parents in the 19th century due to meagre wages were compelled to force their children to work at home or in factories. Bourgeois thinkers presented this issue often as a moral issue, not one of political economy, the working poor, and the exploitation of labour that results in child labour.

Marx discusses as example the impacts of the printing press on educational standards:

> In the English letter-press printing trade, for example, there formerly existed a system, corresponding to that in the old manufactures and handicrafts, of advancing the apprentices from easy to more and more difficult work. They went through a course of teaching till they were finished printers. To be able to read and write was for every one of them a requirement of their trade. All this was changed by the printing machine. It employs two sorts of worker. On the one hand there are adults, tenters, and on the other hand there are boys, mostly from 11 to 17 years of age, whose sole occupation is either to spread the sheets of paper under the machine, or to take from it the printed sheets. They perform this weary task, in London especially, for 14, 15 and 16 hours at a stretch, during several days in the week, and frequently for

36 hours, with only 2 hours' rest for meals and sleep. A great proportion of them cannot read, and they are, as a rule, utter savages and very extraordinary creatures. (615)

The Elementary Education Act 1870 introduced compulsory education for all children aged 5 to 13 in England and Wales. Child labour was largely abolished. But capitalism still has negative impacts on education in the 21st century. One just needs to think of the fact that many countries have university tuition fees that put young people from working-class families at a disadvantage. There have again and again been studies that show that pupils from working-class families tend to perform poorer than those from middle- and upper-class families. One UK study concludes as follows:

> The data shows that at GCSE, 32% of White British pupils eligible for free school meals achieved 5+ A★–C, compared with 65% of pupils who were not eligible. [. . .] The data suggest that White British pupils are the ethnic group most polarised by the impact of socio-economic disadvantage. While poverty makes little difference to the achievements at school of some ethnic groups, it makes a huge difference to White British children on free school meals. In conclusion, the study argues that the worryingly low achievement of many White Working Class pupils has been masked by the success of middle class White children in the English school system, because Government statistics have failed to distinguish the White British ethnic group by social background. Effectively treating White British as a single group is extremely misleading. (Demie 2014, 1)

Education in a Communist Society

Marx argues that a communist society gets rid of the capitalist pressures on education and is therefore likely to improve educational standards and achievements. He acknowledges in this respect the ideas of the social reformer and socialist Robert Owen (1771–1858):

> As Robert Owen has shown us in detail, the germ of the education of the future is present in the factory system; this education will, in the case of every child over a given age, combine productive labour with instruction and gymnastics, not only as one of the methods of adding to the efficiency of production, but as the only method of producing fully developed human beings (614).

Robert Owen was one of the founders of the cooperative movement. He created industrial experiments with good working conditions, such as the New Lanark mill. Owens's ideas, his social and welfare programmes, such as childcare, general education, and the eight-hour day, were far ahead of the times in terms of their progressive social reform content. On educational standards, Owen commented:

> Under this classification and consequent arrangement of society, every individual will be trained and educated to have all his faculties and powers cultivated in the most superior manner known; cultivated too, under a new combination of external objects, purposely formed, to bring into constant exercise the best and most lovely qualities only of human nature. [. . .] They will, therefore, all be equal in their education and condition, and no artificial distinction, or any distinction but that of age, will ever be known among them. (Owen 1991, 350)

The Antagonism between Productive Forces and the Relations of Production

Marx argues that technology in capitalism is highly contradictory: On the one hand it is a capitalist means for exploiting labour, and on the other hand it socialises labour and the means of production and increases productivity, which is a precondition for a society without scarcity and toil, in which humans conduct manifold, self-chosen forms of creative work:

> Modern industry never views or treats the existing form of a production process as the definitive one. Its technical basis is therefore revolutionary, whereas all earlier modes of production were essentially conservative. [. . .] We have seen how this absolute contradiction [between the potentials of modern technology and its capitalist application] does away with all repose, all fixity and all security as far as the worker's life-situation is concerned; how it constantly threatens, by taking away the instruments of labour, to snatch from his hands the means of subsistence, and, by suppressing his specialized function, to make him superfluous. [. . .] This is the negative side. [. . .] That monstrosity, the disposable working population held in reserve, in misery, for the changing requirements of capitalist exploitation, must be replaced by the individual man who is absolutely available for the different kinds of labour required of him; the partially developed individual, who is merely the bearer of one specialized social function, must be replaced by the totally developed individual, for whom the different social functions are different modes of activity he takes up in turn. (617–618)

Marx points out that the structures of capitalism on the negative side cause social problems in capitalism, while on the other side they also have potentials and are nuclei of a more human society that cannot be realised within the confines of class society. The "development of the contradictions of a given historical form of production is the only historical way in which it can be dissolved and then reconstructed on a new basis" (619).

When discussing the division of labour in chapter 14, I pointed out that for Marx and Engels communism enables the sublation of the division of labour so that a well-rounded or totally developed individual can develop in communism. The precondition for this development is a highly productive economy so that toil and scarcity come to an end. The notion of the totally developed individual is a concept that Marx used throughout his life. It cannot just be found in *Capital Volume 1*'s chapter 15, but already in the *German Ideology*, where Marx and Engels (1845) point out that in communism, "nobody has one exclusive sphere of activity but each can become accomplished in any branch he wishes, society regulates the general production and thus makes it possible for me to do one thing today and another tomorrow, to hunt in the morning, fish in the afternoon, rear cattle in the evening, criticise after dinner" (Marx and Engels 1845, 53).

Marx points out in section 15.9 what he terms the antagonism between productive forces and the relations of production: Technology in capitalism on the one hand creates potentials for and seeds of a communist economy and society, but under capitalist class relations enforces crisis, unemployment, and social problems.

Information Technology and the Antagonism between the Productive Forces and the Relations of Production

Also information technology and the Internet in the 21st century are founded on an antagonism of class relations and the now networked productive forces. A good example is that the Internet allows the free sharing of information via peer-to-peer platforms and other technologies, which on the one hand questions the capitalist character of culture and so makes the music and film industry nervous, but on the other hand within capitalism can also constitute problems for artists who depend on deriving income from cultural commodities. Informational networks aggravate the capitalist contradiction between the collective production and the individual appropriation of goods:

> The contradiction between the general social power into which capital develops and the private power of the individual capitalists over these social conditions of production develops

ever more blatantly, while this development also contains the solution to this situation, in that it simultaneously raises the conditions of production into general, communal, social conditions. This transformation is brought about by the development of the productive forces under capitalist production and by the manner and form in which this development is accomplished. (Marx 1894, 373)

Marx says in the *Preface to the Critique of Political Economy* that the "material conditions for the existence" of "new superior relations of production" mature "within the framework of the old society" and that the "productive forces developing within bourgeois society create also the material conditions for a solution of this antagonism" (MECW 29, 263). A comparable formulation of this antagonism is the following one:

> At a certain stage of development, the material productive forces of society come into conflict with the existing relations of production or—this merely expresses the same thing in legal terms—with the property relations within the framework of which they have operated hitherto. From forms of development of the productive forces these relations turn into their fetters. (MECW 29, 263)

In *Capital Volume 1*'s chapter 32, Marx formulates the antagonism between productive forces and relations of production in the following way: "At a certain stage of development, it [the capitalist mode of production] brings into the world the material means of its own destruction. From that moment, new forces and new passions spring up in the bosom of society, forces and passions which feel themselves to be fettered by that society" (928).

The informational networks that form the major productive forces of informational capitalism have turned into fetters of the relations of production. Productive forces that are tied up by existing relations do not necessarily or automatically fully develop. It is in no way assured that they can be freed. They can remain enchained and will remain enchained as long as individuals allow themselves to be enchained. Networks are a material condition of a free association, but the cooperative networking of the relations of production is not an automatic result of networked productive forces. People must struggle for a true network society—a distinctive sublation of network capitalism so that networked communism emerges as "a society composed of associations of free and equal producers, carrying on the social business on a common and rational plan" (MECW 23, 136) and an "association, in which the free development of each is the condition for the free development of all" (MECW 6, 506), and that is based on the principle "[f]rom each according to his abilities, to each according to his needs!" (MECW 24, 87).

The material preconditions for such a society exist. It is, however, not certain if humans can overcome their own enslavement and can to a sufficient degree see through ideologies that perpetuate this enslavement in order to break the chains of capitalism that trap the full development of communism. Networks anticipate a society in which "the antithesis between mental and physical labor has vanished" (MECW 24, 87), "the productive forces have also increased with the all-around-development of the individual" (MECW 24, 87), and "the springs of cooperative wealth flow more abundantly" (MECW 24, 87). Networks are forms of development as well as fetters of capitalism. Paraphrasing a passage from *Capital Volume 1*'s chapter 32, we can say that in informational capitalism "the means of production and the socialization of labour reach a point at which they become incompatible with their capitalist integument" (929).

Marx concludes section 15.9 with a summary in which he says that factory legislation "matures the contradictions and antagonisms of the capitalist form of that process, and therefore ripens both the elements for forming a new society and the forces tending towards the overthrow of the old one" (635).

15.10. Large-Scale Industry and Agriculture

Modern Technology and Agriculture

The rise of modern industry and technology has had huge impacts on rural agricultural regions:

> In the sphere of agriculture, large-scale industry has a more revolutionary effect than else-where, for the reason that it annihilates the bulwark of the old society, the 'peasant', and substitutes for him the wage-labourer. [. . .] Capitalist production collects the population together in great centres, and causes the urban population to achieve an ever-growing preponderance. (637)

In the discussion of section 10.5, I pointed out that urbanisation and flight from the land was not confined to the 19th century, but that, for example, the development in China shows that this development has been continuing up until the 21st century.

The environmental crisis includes phenomena such as oil spills, the depletion of the Ozone layer, deforestation, desertification, nuclear meltdowns, global warming, the extinction of species, the loss of biodiversity, heavy air pollution and smog in metropolises, water shortages and pollution, carcinogenic food, soil and water contamination, etc. It has emerged and intensified as part of the development of modern industry. The destruction of the environment was already visible at the time Marx lived, which is why he argued that capitalist production "only develops the techniques and the degree of combination of the social process of production by simultaneously undermining the original sources of all wealth—the soil and the worker" (638).

15.11. How Not to Theorise Technology: Andrew Feenberg's Dualist Theory of Technology

I have in this chapter argued that the main feature of Marx's philosophy of technology is that he sees technology and modern technology as inherently dialectical. I discussed, for example, how Marx analyses technology as a dialectical system as well as in the context of the dialectic of absolute and relative surplus-value production, the dialectic of essence and appearance, the dialectic of technology and society, the antagonism between productive forces and relations of production, *the dialectical inversion of subject and object and means and ends*, and an antagonism between labour and time and between necessary labour-time and surplus labour-time, as well as how he situates technology in the context of social struggles and crises as dialectical phenomena.

"Critical Theory of Technology": Operational Autonomy and Technical Codes

Andrew Feenberg has created a theory of technology that he terms the "critical theory of technology". It is a good example of how not to theorise technology and how to miss adequately understanding and analysing the dialectical character of technology. In what follows I argue that we need a dialectical critical theory of technology and that Feenberg has merely created a dualist theory of technology.

In his major work *Transforming Technology: A Critical Theory Revisited* (a revision of the 1991 book *Critical Theory of Technology*), Andrew Feenberg (2002) aims to formulate the foundations of a critical theory of technology.

Two key categories for Feenberg are operational autonomy and technical codes: Operational autonomy is the "freedom of management to make independent decisions about how to carry on the activities of the organization it supervises" (Feenberg 2002, 16), and the "power to make strategic choices among alternative rationalizations" (75). A technical code "is the realization of an interest in a technically coherent solution to a general type of problem" (20).

From Marxism to "Radical Critique"

Feenberg is overcritical of Marx and therefore even suggests going from "Marxism to radical critique" as the title of his main book's first part suggests. He argues that there are three critiques of technology in Marx (Feenberg 2002, chapter 2):

(a) A substantivist product critique that sees only technology's bad use as a problem, considers technology as neutral, and argues that the solution is a revolution that changes the class relations, but not technology
(b) A process critique that criticises the production process into which technology is embedded and sees rational planning as the solution
(c) A design critique that Feenberg considers as the source of a critical theory of technology and that argues that "technology is shaped in its design and development by the social purposes of capital" (48), which implies that it can be redesigned away from capitalist interests. The "social impact of technology depends on how it is designed and used" (116)

The trouble is that Feenberg does not substantiate the claim that the first two, rather instrumentalist and determinist views of technology, are immanent in Marx's works. He misses the fact that the crucial aspect of Marx's concept of technology is the dialectic: Marx sees technology in capitalism shaped by antagonisms between classes, the productive forces and the relations of production, use-value and exchange-value, necessary labour and surplus-labour, constant and variable capital, etc. Technology in capitalism exists in a society and economy that is full of antagonisms.

The Design Critique of Technology

Feenberg's design critique of technology argues that technology is ambivalent because it can be designed by different "civilizational projects" (Feenberg 2002, 53): Capitalism and socialism. "Class power determines which of the ambivalent potentialities of the heritage will be realized. An undemocratic power such as that of the capitalist class eliminates institutional and technical innovations that threaten its control. Since, under socialism, workers are in charge, they can change the very nature of technology, which, for the first time in history, concerns a ruling class with an interest in democracy on the workplace" (53). Feenberg certainly does not think that the creation of socialist technology has to wait until the day after the revolution, but rather assumes that it is possible that one can and should start to build, design, and redesign democratic alternative technologies in the here and now. The choice would always be between capitalism and socialism: "In sum, modern technology opens a space within which action can be functionalized in either one of two social systems, capitalism or socialism. It is an ambivalent or 'multistable' system that can be organized around at least two hegemonies, two poles of power between which it can 'tilt'" (Feenberg 2002, 87).

For Feenberg, there is a constant struggle between socialist and capitalist designs and uses of technology. Technology is an "'ambivalent' process of development suspended between different possibilities" (Feenberg 2002, 15). It is a "scene of struggle" and "a social battlefield" (15). "Technological development is a scene of social struggle in which various competing groups attempt to advance their interests and their corresponding civilizational projects" (143).

The Trouble with Feenberg's Theory

The trouble with Feenberg's theory is manifold:

• Feenberg reduces the dialectic to subjective struggles between socialist and capitalist technologies that he considers as inevitable so that he advances a deterministic concept of technological struggles. "Tactics are the inevitable response of the dominated to their domination" (Feenberg 2002, 84). A "different type of autonomy is won by the dominated" (84). Just like celebratory cultural studies has used Michel de Certeau's work for arguing that audiences constantly and necessarily resist and subversively read ideologies and media products, Feenberg based on the same influence ends up with a fetishism of technological struggles that does not see that alternatives and struggles are always potentials, but do not automatically and also not with necessity emerge because struggles can be contained by power asymmetries, ideologies, repression, violence, etc., as critical theorists such as Herbert Marcuse knew. Feenberg overestimates the power of hacking technologies and giving them a subversive rationality. He is a techno-optimist who just like techno-pessimists bases the analysis on undialectical thought.

• Feenberg underestimates the roles of ideology and repression, elements that Herbert Marcuse, the supervisor of Feenberg's PhD dissertation *The Dialectics of Theory and Practice*, always stressed when discussing social movements. So, for example, Marcuse warned against the problems the New Left faced in the early 1970s because of external repression and internal weaknesses:

> About ten years ago, the transcending goals, too, became articulate: the new morality, the emancipation of sensibility, the demand for 'freedom now', the cultural revolution. The Establishment was not prepared. The strategy then could be massive, open, and largely offensive. [. . .] Now the system is prepared-to such an extent that the very survival of the radical movement as a political force is in question. [. . .] How is the movement reacting to these new conditions? It appears to be weakened to a dangerous degree. This is primarily due to the legal and extra-legal aggressive repression on the part of the power structure—a concentration of brutal force against which the Left has no adequate defense. This mobilization of power accentuates the internal weaknesses within the New Left, above all: (1) ideological conflicts within the militant opposition and (2) the lack of organization. (Marcuse 1972, 36)

• Feenberg in a dualistic and nondialectical manner opposes capitalist and socialist technologies to each other. First, he thereby disregards that capitalist technologies and ideologies that frame them understand how to subsume and instrumentalise the concepts, principles, and language of socialism so that principles such as the gift, free access, participation, and cooperation have long become capitalist strategies for the management of labour and technologies.

Second, Feenberg's Manichean (i.e., radical dualist) concept of technology strictly opposes good and evil technologies. He disregards that some aspects of capitalist technologies can be liberating and should continue to be used in a socialist society, whereas others need a redesign, again others should no longer be used because they harm humans and/or nature, and new ones have to be invented. At the same time there is no guarantee that socialist technologies do not adopt a capitalist character and harm humans and/or nature, so that redesign is and will remain a constant challenge. Capitalist technologies can contain socialist Keimformen (germ forms) and socialist technologies can contain potentials to turn into class technologies. Feenberg's dualistic approach cannot grasp this dialectic.

Marx argues, for example, in *Capital Volume 3* that the development of the productive forces "creates the material means and the nucleus ['Keim' in the German original] for relations that permits this surplus labour to be combined, in a higher form of society, with a greater reduction of the overall time devoted to material labour" (Marx 1894, 958). In society, a nucleus does not with necessity result in a new system. It is a mere potential. How a new social system and its technology look is not determined by the nucleus itself, but by the way humans shape and develop it. A technology's real form and content depend on if and how human practices produce something concrete out of the potentials germinating in an older social system.

- Feenberg's theory of technology is also dualist because it does not thoroughly analyse the antagonisms between capitalist technologies and alternative technologies. The first tend to have a privileged position. Because of their embeddedness into the process of capital accumulation and instrumental rationality, they tend to have it easier when it comes to accumulating funding, money, resources, personnel, network contacts, influence, reputation, visibility, attention, etc. Alternative technologies in contrast are based on a noninstrumental logic, which favours democracy, the commons, and the public and tends to be sceptical towards bureaucracy, markets, capital, the commodity form, private ownership, advertising, etc., which in a capitalist world puts them at a strategic disadvantage. Alternative technologies and media are therefore in a capitalist world confronted with an antagonism between political and economic autonomy and the tendency to face resource precarity and voluntary, self-exploitative, precarious work (Sandoval and Fuchs 2010; Fuchs 2010a, 2014b; Fuchs and Sandoval 2015). Feenberg's theory cannot adequately analyse this dilemma and has nothing to say on what left-wing politics can do to help overcome it.

The Fetishism of Chance and Openness

Feenberg sees the ambivalence of technology as "open possibilities that are disputed between dominated and dominating groups" (Feenberg 2002, 79). "Technical mediation, however, has unforeseeable consequences" (86). Technological development would be open and undetermined. Feenberg, however, disregards that although technology is always open for change and contestation, technological struggles are not an automatism and are no necessity because there tend to be power asymmetries within capitalist society. Feenberg tends to fetishise chance, indeterminism, and openness. He ends up with a theory that relies on political voluntarism and the trust in chance alternative designs and uses as well as appropriations of technologies.

Technological Bias

Feenberg introduces the concept of technological bias, by which he means that "technology is not neutral but fundamentally biased toward a particular hegemony" (Feenberg 2002, 63). By formal bias he means "the prejudicial choice of the *time, place and manner of the introduction of a system composed of relatively neutral elements*" (81). Substantive bias means "the application of unequal standards" that "gives the appearance of fairness", but is "most often associated with prejudice, with explicit norms that discriminate between people of different classes, races, sexes, or nationalities" (81).

Feenberg in formulating these confused and obscure concepts adopts liberal language that stresses choices, prejudices, and biases. It is easier to enable more choices, weakening prejudices and biases by strengthening plurality than it is to fundamentally redistribute power towards the dominated and the exploited and to overcome domination and exploitation. Liberalism therefore likes the idea of increasing available choices. The concepts of power, domination, and exploitation, which have a much more political and normative tone than speaking of choices, prejudices, and biases, are missing when Feenberg tries to conceptualise asymmetries. Choice is different from action: To provide more choices does not mean that they are realised because only action transforms potentiality into actuality. It is not enough to aim at increasing and pluralising choices; alternative politics should rather demand and advance actions that make sure socialist projects are realised and empowered to gain resources, influence, and reputation.

So, for example, the fact that celebrities such as Katy Perry or Justin Bieber are the Twitter users with the largest number of followers is not a matter of prejudices such as racism or nationalism, but reflects a fundamental power asymmetry of consumer capitalism, which provides fame, stardom, money, and reputation for the few. Socialist technologies and socialist politics must challenge such power asymmetries and provide alternative policies, technological designs, a redistribution of power, alternative forms of production and ownership, etc., which end the asymmetric accumulation of reputation, visibility, attention, fame, etc.

Feenberg's Dualist Theory of Technology

Feenberg terms an entire book part "The Dialectics of Technology" (Feenberg 2002, 130–190). By the dialectic of technology, he understands a dialectic of "technical orientation" and "action in the world" (175), primary and secondary instrumentalisations, technology and "a larger framework of social relations" (177). Although Feenberg uses the term "dialectic", he has elaborated a nondialectical, dualist theory of technology. It is not sufficient for a theory of technology to be critical; we need a dialectical critical theory of technology. Feenberg falls short of providing a framework that can adequately analyse the dialectic of technology. This may have to do with the lack of grounding of his approach in Hegel's logic and works on the dialectic. Feenberg's main books on the critical theory of technology (Feenberg 1995a, 1999, 2002, 2010) do not contain a single work by Hegel in their bibliographies.

Feenberg's dualistic concept of technology becomes also evident when he tries to apply his approach to computer technology. He opposes the "principle of the conservation of hierarchy" to the "principle of democratic rationalization" (Feenberg 2002, 92). In some instances, the design and use of the computer would result in the first principle in the form of "intensifying surveillance and control", in other cases in the second so that "the drive to computerize has excited and sometimes fulfilled participatory expectations" (92). One here again finds an undialectical, Manichean dualism of good and bad computing that cannot adequately understand the complexities and dialectical antagonisms of capitalist media: The principle of user participation has, for example, been fostered by capitalist social media such as YouTube, Facebook, Pinterest, Instagram, Flickr, etc. that allow users to create and share content, which empowers them culturally. The very same principle of participation has, however, been turned into a possibility for constant surveillance, which is at the heart of the business model of online targeted advertising and has been embraced by secret services such as the NSA and GCHQ; as part of mass surveillance projects such as Prism and XKeyScore these secret services have gained access to user data on Google, Facebook, and other communications platforms. Participation is not opposed to surveillance, as Feenberg wants to make us believe, but has rather become part of surveillance itself.

The prospect for participatory democracy is certainly undermined by the intersection of state and corporate power, which fosters a dialectic of the two principles that Feenberg opposes as dual others. Surveillance in an asymmetric society can also advance socialist goals if a left-wing government, for example, monitors financial transactions and companies suspected of corporate crimes in order to uncover tax avoidance and fraud and expose crime. So here again surveillance and socialism are not opposites. A socialist society certainly will aim at minimising surveillance, but it may have to use certain forms of policing as long as crime cannot be fully overcome because antagonisms remain, although they are likely to occur in a less intensive and less extensive manner.

Facebook and Feenberg's Dualism of Technology

Feenberg's dualistic approach is also evident in his analysis of Facebook. He argues together with Dal Yong Jin that "despite the dispiriting commercialism of SNSs on the Internet, and the role of corporate and government surveillance in stripping us of the last vestiges of privacy, there is another encouraging side to the story. [. . .] it is clear that social networking creates a new kind of democratic public sphere with considerable oppositional potential" (Jin and Feenberg 2015, 58–59). The argument is based on the mistaken techno-deterministic assumption that contemporary protests are

Twitter and Facebook rebellions. The authors argue that Facebook is both a realm of commodification and political activism and that the latter phenomenon is more important. They do not relate the two phenomena to each other and end up with a one-sided techno-optimism that sees struggles everywhere technology is and ignores that struggles face contradictions.

In the case of Facebook, activists using this platform have in many parts of the world also been monitored and violently repressed by secret services, police forces, authoritarian governments. Activists' Facebook groups have been temporarily shut down (with the argument that Facebook does not allow anonymous communication!). Such antagonisms exist precisely because of the fact that Facebook's status as capitalist organisation makes it prone to not sympathising with radical activists, easily handing over control power to state power, etc. A commons-based social network controlled by activists themselves in contrast is less likely to experience such subsumptions. Jin and Feenberg's techno-determinism misses this dialectic of activism. It uncritically celebrates the potentials for activism posed by Facebook. My own study of Occupy activists' use of social media (Fuchs 2014b) has shown (a) a dialectic of online and offline communication (both reinforce each other) and (b) that activists see a contradiction between potentials of corporate social media to reach the public and the commercial and political control they are confronted with when using such platforms. Jin and Feenberg's assessment lacks empirical grounding and is undialectical and one-dimensional.

Online Education and Feenberg's Dualism of Technology

Feenberg also does not understand the complexity of modern technology's dialectic when discussing online education. He asks: "The new computer-based initiatives polarize around two alternative understandings of the computer as an educational technology. Is it an engine of control or a medium of communication?" (Feenberg 2002, 120). Feenberg here again misses the possibility that communication and control are not dual opposites, but in an antagonistic dialectic overgrasp into each other. So, for example, communication has become the principle of economic control on corporate social media that can make more profit the more people communicate online, which allows them to provide and sell more targeted ads. Communication is not the dual opposite of control and community is not the dual opposite of the commodity. Socialism is a society governed by noninstrumental communication and community, but capitalism can also subsume progressive principles.

The State: The Weak and Blind Spot of Feenberg's Theory

I am not arguing that alternatives are not possible, which would be defeatist. My point is rather that we should think about alternative media and technologies in a dialectical manner and discuss the antagonisms they face in capitalism. Alternative participatory designs and social movements that advance them are a necessary component of socialist transition, but they do not suffice because they face antagonisms immanent in the structures of capitalism. The blind spot of Feenberg's theory is the role of the state in socialist transition. When discussing the socialisation of productive resources, democratisation, and alternative innovations as part of the transition to socialism, Feenberg (2002, 147–158) does not mention the potential role and problems of the state, which creates the impression that he speaks of either a purely utopian situation in the future or purely voluntarist projects without demanding legal changes and state support for such projects.

When Feenberg mentions the state, then he does so for stressing that the Soviet state was a problem and that the Left therefore needs nonstatist politics. "The historical experience of communism shows that Marx was wrong to believe that states could be the primary agents of technological transformation" (Feenberg 2002, ix). He speaks of the "illusion of state-sponsored civilizational change" (13) and says that "we need a democratic transformation from below" (17). Feenberg tends to only stress the importance of new social movements (62) and that the working class is not a privileged political subject (61). He argues that to "democratize technology" is "not primarily" a problem "of legal rights but of initiative and participation" (Feenberg 1995b, 18). The authoritarian communist state was a problem, but that it existed does not logically imply that any use of state power is harmful for socialism.

Feenberg likes to stress over and over again the example of the French Minitel system (e.g., Feenberg 2010, chapter 5; 2002, 118–120), which was turned by hackers from an information system that functioned as electronic directory into a communication system. "The cool new information medium was transformed into a hot electronic singles bar" (Feenberg 2012, 7). Feenberg's stress is on how users and civil society appropriated technology and redesigned it. He gives much less stress to the fact that the hardware and infrastructure was introduced by the nationalised communications monopoly Poste, Téléphone, et Télécommunications, which did not have a for-profit imperative. Advertising and commerce therefore did not dominate the system, which is likely to have made it easier for users to develop and establish an alternative design. State and civil society interacted in order to create a public service information system that was put to alternative communicative uses.

There is no doubt that any state contains inherent power asymmetries and that bureaucracies have a tendency to accumulate power and become intransparent. But it is a wrong logical inference to conclude from the realities of the Soviet state that there cannot be a democratic state that helps in the transition from capitalism to socialism. The problems are the capitalist and the authoritarian state, but not any state as such. Socialist politics are at a strategic disadvantage when they do not struggle for power, forming governments, and changing laws within parliamentary democracy. Feenberg speaks, for example, of the "democratization of work" (Feenberg 2002, 17), but simply forming worker and consumer cooperatives won't do. There must also be laws that regulate working conditions and also create a legal framework for self-managed companies, corporate taxation, welfare, minimum wages, and maximum working hours, as well as securing and strengthening the rights of trade unions, etc. Activism and parties can under current conditions not avoid the state; they have at least to make demands to it—otherwise their politics become completely idealist. If a left-wing political mediation of parties and movements, the state and civil society, can be maintained, then the likelihood is greater that in a socialist society the state is not a reified institution, but can be transformed into a participatory democracy as part of the transition process.

Feenberg advances a purely negative, anarchistic notion of the state. I do, however, also not think that states governed by socialist parties are the solution. The Left needs alliances between social movements and political parties, nonparliamentary and parliamentary opposition, civil society and the state as part of a politics of radical reformism that advances legal changes and institutional reforms in order to improve the conditions and resources for social struggles and social movements. A socialist state as part of a socialist transition does not necessarily take on a life of its own. The likelihood that it does can be reduced if both social movements and parties strive to be connected and independent, and in dialogue at the same time.

The point is to work simultaneously inside and outside of the established institutions and to keep constant communication between and networking of the inside and the outside so that one can work inside the institutions to transform them and strengthen the outside so that the institutions turn themselves inside out and open up resources for revolution. The interaction of parties and movements and of organisation and grassroots activity are not sufficient but necessary conditions for revolution and the creation of a society that fully enables democratic politics and democratic technology.

The grassroots character of social movements is part of their prefigurative politics. Given that social movements often lack resources and time (also activists have to work in order to earn a living), grassroots democracy and endless discussions can, however, also be limiting, weaken movements and result in sectarianism, new forms of control and hierarchies. Some form of hierarchy that is democratically elected and accountable can depending on the resource situation therefore also be supportive for social movements when having to organise within the realities of capitalist precarity. Feenberg does not account for the antagonisms that alternative projects and movements face, which is a disservice for radical politics.

Herbert Marcuse: Organised Spontaneity

Feenberg's doctoral advisor Herbert Marcuse understood the importance of a dialectic of movements and parties better than his student. He argued that political spontaneity could only work if it was organised spontaneity. The "process of internal disintegration may well assume a largely decentralized, diffuse, largely 'spontaneous' character, occurring at several places simultaneously or by 'contagion'. However, such points of local dysfunctioning and disruption can become nuclei of social change only if they are given political direction and organization" (Marcuse 1972, 42).

A contemporary reading of Hegel and Marx can inspire us to avoid ending up with a dualist theory of technology and can be a help and foundation for creating dialectical critical theories of technology.

15.12. Conclusion

Chapter 15 is *Capital Volume 1*'s longest chapter. Its 10 sections are a rich source of information and theory that analyses the antagonistic role of technology in the capitalist mode of production.

We can summarise some of the main results of Marx's description of large-scale industry's impacts in capitalism. Modern technology has impacts on all elements of the capital accumulation cycle M–C.. P..C'–M'.

Technology's Impacts on the Whole Capital Accumulation Cycle M—C.. P—C'—M' and Class Relations

- *New economic sectors*: Communications and transport emerged as important economic sectors of capitalism. The machine-producing industry emerged.
- *Class struggles*: Class struggles between capital and labour emerge, such as the Luddite movement, which destroyed machines.
- *Legal and parliamentary demands and changes*: Class struggles result in demands for the legal regulation of working conditions and the limitation of the power of capital. Historically, the Factory Acts improved working, social, educational, and health conditions in the capitalist economy, and these conditions had to be forced upon capital by state power. The welfare state was a historical achievement of the working class' struggles against capital.
- *Capital's evasion of laws that limit its power*: Capital tries to evade laws that limit its power in order to reduce wages and increase the exploitation of labour so that it can increase profits.
- *The antagonism of productive forces and relations of production*: Technology in capitalism is an antagonistic means: It is both a means of exploitation and a means that fosters communist potentials. It is at the heart of the antagonism between productive forces and class relations. Modern technology "ripens both the elements for forming a new society and the forces tending towards the overthrow of the old one" (635).
- *Imperialism and the international division of labour*: Changes of the mode of production induce imperialism and an international division of labour. Colonies are sources of cheap raw materials, cheap labour, and markets for the sale of commodities.
- *Economic crisis*: Modern technology is embedded into the crisis cycle of capitalism; it advances both boom and bust, and thereby the increase and decrease of unemployment. Modern technology both attracts and repulses labour—that is, creates new jobs and destroys existing ones so that workers are thrown into and out of labour.

- *Contradictory effects on the rate of profit*: Increased technology use has antagonistic effects on the organic composition of capital and the rate of surplus-value. Both tend to increase and both have effects on the profit rate.
- *Uprooting of economic sectors based on physical labour*: Home work in the domestic industry and the manufactory were uprooted and substituted by large-scale production that concentrates workers and machines in workshops and brings about a new division of labour in which people operate different machines that are connected to a machine system (cooperation of machines).

Technology's Impact on M—C (Purchase of Labour-Power and the Means of Production)

- *Employment*: New technologies can temporally induce an increasing demand for labour in newly emerging and growing industries. Once the growth potentials are satisfied, these industries stagnate and experience cost-cutting, rationalisation, and downsizing.
- *Say's law is false*: Technologies have contradictory effects on employment and unemployment. It is unlikely that automated labour can be compensated ("Say's law") because the value of newly created labour-power tends to be lower than the one that is put out of work, there are negative rebound effects (reduced consumption as a result of unemployment harms the consumer good industry), and there are skills gaps.
- *Nature and science*: Capital has subsumed the natural forces and science as means of production.
- *Machinery substitutes labour-power*: "The productivity of the machine is therefore measured by the human labour-power it replaces" (513).
- *Child and women's labour*: Machinery makes labour physically less demanding so that more women and children are employed conducting relatively monotonous labour.
- *The inversion of the role of subject and object, labour-power and machinery*: Capitalism is "converting the worker into a living appendage of the machine" (614). The role of subject and object in the production process are inverted: Humans become objects subsumed under capital's control of technology. Technology is then an automaton that alienates humans from the work process.
- *Alienation and de-alienation*: Large-scale industry alienates labour and at the same time develops potentials for the "totally developed individual" (618) and the abolishment of the division of labour.
- *Rural life and agriculture*: Large-scale industry uproots rural life and agriculture, which results in the transformation of peasants into wageworkers; they leave the countryside and move to metropolises, where they become wageworkers, so that urbanisation is an inherent tendency of capitalism.

Technology's Impact on P (Commodity Production)

- *Monotony*: Factory labour is monotonous and intellectually alienating.
- *Transition from absolute to relative surplus-value production*: The introduction of machinery first results in a heavy lengthening of the working day that reaches physical and economic limits. The result is the struggle for legal limits of the working day that fostered the transition from absolute to relative surplus-value production so that productivity increases are achieved by the technification of production.
- *Acceleration and surveillance of production*: Another way capitalists increase the rate of surplus-value in a relative manner is that the speed of labour is accelerated by surveillance, control, and increasing the speed at which machines are running.
- *Health impacts of capitalist production*: Absolute and relative surplus-value productive have negative impacts on workers' health.

- *Overaccumulation and overproduction*: Overinvestment of capital and overproduction of commodities.
- *Nature and work*: Capitalism and capitalist technology advance the exploitation of the worker and the destruction of nature—they undermine "the original sources of all wealth—the soil and the worker" (638).

Technology's Impact on C'—M' (Commodity Sale)

- *Global markets*: Large-scale industry and modern technologies bring about revolutions of the means of transport and communication so that new global and international markets for commodity sales can be developed.
- *Means of transport and the acceleration of sales*: Large-scale industry brings about new means of transport that accelerate the sales process by allowing delivering commodities from one place to another more quickly.
- *Means of communication and the acceleration of circulation*: Large-scale industry brings about new means of communication that allow accelerating not just the production process, but also the sales and distribution process, as the example of Amazon shows.

The Productive Forces

The productive forces are a system in which subjective productive forces (human labour-power) make use of technical productive forces (part of the objective productive forces) in order to transform parts of the natural productive forces (which are also part of the objective productive forces) so that a labour product emerges. The goal of the development of the system of productive forces is to increase the productivity of labour—that is, the output (amount of products) that labour generates per unit of time. Marx therefore defined the concept of the development of the productive forces (= the increase of the productivity of labour) as "an alteration in the labour process of such a kind as to shorten the labour-time socially necessary for the production of a [. . .] [good], and to endow a given quantity of labour with the power of producing a greater quantity of use-value" (431).

Within capitalist relations of production, the productive forces are not just means for producing human wealth and use-values—they are means for the exploitation of the labour of the proletariat and for intensifying this exploitation so that more labour is exploited per unit of time, which results in the production of more commodities in the same time period and in the creation of more surplus-value and more profit. Marx therefore speaks of the capitalist antagonism between the productive forces and the relations of production. Within "the capitalist system all methods for raising the social productivity of labour are put into effect at the cost of the individual worker; [. . .] all means for the development of production undergo a dialectical inversion so that they become means of domination and exploitation of the producers" (799).

Do We Live in an Information Society?

Marx's distinction between productive forces and relations of production can help to better understand the discussion about the information society. Speaking of the emergence of a postindustrial, knowledge, network, or information society describes changes of the productive forces: Knowledge and information technology have become important means for producing commodities that serve the purpose of capital accumulation. It is a mistake to characterise this transformation as radical discontinuity or new society because the economy not only consists of the productive forces but also of the interaction of productive forces and relations of production or what Marx termed the "mode of production".

A main objection to the information society hypothesis, which postulates the emergence of an information society, is that we still live in a class or capitalist society. This objection wants to warn that an explanation that reduces the contemporary economy to the changes of the productive forces obscures the continued existence of capitalist class relations, which are exploitative in character. The argument is that such a reductionism constitutes an ideology that celebrates contemporary society and conceals and denies that changes of the productive forces take place within, advance, and are driven by relations of exploitation.

The General Intellect

Capitalism and the information economy are dialectically connected: The networked and informational productive forces are an outcome of capitalist development and the capitalist drive to increase productivity. Marx knew that capitalism permanently tries to overthrow the productive forces in order to be able to accumulate ever more capital by technically intensifying the exploitation of labour. In the *Grundrisse*, he predicted the emergence of informational productive forces as the result of the development of fixed capital—that is, the increasing technical and organic composition of capital that is characterised by an increase of the role of technology in production at the expense of living labour-power. Marx in this context introduces the notion of the general intellect, by which he means knowledge's social and economic role:

> The development of fixed capital indicates to what degree general social knowledge has become a direct force of production, and to what degree, hence, the conditions of the process of social life itself have come under the control of the general intellect and been transformed in accordance with it. To what degree the powers of social production have been produced, not only in the form of knowledge, but also as immediate organs of social practice, of the real life process. (Marx 1857/1858, 706)

Marx argued that by technological development "the entire production process" becomes "the technological application of science" (Marx 1857/1858, 699). The "transformation of the production process from the simple labour process into a scientific process [...]" appears as a quality of fixed capital in contrast to living labour" (Marx 1857/1858, 700). So for Marx, the rise of informational productive forces was immanently connected to capital's need for finding technical ways that allow accumulating more profits. That society has to a certain degree become informational is just like the discourse about this circumstance a result of the development of capitalism.

Marx stresses in the *Grundrisse* that technology is objectified scientific knowledge and that therefore with the rising organic composition of capital during the course of the development of the productive forces the knowledge character of the economy and society increases:

> The accumulation of knowledge and of skill, of the general productive forces of the social brain, is thus absorbed into capital, as opposed to labour, and hence appears as an attribute of capital, and more specifically of fixed capital, in so far as it enters into the production process as a means of production proper. Machinery appears, then, as the most adequate form of fixed capital, and fixed capital, in so far as capital's relations with itself are concerned, appears as the most adequate form of capital as such. [. . .] Further, in so far as machinery develops with the accumulation of society's science, of productive force generally, general social labour presents itself not in labour but in capital. The productive force of society is measured in fixed capital, exists there in its objective form; and, inversely, the productive force of capital grows with this general progress, which capital appropriates free of charge. (Marx 1857/1858, 694–695)

The Antagonistic Character of Modern Science and Technology

Marx also points out in the *Grundrisse* the antagonistic character of modern science and technology that he discusses in *Capital Volume 1*'s chapter 15. It on the one hand increases the organic composition of capital and makes labour ever more superfluous, but on the other hand capitalism depends on the exploitation of labour so that modern technology calls forth an antagonism between labour and time and between necessary labour-time and surplus labour-time:

> Capital itself is the moving contradiction, [in] that it presses to reduce labour time to a minimum, while it posits labour time, on the other side, as sole measure and source of wealth. Hence it diminishes labour time in the necessary form so as to increase it in the superfluous form; hence posits the superfluous in growing measure as a condition—question of life or death—for the necessary. On the one side, then, it calls to life all the powers of science and of nature, as of social combination and of social intercourse, in order to make the creation of wealth independent (relatively) of the labour time employed on it. On the other side, it wants to use labour time as the measuring rod for the giant social forces thereby created, and to confine them within the limits required to maintain the already created value as value. Forces of production and social relations—two different sides of the development of the social individual—appear to capital as mere means, and are merely means for it to produce on its limited foundation. In fact, however, they are the material conditions to blow this foundation sky-high. (Marx 1857/1858, 706)

This contradiction between the means of production and the capitalist class relations creates communist potentials. Marx imagines how a communist society would look and stresses the importance of technology in it:

> The surplus labour of the mass has ceased to be the condition for the development of general wealth, just as the non-labour of the few, for the development of the general powers of the human head. With that, production based on exchange value breaks down, and the direct, material production process is stripped of the form of penury and antithesis. The free development of individualities, and hence not the reduction of necessary labour time so as to posit surplus labour, but rather the general reduction of the necessary labour of society to a minimum, which then corresponds to the artistic, scientific etc. development of the individuals in the time set free, and with the means created, for all of them. (Marx 1857/1858, 705–706)
>
> Once they have done so—and disposable time thereby ceases to have an antithetical existence—then, on one side, necessary labour time will be measured by the needs of the social individual, and, on the other, the development of the power of social production will grow so rapidly that, even though production is now calculated for the wealth of all, disposable time will grow for all. For real wealth is the developed productive power of all individuals. The measure of wealth is then not any longer, in any way, labour time, but rather disposable time. (Marx 1857/1858, 708)

One of the main insights of Marx in *Capital Volume 1*'s chapter 15 that was already in 1857/1858 formulated in the *Grundrisse* is that modern technology in capitalism extends and intensifies labour, whereas it as the same time fosters communist potentials for the reduction of labour time for all to a minimum. In capitalism, technological changes under capital relations result in the tendency that some work longer hours and others to work precariously or become unemployed. There is a mismatch in the distribution of labour.

Radovan Richta: The Scientific-Technological Revolution

Radovan Richta (1924–1983) was a Marxist philosopher from the Czech Republic. He edited the report "Civilization at the Crossroads" (Richta 1969), which analysed the contradictory role of informatisation in modern society and introduced the notion of the scientific-technological revolution. Richta thereby introduced a Marxist version of the information society hypothesis that was much influenced by Marx's *Grundrisse*:

> In the light of these realities, capital itself appears as a persisting contradiction—on the one hand, it extends work on all sides; on the other, it endeavours to reduce necessary work to a minimum. It mobilizes the forces of science, social combinations, etc., in order to "make the creation of wealth independent of the labour time", while "it wants to measure the enormous social forces so created in terms of labour time". The faster the progress of structural changes in the productive forces, the more the further formation of wealth appears to depend not directly on the amount of labour used, but on the power of factors that are being set in motion in this process and "whose powerful effectiveness itself bears no relationship to the actual labour time required for their production, but depends much more on the general state of science and the progress of technology". (Richta 1969, 82)

The scientific-technological revolution would have negative effects in class societies and require a humanist socialist society as a foundation for having positive effects and being shaped into the right direction:

> By its inner logic the scientific and technological revolution points to the possibility of superseding the old industrial division of labour and replacing it by a conscious organization of human cooperation, where the conflict between operating and managing activity is done away with, the general and prime function of all is the application of science, the split between the intellectual forces of production and labour, between physical and mental work, disappears—where, in short, one and all can affirm themselves through creative activity, whatever form it may assume. (Richta 1969, 127)
>
> When the lives of each and every man reach such a level that the creative self-realization of each, man's development for its own sake, will be a means for the development of others, only then will society overcome the contradiction of means and ends, escape from mere mutual dependence and ultimately be able to convert the universal interconnection and cooperation among human beings into relationships in which the free development of each is the condition for the free development of all—relationships which alone can provide the true communist dimension. (Richta 1969, 164)
>
> Judging by the findings of modern anthropology and psychology, mass participation in the scientific and technological revolution (linking work and education, etc.) could be practicable when the disposable time reaches a level of about 30 hours a week, i.e., three times more than today (and later it would have to be even more). This would mean introducing the 30-hour working week, with about 40 weeks of work a year; and an even more drastic reduction of time expended on reproducing labour power (to about 15 hours a week)—a situation that according to various prognoses, can be expected towards the end of the century. Disposable time would then be the leading component in human life; new powers of man and the community would spring from leisure time, signifying a radical shift in the boundaries of human potentialities and the imperatives of life. (Richta 1969, 174)

The discussion shows that the antagonistic character of modern technology that Marx describes in chapter 15 has historically been of crucial relevance in the emergence of informational/

computerised/networked productive forces that have arisen from the development of the productive forces and the associated rise of the organic composition of capital.

Exercises for Chapter 15

Group exercise (G)
Project exercise (P)

Key Categories: Machine System, Motor Mechanism, Transmission Mechanism, Working Machine, Commons, Moral Depreciation, Dialectic of Absolute and Relative Surplus-Value Production, Inversion of Means and Aims, Luddism, Machine-Breaking, Technological Fetishism, International Division of Labour, Colonies, Means of Communication as Means of Acceleration, Education in Capitalism and Communism, Totally Developed/Well-Rounded Individual, the Antagonism between Productive Forces and Relations of Production, Environmental Destruction

Exercise 15.1 (section 15.1) (G)

Marx in section 15.1 introduces the term "machine system" and also talks about the emergence of new means of communication in the age of large-scale industry.

Work in groups: Conduct a search for different applications of the computer in society. Document the computer's different purposes. After you have come up with a list, classify each purpose/application so that it becomes evident if the computer is used as a means of information, communication, cooperation, production of use-values, or a combination of several of these functions.

Search for literature that defines what a computer is and come up with a concise definition. Think about devices that you use in everyday life—which ones of them are computers? What makes them a computer? What are the necessary elements of a computer?

Exercise 15.2 (section 15.2) (G)

In section 15.2, Marx introduces the idea that knowledge, science, and nature are common goods that cost the capitalist almost nothing, but that s/he uses without payment.

Discuss: How important are the commons in society today? Try to construct a typology of common goods and make a list with examples for each kind of common. What is the role of science and technology in society's commons? What is the connection of the commons and capital?

Are there potentials of knowledge commons that point beyond capitalism? If so, can you give some examples? What contradictions does knowledge face in capitalism?

What is the role of the knowledge commons on the Internet? Does the common encyclopaedic knowledge published on Wikipedia make Wikipedia a communist project? If so, then in which respect is this the case? If not, then why is this not the case? What are characteristics of communist knowledge projects?

Exercise 15.3 (section 15.3) (G)

In section 15.3, Marx introduces the notion of moral depreciation of technologies and commodities.

Work in groups: Each group chooses a communication technology that has high symbolic status. Analyse and document how advertisements (print, text, images, videos, online) for the newest version of this technology present themselves as forward-looking, modern, and future-oriented. What kind of ideologies and symbols are used, and what are the connoted meanings they have? How is the commodity presented as being different from and better than older versions or comparable commodities?

Reflect on how the symbolic reputation of commodities and advertising ideologies contribute to the moral depreciation of technologies and commodities.

Exercise 15.4 (section 15.4) (G)

In section 15.4, Marx describes how technology in capitalism is no longer a means to an end, but how it as part of the end of capital accumulation turns the worker into an appendage of capital and the machine.

The computer enables new forms of workplace control and surveillance.

Work in groups: Conduct a search for a software application that can be used for monitoring what workers do on their computers and on the Internet. Go to the website of the company that produces this software and document how it advertises this product and what kind of ideological language it uses for presenting the surveillance of workers in a positive light.

Present the results.

Exercise 15.5 (section 15.4) (P)

Marx in chapter 15 points out that working conditions in 19th-century factories were very poor. Highly exploitative factory labour still exists in the 21st century, also in the manufacturing and assemblage of communication technologies.

Read the following article, which presents a typology of working conditions and applies this classification for studying labour conditions in the Chinese Foxconn factories that assemble Apple computers and phones:

Sandoval, Marisol. 2013. Foxconned labour as the dark side of the information age: Working conditions at Apple's contract manufacturers in China. *tripleC: Communication, Capitalism & Critique* 11 (2): 318–347.

Work individually or in groups and present the work's results.

The Forbes 2000 list is published annually. It is a ranking of the world's largest companies. Have a look at the dominant transnational corporations that produce computer hardware, consumer electronics, and electronics and make a list of these companies.

China Labor Watch "is an independent not-for-profit organization" that "has collaborated with unions, labor organizations and the media to conduct a series of in-depth assessments of factories in China that produce toys, bikes, shoes, furniture, clothing, and electronics for some of the largest U.S. companies".[4]

Students and Scholars against Corporate Misbehaviour (SACOM) "aims at bringing concerned students, scholars, labor activists, and consumers together to monitor corporate behavior and to advocate for workers' rights. [. . .] We believe that the most effective means of monitoring is to collaborate closely with workers at the workplace level. We team up with labor NGOs to provide in-factory training to workers in South China".[5]

China Labor Watch and SACOM publish reports about the working conditions in large capitalist companies operating in China. Search on the two websites for reports and analyses that are about the ICT, hardware, and electronics companies you found in the Forbes 2000 list. Make a list of poor working conditions that you identify. For each company, classify the working conditions by making use of Marisol Sandoval's typology.

Exercise 15.6 (section 15.5) (G)

In section 15.5, Marx discusses the Luddite movement.

Read Edward P. Thompson's historical analysis of Luddism in Britain:

Thompson, Edward P. 1966. Chapter XIV: An Army of Redressers. In *The making of the English working class*, 472–602. New York: Vintage Books.

Work in groups: Each group identifies one contemporary political movement or group for which modern communication technology plays an important role and that wants to transform technology.

Ask yourself the following questions:

> What problems of modern communication technology does the movement identify?
> Why does it think these problems exist?
> What kind of solutions to these problems does the movement propagate?
> What are commonalities and differences of the analysed movement/group's propagated politics of technology and the Luddite movement?
> What can be features and qualities of 21st-century versions of Luddism? How is it related to the working-class movement?

Each group presents its results.

Exercise 15.7 (section 15.6) (P)

Marx introduces a critique of technological fetishism in section 15.6 that he opposes with the help of a dialectical concept of technology.

Work in groups: Each group analyses one specific business publication (e.g., *Bloomberg*, *Financial Times*, *International Business Times*, *The Economic Times*, *The Economist*, *Wall Street Journal*). Observe the publications' technology/computing/digital media/online section for a week and count how many of the articles are overall technologically fetishist. Analyse why this is the case. Discuss how a dialectical analysis of these media phenomena could look and what needs to happen in order to sublate this technology's antagonism between potentials and existence.

Exercise 15.8 (section 15.9) (G)

Marx points out in section 15.9 how capitalism has negative impacts on educational opportunities. Education in capitalism remains an issue of class in the 21st century.

Search for statistics and analyses of the educational system (primary, secondary, higher education) in the country you currently live in or another country. Document if there are differences in educational attainment that relate to the social class background of young people's families. Discuss where such differences come from, why they exist, and how they can be overcome.

Exercise 15.9 (section 15.9) (G)

In section 15.9, Marx discusses how modern technology constitutes foundations for the emergence of the "totally developed individual" (618) and the abolition of the division of labour's abolition.

Discuss: How could a good life for all look and be organised? What is the role of technology? How could a "totally developed individual" look like today? What hinders humans to be full humans within capitalism? What are the structural barriers that do not allow full human development and flourishing? What is the role of technology in setting up and enforcing such limits? How is the totally developed individual in a communist society related to modern technology and automation?

Exercise 15.10 (section 15.9) (G)

Marx discusses in section 15.9 how the age of modern technology within capitalism "ripens both the elements for forming a new society and the forces tending towards the overthrow of the old one" (635).

Discuss: Which communist forces and seeds exist and germinate within contemporary capitalism? What is the role of technologies in the development of these forces? What limits them? How can these limits be overcome? How would a full development of these forces look in a communist society?

Exercise 15.11 (section 15.9) (P)

In section 15.9, Marx discusses the antagonism between the productive forces and class relations. A 21st-century expression of this antagonism is the conflict between (a) those who argue that culture should be a common good freely available to all and that peer-to-peer sharing on the Internet should therefore be legal and without costs to users, and (b) the music and film industry that wants to commodify culture and has sought to sue sharing platforms such as Napster and the Pirate Bay. Artists take a contradictory role in this conflict because on the one hand they are wageworkers exploited by industry and on the other hand in capitalism depend on income generated by their art form.

Conduct a search and document the positions that representatives of the following four groups hold on this issue:

(a) The music and recording industry
(b) Peer-to-peer and Torrent sharing platforms
(c) Different political parties and groups (including Pirate Parties, left/socialist parties, etc.)
(d) Artists and artists' associations

Document and discuss the differences between these positions. What solutions are there to the antagonism between the networked productive forces of the Internet and capitalist class relations? Why can it not be solved within capitalism? Which of the documented positions capture the full complexity of the antagonism and which ones do not?

Exercise 15.12 (Section 15.10) (G or P)

Work in groups: Conduct a search and document environmental crimes in which transnational corporations have polluted the environment.

Discuss what the sources of these crimes are, how environmental crimes and capitalism are related, and what needs to be done in order to overcome environmental degradation.

Notes

1 Data source: http://www.statista.com/statistics/267468/average-mobile-pc-lifespan/ (accessed on February 12, 2014).
2 http://suicidemachine.org/#faq (accessed on August 13, 2014).
3 https://www.youtube.com/watch?v=CXWJ4GfQ22E (accessed on August 18, 2014).
4 http://www.chinalaborwatch.org/aboutus.html (accessed on August 12, 2014).
5 http://sacom.hk/about-us/ (accessed on August 12, 2014).

PART V

THE PRODUCTION OF ABSOLUTE AND RELATIVE SURPLUS-VALUE

Marx focuses on absolute surplus-value production in part III and analyses relative surplus-value production in section IV. Part V is a dialectical unity of part III and part IV: It discusses the unity, relationship, and combination of absolute and relative surplus-value production.

16

ABSOLUTE AND RELATIVE SURPLUS-VALUE

Absolute and Relative Surplus-Value

In chapter 16, Marx analyses the relationship of absolute and relative surplus-value production. Absolute surplus-value production means the "prolongation of the working day beyond the point at which the worker would have produced an exact equivalent for the value of his labour-power" (645). Relative surplus-value production implies that "the necessary labour is shortened by methods for producing the equivalent of the wage of labour in a shorter time" (645). The first method is focused on the length of the working day; the second "completely revolutionizes the technical process of labour" (645). Marx terms "absolute surplus-value production" also the "formal subsumption of labour under capital and relative surplus-value production" the real subsumption of labour under capital (645).

The Formal and Real Subsumption of Labour under Capital

In formal subsumption, spheres and/or activities that are not under the control of capital become spheres shaped by capitalism, but their content does not change. In real subsumption, already subsumed activities or spaces are substantially changed so that the productivity and intensity of labour is transformed.

Marx discusses the notions of formal and real subsumption in detail in the "Results of the Immediate Process of Production". This text is printed as appendix in the Penguin edition of *Capital Volume*. I refer the reader to it and also to my discussion of it in section 27.2 of this book.

Relative surplus-value production is absolute because there is a part of the working day split off from necessary labour–time—namely, surplus labour-time—so that the working day is absolutely longer than necessary labour-time (646). Absolute surplus-value is relative because it operates with the distinction between necessary and surplus labour-time, which stand in a relation to each other (646). Although there is a dialectic of both absolute and relative dimensions of surplus-value, absolute and relative surplus-value production are two distinct methods of increasing the rate of surplus-value (646). Absolute surplus-value production is the foundation of capitalism and the "starting-point for the production of relative surplus-value" (645). In chapter 15, Marx shows that historically the introduction of large-scale industry for increasing relative surplus-value production by increasing productivity resulted in a lengthening of the working day because capitalists wanted to gain as much surplus-labour as possible in the more productive sectors and so lengthened the working day. Only class struggle and as a consequence state legislation put limits on the length of the working day.

Nature and the Productive Forces

Marx distinguishes between two dimensions of the natural productive forces: (a) "natural wealth in the means of subsistence i.e. a fruitful soil, waters teeming with fish, etc.", and (b) "natural wealth in the instruments of labour, such as waterfalls, navigable rivers, wood, metal, coal, etc." (649). He argues that more favourable natural conditions in a region can result in higher productivity, but also points out that the more industrialisation advances, the less such natural influences play a role.

Marx says that different types of economies have varying sources of wealth: "At the dawn of civilization, it is the first class that turns the scale; at a higher stage of development, it is the second" (648). In a society in which the productive forces are predominantly agricultural (agricultural economy), nature plays a more important role than in one where industry or information play are more relevant. In many 21st century societies, information work has become an important part and sector of the economy. Nature, industry, and information are three important forms of wealth in the 21st century.

Three Levels of Productive Labour

Marx also discusses the notion of productive labour in chapter 16. He discusses three levels or forms of productive labour. He also points out this notion in the "Results of the Immediate Process of Production", a text printed in the appendix of the Penguin edition of *Capital Volume 1*. I therefore refer the reader to the "Results" and my discussion of it in section 27.3 of this book.

Productive labour (1): The first definition of productive labour is that all work that creates use-values is productive: "If we look at the whole process from the point of view of its result, the product, it is plain that both the instruments and the object of labour are means of production and that the labour itself is productive labour" (Marx 1867, 287).

Productive labour (2): Marx's second definition is that labour is productive if it produces surplus-value for the capitalist:

> Yet the concept of productive labour also becomes narrower. Capitalist production is not merely the production of commodities, it is, by its very essence, the production of surplus-value. The worker produces not for himself, but for capital. It is no longer sufficient, therefore, for him simply to produce. He must produce surplus-value. The only worker who is productive is one who produces surplus-value for the capitalist, or in other words contributes towards the self-valorization of capital. (644)

Marx gives an example for productive labour (2): A "schoolmaster is a productive worker when, in addition to belabouring the heads of his pupils, he works himself into the ground to enrich the owner of the school. That the latter has laid out his capital in a teaching factory, instead of a sausage factory, makes no difference to the relation" (644). A teacher working in a public schools, which is tax-funded, is for Marx a productive worker (1), but not a productive labourer (2) because s/he does not create profit for the capitalist. A productive labourer (2) is "capital's direct means of valorization" (644).

One should not forget that Marx in the discussion of productive labour (2) in chapter 15 does not say that wage-labour is a necessary condition of productive labour (2). This means that also unpaid labour in class relations can be productive labour (2) if the outcome is surplus-value and profit. An example is that a capitalist operates within slave class relations—that is, s/he own the bodies and minds of the slaves, and does not pay any wages. Another example is unpaid prosumption (productive consumption), where consumers create value for capitalists, as in the case of Ikea furniture, where consumers assemble the furniture themselves; self-service gas stations, where consumers replace the labour of a filling station attendant; and fast food restaurants such as McDonalds, where the customers are their own waiters. All of these kinds of labour contribute to the creation of value and profit and are completely unpaid.

Productive Labour and the Collective Labourer (*Gesamtarbeiter*)

Productive labour (3) is labour of the combined or collective labourer (what Marx in German calls "Gesamtarbeiter"). It encompasses all labour that contributes to the production of surplus-value and capital. Marx stresses that work is not an individual process. The more cooperative and networked work becomes, which is the consequence of the technification of capitalism and the rise of knowledge in production, the more relevant is Marx's third understanding of productive labour. The more cooperative the labour process and the economy become and the more the division of labour is extended, the more different forms of labour are needed for bringing about one specific commodity. Marx analyses this networked and cooperative dimension of modern labour with the notion of the collective labourer:

> The solitary man cannot operate upon nature without calling his own muscles into play under the control of his own brain. Just as head and hand belong together in the system of nature, so in the labour process mental and physical labour are united. Later on they become separate; and this separation develops into a hostile antagonism.[1] The product is transformed from the direct product of the individual producer into a social product, the joint product of a collective labourer, i.e. a combination of workers, each of whom stands at a different distance from the actual manipulation of the object of labour. With the progressive accentuation of the co-operative character of the labour process, there necessarily occurs a progressive extension of the concept of productive labour, and of the concept of the bearer of that labour, the productive worker. In order to work productively, it is no longer necessary for the individual himself to put his hand to the object; it is sufficient for him to be an organ of the collective labourer, and to perform any one of its subordinate functions. The definition of productive labour given above, the original definition, is derived from the nature of material production itself, and it remains correct for the collective labourer, considered as a whole. But it no longer holds good for each member taken individually. (643–644)

The question that arises is where the collective labourer ends. The boundary could be drawn at the level of an individual factory, an industry, or society as a whole. The latter is stressed by Autonomist Marxists, who speak of the emergence of a social factory, a notion that was first introduced by Mario Tronti (1962).

The Collective Labourer and the *Grundrisse*

The notion of the collective labourer becomes more important with the development of fixed capital and productivity. With rising productivity, a growing "part of production time is sufficient for immediate production" (Marx 1857/1858, 707). It therefore becomes possible for society "to employ this part for labour which is not immediately productive (within the material production process itself). This requires a certain level of productivity and of relative overabundance, and, more specifically, a level directly related to the transformation of circulating capital into fixed capital" (Marx 1857/1858, 707). Surplus labour can be used for the production of fixed capital and circulating capital, for example, "to build railways, canals, aqueducts, telegraphs etc." (Marx 1857/1858, 707).

The socialisation of labour that is expressed in the collective labourer expresses itself in the antagonism of the productive forces and the relations of production that anticipates the emergence of communism, in which disposable time is the measure of wealth: Once the "mass of workers [...] appropriate their own surplus labour", "disposable time will grow for all. For real wealth is the developed productive power of all individuals. The measure of wealth is then not any longer, in any way, labour time, but rather disposable time" (Marx 1857/1858, 708). Only human practice can realise the potential for communism. There is no automatism of history because capitalism's "tendency [is] always, on the one side, to create disposable time, on the other, to convert it into surplus labour" (Marx 1857/1858, 708).

If there is labour that is productive, then there must also be some that is "unproductive". The distinction between productive and unproductive labour is not just an analytical but also a political tool that identifies important and unimportant actors in class struggles that can bring about transformations of society. The notion of unproductive labour carries the connotation that those who are signified as such are unimportant, peripheral, or even parasitic elements in political change processes that are necessary for overcoming capitalism.

Marxist Feminism, Reproductive Labour, and Productive Labour

Marxist feminists have long resisted the reduction of housework to peripheral, secondary, or unproductive activities. They have argued that reproductive work in capitalism is productive labour. A few examples shall illustrate this circumstance, although this chapter does not allow space for a detailed discussion. The Marxist feminists Mariarosa Dalla Costa and Selma James (1972, 30) challenged the orthodox Marxist assumption that reproductive work is "outside social productivity". In contrast a socialist feminist position would have to argue that "domestic work produces not merely use values, but is essential to the production of surplus value" and that the "productivity of wage slavery" is "based on unwaged slavery" in the form of productive "social services which capitalist organization transforms into privatized activity, putting them on the backs of housewives" (Dalla Costa and James 1972, 31). The Marxist feminist Zillah Eisenstein (1979, 31) argues that the gender division of labour guarantees "a free labor pool" and "a cheap labor pool".

The Marxist feminist Maria Mies (1986, 37) says that women are exploited in a triple sense: "they are exploited [...] by men and they are exploited as housewives by capital. If they are wage-workers they are also exploited as wage-workers". Capitalist production would be based on the "*superexploitation* of non-wage labourers (women, colonies, peasants) upon which wage labour exploitation then is possible. I define their exploitation as super-exploitation because it is not based on the appropriation (by the capitalist) of the time and labour over and above the 'necessary' labour time, the *surplus* labour, but of the time and labour *necessary* for people's own survival or subsistence production. It is not compensated for by a wage" (Mies 1986, 48).

Mies also reminds us that female productivity is the precondition of male productivity in the sense that "women *at all times* will be the producers of new women and men, and [...] without this production all other forms and modes of production lose their sense" (Mies 1986, 58). Subsistence production would create the basic use-values for human survival—it would produce life itself. It would largely be women's nonwage labour that produces life and is thereby productive for capital (Mies 1986, 50).

Leopoldina Fortunati (1995) argues that reproductive labour is productive because "it produces and reproduces the individual as a commodity" (70) by "producing and reproducing labor-power" (70) and "the use-value of labor-power" (69).

The notion of the collective labourer [productive labour (3)] stresses the importance of reproductive and other unpaid labour for the existence of capitalism. Reproductive labour reproduces labour-power. If capital had to pay for all the labour performed in the household and financed by the state (that is in most countries predominantly financed out of taxes on wages and not profits), then its profits would be much lower. Unremunerated reproductive labour drives up the profits of capital; it is a gratis resource that capital exploits, but that it does not or hardly pay for.

The Role of Reproductive Labour: An Example

Value is the average amount of time it takes to produce a commodity. Labour-power is a necessary constituent for the existence of value, the commodity, and profit. It does not simply exist, but needs to be permanently reproduced by reproductive labour. The average number of hours required for the reproduction of labour power must therefore be taken into account when calculating the value of a commodity. An example is as follows: It takes on average 10 labourers working each an hour to produce a car. We assume they have an average hourly wage of £10 and that the average profit that can be achieved per car is £900. The relationship of surplus to necessary labour is therefore 900 / 100 = 9. This shows that unpaid labour is in this case nine times as large as paid labour. Going back from the price to the value level, this means that in the example only 6 minutes per hour are paid and 54 minutes are unpaid. Given the combined labour of 10 workers needed for the production of one car, we have a total of 540 minutes of unpaid labour for the production of one car. We also assume that they all have families in which women are responsible for all the housework. So the capitalist not just consumes 540 minutes of unpaid labour for the production of one car, but also 10 times 1 hour = 10 hours of unpaid reproductive labour, which constitutes and re-creates the labour power of the 10 workers. Therefore the total production time for one car is not 10 hours of working time, but 20 hours or 1,200 minutes. Out of these 1,200 minutes, only 60 minutes are paid working time, whereas 1,140 minutes are unpaid labour time of wageworkers and reproductive workers.

It could, however, be the case that in a household the total reproductive labour sustains not just one, but two or several wageworkers. In this case the total number of reproductive labour hours needs to be divided by the number of wageworkers in the household.

Unpaid Information Labour and Productive Labour: Dallas Smythe's Approach

What about unpaid information labour that is conducted in the context of capitalist media? Is it productive labour (1), (2), (3)? Or not? Or some of it? A good example is the usage of capitalist social media platforms such as Facebook, Twitter, Google/YouTube, Baidu, or Sina Weibo (for a detailed analysis, see also Fuchs 2014a, 2014c, 2015).

Dallas Smythe (1907–1992) was a Canadian political economist of media and communication. He is also one of the founding figures of this field and as such played a crucial role in its development. Smythe (1977, 1981) introduced the notion of the audience commodity for analysing media advertisement models in which the audience is sold as a commodity to advertisers: "Because audience power is produced, sold, purchased and consumed, it commands a price and is a commodity. [. . .] You audience members contribute your unpaid work time and in exchange you receive the program material and the explicit advertisements" (Smythe 1981, 26, 233). Audiences "work to market [. . .] things to themselves" (Smythe 1981, 4). The "main function of the mass media [. . .] is to produce audiences prepared to be dutiful consumers" (Smythe 1994, 250). Work would not necessarily be wage labour, but a general category—"doing something creative" (Smythe 1981, 26).

Smythe asked the question, Who produces the commodity of the commercial, advertising-financed media?

> I submit that the materialist answer to the question—What is the commodity form of mass-produced, advertiser-supported communications under monopoly capitalism?—is audiences and readerships (hereafter referred to for simplicity as audiences). The material reality under monopoly capitalism is that all non-sleeping time of most of the population is work time. This work time is devoted to the production of commodities-in-general (both where people get paid for their work and as members of audiences) and in the production and reproduction of labor power (the pay for which is subsumed in their income). Of the off-the-job work time, the largest single block is time of the audiences which is sold to advertisers. (Smythe 1977, 3)

> The work which audience members perform for the advertiser to whom they have been sold is to learn to buy particular 'brands' of consumer goods, and to spend their income accordingly. In short, they work to create the demand for advertised goods which is the purpose of the monopoly capitalist advertisers. While doing this, audience members are simultaneously reproducing their own labor power. (Smythe 1977, 6)

Smythe stressed the importance of reproductive labour for capitalism and that the engagement with commercial media and culture in consumer capitalism is an important form of reproductive labour: The "material reality under monopoly capitalism is that all non-sleeping time of most of the population is work time. [. . .] Of the off-the-job work time, the largest single block is time of the audiences, which is sold to advertisers. [. . .] In 'their' time which is sold to advertisers workers (a) perform essential marketing functions for the producers of consumers' goods, and (b) work at the production and reproduction of labour power" (Smythe 1977, 3).

Four purposes of the commercial mass media are

1.   The supply of consumers,
2.   The diffusion of the ideology of possessive individualism,
3.   The attempt to create support for state politics, and
4.   The attempt to maintain mass media as profitable enterprises (Smythe 1977, 20).

Smythe's approach has resulted in a sustained debate on the nature of commercial media within the field of the critical political economy of media and communication. This debate has also become known as the Blindspot Debate (for important contributions, see Smythe 1977; Murdock 1978; Smythe 1978; Livant 1979; Meehan 1984; Jhally 1987; Jhally and Livant 1986/2006; for a discussion of these and other contributions, see Fuchs 2012; McGuigan and Manzerolle 2014).

Graham Murdock (1978) pointed out in the "blindspot-debate" that the audience commodity is just one of several political economies of the media besides the sale of content and a strong public service tradition in Europe. He also stressed that corporate media have an ideological role in capitalism. In a contribution written in 2014, he reflects on his debate with Dallas Smythe (Murdock 2014a). He points out that he grew up in Britain where everyone was accustomed to the BBC as a strong public service institution. Public service would, however, not have been taken for granted in North America and Dallas Smythe was involved in struggles for strengthening its role in the media landscape. The notion of the audience commodity is of crucial relevance for understanding exploitation in the digital age. The digital media landscape is, however, not just shaped by commodification, but has huge potentials for the emergence of digital commons. Graham Murdock points out the importance of reconsidering the notions of the audience commodity and audience labour in the context of digital media.

Criticisms of Smythe

The orthodox-Marxist theorist Michael Lebowitz (1986) criticises Dallas Smythe's approach. Lebowitz (1986, 165) argues that Smythe's approach is only a "Marxist-sounding communications theory". Marxism would assume that "surplus value in capitalism is generated in the direct process of production, the process where workers (having surrendered the property rights over the disposition of their labour-power) are *compelled* to work longer than is necessary to produce the equivalent of their wage. Perhaps it is for this reason that there is hesitation in accepting the conception that audiences work, are exploited, and produce surplus value—in that it is a paradigm quite different to the Marxist paradigm" (Lebowitz 1986, 167). Media capitalists compete "for the expenditures of competing industrial capitalists", help to "increase the commodity sales of industrial capitalists" and their profits are "a share of the surplus value of industrial capital" (Lebowitz 1986, 169). Smythe's audience commodity approach advances an "entirely un-Marxian argument with un-Marxian conclusions" (Lebowitz 1986, 170).

A specific version of the labour theory of value argues that only wageworkers in factories are productive workers, which implies that they are the only people exploited in capitalism and the only ones capable of making a revolution. Dallas Smythe wrote his "Blindspot" article also as a criticism of this approach that ignored aspects of communication. This is evident when he says that Paul A. Baran (1909–1964) and Paul M. Sweezy (1910–2004), who developed the monopoly capitalism approach, in an idealist manner reduce advertising to a form of manipulation in the sales effort and when he criticises them for "rejecting expenses of circulation as unproductive of surplus" (Smythe 1977, 14). Baran and Sweezy put the main focus on monopolies rather than the exploitation of labour. Consequently, they reduce advertising to an unproductive attribute of monopoly—"the very offspring of monopoly capitalism" (Baran and Sweezy 1966, 122), which is one form of "surplus eaters" (127) and "merely a form of surplus absorption" (141). Smythe concluded that the "denial of the productivity of advertising is unnecessary and diversionary: a cul de sac derived from the pre-monopoly-capitalist stage of development, a dutiful but unsuccessful and inappropriate attempt at reconciliation with Capital" (Smythe 1977, 16).

Lebowitz's criticism of Smythe bases its argument on three specific assumptions:

1. Industrial capital is the central form of capital.
2. Only work performed under the command of industrial capital is productive labour and creates surplus-value.
3. Only wage labour can be exploited.

The immediate theoretical and political consequences of this logic of argumentation are the following ones:

1. Commercial media are subsumed to industrial capital.
2. Slaves, house workers, and other unpaid workers are not exploited.
3. The wage and nonwage labour performed under the command of media capital is unproductive. Media companies cannot exploit workers because they create products and services that are part of the circulation sphere of capitalism.

The political question that Lebowitz's argument poses is if one wants to share the implications of a wage-centric theory of value, that unpaid workers cannot be exploited.

Corporate Internet Platforms

Forty years after the "blindspot debate", Smythe's notion of the audience commodity has been used for explaining the political economy of social media platforms that use targeted advertising as capital accumulation model (see McGuigan and Manzerolle 2014; Fuchs 2009, 2012a, 2014a, 2015).

Tiziana Terranova (2000) used the term "free labour" for characterising unpaid value-generating labour conducted on Internet platforms. In order to understand the political economy of Facebook and similar online platforms, some scholars found it useful to introduce the notion of digital labour (see the contributions in Scholz 2013). The connection of Smythe's concept of the audience labour and the concept of digital labour emerged partly in this debate, but the concept of digital labour took on a more general meaning, encompassing all forms of labour engaged in the production of digital technologies and digital content (Fuchs 2014a, 2015).

The notion of the audience commodity is relevant for capitalist media that are funded by advertising. Given that large capitalist Internet companies such as Facebook, Google, Twitter, Sina Weibo, and Baidu make profits to large degrees with the help of targeted advertising, Smythe's notion is suited for the analysis of the political economy of the part of the Internet that is commercial and advertising-based.

Dallas Smythe argued that it is a specific feature of audience labour that audiences "work to market [. . .] things to themselves" (Smythe 1981, 4). Facebook users constantly work and constantly market things to themselves. Their usage behaviour constantly generates data that is used for targeting ads. All Facebook usage is productive labour, with the exception of those cases where users block advertising with the help of ad block software. Facebook usage labour adds value to the commodity that is sold by Facebook's ad clients. Practically this means that a lot of companies want to advertise on Facebook and calculate social media advertising costs into their commodity prices. Facebook usage and similar social media platforms create a use-value: communication and social relations. It is therefore productive labour (1). It also creates a data commodity that is sold to advertisers, who in return can offer targeted ads to users. It is therefore productive labour (2). Different forms of labour are involved Facebook's capital accumulation: unpaid user-labour and the paid labour of software engineers, advertising workers, secretaries, etc. at Facebook. Together these workers form a collective labourer whose labour is productive (3). Facebook and other means of communication are embedded into different social systems in the capitalist economy, households, the political system, public life, etc. Communication is a means for organising economic, political, and cultural life. Facebook, Twitter, and other social media have become important tools of corporate communication among employees, employees and managers, companies and freelancers who work for them, companies and customers, companies and the public. Facebook usage therefore also is part of the collective labourer in companies that use social media for internal and external organisational communication and is also in this respect productive labour (3).

The Difference between Audience Labour in Commercial Broadcasting and Digital Labour on Commercial Internet Platforms

Social media users are partly audiences who read texts, comments, or e-mails; watch videos or images; listen to music; etc. They tend, however, also to be prosumers in that they create texts, comments, e-mails, videos, images, or music. Prosumer labour on social media differs in a number of respects from audience labour in broadcasting:

- *Creativity and social relations*: Broadcasting audiences produce meanings of programmes, whereas social media prosumers not just produce meanings, but also content, communications with other users, and social relations. Users of social media do not always create content, but to a specific degree behave as audiences watching content.
- *Surveillance*: Broadcasting requires audience measurements, which are approximations, in order to sell audiences as commodities. Social media corporations monitor, store, and assess all online activities of users on their platforms and also on other platforms. They have very detailed profiles of users' activities, interests, communications, and social relations. Constant real-time surveillance of users is an inherent feature of prosumers' labour on capitalist social media. Personal data is sold as a commodity. Measuring audiences has in broadcasting and print traditionally been based on studies with small samples of audience members. Measuring and monitoring user behaviour on social media is constant, total, and algorithmic.
- *Targeted and personalised advertising*: Advertising on capitalist social media can therefore more easily target user interests and personalise ads, whereas this is more difficult in commercial broadcasting.

- *Algorithmic auctions*: Algorithms organise the pricing of the user data commodity in the form of auctions for online advertising spaces on the screens of a specific number of users. The ad prices on social media vary depending on the number of auctioneers, whereas the ad prices in newspapers and on radio and TV are set in a relatively fixed manner and are publicly advertised. User measurement uses predictive algorithms (if you like A, you may also like B because 100,000 people who like A also like B).

House workers, slaves, and Facebook users have in common that they are unpaid workers (1, 2, 3) who are exploited by capital. Forms of unpaid labour differ qualitatively: Slaves are threatened with death if they stop working. House workers in patriarchal relations are partly coerced by physical violence and partly by commitments. Facebook user-workers are coerced by the threat of missing social advantages (such as being invited to a friends' party) and monopoly power.

The Patriarchal Character of the Soviet System

There is a historical reason why I think one should not characterise Facebook users, slaves, and house workers as unproductive or minor productive: Soviet Marxism. In the Soviet Union, the notions of productive and unproductive labour were at the heart of the calculation of national wealth. The Material Product System (MPS) was the Soviet equivalent of the Gross Domestic Product (GDP). The MPS was introduced under Stalin in the 1920s (Árvay 1994). It only considered physical work in agriculture, industry, construction, transport, supply, and trade as productive, whereas services, administration, public services, education, culture, and housework were seen as unproductive forms of work because they do not contribute to national income, but rather consume it (Noah 1965). Women had especially high employment shares in medicine (physicians, nurses), schools, light industry (e.g., textiles), childcare, culture, retail, and catering (Katz 1997).

The Soviet wage system privileged domains such as heavy industry, construction, energy, metalwork, and mining because the MPS system considered them to contribute strongly to national wealth and productivity (Katz 1997). The feminised employment sectors just mentioned were seen as secondary and unproductive and thus had lower wage levels. A gender bias was "built into perceptions of productivity" (Katz 1997, 446). The gender division of labour and wages was "hidden behind a screen of officially proclaimed 'equal participation in the national economy'" (Katz 1997, 446). The reality was that "the Soviet wage-structure [. . .] was in itself male-biased" (Katz 1997, 446).

The notion of unproductive labour has historically been used for signifying reproductive work, service work, and feminised work as secondary and peripheral. It has thereby functioned as ideological support mechanism for the discrimination of women. This circumstance should caution us to be careful about which people we analytically characterise as "unproductive"—that is, not creating surplus-value in the capitalist production process.

Un/Productive Labour and Power

Conceptualising somebody as "unproductive" is not just an analytical term, it is also a slur and quite emotive. Nobody wants to be called unproductive as it carries the connotation of being useless and parasitic. Saying that Facebook users or house workers do not create value and that Facebook is a rentier company that consumes the value produced by wageworkers who are employed by other companies politically implies that users are unimportant in class struggles in the digital age. Wageworkers in the nondigital economy are seen as the true locus of power. Hence recommended political measures to be taken focus on how to organise these workers in unions, parties, or other organisations and on struggles for higher wages and better wage labour conditions. Users and Facebook are seen as being outside the locus of class struggle or only as something that unions and parties can also use in wage labour struggles.

In the case of Facebook, there are also paid employees who produce and maintain the software platform, the servers storing data, public relations, etc. These workers are, however, much less powerful than the users: If they go on strike and leave the workplace, the platform is likely to be still online and to generate profits by selling targeted ads because the actual sales process is based on the data generated by users and auctions for ad space, which is organised by an algorithm. If, however, the users go on strike and stop using the platform, Facebook can no longer make any profits because no new data is generated and nobody watches and clicks on the targeted ads. On corporate social media, users have tremendous power to bring profit-making to an end, which shows that their consumption work is crucial in the process of value-generation.

That Facebook users are productive workers (1, 2, 3) means that they have the power to bring corporate social media to a standstill. If users go on strike, then Facebook immediately loses money. If Facebook's wageworkers go on strike, the platform is still online and can be further operated for exploiting users. Users are economically powerful because they create economic value. Organising a collective Facebook strike or shifting to alternative noncommercial platforms is a refusal of digital labour.

Marx's concept of the collective labourer, which he introduces in chapter 15, has political importance. It shows that class struggles need to extend from factories and offices to the household, developing countries, and media spaces. There are many spaces and fields of capitalist exploitation in which humans experience different class relations. If they all unite as a class in struggle against capital, then there is a chance that capitalism can come to an end.

Exercises for Chapter 16

Group exercise (G)
Project exercise (P)

Key Categories: Absolute Surplus-Value Production, Relative Surplus-Value Production, Productive Labour, Collective Labourer (Gesamtarbeiter), Natural Wealth

Exercise 16.1 (G)

In chapter 16, Marx introduces the notion of the collective labourer in order to stress the connected and cooperative form of labour and exploitation in capitalism.

After reading Marx's chapter 16, read the following two texts:

Smythe, Dallas W. 1977. Communications: Blindspot of Western Marxism. *Canadian Journal of Political and Social Theory* 1 (3): 1–27.

Dalla Costa, Mariarosa and Selma James. 1972. *The power of women and the subversion of community.* Bristol: Falling Wall Press.

Discuss: What are the commonalities and differences of reproductive labour in household and audience labour?

How can the role of both forms of labour in capitalism be explained with the help of Marx's concept of the collective labourer?

Given that capital exploits the collective labourer, what can be done in order to overcome capitalism? What role can in this context house workers and media users have in class struggles? How can they best resist the rule of capital?

Exercise 16.2 (G)

Read the following text, which discusses the importance of Dallas Smythe's theory for understanding the role of unpaid digital labour in social media in capitalism:

Fuchs, Christian. 2012. Dallas Smythe today: The audience commodity, the digital labour debate, Marxist political economy and critical theory. Prolegomena to a digital labour theory of value. *tripleC: Communication, Capitalism & Critique* 10 (2): 692–740.

Discuss: What are differences between audience labour and digital labour? How do both concepts relate to Marx's notion of the collective labourer?

What is the role of advertising and commercial culture in capitalism?

What are the problems and dangers of advertising?

What are the most effective strategies for struggles against advertising? Look for examples and discuss them.

Exercise 16.3 (G)

Marx introduces the notion of natural wealth in chapter 16 (648).

Discuss: What are differences among agricultural, industrial, and information economies? What is wealth in a society in which information and technology play important roles?

Is the distinction among agricultural, industrial, and information economies feasible within a Marxist theory framework? Why and how? Or respectively, Why not?

Have humans today become more dependent and/or independent from nature? An in what respects?

In the *Grundrisse*, Marx discusses the transformation of wealth in a communist society:

> [T]he mass of workers must themselves appropriate their own surplus labour. Once they have done so—and disposable time thereby ceases to have an antithetical existence—then, on one side, necessary labour time will be measured by the needs of the social individual, and, on the other, the development of the power of social production will grow so rapidly that, even though production is now calculated for the wealth of all, disposable time will grow for all. For real wealth is the developed productive power of all individuals. The measure of wealth is then not any longer, in any way, labour time, but rather disposable time. (Marx 1857/1858, 708)

Discuss: How do the sources of wealth differ in capitalism and communism? What is the role of information and technology in relation to wealth in capitalism and communism?

Note

1   Marx here stresses a point that I have already highlighted several times in the discussion of previous chapters: All work requires a combination of the brain and the body. There are, however, qualitative differences that as part of the capitalist division of labour create a hierarchy between those who control, own, and command production and those who have to follow the given orders, so that a class relation shapes ownership and management of capitalist companies.

17

CHANGES OF MAGNITUDE IN THE PRICE OF LABOUR-POWER AND IN SURPLUS-VALUE

In chapter 17, Marx discusses the relationship of three factors that influence the rate of surplus-value:

(a) The length of the working day
(b) The intensity of labour (the amount of activities that a worker has to perform per unit of time)
(c) The productivity of labour (the production of a specific quantity of commodities per unit of time)

Changes of Surplus-Value and Variable Capital

The intensity of labour increases if one worker has to perform more activities per hour than before or if fewer workers have to perform the same amount of activities per hour as a larger number did before. There is no technological increase of productivity; the relationship between constant and variable capital remains constant. But just as in the case of increased productivity, there is an increased output of commodities produced per hour if the workers can keep up with the increased demands on their labour-power. Taylorism is a method that studies the movements of workers and tries to increase the speed of their performance.

Marx analyses four cases that result in changes of surplus-value and variable capital:

1. The length of the working day and labour intensity are constant; productivity is variable.
2. The length of the working day and productivity are constant; labour intensity is variable.
3. Productivity and labour intensity are constant; the length of the working day is variable.
4. There are simultaneous variations in the duration, productivity, and intensity of labour.

The Rate of Profit

Marx also formally introduces the concept of the rate of profit in chapter 17. It is defined as the ratio of profit p to invested capital (660):

$$rate\ of\ profit: rp = \frac{p}{c+v}$$

The invested capital is the sum of constant capital c and variable capital v. The rate of profit can be calculated for a company, a branch of the economy, an industry, a sector (e.g., the agricultural sector, manufacturing sector, information sector), a national economy, or the global economy. The used data must refer to a specific time period, typically a full year or a quarter of a year. Marx devotes chapter 2 in *Capital Volume 3* (Marx 1894) to the discussion of the rate of profit.

Marx gives one example (660): c = £400, v = £100, p = £100.

$$\text{rate of profit}: rp = \frac{p}{c+v} = \frac{£100}{£400 + £100} = \frac{£100}{£500} = 20\%$$

The Organic Composition of Capital and the Rate of Surplus-Value: Two Contradictory Forces that Influence the Rate of Profit

The rate of profit can be transformed by dividing its numerator and denominator by variable capital v, which results in the following formula:

$$\text{rate of profit}: rp = \frac{p}{c+v} = \frac{\dfrac{p}{v}}{\dfrac{c}{v}+1}$$

The transformed formula shows that the rate of profit rp is influenced by the levels of the rate of surplus-value rs = p/v and the organic composition of capital oc = c/v. The rate of surplus-value is directly proportional to the rate of profit. The organic composition is inversely proportional to the rate of profit. The higher the rate of surplus-value, the higher the rate of profit. The higher the organic composition, the lower the rate of profit.

The rate of surplus-value and the organic composition exert contradictory upward and downward pressures on the rate of profit. Technology plays a role in setting both the rate of surplus-value and the organic composition because it influences productivity and the usage of technology in production. It is therefore embedded into the contradictory economic structures of capitalism and not just a means for the production of surplus-value and for automating labour, but also a means that under capitalist conditions reflects and enforces the antagonisms that result in capitalism's inherent crisis tendencies.

Calculation of the Rate of Profit, the Organic Composition, and the Rate of Surplus-Value Based on Existing Macroeconomic Data

In many countries, companies listed on the stock market (so-called public companies, which does not stand for publicly owned, but publicly listed on the stock market) have to publish an annual financial report. In the USA, there is a standardised format for these reports that are submitted to the US Securities and Exchange Commission (SEC) and are published as so-called SEC filings. SEC filing 10–K is the annual financial report, and 10–Q the quarterly financial report. The annual proxy statement contains information on the board of directors and the largest shareholders and their voting power. Rankings such as the annual Forbes 2000 list of the world's largest transnational companies and the Fortune Global 500 list of the world's top 500 corporations provide financial information on large capitalist companies.

Such data sources tend to contain information on revenue/sales and net income/profit. The net income is a company's profit after taxes and deductions, whereas the gross income is the profit before deductions and taxes. Often data on total wage costs are not readily available. Profit rates can, however, still be obtained by calculating the total investment costs as sales minus profit.

Macroeconomics is concerned with the analysis of entire economies at a high level of aggregation. Macroeconomic statistics provide data for entire countries.

Such macroeconomic data is for various countries, for example, available in the OECD Stats Structural Analysis (STAN) Database and the EU's Annual Macro-Economic Database (AMECO). Figure 17.1 shows as an example approximations for the development of the rate of profit, the rate of surplus-value, and the organic composition of capital in the UK's economy. I obtained the data from the AMECO[1] database. The following variables were used and its values downloaded for the years 1960 through 2015:

Net operating surplus: total economy (UOND)
Net Operating Surplus = Gross Value Added – Consumption of Fixed Capital – Compensation
    of Employees – Indirect Taxes (VAT) + Subsidies
Compensation of employees: total economy (UWCD)
Taxes linked to imports and production minus subsidies: total economy (UTVN)
Consumption of fixed capital at current prices: total economy (UKCT)

I calculated the following variables:

Gross Value Added GVA = UOND + UWCD + UTVN + UKCT
Rate of Profit RP = UOND / GVA
Rate of Surplus-Value RSV = UOND / UWCD
Organic Composition OC = UKCT / UWCD

An Example Calculation: The Development of the Rate of Profit, the Organic Composition, and the Rate of Surplus-Value in the UK Economy

The data shows that in the early 1960s the organic composition was relatively low and the rate of surplus-value high, which resulted in a rate of profit of 31.7% in 1960. Until the middle of the 1970s, the organic composition continuously increased, whereas the rate of surplus-value continuously decreased, which resulted in a falling rate of profit. The organic composition further rose to closely 25% and then until the middle of the 1990s stabilised at this value. At the same time, the rate of surplus-value steeply increased from a low of 23.2% in 1975 to values between 35% and 50%. In the 1980s, the rate of profit fluctuated because the organic composition continued to increase. A slight decrease of the organic composition to values around 20% and a steep increase of the rate of surplus-value resulted between the early 1990s and 2015 when the date ends in an increased rate of profit at values between 25% and 35%.

Two very significant developments in these 55 years were the increase of the organic composition of capital from levels around 15% in the early 1960s to levels of 20% to 25% and the increase of the rate of surplus-value. This increase of the organic composition is likely to be the result of the microelectronic revolution—that is, the rise of computing and the networked computer in the capitalist economy. The second tendency was due to increased productivity and wage repression. Wage repression means that the share of the wage sum in the total economy decreased. The wage share (the share of employee compensation in gross value added) was in the years 1960 through 1976 at a level between 57% and 65%. In the years 1983 through 2015 it had significantly decreased to 50% to 55%. Whereas an increasing rate of surplus-value has a positive effect on the rate of profit, an increasing organic composition has a negative effect. Both tendencies stand in contradiction to each other and exert opposing pressures on the rate of profit. As a result, the rate of profit in the UK developed in a rather unpredictable and fluctuating manner.

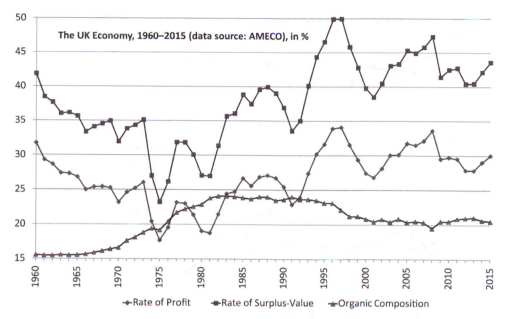

FIGURE 17.1   The development of the UK economy, 1960–2015

A Second Example Calculation: The Development of the UK Computer Industry in the Years 1992–2004

Figure 17.2 shows the economic development of the UK computer industry in the years 1992 to 2004. The data are from the OECD STAN database, where they are not available for the time before 1992 and after 2004. The economic sector is one called "computer and related activities", as defined in the International Standard Industrial Classification of All Economic Activities (ISIC), version 3.1. According to this classification of industries, division 72 "computer and related activities" includes the production and sale of the following economic services and goods: 721 hardware consultancy; 722 software publishing, consultancy, and supply; 723 data processing; 724 database activities and online distribution of electronic content; 725 maintenance and repair of office, accounting, and computing machinery; 729 other computer-related activities.

I obtained the following variables from OECD STAN for the UK's computer industry:

VALU Gross Value Added
LABR Compensation of Employees
GFCF Gross Fixed Capital Formation
OTXS Other Taxes Less Subsidies on Production
GOPS Gross Operating Surplus

Net operating surplus (NOPS) data was not available for the UK's computer industry. Net operating surplus can, however, be calculated as follows:

NOPS = GOPS—GFCF

I calculated the following variables, which are displayed in figure 17.2:

Rate of Profit RP = NOPS / VALU
Rate of Surplus-Value = NOPS / LABR
Organic Composition = GFCF / LABR
Wage Share = LABR / VALU

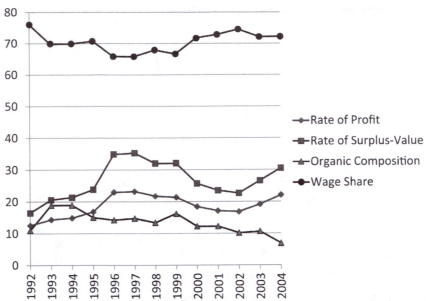

Development of the UK computer industry, 1992-2004 (data source: OCED STAN), in %

FIGURE 17.2 The development of the UK's computer industry in the years 1992–2004

The data shows that the UK's software and computer industry had a relatively low organic composition of capital of around 10% and a very high wage share of around 70% during the analysed time period. Software engineers tended to have fairly high wages. They formed a kind of labour aristocracy (for a detailed analysis, see Fuchs 2014a, chapter 9).

Friedrich Engels describes in the 1892 preface to the English edition of *The Condition of the Working Class in England* that in 1885 in the UK there were workers whose "state of misery and insecurity in which they live now is as low as ever" (MECW 27, 266), but there was also "an aristocracy among the working-class" (engineers, carpenters, joiners, bricklayers) that had "succeeded in enforcing for themselves a relatively comfortable position" (MECW 27, 266). The date in figure 17.2 shows that the UK's software and computer industry had a relatively constant rate of profit of around 15%–20% in the years 1992–2004.

A Third Example Calculation: The Development of the US Computer Industry

Figures 17.3 and 17.4 visualise similar economic data for the development of the US computer industry in the years 1987 through 2009.

The organic composition of capital was in the US computer industry on average 16.2% in the years 1987 through 2009. In the same time period, the wage share was 80.5%. So the US computer industry shows the same tendencies as the one in the UK. The US computer industry experienced a deep crisis in 2000 and 2001 when the industry in total experienced very large losses.

The Dot-Com Crisis in the Internet Economy

The cause was the so-called dot-com crisis, which was an outcome of the Internet economy's financialisation: Venture capital firms work in such a way that they invest large sums of money into start-up companies and thereby acquire specific roles, influences, and shares in these companies. As investors they compel firms to find commodification strategies in order to be profitable. Often an

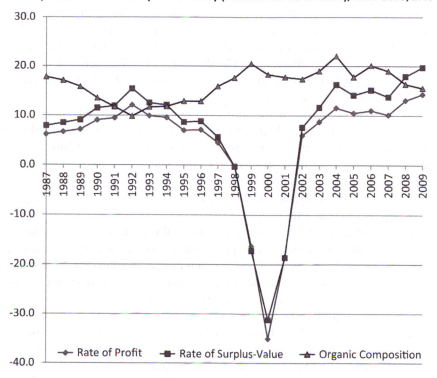

FIGURE 17.3 The development of the US computer industry, 1987–2009

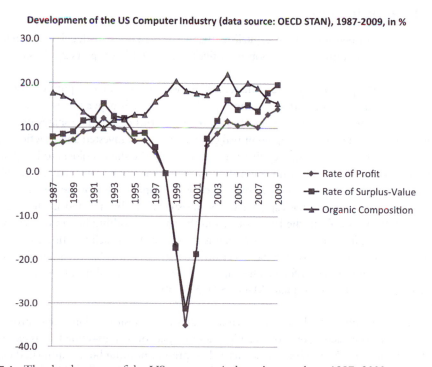

FIGURE 17.4 The development of the US computer industry's wage share, 1987–2009

influx of venture capital results in companies becoming listed on the stock market because they have acquired the necessary capital for doing so. Financialisation can, however, drive up market values on stock markets without actual growth of monetary profits if the expectation is created that a company will become very profitable in the future. Divergences between share values and profits can as aggregated phenomenon create financial bubbles that burst when investors lose confidence, which occurs typically upon the failure of specific corporations so that massive doubts and uncertainties are triggered and spread in the financial economy.

eToys.com is an online toy retail website that was founded in 1997. Based on large venture capital injections by investors such as Highland Entrepreneurs' Fund III Limited Partnership, DynaFund L.P., idealab! Capital Partners, Bessemer Venture Partners, Sequoia Capital Moore Global Investments Ltd., Remington Investment Strategies L.P., and Multi-Strategies Fund it made an Initial Public Offering (IPO) on the stock market in 1999. It made huge losses of up to $200 million and had to file for chapter 11 bankruptcy in 2001. It is just one of many Internet corporations that exploded during the 2000 dot-com crisis.

The new economy crisis of 2000/2001 made financial capitalists reluctant to invest into new Internet companies. Web 2.0 and later social media were ideological strategies to create the impression that the Internet had been reinvented and was entirely new and thus that new business opportunities had emerged. Social media was founded as an ideology aimed at convincing finance capitalists to invest in Internet companies and to attract advertising clients.

The US computer industry's rate of profit was at the end of the 1980s and for most of the 1990s relatively stable around 10%. It then absolutely collapsed and took on negative values due to massive losses in the entire industry during the dot-com crisis and then stabilised again around 10% in the years 2003 through 2010. The example of the US computer industry shows that even industries that are considered to have high growth potentials and to bring about technological innovations to transform the entire economy are under capitalist conditions prone to crisis.

What Is Financialisation?

Financialisation is a phenomenon of capitalism that Marx discusses in detail in *Capital Volume 3* (Marx 1894), where he introduces the notion of fictitious capital in chapters 26 through 32.

> Even when the promissory note—the security—does not represent a purely fictitious capital, as it does in the case of state debts, the capital value of such paper is still pure illusion. [. . .] Securities purport to be ownership titles representing this capital. The shares in railway, mining shipping companies, etc. represent real capital, i.e. capital invested and functioning in these enterprises, or the sum of money that was advanced by the share-holders to be spent in these enterprises as capital. It is in no way ruled out here that these shares may be simply a fraud. But the capital does not exist twice over, once as the capital value of the ownership titles, the shares and then again as the capital actually invested or to be invested in the enterprises in question. It exists only in the latter form, and the share is nothing but an ownership title, *pro rata*, to the surplus-value which this capital is to realize. A may sell this title to B, and B to C. These transactions have no essential effect on the matter. A or B has then transformed his title into capital, but C has transformed his capital into a mere ownership title to the surplus-value expected from this share capital. (Marx 1894, 597–598)

Financial investments in stocks and financial derivatives are transformed into operative capital, but they are not capital themselves, only ownership titles to a part of surplus-value that is expected to be produced in the future. "All these securities actually represent nothing but accumulated claims, legal titles, to future production" (Marx 1894, 599). If the company collapses or has falling profit rates, then the invested money is not paid back—the investors lose money. The value of shares is therefore speculative and not connected to the actual profits of the company; it is only the expectations about future profits that determine buying and selling decisions of stock investors.

> The market value of these securities is partly speculative, since it is determined not just by the actual revenue but rather by the anticipated revenue as reckoned in advance. [. . .] the rise or fall in value of these securities is independent of the movement in the value of the real capital that they represent. (Marx 1894, 598, 599, see also 608, 641)

Fictitious Capital and Crises

The result is a high-risk system of speculation, which resembles gambling: "Profits and losses that result from fluctuations in the price of these ownership titles [. . .] are by the nature of the case more and more the result of gambling" (Marx 1894, 609). For Marx, the system of fictitious capital, which produces a relative independence of stock values and profits, is inherently crisis-prone:

> In a system of production where the entire interconnection of the reproduction process rests on credit, a crisis must evidently break out if credit is suddenly withdrawn and only cash payment is accepted, in the form of a violent scramble for means of payment. At a first glance, therefore, the entire crisis presents itself as simply a credit and monetary crisis. And in fact all it does involve is simply the convertibility of bulls of exchange into money. The majority of these bills represent actual purchases and sales, the ultimate basis of the entire crisis being the expansion of these far beyond the social need. On top of this, however, a tremendous number of these bills represent purely fraudulent deals, which now come to light and explode; as well as unsuccessful speculations conducted with borrowed capital, and finally commodity capitals that are either devalued or unsaleable, or returns that are never going to come in. (Marx 1894, 621)

Marx says that this is an "artificial system of forced expansions" (621) of accumulation that must ultimately enter crisis. "Monetary crises, independent of real crises or as an intensification of them, are unavoidable" in capitalism (Marx 1894, 649). He writes on monetary crises that "the pivot of these crises is to be found in money capital, and their immediate sphere of impact is therefore banking, the stock exchange and finance" (Marx 1867, 236).

Marx writes that "credit also enables the acts of buying and selling to take a longer time, and hence serves as a basis for speculation" (Marx 1894, 567). In relation to the stock market, he speaks of "an entire system of swindling and cheating with respect to the promotion of companies, issues of shares and share dealings" (Marx 1894, 569). Speculation is built into the credit system "because a great part of the social capital is applied by those who are not its owners, and who therefore proceed quite unlike owners" (Marx 1894, 572). Credit therefore "accelerates the violent outbreaks of this contradiction, crises, and with these the elements of dissolution of the old mode of production" (Marx 1894, 572).

For Marx, financial crises are not avoidable by regulated financial markets or moral rules that limit greed because greed is for him a necessary structural feature of capitalism that derives from the necessity of capitalists to accumulate evermore capital and to increase profit rates or perish. Competition among capitals and the need to expand accumulation result in attempts to create "financial innovations" that have a high risk, but promise very high short-time revenue rates. The fictitious value of commercial papers stands in no direct relation with the actual value created in the companies. The fictitious value signifies the actual value, but can largely deviate from it. Financial bubbles are the result—that is, share prices that do not reflect the actual profitability and that fall heavily once a burst of the financial bubble is triggered by events that destroy the investors' expectations for high future returns. For Marx, a financial crisis does not signal the need for more regulation, but the inherent defectiveness of capitalism. Financial crises speak in favour of socialism instead of capitalism.

Productivity Increases under the Condition of Asymmetric Power

Marx also points out in chapter 17 that historically the productivity of labour has increased, which in principle means an increase of "the time at society's disposal for the free intellectual and social activity of the individual" (667). Power is in capitalism, however unequally distributed, so that increases in productivity do not automatically result in a shortening of the working day and an even distribution of labour among all. The dominant class holds the power to "shift the burden of labour [...] from its own shoulders to those of another social stratum. [...] In capitalist society, free time is produced for one class by the conversion of the whole lifetime of the masses into labour-time" (667).

Capitalism has a tendency to convert productivity increases unequally so that some people lose their jobs, others work longer hours, and again others have insecure and precarious working conditions. Decreasing the normal working week for all while holding wages constant is a measure that capitalists do not like because they prefer to let a reduced number or the same amount of workers work for the same number of hours per week as before under higher productivity standards, which promises a larger increase of profits.

Exercises for Chapter 17

Group exercise (G)
Project exercise (P)

Key Category: Rate of Profit

Exercise 17.1 (P)

In chapter 17, Marx introduces the concept of the rate of profit, which is shaped by the rate of surplus-value and the organic composition of capital. I have given an example of how to calculate these three ratios that shape the development of the capitalist economy (Figure 17.1).

Work in groups: Each group calculates the rate of profit, the organic composition, the rate of surplus-value, and the wage share for a specific country's economy during a particular period of time. Consult databases such as AMECO, OECD STAN, and others for obtaining the data.

Present and visualise the results.

Exercise 17.2 (P)

In chapter 17, Marx introduces the concept of the rate of profit, which is shaped by the rate of surplus-value and the organic composition of capital. I have given two examples from the information economy in order to show how to calculate these three ratios that shape the development of the capitalist economy: the US's and the UK's computer industries (Figures 17.2, 17.3, 17.4).

Work in groups: Each group calculates the rate of profit, the organic composition, the rate of surplus-value, and the wage share for a specific country's media and information sectors during a particular period of time. Consult databases such as OECD STAN for obtaining the data. You have to consult the different versions of the International Standard Industrial Classification of All Economic Activities (ISIC) that are used in this database in order to find out which industries are media and information industries and if data is available for them.

Present and visualise the results.

Note

1   Similar variables are available in the OECD Stat STAN database:
VALU: Value Added at Current Prices (= Gross Value Added)
NOPS: Net Operating Surplus
CFCC: Consumption of Fixed Capital (or GFCC: Gross Fixed Capital Formation)
LABR: Labour Costs, Compensation of Employees
OTXS: Other Taxes Less Subsidies on Production

18

DIFFERENT FORMULAE FOR THE RATE OF SURPLUS-VALUE

Classical Political Economy's Formula for the Rate of Surplus-Value

Marx criticises the classical political economy's mathematical formula for the rate of surplus-value and provides his own version of it. The classical political economy defines the rate of surplus-value the following way:

$$rs = \frac{Surplus\, labour}{Working\, day} = \frac{Surplus-value}{Total\, product} = \frac{Surplus\, product}{Total\, product}$$

Marx's Formula for the Rate of Surplus-Value

Marx in contrast defines the rate of surplus-value as follows:

$$rs = \frac{Surplus-value\, s}{Variable\, capital\, v} = \frac{Surplus-value}{Value\, of\, labour-power} = \frac{Surplus\, labour}{necessary\, labour}$$

$$= \frac{Unpaid\, labour}{Paid\, labour}$$

Marx says that in his formulation, the first two versions are rations of "values", whereas the third one is a "ratio of the times during which those values are produced" (668). In capitalism, workers are compelled to produce commodities during a specific period of labour-time. Capitalists own these commodities. They sell them on markets in order to accumulate capital and they own these commodities.

A commodity is in the production process a physical or nonphysical good that embodies parts of the means of production and the workers' labour-time that it takes to create it. In the sphere of circulation, the commodity is sold, and so capital is turned from the commodity-form into the money-form. Value therefore takes on both the form of labour-time and money. If one thinks of a rock concert, a haircut, or a theatre play, then it becomes evident that there are commodities that are produced and consumed at the same time, so production, circulation, and consumption of the commodity are organised under the conditions of temporal synchronicity and spatial co-presence.

If a commodity is, however, not sold because there is a crisis in a company, an industry, or the economy, then the workers have already expended labour-time, and they have already been exploited.

The commodity exists without being sold. The way Marx formulates the rate of surplus-value shows that he thinks about value on the level of labour-time and money. This also becomes evident in chapter 18 and throughout *Capital* by the fact that he frequently uses examples, in which he mentions both monetary units and labour-times.

Value at the Level of Labour-Time and Prices

Marx uses the term "surplus-value" interchangeably with "unpaid labour-time" and "monetary profit". This usage is a bit confusing, but it shows that for Marx value has both a level of labour-time and one of money.

The individual commodity stands in a relationship to the average commodity produced in a company, which stands in a relationship to the average commodity produced in the entire industry or economic sector, which stands in a relationship to the average commodity produced in a national economy, which stands in a relationship to the average commodity produced on the world scale. Commodity production is organised on different levels: the individual commodity, the company, the industry/sector, the national economy, and the global economy. Each level above the individual one is an aggregation of many different producers and commodities so that an average production time, an average price, an average profit, an average wage, average constant capital, an average rate of surplus-value, an average organic composition, and an average rate of profit emerge. These average magnitudes are not constant, but change as the conditions of production change because the capitalist economy is a complex and dynamic system founded on capital accumulation and the exploitation of labour. The average commodity value at each level can stand at, above, or below the average level of the next higher level. Given the interconnection of levels, one can calculate commodity values at each level in monetary units and units of labour-time. So, for example, at the level of the company, annual production has an average value that takes an average number of hours per commodity and yields an average monetary profit.

If one knows the total profit and the total working hours at the industry level, then one can calculate a measure of how much monetary profit is on average generated per hour. Some Marxist political economists call this measure the Monetary Expression of Labour Time (MELT) (Freeman, Kliman, and Wells 2004; Kliman 2007; Freeman 2010). The industry-wide MELT allows transforming a company's profits, constant capital, and variable capital, as well as the commodity-value, the rate of surplus-value, the organic composition, and the rate of profit from company averages into units calculated at the level of the entire industry. This procedure allows comparing commodity-values measured in monetary units/prices to the average industry-wide levels so that one can see if the company produces at, below, or above the average. MELT can also be calculated for national economies and the global economy and the same kind of calculations can be applied.

An Example Calculation: The Classical and the Marxian Rate of Surplus-Value

An example can show the difference between the two rates of surplus-value:

Surplus labour-time = 4 hours per day, necessary labour-time = 4 hours per day, profit = £300, wages = £300.

Marx's rate of surplus-value = £300 / £300 = 4h / 4h = 100%.
Classical political economy's rate of surplus-value = £300 / £600 = 4h / 8h = 50%.

Marx's criticism is that classical political economy's understanding of surplus-value underestimates the level of exploitation. The "actual degree of exploitation of labour, or the rate of surplus-value, is falsely expressed" (668). As a consequence, classical political economists "conceal the specific character of the capital-relation, namely the fact that variable capital is exchanged for living labour-power, and that the worker is accordingly excluded from the product" (670).

Exploitation and Alienation

Marx's formula allows us in contrast to see that the rate of surplus-labour is the relationship of unpaid labour and paid labour and that capitalism is founded on capital's exploitation of the workers' unpaid labour-time, which yields surplus-value and profit:

> During one period, the worker produces a value that is only equal to the value of his labour-power, i.e. he produces its equivalent. [...] During the other period, the period of surplus labour, the utilization of the labour-power creates a value for the capitalist without costing him any value in return. Capital, therefore, is not only the command over labour, as Adam Smith thought. It is essentially the command over unpaid labour. All surplus-value, whatever particular form (profit, interest or rent) it may subsequently crystallize into, is in sub- stance the materialization of unpaid labour-time. The secret of the self-valorization of capital resolves itself into the fact that it has at its disposal a definite quantity of the unpaid labour of other people *[fremder Arbeit]*. (671–672)

Marx here summarises one of his main insights in chapter 18—namely, that capital accumulation is founded on the exploitation of the workers' unpaid labour, which is alienated because the capitalists own the products (surplus-value, monetary profit, commodities). Labour and products thereby become alien labour and alien products. The insight that capitalism is founded on capital's exploitation of workers' unpaid labour is for Marx not just a structural feature, but also a political issue: Exploitation and unpaid labour are fundamental injustices built into the capitalist system; this calls for overthrowing capitalism and replacing it with a fair and just society in which all people control and shape the economy and the political system in common.

Facebook and the Rate of Surplus-Value

All labour in class societies involves unpaid labour and is therefore exploitative. The degree of exploitation varies from circumstance to circumstance. I have discussed in previous chapters that there are capitalist business models in which consumers become producers (prosumers) of value and surplus-value. In many of these models, prosumption is completely unremunerated. A good example is Facebook:

Facebook SEC filings form 10-Q from July 2014
January to June 2014: net income—US$1,433 billion
1.3 billion monthly active users
All revenue is generated from advertising.

According to statistics, the average user spends around 8.3 hours per month on Facebook.[1]
Total number of hours spent by Facebook users on average on the platform in the period January to June 2014: 1.3 billion * 8.3 = 10.8 billion hours.
The Marxian rate of surplus-value is calculated as surplus labour-time divided by necessary labour-time. If labour is completely unpaid, then surplus-labour time is maximised to 100% and necessary labour-time is minimised to 0%:

$$rs = \frac{surplus\ labour-time}{necessary\ labour-time} = \frac{10.8 * 10^9}{0} \rightarrow \infty$$

All labour conducted under capitalist or other class relations is at least partly unpaid and therefore exploited. If surplus labour-time is maximised so that it takes all labour-time, then exploitation converges towards infinity (Fuchs 2014a, 2015). A position sometimes brought up against this argument is that Facebook users are paid by gratis access to the platform. Such a logic disregards that money is the universal commodity that allows you to purchase all other commodities. One can buy food, clothes, and computers with money, but one cannot buy anything by having access to Facebook. Facebook access is therefore not a form of wage. The wage is the monetary expression of the price of labour-power.

Exercise for Chapter 18

Group exercise (G)
Project exercise (P)

Key Categories: Rate of Surplus-Value, Paid Labour, Unpaid Labour

Exercise 18.1 (G)

Marx discusses different formulations for the rate of surplus-value in chapter 18. The key issue is that this rate can be expressed in monetary units or units of labour-time, and that capitalism is based on the exploitation of unpaid labour-time, which yields surplus-value and profit.

Work in group: Each group selects one specific media company and tries to find statistical data (profits, labour-times, usage times, number of users, wages, etc.) that is necessary for calculating the rate of surplus-value for a specific time period (e.g., one month, six months, one year). Take into account that in the case of advertising-funded media, the users or audiences create a specific part of the surplus-value and profit. Therefore before searching for statistical data, discuss and clarify what capital accumulation model the selected company uses, the commodity it sells, and who exactly creates the value of this commodity.

Calculate the rate of surplus-value and present the results.

Note

1   http://www.dazeinfo.com/2014/01/03/facebook-inc-fb-users-vital-marketers-average-8–3hrsmonth-spent-per-user-total-number-connections-exceed-150-billion-infographic/ (accessed on September 8, 2014).

PART VI

WAGES

In section VI (chapters 19–22), Marx discusses the concept of the wage.

19

THE TRANSFORMATION OF VALUE (AND RESPECTIVELY THE PRICE) OF LABOUR-POWER INTO WAGES

"The Value and Price of Labour"

Marx argues that classical political economists such as Samuel Bailey (1791–1870), Edward Gibbon Wakefield (1796–1862), Jean Charles Léonard de Sismondi (1773–1842), and Jean-Baptiste Say (1767–1832) spoke of the "value of labour" and the "price of labour". This terminology is "imaginary" (677), "uncritical" (679), and "irrational" (679):

> It is not labour which directly confronts the possessor of money on the commodity-market, but rather the worker. What the worker is selling is his labour-power. As soon as his labour actually begins, it has already ceased to belong to him; it can therefore no longer be sold by him. Labour is the substance, and the immanent measure of value, but it has no value itself. (677)

What Is a Wage?

Therefore for Marx the correct terms are "value of labour-power" and "price of labour-power". The value of labour-power is the average amount of labour necessary to produce the means required for sustaining labour-power. The wage is the monetary price of labour-power. In 1849, Marx published a piece called *Wage Labour and Capital*. Already in this piece, he asked the question, "What are wages?" (Marx 1849) and answered as follows: "wages are the amount of money which the capitalist pays for a certain period of work or for a certain amount of work. [. . .] Wages therefore are only a special name for the price of labour-power, [. . .] it is the special name for the price of this peculiar commodity, which has no other repository than human flesh and blood" (Marx 1849). So Marx here clarifies that the wage is the price of labour-power expressed in money.

In June 1865, Marx made a speech titled "Value, Price and Profit" at the meeting of the International Working Men's Association. In this talk, he pointed out that "there exists no such thing as the *value of labour*", only "the value of labouring power" (Marx 1865). The "*value or price of the labouring power* takes the semblance of the *price or value of labour itself*, although, strictly speaking, value and price of labour are senseless terms" (Marx 1865). Marx (1865) says that "value of labour" and "price of labour" are "popular slang" terms for the "value of labour-power" and "price of labour-power".

The commodity value is not set "by the quantity of labour actually objictified in it, but by the quantity of living labour necessary to produce it" (677). If a commodity is produced on average in six hours, but is stored for 10 years before it is offered on the market and in the meantime the average productivity has increased to such an extent that the same commodity can on average be produced in three hours, then its value has dropped to "3 hours of socially necessary labour instead of the 6 formerly required" (677).

The Value and Price of Labour-Power

Let us assume a worker labours for eight hours a day and receives a wage of £80. In Marx's theory, if it takes on average four hours per day to produce all the means of subsistence that a person needs to survive, then both the necessary labour and the surplus labour are four hours long. The value of labour-power is therefore four hours. If we assume that one worker produces one commodity per day that is sold at a price of £180 (constant capital c = £20), then it becomes evident that the worker has in the eight labour hours reproduced the value of his/her labour-power, transferred the value of the necessary means of production, and created a surplus-value. The price of labour-power is £80 and the profit £80. The value of labour-power is four hours. The surplus labour of four hours represents a profit of £80. Marx points out that the value of labour-power can differ from its price (679). If the average wage in the entire economy is £100 per working day and it takes four hours to produce the means that sustain labour-power, then the labour-power in our example has been sold £20 below its value. The price of labour-power is then lower than its value. Value and price of a commodity do not have to coincide.

In our example, common sense logic is that £80 is the wage for eight hours of labour and that eight hours of labour have been paid. Marx points out that this impression is a fetishism created by the wage-form, which "extinguishes every trace of the division of the working day into necessary labour and surplus labour, into paid labour and unpaid labour. All labour appears as paid labour" (680). Even "surplus labour, or unpaid labour, appears as paid" (680).

Imagine two situations:

S1. There is only one company in the world producing computers and there is a significant demand for this type of good. There is almost unlimited supply of the workforce and a securitisation of work by military means: Workers who resist working are shot. There is no labour legislation—that is, the owners of the computer company are free to choose the standard work time, wages, rest times, etc. It takes on average 15 minutes to assemble one computer and the price of one computer is £500. There are fixed constant capital costs of £100. The price depends on the investment costs. Given that the labour supply is limited, capitalists will try to reduce the labour costs to a minimum in order to maximise profits. In the example, they can due to the fascist conditions of production, enslave the workers, pay no wages, and thereby maximise the profit to the possible maximum of £400.

S2. There is a regime change and labour legislation is introduced. There is now a minimum wage that requires the capitalist in our example to pay £200 in wage costs for the production of one computer. The production conditions remain unchanged; the constant capital costs are still £100. The capitalist is used to making £400 profit per computer; s/he has based on the calculation that s/he makes a profit of 400% per computer acquired a luxurious lifestyle that he does not want to give up. If s/he demands the same price for each computer, the profit per commodity will half from £400 to £200. Given that there is no competition, but a high demand for computers, he decides to increase the price of one computer from £500 to £700, which allows him continuing to achieve a profit of £400.

Class Struggle, the Price of Labour-Power, and the Sociopolitical Concept of the Wage

The example aims to show that the price of labour-power (the wage) cannot simply be derived and calculated from the value of labour-power, but depends on the politics of class struggle. The French

Marxist philosopher Jacques Bidet (2009) therefore speaks of the sociopolitical concept of value, which is coupled to the political-economic concept of value. In capitalism, labour as the substance of value is coupled to "the social compulsion" for the expenditure of labour that is "exercised over the workers by the capitalist class" (Bidet 2009, 51). Labour is therefore a class concept and value is connected to labour's class relation to capital. Capital has to secure the command over labour, which is a political task. Labour can try to resist this command, which is a political answer to this command. If "the substance of value is abstract labour, expenditure, it is coupled in the mode of production with its correlative, the social compulsion for this expenditure (a market compulsion exercised over the workers by the capitalist class), with which it forms, in the unity of the concept, a social and class relationship" (Bidet 2009, 51). The concepts of value and abstract labour are therefore simultaneously an expression of political economy and sociopolitical class struggle.

Also Marx stressed this connection in relation to the value and price of labour-power:

> During the time of the anti-Jacobin war, undertaken, as the incorrigible tax-eater and sine-curist, old George Rose, used to say, to save the comforts of our holy religion from the inroads of the French infidels, the honest English farmers, so tenderly handled in a former chapter of ours, depressed the wages of the agricultural labourers even beneath that *mere physical minimum*, but made up by Poor Laws the remainder necessary for the physical perpetuation of the race. This was a glorious way to convert the wages labourer into a slave, and Shakespeare's proud yeoman into a pauper. (Marx 1865)

The sociopolitical concept of class and the wage has led Bidet (2007) to stress that capitalism "really poses the market *and the organization*, the two mediations, the two forms of rational-reasonable coordination at social scale, as its logical presuppositions. It poses them while turning them into the two *class factors* which are combined in the modern *class relation*". Although coming from another background, namely Autonomous Marxism, Harry Cleaver (2000) argues like Bidet for a political reading of Marx's *Capital*. Like Bidet, also Cleaver sees class relations as an important aspect of value.

The exchange-value of labour-power is, as we have seen, the money that the working class receives for its sale. Yet for the working class this exchange-value is at once income and a source of power in its struggle with capital, while for the latter it is a cost and a deduction from total value produced, a threat to surplus-value and thus to capital's power. Because of these differences there is often a struggle over the form in which the working class will receive the exchange-value of its labour-power: money wages, wages in kind, social services, welfare, unemployment benefits, pensions, and so forth (Cleaver 2000, 101).

The Value of Labour-Power

What is the value of labour power? In *Capital Volume 1*'s chapter 6, Marx argues: "The value of labour-power is determined, as in the case of every other commodity, by the labour-time necessary for the production, and consequently also the reproduction, of this specific article. [. . .] the value of labour-power is the value of the means of subsistence necessary for the maintenance of its owner" (Marx 1867, 274). The means of reproduction of a worker include his/her own subsistence costs, the ones of her/his family, education for obtaining skills, and health care for maintaining a physical and mental status that allows the continuance of work. Harry Cleaver stresses the Autonomist Marxist notion of the social worker and the social factory: "Both housework and schoolwork are intended to contribute to keeping the value of labour-power low" (Cleaver 2000, 123). The more unpaid labour-time is available in the reproduction of labour-power, the more the "amount of variable capital necessary for the reproduction of the working class" decreases, so that the social worker in the social factory contributes "to the expansion of surplus value" (Cleaver 2000, 123).

The price of labour-power (wages) depends on the politically set working conditions, which are the actual, temporal, and dynamically changing result of the class struggle between capital and labour. Marx argues in *Capital Volume 1*'s appendix called "Results of the Immediate Process of Production" that organisations of the working class, such as the trade unions, "aim at nothing less than to prevent the *reduction of wages* below the level that is traditionally maintained in the various branches of industry. That is to say, they wish to prevent the *price* of labour-power from falling below its *value*" (1069).

In the first example S1, the wages are driven by the power of capital in the class struggle to an absolute minimum, below the subsistence level of labour-power—that is, below its value. In the second example, class struggle empowers worker organisations and allows them to raise the price of labour-power. The examples show that "value is established in a class struggle defined by the question of the price of labour-power" (Bidet 2009, 101). "By comparing the standard wages or values of labour in different countries, and by comparing them in different historical epochs of the same country, you will find that the *value of labour* itself is not a fixed but a variable magnitude, even supposing the values of all other commodities to remain constant" (Marx 1865).

Exercises for Chapter 19

Group exercise (G)
Project exercise (P)

Key Category: Wages, Value of Labour-Power, Price of Labour-Power

Exercise 19.1 (P)

Marx in chapter 19 discusses the notion of wages. The task of this exercise is to compare the wages of various information and service jobs across countries.

National Labour Force Surveys[1] and the International Labour Organization's Statistical Database (ILOSTAT, called LABORSTA for data until 2009) provide data on average or mean weekly or monthly wages in various industries and for various occupations.

Work in groups: Each group selects one country. Search in databases for the latest available average wages in various media, information, cultural, and communication industries and occupations. Compare the wage levels to each other. Present and interpret the results. Compare the wage levels in similar industries and occupations across countries and interpret the results.

Such databases use industry classifications such as the International Standard Industrial Classification of All Economic Activities that has different versions (called revisions; e.g., ISIC Rev. 4, ISIC Rev. 3) or the International Standard Classification of Occupations (ISCO) that also has different versions (such as ISCO-88, ISCO-08). So, for example, the UK Office for National Statistics publishes as part of the regular Labour Force Survey average wages by industry and occupation.

In 2014, the classification of industries included among others the following sectors:

J: Information and Communication
M: Professional, Scientific, and Legal Activities
N: Administrative and Support Service Activities
P: Education
R: Arts, Entertainment, and Recreation

These classifications are based on the UK Standard Industrial Classification 2007 (SIC07), which corresponds to ISIC Rev 4. The occupations in 2014 included among others the following labour activities:

Managers and Senior Officials
Professional Occupations
Associate Professional and Technical Occupations
Administrative and Secretarial Occupations (Clerical Support Workers)

These classifications are based on the UK Standard Occupational Classification 2000, which corresponds to ISCO-08.

Exercise 19.2 (P)

Glassdoor.com is a platform where employees anonymously review working conditions in various companies. In 2014, it described itself the following way: "Glassdoor holds a growing database of 6 million company reviews, CEO approval ratings, salary reports, interview reviews and questions, benefits reviews, office photos and more. Unlike other jobs sites, all of this information is entirely shared by those who know a company best—the employees. Add to that millions of the latest jobs—no other community allows you to see which employers are hiring, what it's really like to work or interview there according to employees, and how much you could earn" (source: http://www.glassdoor.com).

To get access, one must submit one review of an employer.

Work in groups: Each group selects one information job. Take care that each group focuses on a different occupation and that there is a broad range of different occupations, including low-skill, medium-skill, and high-skill labour jobs. Each group creates a list of 20 large companies that employ the kind of information workers it is analysing. Get access to Glassdoor.com and use the function "Salaries", which allows you to search for average salaries in these companies. Take care to select data for the right kind of information work (there may be different ones listed for each company). Compare the average salaries across companies.

Present the results and compare the average wage levels for the various jobs that different groups analysed. Interpret the results of this comparison.

Note

1   For links see, for example, http://www.ilo.org/dyn/lfsurvey/lfsurvey.home, (accessed on August 21, 2014).

20
TIME-WAGES

What Is a Time-Wage?

Marx discusses one of the "two fundamental forms" (682) of the wage in chapter 20: the time-wage. He analyses the second one, the piece-wage, in chapter 21.

> The sale of labour-power, as will be remembered, always takes place for definite periods of time. The converted form in which the daily value, weekly value, etc. of labour-power is directly presented is hence that of time-wages, therefore day-wages, etc. (683)

The time-wage per week or month may vary between one company and another in the same industry. It is therefore feasible to calculate the average wage of an industry and of an entire national economy in order to be able to compare wage levels.

The Average Wage

The average hourly wage can be calculated as follows:

$$Average\ hourly\ wage = \frac{Daily\ wage}{Number\ of\ daily\ working\ hours}$$

The same calculation can be made in order to obtain the magnitudes of the average weekly, monthly, and annual wage:

$$Av.\ weekly\ wage = \frac{Monthly\ wage}{Number\ of\ weeks\ worked\ /\ month}$$

$$Av.\ monthly\ wage = \frac{Annual\ wage}{Number\ of\ months\ worked\ /\ year}$$

Marx argues that the wage is inversely proportional to the number of hours worked and directly proportional to the hourly wage. If, for example, the absolute wage remains the same, but the working time is by absolute surplus-value production prolonged, then the hourly wage drops. If, for example, the weekly wage is £600 and corresponds to 30 hours per week, then the hourly wage is £600/30 = £20. If the normal working time increases to 40 hours per week without a wage increase, then the hourly wage drops to £600/40 = £15. A "mere prolongation of the working day lowers the price of labour, if no compensatory factor enters" (689).

Marx argues that capitalists tried to introduce payment by hourly wages with variable weekly working hours in London's building industry, which resulted in a strike in 1859/1860 (686).

Overtime

Marx also introduces the concept of overtime: Working beyond a specific number of hours per day or week is considered abnormal and all hours beyond the standard working time are therefore remunerated at a "better hourly rate ('extra pay')" (687). Marx explains that in the middle of the 19th century it was fairly common in Britain that "normal hours" were compensated at a very low rate, so that workers in various industries, such as bleaching and bookbinding (687), were forced to work overtime in order to survive.

The Software Industry: A Labour Aristocracy with Huge Amounts of Overtime

The software industry is an industry that is known for the circumstance that workers tend to work very long hours (see Fuchs 2014a, chapter 9). Software engineers tend to be highly paid and highly stressed. They typically work on software projects that have set deadlines, which results in phases with very long working hours. In the USA, making IT professionals work unpaid overtime is legal: The US's Fair Labor Standards Act [Section 13 (a) 17] provides an exemption from overpay for computer systems analysts, software engineers, or similar workers if they earn at least $27.63 an hour or $455 per week.

I argued supported by statistical data in chapter 19 that software/ICT professionals form a labour aristocracy that has relatively high hourly and total annual wages. This wealth of income comes, however, along with specific forms of poverty: Long working hours mean poverty of leisure; high stress means poverty of rest; a relative high turnover of labour in the software industry means poverty of stability in life; bad work–life balance means poverty of leisure and social relations.

Friedrich Engels describes in the 1892 preface to the English edition of *The Condition of the Working Class in England* that in 1885 in the UK there were workers whose "state of misery and insecurity in which they live now is as low as ever" (MECW 27, 266), but there was also "an aristocracy among the working-class" (engineers, carpenters, joiners, bricklayers) that has "succeeded in enforcing for themselves a relatively comfortable position" (MECW 27, 266). In the 21st century, software and computer professionals form such a labour aristocracy. Also Lenin (1920), based on Engels, spoke of a labour aristocracy that consists of "workers-turned-bourgeois", "who are quite philistine in their mode of life, in the size of their earnings and in their entire outlook" and are "the real *agents of the bourgeoisie in the working-class* movement, the labour lieutenants of the capitalist class". Many software and computer workers earn much higher wages and get more privileges than other workers, which makes it also more unlikely to resist capitalist rule. The lack of resistance is according to Engels typical for the labour aristocracy: "they are very nice people indeed nowadays to deal with, for any sensible capitalist in particular and for the whole capitalist class in general" (MECW 27, 266).

In the *Grundrisse*, Marx describes conditions of production, such as a high demand of labour in one specific industry, in which certain workers gain "surplus wages", which represent a "small share of [. . .] surplus labour" (Marx 1857/1858, 438). Martin Nicolaus therefore writes in the foreword that Marx shows that it is "theoretically possible, quite apart from the question of the economic cycle, for one fraction of the working class (but not the whole) to receive, via the mechanisms of the distribution of profit among the different capitalists, 'an extremely small share of' the surplus value produced by themselves in the form of 'surplus wages'" (Marx 1857/1858, 48). Software and computer professionals have in contrast to many other workers relatively high wages—they have surplus wages. They are, however, not just highly paid, but also highly stressed.

Marx describes in *Capital Volume 1* that in the early days of British capitalism the lengthening of the working day was achieved by control, surveillance, disciplinary measures, and legitimation by state laws. The price was an increase of class struggles that pressed for reducing working hours. The ICT industry's main way of increasing surplus-value production is also absolute surplus-value production—that is, the lengthening of the working day—but it takes a different approach: the coercion makes use of the law, but is also ideological and social: It is built into the company's culture of fun, playbour (play labour), employee services, and peer pressure. The result is that the total average working time and unpaid working hours per employee tend to increase. Marx described this case as a specific method of absolute and relative surplus-value production in which the productivity and intensity of labour remain constant, whereas the length of the working day is variable: If the working day is lengthened and the price of labour (wages) remains the same, "the surplus-value increases both absolutely and relatively. Although there is no absolute change in the value of labour-power, it suffers a relative fall. [...] Here, [...] the change of relative magnitude in the value of labour-power is the result of the change of absolute magnitude in surplus-value" (663).

What Marx explains in this passage is that the wages tend to relatively decrease the more hours employees work unpaid overtime because they then create additional surplus-value and profit. Labour contracts that make overwork unpaid are nowadays not uncommon in the ICT industry as the case of US labour legislation that enables such practices shows. This also means that in ICT companies that have all-inclusive contracts, where overtime is not paid extra, pressure to work long hours drives down the average hourly wage, and the more hours of overtime employees work, the more absolute surplus-value they produce and the higher the rate of surplus-value becomes.

Exercise for Chapter 20

Group exercise (G)
Project exercise (P)

Key Categories: Time-Wages, Overtime

Exercise 20.1 (G, P)

G: Work in groups: Conduct a search for statistics, research reports, academic studies, journal articles, books, book chapters, and journalistic reports that document the working conditions in specific digital media/software/Internet companies or the entire ICT sector. Analyse, interpret, and present the results. Pay particular attention to the level of wages per unit of time, if long hours are being worked that go beyond a regular working week of 35 to 40 hours, and if overtime is paid, only partly paid, or not paid at all.

P: You can also think of conducting a survey or interviews with workers in the ICT industry who live in your region about their working conditions.

21
PIECE-WAGES

What Is a Piece-Wage?

In chapter 21, Marx discusses the form that is besides the time-wage the major type of wage in capitalism: the piece-wage. Whereas in a time-wage relationship, workers are paid by the hour, day, week, or month, in a piece-wage system they are paid a wage per produced commodity.

> Piece-wages are not in fact a direct expression of any relation of value. It is not, therefore, a question of measuring the value of the piece by the labour-time incorporated in it. It is rather the reverse: the labour the worker has expended must be measured by the number of pieces he has produced. In time-wages the labour is measured by its immediate duration, in piece-wages by the quantity of products in which the labour has become embodied during a given time. The price of labour-time itself is finally determined by this equation: value of a day of labour = daily value of labour-power. The piece-wage is therefore only a modified form of the time-wage. (694)

Marx argues that the time-wage and the piece-wage "exist side by side", not just in capitalism, but also in "the same branches of industry" (692). He mentions, for example, London's compositors, shipwrights, and saddler workers, who were confronted with both wage-forms.

Piece-wages are "the most fruitful source of reductions on wages, and of frauds committed by the capitalists" (694). Under the piece-wage system, those who are not productive and fast enough tend to be quickly dismissed (694). The speed of labour controls performance so that there is a tendency for less surveillance in piece-labour than time-labour (695). Labour-speed controls performance because low speed results in small wages so that control is directly built into the wage system. Piece-wages tend to result in both relative and absolute surplus-value production: Workers tend to work as fast as possible and they tend to favour long working days in order to increase their wages:

> Given the system of piece-wages, it is naturally in the personal interest of the worker that he should strain his labour-power as intensely as possible; this in turn enables the capitalist to raise the normal degree of intensity of labour more easily. Moreover, the lengthening of the working day is now in the personal interest of the worker, since with it his daily or weekly wages rise. (695–696)

The Piece-Wage and the Rate of Surplus-Value

If both absolute and relative surplus-value production take place at the same time, then the rate of surplus-value tends to significantly increase. The piece-wage is therefore an attempt to dramatically increase the exploitation of labour.

Marx argues that the piece-wage goes back to the French and English economies in the 14th century, but only became widely used during the period of the manufactory, especially from 1797 until 1815, when "it served as a lever for the lengthening of the working day and the lowering of wages" (698). But the piece-wage was not limited to the 19th century and the time of the manufacture, but has remained an important element of the capitalist wage-system. It continues to exist in 21st-century informational capitalism.

Online Freelancing: A 21st-Century Piece-Wage System

In the 21st century, online platforms such as Amazon Mechanical Turk, PeoplePerHour, Upwork (eLance-ODesk), and Freelancer.com have emerged, where especially freelance information workers offer their services. In the UK, PeoplePerHour has for some time been the most widely used online freelance platform. It describes itself on its website as a platform that wants "to help people start and build their own businesses and live their dream of being independent", as "empowering [the] 'citizen entrepreneur'". "And we strongly believe that some time in the not so distant future, more people will be working on PPH than for the world's largest governments or for the largest FTSE companies just like the one I started my career in and in an very ironic way set off to 'free myself' from". PeoplePerHour offers the freelance categories of design, writing, and translation; video, photo, and audio; business support, social media, sales and marketing, software development, and mobile and web development. So it is a platform predominantly focused on information work.

Freelancers can post job offers, and people who need to get something done can post jobs that freelancers can apply for. Payment is possible either at a fixed price (piece-wage) or per hour (time-wage). According to statistics, there were 1.56 million freelancers in the UK in 2012, around 6% of the total workforce (Kitching and Smallbone 2012). The largest group of freelancers—around 265,000 or 17%—worked in art, literature, and the media (Kitching and Smallbone 2012). This group of freelancers made up 64.4% of all people working in this sector in the UK. There were 93,300 (6%) IT and telecommunications freelance professionals in 2011 (Kitching and Smallbone 2012). Freelancers generated around 8% of the private sector's turnover (Kitching and Smallbone 2012). Thirty-eight percent of UK freelancers worked from home and other places, 26% only at home, 33% only outside of the home (Kitching and Smallbone 2012). So 64% of UK freelancers worked at or from home. Their home is at the same time the household for free time and their work place for labour-time. It is a liquid space. Broadcast Now conducted a UK Freelancer Survey in the media and cultural industries in 2012 (N = 656).[1] Twenty-one percent of the respondents worked more than 60 hours a week, nearly 50% more than 50 hours, and 56% 10 hours or more a day. Forty-seven percent earned less than £25,000.

These data indicate that freelancers tend to work long hours. The liquefaction of the boundaries between the home and the work place and between working time and leisure time they experience tends to be dominated by more time being occupied by labour. At the same time liquefaction has not resulted in a high income for most freelancers. Connected to the freelance economy is a crowd-sourcing economy, in which companies try to find cheap or unpaid labour on the Internet with the help of platforms such as Amazon Mechanical Turk, eLance, oDesk, or PeoplePerHour.

PeoplePerHour and similar platforms advertise online freelancing as freedom and citizen entrepreneurship. The reality shows that freelancers in the information sector tend not to be rich entrepreneurs, but part of a young, urban precariat that is part of the 21st-century proletariat. They work long hours for little income, do not own capital, and depend on short-term contract work that is often paid by a piece-wage.

Here are some examples for piece-wage labour offered by freelancers on PeoplePerHour:[2]

- "I can design and build WordPress website for £48".
- "I can write SQL programs for you for £10".
- "I can provide the best PHP programming for £6".
- "I can setup your Wordpress Website for £21".
- "I can design your Logo for £24".
- "I can do your data analysis using programming languages for £18".
- "I can design eye catching magazine cover for £6".
- "I can call 50 potential customers/clients for £20".
- "I can write two personalized love poems and flower photo for £6".
- "I can write a 450–600 word high-quality article on a wide variety of topics for £6".
- "I can translate 1000 words from German to English and vice versa for £6".
- "I can add 100 YouTube Likes in your Video for £6".
- "I can add you 3000 Instragram followers for £6".
- "I can give 1000 plus facebook likes And 50+ Daily likes as bonus for your fan page for £6".
- "I can provide real 2000 Youtube views safe guaranteed 100% for £6".
- "I can give 200 retweets to your tweet in LESS than 24 hours for £6".
- "I can deliver 250 HIGH quality Youtube likes to your video for £6".
- "I can deliver 500 Facebook fans to your fan page in less than 24 hours for £6".
- "I can deliver 10.000 hits to your website in LESS than 24 hours for £6".

PeoplePerHour and comparable online platforms organise relations of exploitation that are grounded in the piece-wage. The piece-wage relationship is both a method of absolute and relative surplus value production: Workers may have to work long hours in order to achieve a wage that guarantees their survival. This is especially the case with platforms such as PeoplePerHour or Amazon Mechanical Turk, that are designed to crowdsource labour in order to reduce investment costs. At the same time the online freelancers will try to work as fast as possible because they do not have a guaranteed hourly wage. The result of crowdsourcing platforms is a tendency toward fewer jobs and low payment. The piece-wage is, as Marx pointed out, "the most fruitful source of reductions in wages, and of frauds committed by the capitalists" (694).

Performance-Based Payment in Call Centres

The Global Call Centre Project studied working conditions in call centres in 17 countries (for an analysis of the political economy of call centres, see Fuchs 2014a, chapter 10). The aggregated results (N = 2,477 companies in 17 countries) showed that 15.3% of the conducted labour was performance-based (Holman, Batt, and Holtgrewe 2007). Payment by individual performance was particularly high in the Netherlands, where 41% of all call centres in the study used it (Holman, Batt, and Holtgrewe 2007). In South Korea, 60% of the employees had part-time contracts. The level was 48% in Israel, 46% in the Netherlands, and 44% in Spain. In the UK (N = 100), 21% of the call centres used individual performance-related pay and 18% group-based performance pay (Holman, Wood, and Stride 2005).

Performance-based payment is a form of piece-wage: Employees are paid per sold commodity or successfully conducted conversation (e.g., participation in a survey, etc.). Such performance measurement puts pressure on call centre agents to use dubious tactics and to lie about who they are, what they are selling, what people are actually buying, and the qualities the sold commodities have.

Günter Wallraff as Undercover Call Centre Worker

Günter Wallraff is a German investigative journalist who became well-known when he worked undercover in the 1970s as the journalist "Hans Esser" for Germany's major tabloid *Bild* and documented how stories were partly invented. For his investigative reporting he also disguised himself, for example, as Turkish immigrant worker at McDonald's and other companies, as a black person in Bavaria, and as a call centre agent, and reported on his experiences.

For his investigative report on call centre labour, Wallraff, for example, worked undercover at the call centre ZIU-International, which sold signboards displaying the German Youth Protection Act to immigrant owners of small restaurants and snack stands who did not know the German law well. The call centre agents had to lie and say that they called on behalf of the youth protection authorities. If the shop owners did not want to buy a signboard, they said that they would send inspectors. Wallraff reported on the use of performance measurement: "In order not to be laid off immediately, I had to meet my target: at least five sales per day".[3]

Wallraff writes about the labour conditions in the call-centres he worked in:

> 60 computer workstations are installed in a confined space. The setting: a flat screen, a headset, and software that calls stored numbers after a mouse click. As soon as a connection is established, the address of the participant and the origin of the addresses are displayed. [. . .] I ask myself: Why do these workers stoop to do this? Who forces them? The woman at Cal-lOn who left ZIU had defended her former colleagues: They are often desperate people who were unemployed for a long time and clutch at the last straw. They now must convey energy and good spirits on the phone although they have a hard time. But what consequences does such labour have for the employees? [. . .] Already the furnishing of the office gives an answer: A board hangs on the wall, on which sales are recorded by name. If somebody has brought about a new deal, s/he goes to the front and notes it. This automatically creates a pressure to success and competition.[4]

The examples show that the piece-wage continues to exist and to be a source of high rates of exploitation in capitalism in the information age. The feminist political economist of communication Catherine McKercher concludes in an analysis of freelancing in the culture industry that women freelancers are particularly affected by piece-work and precarious labour. "Piece work allows owners to assert moral rights to a creator's work, frees owners from any responsibility to the creator beyond a one-off payment for the product, and permits owners to encourage competition among workers over who will accept the lowest rate" (McKercher 2014, 227).

Exercise for Chapter 21

Group exercise (G)
Project exercise (P)

Key Category: Piece-Wage

Exercise 21.1 (G, P)

Marx analyses the piece-wage in chapter 21.

(G) Work in groups: Search for reports and analyses of piece-wages in the media, cultural, digital, and information industries. Have especially a look at what kind of pressure piece-wages put on information workers and how they report about these pressures.

Document and present the results.

(P) You can also consider conducting interviews with piece-workers in the information industries. Discuss what the piece-wage's specific characteristics are in the capitalist information economy.

Notes

1 http://www.broadcastnow.co.uk/freelancer/freelancer-survey-2012-i-cant-do-this-much-longer/5043075.article (accessed on December 12, 2013).
2 Accessed on August 22, 2014.
3 Translation from German: "Um nicht sofort entlassen zu werden, muss ich mein Soll erfüllen: mindestens fünf Abschlüsse am Tag" (Undercover—Bei Anruf Abzocke, http://www.dokumax.com/gunter-wallraff-undercover-bei-anruf-abzocke-doku-video_24fe964b2.html [accessed on August 22, 2014]).
4 Translation from German:

> Auf engstem Raum sind hier 60 Computerarbeitsplätze installiert. Die Ausstattung: Flachbildschirm, Headset und Software, die gespeicherte Nummern nach Mausklick anwählt. Sobald eine Verbindung zustande kommt, erscheinen auf dem Bildschirm die Anschrift des Teilnehmers und die Herkunft der Adresse. [. . .] Ich frage mich: Warum geben sie sich dafür her? Wer zwingt sie dazu? Die Frau bei CallOn, die bei ZIU ausgestiegen war, hatte ihre früheren Kollegen in Schutz genommen: Es seien oft Verzweifelte, die über lange Zeit arbeitslos gewesen seien und sich an den letzten Strohhalm klammerten. Die nun am Telefon Energie und gute Laune versprühen müssten, obwohl es ihnen dreckig gehe. Aber welche Auswirkungen hat eine solche Arbeit auf die Beschäftigten? Einmal unterstellt, dass hier keine Betrüger am Werke sind, die lustvoll andere ausnehmen. Schon die Einrichtung des Büros gibt eine Antwort: An der Wand hängt eine Tafel, auf der die Verkaufsabschlüsse namentlich erfasst werden. Wer einen neuen Abschluss zustande gebracht hat, geht nach vorn und notiert das. So entsteht automatisch Erfolgs- und Konkurrenzdruck. (Wallraff 2007)

22

NATIONAL DIFFERENCES IN WAGES

In chapter 22, Marx deals with the question of how wages compare to each other internationally. He says that important factors that shape wage-levels are the natural conditions of production, the price of the means of production, the cost of education, the influence of cheap labour, the productivity of labour, and the role of absolute and relative surplus-value production (701).

Universal Labour

Marx speaks of "universal labour" (702, in German, "universelle Arbeit") as the international average standard of labour—that is, labour with an average international level of wages, productivity, intensity, extensity, etc. "The more intense national labour, therefore, as compared with the less intense, produces in the same time more value, which expresses itself in more money" (702).

Marx says that the law of value operates in a modified form on the international level and the world market, where more productive nations (702) enjoy advantages: "The different quantities of commodities of the same kind, produced in different countries in the same working time, have, therefore, unequal international values, which are expressed in different prices, i.e. in sums of money varying according to international values" (702). The more productive nation will produce at lower values and be able to sell at lower prices and to attain competitive advantages. Marx argues that the wages tend to be higher in such nations, whereas the rate of exploitation/surplus-value tends to be higher in less productive nations.

Samir Amin: The Law of Worldwide Value

Especially theories of imperialism, such as world systems theory, have within Marxist theory analysed international political-economic relations. I have in chapter 12 pointed out that in world systems theory, Samir Amin has described the law of worldwide value, which results in a transfer of value from the periphery to core countries and regions (see chapter 12).

There are often big *differences in productivity* and therefore in wages in peripheral regions' various economic sectors (Amin 1976, 215–218). There are quite often great disparities in wages between urban and rural areas as well as better and lesser-trained labour forces (Amin 1976, 221). There are also differences in productivity between the cores and the periphery to the disadvantage of the periphery. Less productive nations' commodities tend to have higher values; the commodities require more labour-power to be produced. The more competitive and productive nations' commodities tend to have lower values, which allows lower prices, and they thus set the levels at the world market. They compel producers in less productive nations to sell at the international market-level set by the more productive companies. Therefore wage levels in the less productive countries have to be lowered in order to be competitive.

Connected to the differences in productivity is an *unequal economic structure*: The economies of the peripheral regions often have a high proportion of agriculture and the service sector in their value and employment structures, while the newest economic developments take place in the centres (Amin 1976, 239–246). The industries in peripheral regions often have difficulty competing with companies in the centres. The services in the periphery often have low productivity. There has been more industrialisation in the periphery since 1945, but it is nevertheless an unequal industrialisation relative to the core (Amin 1997, 2).

The law of worldwide value (Amin 2010) by which value is transferred from the periphery to the centres is enabled by five monopolies: the monopoly on technology, of the financial markets, on access to natural resources, of media and communication, and on weapons of mass destruction (Amin 1997, 4–5). The average global value of goods and labour play a key role because through them arise the disadvantages of the periphery and the advantages of the centres (Amin 2010, 83–86). The goods from the periphery contain more hours of labour than those of the centres, but are often sold at below the global average value, which is set in the centres, which take advantage of their higher productivity.

Global Differences in Productivity

In chapter 22, Marx argues that more productive countries tend to have higher profits and wages and less productive ones higher rates of exploitation. Detailed international macroeconomic statistics did not exist at the time of Marx, so he cites anecdotal evidence for his analysis. Today there are a lot more international comparative macroeconomic statistics available. Macroeconomics does, however, not tailor its data to Marx's theory because economics is in general dominated by non-Marxist approaches. Therefore some of the data required for Marxist calculations are simply not available.

The UN World Productivity Database provides data for the total factor productivity for a selection of countries. Total factor productivity is a measure that takes into account the impact of technological innovations on productivity. In the UN database, measures are given relative to the USA. So a value of 0.900 means, for example, a productivity that is 10% lower than in the USA.

One measure for national wealth is the gross domestic product (GDP) per capita. It combines profits, wages, and constant capital in one variable and therefore says nothing about the distribution of wealth. It can nonetheless for statistical purposes be used as a measure for general wealth.

There is no indicator for all countries available that measures the rate of surplus-value. The International Labour Organization provides, however, wage share–data for many countries. The wage share is the total wages' share in the GDP. It is a measure that shows the power of labour in relation to the overall value. A low wage share is no proof for a high rate of surplus-value because also profits and constant capital play a role in the denominator. The wage share can, however, measure the relative power and wealth of labour.

Data on Total Factor Productivity

Table 22.1 shows these three variables (total factor productivity, GDP per capita rank, unadjusted wage share) for 66 countries. The data stems from three different databases. The number of 66 countries emerged from combining data from all three databases and only leaving those entries for which all three data items were available.

TABLE 22.1 Productivity, GDP rank, and wage share for 66 countries (data sources: total factor productivity: UN World Productivity Database, year: 2010; GDP per capita rank: Human Development Report, year: 2014; wage share: International Labour Organization: Global Wage Report 2012/2013); for each country the latest available data was selected

Country	Total factor productivity	GDP per capita rank	Unadjusted wage share
Ireland	1.280	28	45.9
Belgium	1.092	22	52.9
USA	1.000	11	55.7
Hong Kong (China)	0.840	10	51.6
Austria	0.809	15	55.0
Netherlands	0.801	17	52.1
Norway	0.800	6	46.7
Mauritius	0.793	66	33.8
Canada	0.785	19	53.6
Denmark	0.782	16	58.7
UK	0.776	27	55.5
France	0.775	25	52.7
Italy	0.745	29	42.9
Finland	0.740	23	50.6
Cyprus	0.726	37	46.1
Israel	0.726	34	48.7
Switzerland	0.723	9	65.9
Sweden	0.718	13	53.7
New Zealand	0.681	30	43.7
Spain	0.676	32	49.0
Japan	0.640	24	53.2
Korea, Republic of	0.637	33	49.9
Greece	0.632	40	37.7
Portugal	0.612	43	51.1
Trinidad and Tobago	0.585	39	43.2
Chile	0.577	54	40.6
Iran, Islamic Republic of	0.572	79	20.7
Argentina	0.554	63	42.9
Botswana	0.539	74	23.4
Uruguay	0.537	61	34.4
South Africa	0.529	84	45.2
Gabon	0.526	65	21.1
Dominican Republic	0.491	92	30.6
Mexico	0.486	70	29.2
Egypt	0.460	94	24.9
Venezuela	0.448	64	32.3
Tunisia	0.428	93	36.1
Namibia	0.408	106	40.7
Guatemala	0.406	117	30.6
Costa Rica	0.398	81	50.5
Fiji	0.396	114	38.0
Jordan	0.395	89	40.4
Colombia	0.382	87	32.2
Panama	0.365	68	30.0
Sri Lanka	0.292	103	53.7
Cameroon	0.283	157	19.9
Philippines	0.275	119	28.6
Bolivia, Plurinational State of	0.275	124	26.5

Country	Total factor productivity	GDP per capita rank	Unadjusted wage share
Morocco	0.252	115	30.8
Côte d'Ivoire	0.245	153	22.0
Papua New Guinea	0.241	158	15.1
China	0.227	88	48.0
Jamaica	0.226	110	45.0
India	0.225	131	29.9
Honduras	0.201	140	44.5
Senegal	0.193	161	20.0
Nepal	0.180	160	35.3
Mozambique	0.169	184	25.5
Lesotho	0.161	152	16.4
Sierra Leone	0.156	164	34.9
Kenya	0.148	162	35.4
Niger	0.137	185	14.8
Burkina Faso	0.086	169	20.3
Nigeria	0.085	126	4.1
Burundi	0.077	187	22.8
Tanzania, United Republic of	0.054	166	12.8

TABLE 22.2 Correlation analysis

	Wage share	GDP per capita rank
Productivity	0.69, significance < 0.001	−0.90, significance < 0.001

Conducting correlation analysis allows us to analyse if there is a statistical relationship between productivity and the other two variables. Table 22.2 shows the results of the correlations that was carried out with the software PSPP.

There is a strong positive correlation between productivity and the wage share and a strong negative correlation between productivity and the GDP per capita in the 66 analysed countries. Sixty-six countries is a good sample as it constitutes about one-third of the countries in the world. The statistical results show a tendency that the higher a country's productivity, the higher its wage share and the lower its GDP rank (which means the higher its GDP per capita).

The data provide some mathematical indication for a confirmation of Marx's analysis in chapter 22—namely, that countries with higher productivity tend to have higher wage levels and lower rates of exploitation and that countries with lower productivity tend to have lower wage levels and higher rates of exploitation. The rate of exploitation does of course not correspond to the wage share, but we can at least say that higher productivity in a country tends to empower workers in making demands for wage increases in class struggles and to disempower workers in less productive countries. Capitalists in poor countries with low rates of productivity are forced to increase profits by lowering wages so that they can compete with the commodity prices set by productive nations and companies on the world market.

In the 20th century's last quarter and in the 21st century, computers have played an important role in economies and were part of the informatisation of the economy and society. We can therefore assume that in the nations with the highest levels of productivity the computerisation of production are the most advanced. Table 22.1 shows that in the first 10 years of the 2000s, total factor productivity was highest in Ireland, Belgium, and the USA. Looking at the available data in the UN World Productivity Database shows that during the same years total factor productivity was also very high in Luxembourg, Barbados, and Mauritius.

According to the data, there seems to be a tendency that highly productive countries are located in the West and less productive ones in the rest of the world. The correlations do not imply that high productivity brings about very high wage shares in the West; it rather shows a difference between Western and non-Western countries. Ireland, for example, has high productivity, but at the same time for a Western country a relatively low wage rate and therefore a rather weak working class. High productivity also does not imply endless economic growth. In Ireland, high profits, which stemmed from high productivity and exploitation, seem to have been invested into speculative finance, especially in the housing market. At the same time, the relatively low wages compelled workers to take out loans and mortgages in order to sustain themselves. An Irish credit and property bubble built up. It exploded in 2008 and plunged Ireland into a very deep crisis.

Exercise for Chapter 22

Group exercise (G)
Project exercise (P)

Key Categories: National Wage-Differences, International Law of Value

Exercise 22.1 (G)

Work in groups: Identify a list of 10 countries that differ in location and general wealth. Each group selects one occupation in the information/media/cultural/digital industries. Collect data about average wage-rates in these occupations and conduct an international comparison. Possible data sources are personal contacts in these countries, statistics, research reports, academic publications, interviews with experts and workers.

Present and compare the results.

PART VII

THE PROCESS OF ACCUMULATION OF CAPITAL

The capital accumulation process as a whole

In part VII (chapters 23–25), Marx draws together the analysis of the previous chapters and focuses on the capital accumulation process as a whole:

$$M–C \ (c, v).. \ P.. \ C' \ (s)–M' \ (p).$$

Marx argues that the capital accumulation process consists of three parts (709):

1. The purchase of means of production and labour-power (M–C)
2. The production of a new commodity that contains surplus-value (P..C')
3. The selling of this commodity that yields profit p (C'–M')

The crucial aspect is that money M needs to be turned into capital M' and parts of it need to be reinvested.

Surplus-value is split up into profit, interest, and rent. Marx (1894) discusses this distinction in *Capital Volume 3*.

23

SIMPLE REPRODUCTION

Production and Reproduction

Marx argues that economic production and consumption must be repeated in all societies as a matter of economic existence. Economic production would therefore be an important part of the reproduction of the existence of humans and society (711): "every process of production is at the same time a process of reproduction" (711). We can add that the economic production of basic use-values not just involves housing and food, but also information goods such as education, and communication that sustains social relations, morality, and norms.

In capitalism, economic production not just reproduces means of subsistence, but also reproduces and increases capital. Capitalism and all capitalist companies must continuously reproduce and repeat "the periodic increment of the value of the capital" (712).

Simple Reproduction

Simple reproduction means according to Marx that capitalists use the whole surplus-value or profit p ($M' = M + p$) "as a fund to provide for his consumption" (712). In this case, the initially invested sum of money $M = c + v$ is not increased. It remains constant "on the same scale as before" (712). Capital is reproduced, but not increased and accumulated. "Expanded reproduction" is a term that Marx in contrast uses for the accumulation of capital (Marx 1885, chapter 17). The sum of invested capital M_n in period n is increased beyond the invested sum M_{n-1} in the previous period n–1. Capital *expands*.

Marx argues that the "worker is not paid until after he has expended his labour-power, and realized both the value of his labour-power and a certain quantity of surplus-value in the shape of commodities" (712). The wages of the worker are paid out of the capital s/he previously created. "It is his labour of last week, or of last year, that pays for his labour-power this week or this year" (713). It is therefore a bourgeois ideological illusion that the capitalist pays for the worker; the worker rather produces the capital, out of which her/his labour-power is paid. In the German language, a related ideology is that the employer gives labour ("employer" means "Arbeitgeber" in German, which is literally translated as "labour-giver") and the employee takes labour ("Arbeitnehmer" = "labour-taker"). Rather, the employee gives unpaid labour-time to the employer, who takes and steals it without payment and so derives a profit from it.

Primitive Accumulation

Marx introduces the notion of the primitive accumulation of capital in chapter 23, by which he means the way "the capitalist, once upon a time, became possessed of money" (714) and the means of production. He analyses "primitive accumulation" in detail in part VIII, but it is good to note that he first introduces the term in chapter 23. In this starting point, the capitalist becomes the owner of the means of production and the worker becomes compelled to sell his/her labour-power in order to survive. Reproduction also means the constant renewal and perpetuation of this class relationship: "The capitalist process of production, therefore, seen as a total, connected process, i.e. a process of reproduction, produces not only commodities, not only surplus-value, but it also produces and reproduces the capital-relation itself; on the one hand the capitalist, on the other the wage-labourer" (724).

The Reproduction of Alienation

Capitalism also permanently reproduces the alienation of the workers—that is, their non-ownership of the means of production and the products they create. I have already cited in chapter 7 an important passage from chapter 23 (716) where Marx speaks of the reproduction of alienation in the more detailed discussion of alienation, so I do not reproduce it here a second time, but advise the reader to now go back to chapter 7 of this book and have a look at my discussion of how Marx discusses alienation.

Individual and Productive Consumption

Marx points out that workers are involved in two forms of consumption: They consume the means of production in order to produce commodities and surplus-value (productive consumption), and they consume the means of subsistence they buy with their wages in order to survive and sustain their labour-power (individual consumption) (717).

> The worker's productive consumption and his individual consumption are therefore totally distinct. In the former, he acts as the motive power of capital, and belongs to the capitalist. In the latter, he belongs to himself, and performs his necessary vital functions outside the production process. The result of the first kind of consumption is that the capitalist continues to live, of the second, that the worker himself continues to live. (717)

Both the workers' individual and productive consumption stand under the control of capital and help capital accumulation—the latter by creating commodities, the former by reproducing labour-power. Workers help in the production "of wealth for other people" (719)—that is, for the capitalists. The worker has to rebuy means of subsistence in order to survive, which compels him/her to continuously enter the wage-labour relationship. "The Roman slave was held by chains; the wage-labourer is bound to his owner by invisible threads" (719). It is not Adam Smith's invisible hand that coordinates the emergence of general wealth from egoistic capitalist practices, but rather Marx's invisible threat of class structures that compels workers to let capitalists exploit them so that capital can continuously be accumulated. "Capitalist production therefore reproduces in the course of its own process the separation between labour-power and the conditions of labour. It thereby reproduces and perpetuates the conditions under which the worker is exploited" (723).

The Dimensions of Reproduction in Capitalism

I have pointed out in chapters 6 and 16 the importance of reproductive labour in the household, as it helps sustain labour-power. Reproductive labour includes, for example, housework, education, public services, care, sexuality, the provision of public means of communication and transport, etc. Marx says that means of subsistence "have to be consumed to reproduce the muscles, nerves, bones and brains of existing workers, and to bring new workers into existence" (717). One needs to add that means of subsistence are only partly bought on the market. Unpaid house workers and tax-funded public service workers produce other parts of it.

Marx shows in chapter 23 that capitalism is based on the constant reproduction of productive consumption, individual consumption, the production of commodities, and the increase of capital, which is brought about by structural violence exerted against the non-owners of capital so that the class relationship between capital and labour is reproduced. Capitalist production is reproduction in multiple senses:

- It involves the constant production and consumption of commodities C and C′.
- It involves the reproduction of labour-power by reproductive labour.
- It is a constant repetition of capital accumulation on a larger scale M–C..P..C′–M′.
- It is the reproduction of the exploitation of labour and the class relationship between capital and labour.

Given that the "capitalist continues to live" (717) by the exploitation of labour and the workers' productive consumption, workers have a powerful role: If they collectively go on strike; refuse to work; or occupy factories, offices, land, and means of communication and transport, then capital's breath of life is seriously disrupted. The workers' important role in the reproduction process does not just make them "an appendage of capital" (719), but also gives them in essence the power to overthrow capitalism and to substitute it with a worker-controlled economy and a citizen-controlled society.

Exercise for Chapter 23

Group exercise (G)
Project exercise (P)

Key Categories: Reproduction, Simple Reproduction of Capital, Expanded Reproduction of Capital, Primitive Accumulation

Exercise 23.1 (P)

Marx explains in chapter 23 that there is an original state of capital ownership and a constant reproduction of the various structures that enable and reproduce capitalism. He calls all of this together the reproduction of capitalism.

The Forbes list of the world's billionaires is published annually and documents data on the world's richest people and their wealth.

Work in groups: Identify media billionaires in the current Forbes list. Each group selects one media billionaire, traces the development of his/her wealth over the past years by backtracking the data in the Forbes lists of previous years, and searches for information and critical reports on how s/he became rich. Such stories of individual wealth are often related to company histories, so also have a look at who provided the initial capital for the companies that media billionaires founded or in which they are directors/managers.

Discuss: Why is the idea of the American dream that everyone can advance from a dishwasher to a millionaire mistaken and ideological? How are riches produced and distributed in capitalism?

24

THE TRANSFORMATION OF SURPLUS-VALUE INTO CAPITAL

The Accumulation of Capital

Marx defines the accumulation of capital (or the extended reproduction of capital) as the "employment of surplus-value as capital, or its reconversion into capital" (725). "Accumulation requires the transformation of a portion of the surplus product into capital" (726).

Surplus-labour creates a surplus product and surplus-value; these are, when the commodity is sold, transformed into monetary profits. Parts of the profit (after deductions for the payment of interest, salaries of managers and capitalists, dividends) are reinvested so that the profit is laid out for additional constant and variable capital—that is, for the "production of additional means of production and subsistence" (727). Accumulation is therefore "production of capital on a progressively increasing scale" (727). It is grounded in the "separation of property from labour" (730).

Capital accumulation means that capitalists are compelled to try to increase their capital:

$M-M'(>M)-M''(>M')-M'''(>M'')-\ldots$
$M-M'$ is just an abbreviation for the full process M–C (c, v).. P.. C'–M'.

Visualisation of the Cycle of Capital Accumulation

Marx summarises the process of capital accumulation in section 24.1. I have visualised this process in figure 24.1.

The capitalist invests money M for purchasing two commodities: means of production (constant capital c) and labour-power (variable capital). In the production process P, the workers transfer the value of the means of production to the product and create the value of their own labour-power and a surplus-value. These values are objectified in a new product C', which has a larger value than the combination of the initial commodities the capitalist bought and brought into the production process. The commodity C' is sold for a sum of money M' that is larger than M. It contains a profit. The new capital is reinvested in order to produce more commodities, which can then yield more profit.

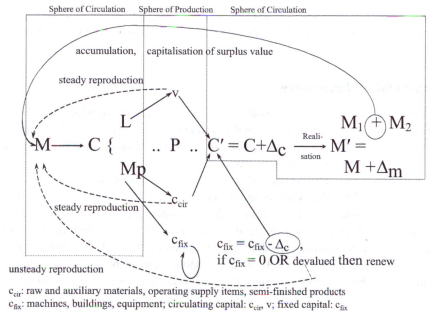

FIGURE 24.1 The process of capital accumulation

Three Results of the Transformation of Money into Capital

Marx argues that there are three results of the transformation of money into capital. The result is

1. that the product belongs to the capitalist and not to the worker;
2. that the value of this product includes, apart from the value of the capital advanced, a surplus-value, which costs the worker labour but the capitalist nothing, and which nonetheless becomes the legitimate property of the capitalist;
3. that the worker has retained his labour-power and can sell it anew if he finds another buyer (731).

So these three characteristics are the workers' nonownership/alienation; surplus-value; and double-"free" wage-labour. Wealth as a consequence is "the property of those who are in a position to appropriate the unpaid labour of others over and over again" (733). Exploitation is inherently built into all class societies and is their constituent principle.

Profit's Different Parts

Marx criticises (734–738) Adam Smith, David Riccardo, John Stuart Mill, and other political economists' assumption that all profit is transformed into wages. Their argument is erroneous because the capitalist who has an increased sum of capital available and wants to produce more commodities than before does not just needs more labour-power, but also more means of production.

Marx distinguishes the part of the revenue that the capitalist takes for his/her own subsistence and for buying luxury goods as revenue and the other part as accumulated capital (738–746). To be precise, one needs to add that in corporations dividends are part of revenue, and if the corporation must pay back a loan to a bank, then also interest payments are deduced from capital. Marx, however, also uses the term "revenue" for designating surplus-value (738, footnote 21). Profit is divided into different parts: reinvested capital, interest payments, owners' and shareholders' dividends, bonus payments, and compensation.

The Accumulation Imperative

The capitalist "shares with the miser an absolute drive towards self-enrichment" (739). This drive derives from a "social mechanism" in which the capitalist "is merely a cog" (739). Whereas the miser wants to divest as much money from economic circulation as possible, the capitalist has to strive to keep ever-larger amounts of capital in circulation.

Marx summarises the imperatives and convictions of corporations in the following words: "Accumulate, accumulate! That is Moses and the prophets! [...] Therefore, save, save—that is, reconvert the greatest possible portion of surplus-value or surplus-product into capital! Accumulation for accumulation's sake, production for production's sake: this was the formula in which classical economics expressed the historical mission of the bourgeoisie" (742). The accumulation imperative stops at nothing. Marx here deliberately alludes to Moses because he wants to express that capital accumulation is just like religion a fetishism that makes reality appear in a distorted form.

Four Factors that Influence Capital Accumulation

Marx points out that four factors influence the amount of capital that is accumulated (747–757):

- the degree of exploitation of labour-power, including increases achieved by the lengthening of the working day and wage repression so that labour-power is remunerated below its value
- the productivity of labour arising from scientific and technological advances
- the more scientifically and technologically advanced capitalism becomes, the more it makes use of the "free service of past labour" (757) that developed scientific knowledge and technological progress as well as the gratis use of natural resources and reproductive labour
- the total number of workers employed, which tends to increase with the growth of capital

Exercise for Chapter 24

Group exercise (G)
Project exercise (P)

Key Categories: Accumulation of Capital, Revenue

Exercise 24.1 (G)

Identify various forms of capital accumulation in the media, digital, and cultural industries (they are commonly called "business models"). Discuss for each form how capital accumulation works. What kinds of labour are involved, and how are they organised? What is the commodity? How is the commodity sold? What is specific for capital accumulation in the media, digital, and cultural industries, and how do they differ from other capital accumulation models?

25

THE GENERAL LAW OF CAPITALIST ACCUMULATION

The Technical and the Organic Composition of Capital

Marx introduces the notion of the organic composition of capital, the relationship of constant capital and variable capital $\frac{c}{v}$, in chapter 25:

> The composition of capital is to be understood in a twofold sense. As value, it is determined by the proportion in which it is divided into constant capital, or the value of the means of production, and variable capital, or the value of labour-power, the sum total of wages. As material, as it functions in the process of production, all capital is divided into means of production and living labour-power. This latter composition is determined by the relation between the mass of the means of production employed on the one hand, and the mass of labour necessary for their employment on the other. I call the former the value-composition, the latter the technical composition of capital. There is a close correlation between the two. To express this, I call the value-composition of capital, in so far as it is determined by its technical composition and mirrors the changes in the latter, the organic composition of capital. Wherever I refer to the composition of capital, without further qualification, its organic composition is always understood. (762)

Calculating the Organic Composition of Capital: An Example

So Marx distinguishes between the technical and the organic composition of capital. Let us, for example, assume that a software company has 10 employees, each of whom use one computer as a means of production. They all use Microsoft Visual Studio as software development kit, so the company pays for 10 developer licenses, which are annually renewed. All 10 employees work in an office that the company rents. In the software production process, there is a technical composition of capital that consists of 10 computers. Each computer runs one licensed version of Visual Studio. Also a rented office forms part of the constant capital. Ten workers' labour-power makes up the variable capital. Let us assume that new computers are bought all two years and one computer costs £1,000. So the annual wear and tear of one computer is £500. The software licenses have to be renewed annually and each one costs £500 per year. The office rent is £10,000 per month or £120,000 per year. The average annual salary is £40,000.

The calculation of the organic composition of capital must be related to a specific period of time, such as one year. In our example, given a period of one year, the average organic composition of capital is

$$oc = \frac{c}{v} = \frac{£500 \star 10 + £500 \star 10 + £120,000}{£40,000 \star 10} = \frac{£5,000 + £5,000 + £120,000}{£400,000}$$

$$= \frac{£130,000}{£400,000} = 32.5\%$$

I have discussed aspects of the organic composition in chapters 12 (in the context of relative surplus-value), 15 (in the context of machinery), 17 (in the context of the rate of profit), and 18 (in the context of the rate of surplus-value). In chapter 17, I showed with the example of the UK economy and the UK computer and software industry how the organic composition can be approximated with the help of macroeconomic statistical data.

Two Distinct Cases of How the Organic Composition Can Develop: Case 1

Marx discusses two distinct cases of how the organic composition can develop.

First, he has a look at what happens if the demand for labour increases (section 25.1).

If in our example, an additional worker is employed as a freelancer who pays for his/her own means of production and works from home, but achieves the same annual wage; then the constant capital costs remain equal, but the variable capital costs increase so that the result is a drop in the organic composition:

$$oc = \frac{c}{v} = \frac{£500 \star 10 + £500 \star 10 + £120,000}{£40,000 \star 11} = \frac{£5,000 + £5,000 + £120,000}{£440,000}$$

$$= \frac{£130,000}{£440,000} = 29.5\%$$

The wage sum has increased. Marx points out that such an increase can also result from demands in wage increases, if, for example, there is a strong union that negotiates an increase of the 10 workers' annual wage from £40,000 to £44,000. If no additional workers are employed, then this results in the same drop of the organic composition to 29.5%. If surplus-value s and profit p do not absolutely increase, then an increase of the wage sum will result in a drop of the rate of profit. The rate of profit is directly proportional to the organic composition and inversely proportional to the rate of surplus-value:

$$rate\ of\ profit : rp = \frac{p}{c + v} = \frac{\frac{p}{v}}{\frac{c}{v} + 1} = \frac{organic\ composition}{rate\ of\ surplus-value + 1}$$

Let us assume that the annual profit the 10 workers in the example create is £100,000, that their union negotiates an average wage increase from £40,000 to £44,000, and that constant capital does not change. Let us see how the organic composition, the rate of surplus-value, and the rate of profit develop. In the initial situation, we get

$$oc1 = 32.5\%, rs1 = \frac{p}{v} = \frac{£100,000}{£400,000} = 25\%,$$

$$rp1 = \frac{p}{c+v} = \frac{£100,000}{£130,000 + £400,000} = 18.9\%$$

At the second point of time, variable capital increases to v = £440,000, whereas constant capital c and profit p do not change:

$$oc2 = 29.5\%, rs2 = \frac{p}{v} = \frac{£100,000}{£440,000} = 22.7\%,$$

$$rp2 = \frac{p}{c+v} = \frac{£100,000}{£130,000 + £440,000} = 17.5\%.$$

In the example, both the rate of surplus-value and the organic composition have dropped. The organic composition's fall can in the example not offset the drop of the rate of surplus-value so that the rate of profit drops from 18.9% to 17.5%.

Given that such a development threatens profitability, Marx argues that an increase of the wage sum or a decrease of the rate of exploitation can very likely result in reactions by capital that aim at weakening the workers and their unions' power (771).

Two Distinct Cases of How the Organic Composition Can Develop: Case 2

Second, Marx discusses a relative decrease of variable capital v (section 25.2). He speaks in this context of a "law of the progressive growth of the constant part of capital in comparison with the variable part" (773). The "growing extent of the means of production, as compared with the labour-power incorporate in them, is an expression of the growing productivity of labour" (773). So Marx argues that there is a tendency that with scientific and technological progress, the organic composition of capital tends to rise.

Let us assume in the case of the example software company that a new software engineering developer's kit allows an increase in the productivity of labour so that the company owners lay off one worker. An annual licence for this tool costs double the price of Visual Studio—that is, £1000. Given that there are now just nine workers, there are also only nine computers (each costing £500 per year) and nine licences as means of production. The annually produced profit remains constant at p = £100,000. Office rent remains unchanged at £120,000. Let us see how the organic composition, the rate of surplus-value, and the rate of profit develop:

$$oc = \frac{c}{v} = \frac{9 * £1,000 + 9 * £500 + £120,000}{9 * 40,000} = \frac{£133,500}{£360,000} = 37.1\%$$

$$rs = \frac{p}{v} = \frac{£100,000}{£360,000} = 27.8\%,$$

$$rp = \frac{p}{c+v} = \frac{£100,000}{£133,500 + £360,000} = 20.3\%$$

The organic composition of capital oc has increased from 32.5% to 37.1%. The rate of exploitation rs has simultaneously increased from 25% to 27.8%. The total effect is that the rate of profit rp increases from 18.9% to 20.3%.

The Dialectic of the Repulsion and Attraction of Capitals

Marx also speaks of a dialectic of the repulsion and attraction of capitals. New capitals emerge in the accumulation process; there is "repulsion of many individual capitals from one another" (777). More productive labour can produce at lower values, which allows their companies to sell commodities at cheaper prices, whereas companies with less productive labour have problems competing (777). The credit system tends to favour specific capitals that as a result are enabled to buy more productive technologies (777–778). Competition and credit are the two "most powerful levers of centralization" (779). Centralisation of capital means the "expropriation of capitalist by capitalist, transformation of many small into few large capitals" (777). Capital centralisation is the "attraction of capitals", the "destruction of their individual independence" (777).

I explained in section 1.3 of chapter 1 Hegel's dialectic of attraction and repulsion, which Marx uses for analysing the dialectic of the value-forms in *Capital Volume 1*'s section 1.3, the dialectic of the single worker and many workers in the cooperation process in chapter 13 (section 13.1), and the attraction and repulsion of workers by technology in chapter 15 (section 15.7). I refer the reader to my explanations in chapter 1 about Hegel's understanding of this dialectic and to chapters 1 (1.3), 13 (13.1), and 15 (15.7) for Marx's application of it. In chapter 25 (section 25.2), Marx adds another example of this dialectic: the dialectic of the attraction and repulsion of capitals. The growth of capital can repulse capitals so that additional capitals enter the market. There are many capitals. One capital is therefore not just a capital in-itself, but stands in a competitive relationship with many other capitals; it is one of many capitals.

The peculiar structures of competition, value production, science, technology, and credit result, however, in the tendency to sublate the contradiction between one capital and many capitals so that the centralisation of capital emerges as a negation of the negation of this contradiction. Many capitals

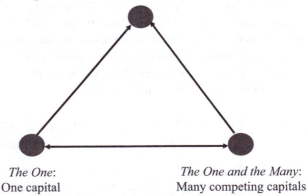

Attraction through repulsion of capitals: Centralisation of capital
(one capital asserts itself and destroys other capitals)

The One:
One capital

The One and the Many:
Many competing capitals

FIGURE 25.1 The dialectic of the attraction and repulsion of capitals

repulse each other because they compete, but at the same time attract each other because they are all capitals subject to the laws of capitalism. Their contradiction is sublated when one (or several) capital(s) centralise(s) production and markets and destroy(s) others. A special form of attraction through repulsion, the centralisation of capital, emerges: One capital attracts the others and repulses them by destroying them so that it becomes more powerful. Figure 25.1 visualises the dialectic of the attraction and repulsion of capitals.

The Unemployment Tendency

Marx discusses in section 25.3 that the tendency of the organic composition to rise results in a tendency for the production of unemployment. The increase of constant capital and the reduction of variable capital induce unemployment. Marx terms the unemployed also the "surplus population" and the "industrial reserve army" (784) because this part of the population is a "human material always ready for exploitation by capital" (784). "The working population therefore produces both the accumulation of capital and the means by which it is itself made relatively superfluous" (783).

Marx describes the cycle of capitalist development the following way (785, 790–791):

*   There is a drive to increase productivity.
*   => New technologies emerge that induce demand for additional labour in new industries and transformed existing industries.
*   => Productivity increases.
*   => Increases of productivity allow producing the same or more commodities in less time.
*   => Fewer workers are needed so that in some industries employees are laid off and become unemployed.
*   Productivity growth reaches limits so that there is a tendency for the overproduction of commodities and capital; unemployment has negative rebound effects on consumption and specific industries.
*   => A crisis emerges that results in a drop of the average rate of profit.
*   => There is an increased pressure for increasing productivity and profitability.
*   => There is pressure for adopting new technologies that allow increasing productivity.

This cycle involves both the "absorption [. . .] and the re-formation of the industrial reserve army" (785), which means that unemployment is a variable that depends on capitalist development. Given that capitalism is an inherently antagonistic and therefore crisis-ridden system, rising unemployment is a recurrent phenomenon of capitalism. Given that crisis means increasing misery (unemployment), capitalism is an inherently misery-creating system. This misery can hit anyone, not just workers, but also capitalists, who may as a consequence of the centralisation of capital have to close their businesses. It is unpredictable which workers and capitalists are turned into surplus population at which point of time. Given that humans do not want to live in misery and that capitalism produces uncertainty and potential misery, there are good reasons why capitalism should be replaced by a system that is able to foster the wealth of all humans.

Floating, Latent, and Stagnant Surplus Population

Marx distinguishes between floating, latent, and stagnant surplus populations (794–797). Floating unemployment means that in specific industries the rate of unemployment rises and falls with the development of the economic cycle. Latent unemployment means that there is a tendency in capitalism that people living in the countryside are worse off than people in larger cities. Unemployment tends to more affect the rural than the urban population, so it is a constant latent threat for them. A specific part of them therefore seeks opportunities to move to larger cities, which advances urbanisation. Stagnant unemployment means that there is a part of the unemployed that finds work for a short time, but then tends to become unemployed again. Marx also mentions that there is one part of the unemployed, the lumpenproletariat (797), that lives in total misery and poverty. As a result, its members are driven into crime, prostitution, or illness.

The General Law of Capitalist Accumulation

In section 25.4, Marx formulates the *general law of capitalist accumulation*. This law says that accumulation "of wealth at one pole is [. . .] at the same time accumulation of misery, the torment of labour, slavery, ignorance, brutalization and moral degradation at the opposite pole, i.e. on the side of the class that produces its own product as capital" and that "in proportion as capital accumulates, the situation of the worker, be his payments high or low, must grow worse" (799).

The most well-known formulation of the general law of capitalist accumulation is the following one:

> The greater the social wealth, the functioning capital, the extent and energy of its growth, and therefore also the greater the absolute mass of the proletariat and the productivity of its labour, the greater is the industrial reserve army. The same causes which develop the expansive power of capital, also develop the labour-power at its disposal. The relative mass of the industrial reserve army thus increases with the potential energy of wealth. But the greater this reserve army in proportion to the active labour-army, the greater is the mass of a consolidated surplus population, whose misery is in inverse ratio to the amount of torture it has to undergo in the form of labour. The more extensive, finally, the pauperized sections of the working class and the industrial reserve army, the greater is official pauperism. *This is the absolute general law of capitalist accumulation.* (798)

Technology and the General Law of Capitalist Accumulation

Marx stresses the important role that technology plays as "methods for the production of surplus-value" (799) in the general law of capitalist accumulation: Technology is a "means of domination and exploitation of the producers" that "distort[s] the worker into a fragment of a man" and "degrade[s] him to the level of an appendage of a machine" (799).

Technologies in production, such as the computer in computerised production, are means that foster the tendency of the organic composition to rise. The American Marxist political economist Harry Braverman (1920–1976) observed therefore already in the 1970s that "with the economies [i.e., rising productivity] furnished by the computer system and the forcing of the intensity of labor come layoffs" (Braverman 1974/1998, 231). The critical theorist and historian of technology David F. Noble (1945–2010) summarises his analysis of the effects of the computer in capitalism:

> Computer-aided manufacturing, robotics, computer inventories, automated switchboards and tellers, telecommunications technologies—all have been used to displace and replace people, to enable employers to reduce labour costs, contract-out, relocate operations. From the factory to the farm, from the oil refinery to the office, no workplace has been immune to this assault. (Noble 1995, XIII)

In section 25.5, Marx illustrates unemployment in Britain and Ireland with historical examples and so underpins his theoretical analysis empirically.

Why the General Law of Capitalist Accumulation Is Not a Theory of Immiseration and Breakdown

Critics of Marxism have argued that Marx has formulated a theory of immiseration (the continuous increase of absolute misery) and breakdown in *Capital Volume 1*'s parts VII and VIII, including chapter 25. So, for example, the Austrian-British philosopher Karl Popper (1902–1994), who in his criticism of Marx in the book *The Open Society and its Enemies* directly refers to and quotes from chapter 25 (Popper 1945, 490–391), writes: "Marx undoubtedly believed that misery was growing both in extent and in intensity" (Popper 1945, 375). Popper says that Marx's work deserves respect for the analysis of exploitation and unemployment (Popper 1945, 383–384), but was defective:

> [Marx's] law that misery must increase together with accumulation does not hold. Means of production have accumulated and the productivity of labour has increased since his day to an extent which even he would hardly have thought possible. But child labour, working hours, the agony of toil, and the precariousness of the worker's existence, have not increased; they have declined. [. . .] Experience shows that Marx's prophecies were false. (Popper 1945, 391–392)

The Polish philosopher Leszek Kołakowski (1927–2009), who turned from a Marxist humanist into a critic of Marx and Marxism, stresses in his book *Main Currents of Marxism* the important role of technology in the rise of the organic composition and, similar to Popper, holds that Marx assumed that the process through which "technology progresses and the amount of constant capital increases" must result in "the inevitable collapse of capitalism" (Kołakowski 2005, 244). He says Marx had the "hope that capitalism would be destroyed by its own inconsistencies" (Kołakowski 2005, 245).

In the first sentence of the passage cited above (on page 798 in *Capital Volume 1*) ("The greater the social wealth, the functioning capital, the extent and energy of its growth, and therefore also the greater the absolute mass of the proletariat and the productivity of its labour, the greater is the industrial reserve army"), Marx says nothing more than that in the expansion of capital, there are phases in which employment increases ("the absolute mass of the proletariat") and phases where unemployment increases ("the greater is the industrial reserve army") and that employment and unemployment are dialectically connected. Marx argues that the "relative mass of the industrial reserve army [. . .] increases with the potential energy of wealth". What he stresses here is that if the total capital that is made up of constant capital c, variable capital v, and profits p grows, then the sum of variable capital at point of time t_2 tends to be larger than at the previous point of time t_1. Therefore if a crisis of capitalism emerges at t_2, more variable capital can potentially be put out of work in relation to point of time t_1.

What should one make of Marx's following formulations in chapter 25?

- "[T]he higher the productivity of labour, the greater is the pressure of the workers on the means of employment, the more precarious therefore becomes the condition for their existence" (798).
- "It follows therefore that in proportion as capital accumulates, the situation of the worker, be his payment high of low, must grow worse" (799).
- "Accumulation of wealth at one pole is, therefore, at the same time accumulation of misery" (799).
- "[A]ccumulation of misery" is "a necessary condition, corresponding to the accumulation of wealth" (799).

Capitalism is a system in which the growth is capital's *conditio sine qua non*. Stagnating or declining capital is unlikely to survive and will be eaten up and crushed by the more productive and powerful capital. Labour produces capital, but does not own it. So the more capital grows, the more capital labour has produced that it does not own. There is an absolute increase of the working class' non-ownership of capital. Marx expresses this circumstance by arguing that capital accumulation advances precariousness and misery of the working class. His formulations do not exclude the logical possibility of absolute decline of capital in crises. Mostly such a decline results, however, also in an increase of unemployment.

Interpreted this way, Marx has not formulated a breakdown law of capitalism, but rather shows that capital accumulation requires a permanent reproduction of the class relation between capital and labour so that workers are non-owners of capital.

Poverty: The Dialectic of Ownership and Non-Ownership

Marx formulates this dialectic of capitalists' ownership of capital and workers' non-ownership most powerfully in the *Grundrisse* as the concept of the working class' poverty:

> Separation of property from labour appears as the necessary law of this exchange between capital and labour. Labour posited as not-capital as such is: (1) not-objectified labour [nicht-vergegenständlichte Arbeit], conceived negatively (itself still objective; the not-objective itself in objective form). As such it is not-raw material, not-instrument of labour, not-raw-product: labour separated from all means and objects of labour, from its entire objectivity. This living labour, existing as an abstraction from these moments of its actual reality (also, not-value); this complete denudation, purely subjective existence of labour, stripped of all objectivity. Labour as absolute poverty: poverty not as shortage, but as total exclusion of objective wealth. Or also as the existing not-value, and hence purely objective use value, existing without mediation, this objectivity can only be an objectivity not separated from the person: only an objectivity coinciding with his immediate bodily existence. Since the objectivity is purely immediate, it is just as much direct not-objectivity. In other words, not an objectivity which falls outside the immediate presence [Dasein] of the individual himself. (2) Not-objectified labour, not-value, conceived positively, or as a negativity in relation to itself, is the not-objectified, hence non-objective, i.e. subjective existence of labour itself. Labour not as an object, but as activity; not as itself value, but as the living source of value. [Namely, it is] general wealth (in contrast to capital in which it exists objectively, as reality) as the general possibility of the same, which proves itself as such in action. Thus, it is not at all contradictory, or, rather, the in-every-way mutually contradictory statements that labour is absolute poverty as object, on one side, and is, on the other side, the general possibility of wealth as subject and as activity, are reciprocally determined and follow from the essence of labour, such as it is pre supposed by capital as its contradiction and as its contradictory being, and such as it, in turn, presupposes capital. (Marx 1857/1858, 295–296)

The general law of capitalist accumulation says precisely that labour is "absolute poverty" = "total exclusion of objective wealth" (Marx 1857/1858, 296). At the same time, Marx importantly points out that this poverty of the working class' labour is not just "absolute poverty as object", but also on the other side "the general possibility of wealth as subject and as activity" (Marx 1857/1858, 296). Capitalism's absolute law is that every accumulation process deepens the working class' absolute poverty, but also constitutes its power to overthrow capital because capital is dependent on exploiting labour and labour can in collective action refuse its exploitation and bring accumulation to a standstill.

The tendency of the rise of the organic composition of capital is an important factor in what Marx terms in *Capital Volume 3* (chapters 13–15) the "tendency of the rate of profit to fall". I want to therefore refer the reader also to these chapters in *Volume 3* and recommend that s/he studies them. Marx's basic argument is that if the organic composition of capital rises due to technological progress and this growth is not offset by a growing rate of surplus-value, the rate of profit falls. This law is, however, not a breakdown law of capitalism because there can be countervailing tendencies, especially the lowering of wages, the usage of the methods of absolute and relative surplus–value production, the cheapening of constant capital, foreign trade, the sale of commodities above their value, high exploitation rates of labour in colonies, the devaluation of fixed constant capital, increasing speed of the turnover of capital, and violent devaluation of capital by war or crises.

The Role of the Rate of Surplus-Value and the Organic Composition in the Rate of Profit

The rate of profit is the relationship of profit and investment or of the monetary expression of surplus–value and the value of the means of production and labour-power (constant and variable capital).

$$ROP = \frac{s}{c + v}$$

If we divide the numerator and the denominator by v, then we get the following:

$$ROP = \frac{\dfrac{s}{v}}{\dfrac{c}{v} + 1}$$

This formula shows that the rate of profit depends (a) on the rate of surplus–value, which Marx also calls the rate of exploitation because it described the relationship of unpaid and paid labour, and (b) the organic composition of capital, which represents the relationship of dead and living labour, constant and variable capital, the value of machinery/resources and labour-power. The rate of profit is directly proportional to the rate of surplus–value and indirectly proportional to the organic composition of capital.

Technology and the Rate of Profit

New technology has the potential to both increase the rate of surplus–value and the organic composition of capital. The effects of new technology on the rate of profit depend on the relationship between the rate of surplus–value and the organic composition. If the organic composition increases more than the rate of surplus–value, then a fall of the rate of profit emerges. Vice versa, if the rate of surplus–value increases more than the organic composition, then the rate of profit increases. An important factor in this respect is class struggle, which influences the absolute value of variable capital v. In any case, the formula for the rate of profit shows that technification has contradictory potentials: It can increase productivity, technological intensity, and the exploitation of labour.

Technification is a method of relative surplus–value production. So raising the organic composition can increase the rate of surplus–value. There is, however, no guarantee that this increase is larger than the increase of the organic composition and so capitalists will tend to try to reduce wage costs in order to increase profitability. Methods of absolute and relative surplus–value production are, however, contested, as Marx knew. Workers have the capacity to resist capitalists' attacks so that the rate of surplus–value is also shaped by the outcomes of class struggle. If workers' struggles are successful, the rate and therefore their exploitation decrease. If they are not, capitalists triumph and increase the rate of exploitation. The increase of the organic composition as a structural tendency of capital stands in a contradiction with class struggles. The outcomes of this contradiction cannot be predicted in advance, but depend on historical circumstances. If the organic composition increases and there are no or unsuccessful workers' struggles so that the wage sum decreases, then the rate of profit can increase. If, however, workers' struggles are successful and they resist layoffs and achieve wage increases, the profit rate is more likely to fall.

The Development of the Rate of Profit, the Organic Composition, and the Rate of Surplus-Value in the USA and the EU

Let us as an example have a look at the development of the organic composition and some other macroeconomic variables in the aggregate of the economies of the USA and the EU15 countries (Austria, Belgium, Denmark, Finland, France, Germany, Greece, Ireland, Italy, Luxembourg, Netherlands, Portugal, Spain, Sweden, UK).

I obtained data for the following variables (time period, 1960–2015) from the AMECO database:

Net operating surplus: total economy (UOND)
Compensation of employees: total economy (UWCD)
Taxes linked to imports and production minus subsidies: total economy (UTVN)
Consumption of fixed capital at current prices: total economy (UKCT)
Unemployment rate (ZUTN)
I calculated the following variables:
Gross Value Added GVA = UOND + UWCD + UTVN + UKCT
Rate of Profit RP = UOND / GVA
Rate of Surplus-Value RSV = UOND / UWCD
Organic Composition OC = UKCT / UWCD
Wage Share = UWCD / GVA
Capital Share = (UOND + UKCT) / GVA

Figures 25.2 and 25.3 show the development of the rate of profit, the organic composition, and the rate of surplus-value in the USA and the EU15 countries.

The Rate of Profit, Organic Composition, and Rate of Surplus-Value in the USA, in % (data souce: AMECO)

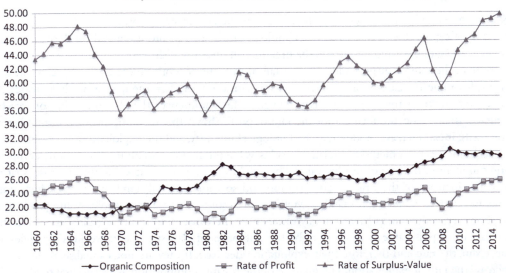

FIGURE 25.2 Economic development in the USA

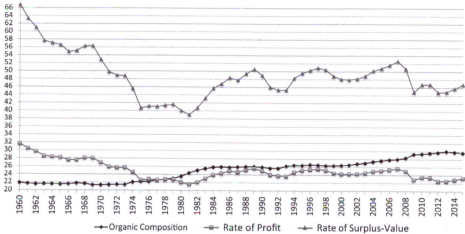

The Rate of Profit, Organic Composition, and Rate of Surplus-Value in the EU15 countries, in % (data souce: AMECO)

FIGURE 25.3 Economic development in the EU15 countries

The rate of surplus-value—that is, the degree of exploitation—decreased in the 1960s and was relatively low in the 1970s in both the USA and the EU15. This is an indication that the working class' struggles were relatively successful in this time period and resulted in relative wage increases. In the early 1980s, the time of the rise of neoliberal politics such as Reagonomics and Thatcherism, the degree of exploitation started a long-term increase caused by wage repression.

The time period (1960–2015) is one, in which the computer has arisen, shaped, and transformed capitalist economies. As a result, both in the USA and the EU15 countries the organic composition has in this period, covering 55 years, increased from around 20% to almost 30%, which confirms Marx's analysis that there is a tendency of the organic composition to rise as a result of the technification and scientification of production. The rate of profit in both the US and the EU countries dropped as a result of increasing wages and the working class' struggles in the 1960s until the middle of the 1970s, the time of a large global economic crisis. In the decades following the mid 1970s, the increasing organic composition put a downward pressure and the increasing rate of surplus–value an upward pressure on the rate of profit. The microelectronic revolution extended and intensified the role of technology in capitalism and financing computerisation accounted for a growing share of total capital. As a result, the rate of profit both in the EU and the USA fluctuated and never returned to the rates it had reached in the 1960s.

The Development of the Wage Share in the USA and the EU

In 2008, a new world economic crisis of capitalism started, which resulted in significant drops of the rate of profit in both the USA and the EU. In the USA, the effect was that the capitalist class heavily intensified exploitation in order to drive up the rate of profit. In the EU, the economy stagnated and the rate of profit remained at a low rate in the years after the crisis started in 2008.

The wage share is the share of the total wages in the gross domestic product, whereas the capital share is the share of capital (profits and constant capital) in the GDP. These two shares are indicators for the power of labour and capital. Figures 25.4 and 25.5 show the development of these two variables in the USA and the EU.

From the early 1960s until the mid-1970s, the wage share increased in both the USA and the EU, which signified an increasing power of the working class and relatively successful class struggles

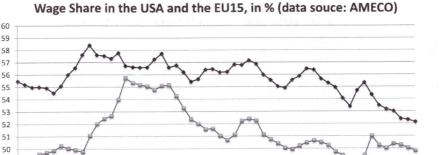

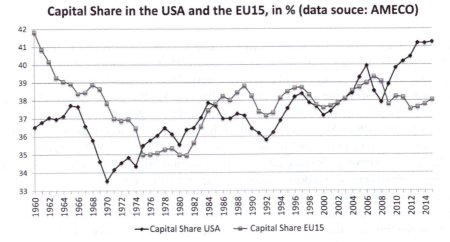

FIGURE 25.4 The development of the wage share in the USA and the EU

FIGURE 25.5 The development of the capital share in the USA and the EU

during this period, which compelled capital to increase wages. In the mid-1970s a period of wage repression started in both the EU and the US, which resulted in significant drops of the wage share. At the same time, the share of capital in the total economy increased. The data empirically validate the core of Marx's general law of capitalist accumulation—namely, that the working class produces all capital, but is expropriated from its ownership. Class struggle determines how large the working class' exploitation and its poverty (understood as non-ownership) is and which share of the economy it can control. The period that started in the mid-1970s saw a defeat of the working class and as a result an increasing level of its expropriation. Marx stresses in his general law of capitalist accumulation that the capitalist class must constantly seek to expropriate the working class in order to be able to accumulate capital. The working class has the power the resist, but does not automatically organise collectively and does not automatically win battles.

The Development of the Unemployment Rate in the USA and the EU

Figure 25.6 shows the development of the unemployment rate in the USA and the EU.

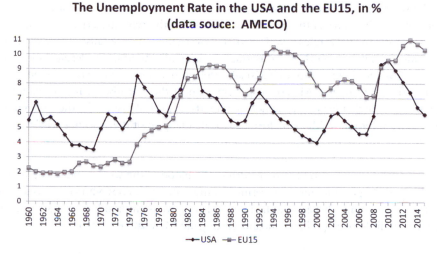

FIGURE 25.6 The development of the unemployment rates in the USA and the EU

In the EU, one can observe a long-term increase of the level of unemployment. Marx's assumption is that such a development has to do with the increase of the organic composition of capital and the increasing technification of the economy. The age of computerisation or what is called the information age has clearly not brought about stability and jobs for all in Europe. In the USA, the unemployment rate fluctuated much more than in the EU, showing increases in the 1970s, an overall decrease in the 1980s and 1990s, and an increase in the first decade of the second millennium. These data are, however, somehow deceptive because the USA has seen a large increase of the working poor and people having multiple jobs.

The Precariat

In 2014, 4.6% of all US employees had multiple jobs. In the same year 19.2% of all employees had part-time jobs. In-work poverty was in 2012 11.1% among single-person families (so-called "unrelated individuals") and 8.2% among the families of employees (source for all data: US Bureau of Labor Statistics). So, while the data in Figure 25.6, that shows that the US unemployment rate was between 4% and 5% in the years 1997 through 2007, is statistically correct, it is misleading because at the same time there was a strong growth of the working poor and precarious workers. Being led to believe that low unemployment rates correspond to workers are doing well is misleading. This increase of the precariat is also reflected in a drop of the wage-share in these years (see Figure 25.4). Also in the EU precarity plays a significant role: In 2012, 9.1% of all employees in the EU28 countries were at risk of poverty. Also in 2012, 24.8% of all individuals were at risk of poverty. In 2013 20.3% of employees were part-time workers (data source: Eurostat).

Ya Basta!

Marx discusses the organic composition of capital and the general law of capitalist accumulation in chapter 25. He describes a tendency of the organic composition to rise as a result of scientific and technological progress. Statistical data show that in the age of information technology, this tendency has asserted itself in many countries with the rise of the computer in capitalism. At the same time Marx argues in the general law of capitalist accumulation that capitalism is founded on the working class' poverty (non-ownership of capital). Capital accumulation is only possible by expropriating workers from the fruits of their labour. Statistical data has confirmed that there is a constant conflict between the working class and the capitalist class about the control of the economy. Capital can only grow if it successfully represses the power and interests of the working class. In turn, the working class has the power to strike, refuse work, and take over companies because it creates capital, value, and commodities. It if says "Ya Basta!" ("Enough is enough!"), then it can defeat capital and abolish the capitalist class and thereby also itself and all classes so that a classless society can emerge.

Subcomandante Insurgente Marcos, a spokesperson of the Zapatista Army of National Liberation, which has struggled for peace, democracy, liberty, land, and justice for the indigenous people in Chiapas (a poor region in Mexico), formulated the dialectic of the working class' power the following way:

> The powerful becomes so because he drinks the blood of the weak. And so the weak become weaker and the powerful more powerful. But there are weak ones who say, "Enough is enough! *Ya Basta!*" and who rebel against the powerful and give their blood, not to fatten the great but to feed the little ones. (Subcomandante Insurgente Marcos 2001, 359)

Exercises for Chapter 25

Group exercise (G)
Project exercise (P)

Key Categories: Composition of Capital, Organic Composition of Capital, Technical Composition of Capital, Centralisation of Capital, Surplus Population, Industrial Reserve Army, Lumpenproletariat, General Law of Capitalist Accumulation

Exercise 25.1 (G)

Search for statistics that show how employees and freelancers in the media/digital/cultural industries have been affected by unemployment, working poverty, part-time labour, temporary labour, and precarious labour in different countries. If you work in groups, then each group can focus on one country. Have a look at how the available data developed over the years and decades.

Present and interpret the results. How are a precarious life and precarious labour connected to what Marx terms the "general law of capitalist accumulation"? What are their causes? How can they be overcome?

Exercise 25.2 (P)

Marx discusses the organic composition of capital's role in capitalism in chapter 25. I have shown in the discussion how this variable can be calculated with the help of macroeconomic data and that it is related to the rate of profit and the rate of surplus-value.

Work in groups: Each group chooses one country for which the macroeconomic data needed for calculating the organic composition, the rate of surplus-value, and the rate of profit are available. Look into databases such as OECD STAN and AMECO, as well as national statistical offices' databases for obtaining the required information. Calculate the shares analogous to the examples I provided in chapter 25.

Present and interpret your results. How is the organic composition related to the rate of surplus-value and the rate of profit? How have these shares and their relations developed in your example cases, and why have they developed in specific ways? What have been the role of the microelectronic revolution and the rise of the computer in the analysed countries' economies?

PART VIII
SO-CALLED PRIMITIVE ACCUMULATION

26

PART VIII: SO-CALLED PRIMITIVE ACCUMULATION

Part VIII consists of eight shorter chapters that focus on primitive accumulation, the historical development of capitalism, and colonialism. In the German edition, Marx summarised chapters 26 through 32 as one overall chapter called "24: So-Called Primitive Accumulation", which has 7 sections. Chapter 33 forms a separate short chapter in the German edition (chapter 25). So this section covers chapters 24 and 25 in the German edition and chapters 26 through 33 in the English edition of *Capital Volume 1*.

The following chapters make up the English edition of *Capital Volume 1*'s part VIII:

Chapter 26: The Secret of Primitive Accumulation
Chapter 27: The Expropriation of the Agricultural Population from the Land
Chapter 28: Bloody Legislation against the Expropriated since the End of the Fifteenth Century. The Forcing Down of Wages by Act of Parliament
Chapter 29: The Genesis of the Capitalist Farmer
Chapter 30: Impact of the Agricultural Revolution on Industry. The Creation of a Home Market for Industrial Capital
Chapter 31: The Genesis of the Industrial Capitalist
Chapter 32: The Historical Tendency of Capitalist Accumulation
Chapter 33: The Modern Theory of Colonization

Given that these chapters are connected, that they are rather short, and that Marx put seven of them together to form chapter 24 in the original German edition of *Capital Volume 1*, it is feasible to discuss them all together.

How Does Marx Conceptualise Primitive Accumulation?

Marx conceives of primitive accumulation as a phase that "precedes capitalist accumulation" (873), "the pre-history of capital" (875), and as the latter's "point of departure" (873), in which "conquest, enslavement, robbery, murder, in short, force, play the greatest part" (874). It is a phase in which resources are transformed into capital and humans into proletarians depending on being exploited by capitalists in order to survive. Primitive accumulation is "the historical process of divorcing the producer from the means of production" (875).

Double-Free Labour

Marx argues that historically this phase has involved the emergence of capitalist and wageworkers. The latter would be double-free labour:

> Free workers, in the double sense that they neither form part of the means of production themselves, as would be the case with salves, serfs, etc., nor do they own the means of production, as would be the case with self-employed peasant proprietors. The free workers are therefore free from, unencumbered by, any means of production of their own. (874)

Proletarians' minds and bodies are not the private property of the dominant class, as slaves are. They are rather compelled by the "silent compulsion of economic relations" (899), i.e. by the violence of the market that makes ordinary people die if they do not obtain money in order to buy commodities, which compels many to become wageworkers. Marx uses the concept of "freedom" in the term "double free labour" in a rather ambiguous and cynical way. He does not think that wage-labour and capitalism are forms of freedom, but rather that the bourgeois revolution has liberated people from the rule of the aristocracy, the monarch, and the church, but has installed new forms of domination and exploitation, so that one form of unfreedom was substituted by another one.

From Feudalism to Capitalism: Blood and Fire

Marx describes how small landowners have been robbed of their land and how communal land was turned into private property so that feudalism turned into capitalism. The history of people's expropriation "is written I the annals of mankind in letters of blood and fire" (875). Great "masses of men are suddenly and forcibly torn from their means of subsistence, and hurled onto the labour-market as free, unprotected and rightless proletarians. The expropriation of the agricultural producer, of the peasant, from the soil is the basis of the whole process" (876). Marx's example case is the UK. He argues that capitalism emerged in the 16th century (876).

Marx shows that since the late 14th century, many English peasants owned small amounts of arable land and had the right to use the common land as pasture and source of wood, etc. (877). In the late 15th and the 16th centuries, many peasants were expropriated and common land was turned into private property (one also speaks of the enclosure of the commons). They lost ownership of their land. Many of the Catholic Church's monasteries were dissolved in the Reformation period and its land privatised by selling it cheaply to farmers and townsmen so that people formerly cultivating this land were turned into proletarians (881–882). Expropriation and the privatisation of common and state property were greatly advanced under Charles II's (1660–1665), James II (1685–1688), and William III of Orange (1689–1702), who with the "Glorious Revolution" ended Catholic rule in England (883–884).

Enclosures of the Land

Since the early 17th century until the early 20th century, various Enclosure Acts legally enabled landowners to turn common land and fields into private property. They were "decrees of expropriation of the people" (885). Commoners were thereby excluded from the use of the land and as a consequence had to find another activity in order to survive. Many of them were thereby turned into wage-labourers.

So, for example, the Enclosure Act 1773 enabled landowners to enclose commons by putting notices on the door of the local church and building a fence around the common land in order to privatise it. A decisive passage in this Act was the following one:

How arable land shall be fenced: In every parish or place in this kingdom where there are open or common field lands, all the tillage or arable lands lying in the said open or common fields shall be ordered, fenced, cultivated and improved in such manner by the respective occupiers thereof, and shall be kept, ordered and continued in such course of husbandry, and be cultivated under such rules, regulations and restrictions, as three-fourths in number and value of the occupiers of such open or common field lands in each parish or place, cultivating and taking the crops of the same, and having the consent of the owners in manner hereinafter mentioned, and likewise the consent of the rector, impropriator or tithe owner, or the lessee of either of them respectively, first had in writing, shall, at a meeting (in pursuance of notice for that purpose in writing under the hands of one-third of such occupiers, to be affixed on one of the principal doors of the parish church, chapel or place where meetings have been usually held for such parish or place respectively, twenty one days at least before such meeting, specifying the time and place of such meeting), by writing under their hands, constitute, direct and appoint, and which notice any of such occupiers are hereby authorised and impowered to give.[1]

Enclosures were militarily enforced by the so-called "clearing of estates", in which commoners were violently driven from the land (889–893):

As an example of the method used in the nineteenth century, the "clearings" made by the Duchess of Sutherland will suffice here. This person, who had been well instructed in economics, resolved, when she succeeded to the headship of the clan, to undertake a radical economic cure, and to turn the whole county of Sutherland, the population of which had already been reduced to 15,000 by similar processes, into a sheep-walk. Between 1814 and 1820 these 15,000 inhabitants, about 3,000 families, were systematically hunted and rooted out. All their villages were destroyed and burnt, all their fields turned into pasturage. British soldiers enforced this mass of evictions, and came to blows with the inhabitants. One old woman was burnt to death in the flames of the hut she refused to leave. (891)

Many dispossessed peasants became poor, beggars, criminals, or vagabonds. Marx documents in chapter 28 repressive state laws against such people that were passed under the rule of Henry VIII (ruler of England from 1509–1547), Edward VI (1547–1553), Elizabeth I (1558–1603), and James I (1603–1625). Legal measures against the refusal to work and against begging and vagrancy included imprisonment, whipping, cutting off limbs such as ears and hands, execution, branding of the forehead or chest. "Thus were the agricultural folk first forcibly expropriated from the soil, driven from their homes, turned into vagabonds, and then whipped, branded and tortured by grotesquely terroristic laws into accepting the discipline necessary for the system of wage-labour" (899).

Law-and-Order Politics and Right-Wing Ideology

Marx's discussion shows that law-and-order politics that see criminals and the poor not as the consequence but the source of social problems and therefore use harsh punishments against them, are nothing new. Right-wing ideology comes along with class rule. The Code of Hammurabi is a legal text from Babylonia that was written around 1750 BC. It included, for example, capital punishment for theft: "If any one is committing a robbery and is caught, then he shall be put to death" (§22).[2] Babylonia was an ancient class society consisting of an upper class, a lower class, and slaves. Already in ancient times, class rule was accompanied by right-wing ideologies such as law-and-order politics.

Such ideologies have not ceased to exist in the 21st century. Right-wing politicians, media, commentators, and citizens often present immigrants, black youth, the unemployed, lower class people ("chavs"), welfare benefit recipients, and others as sources of social problems and demand law-and-order legislation, including large-scale surveillance of public spaces and transport systems; censorship, control and surveillance of the Internet and other communications, draconian prison sentences, capital punishment, heavily armed police that is all-present, etc. Law-and-order politics mistakes consequences for causes of social problems and suggests superficial measures. Property-related crime has reasons and causes, including inequality and deprivation caused by class relations and capitalism. Law-and-order politics are an ideology that distracts from the complex societal and political-economic causes of social problems. They legitimate, defend, and cement capitalism, class rule, exploitation, and inequality. Law-and-order ideology typically opposes left-wing ideas such as taxing capital, redistributing wealth from the rich to the poor, and abolishing capitalism.

Right-Wing Ideology on Reality TV: *Benefits Street*

In 2014, Channel 4, a British TV station, broadcast the first season of the reality TV documentary *Benefits Street*. It showed life on James Turner Street, a deprived neighbourhood in Birmingham. Many residents living in the street are recipients of welfare benefits. The residents were presented as criminals, losers, alcoholics, drug dealers, and social "parasites" who do not want to work and are financed by the taxpayer. Residents said Channel 4 deceived them by presenting false goals of the programme. One of the residents reported: "They told me it was about living as a community and how we all got along. But the actual programme doesn't show any of that. If they had said it was about benefits and making the street look bad I would not have taken part. They tricked us".[3]

Channel 4 and the regulation authority Ofcom received thousands of complaints. Tens of thousands of people signed an online petition on change.org that called for "Channel 4 to stop any further episodes of this horrible program being broadcast and make a donation to a relevant charity for the harm done" and argued: "*Benefits Street* has portrayed people on benefits as scroungers and it's wrong. [. . .] Channel 4 [. . .] is creating a skewed image of a section of society and stirring up hatred". Here is an excerpt from the commentary in the first episode:

> James Turner Street in Birmingham is not your average street: There are 99 houses, 13 nationalities, and most of the residents are claiming benefits. [. . .] On James Turner Street there is money to be made—if you bend the rules. [. . .] Fungi's best mate Danny has only been out of jail a day. And he has already been out "shopping". [. . .] Danny is getting ready to go out to "work" with Fungi. [. . .] Danny is off to "work". And an ASBO [antisocial behaviour order] for city centre shoplifting is not going to stop him. While Danny spends an hour in the shopping centre, Fungi has his own scheme to make some quick cash. [. . .] Together Danny and Fungi have cleared £200. It is time to call the local dealers. [. . .] Fungi and shoplifter Danny are broke. £200 from selling stolen jackets has been spent [Fungi is shown drinking a beer].

Such distorted programmes and reporting that focus on the surface of social problems and ignore its causes are not just ideological in themselves, but opportunities for the state and right-wing politicians to advance law-and-order politics. So, for example, the UK Work and Pensions Secretary Iain Duncan Smith (Tories) shared his views about *Benefits Street* with the public and took the opportunity for introducing benefits caps: "Many people are shocked by what they see. [. . .] The reality is that is why the public backs our welfare reform package, to get more people back to work, to end these abuses".[4]

Also the leader of the far-right UK Independence Party, Nigel Farage, called for banning immigrants from receiving welfare benefits for five years and communicated the racist stereotype that immigrants take away British workers' jobs: "We must be completely mad, as a country, to be giving people from Eastern Europe in-work benefits. [. . .] some things are more important than money, namely the shape of our society and giving our own youngsters a chance to work".[5]

Capitalism and the Modern State

Law-and-order politics and the ideological scapegoating of the poor and immigrants go hand in hand, especially in times of societal and economic crises. They deflect public attention from discussing issues such as the wrongs of capitalism, inequality, social justice, or measures for redistribution. The modern state is deeply entrenched into capitalism.

In his work *The Civil War in France*, Marx describes the modern state as "public force organized for social enslavement, [. . .] an engine of class despotism" (MECW 22, 329), as "the instrument of class despotism, the political engine for forcibly perpetuating the social enslavement of the producers of wealth by its appropriators", "the economic rule of capital over labour" (MECW 22, 535). In *Capital Volume 1*'s section VIII, he shows how historically state laws have been used for enforcing and enabling capitalist rule.

The capitalist class does not necessarily rule the state directly. Its interests are rather in a complex manner entangled with the ones of political elites who compete for ruling the state. The state is a field of power forces and not a monolithic and homogenous apparatus or machine of the ruling class for dominating the ruled class. First, there are factions of the capitalist class (e.g., transnational corporations, small and medium enterprises, finance capital, commercial capital, manufacturing capital, cultural capital, etc.) that compete for shares of capital and power and therefore have to a certain degree conflicting interests. Second, although there are overlaps of the capitalist class and the political elite (e.g., when managers become politicians or bureaucrats become consultants for companies or when private-public partnerships are established as part of neoliberal governance systems), their activities, personnel, and interests are not coextensive. The differentiation of the state and the capitalist economy in modern society has also brought about a division of labour between capitalists and politicians. Third, the state's class power can be challenged by left-wing political movements that want to establish a transitory state that drives back capitalist interests and advances welfare and social benefits for all. It is of course doubtful in this context that a socialist state can exist in a capitalist society and that state power is necessary in all forms of society, but at the same time progressive movements' goal to conquer state power is not necessarily a social democratic-reformist strategy, but can be based on a politics of radical reformism that is politically immanent and transcendental at the same time. The state is, however, not just challenged and reproduced by political parties, but also by social movements organised in civil society.

The State as a Power Bloc

Given these complexities and contradictions of the state, it can only be conceived as a contradictory force field with temporal unity—a power bloc—between conflicting interests that form political alliances. The state is according to the Greek-French Marxist state theorist Nicos Poulantzas (1936–1979) an "institutional crystallization", "the material condensation of a relationship of forces", "a strategic field and process of intersecting power networks, which both articulate and exhibit mutual contradictions and displacements" (Poulantzas 1980, 136). The state does not directly map or mirror the interests of the capitalist class, but rather crystallises the complexities of the class structure in contradictory ways. By the articulation of complex factions and oppositions, dominant interests are transposed from economic power into state power and in a dialectical reversal back from state power to economic power. The "state crystallizes the relations of production and class relations. The modern political state does not translate the 'interests' of the dominant classes at the political level, but the relationship between those interests and the interests of the dominated classes—which means that it precisely constitutes the 'political' expression of the interests of the dominant classes" (Poulantzas 2008, 80).

The British Marxist thinker Ralph Miliband (1924–1994) notes in a similar manner to Poulantzas that "'the state' is not a thing, that it does not, as such, exist. What 'the state' stands for is a number of particular institutions which, together, constitute its reality, and which interact as parts of what may be called the state system" (Miliband 1969, 46). The state includes according to Max Weber the "monopoly of legitimate use of physical force within a given territory" (Miliband 1969, 47). Citing Karl Kautsky, Miliband says that the corporate elite "'rules but does not govern', though he added immediately that 'it contents itself with ruling the government'" (Miliband 1969, 51).

Corporations are "distinct groupings and interests, whose competition greatly affects the political process" (Miliband 1969, 44–45). However, such competition does not "prevent the separate elites in capitalist society from constituting a dominant economic class, possessed of a high degree of cohesion and solidarity, with common interests and common purposes which far transcend their specific differences and disagreements" (Miliband 1969, 44–45).

The state's roles in modern society include the regulation of the economy and society (by laws and taxation), control and exertion of the monopoly of the means of internal and external violence, the legitimisation of this monopoly, information-gathering about citizens for the purposes of administration and policing, the legal individualisation of humans into specific roles (such as workers, voters, consumers, owners, etc.), the definition and control of membership and boundaries/closure of society, the self-description of society in the form of imaginarily constructed narratives termed "national identities" (connected to nationalist, patriotic and racist ideologies), as well as population policies for fostering the reproduction of citizens and the workforce (Fuchs 2008, 76–89).

Marx saw the Paris Commune, a revolutionary-socialist rule of Paris that lasted from March 18 until May 28, 1871, as a "Revolution against the State itself" (MECW 22, 486) and "a Revolution to break down this horrid machinery of Class domination itself" (MECW Volume 22, 486). Engels commented that for Marx the Commune was a "shattering [*Sprengung*] of the former state power and its replacement by a new and truly democratic one" (MECW 27, 190).

Colonies and Primitive Accumulation

Marx argues that also the enslavement of people in and from colonies as well as the robbery of colonies is part of primitive accumulation:

> The discovery of gold and silver in America, the extirpation, enslavement and entombment in mines of the indigenous population of that continent, the beginnings of the conquest and plunder of India, and the conversion of Africa into a preserve for the commercial hunting of blackskins, are all things which characterize the dawn of the era of capitalist production. (915)

Violence was used in order to rob colonies. "The treasures captured outside Europe by undisguised looting, enslavement and murder flowed back to the mother-country and were turned into capital there" (918). The colonies were also markets for the sale of commodities (918). Colonialism shows that capital is "dripping from head to toe, from every pore, with blood and dirt" (926).

Primitive Accumulation: The British Rule of India

Marx mentions the British rule of India as example of primitive accumulation. The critical theorist Edward Said (1935–2003) argues that Karl Marx in his works on India wrote that "in destroying Asia, Britain was making possible there a real social revolution" and thereby accepted "the sufferings of Orientals while their society is being violently transformed" as "historical necessity" (Said 1978, 153). Kevin Anderson (2010, 20) acknowledges that there are problems with Marx's view that all societies are likely to have the same development path as the West and the view that the latter's pathway is the ultimate model of development, but this "in no way implies a lack of sympathy for the human beings suffering". Marx in his articles on India indeed wrote that "the English interference" destroyed Indian communities and their economy and thereby brought about "the only social revolution ever heard of in Asia" (MECW 12, 131–132). Marx also said that "England has to fulfil a double mission in India: one destructive, the other regenerating the annihilation of old Asiatic society, and the laying the material foundations of Western society in Asia" (MECW 12, 217).

But this is not the whole reality of Marx's 1853 articles on India. He says that the bourgeoisie is, in India and wherever it is active, "dragging individuals and people through blood and dirt, through misery and degradation" (MECW 12, 221). And he concludes: "The Indians will not reap the fruits of the new elements of society scattered among them by the British bourgeoisie, till in Great Britain itself the now ruling classes shall have been supplanted by the industrial proletariat, or till the Hindoos themselves shall have grown strong enough to throw off the English yoke altogether" (MECW 12, 221). This passage shows that Marx anticipated and was in favour of the "rise of an Indian liberation movement" (Anderson 2010, 24) and that he felt sympathy for such a perspective. He did not conceive of the Indian people as passive and incapable of revolution, but rather thought that all rule of the bourgeoisie results in misery, blood, dirt, and degradation and that this is shown by the Indian case. He furthermore said that Indians would not benefit from this capitalist and colonial rule. Given capitalism's exploitative and imperialistic character, social revolutions would be needed in India, Britain, and the world in order to attain a humane society. This is the ultimate conclusion of Marx's writings on India.

Methods of Primitive Accumulation

Methods of primitive accumulation that Marx discusses include "the theft of the common lands, the usurpation of feudal and clan property and its transformation into modern private property under circumstances of ruthless terrorism" (895), bloody state legislation that disposes individuals of property and uses law-and-order politics against them, and colonialism.

Rosa Luxemburg: Original and Ongoing Primitive Accumulation

A tradition within Marxist theory and politics that goes back to the German Marxist theorist and activist Rosa Luxemburg (1871–1919) has interpreted Marx's concept of primitive accumulation by arguing that primitive accumulation has not ended, but is an ongoing process by which capitalism creates milieus that can be exploited to a particularly high degree. There are two forms: original and ongoing primitive accumulation. Original primitive accumulation created the foundations of capitalism, whereas ongoing primitive accumulation is a method by which capital seeks to find new spheres of accumulation and exploitation in order to offset or overcome crises. Luxemburg argues that capital accumulation feeds on the exploitation of milieus that are drawn into the capitalist system: "capital feeds on the ruins of such organisations, and, although this non-capitalist milieu is indispensable for accumulation, the latter proceeds, at the cost of this medium nevertheless, by eating it up" (Luxemburg 1913/2003, 363). Capitalism "needs non-capitalist social organisations as the setting for its development, that it proceeds by assimilating the very conditions which alone can ensure its own existence" (Luxemburg 1913/2003, 346). As a result, "capital must go all out to obtain ascendancy over [. . .] territories and social organizations" (Luxemburg 1913/2003, 346). If such milieus were only markets for commodity sales, then one would end up with an underconsumption theory of crisis. Colonies are, however, also spheres for the exploitation of labour so that they can both be realms of commodity production and sales.

Patriarchy, Milieus of Primitive Accumulation, and Inner Colonies of Capitalism

Marxist feminists have used Luxemburg's theory in order to argue that unpaid reproductive labour can be considered as an inner colony and milieu of primitive accumulation of capitalism (Mies 1986;

Mies, Bennholdt-Thomsen, and Werlhof 1988; Werlhof 1991). Nonwage labour "ensures the repro-duction of labour power and living conditions" (Mies, Bennholdt-Thomsen, and Werlhof 1988, 18). It is labour spent "in the production of life, or subsistence production" (Mies, Bennholdt-Thomsen, and Werlhof 1988, 70). Primitive accumulation "is overt violence, with the aim of robbery wherever, whenever, and against whomever this is 'economically' necessary, politically possible and technically feasible" (Mies, Bennholdt-Thomsen, and Werlhof 1988, 102). "Women, colonies and nature" are "the main targets of this process of ongoing primitive accumulation" (Mies, Bennholdt-Thomsen, and Werlhof 1988, 6).

In neoliberal capitalism, the inner colonies of capitalism have been expanded so that profits rise by generating milieus of low-paid and unpaid labour. The formation of these colonies is a form of ongoing primitive accumulation that uses violence for expropriating labour. This phenomenon has been termed "housewifisation" (Mies 1986; Mies, Bennholdt-Thomsen, and Werlhof 1988): more and more people live and work under precarious conditions that have traditionally been charac-teristic for patriarchal relations. People working in such relations are like housewives a source of uncontrolled and unlimited exploitation. Housewifisation transforms labour so that it "bears the characteristics of housework, namely, labour not protected by trade unions or labour laws, that is avail-able at any time, for any price, that is not recognized as 'labour' but as an 'activity', as in the 'income generating activities', meaning isolated and unorganized and so on" (Mies, Bennholdt-Thomsen, and Werlhof 1988, 10). Housewifised labour is characterised by "no job permanency, the lowest wages, longest working hours, most monotonous work, no trade unions, no opportunity to obtain higher qualifications, no promotion, no rights and no social security" (Mies, Bennholdt-Thomsen, and Werlhof 1988, 169). Such informal work is "a source of unchecked, unlimited exploitation" (Mies 1986, 16). Housewifised labour is "superexploitation of non-wage labourers [...] upon which wage labour exploitation then is possible" (Mies 1986, 48) because it involves the "externalization, or ex-territorialization of costs which otherwise would have to be covered by the capitalists" (Mies 1986, 110).

David Harvey: The New Imperialism and Primitive Accumulation

The Marxist geographer David Harvey bases his understanding of what he terms the "new imperial-ism" on Rosa Luxemburg's and Hannah Arendt's works.

> The disadvantage of these assumptions is that they relegate accumulation based upon preda-tion (Raub), fraud (Betrug), and violence to an "original stage" that is no longer relevant or, as with Luxemburg, as being somehow "outside of" capitalism as a closed system. A general re-evaluation of the continuous role and persistence of the predatory practices of "primitive" or "original" accumulation within the long historical geography of capital accumulation is, therefore, very much in order, as several commentators have recently observed. Since it seems peculiar to call an ongoing process "primitive" or "original" I shall, in what follows, substitute these terms by the concept of "accumulation by dispossession". (Harvey 2003, 144)

Harvey argues that various forms of continuous primitive accumulation based on colonising spaces are needed for overcoming capitalist crises of overaccumulation. This takes on the form of spatiotemporal fixes—that is, "temporal deferral and geographical expansion" (Harvey 2003, 115). Overaccumulation produces capital surpluses that cannot be invested within existing boundaries; as a result, "profitable ways must be found to absorb the capital surpluses" (Harvey 2005, 88) by "tem-poral displacement through investment in long-term capital projects or social expenditures (such as education and research that defer the re-entry of capital values into circulation into the future)" and/or "spatial displacements through opening up new markets, new production capacities, and new resource, social and labour possibilities elsewhere" (Harvey 2003, 109). Capital accumulation, therefore, in search of profitable spheres, produces spaces and thereby creates uneven geographical development. New imperialism is for Harvey a specific form of primitive accumulation that developed after 1970: Neoliberal imperialism (Harvey 2003, 184, 188, 190), or "imperialism as accumulation by dispossession" (Harvey 2003, 137–182).

Four Strategies of Accumulation by Dispossession

For Harvey, new imperialism is a revisiting of the old, robbery-based imperialism of the 19th century in a different place and time (Harvey 2005, 182). Accumulation by dispossession employs four strategies for turning assets into profitable use—that is, the commodification of everything (Harvey 2005, chapter 6):

1. the privatisation and commodification of public assets and institutions, social welfare, knowledge, nature, cultural forms, histories, and intellectual creativity (the enclosure of the commons);
2. financialisation, which allows the appropriation of assets by speculation, fraud, predation, and thievery;
3. the creation, management, and manipulation of crises (e.g., the creation of debt crises that allow the intervention of the IMF with structural adjustment programs so that new investment opportunities, deregulations, liberalisations, and privatisations emerge); and
4. state redistributions, which favour capital at the expense of labour (Harvey 2005, 160–165; 2006, 44–50).

Primitive Accumulation in the Media, Communications, and Culture Industry

Media and culture have just like other realms of the commons been battlefields, where primitive accumulation has been implemented and challenged. Examples are the creation of forms of low-paid precarious freelance labour in the media and cultural industries; capital accumulation models that are based on unpaid user or audience labour; the creation of specific media company's capital accumulation models that crowdsource labour via the Internet in order to minimise wage costs, which creates precarious and unregulated forms of labour; the use of state laws for criminalising file-sharing and content-sharing platforms (e.g., Napster, Pirate Bay, Megaupload, library.nu/gigapedia.com, LimeWire, etc.) that try to turn culture into a common good and thereby question the capitalist interests of the culture industry and its interest organisations such as the Recording Industry Association of America and the Motion Picture Association of America; the privatisation of formerly state-owned media industries (such as telecommunications and broadcasting in many European countries); public value tests that assess if public service media's technologies and online platforms "distort" competition (if so, then such services are not allowed to be started or have to be abolished as was the case with, e.g., BBC Video Nation and BBC Jam); or the transformation of the World Wide Web from a common resource for communication that was released by its inventor Tim Berners-Lee to the public without charge in 1989 into a sphere dominated by commerce, companies, shopping, marketing, and economic and political surveillance.

In the 20th century, many European states held telecommunications and broadcasting monopolies. The basic idea was that there should be universal communications services for all citizens: The same kind of quality for all citizens no matter where they live and cheap access independent from income and wealth. The EU's Directive 98/10/EC liberalised the telecommunications markets of all member states in 1998. It spoke of creating "an environment of open and competitive markets". The EU's Directive 89/552/EEC Television without Frontiers liberalised the television provision in the EU member states by implementing the "free movement of broadcasts within the Community" so that "competition in the common market is not distorted". These formulations imply that markets and capitalism mean freedom and that markets guarantee competition and diversity of information. In reality, media markets and other markets tend to result in monopolies and to give power to large capitalist corporations, which in the case of the media means not just the financial dominance of private enterprises, but also the ideological dominance of partial interests.

In the UK, the state ownership of telecommunications ended in 1981 when Post Office Telecommunications became British Telecommunications. The Telecommunications Act 1984 liberalised the British telecommunications market. Whereas the BBC has remained largely advertising-free throughout its history, commercial television started in the UK in 1955 when ITV went on air. "The first TV ad broadcast in the UK was on ITV on 22 September 1955, advertising Gibbs SR toothpaste".[6]

The examples show how states have used the law in order to destroy true universal service and to create milieus of primitive accumulation that turned communications or parts of the communications realm into a profitable business dominated by commerce, advertising, commodity logic, the exploitation of audience labour, and the fast-paced logic of consumer culture.

The Commodification of the Commons: A Process of Ongoing Primitive Accumulation

Goods and services that all people need in order to survive or that they all produce together, such as nature, air, education, knowledge, communications, culture, and social welfare, should be commons, goods that are available to all without payment. The main commons are the natural commons, the communication and cultural commons, and the social commons. If these goods turn into commodities, then those who are economically more powerful will be able to afford better access, which will result in inequalities and the destruction of the survival capacities of a specific share of individuals and families. Every good can be turned into a common and in a communist society, all means of production and consumption are common goods available without payment. I have discussed the notion of the commons in more detail in chapter 15. We can here add the idea that the privatisation of commons is a form of ongoing primitive accumulation.

Raymond Williams (1983, 70–72) points out that the term "commons" stems from the Latin word "communis", which means that something is shared by many or all. The notion has to do with the generality of mankind and that something is shared. Williams (1983, 73) argued that there are affinities and overlaps between the words "communism" and "commons". The notion of the commons is also connected to the word "communication" because to communicate means to make something "common to many" (Williams 1983, 72).

Communication is an essential feature of human society. There can be no society without communication. Humans create and maintain social relationships by communication and thereby continuously reproduce their social existence. Media, such as the Internet, are means of communication. They are tools that enable the production of communication and human sociality. Means of communication are therefore essential necessary features of human society, just like nature, education, love, care, knowledge, technology, affects, entertainment, language, transportation, housing, food, cities, cultural goods and traditions, etc. Communication and the means of communication are part of the commons of society. All humans continuously create, reproduce, and use them in order to exist. Denying humans community and communication is like denying them to breathe fresh air. The denial of the fresh air of sociality undermines the conditions of human survival. Therefore the commons of society should be available for free (without payment or other access restrictions) for all and should not be privately owned by a class. Private ownership of the commons enables the owning class to limit access to the essence of society for other members of society and will therefore severely limit the quality of life of humans. Marx and Engels stressed that the economic means of production that are used for producing goods that satisfy human needs (use-values) are also parts of the commons of society, but are in capitalist society privately owned by the capitalist class. Capitalism has since its very beginning been based on the private ownership of parts of the commons. In recent decades, neoliberalism has resulted in the further commodification and privatisation of parts of the commons. The commons have again and again been enclosed and dispossessed in processes of original and ongoing primitive accumulation.

The Historical Tendency of Capitalist Accumulation

Marx devotes chapter 32 to what he terms the "*historical tendency of capitalist accumulation*". He argues that capitalist development inherently results in the centralisation of capital, but at the same time brings about social and cooperative forms of production, an internationalisation of the economy, and germs of a communist society that ripen within capitalism:

> At a certain stage of development, it brings into the world the material means of its own destruction. From that moment, new forces and new passions spring up in the bosom of society, forces and passions which feel themselves to be fettered by that society. It has to be annihilated; it is annihilated. Its annihilation, the transformation of the individualized and scattered means of production into socially concentrated means of production, the transformation, therefore, of the dwarf-like property of the many into the giant property of the few, and the expropriation of the great mass of the people from the soil, from the means of subsistence and from the instruments of labour, this terrible and arduously accomplished expropriation of the mass of the people forms the pre-history of capital. (928)

The centralisation of capital would be immanent to capitalism:

> What is now to be expropriated is not the self-employed worker, but the capitalist who exploits a large number of workers. This expropriation is accomplished through the action of the immanent laws of capitalist production itself, through the centralization of capitals. One capitalist always strikes down many others. (928–929)

Marx (1894) argues in *Capital Volume 3* that on the one hand credit and financialisation give "rise to monopoly in certain spheres and hence provokes state intervention", reproduce "a new financial aristocracy", create "an entire system of swindling and cheating with respect to the promotion of companies, issue of shares and share dealings" and monopoly as "the abolition of the capitalist mode of production within the capitalist mode of production" (Marx 1894, 569), which on the other hand accelerate "the violent outbreaks of this contradiction, crises" (Marx 1894, 572).

Capital Concentration

The centralisation of capital is a topic that in relation to the media is often discussed as media monopolisation and media concentration. Media concentration means "an increase in the presence of one or a handful of media companies in any market as a result of various possible processes: acquisitions, mergers, deals with other companies, or even the disappearance of competitors" (Sánchez-Tabernero 1993, 7).

Capital concentration is an inherent feature and outcome of capital accumulation. Competition has monopolistic tendencies; the very logic of competitive markets and exchange drives corporations to search for strategies that allow them to reduce investment costs and increase productivity so that they can produce cheaper than competitors, which in the long run results in bankruptcy of the less productive corporations and a tendency for capital concentration.

Marx argues in *Capital Volume 1* that the cause of capital concentration is capital's inherently competitive character and the drive of having to cheapen and accelerate production:

> The battle of competition is fought by the cheapening of commodities. The cheapness of commodities depends, all other circumstances remaining the same, on the productivity of labour, and this depends in turn on the scale of production. Therefore the larger capitals beat the smaller. It will further be remembered that, with the development of the capitalist mode of production, there is an increase in the minimum amount of individual capital necessary to carry on a business under its normal conditions. The smaller capitals, therefore, crowd into spheres of production which large-scale industry has taken control of only sporadically or incompletely. Here competition rages in direct proportion to the number, and in inverse proportion to the magnitude, of the rival capitals. It always ends in the ruin of many small capitalists, whose capitals partly pass into the hands of their conquerors, and partly vanish completely. Apart from this, an altogether new force comes into existence with the development of capitalist production: the credit system. In its first stages, this system furtively creeps in as the humble assistant of accumulation, drawing into the hands of individual or associated capitalists by invisible threads the money resources, which lie scattered in larger or smaller amounts over the surface of society; but it soon becomes a new and terrible weapon in the battle of competition and is finally transformed into an enormous social mechanism for the centralization of capitals. (777–778)

The Liberal and the Marxist Critique of Capital Concentration

The aim of a Marxist critique of capitalist concentration tendencies is in contrast to liberal criticisms not to argue for plural markets because markets in the long run always bring about concentration and monopolies. The task is rather to show that capitalism is an inherently antagonistic system that brings disadvantages to workers as well as to many capitalists, who have to permanently fear the effects of heavy competition and the potential threat of bankruptcy. The American political economist of communication Robert McChesney argues in this context that the "problem with market regulation is not merely a matter of economic concentration—even competitive markets are problematic. Perhaps we should not even expect the market to be the appropriate regulator for the media system" (McChesney 2004, 175).

The Marxist critique of capital concentration shows that there is an inherent tendency in capitalism that a small group of owners controls an increasing amount and share of capital and wealth; in this way, class divisions are maintained, reproduced, and deepened. The Marxist critique of capital concentration aims to show the contradictions of capitalism, such as the antagonism between competition and centralisation, in order to give rational grounds to the ideas of self-managed companies (owned by workers) and common and public ownership of the means of production in general and the means of communication in particular. Liberal or even conservative critics of media concentration argue that media power and concentration can be tamed by, for example, measures such as unbundling, asset stripping, public services, and government aid for small suppliers. Marxists in contrast argue that the principles of competition and profit have to be overcome.

Apologetic-Normative Theories of Media Competition and Critical-Empirical Theories of Media Concentration

The Marxist political economist of the media Manfred Knoche (2005) distinguishes between an apologetic-normative theory of competition and a critical-empirical theory of concentration. The first would argue that competition is a normative goal and that concentration is an exception from the competitive rule that can be avoided, whereas the second would see "actual economic competition that is connected to profit maximization" as the "systematic, regular cause of concentration processes that has negative consequences for the freedom and plurality of information and expression of the media" (Knoche 2005, 125). Capital concentration and market concentration would be the rule of capitalism, not an exception from the rule (Knoche 2005, 125; see also Knoche 2013).

For the political economist Nicholas Garnham (2000, 57–58), media monopolies in capitalism arise from the circumstance that media are public goods that need to be artificially turned into commodities. The law helps to erect "artificial barriers to consumption" and thus to turn "a public into a private good" (Garnham 2000, 58). The media's "economic survival under market conditions depends upon the exploitation of monopolies" (Garnham 2000, 58). The public good character of the media (nonrivalry and nonexcludability of consumption, need to permanently innovate, low reproduction costs) results in a "drive to audience maximization" (Garnham 1990, 160) that lets media organisations strive to establish "oligopolistic controls over distribution channels" (160), which in turn fosters a "tendency towards a high level of concentration" (159–160). The "mass media are, by their very nature, for better or worse the products of economies of scale and scope and thus are by their very nature concentrated. Diversity and mass media are simply contradictions in terms" (Garnham 2004, 100).

Media Concentration: The Advertising-Circulation-Spiral

Capital concentration in the realm of the media has a peculiar characteristic: the advertising–circulation–spiral (Furhoff 1973). Media with larger audiences tend to attract more advertising clients. More ads mean more profits for them and the possibility to make capital reinvestments that allow larger circulation, which again can attract more advertisers, etc.

The economist Edward Herman and the political analyst Noam Chomsky describe the advertising–circulation–spiral in their book *Manufacturing Consent. The Political Economy of the Mass Media* the following way:

> A market share and advertising edge on the part of one paper or television station will give it additional revenue to compete more effectively—promote more aggressively, buy more saleable features and programs—and the disadvantaged rival must add expenses it cannot afford to try to stem the cumulative process of dwindling market (and revenue) share. (Herman and Chomsky 1994, 15)

Manfred Knoche (2013) distinguishes in his approach to studying media concentration between the measurement of capital and market concentration (absolute: number of corporations; relative: share of turnover, profits) on the one hand and journalistic concentration (absolute: number of journalistic units; relative: circulation rate, audience rate) on the other hand.

Why Is Media Concentration a Problem?

There are several possible effects of media monopolies and media concentration processes:

- Ideological power: Corporations that produce or organise content have the power to provide material that aims to influence what people consider as correct and valuable views of reality and as truth. Corporate monopolies hence have an ideological function; they can potentially lead to the simplification of complex realities.
- Labour standards: Monopoly corporations can set low labour standards (especially concerning wages) in their industry sector.

- Political power: In capitalism, money is entangled with political power; hence monopolies enable huge political influence of small groups of people.
- Control of prices: Monopolies have the economic power to control prices of goods and services.
- Control of technological standards: Monopolies have the power to define and control technological standards.
- Dependency of customers: Controlling the power to define technological standards also means that the need of customers to buy evermore media technologies in order to remain up to date can be generated. Hence a potential result is an increasing dependency on commodities produced by one corporation and increasing monopoly profits.
- Economic centralisation: Monopoly capital deprives others of economic opportunities.
- Quality: A monopolist might care less about quality because there are no alternatives to choose from for consumers.
- Consumer surveillance and censorship: If content and applications are monopolised—that is, most users have to rely on certain products of single media companies—operations of surveillance (i.e., monitoring, statistically evaluating, and recording audience and user behaviour, which content they create and consume, and how and what they communicate) and censorship can be carried out easier and more completely than in the case of several competing companies. This concerns especially communication technologies, such as phones and the Internet.

Measuring Concentration: The C4 Index and the Herfindahl-Hirschman Index

Two commonly used measures of concentration are the C4 index, which measures the market share of the four largest companies and the Herfindahl–Hirschman index.

C4 ratio:

$$C4_j = \sum_{i=1}^{4} S_{ij}.$$

S_i = firm i's market share of a given industry j.

Herfindahl–Hirschman Index:

$$HHI_j = \sum_{i=1}^{f} S_{ij}^{2}.$$

f = number of firms participating in an industry;
S_{ij} = each firm i's market share in the industry j.

Interpretation (Noam 2009, 48) is as follows:

HHI < 1 000: low concentration
1 000 < HHI < 1 800: medium concentration
HHI > 1 800: high concentration

Media Concentration: An Example Calculation

Here is an example calculation of media concentration using the C4 ratio and the Herfindahl-Hirschman index.

TABLE 26.1 Average daily readers of UK newspapers, in 1,000s (data source: National Readership Survey, July 2013–June 2014)

Newspaper	Owner	Type	Average daily readers (1,000s)	Share
The Sun	News UK	Tabloid	5,508	30.0%
Daily Mail	Daily Mail and General Trust	Tabloid	3,866	21.0%
Daily Mirror/Record	Trinity Mirror	Tabloid	2,893	15.8%
Daily Telegraph	Telegraph Media Group	Quality	1,261	6.9%
The Times	News UK	Quality	1,110	6.0%
Daily Star	Northern & Shell Media	Tabloid	1,039	5.7%
Daily Express	Northern & Shell Media	Tabloid	1,097	6.0%
The Guardian	Guardian Media Group	Quality	748	4.1%
i	Alexander and Evgeny Lebedev	Quality	584	3.2%
The Independent	Alexander and Evgeny Lebedev	Quality	261	1.4%
			Total: 18,367	100.0%

TABLE 26.2 Average daily readers attracted by UK newspaper ownership groups, in 1,000s (data source: National Readership Survey, July 2013–June 2014)

Owner	Readers	Share
News UK	6,618	36.0%
Daily Mail and General Trust	3,866	21.0%
Trinity Mirror	2,893	15.8%
Northern & Shell Media	2,136	11.6%
Telegraph Media Group	1,261	6.9%
Alexander and Evgeny Lebedev	845	4.6%
Guardian Media Group	748	4.1%
	Total: 18,367	100.0%

In order to calculate market concentration, the data need to be sorted and organised taking ownership into account. Table 26.2 gives an overview of the reorganised data.

Herfindahl–Hirschman index HHI: $36.0^2 + 21.0^2 + 15.8^2 + 11.6^2 + 6.9^2 + 4.6^2 + 4.1^2 = 2209.6$.

C4-ratio of the British newspaper industry: $36.0\% + 21.0\% + 15.8\% + 11.6\% = 84.5\%$.

The four largest owners controlled in 2014 84.5% of the British newspaper market. The Herfindahl–Hirschman index is with 2,209.6 larger than 1,800, which is an indication that the British newspaper market is very highly concentrated. The Murdoch group's News UK, which is known for its conservative and right-wing tabloid media, accounts, with a 36.0% share, for the largest audience share. This is an indication that right-wing ideology backed by financial power plays a crucial role in the British media landscape.

Socialisation and the Foundations of a Communist Economy: The Antagonism between Productive Forces and Relations of Production

Marx argues that centralisation would be accompanied by the socialisation, scientification, technification, and globalisation of production, which constitute foundations of a communist economy without scarcity and toil and with free activities and free goods instead of forced labour and commodities. Class relations would, however, hinder the realisation of such a society and result in the antagonism between productive forces and relations of production, which is one of the sources of capitalist crises:

Hand in hand with this centralization, or this expropriation of many capitalists by a few, other developments take place on an ever-increasing scale, such as the growth of the co-operative form of the labour process, the conscious technical application of science, the planned exploitation of the soil, the transformation of the means of labour into forms in which they can only be used in common, the economising of all means of production by their use as the means of production of combined, socialized labour, the entanglement of all peoples in the net of the world market, and, with this, the growth of the international character of the capitalist regime. Along with the constant decrease in the number of capitalist magnates, who usurp and monopolize all the advantages of this process of transformation, the mass of misery, oppression, slavery, degradation and exploitation grows, but with this there also grows the revolt of the working class, a class constantly increasing in numbers, and trained, united and organized by the very mechanism of the capitalist process of production. The monopoly of capital becomes a fetter upon the mode of production which has flourished alongside and under it. The centralization of the means of production and the socialization of labour reach a point at which they become incompatible with their capitalist integument. This integument is burst asunder. The knell of capitalist private property sounds. The expropriators are expropriated. (929)

The historical tendency of capitalism is that it is a schizophrenic system that fosters at the same time ever-newer forms of exploitation and centralisation supported by science and technology, which within private property relations stand in a contradiction to the cooperative and social potentials they enable. This antagonism between private property and class relations on the one side and social and collaborative production on the other side results in capitalism's proneness to crisis. Marx argues that exploitation and crises show the problematic nature of capitalism and can be an incentive for people to conduct a revolution that creates a communist society. For this to happen, "the expropriation of a few usurpers by the mass of the people" must take place.

The Historical Tendency of Capitalist Accumulation: Did Marx Formulate a Breakdown Law Of Capitalism? No!

Do the passages in chapter 32 mean that Marx thinks that capitalism will by "a natural process" (929) due to its contradictions automatically break down because workers are necessarily driven to conduct a revolution? Does Marx have a linear and mechanical concept of history?

The Marxist literary and cultural theorist Terry Eagleton summarises frequently heard criticisms of Marx's concept of history the following way:

> Marxism is a form of determinism. It sees men and women simply as the tools of history, and thus strips them of their freedom and individuality. Marx believed in certain iron laws of history, which work themselves out with inexorable force and which no human action can resist. Feudalism was fated to give birth to capitalism, and capitalism will inevitably give way to socialism. As such, Marx's theory of history is just a secular version of Providence or Destiny. It is offensive to human freedom and dignity, just as Marxist states are. (Eagleton 2011, 30)

Eagleton's own view is that Marx did not hold the view that "men and women were the helpless playthings of history" (Eagleton 2011, 238) and that such criticisms travesty Marx.

Marx and Engels have distinguished different modes of production, such as slavery, feudalism, capitalism, and communism. Only communism is a classless society. Table 26.3 gives an overview of various modes of production.

But how are modes of production related to each other? In a historical way, where they supersede each other, or in a historical-logical way within a specific social formation that sublates older formations, but encompasses older modes of production in itself? The Marxist theorist Jairus Banaji (2011) argues that Stalinism and vulgar Marxism have conceptualised the notion of the mode of production

TABLE 26.3 The main forms of ownership in various modes of production

	Owner of labour power	Owner of the means of production	Owner of the products of work
Patriarchy	Patriarch	Patriarch	Family
Slavery	Slavemaster	Slavemaster	Slavemaster
Feudalism	Partly self-control, partly lord	Partly self-control, partly lord	Partly self-control, partly lord
Capitalism	Worker	Capitalist	Capitalist
Communism	Self	All	Partly all, partly individual

based on the assumption that a specific mode contains only one specific historical form of labour and surplus-value appropriation and eliminates previous modes so that history develops in the form of a linear evolution: slavery => feudalism => capitalism => communism. So, for example, Althusser and Balibar (1970) argue in their book *Reading Capital* that the historical development of society is non-dialectical and does not involve sublations, but rather transitions "from one mode of production to another" (Althusser and Balibar 1970, 307) so that one mode succeeds the other. This concept of history is one of the reasons why the Marxist historian Edward P. Thompson (1978, 131) has characterised Althusser's approach as "Stalinism at the level of theory". The Stalinist "metaphysical–scholastic formalism" (Banaji 2011, 61) has been reproduced in liberal theory's assumption that there is an evolutionary historical development from the agricultural society to the industrial society to the information society so that each stage eliminates the previous one (as, e.g., argued by Bell 1974 and Toffler 1980), which shows that in the realm of theory the liberals of today are contemporary Stalinists (see Fuchs 2014a, Chapter 5, for a Marxist discussion of information society theory).

Marx discusses aspects of his concept of history in chapters 32 and 25 (see also my discussion of chapter 25). One must bear in mind that Marx in these chapters wants to appeal to those opposed to and suffering under capitalism to make a revolution. The chapters contain a combination of normative, structural, and agency-focused formulations. So he, for example, argues that there are structures in capitalism that point beyond capitalism and are "fettered by that society" (928) so that a structural antagonism between private ownership and socialised structures exists. Marx here applies a structural logic. When he writes that capitalism "has to be annihilated; it is annihilated" (928), then he puts the normative statement that it has to be annihilated first. He thereby expresses that there is something fundamentally wrong with capitalism and that people should get rid of it and replace it by a communist society. When he says that capitalism "is annihilated", he takes an agency position of revolutionaries and imagines and describes the situation in which humans bring down capitalism by revolutionary action. Marx's concluding thoughts and chapters in *Capital Volume 1* are also a political appeal to workers to engage in class struggles that challenge capitalism.

In another passage Marx says that with capitalist development misery grows (929). I have discussed in chapter 25 that he by misery and poverty means that the more capital is accumulated, the more absolute wealth that is not owned by the working class exists so that its "absolute poverty as object", understood as non-ownership, exists, which is at the same time "the general possibility of wealth as subject and as activity" (Marx 1857/1858, 296) because the working class creates all wealth and therefore has the power to bring capitalism to an end and to replace it.

Given the existence of ideology and various forms of repression, struggles can be contained and are therefore always a possibility, but not always a reality. So there is no guarantee that with capitalist development "grows the revolt of the working class" (929). In the sentences that follow, Marx stresses first by using a structural logic that the "monopoly of capital becomes a fetter upon the mode of production which has flourished alongside and under it. The centralization of the means of production and the socialization of labour reach a point at which they become incompatible with their capitalist integument" (929). He here, however, does not assume that capitalism automatically breaks down because he does not write that capitalism bursts asunder, but rather that capitalism "is burst asunder" and that the "expropriators are expropriated" (929). The use of the passive form in these formulations means that there is an active subject—the proletariat—bursting capitalism asunder in expropriating the expropriators in the process of social revolution. As human agency is not programmed or predetermined, the logic that Marx uses here implies that he imagines that the exploited class collectively decides to conduct a revolution. Marx describes this very situation and ends Chapter 32 on a positive and hopeful note by writing in the final sentence that such a revolution means "the expropriation of a few usurpers by the mass of the people" (930), by which he reminds people that change is possible, that capitalism is not the end of history and not an endless necessity, but that they can be the change that humanises society by implementing a democratic-communist system in which there is wealth for all, the abolishment of toil, well-rounded individuality, "associations of free and equal producers, carrying on the social business on a common and rational plan" (MECW 23, 136) and producing according to the principle "From each according to his abilities, to each according to his needs!" (MECW 24, 87).

Vera Zasulich's Letter to Marx: The Historical Tendency of Capitalist Accumulation and Russia

The Russian socialist Vera Zasulich (1849–1919) wrote in 1881 to Marx and asked him how the *historical tendency of capitalist accumulation* that Marx sets out in chapter 32 shall be interpreted for an agricultural society such as Russia:

> You would be doing us a very great favour if you were to set forth Your ideas on the possible fate of our rural commune, and on the theory that it is historically necessary for every country in the world to pass through all the phases of capitalist production. [. . .]
>
> What you probably do not realise is the role which your *Capital* plays in our discussions on the agrarian question in Russia and our rural commune. You know better than anyone how urgent this question is in Russia. [. . .] In one way or another, even the personal fate of our revolutionary socialists depends upon your answer to the question. For there are only two possibilities. Either the rural commune, freed of exorbitant tax demands, payment to the nobility and arbitrary administration, is capable of developing in a socialist direction, that is, gradually organising its production and distribution on a collectivist basis. In that case, the revolutionary socialist must devote all his strength to the liberation and development of the commune.
>
> If, however, the commune is destined to perish, all that remains for the socialist, as such, is more or less ill-founded calculations as to how many decades it will take for the Russian peasant's land to pass into the hands of the bourgeoisie, and how many centuries it will take for capitalism in Russia to reach something like the level of development already attained in Western Europe. Their task will then be to conduct propaganda solely among the urban workers, while these workers will be continually drowned in the peasant mass which, following the dissolution of the commune, will be thrown on to the streets of the large towns in search of a wage. (Zasulich 1881)

Vera Zasulich asked Marx if an agricultural society first needs to introduce capitalism in order to achieve communism or if it immediately can introduce communism and can leapfrog capitalism. Given that she asked this question in the context of Russia, where the 20th century's largest communist revolution took place, Marx's answer is of particular interest. Responding was not easy for him. He first made three drafts of the answer letter and then replied with a fourth, shorter version.

Marx's Answer to Vera Zasulich's Letter

In the letter that he actually sent to Zasulich, Marx writes that he had said in chapter 32 when describing the historical development from feudalism to capitalism to communism that the private "property [of feudalism] which is personally earned—that is, which is based, as it were, on the fusing together of the isolated, independent working individual with the conditions of his labour, is supplanted by capitalist private property, which rests on the exploitation of alien, but formally free labour" (*Capital Volume 1*, 928).

This development would be "expressly limited to the countries of Western Europe" (MECW 24, 370) because the European development had been from feudal private property to capitalist private property, whereas in Russia communal property prevailed (MECW 24, 371), which posed a different context.

In the three drafts of the letter (MECW 24, 346–369), Marx explains his analysis in more detail. Other than in Europe, where communal property was fully destroyed, Russia had a long ongoing history of such property. "Russia is the sole European country where the 'agricultural commune' has kept going on a nationwide scale up to the present day" (MECW 24, 352). The Russian peasants would already have been familiar with collective labour. Furthermore the nearness, contemporaneity, and trade relations with Europe would allow Russia to apply scientific and technological progress as well as modern machinery to Russian agriculture. The good quality of the Russian soil would be conducive to the introduction of modern machinery. "The physical lie of the land in Russia invites agricultural exploitation with the aid of machines, organised on a vast scale and managed by cooperative labour" (MECW 24, 356). The situation of India would be different than the one of Russia because the British conquered and ruled it. "As for the East Indies, [. . .] the suppression of communal landownership out there was nothing but an act of English vandalism, pushing the native people not forwards but backwards" (MECW 24, 365). A problem Marx saw was that Russian villages were relatively isolated and unconnected to each other.

The danger for Russia according to Marx was that capitalists already had appropriated agriculture and were supported by the state. "To save the Russian commune, a Russian revolution is needed" (MECW 24, 359).

So Marx argues that there is no historical necessity that communism is established via capitalism and capitalist industry. Given specific preconditions, there could also be a direct development from other forms of society to communism. His letter to Vera Zasulich and its three drafts are further indications that Marx did not have a deterministic and mechanistic concept of history, but that his version of historical materialism is dynamic, complex, contextual, and based on a dialectic of object and subject.

The Dialectical Articulation of Modes of Production

According to Jairus Banaji, capitalism often intensified feudal or semi-feudal production relations. In parts of Europe and outside, feudalism only developed as a "commodity-producing enterprise" (Banaji 2011, 88). In the Islamic world, capitalism developed without slavery and feudalism (Banaji 2011, 6).

Banaji advances in contrast to formalist interpretations a complex reading of Marx's theory, in which a mode of production is "capable of subsuming often much earlier forms" (Banaji 2011, 1) and "similar forms of labour-use can be found in very different modes of production" (6); also capitalism is "working through a *multiplicity* of forms of exploitation" (145) and is a combined form of development (358) that integrates "diverse forms of exploitation and ways of organising labour in its drive to produce surplus value" (359).

A mode of production is a unity of productive forces and relations of production (Marx and Engels 1845, 91). If these modes are based on classes as their relations of production, then they have specific contradictions that result in the sublation (*Aufhebung*) of one mode of production and the emergence of a new one. The emergence of a new mode of production does not necessarily abolish, but rather sublate (*aufheben*) older modes of production. This means that history is for Marx a dialectical process precisely in Hegel's threefold meaning of the term "Aufhebung" (sublation): (1) uplifting, (2) elimination, (3) preservation: (1) There are new qualities of the economy, (2) the dominance of an older mode of production vanishes, (3) but this older mode continues to exist in the new mode in a specific form and relation to the new mode. The notion of ongoing primitive accumulation that I discussed earlier in this chapter stresses that noncapitalist and capitalist class relations can be created within capitalism in order to outsource labour to them so that capitalists can reduce wage-costs and increase profits. The rise of capitalism did not bring an end to patriarchy, but the latter continued to exist in such a way that a specific household economy emerged that fulfils the role of the reproduction of modern labour power. Also various forms of slavery have continued to exist within capitalism.[7] A sublation can be more or less fundamental. A transition from capitalism to communism requires a fundamental elimination of classes; the question is, however, if this is immediately possible. Elimination and preservation can take place to differing degrees. A sublation is also no linear progression. It is always possible that relations that resemble earlier modes of organisation are created.

Capitalism is at the level of the relations of production organised around relations between capital owners on the one side and paid/unpaid labour and the unemployed on the other side. On the level of the productive forces, it has developed from industrial to informational productive forces. The informational productive forces do not eliminate, but sublate (aufheben) other productive forces (Adorno 1968/2003, chapter 5 in Fuchs 2014a): In order for informational products to exist a lot of physical production is needed, which includes agricultural production and mining and industrial production. The emergence of informational capitalism has not virtualised production or made it weightless or immaterial, but is grounded in physical production. Whereas capitalism is a mode of production, the terms "agricultural society", "industrial society", and "information society" characterise specific forms of the organisation of the productive forces (Adorno 1968/2003; Fuchs 2014a, chapter 5).

The Dialectics of Structure and Agency, Necessity and Freedom, Object and Subject

Necessity is the German translation of "Notwendigkeit", which means the need to turn. When Marx speaks of "necessity", he does not mean that something breaks down automatically, but that there is a normative and political need that humans act collectively in order to create a fair and just society. Marx points out in *Capital* that there are structural antagonisms of capitalism that again and again result in crisis and misery and that humans have the power to conduct protests, revolts, and a revolution in order to overcome capitalism.

The Marxist philosopher and critical theorist Herbert Marcuse (1898–1979) has in his book *Reason and Revolution* summarised Marx's dialectics of structure and agency, necessity and freedom, object and subject:

> The negativity and its negation are two different phases of the same historical process, straddled by man's historical action. The 'new' state is the truth of the old, but that truth does not steadily and automatically grow out of the earlier state; it can be set free only by an autonomous act on the part of men, that will cancel the whole of the existing negative state. [...] Not the slightest natural necessity or automatic inevitability guarantees the transition from capitalism to socialism. [...] The revolution requires the maturity of many forces, but the greatest

among them is the subjective force, namely, the revolutionary class itself. The realization of freedom and reason requires the free rationality of those who achieve it. Marxian theory is, then, incompatible with fatalistic determinism. (Marcuse 1941, 315, 318–319)

Exercises for Chapters 26–33

Group exercise (G)
Project exercise (P)

Key Categories: Primitive Accumulation, State Power, Colonialism, Centralisation of Capital, Historical Tendency of Capitalist Accumulation

Exercise 26.1 (G)

One of the issues that Marx discusses in section VIII is the role of the state and the law in capitalism.

Work in groups: Each group searches for, documents, and analyses an example in which both media and politicians scapegoat certain groups in society, blame them for social problems, and imply the need for law-and-order politics.

Present and discuss the results. Ask yourself: What is law-and-order politics? What is wrong about it? What would Marx say about your examples? What solutions for social problems would he suggest today?

Exercise 26.2 (G)

Marx in section VIII discusses the notion of primitive accumulation. Marxists such as Rosa Luxemburg, Maria Mies, and David Harvey have argued that primitive accumulation is not a historically unique stage at the beginning of capitalism, but an ongoing process of accumulation by dispossession.

Work in groups: Document cases where media and communications have been turned into realms of capital accumulation. Observe the arguments that have been used for advancing liberalisation, privatisation, commodification, and capitalisation.

Present you examples. Ask yourself and discuss: In which respect are these examples forms of ongoing primitive accumulation? What ideologies have been used for justifying primitive accumulation and how can they be criticised? What are the alternatives to capitalist media, and how can they be achieved and sustained?

Exercise 26.3 (G)

Marx shows in section VIII that in the UK, Bills for the Enclosures of Commons have resulted in the privatisation of land as part of the process of original primitive accumulation.

Knowledge, culture, technology, media, and communications are also commons of society that have been commodified and capitalised.

Work in groups: Search for examples of the commodification of the communication and cultural commons. Present the examples.

Discuss: What are specific qualities of the commodification of the communication and cultural commons? Should all knowledge, culture, technology, and media be available for all without payment? Why respectively why not? What problems and antagonisms can emerge if such attempts are made within capitalism? What is the role of the commons in general and of the communication commons in particular in a democratic-communist society? What is in contrast the role of the commons in capitalism and in a social-democratic welfare capitalist system?

Exercise 26.4 (P)

Marx discusses in chapters 32 and 25 the centralisation of capital. I have shown how the Herfindahl-Hirschman index (HHI) and the C4 ratio can be used for calculating how strongly a market is concentrated.

Work in groups: Each group selects one specific media market in a particular country, searches for available profit and audience data, and calculates the HHI and the C4 ratio. Present the results.

Discuss: What is the difference between a Marxist and a non-Marxist approach to media concentration? Why does Marx think that a competitive market is an illusion? What is for Marx the alternative to markets? How could alternatives to capitalism look like in the media world? How can they be achieved?

Notes

1   Inclosure Act 1773. http://www.legislation.gov.uk/apgb/Geo3/13/81 (accessed on August 28, 2014).
2   http://eawc.evansville.edu/anthology/hammurabi.htm (accessed on August 28, 2014).
3   "Benefits Street": Channel 4 documentary sparks anger and threats of violence. The Independent Online. January 7, 2014.
4   Iain Duncan Smith suggests hit show Benefits Street justifies savage welfare cuts. Daily Mirror Online. January 13, 2014.
5   Nigel Farage calls for five-year ban on migrant benefits. BBC Online. January 7, 2014.
6   http://en.wikipedia.org/wiki/Television_advertisement (accessed on August 28, 2014).
7   The Global Slavery Index report has estimated that in 2014 there were 30 million slaves in the world. http://www.globalslaveryindex.org.

27

APPENDIX

"Results of the Immediate Process of Production"

What Is the "Results of the Immediate Process of Production"?

"Results of the Immediate Process of Production" is not part of the German version of *Capital Volume 1*. It is, however, included as an appendix to the English Penguin edition.

Marx conducted and wrote several pre-studies for *Capital Volume 1*, including the *Grundrisse*, *A Contribution to the Critique of Political Economy*, *Theories of Surplus-Value*. "Results of the Immediate Process of Production" is also a pre-study. It is not entirely clear when it was written. Ernest Mandel dates it in his introduction to the time between June 1863 and December 1866 (944). The "Results" was first published in German and Russian in 1933.

The "Results" is a more than 130-page text that partly repeats and partly complements *Capital Volume 1* and is therefore much worth reading. I want to focus here especially on four aspects that Marx addresses in the "Results" that I consider particularly relevant:

* Ideology and fetishism
* Formal and real subsumption of labour under capital
* Productive labour
* Trade unions

Continuous and Discrete Commodities

Marx argues that the commodity is both a precondition and a result of capitalism (949). The commodity, money, and markets are older than capitalism, but in capitalism they are fused into a new unity so that commodity production becomes the "*universal elementary form of wealth*" (951). Capitalism is the first economy, where the commodity form takes on a general form and dominates the economy (951).

Marx distinguishes between continuous and discrete commodities. He argues that there are "individual commodities such as railways, large building complexes, etc. which are so continuous in nature and on such a grand scale that the entire product of the capital invested appears to be a single product" (955). He calls these commodities continuous commodities. Think of software: It appears that the commercial software (such as Microsoft Office, Microsoft Windows, Macintosh OS X, SPSS, Adobe Photoshop, etc.) you have on your computer is an individual commodity for which you pay an individual price. What you pay for is, however, only an individual copy of a master version, into which many thousands of labour hours are invested per year. Software is developed in versions, so it is never complete and final, but tends to be changed by additional labour year by year. Software only appears to take on the form of many single commodities, but is in fact a continuous and total commodity. Calculating the required labour hours, profit, wages, etc. should in the case of software therefore not be conducted for a single copy, but for an entire version or over a period of a year.

I have pointed out that Marx in section 15.4 discusses how in capitalism, subject and object are inverted so that it is not the worker who controls technology, but rather technology in the hands of capitalists controls the worker. In the "Results", Marx calls this process explicitly an "inversion of subject into object and *vice versa*" and says that the "same situation" can be found in "*religion* at the ideological level" (990).

Alienation

The notion of alienation is quite prevalent in the "Results". Marx speaks, for example, of alien cooperation, alien nature, alien products of labour, alien machinery (1054), "*alien labour*" (1016), "alienation of the product" (951), alien subjective and objective conditions (1056), alien value (988), "alien world" (1062), "alien property" (1003, 1006, 1026), alienation of labour-power (1066), alien-ation of the commodity (1066), labour alienated from capital (1025), "*alienation* of man from labour" (990), alienated machinery/science/invention (1058). The prevalence of the usage of the notion of alienation in the "Results" confirms the analysis that the assumption of Louis Althusser (1969, 34) and others that there is an "epistemological break" between Marx's early and late works is wrong. The notion of alienation is not, as assumed by Althusser, confined to the early works, but also plays a prominent role in Marx's late works. Alienation was a concept that was important for Marx through-out his life. I have analysed the role of the notion of alienation in *Capital Volume 1* and why Althusser is wrong in more detail in chapter 7.

27.1. Ideology and Fetishism

Examples that Illustrate Commodity Fetishism

Marx's section on commodity fetishism (section 1.4) is rather brief (14 pages) and abstract. Many people who read it for the first time find it difficult to understand. In the "Results", Marx discusses some concrete examples that help to illustrate commodity fetishism.

Marx argues that because means of production are capital in the capitalist mode of production, many classical political economists see capital as "a necessary feature of the *human work* ['labour' in the original English translation] *process as such*, irrespective of the historical form it has assumed" (981). It would be a mistaken logic to assume that because money is gold, all gold is always money (982). Or to assume that because "wage-labour is labour, all labour is necessarily wage-labour" (982). Classical political economists would see capital as a thing (982), not a historical social relationship between two classes. Marx also says that given that the worker was a slave in antiquity, one cannot infer from this fact that being a slave is the worker's nature (997).

Capital as Fetish in Classical Political Economy

Marx cites examples for the argument that capital is a quality of all societies from the works of David Ricardo (1772–1823), Robert Torrens (1780–1864), Nassau W. Senior (1790–1864), Hein-rich Friedrich von Storch (1766–1835), Pellegrino Rossi (1787–1848), Antoine-Elisée Cherbuliez (1797–1869), John Stuart Mill (1806–1873), Claude Frédéric Bastiat (1801–1850), and Pierre Joseph Proudhon (1809–1865).

So, for example, David Ricardo (1819, 95) argues in his famous book *On the Principles of Politi-cal Economy and Taxation* that capital "is that part of the wealth of a country which is employed in production, and consists of food, clothing, tools, raw materials, machinery, etc. necessary to give effect to labour".

John Stuart Mill in his book *Principles of Political Economy* gives a similar definition:

> It has been seen in the preceding chapters that besides the primary and universal requisites of production, labor and natural agents, there is another requisite without which no productive operations beyond the rude and scanty beginnings of primitive industry are possible—namely, a stock, previously accumulated, of the products of former labor. This accumulated stock of the produce of labor is termed Capital. What capital does for production is, to afford the shelter, protection, tools, and materials which the work requires, and to feed and otherwise maintain the laborers during the process. These are the services which present labor requires from past, and from the produce of past, labor. Whatever things are destined for this use—destined to supply productive labor with these various prerequisites—are Capital. (Mill 1884, 65)

Adam Smith takes a somewhat different position: He argues in his famous book *The Wealth of Nations* that there is no capital in societies that do not have a division of labour (Smith 1776, 267). He defines capital as specific part of a stock of things. "That part which he [a person possessing more stock than needed for individual survival] expects is to afford him this revenue is called capital. The other is that which supplies his immediate consumption" (Smith 1776, 270).

So for Ricardo and Mill, capital is a stock of things such as machines, tools, shelter, food, clothing, and raw materials that enables production. For Smith, capital is also a stock, but only that part which is employed for creating profits. So Smith relates the notion of capital to capitalism, whereas Ricardo and Mill completely naturalise capital by defining it is aspect of all economies in all societies. However, also for Smith, capital is a thing.

Marx in contrast sees capital as a social relationship between the capitalist and the worker that requires the exploitation of labour and enables accumulation. The production of surplus-value, and therefore the exploitation of labour, is "the determining purpose, the driving force and the *final result* of the capitalist process of production" (976). Labour in capitalism is a "*fluens* that creates a fluxion" (994) in the process of the self-valorisation of capital.

Labour Fetishism

Marx argues that many bourgeois economists confuse "the appropriation of the labour process by capital with the work [labour in the original translation] process itself" (998). They reproduce the fetishist—that is, naturalising—appearance of capital in their analyses. The result is an ideology that proclaims that capitalism is the natural state of society and a condition for the survival of humans. The problem is that thereby the limits of capitalism, such as its crisis-tendencies and inherent inequalities, are theoretically justified and legitimised.

Marx points out that his political economic analysis in contrast to bourgeois political economy names on the one hand "the elements of the labour process combined with the *specific characteristics* peculiar to them in a given *historical* phase" and on the other hand elements of the economy that are "independent of any particular social formation" and are part of the eternal relationship "between man and nature" (998).

Essential and Historic Categories

Marx indicates that his method not just develops categories that critically analyse capitalism, but relates these categories to other categories that take on specific expressions in capitalism, but at the same time reflect underlying essential social relations characteristic for all societies. Marx wrote both

TABLE 27.1 Marx's description of the dual character of capitalism and social theory

Essential categories	Historic categories
Work	Labour
Use-value	Exchange value
Concrete labour	Abstract labour
Work process	Valorisation process
Necessary labour	Surplus labour

a critique of capitalism and an economic theory in the same book. These two levels have resulted in two series of categories that are both constituents of capitalism, but represent on the one hand that which is specific for capitalism and on the other hand that which forms the essence of all economies (and therefore also exists in capitalism) and interacts dialectically with capitalism's historic reality. Some of these categories are shown in Table 27.1 and constitute for Marx the dual character of capitalism. The problem of fetishist thought, as found in the works of many bourgeois political economists, is that it reduces historic categories to essential categories.

The Marxist philosopher Herbert Marcuse (1898–1979) argues that the two rows of Marx's categories express the dialectic of essence and appearance. He says that both

> groups of concepts are equally necessary to the understanding of the antagonistic reality; nevertheless, they are not on the same level. In terms of dialectical theory, the second group of concepts, which has been derived from the totality of the social dynamic, is intended to grasp the essence and the true content of the manifestations which the first group describes as they appear. (Marcuse 1936/1988, 85–86)

Marcuse says that this dialectic of essence and appearance in Marx's categories has a political purpose: Marx wants to point towards the possibility of a classless society:

> The dialectical concepts transcend given social reality in the direction of another historical structure which is present as a tendency in the given reality. [. . .] If, for instance, it is said that concepts such as wages, the value of labor, and entrepreneurial profit are only categories of manifestations behind which are hidden the 'essential relations' of the second set of concepts, it is also true that these essential relations represent the truth of the manifestations only insofar as the concepts which comprehend them already contain their own negation and transcendence—the image of a social organization without surplus value. All materialist concepts contain an accusation and an imperative. (Marcuse 1936/1988, 86)

27.2. The Formal and Real Subsumption of Labour under Capital

Marx introduces the terms "formal subsumption of labour" and "real subsumption of labour" in the "Results". These categories relate to the concepts of absolute and relative surplus-value as set out in *Capital Volume I*'s parts III, IV, and V.

The Formal Subsumption of Labour under Capital

Formal subsumption is the "general form of every capitalist process of production", but also a particular form of capitalism (1019). In it, the "labour process is subsumed under capital" (1019)—that is, there is a class relationship between workers and capitalists that constitutes a process of labour's exploitation.

Formal subsumption of labour under capital means that a production process is incorporated into capitalist relations in a form of original or ongoing primitive accumulation (see chapter 26 in this book and part VIII of *Capital Volume 1*). It is the "takeover by capital of a mode of labour developed before the emergence of capitalist relations" (1021). More surplus-value is in formal subsumption created by the lengthening of the working day—that is, by absolute surplus-value production (1021).

Marx speaks of *formal* subsumption because this kind of production is

> only *formally* distinct from earlier modes of production on whose foundations it arises spontaneously (or is introduced). [. . .] There is no change as yet in the mode of production itself. *Technologically speaking*, the *labour process* goes on as before, with the provision that it is now *subordinated* to capital. (1025–1026)

The Real Subsumption of Labour under Capital

In the real subsumption of labour under capital, there is a revolution of the "actual mode of labour" (1023) with the help of technology, scientific knowledge, the division of labour, cooperation (1024)—a "revolution takes place in the mode of production, in the productivity of the workers and in the relations and in the relations between workers and capitalists" (1035). The technological, natural, and scientific forces are subsumed under capital in order to increase productivity. A qualitative change of the labour process emerges. "If the production of absolute surplus-value was the material expression of the formal subsumption of labour under capital, then the production of relative surplus-value may be viewed as its real subsumption" (1025).

Marx argues that one specific mode of dominant real subsumption tends to transform other industries so that they also become subsumed in the same way (1036). The microelectronic revolution is a specific example: The concept of the computer goes back to Charles Babbage, an English engineer (whom Marx cites several times in *Capital Volume 1* when discussing the concepts of machinery and large-scale industry), in the 19th century (he called his concepts the differential engine and the analytical engine).

The first computers were built in the late 1930s—for example, by Konrad Zuse in Germany. During World War II, computers were used as encryption and deciphering machines—for example, in the UK ("Colossus), and Nazi Germany ("Enigma"). The first electronic computer was built in 1945 in the USA ("ENIAC"). The UNIVAC was the first commercial computer. Its sale started in the early 1950s. To computing's application in the military realm an economic role was added. At around the same time, IBM introduced the IBM 701 as its first commercially available computer. Computer and software production emerged as a new industry that subsequently transformed other capitalist industries.

The first industry in which computer-based real subsumption took place was probably the car industry, in which computer-aided manufacturing was introduced (first at Renault in France) in the 1960s. Computer-based automation and rationalisation subsequently affected many manufacturing industries such as the chemical industry, machine production, the food and beverage industry, the textile industry, etc. All manufacturing industries have their own specific histories of the introduction of the computer and its effects. Computerisation is not limited to manufacturing, but in a second stage has also affected the service and information sector. Today there are hardly sectors of advanced economies in which the computer is not used and in which there have not been major debates or even struggles about the effects of computer use.

27.3. Productive Labour

In the "Results", Marx also takes up the discussion of productive labour, which he in detail conducts in *Capital Volume 1*'s chapter 16 (see my discussion in chapter 16 of this book).

The Concept of Productive Labour in the "Results"

Marx says that labour is productive if it "creates *surplus-value* directly" (1038), if it "creates surplus-value" (1039). This surplus labour appears in "surplus produce, i.e. an *additional increment of a commodity* on behalf of the monopolizer of the means of labour, the capitalist" (1039). Marx also argues that productive labour creates commodity (1039). "The *worker* who performs *productive work* is *productive* and the work he performs is productive if it directly creates *surplus-value*, i.e. if it *valorizes* capital" (1039). "Labour remains productive as long as it objectifies itself in *commodities*, as the unity of exchange-value and use-value" (1039).

This definition of productive labour does not imply that one has to be a wageworker for being a productive worker. A consumer of commercial media and a Facebook user produce a commodity—namely, the audience commodity (Smythe 1977, 1981) and a data commodity (Fuchs 2014a, 2014c, 2015), respectively—without earning a wage. Also reproductive workers in the household produce and reproduce a commodity, namely labour-power, and are therefore in the understanding that Marx advances productive workers.

The Collective Worker (*Gesamtarbeiter*)

Marx also again discusses just like in chapter 16 the notion of the combined, aggregate, or collective worker (Gesamtarbeiter). He stresses that this worker emerges from the real subsumption of labour under capital (1039):

> An ever increasing number of types of labour are included in the immediate concept of productive labour, and those who perform it are classed as productive workers, workers directly exploited by capital and subordinated to its process of production and expansion. If we consider the aggregate worker, i.e. if we take all the members comprising the workshop together, then we see that their combined activity results materially in an aggregate product which is at the same time a quantity of goods. And here it is quite immaterial whether the job of a particular worker, who is merely a limb of this aggregate worker, is at a greater or smaller distance from the actual manual labour. But then: the activity of this aggregate labour-power is its immediate productive consumption by capital, i.e. it is the self-valorization process of capital, and hence, as we shall demonstrate, the immediate production of surplus-value, the immediate conversion of this latter into capital.

The question that arises is where the collective worker ends. The boundary could be drawn at the level of an individual factory, an industry, or society as a whole. Autonomist Marxism stresses the latter. The notion of the collective or socially combined worker is a concept that allows us to distinguish different levels of organisation of labour and the fact that labour in capitalism has undergone a process of growing socialisation that has developed together with the scientification, technification, and informatisation of production.

Paid and Unpaid Labour

Marx argues that every "productive worker is a wage-labourer, but not every wage-labourer is a productive worker" (1041). He mentions as example that a wageworker in public services funded by the state is not a productive worker (1041).

The question that arises is if one needs to necessarily earn a wage to be a productive worker. Most of Marx's definitions of productive labour are much more general and include both paid and unpaid labour. Marxist feminists have argued against a focus on wage-labour by pointing out that capital also exploits unpaid houseworkers.

The one quote just mentioned, however, exclusively focuses on wage-labour. In contemporary capitalism, there is a tendency that parts of wage-labour are outsourced to unpaid prosumer labour. Examples are self-service gas stations, self-assembled IKEA furniture, fast-food restaurants (where customers are their own waiters), and corporate social media usage. Unpaid labour here creates parts of the use-value and value of the commodity. These phenomena fall into Marx's more general definition of productive labour (2) and are not antithetical to the ones just mentioned if we assume that in these cases the wage is zero so that surplus labour time is 100% of the total labour time. Capitalists have to structurally strive to reduce investment costs in order to maximise profits and to survive in competition. Therefore to reduce the wage costs to zero is the dream of all capitalists. It has come true in prosumer labour, a form of productive labour (2).

Marx discusses the examples of a writer ("Milton, who wrote *Paradise Lost*"), a singer, and a teacher who become productive workers if they produce commodities (1044). He says that at the time of writing, "work of this sort [information work] has scarcely reached the stage of being subsumed even formally under capital, and belongs essentially to a transitional stage" (1044). In times of the Internet, the computer, and knowledge work, the situation has of course quite profoundly changed.

Two Forms of Knowledge Work

Marx also distinguishes two forms of knowledge work:

1. "[N]on-material production" (1047): "It results in commodities which exist separately from the producer, i.e. they can circulate in the interval between production and consumption as commodities, e.g. books, paintings and all products of art as distinct from the artistic achievement of the practising artist" (1049).
2. "The product is not separable from the act of producing" (1048).

Marx saw the possibility of productive knowledge work, but stressed that it was limited at his time. One hundred fifty years later both forms of knowledge work had become very important in advanced capitalist societies.

27.4. Trade Unions

What Is a Trade Union?

Marx deals explicitly with the trade unions in the "Results". "The *trade unions* aim at nothing less than to prevent the *reduction of wages* below the level that is traditionally maintained in the various branches of industry. That is to say, they wish to prevent the *price* of labour-power from falling below its *value*" (1069).

In a trade union, "workers *combine* in order to achieve *equality* of a sort with the capitalist in their *contract concerning the sale of their labour*" (1070). Trade unions are "insurance societies formed by the workers themselves" (1070).

Atypical and Freelance Labour and the Unions

Late 20th and 21st century capitalism have been shaped by many different forms of atypical labour, including, for example, precarious freelancers in the media/cultural/digital industries and other sectors. They do not earn a lot of money, have high individual risks, and tend to work atypical and at times very long hours in order to survive.

The International Trade Union Confederation (ITUC), a large international federation of trade unions, had up until 2014 nothing in particular to say about the situation of freelancers. It rather meshes them together with other workers: "Part-timer, full-timer, trainee, temp, freelancer, student, white collar, blue collar, T-shirt or turtleneck, it doesn't really matter—anyone who's looking for work or trying to keep their job these days likely has one thing in common—they're stressed" (ITUC 2010, 3)

Freelancers are not traditional workers and tend not to define their identity as being workers. An organisation such as the ITUC, which defines itself as "the global voice of the world's working people", is therefore not automatically appealing to freelancers. Furthermore, there are many forms of unpaid labour today, such as housework and prosumption, that are also atypical and diffusely organised. Many freelancers own their means of production, but hardly any capital. They are quite special and peculiar workers, which is why many trade unions tend to have problems organising them. Many freelancers do not see themselves as classical workers. Intelligent strategies are required for organising freelance trade unions.

Important developments have, for example, been the International and European Federations of Journalists' Charter of Freelance Rights, which calls for improved legal protection of freelancers, as well as the emergence of unions focusing entirely on freelancers, such as the Freelancers Union in the USA and the Canadian Freelance Union.

There are, however, also unremunerated workers, such as houseworkers, audience workers, and digital workers, who also need unions in order to represent their interests as workers exploited by capital.

Exercises for Chapter 27

Group exercise (G)
Project exercise (P)

Key Categories: Formal Subsumption of Labour under Capital, Real Subsumption of Labour under Capital, Productive Labour, Trade Unions

Exercise 27.1 (P)

Marx introduces the notions of formal and real subsumption of labour under capital in the "Results of the Immediate Process of Production" and discusses that new modes of real subsumption tend to reshape various industries and the entire capitalist economy. I discussed the example of the micro-electronic revolution.

Work in groups: Each group chooses one industry and documents how the computer has transformed this industry, which problems have emerged, and how trade unions have discussed this transformation. Ask yourself the following: What are the specific contradictions of computerisation in this industry? How can the associated problems be overcome?

Exercise 27.2 (G)

Marx discusses the relevance of trade unions in the "Results of the Immediate Process of Production". Identify a list of important trade unions that deal with media/cultural/information/digital labour in various countries.

Work in groups: Each group analyses how one of these unions has analysed the role of freelancers, audience labour, digital labour, house workers and other forms of unpaid or precarious labour.

Present the results. Ask yourself the following: What is the relevance of trade unions for freelancers, digital labour, audience labour, and house workers, and what is the best strategy for organising the interest of such people against the interests of capital?

28
CONCLUSION

Marx's Achievements

At Karl Marx's funeral on March 17, 1883, his long-time friend and comrade Friedrich Engels pointed out two aspects that are of particular importance:

- Marx "discovered the special law of motion governing the present-day capitalist mode of production and the bourgeois society that this mode of production has created. The discovery of surplus value suddenly threw light on the problem, in trying to solve which all previous investigations, of both bourgeois economists and socialist critics, had been groping in the dark" (MECW 24, 468).
- "For Marx was before all else a revolutionist. His real mission in life was to contribute, in one way or another, to the overthrow of capitalist society and of the state institutions which it had brought into being, to contribute to the liberation of the modern proletariat, which he was the first to make conscious of its own position and its needs, conscious of the conditions of its emancipation. Fighting was his element. And he fought with a passion, a tenacity and a success such as few could rival. His work on the first Rheinische Zeitung (1842), the Paris Vorwärts! (1844), Brüsseler Deutsche Zeitung (1847), the Neue Rheinische Zeitung (1848–49), the *New-York Tribune* (1852–61), and in addition to these a host of militant pamphlets, work in organisations in Paris, Brussels and London, and finally, crowning all, the formation of the great International Working Men's Association—this was indeed an achievement of which its founder might well have been proud even if he had done nothing else" (MECW 24, 468).

Marx's achievement was that he uncovered how exploitation works in capitalism and that he was concerned with the political question of how to overthrow capitalism. It is important to see that Engels mentions in this speech that writing and journalism were for Marx part of this struggle. Science, theory, and journalism matter for the Marxist class struggle insofar as they can denounce and deconstruct capitalism.

Marx Is Alive after His Death

Marx's funeral was not his death because his works continue to attract people who think about how to understand and abolish capitalism. At the same time there are also still many who try to overcome Marx by denouncing his work as outdated or wrong. Marx is, as Engels said in this speech, the "best-hated and most calumniated man of his time". This is true not just "of his time" (MECW 24, 469).

The goal of this book is to inspire people to use Marx's works as an anchor point for thinking about the role of communication in capitalism and communication in society, and how to create democratic informational communism. The book wants to inspire people, especially younger ones and students, to read *Capital Volume 1* from a media and communication studies perspective.

I hope that for many readers of this book it has become evident that Marx analysed communications in his time and that his approach was forward-looking and anticipatory and therefore has much to offer for critically understanding communications today.

Marx and the Media

Jean Baudrillard, one of the main French postmodern thinkers, was wrong in arguing that "the Marxist theory of production is irredeemable partial, and cannot be generalized" to culture and the media and in saying that "the theory of production (the dialectical chaining of contradictions linked to the development of productive forces) is strictly homogenous with its object—material production—and is non-transferable, as a postulate or theoretical framework, to contents that were never given for it in the first place" (Baudrillard 1981, 214). Also the Canadian media philosopher Marshall McLuhan (1964/2001, 41) was wrong when he argued that Marx and his followers did not "understand the dynamics of the new media of communication. Marx based his analysis most untimely on the machine, just as the telegraph and other implosive forms began to reverse the mechanical dynamic".

There are many aspects of how communication relates to commodities (part I), money (part I), capital (part II), absolute surplus-value (parts III, V), relative surplus-value (parts IV, V), wages (part VI), accumulation (part VII), and primitive accumulation (VIII). The specific chapters in Marx's book and in its discussion in the work at hand stand by themselves. In this conclusion, I want to merely introduce a model that points out some of the aspects of communications in capitalism (for details of this model see Fuchs 2009b).

The model in Figure 28.1 visualises the capitalist information economy. It summarises the connection of four roles of the media in the capitalist economy: (1) the commodity form of the media,

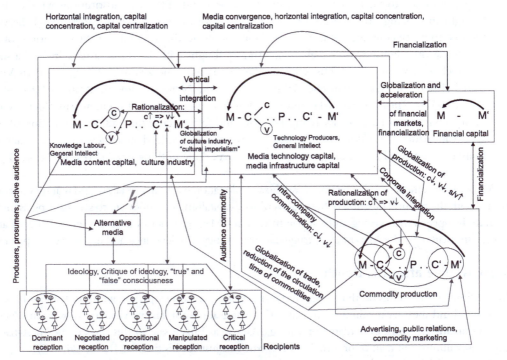

FIGURE 28.1 The capitalist information economy = the processes of media production, circulation, and consumption in the capitalist economy and society

(2) the ideological form of the media, (3) media reception, (4) alternative media. It focuses on the role of the media in the production, circulation, and consumption processes of the economy, not on the relations to the political system (state, civil society, laws, etc.) and cultural institutions (education, family, religion, etc.). Capital accumulation within the media sphere takes place in both the media content sphere and the media technology sphere. These two realms together form the sphere of media capital. The Marxian circuit of capital is shown for each of the two realms, which indicates that they are oriented on capital accumulation.

The Media and the Commodity Form

The commodity aspect of the media can be visualised as the following processes, which are shown in Figure 28.1: vertical and horizontal integration; media concentration; media convergence; media globalisation; the integration of media capital and other types of capital; the rationalisation of production; the globalisation of production, circulation, and trade; intra-company communication, advertising, and marketing. Processes of vertical integration make the boundaries between the two systems fuzzy. Concentration and capital concentration processes and horizontal integration, which are inherent features of capital accumulation, shape each of the two spheres. Media convergence is a specific feature of media infrastructure capital. The two realms together are factors that influence the globalisation of the culture industry.

The Media Industries

The realm of the economy that is shown at the bottom right of Figure 28.1 is the one of capital accumulation in nonmedia industries and services. It is partly integrated with the media sector due to corporate integration processes. Media technologies advance the rationalisation of production in this realm as well as in the media content industry. Furthermore they further the globalisation of production, circulation, and trade. These globalisation processes are also factors that in return advance the development of new media technologies. Media technologies are also used for intra-company communication. Rationalisation, globalisation, and intra-company communication are processes that aim at maximising profits by decreasing the investment cost of capital (constant and variable capital) and by advancing relative surplus value production (more production in less time). The media content industry is important for advertising and marketing commodities in the circulation process of commodities, which is at the same time the realisation process of capital, in which surplus value is transformed into money profit.

The Media and Ideologies

The ideology aspect of the media is visualised in Figure 28.1 by media content capital and its relation to recipients. Media content that creates false consciousness is considered as ideological content. Media content depends on reception. The reception hypothesis is visualised in the lower left part of the figure. Reception is the realm where ideologies are reproduced and potentially challenged.

Alternative Media

Alternative media is a sphere that challenges the capitalist media industry. Alternative media are visualised in Figure 28.1 by a separate domain that stands for alternative ways of organizing and producing media that aim at creating critical and alternatively organised technologies and contents. Alternative media is a sphere that challenges the capitalist media industry. These are alternative ways of organizing and producing media that aim at creating critical content that challenges capitalism. Media content depends on reception. Five forms of reception are distinguished in the left lower left part of Figure 28.1 (for details see Fuchs 2009b). Reception is the realm where ideologies are reproduced and potentially challenged. In some types and parts of media content capital, capital is accumulated by selling the audience as commodity to advertising clients. Dallas Smythe (1977, 1981) spoke in this context of the audience commodity. As advertising profits are not a general feature of all media capital, there is a dotted line in Figure 28.1 that signifies the audience commodity. In recent times, recipients have increasingly become an active audience that produces content and technologies. In this context, the notion of produsers (producer + user) and prosumers (producer + consumer) can be employed. Produsage and prosumption can both advance media capital accumulation and alternative media production.

The Multilevel Political Economy of the Media

The use-value of media and media technologies is that they allow humans to inform themselves and to communicate. In capitalist society, use-value is dominated by the exchange value of products, which become commodities. The media take on commodity form; their use-value only becomes available for consumers through exchanges that accumulate money capital in the hands of capitalists. Media and technologies as concrete products represent the use-value side of information and communication, whereas the monetary price of the media represents the exchange value side of information and communication. The commodity hypothesis discusses the exchange value aspect of the media. The ideology hypothesis shows how the dominance of the use-value of the media by exchange value creates a role of the media in the legitimatization and reproduction of domination. The two hypotheses are connected through the contradictory double character of media as use-values and exchange values. The media as commodities are in relation to money use-values that can realise their exchange value—that is, their price, in money form. Money is an exchange value in relation to the media. It realises its use-value in the media commodities. Consumers are interested in the use-value aspect of media and technology, whereas capitalists are interested in the exchange value aspect, which helps them to accumulate money capital. The use-value of media and technology only becomes available to consumers through complex processes in which capitalists exchange the commodities they control with money. This means that the use-value of media and technology is only possible through the exchange value that they have in relation to money. Commodification is a basic process that underlies media and technology in capitalism. Use-value and exchange value are "bilateral polar opposites" (MECW 29, 326) of media and technology in capitalist society. Once media and technology reach consumers, they have taken on commodity form and are therefore likely to have ideological characteristics. The sphere of alternative media challenges the commodity character of the media. It aims at a reversal so that use-value becomes the dominant feature of media and technology by the sublation of their exchange value. Processes of alternative reception that can also be part of social movements, alternative parties, and protests, can transcend the ideological character of the media—the recipients are empowered in questioning the fetish character of the world they live in.

Capital Matters Today

In 1868, Friedrich Engels published a review of *Capital Volume 1* in which he said something that in the age of information and digital media remains absolutely crucial:

> As long as there have been capitalists and workers on earth no book has appeared which is of as much importance for the workers as the one before us. [. . .] [with it] the whole field of modern social relations can be seen clearly and in full view just as the lower mountain scenery is seen by an observer standing on the top-most peak. (MECW 20, 231)

APPENDIX 1

Thomas Piketty's Book *Capital in the Twenty-First Century*, Karl Marx, and the Political Economy of the Internet

Acknowledgement: This chapter was first published as article in the journal tripleC: Communication, Capitalism & Critique (http://www.triple-c.at) and is re-printed with kind permission: Fuchs, Christian. 2014. Thomas Piketty's Book "Capital in the Twenty-First Century", Karl Marx and the Political Economy of the Internet. /tripleC: Communication, Capitalism & Critique/ 12 (1): 413–430.

> *The daily struggle for reforms, for the amelioration of the condition of the workers within the framework of the existing social order, and for democratic institutions, offers to the social democracy the only means of engaging in the proletarian class war and working in the direction of the final goal-the conquest of political power and the suppression of wage labor. Between social reforms and revolution there exists for the social democracy an indissoluble tie. The struggle for reforms is its means; the social revolution, its aim.*
>
> *(Rosa Luxemburg 1899, 41)*

1. Three Kinds of Reactions to Thomas Piketty's Book

In the reactions to and discussions of Thomas Piketty's (2014) monograph *Capital in the Twenty-First Century*, one can identify three ways how commentators position this book in relation to Karl Marx's works: (1) dignification, (2) denigration of the work's integrity, (3) denial of any parallel to Marx.

The Adulation of Piketty

The *first* group of commentators *dignifies* Piketty's work and argues that he shows the topicality of Marx's works and has written the 21st-century equivalent of Marx's (1867) *Capital*. James Pethokoukis (2014) calls the book a version of "new Marxism" that shows that "now Marxism's fundamental truth" that "private capital accumulation inevitably leads to the concentration of wealth into ever-fewer hands [. . .] is reasserting itself with a vengeance". Daniel Shuchman (2014) wrote that Piketty "revives Marx for the 21st Century".

The *New York Times* published a review that argued that Piketty's book shows that "Karl Marx is back from the dead. [. . .] Piketty himself is a social democrat who abjures the Marxist label. But as his title suggests, he is out to rehabilitate and recast one of Marx's key ideas: that so-called 'free markets', by their nature, tend to enrich the owners of capital at the expense of people who own less of it" (Douthat 2014). A *New York Times* op-ed piece concluded: "Like Marx, he is fiercely critical of the economic and social inequalities that untrammeled capitalism produces—and, he concludes, will continue to worsen" (Erlanger 2014). Around the same time as the English version of Piketty's book came out, the *New York Times* published a feature that asked: "Was Marx right?" (*New York Times* 2014). In it, Doug Henwood (editor of *Left Business Observer*), Michael R. Strain (American Enterprise Institute), Yves Smith (author of the blog Naked Capitalism), Tyler Cowen (professor of economics at George Mason University), and Brad DeLong (professor of economics at University of California, Berkeley) discussed whether Marx's works are topical or not.

Thomas Shenk (2014) argued in *The Nation* that Piketty shows the topicality of the critique of capitalism: "Though not a Marxist, Piketty is firmly of the left". Piketty's hostility to Marx(ism) is unnecessary:

> The hostility matches the temper among French intellectuals after their widespread turn against Marxism in the 1970s, but it is troubling to watch him snarling at prospective allies when the scale of the challenge facing advocates of equality is so daunting". There would be strong parallels between Marxism and Piketty's work: "Marxism is one kind of socialism, but history suggests a much richer set of possibilities, along with some grounds for hope. So does a work like Capital in the Twenty-First Century—a sign that another lost tradition, the postcapitalist visions in abeyance since the 1970s, could be poised for a return. (Shenk 2014)

Paul Krugman (2014b) wrote in a review: "It's not just the obvious allusion to Marx that makes this title so startling. By invoking capital right from the beginning, Piketty breaks ranks with most modern discussions of inequality, and hearkens back to an older tradition". He concluded: "Piketty has transformed our economic discourse; we'll never talk about wealth and inequality the same way we used to".

The Neoliberal Critique of Piketty

A *second* group of commentators holds that Piketty is just like Marx wrong and that his ideas are similarly dangerous. They try to *denigrate* the integrity of the book. *The Economist* wrote that Piketty is "bigger than Marx" (The Economist 2014) and that he just like Marx "glosses over the question of whether attempts to redistribute wealth will weaken growth". *The Spectator* concedes that "Piketty has resurrected Marx from the ash-heap of history by proving that his central argument was true: the capitalist system is rigged to make the rich grow ever richer while ordinary classes sink into penury" (Mount 2014). It concludes, however, that Piketty's political vision is as repressive as the one Marx imagined: "this decaff Marxism would be just oppressive and intrusive as the old variety" (Mount 2014).

The most sophisticated attack has been launched by the *Financial Times* (Giles and Giugliano 2014). It is sophisticated because it does not challenge Piketty on political, but on academic grounds. The intention is obviously political—namely, to defend capitalist interests against the idea that the taxation of wealth and capital should be increased—but remains hidden. *The Financial Times* argues that it found "numerous mistakes in Prof Piketty's work: simple fat-finger errors of transcription; suboptimal averaging techniques: multiple explained adjustments to the numbers; data entries with no sourcing; unexplained use of different time periods; and inconsistent use of source data" (Giles and Giugliano 2014, 5). Correcting the data would show that "the European results do not show any tendency towards rising wealth inequality after 1970" and that the US data do not support "the view that the wealth share of the top 1 per cent has increased in the past few decades", although there "is some evidence of a rise in the top 10 per cent wealth share since 1970" (Giles and Giugliano 2014, 5).

The *Financial Times'* criticism concerns data for what Piketty terms "wealth inequality" in Britain (Piketty 2014, 344, Figure 10.3) and the USA (Piketty 2014, 348, Figure 10.5). Piketty uses the term "wealth" interchangeably with the term "capital" (Piketty 2014, 47) and includes in it "everything owned by the residents and government of a given country at a given point in time, provided that it can be traded on some market" (Piketty 2014, 48). Capital therefore comprises for him "nonfinancial assets (land, dwellings, commercial inventory, other buildings, machinery, infrastructure, patents, and other directly owned professional assets) and financial assets (bank accounts, mutual funds, bonds, stocks, financial investments of all kinds, insurance policies, pension funds, etc.), less the total amount of financial liabilities (debt)" (Piketty 2014, 48).

Notwithstanding the question of if capital is a stock or a social relation, it becomes evident that the two figures the *Financial Times* questions are about the distribution of owned assets within the property-owning class. It does not concern the question of how the surplus-product is distributed between capital and labour because labour-power is excluded from these specific statistics. Chapter 10 of Piketty's book, in which there are the two figures that the *Financial Times* criticises, is focused on the "inequality of capital ownership", as the chapter title says. It is about the question of how capital concentration has developed. So we are talking about capital concentration and not income inequality or the relationship between capital and labour. No matter if capital is more or less concentrated, capital as a totality, i.e. the collective capitalist, exploits labour and excludes it from ownership. Labour is not-capital: It creates, but does not own capital. Marx stresses that labour is "not-value", "not-capital", "not–raw material", "not–instrument of labour", "not-raw-product" (Marx 1857/1858, 295): It is "absolute poverty", which means an "exclusion from objective wealth" (Marx 1857/1858, 296), and at the same time the constitution of labour as the "living source of value", the "general possibility" of wealth (Marx 1857/1858, 296).

Piketty discusses the question of the capital–labour relationship in chapter 6 and shows sustained inequality deriving from capital's exploitation of labour. The *Financial Times* concludes on the front page of its weekend edition published on May 24/25, 2014, in one of the headlines that "Piketty did his sums wrong in bestseller that tapped into the inequality zeitgeist". It wants to communicate that inequality is no contemporary problem and that Piketty is all wrong. Piketty's concept of wealth is somewhat misleading because it does not focus on the capital–labour relationship and Marx's insights that labour creates capital and that work is the source of wealth. He nonetheless provides important data about the capital–labour relationship that is not refuted by the *Financial Times*. Paul Krugman (2014a) commented that the *Financial Times*' claim of "stable wealth concentration in the United States is at odds with many sources of evidence". Thomas Piketty: "Where the *Financial Times* is being dishonest is to suggest that this changes things in the conclusions I make, when in fact it changes nothing. More recent studies only support my conclusions, by using different sources" (Rankin 2014a).

Marxist Critiques of Piketty

A *third* group of commentators holds that Piketty's analysis is not Marxist at all and that Marx and Marxist theory provide superior analyses. They *deny* parallels to Marx. Piketty himself positions his work partly against Marx, especially when he associates Marx's ideas of the abolishment of private property and the creation of the collective ownership of the means of production with "the Soviet experiment", "totalitarian experiments" (Piketty 2014, 531), and the "human disasters caused by Soviet-style centralized planning" (532).

> I belong to a generation that came of age listening to news of the collapse of the Communist dictatorships and never felt the slightest affection or nostalgia for those regimes or for the Soviet Union. I was vaccinated for life against the conventional but lazy rhetoric of anticapitalism, some of which simply ignored the historic failure of Communism and much of which turned its back on the intellectual means necessary to push beyond it. I have no interest in denouncing inequality or capitalism per se—especially since social inequalities are not in themselves a problem as long as they are justified. (Piketty 2014, 31).

One cannot blame Marx for Stalin. Stalin was just four years old when Marx died, in 1883, which did not allow Marx to account for and comment on what Stalin did as Soviet dictator. Marx furthermore stressed that communism is the "struggle for democracy" (Marx and Engels 1848b, 481). Marx would have disapproved of Stalin's presentation of Soviet state capitalism as a socialist society that was on a path towards communism simply because the workers were not in control of production and were dominated by bureaucracy.

Piketty's scepticism towards Marx explains why Marxist authors tend to be sceptical of Piketty. Andrew Kliman (2014) commented that "the disproportionate concern over inequality [in Piketty's book] can divert attention from major economic problems like the economy's failure to rebound from the Great Recession, and what to do about that". David Harvey (2014) criticised that Piketty's book "does not tell us why the crash of 2008 occurred" and that, although his empirical data would be valuable and his suggestions for progressive taxation of wealth, inheritance, and capital thoughtful, he would not provide a theory of capitalism in the 21st century so "that we still need Marx or his modern-day equivalent".

Harvey (2014) also questions Piketty's definition of capital as too broad: "Money, land, real estate and plant and equipment that are not being used productively are not capital". Hans Despain (2014) stresses:

> Piketty's definition of capital is highly problematic. Piketty defines capital as all physical equipment, land, housing, money, financial assets, and other valuables. To his credit he excludes so-called 'human capital'. To count and aggregate these heterogeneous capitals Piketty estimates market prices. Thus, for Piketty capital is strictly monetary and financial. [. . .] Marx attempted a far more philosophical definition of capital as value. Marx's notion of value captures the philosophical, moral, sociological, psychological, political economic, and monetary and financial aspects of capital. In this definition, capital is a social relationship that establishes the relations of production. This places Marx's argument purposefully in the sphere of production. Piketty's definition leaves his argument in the sphere of distribution. The book is not directly about capital, at least not capital in the Marxian sense. Rather the book concerns the accumulation of wealth and financial assets.

James Galbraith (2014) makes a similar point from a neo-Keynesian perspective: He argues that Piketty "conflates physical capital equipment with *all* forms of money-valued wealth, including land and housing, whether that wealth is in productive use or not". Galbraith concludes that the "book is not the accomplished work of high theory that its title, length, and reception (so far) suggest".

For Marx (1885, chapter 8), resources such as equipment, land, and houses become capital if they are employed as means of production for the creation of commodities in the capital accumulation process. He speaks in this context of fixed constant capital that remains in the production process for a longer time. If a person owns a house and a garden for private living, then these assets are for Marx not capital. If s/he rents it out, then s/he earns rent that is paid out of wages or profits. If the renter is a company that turns the garden and the house into an office or a factory for the production of commodities, then both the land and the house become means of production and fixed constant capital. Capital implies social relations between capital and labour, competing capitalists, capitalists and banks, rentiers and renters. So if land becomes capital this implies that labour standing in class relations uses it as a means of production in order to produce capital and that the land must have either been bought or rented by a company, which implies a sales relationship.

Marx pinpoints the difference between capital conceived as thing and social relation:

> But capital is not a thing, it is a definite social relation of production pertaining to a particular historical social formation, which simply takes the form of a thing and gives this thing a specific social character. Capital is not the sum of the material and produced means of production. Capital is the means of production as transformed into capital, these being no more capital in

themselves than gold or silver are money. It is the means of production monopolized by a particular section of society, the products and conditions of activity of labour-power, which are rendered autonomous vis-à-vis this living labour-power and are personified in capital through this antithesis (Marx 1894, 953)

Paul Mason rejects the comparison of Piketty to Marx:

Is Piketty the new Karl Marx? Anybody who has read the latter will know he is not. Marx's critique of capitalism was not about distribution but production: for Marx it was not rising inequality but a breakdown in the profit mechanism that drove the system towards its end. Where Marx saw social relationships—between labour and managers, factory owners and the landed aristocracy—Piketty sees only social categories: wealth and income. Marxist economics lives in a world where the inner tendencies of capitalism are belied by its surface experience. Piketty's world is of concrete historical data only. So the charges of soft Marxism are completely misplaced. (Mason 2014)

Some Marxist scholars also question Piketty's political conclusions. Harvey (2014) says his "remedies for the inequalities are naïve if not utopian". Sean Collins concludes that Piketty's book is a "navel-gazing distraction with zero progressive content" (Collins 2014).

Despain (2014) argues even that they are reactionary:

Piketty's policy recommendations are impressively anemic and aimed at perpetuating exploitation of the economically vulnerable populations. In the end Piketty wants to take the 'hyper' out of hyperexploitation and reestablish good old-fashion exploitation with higher minimum wages, taxes on capital, progressive income tax, and limits on inheritance. [. . .] Piketty's policy recommendations can be described as hyperliberalism. [. . .] Nonetheless, there is no acknowledgement that democracy should be extended into the totalitarian workplaces of capitalism. He theorizes an entire chapter on the 'utopian' notion of a progressive 'global' tax capital as at least a reference point for more practical policy. Why not offer a gesture toward democratizing the workplace for income distribution? Why not acknowledge the self-directed worker enterprises, such as the Mondragon Corporation of Spain, that have successfully reduced inequality between employees?

Dignification, denigration, and denial do not seem to be adequate responses to Piketty's work to me. Whereas the first position is rather purely affirmative and celebratory, the latter two tend to be purely dismissive. My own assessment is in contrast that Piketty's book is neither completely different from Marx's approach nor unrelated.

2. Piketty and Marx

Inequality

Piketty's main assumption, which he tries to show empirically, is that inequality emerges in capitalism when "the rate of return on capital exceeds the rate of growth of output and income" (Piketty 2014, 1). Piketty (2014, 9) argues that Marx predicted "an apocalyptic end to capitalism: either the rate of return on capital would steadily diminish (thereby killing the engine of accumulation and leading to violent conflict among capitalists), or capital's share of national income would increase indefinitely (which sooner or later would unite the workers in revolt)". He here combines a specific interpretation of Marx's theorem of the tendency of the profit rate to fall with the claim that

Marx assumed that capitalism implies absolute immiseration of workers. Piketty (2014, 9) argues that by the end of the 19th century wages began to increase and that increasing productivity and technological progress can act against capital concentration. He, however, overlooks that for Marx the first tendency was not a deterministic law because he identified countervailing tendencies (Marx 1894, chapter 14) and that for Marx the wealth gap between capital and labour need not necessarily become ever larger in absolute terms. Marx did not predict the breakdown of capitalism. It is simply not true that Marx's "principle of infinite accumulation" implies apocalypse because he "implicitly relies on a strict assumption of zero productivity growth over the long run" (Piketty 2014, 27).

The General Law of Capitalist Accumulation

In chapter 25 of *Capital Volume 1*, Marx (1867) describes what he terms the "general law of capitalist accumulation". "But all methods for the production of surplus-value are at the same time methods of accumulation, and every extension of accumulation becomes, conversely, a means for the development of those methods. It follows therefore that in proportion as capital accumulates, the situation of the worker, be his payment high or low, must grow worse" (Marx 1867, 799).

This key passage can easily be misread as capital accumulation implying absolute immiseration. Marx stresses, however, that with capital accumulation the worker's situation "must grow worse" no matter if his/her payment is "high or low". This formulation implies that accumulation does not necessarily bring about an absolute lowering of wages or the wage-sum, but that even if capitalists at point t+1 pay higher wages than at point t because profits have increased, the workers do not own the monetary profits and commodities they produced. If a company or economic sector is not struck by crisis, it successfully increases its capital. This constant increase and reinvestment for further increasing capital is only possible if the workers do not own the monetary profit. As capital grows, the workers' situation grows worse because the absolute amount of capital that they do not own increases.

Piketty measures inequality between capital and labour in relative terms. He shows that capitalism's history has been a history of capitalists trying to increase their profits at the expense of labour. Marx's general law of capitalist accumulation describes that all capital accumulation dispossesses workers of surplus and profits and that therefore inequality of ownership is inherently built into capitalism. For Marx, there can be no just form of capitalism. Marx did, however, not assume, as incorrectly stated by Piketty, that inequality results in a necessary breakdown of capitalism. If capitalism breaks down is for Marx a question of social action—that is, of class struggles and revolution.

Crises and capitalist contradictions condition the possibilities for working class struggles. The overthrow of the system can, however, only be an act of agency. This becomes evident when Marx, for example, stresses that "the greatest productive power is the revolutionary class itself" (MECW 6, 211), that "all social life is essentially practical" (MECW 5, 5), and that the "coincidence of the changing of circumstances and of human activity or self-change can be conceived and rationally understood only as revolutionary practice" (MECW 5, 4). Decisive is the "historical self-initiative ['self' is missing in the English translation although it can be found in the German original, CF]" (Marx and Engels 1848b, 490) of the dominated and that history is "the history of class struggles" (Marx and Engels 1848b, 462).

In the famous passage in *Capital Volume 1* in which Marx describes revolution, he does not describe it as a systemic necessity, but as a structural development that conditions an active process of the proletariat: "The monopoly of capital becomes a fetter upon the mode of production which has flourished alongside and under it. The centralization of the means of production and the socialization of labour reach a point at which they become incompatible with their capitalist integument. This integument is burst asunder. The knell of capitalist private property sounds. The expropriators are expropriated" (Marx 1867, 929).

Marx here does not say the capitalism "bursts asunder", but that it "is burst asunder". He does not say that the capitalist system expropriates capitalists via its own breakdown, but that they "are expropriated" by the proletarians. This implies revolutionary agency on behalf of the proletariat. Marx imagines that this situation happens and describes it in a lively manner. He does not assume that it occurs with necessity. Piketty underestimates the dialectic of structure and agency, capitalist contradictions and class struggles, in Marx's works.

Piketty, however, also concedes that Marx correctly identified accumulation as being dialectically connected to the workers' expropriation and resulting inequalities when saying that relatively rising inequality as in contemporary capitalism "directly reflects the Marxian logic" (Piketty 2014, 11). So Piketty does not dismiss Marx, but misinterprets him, which is not a surprise because when being asked about Karl Marx, Piketty said: "I never managed really to read it" (Chotiner 2014).

Sources of Contemporary Inequality

Piketty (2014) identifies as sources of contemporary inequality high remunerations of managers (24, 314–315); the high growth of profits, dividends, interests and rents (25); long-term slow growth coupled with high savings (173); the privatisation of public assets (173); a skills gap (304–307, 315); low taxation of profits and income (355); and inherited wealth (424–429). Piketty's main variables for analysing the consequences and realities of inequality are the capital/income share (chapter 5), the capital-labour split (chapter 6), the distribution of labour income (chapter 9), and the concentration and distribution of capital and wealth (chapter 10). He thereby shows the historical realities of inequality between capital and labour as well as capital concentration. The typical development of the capital-labour split, labour incomes, and capital concentration takes on U-shaped curves with especially high levels of inequalities in the 19th and early 20th centuries and since the 1970s or 1980s.

The Tendency of the Profit Rate to Fall

Piketty discusses Marx's law of the tendency of the profit rate to fall: "Marxist analysis emphasizes the falling rate of profit—a historical prediction that turned out to be quite wrong" (Piketty 2014, 52). The profit rate would in the long run be relatively stable but would have decreased from levels of 4% to 5% in the 18th and 19th centuries to 3% to 4% today (Piketty 2014, 206). Piketty argues that Marx's law of the tendency of the profit rate to fall means that "the bourgeoisie digs its own grave" (227) because Marx would have assumed that he average profit rate evermore diminishes. Marx would have overlooked the growth of productivity and population (228) and the diffusion of knowledge (234).

Here again Piketty's reading of Marx is not thorough enough. Marx spoke of a "tendency" of the profit rate to fall and not an automatism. This tendency would derive from the increasing role of constant capital, especially technology, in production so that the organic composition of capital c / v (the relationship of constant and variable capital—that is, the monetary value of means of production and labour power) increases. Marx (1894, chapter 14) furthermore identified countervailing tendencies, such as the lowering of wages, the usage of the methods of absolute and relative surplus-value production, the cheapening of constant capital, foreign trade and the sale of commodities above their value, high exploitation rates of labour in colonies, the devaluation of fixed constant capital, increasing speed of the turnover of capital, and violent devaluation of capital by war or crises. Ernest Mandel commented in his introduction to *Capital Volume 3*: "To be sure, Marx explicitly speaks about a tendency, not an uninterrupted linear development. He stresses that there are powerful countervailing forces at work under capitalism. The most important countervailing force is the possibility for the capitalist system to increase the rate of surplus-value" (in Marx 1894,

31). Marx (1894, 339–342) stresses that methods of absolute and relative surplus value production increase the rate of exploitation and so the "law [of the tendency of the profit rate to fall] operates more as a tendency, i.e. as a law whose absolute realization is held up, delayed and weakened" (Marx 1894, 341).

Dogmatism, Orthodoxy, and Sectarianism

Within Marxist theory, there have been quite fierce battles about the validity or faultiness of Marx's tendency of the profit rate to fall (see Ebermann, Heinrich, Kurz, and Vogl 2011; Carchedi and Roberts 2013; Heinrich 2013a, 2013b; Kliman, Freeman, Potts, Gusev, and Cooney 2013;, Mage 2013, Moseley 2013). Scholars involved in these academic battles will of course always reject and deny the claim that these debates tend to be sectarian and dogmatic because they always perceive the others as sectarians and never themselves. The problem often is not just the aggressive language used in such debates, but also that those involved tend to lose sight of the forest for the trees. They tend to get so invested in stressing differences and that other Marxists are wrong, interpret Marx falsely, etc., and that they have the only valid interpretation of Marx that they lose the sense for a big commonality—namely, the interest in Marx's theory and the political opposition to capitalism. They lose sight of how important it is to together tackle the enemy in theory and politics. In the course of the ongoing capitalist crisis, the camp of conservatives, right-wingers, and fascists will definitely be thankful for such inward-directed theoretical and political wars.

All of this is dogmatism, orthodoxy, and sectarianism. But of course those involved will never admit to it. Hopefully the time will come that they at least change their strategy. If so, then it will most likely be done without them admitting to their own sectarianism. David Harvey is arguably the most well-known Marxist theorist today. But of course the sectarians will deny this fact, will stress how wrong Harvey is, that they are right, have the correct interpretation of Harvey, etc. Such claims are, however, nothing more than uninteresting and a waste of time. When Harvey says that we still need Marx's "modern-day equivalent" instead of Piketty, then psychoanalytically he may project himself into this position. But may it not be that besides all the repression, institutional, and structural discrimination Marxists have to face in capitalist society, which much limits the attention and visibility they get, a factor that contributes to the fact that Marxists don't have a figure with the same media and public presence as Piketty may be that they invest too much time in internal battles instead of in outward-oriented struggles?

Debates about Marx's law of the tendency of the profit rate to fall often centre around the question of if Marx's crisis theory is more a structural or an agency-focused theory that is determined either by structural antagonisms or class struggles. The basic question is if the profit rate varies because of a structural historical increase of the organic composition of capital or because of the outcomes of struggles between capital and labour that are reflected in the relationship of the profit and wage share.

The Marxian Rate of Profit

The rate of profit (ROP) is the relationship of profit and investment or of the monetary expression of surplus-value and the value of the means of production (constant and variable capital).

$$ROP = \frac{s}{c+v}$$

If we divide the numerator and the denominator by v, then we get:

$$ROP = \frac{\dfrac{s}{v}}{\dfrac{c}{v}+1}$$

This formula shows that the rate of profit depends (a) on the rate of surplus-value that Marx also calls the rate of exploitation because it describes the relationship of unpaid and paid labour and (b) on the organic composition of capital, which represents the relationship of dead and living labour, constant and variable capital, and the value of machinery/resources and labour power. The rate of profit is directly proportional to the rate of surplus-value and indirectly proportional to the organic composition of capital.

Capitalists have to constantly strive to increase productivity in order to survive and produce more commodities in less time. So they strive to invest in more efficient production technologies and to speed up production and circulation. The rise of computing in production or what some term the "information economy" and "information society" is grounded in the technification of production and the development of the productive forces. As a result, science and knowledge in production and society have historically increased their importance. Technification as means for raising productivity is likely to bring about an increase of the organic composition of capital because more money tends to be spent on technology. It, however, also tends to increase the rate of surplus-value because technology in production is according to Marx (1867) a means of relative surplus-value production resulting in the production of more value in less or the same time. So the same amount of labour measured in hours suddenly produces more surplus-value than before. It is clear that if the rate of surplus-value remains constant, while the organic composition rises, the rate of profit decreases.

The Contradiction between the Rate of Surplus-Value and the Organic Composition of Capital

There is a contradiction between the rate of surplus-value, which is directly proportional to the rate of profit, and the organic composition of capital, which is indirectly proportional to it. In a situation of technological innovation in which new technologies are adopted by many companies and so widely diffuse into the capitalist economy, additional constant capital investments tend to be made. If technologies are not cheapened, then this will result in an increase of the organic composition. The question is how capitalists will react to this downward pressure on their profits. It is likely that many of them attempt to mobilise countervailing tendencies, such as laying off labour, reducing wages, outsourcing labour, making employees work more for the same or lower wages, etc. They aim to always further increase the rate of surplus-value by various methods of absolute and relative surplus-value production. Technification is a method of relative surplus-value production itself, so raising the organic composition can increase the rate of surplus-value. There is, however, no guarantee that this increase is larger than the increase of the organic composition and so capitalists will tend to try to continuously reduce wage costs in order to increase profitability.

Class Struggles

Methods of absolute and relative surplus-value production are, however, as Marx knew, contested. Workers' struggles are not an automatism, but always a possibility. Workers have the capacity to resist capitalists' attacks so that the rate of surplus-value is also shaped by the outcomes of class struggles. If workers' struggles are successful, the rate and therefore their exploitation tend to decrease. If they are not successful, capitalists triumph and increase the rate of exploitation. The increase of the organic composition as structural tendency of capital stands in a contradiction to class struggles. The outcomes of this contradiction cannot be predicted in advance, but depend on historical circumstances. If the organic composition increases and there are no or unsuccessful workers' struggles so that the wage sum decreases, then the rate of profit can increase. If, however, workers' struggles are successful and they resist layoffs and achieve wage increases, the profit rate is more likely to fall.

Marx argues that capitalism is a vampire-like machine that sucks out labour: "Capital is dead labour which, vampire-like, lives only by sucking living labour, and lives the more, the more labour it sucks" (Marx 1867, 342). Capitalism's very structure compels capitalists to try to exploit labour as much as possible in order to survive in the competitive race and to increase its profits. So there is a necessary class struggle from above in capitalism. If capital could, then it would reduce wages as far as possible towards zero in order to increase profits. If it had unlimited supply of, access to, and coercive power over labour power, it would pay no wages at all and make workers toil for 24 hours a day in order to maximise profits. Capital has inherently fascist potentials. The question is if labour reacts to exploitation with struggles or is blinded by ideologies. Two means of capitalist class struggle for increasing exploitation are absolute and relative surplus-value production.

One can sometimes hear that the early Marx was more a humanist focusing on agency and the old Marxist a functionalist describing capital's structural contradictions. This assumption is, however, odd, just like the claim that there has been an epistemological break in the work of the young "esoteric" and the old "scientific" Marx. Marx in contrast describes in detail in *Capital Volume 1* how workers struggled against and resisted absolute and relative surplus-value production. Capital's attempts to prolong the working day resulted in counter-struggles of the proletariat. In "the history of capitalist production, the establishment of a norm for the working day presents itself as a struggle over the limits of that day, a struggle between collective capital, i.e. the class of capitalists, and collective labour, i.e. the working class" (Marx 1867, 344). "The establishment of a normal working day is [. . .] the product of a protracted and more or less concealed civil war between the capitalist class and the working class" (Marx 1867, 412–413).

Technification as method of relative surplus-production just like the intensification of control, surveillance, and the speed of production as comparable methods can call forth resistance of workers who are concerned about layoffs, quality of work and life, and absolute or relative decreases of wages. "In general, relative surplus-value is produced by raising the productivity of the worker, and thereby enabling him to produce more in a given time with the same expenditure of labour" (Marx 1867, 534). Workers' struggles against relative surplus-value production often contest the implications of the introduction of new technologies, such as layoffs, an increased pace of work, the standardisation of work routines, deskilling, etc. "The struggle between the capitalist and the wage-labourer starts with the existence of the capital-relation itself. It rages throughout the period of manufacture. But only since the introduction of machinery has the worker fought against the instrument of labour itself, capital's material mode of existence. He is in revolt against this particular form of the means of production because it is the material foundation of the capitalist mode of production" (Marx 1867, 553–554).

Marxist Theories of Crisis

Some Marxists tend to argue that a revolutionary approach is only possible based on the assumption that capitalist development is governed by *one* structural law that with necessity brings about crises and over time brings us close to the end of capitalism. Along comes often the argument that class struggle explanations of crises are underconsumptionist, distributionist, and reformist, that they ignore the structural contradictions of capitalism, aim at making capitalism work better, and assume that an equal distribution is possible within capitalism. Underconsumption can also be framed as overproduction. Class conflict and struggle over the distribution of surplus-value is a structural contradiction of capitalism itself. It cannot be overcome as long as capitalism exists. Capitalists again and again try to drive down wage costs in order to increase profits and thereby foster capitalist contradictions. If this class struggle from above is, however, structural, then no fair distribution of capital and wealth is possible within capitalism. Capitalists have to exploit workers and therefore create inequality understood as an antagonism between those who own the means of production and the poverty (that Marx understood in the *Grundrisse* as non-ownership) of the working class as a structural feature of capitalism.

It is not feasible to assume that there is only one antagonism of capitalism and that it is always the same contradiction that calls forth crises because capitalism is a complex, dynamic system (Fuchs 2002, 2004). Deterministic and one-dimensional crisis theories fail to account for this nature of capitalism. It is rather more feasible to assume that capitalism has a set of inherent antagonisms revolving around the dialectic of capital and labour and that a specific crisis is a manifestation of an interaction of several antagonisms (Fuchs 2002, 2004; Fuchs and Sandoval 2014b). For Marx, capitalism's antagonisms include the ones between classes; producers and the means of production, necessary and surplus labour, use-value and exchange-value, productive forces and the relations of production, single production and social need; socialised production and capitalistic, private appropriation; the fictitious value of financial capital and the actual profits that capital achieves on the commodity markets; etc. The task is then to analyse how capitalism's antagonisms interact and develop historically and in specific crisis situations.

Marx Is a Communist Soldier, not an Apocalyptic Rider

Back to Piketty's book, we can based on the preceding discussion argue that he fails to see the complexity and manifoldness of Marx's crisis theory and capitalism's dialectic of structure and agency. Marx is not an apocalyptic rider, but a communist soldier engaged in waging war against capitalism. One of Piketty's basic arguments is that historically there have been "numerous shocks to capital", but that capital has managed to again and again grow in the long-term by increasing inequality. Marx's insight was that this inequality is a structural feature of class society that in capitalism takes on the form of private property ownership of capital and the exploitation of labour. Piketty shows the ups and downs of capitalist development, which not just shows capital's capacity to restore growth by increasing and extending the exploitation of labour, but also its inherent crisis-proneness. Marx showed that there are inherent crisis-tendencies of capital that result again and again in crisis and that the growth, stagnation, and decline of capital are conditioned by structural antagonisms and class struggles.

Marx saw the concentration of capital as an inherent tendency of capitalism that arises from the drive that capitalists have to increase productivity. The progress of the use of technology and the rise of productivity tend to be distributed asymmetrically so that some companies can produce more cheaply than others. Competition reverts in capitalism into the tendency of capital concentration.

> This expropriation is accomplished through the action of the immanent laws of capitalist production itself, through the centralization of capitals. One capitalist always strikes down many others. Hand in hand with this centralization, or this expropriation of many capitalists by a few, other developments take place on an ever-increasing scale, such as the growth of the co-operative form of the labour process, the conscious technical application of science, the planned exploitation of the soil, the transformation of the means of labour into forms in which they can only be used in common, the economising of all means of production by

their use as the means of production of combined, socialized labour, the entanglement of a 11 peoples in the net of the world market, and, with this, the growth of the international character of the capitalist regime. (Marx 1867, 929)

The Inequality of Capital Ownership: The Concentration and Centralisation of Capital

Marx explained the tendency that Piketty (2014, chapter 10) calls the "inequality of capital ownership". Marx spoke of the concentration and centralisation of capital.

The concern about capitalism's inequalities unites Piketty and Marx more than Piketty and the contemporary Marxist, liberal, and conservative commentariat tends to realise. At the same time their perspectives also diverge because Piketty takes a predominantly empirical and Marx a predominantly theoretical approach, and Piketty draws the conclusion that inequalities cannot be overcome in capitalism, but be tamed and justified. Marx in contrast argues that capitalist antagonisms result again and again in crises that bring about human misery so that overcoming capitalism is the main political goal for the political left.

3. Capitalism and the Internet

Thomas Piketty and the Internet

Thomas Piketty's (2014) references to the Internet and digital media are scarce. On the one hand this industry is of course just one among many and one should not overestimate its size. On the other hand, quite a few IT and telecommunications companies are among the world's largest companies. References to digital media are threefold in Piketty's book: He discusses the fetishism of Internet capitalism, changes brought about by technological progress, and the example of the new economy crisis in 2000.

First, Piketty discusses that there is a fetishism of the rich that disregards the social relations underlying this richness and the success and reputation of companies such as Microsoft, Apple, Facebook, and Google. "Bill Gates, the former number one, who is seen as a model of the meritorious entrepreneur. At times one almost has the impression that Bill Gates himself invented computer science and the microprocessor. [. . .] No doubt the veritable cult of Bill Gates is an outgrowth of the apparently irrepressible need of modern democratic societies to make sense of inequality" (Piketty 2014, 444). "Steve Jobs, who even more than Bill Gates is the epitome of the admired and talented entrepreneur who fully deserves his fortune" (Piketty 2014, 440). Piketty stresses that monopolies and the exploitation of labour are crucial for the success of these companies:

> [I]t seems to me that Bill Gates also profited from a virtual monopoly on operating systems (as have many other high-tech entrepreneurs in industries ranging from telecommunications to Facebook, whose fortunes were also built on monopoly rents). Furthermore, I believe that Gates's contributions depended on the work of thousands of engineers and scientists doing basic research in electronics and computer science, without whom none of his innovations would have been possible. (Piketty 2014, 444)

Second, Piketty foregrounds that technological progress changes lifestyles, society, and consumption as evidenced by the rise of the Internet and mobile phones. Annual growth of 1% would bring about major changes, as evidenced by the fact that in "1980 there was no Internet or cell phone network" (Piketty 2014, 95).

Third, Piketty discusses the 2000 new economy crisis as an example of bursting financial bubbles (Piketty 2014, 49, 172, 190, 295f). "To be sure, the price that the financial markets sets on a company's or even a sector's immaterial capital at any given moment is largely arbitrary and uncertain. We see this in the collapse of the Internet bubble in 2000, in the financial crisis that began in 2007–2008, and more generally in the enormous volatility of the stock market" (Piketty 2014, 49). "[T]he bursting of the Internet bubble in 2000–2001, which caused a particularly sharp drop in the capital/income ratio in the United States and Britain" (Piketty 2014, 172).

The Political Economy of the Internet

The political economy of the Internet is complex and involves a manifoldness of dimensions and problems such as the exploitation of digital labour; the surveillance-industrial complex; struggles around intellectual property; an antagonism between knowledge commons and knowledge commodities; the role of the Internet in social struggles; the political economy of online attention, voice, and visibility; complex relations between the public and the private; the creation, limitation, and destruction of online public spheres; the rise of new forms of collaboration; etc. (see Fuchs, Boersma, Albrechtslund, and Sandoval 2012; Fuchs and Mosco 2012; Fuchs 2008, 2014a, 2014c; Fuchs and Sandoval 2014a).

One of course does and should not expect from a general economist like Piketty to work out a political economy of the Internet. It rather makes sense to ask if there are elements in his approach that can help us in this task of better understanding the digital media economy in contemporary capitalism.

Capital Taxation and the ICT Industry

In the EU's 28 countries, capital taxes accounted in 2014 for only 0.3% of the GDP (data source: AMECO). In the United States the value was 0.2% (AMECO). The projections for 2015 are 0.2% both for the EU and the USA (AMECO). This means that treated as a collective capitalist, companies hardly pay taxes. The lowering of capital taxation to almost nothing has since the 1970s come along, as Piketty (2014) shows in his book, with an increasing capital share and a decreasing wage share in most capitalist economies. If wages decrease while profits continue to increase, the exploitation of labour rises. Capital taxation is in principle a way of using state power for distributing wealth away from capital towards the general public by investing in public services that are available to all. The lowering of capital taxes helps further increasing profits and therefore increases the level of capitalism's inherent inequality between capital and labour.

> [The] recent rise of tax competition in a world of free-flowing capital has led many governments to exempt capital income from the progressive income tax. This is particularly true in Europe, whose relatively small states have thus far proved incapable of achieving a coordinated tax policy. The result is an endless race to the bottom, leading, for example, to cuts in corporate tax rates and to the exemption of interest, dividends, and other financial revenues from the taxes to which labor incomes are subject. (Piketty 2014, 496)

Transnational corporations tend to make use of financial outsourcing, tax havens, and tax loopholes in order to avoid paying taxes.

> The problem with the current system is that multinational corporations often end up paying ridiculously small amounts because they can assign all their profits artificially to a subsidiary located in a place where taxes are very low; such a practice is not illegal, and in the minds of many corporate managers it is not even unethical. (Piketty 2014, 561)

Amazon had in 2012 15,000 employees in the UK, but its headquarters are in Luxembourg, where it had just 500 employees in the same year.[1] In 2011, it generated revenues of £3.3 billion in the

UK, but only paid £1.8 million corporation tax (0.05%).[2] In 2013, it paid £4.2 million in corporation tax (0.1%) on sales of £4.3 billion.[3] Facebook paid £238,000 corporation tax on a UK revenue of £175 million (0.1%) in 2011.[4] Google had a UK turnover of £395 million in 2011, but only paid taxes of £6 million (1.5%).[5] The House of Commons' Public Accounts Committee under its Chair MP Margaret Hodge started an inquiry about corporate tax avoidance in 2012. Tax avoidance concerns not just Internet companies, but also other transnational corporations such as Starbucks. The Internet is a global space. Companies selling commodities online (services, content, access to platforms, users) therefore operate on a global scale automatically and are likely to have customers outside the country where their headquarters are located. It is therefore no surprise that among those companies that avoid paying taxes there are many Internet corporations. They outsource their finances in a complex manner to tax havens such as Luxembourg, the Bermuda Islands, the Cayman Islands, or the Virgin Islands and argue that they don't have to pay taxes in those countries where their users or customers are located because the intellectual property for their platforms and/or their headquarters are registered in tax havens where they either have to pay no or only very low capital taxes.

In its inquiry, the Public Accounts Committee concluded the following:

> Google defends its tax position by claiming that its sales of advertising space to UK clients take place in Ireland—an argument which we find deeply unconvincing on the basis of evidence that, despite sales being billed from Ireland, most sales revenue is generated by staff in the UK. It is quite clear to us that sales to UK clients are the primary purpose, responsibility and result of its UK operation, and that the processing of sales through Google Ireland has no purpose other than to avoid UK corporation tax. [. . .] HMRC needs to be much more effective in challenging the artificial corporate structures created by multinationals with no other purpose than to avoid tax. [. . .] International tax rules are complicated and have not kept pace with the way businesses operate globally and through the internet. [. . .] it is far too easy for companies to exploit the rules and set up structures in low-tax jurisdictions, rather than pay tax where they actually conduct their business and sell their goods and services. We are also particularly concerned about the out-of-date tax frameworks covering international internet based commerce which rely on a fully automated process. [. . .] HMRC and HM Treasury should push for an international commitment to improve tax transparency, including by developing specific proposals to improve the quality and credibility of public information about companies tax affairs, and use that information to collect a fair share of tax from profits generated in each country. This data should include full information from companies based in tax havens. (House of Commons Committee of Public Accounts 2013, 5–6)

The Welfare State

Thomas Piketty (2014, 479) argues that the welfare state's funding of public services means that for services such as education and health there can be "real equality of access for everyone regardless of income (or parents' income), at least in principle". The welfare state certainly has the role of reproducing labour power so that it can be better exploited by capital. It, however, was also the outcome of long struggles of the working class and is therefore a working-class achievement that has in the past decades been increasingly privatised, commodified, and destroyed. Services of the welfare state that are available to all independent of income are an element of communism within capitalism. Modern society contains both elements of communism and capitalism, which stand in a dialectical-contradictory relationship to each other. So communism is not something completely distant, but has its own realities and germ forms already today. The task of the political left is to question and struggle against the dismantling of communist elements and their replacement by elements of capitalism.

A Global Progressive Tax on Capital and Income

Piketty (2014, 494) argues that flat taxes such as consumption taxes "are often the most hated of all" because they put "the heaviest burden on the lower class". He suggests the introduction of a global progressive tax on capital and income for realising a 21st-century social state. The "capital tax I am proposing is a progressive annual tax on global wealth. The largest fortunes are to be taxed more heavily, and all types of assets are to be included: real estate, financial assets, and business assets—no exceptions" (Piketty 2014, 517). The problem is of course how to implement such a tax and to avoid capital flight. The problem is that taxation tends to be national, whereas capital is often global. It is, however, inappropriate to dismiss Piketty's suggestions as utopian and unrealistic (Harvey 2014; Žižek 2014). One should rather think about institutional reforms that need to be implemented along with a unified global progressive tax on capital.

The tax that Piketty (2014, 528, 572) suggests is certainly too modest: 0% or 0.1% or 0.5% on wealth below €1 million, 1% between €1 and €5 million, and 2% above €5 million. He also leaves open how high the global progressive tax on profits should be. If the same rates of 0%, 1%, and 2% applied, then this would be a further tax relief for many companies and have no or negative redistributive effects that would further support capitalist interests. Corporate taxation should have much higher levels and could above a specific tax bracket be 100%—that is, a confiscatory tax—for that part of all annual profits that exceed a specific level. Piketty (2014, 505–508) himself shows that confiscatory taxes have historically played an important role especially in the USA and the UK.

"For collective action, what would matter most would be the publication of detailed accounts of private corporations (as well as government agencies)" (Piketty 2014, 570). Piketty here hints at the fact that implementing a global progressive tax on capital requires not just institutions for a global tax system, but also a system that makes global financial flows and companies' revenues transparent to the public. This requires abolishing bank secrecy, or what some term "financial privacy", of all companies in the world. Piketty (2014, 521–524) suggests a system that automatically transmits banking information to public tax authorities. Global computer networks are an indispensable tool for financial tracking and monitoring. One problem of taxing capital is indeed the in transparency of revenues and capital flows. One could therefore make the even more radical suggestion that all capital flows and corporate revenues should be transparent to everyone in the world. I imagine an open Internet system that allows everyone to track the annual revenues, profits, and taxes of each company in the world broken down by geographic regions.

Alternative Media, Alternative Internet

Alternative, noncommercial Internet and media platforms face the problem that dominant media and Internet corporations have often de facto monopolies of audiences, users, attention, visibility, and voices. The public sphere is in capitalism therefore necessarily undemocratic and unfree (Fuchs 2014d). I have suggested in another paper that it is crucial to provide and organise a resource base, visibility, voice, and attention of alternative, noncommercial, nonprofit Internet platforms, and media in order to strengthen democracy in the digital and media age (Fuchs 2014d). The Internet is today highly controlled by capitalist corporations that exploit the digital labour of users. It is also controlled by state institutions that make use of surveillance systems such as the Prism and XKeyScore systems, whose existence Edward Snowden unveiled. The Internet is today highly controlled, unfree, and undemocratic. An alternative Internet is urgently needed. Making the Internet noncapitalist would certainly require and constitute an Internet revolution. But the problem is how to start and how to support projects that are based on worker-user cooperatives and don't want to accumulate capital, but still need a resource base in order to exist.

Piketty argues for extending and modernising the social state in the 21st century. He suggests that the public sector should involve "new decentralized and participatory forms of organization" (Piketty 2014, 482) and intermediary forms in which foundations and association cooperate with the state. The cultural and media sector would be a good realm for such forms (Piketty 2014, 483). I have suggested such reforms for the media and Internet sector (Fuchs 2014d): A politically progressive measure is to tax large media and other corporations based on a global corporation tax and to channel this income into noncommercial media, and to combine this measure with elements of participatory budgeting, which allows every citizens to receive and donate a certain amount per year to a noncommercial media project (Fuchs 2014d). Elements of state action and civil society action could be combined: The power of the state would guarantee taxation of large companies; the distribution of this income to media projects would, however, be decentralised and put in the hands of citizens.

Google, Facebook, and other large online media companies hardly pay taxes in many countries. The insight that users are digital workers and create economic value on corporate social media that are financed by advertising allows changing global tax regulations: Corporate social media platforms should have to tax in a specific country that share of their revenues that corresponds to the share of users or ad-clicks/views they have in the same country. Such a measure reflects Piketty's insight that it "makes more sense to give up the idea that profits can be pinned down to a particular state or territory; instead, one can apportion the revenues of the corporate tax on the basis of sales or wages paid within each country" (Piketty 2014, 561). Implementing such a tax system requires, as Piketty suggests, the global monitoring and transparency of company revenues and their financial flows, for which computer networks and the Internet are, as suggested above, excellent tools.

The Participatory Media Fee

The licence fee—a tool of the broadcast age—could be developed into a media fee paid by citizens and companies. It could be made more socially just than the licence fee by implementing it not as a flat but a progressive fee that varies based on salary and revenue levels. It is a matter of fairness that those who earn more contribute more to the organisation of the common interest and public good.

The media fee could partly be used for directly funding public service media's online presence and partly be used in the form of participatory budgeting to provide an annual voucher to every citizen that s/he must donate to a nonprofit, noncommercial media organisation. So participatory budgeting should not be used for deciding if the BBC receives the full funding it needs for its operations. Additional income from the media fee could, however, be distributed to alternative media projects with the help of participatory budgeting. Nonprofit versions of Twitter, YouTube, and Facebook run by civil society organisations and public institutions could, based on such a model, serve the purpose of the public sphere and strengthen the democratic character of communications.

Capital Taxation and the Left

The suggestion to tax capital is always likely to arouse among Marxists the reaction that such measures are just social-democratic reformism that does not abolish but rather stabilise capitalism. There is no doubt that Piketty (2014) does not want to abolish capitalism, but to establish "control of capitalism" (532), "to regulate capitalism" (518), and "to stop the indefinite increase of inequality of wealth" (518). This does, however, not mean that a global progressive tax on capital cannot be part of a radical-reformist political agenda of the left that tries to foster better conditions for the overcoming of capitalism. It is political idealism to think that the only thing we can do now is to build revolutionary movements and wait with the creation of democratic communism until the day after the revolution. We must start in the here and now with roots and seeds of democratic communism—that is, participatory democracy. And such seeds need resources and have their own political economy. Channelling resources towards alternatives requires state power, state action, the interaction of progressive political parties and social movements, and the interaction of the state and civil society. A global progressive tax on capital should be part of a strategy of a New Left to improve the living conditions of workers, consumers, and users by weakening capitalism and capitalist interests. If implemented the right way together with other measures it could be a good tool of class struggle for a noncapitalist Internet.

Taxing Google, Facebook, Apple, Amazon, etc. more effectively, efficiently, and transparently does certainly not abolish the exploitation of workers, prosumers, and users. The important step is to establish noncapitalist digital media. Doing so requires resources. And these resources should be taken from large corporations. So effectively, efficiently, and transparently taxing the likes of Google, Facebook, and Apple is not a substitution for creating alternatives, but can become a means for fostering, creating, building, and enlarging noncapitalist digital media and a way towards a noncapitalist Internet.

Marx and Engels: Communism and Progressive Taxation

The second congress of the Communist League took place at the Red Lion pub in London from November 29 to December 8, 1847 (Briggs and Callow 2008, 35). As a result of it, "Marx and Engels were given the task of writing a Manifesto to publicise the doctrines of the League" (McLellan 2006, 161). One of 10 concrete measures that the *Communist Manifesto* advocates is a "heavy progressive or graduated income tax" (Marx and Engels 1968, 51). A draft of the *Manifesto* titled *Principles of Communism* called for the "[l]imitation of private ownership by means of progressive taxation" (Engels 1847, 350). A leaflet of the Communist Party in Germany that was written by Marx and Engels and signed by Marx, Engels, Karl Schapper, Heinrich Bauer, Joseph Moll, and Wilhelm Wolff identified 17 demands, including the "[i]ntroduction of strongly progressive taxes and abolition of taxes on consumption" (Marx and Engels 1848a).

Engels already in 1845 suggested the introduction of public services financed by progressive taxes. In order to raise the money for public services and

> at the same time replace all the present, unjustly distributed taxes, the present reform plan proposes a general, progressive tax on capital, at a rate increasing with the size of the capital. In this way, the burden of public administration would be shared by everyone according to his ability and would no longer fall mainly on the shoulders of those least able to bear it, as has hitherto been the case in all countries. For the principle of taxation is, after all, a purely communist one, since the right to levy taxes is derived in all countries from so-called national property. (Engels 1845)

The idea of progressive taxation remained important for Marx and Engels throughout their lives, as evidenced by the fact that Engels in 1891 commented on the draft of the German Social-Democratic Party's programme that progressive tax should "cover all expenditure of the state, district and community, insofar as taxes are required for it. Abolition of all indirect state and local taxes, duties, etc." (Engels 1891).

Marx and Engels did not reject parliamentary democracy, elections, and state power, but saw them rather as a "means for putting through measures directed against private property and ensuring the livelihood of the proletariat" (Engels 1847). They recommended that "workers' candidates are nominated everywhere in opposition to bourgeois-democratic candidates" (Marx and Engels 1850). Elections and parliamentary democracy are for Marx and Engels (1850) part of the proletariat's "battle-cry [. . .]: The Permanent Revolution". They argued that the workers must drive the proposals of the democrats to their logical extreme (the democrats will in any case act in a reformist and not a revolutionary manner) and transform these proposals into direct attacks on private property. If, for instance, the petty bourgeoisie propose the purchase of the railways and factories, the workers must demand that these railways and factories simply be confiscated by the state without compensation as the property of reactionaries. If the democrats propose a proportional tax, then the workers must demand a progressive tax; if the democrats themselves propose a moderate progressive tax, then the workers must insist on a tax whose rates rise so steeply that big capital is ruined by it; if the democrats demand the regulation of the state debt, then the workers must demand national bankruptcy. The demands of the workers will thus have to be adjusted according to the measures and concessions of the democrats. (Marx and Engels 1850)

Marx and Engels would today not reject, but embrace and radicalise the idea of a global progressive tax on capital. They saw progressive taxation as a communist measure. If we want to establish a noncapitalist Internet that benefits all humans as a commons, then fostering alternative Internet platforms and making use of elections, the state, governments, parliament, institutional reforms, and progressive taxation is crucial.

Rosa Luxemburg and Thomas Piketty

Thomas Piketty's book *Capital in the Twenty-First Century* should neither be dignified nor denigrated. Neither should its importance be denied. Those interested in the creation of a New Left should constructively and critically engage with the book's ideas, which can help foster a discourse about how left politics can look today. Books like Piketty's *Capital* are a welcome intervention. Activists, scholars, users, and citizens struggling for an alternative Internet can gain insightful stimuli from it that can be further developed and radicalised. This is what Marx and Engels would have done. Radical reforms of the Internet are a crucial task today. A New Left is urgently needed. An alternative Internet is needed. The latter cannot be achieved without the first. And the first should take politics and struggles that help establishing the latter quite serious.

Rosa Luxemburg's words are in the age of the Internet more relevant than ever and should not be forgotten:

> The daily struggle for reforms, for the amelioration of the condition of the workers within the framework of the existing social order, and for democratic institutions, offers to the social democracy the only means of engaging in the proletarian class war and working in the direction of the final goal-the conquest of political power and the suppression of wage labor. Between social reforms and revolution there exists for the social democracy an indissoluble tie. The struggle for reforms is its means; the social revolution, its aim. (Luxemburg 1899, 41)

Exercises for Appendix 1

Group exercise (G)
Project exercise (P)

Exercise Appendix 1.1 (P)

Search for both Marxist and liberal or conservative reviews of Thomas Piketty's book *Capital in the Twenty-First Century*.

Ask yourself the following questions:

> What are commonalities and differences between these types of reviews?
> How do they discuss the relationship of Piketty and Marx?
> How do you assess Piketty's book in relationship to Marx's book *Capital*?

Exercise Appendix 1.2 (G)

Search in Thomas Piketty's book *Capital in the Twenty-First Century* for passages where he discusses aspects of technology, the media, and the Internet. Compare these passages to quotes from *Capital Volume 1* in which Marx discusses aspects of technology (e.g., in chapter 15).

Discuss the following questions:

What are commonalities and differences between the way Piketty and Marx analyse the role of technology in capitalism?

What are political implications of Marx's analysis of technology? What are the political implications of Piketty's analysis of technology? What commonalities and differences are there of these analyses? What's your own assessment of them?

Notes

1 Starbucks, Google and Amazon grilled over tax avoidance. BBC Online. November 12, 2012. http://www.bbc.co.uk/news/business-20288077 (accessed on July 28, 2015).
2 Amazon: £7bn sales, no UK corporation tax. The Guardian Online. April 4, 2012. http://www.guardian.co.uk/technology/2012/apr/04/amazon-british-operation-corporation-tax. Google, Amazon, Starbucks: The rise of "tax sharing". BBC Online. December 4, 2012. http://www.bbc.co.uk/news/magazine-20560359 (accessed on July 28, 2015).
3 Amazon boycott urged after retailer pays just £4.2m in tax. The Guardian Online. May 9, 2014. http://www.theguardian.com/business/2014/may/09/margaret-hodge-urges-boycott-amazon-uk-tax-starbucks (accessed on July 28, 2015).
4 Should we boycott the tax-avoiding companies? The Guardian Online. Shortcuts Blog. October 17, 2012. http://www.guardian.co.uk/business/shortcuts/2012/oct/17/boycotting-tax-avoiding-companies (accessed on July 28, 2015).
5 Starbucks, Google and Amazon grilled over tax avoidance. BBC Online. November 12, 2012. http://www.bbc.co.uk/news/business-20288077 (accessed on July 28, 2015).

APPENDIX 2

Knowledge, Technology, and the General Intellect in the *Grundrisse* and Its "Fragment on Machines"

1. Introduction

Media Companies

Of the world's 2,000 largest transnational corporations, 232 or 11.6% were in 2014 located in the realm of communications and digital media, which is comprised of advertising, broadcasting, communications equipment, computer and electronic retail, computer hardware, computer services, computer storage devices, consumer electronics, electronics, Internet shopping and distribution, printing and publishing, semiconductors, software and programming, telecommunications (data source: Forbes 2000, 2014 list). Digital and information capitalism is one dimension of contemporary capitalism. It reflects the growing importance of science, communication, knowledge, computing, the Internet, and information labour in production. Scholarship has in recent years stressed that Marx in the *Grundrisse*, especially in the so-called "Fragment on Machines" and with the category of the general intellect, anticipated such developments.

The Grundrisse

This chapter is a reflection on the *Grundrisse* in the age of digital capitalism and digital labour. It contributes to recent studies on the *Grundrisse* that have largely neglected issues such as advertising, the Internet, and the digital world. It is, for example, telling that on a total of 736 pages, the two collected volumes *In Marx's Laboratory: Critical Interpretations of the Grundrisse* (Bellofiore, Starosta, and Thomas 2014b) and *Karl Marx's Grundrisse: Foundations of the Critique of Political Economy 150 Years Later* (Musto 2008) do not a single time mention the terms "digital", "Facebook", or "Twitter", and that the terms "Internet" and "advertising" occur only twice. Although such works provide extremely interesting insights into Marx's philosophy, they in contrast to some other recent publications (e.g., Fuchs and Mosco 2012, 2015a, 2015b) remain completely idealist, ignorant, and abstract when it comes to applying Marx to popular culture and communications.

This chapter provides a reading of Marx's *Grundrisse* by discussing advertising and productive labour in the context of social media (section 2) and by focusing on the "Fragment of Machines" (section 3) and its connection to other parts of the *Grundrisse* (section 4), as well as situating cultural and digital labour in the context of the Marxist debate on the "Fragment" and the general intellect (section 5).

Marx wrote the *Grundrisse* in the time from October 1857 until May 1858 (MEW 42,V). For some, the *Grundrisse* is an interesting and important draft of *Capital* that helps to understand the latter's genesis (Rosdolsky 1977), whereas for others it is "the central point in the development of Marx's theory" (Negri 1988, 87) and "an original work in its own right" (86) that stands independent of *Capital* and "represents the high point of Marx's revolutionary thinking" (88). Setting apart *Capital* and the *Grundrisse* served at the time of the Soviet Union often the purpose to question orthodoxy and Stalinism. Today it is much easier to see the complementarities and continuities between the two works—that is, not to read Marx against and beyond Marx, but Marx with Marx. The *Grundrisse* is "a veritable 'laboratory' in which we can observe Marx in the very process of unfolding his dialectical investigation of the movement of capitalist social and economic forms" (Bellofiore, Starosta, and Thomas 2014b, 3). All of Marx's works and categories are dialectical in character. In the *Grundrisse* the grounding in Hegel's logic is more explicit than in *Capital*, although both employ the same dialectical method of analysis and development.

2. Advertising, Circulation, and Productive Labour in the Age of Social Media

Dallas Smythe on Advertising

The Canadian Marxist political economist Dallas Smythe (1977) argued in his article "Communications: Blindspot of Western Marxism" that in advertising-financed media, the audience's labour produces attention as an audience commodity, which is sold to advertising clients. He wrote that it is a theoretical and political mistake to assume, such as the critics of the audience labour thesis do (for a prototypical example, see Lebowitz 1986), that advertising and audience labour are unproductive attributes of the sphere of circulation that eat up surplus value created in other parts of the economy. The most important online and social media, such as Google/YouTube/Blogspot, Facebook, Twitter, Weibo, and Baidu, use targeted advertising-based capital accumulation models. In their case, audience labour is users' digital labour, which creates data and meta-data that is sold as commodity to the platforms' ad clients. Google, Facebook, and the like are the world's largest advertising agencies (Fuchs 2014a, 2015).

The difference between audience commodification in commercial broadcasting and user commodification on corporate social media is that the in the latter case online activities generate data that can be monitored in real time; that data is networked across the Internet; that ads can be individually targeted based on interests and profiles, the audience size, composition; that behaviour is due to constant online surveillance not an estimation, but exactly known; and that commodification affects the convergence of users' various social roles. Can the *Grundrisse* help us to better understand the political economy of online advertising?

Marx on Productive Labour in the Grundrisse

Marx argues that productive labour "is only that which produces *capital*. [...] *Labour becomes productive by producing its own opposite*" (Marx 1857/1858 [English], 305). "Actors are productive workers, not in so far as they produce a play, but in so far as they increase their employer's wealth. But what sort of labour takes place, hence in what form labour materializes itself, is absolutely irrelevant for this relation" (328–329). "A. Smith was essentially correct with his productive and unproductive labour, correct from the standpoint of bourgeois economy. [...] The capitalist obtains labour itself, labour as valuepositing activity, as productive labour; i.e. he obtains the productive force which maintains and multiplies capital, and which thereby becomes the productive force, the reproductive force of capital, a force belonging to capital itself" (273–274).

An argument against audience and digital labour theory is that only wage-labour is productive, surplus–value generating labour (see, e.g., Lebowitz 1986). Marx's concept of productive labour in the *Grundrisse* (just like the one in *Capital Volume 1*'s chapter 16) does not confirm such an assumption. Rather he understands productive labour as labour that produces capital, which does not logically presuppose a wage-labour relationship. Facebook's and Google's wageworkers do not create a commodity, but rather a platform that users access as "free lunch", whereas users' activities create a data commodity that is sold in order to generate profit and enable the accumulation of capital.

Transport Costs

Marx (1885, 225–229) discusses transport costs especially in *Capital Volume 2*, chapter 3, section 3. Also in the *Grundrisse* he makes a similar argument—namely, that transport costs and transport labour produce surplus-value. So although the "*costs of circulation* proper (and they achieve a significant independent development in the money trade) are not reducible to productive labour time" (Marx 1857/1858 [English], 624–625), transport costs are of a different nature:

> Transport to market (spatial condition of circulation) belongs in the production process. [. . .] Circulation proceeds in space and time. Economically considered, the spatial condition, the bringing of the product to the market, belongs to the production process itself. The product is really finished only when it is on the market. The movement through which it gets there belongs still with the cost of making it. It does not form a necessary moment of circulation, regarded as a particular value process, since a product may be bought and even consumed at the point of its production. But this spatial moment is important in so far as the expansion of the market and the exchangeability of the product are connected with it. (Marx 1857/1858, 533–534)
>
> [Transport] gives the product a new use value (and this holds right down to and including the retail grocer, who weighs, measures, wraps the product and thus gives it a form for consumption), and this new use value costs labour time, is therefore at the same time exchange value. Bringing to market is part of the production process itself. The product is a commodity, is in circulation only when it is on the market. (Marx 1857/1858, 635)

Ideological Transport and the Media

Commercial media link commodity ideologies to consumers—they "transport" ideologies to consumers—although it is unclear and not determined how the latter react and if the confrontation with commodity ideologies results in actual purchases. Facebook and other corporate social media are advertising companies that sell advertising space and user data as commodities to clients who want to present commodity ideologies to users and hope that the latter buy their commodities.

Most commodities have independent from their physical or informational nature a cultural component that is created by the cultural labour performed in advertising departments and agencies. The cultural dimension of a commodity is necessary ideological: It appeals to consumers' imagination and wants to make them connote positive images and feelings with the idea of consuming this commodity. Wolfgang Fritz Haug (1986) speaks in this context of the commodity's use-value promise: The sales and advertising ideology associated with a commodity promises specific positive life enhancement functions that the commodity brings with it and thereby conceals the commodity's exchange-value behind promises. The symbolic commodity ideology promises a use-value beyond actual consumption, an imaginary surplus and surplus enjoyment. These promises are detached from the actual use-value and are therefore a fictitious form of use-value. Capitalism's antagonism between use-value and exchange-value takes in the realm of the commodity aesthetic the form of a contradiction between use-value and appearances of use-value: As long as the consumer has not purchased a commodity, s/he can only imagine how using it actually is. Advertising makes use-values appear to be specific forms and promises specific qualities—it communicates the commodity aesthetic. The

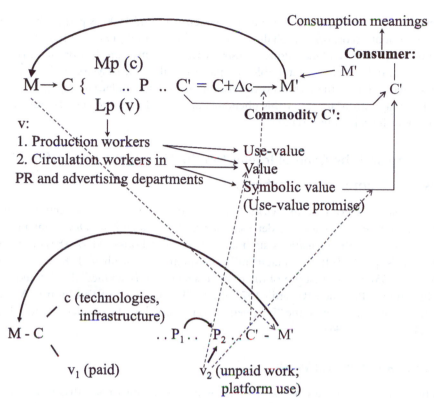

FIGURE A2.1 The economic relationship of Facebook and its advertising clients

commodity's appearance becomes more important than its being and is an instrument for capital accumulation. "The aesthetics of the commodity in its widest meaning—the sensual appearance and the conception of its use value—becomes detached from the object itself" (Haug 1986, 16–17).

Commercial media link commodity ideologies to consumers; they "transport" ideologies to consumers. Facebook and other corporate social media are advertising companies that sell advertising space and user data as commodities to clients who want to present commodity ideologies to users and hope that the latter will buy their commodities. The users' constant online activity is ideological transport labour necessary for running the targeting algorithms and for generating viewing possibilities and attention for ads' use-value promises. They do not transport a commodity in physical space from A to B; they rather organise a communication space that allows advertisers to communicate their use-value promises to potential customers. Figure A2.1 visualises the economic relationships of targeted advertising–based platforms such as Facebook and its advertising clients.

The Transport of Commodities

The transport of a commodity has two parts:

1. The commodity's physical transport: In the case of information this means data transmission via cables, telecommunications networks, radio signals, satellite transmission, etc.
2. Informational transport: The transport of the information that the commodity exists and why it should be bought by the consumer. Advertising plays a crucial role in this form of transport.

The modern advertising industry came into existence around 1890 as part of the emergence of the "new 'monopoly' (corporate) capitalism" (Williams 1960/1969, 177) and took full effect in the 20th century with the rise of the culture industry, mass media, mass production, and mass consumption. Advertising did not play a central role in capitalism at the time of Marx, which is the reason he hardly discussed it. Given this fact, however, also means that for understanding advertising culture, we have to think with Marx about this phenomenon. The idea of audience labour as ideological transport labour is such an undertaking.

3. Machinery and the General Intellect in the "Fragment on Machines"

What Is the "Fragment on Machines"?

What some Marxist scholars term Marx's "Fragment on Machines" is the section "Fixes Kapital und Entwicklung der Prodktivkräfte der Gesellschaft" (Capital and the Development of Society's Productive Forces) in the *Grundrisse*'s sixth and seventh notebooks (Marx 1857/1858 [German], 590–609; [English], 690–714). The "Fragment" was written in the first half of 1858 (Marx 1857/1858 [English], 697, 555). The earliest use of the term "Fragment on Machines" that I could trace in the English literature is Pier Aldo Rovatti's 1973 article "The Critique of Fetishism in Marx's 'Grundrisse'". An Italian translation of the "Fragment" was published in 1964 under the title "Frammento sulle Macchine" (Marx 1964).

Knowledge and General Work

Marx interprets in the "Fragment" technology as fixed constant capital that is an "alien power" (Marx 1857/1858 [English], 693) to the worker. He terms "science", "knowledge", and "technology" in production as part of fixed constant capital, the "accumulation of knowledge and of skill, of the general productive forces of the social brain" ([English], 694, in German: "Akkumulation des Wissens und des Geschicks, der allgemeinen Produktivkräfte des gesellschaftlichen Hirns", [German], 594; "gesellschaftliches Hirn" can more precisely be translated as "societal brain", but has been translated as "social brain", which has a more micro-sociological connotation) and "general social labour" ([English], 694). The "transformation of the production process from the simple labour process into a scientific process [...] appears as a quality of fixed capital in contrast to living labour" (Marx 1857/1858 [English], 700).

Marx here takes up the issue of knowledge and scientific work as general work, which he also discusses in *A Contribution to the Critique of Political Economy* (Marx 1859, 278) and *Capital Volume 1* (Marx 1867, 667) and *Volume 3* (Marx 1894, 199; MEW 25, 113–114). General work is general because its results are not just consumed in one specific company or branch of industry, but throughout the entire economy. General work has "a scientific and at the same time general character" (Marx 1857/1858 [English], 612). Marx writes in the German version of the *Grundrisse* that "materielle Produktion" is "zugleich allgemeine Arbeit" when it has "wissenschaftlichen Charakter[s]" (Marx 1857/1858 [German], 512). The English translation of this passage is that "material production" is of "a scientific and at the same time general character" (Marx 1857/1858 [English], 612). It is misleading because it presents scientific and general work as two different activities, whereas Marx in the German original wrote that "material production" is "at the same time general work" when it has "a scientific character".

Marx Anticipated the Emergence of an Information Economy

Marx anticipated the emergence of the important role of knowledge, science, and highly productive technologies such as the computer in production by arguing that capital's inherent need to develop the productive forces not just makes technology in production ever more important, but also results in a scientification of production and an increasing importance of knowledge labour: "machinery develops with the accumulation of society's science, of productive force generally" ([English], 694). Wolfgang Fritz Haug (2010, 211) argues in this context that Marx's concept of the general intellect was "prognostic-descriptive" of the emergence of computerisation and high-tech capitalism.

Radovan Richta: The Scientific-Technological Revolution

Radovan Richta (1969) has based on Marx termed "general labour" the scientific and technological revolution. "Science is now penetrating all phases of production and gradually assuming the role of the central productive force of human society and, indeed, the 'decisive factor' in the growth of the productive forces" (Richta 1969, 28). "Logically, then—from the standpoint of the deeper linkages of the model—the chances of carrying out the scientific and technological revolution to the full lie with a society advancing towards communism" (Richta 1969, 53–54). Richta (1969) coined the notion of the scientific and technological revolution in the context of hopes for a democratic form of communism in light of the Prague Spring. The rise of the important role of science and the computer in production would constitute a scientific-technological foundation for the transition of capitalism to communism and the transition from authoritarian to human-centred communism.

The idea of the scientific and technological revolution can already be found in the *Grundrisse*. "But to the degree that large industry develops, the creation of real wealth comes to depend less on labour time and on the amount of labour employed than on the power of the agencies set in motion during labour time, whose 'powerful effectiveness' is itself in turn out of all proportion to the direct labour time spent on their production, but depends rather on the general state of science and on the progress of technology, or the application of this science to production" (Marx 1857/1858, 704–705). As a consequence of technological development, "the entire production process" becomes "the technological application of science" (Marx 1857/1858, 699).

The Antagonism between Productive Forces and Relations of Production in the "Fragment"

The "Fragment on Machines" shows how modern technology reduces necessary labour time and thereby creates conditions for communism, free individuality, and a life based on free time as a source of wealth, but at the same time is embedded into capitalist class relations that have to set labour-time as the source of wealth so that the antagonism between the evermore socialised productive forces and the relations of production deepens the crisis-proneness of capitalism, the enslavement of labour, unemployment, and precarity:

[Under the conditions of capitalist technology, the worker] "steps to the side of the production process instead of being its chief actor. [. . .] as the great foundation-stone of production and of wealth. The theft of alien labour time, on which the present wealth is based, appears a miserable foundation in face of this new one, created by large-scale industry itself. As soon as labour in the direct form has ceased to be the great well-spring of wealth, labour time ceases and must cease to be its measure, and hence exchange value [must cease to be the measure] of use value. The surplus labour of the mass has ceased to be the condition for the development of general wealth, just as the non-labour of the few, for the development of the general powers of the human head. With that, production based on exchange value breaks down, and the direct, material production process is stripped of the form of penury and antithesis. The free development of individualities, and hence not the reduction of necessary labour time so as to posit surplus labour, but rather the general reduction of the necessary labour of society to a minimum, which then corresponds to the artistic, scientific etc. development of the individuals in the time set free, and with the means created, for all of them. (Marx 1857/1858, 705–706)

The Antagonism between Necessary Labour and Surplus Labour

Marx continues his analysis by describing a capitalist antagonism between necessary labour (that technology evermore reduces) and surplus labour (that capital tries to evermore increase):

> Capital itself is the moving contradiction, [in] that it presses to reduce labour time to a minimum, while it posits labour time, on the other side, as sole measure and source of wealth. Hence it diminishes labour time in the necessary form so as to increase it in the superfluous form; hence posits the superfluous in growing measure as a condition—question of life or death—for the necessary. On the one side, then, it calls to life all the powers of science and of nature, as of social combination and of social intercourse, in order to make the creation of wealth independent (relatively) of the labour time employed on it. On the other side, it wants to use labour time as the measuring rod for the giant social forces thereby created, and to confine them within the limits required to maintain the already created value as value. Forces of production and social relations—two different sides of the development of the social individual—appear to capital as mere means, and are merely means for it to produce on its limited foundation. In fact, however, they are the material conditions to blow this foundation sky-high. (Marx 1857/1858, 706)

Technology, Time, Capitalism, Communism

Marx ascertains a capitalist antagonism between the tendency of technology to reduce necessary labour time and the capitalist tendency to turn all labour time into surplus labour and argues that modern technology creates the foundation of a communist society in which free time and free activity beyond necessity is maximised and the source of wealth:

> [Capital] increases the surplus labour time of the mass by all the means of art and science [. . .] It is thus, despite itself, instrumental in creating the means of social disposable time, in order to reduce labour time for the whole society to a diminishing minimum, and thus to free everyone's time for their own development. But its tendency always, on the one side, to create disposable time, on the other, to convert it into surplus labour. If it succeeds too well at the first, then it suffers from surplus production, and then necessary labour is interrupted, because no surplus labour can be realized by capital. The more this contradiction develops, the more does it become evident that the growth of the forces of production can no longer be bound up with the appropriation of alien labour, but that the mass of workers must themselves appropriate their own surplus labour. Once they have done so—and disposable time thereby ceases to have an antithetical existence—then, on one side, necessary labour time will be measured by the needs of the social individual, and, on the other, the development of the power of social production will grow so rapidly that, even though production is now calculated for the wealth of all, disposable time will grow for all. For real wealth is the developed productive power of all individuals. The measure of wealth is then not any longer, in any way, labour time, but rather disposable time. (Marx 1857/1858 [English], 708)

Marx adds that "[r]eal economy [. . .] consists of the saving of labour time" so that there can be "an increase of free time, i.e. time for the full development of the individual" (Marx 1857/1858 [English], 711). Marx ascertains in the *Grundrisse* that communism requires a technological foundation so that society can be based on the principle "From each according to his abilities, to each according to his needs!" (Marx 1875, 87), which he in 1875 formulated in the *Critique of the Gotha Programme*. Roman Rosdolsky (1977, 427–428) comments in his study of the *Grundrisse*:

> It is hardly necessary today—in the course of a new industrial revolution—to emphasise the prophetic significance of this enormously dynamic and essentially optimistic conception. For the dreams of the isolated German revolutionary in his exile in London in 1858 have now, for the first time, entered the realm of what is immediately possible. Today, for the first time in history, thanks to the developments of modern technology, the preconditions for a final and complete abolition of the 'theft of alien labour-time' actually exist; furthermore, the present period is the first in which the development of the productive forces can be carried so far forward that, in fact, in the not too distant future it will be not labour-time, but rather disposable time, by which social wealth is measured.

The General Intellect

The General Intellect Is the Crucial Concept in the "Fragment"

> Nature builds no machines, no locomotives, railways, electric telegraphs, self-acting mules etc. These are products of human industry; natural material transformed into organs of the human will over nature, or of human participation in nature. They are organs of the human brain, created by the human hand; the power of knowledge, objectified. The development of fixed capital indicates to what degree general social knowledge has become a direct force of production, and to what degree, hence, the conditions of the process of social life itself have come under the control of the general intellect and been transformed in accordance with it. To what degree the powers of social production have been produced, not only in the form of knowledge, but also as immediate organs of social practice, of the real life process. (Marx 1857/1858 [English], 706)

Already Rosdolsky wrote in his book *The Making of Marx's "Capital"*, which was published in 1968, that the general intellect passage shows that "the development of machinery—although leading under capitalism only to the oppression of workers—offers, in fact, the surest prospect for their future liberation, by facilitating that radical reduction of working time, without which the abolition of class society would remain mere words" (Rosdolsky 1977, 243).

The "Fragment" anticipated many ideas that Marx (1867, 492–639) formulated in *Capital Volume 1*, chapter 15, "Machinery and Large-Scale Industry": technology as fixed constant capital; the concept of the machine system; technology as means of alienation and rationalisation in capitalism and material foundation of communism; the dialectic of modern technology; technology in the context of the antagonism between productive forces and relations of production, technology, and crises.

4. The Connection of the "Fragment" to Other Sections in the *Grundrisse*

Aspects of knowledge and technology are in the *Grundrisse* not just limited to the "Fragment", but also occur outside of it. This section discusses some examples.

Marx first mentions the antagonistic relationship of machinery and labour time not in the "Fragment on Machines" (which can be found in "Notebooks VI/VII"), but in the section on "Surplus-Value and Profit" of "Notebook IV" (Marx 1857/1858 [English] 389, 398–401; Marx 1857/1858 [German], 303, 312–315).

In the section on the "Circuit of Capital" in "Notebook V", Marx introduces the notion of the *"general conditions of production"* (530) and argues that capital only organises them if it is profitable and not too expensive to do so and otherwise "shifts the burdens on the shoulders of the state" (531). They include the "means of communication" that are "physical conditions of circulation" (533). Marx here basically introduces the ideas of the commons, including the communication commons, and of the commodification of the commons (public works' "migration into the domain of the works undertaken by capital", 531).

In "Notebook IV", Marx introduces the dialectical idea that capital finds in itself and sets itself barriers that it has to strive to overcome (Marx 1857/1858 [English], 405–423; [German], 318–338). Capital faces barriers such as necessary and surplus labour time, national borders and regulations, circulation time, consumption capacities, and money and exchange value that limit use-value. The effects are crises that capital tries to overcome, which creates new limits and conditions of crisis. Capital's "production moves in contradictions which are constantly overcome but just as constantly posited". It drives "towards its own suspension" and "encounters barriers in its own nature" (Marx 1857/1858 [English], 410). In "Notebook V", Marx argues that capitalism's dialectic of boundaries also concerns the productive forces, including the production of knowledge: "Capital posits the production of wealth itself and hence the universal development of the productive forces, the constant overthrow of its prevailing presuppositions, as the presupposition of its reproduction. [. . .] every degree of the development of the social forces of production, of intercourse, of knowledge etc. appears to it only as a barrier which it strives to overpower" (Marx 1857/1858 [English], 541; [German], 447).

Marx also discusses the antagonistic character of technology in the section "Das Kapital als Frucht bringend" (Capital as Fructiferous) of "Notebook VII" (Marx 1857/1858 [German], 637–669; [English], 745–778), where he says that the antagonism between technological development of the productive forces and the capitalist relations of production results in "explosions, cataclysms, crises" ([English], 750), "bitter contradictions, crises, spasms" ([English], 749).

In the next section I will reflect on debates about the "Fragment".

5. Cultural and Digital Labour in the Context of the Marxist Debate on the "Fragment" and the General Intellect

The debate about the "Fragment" and the general intellect has especially focused on (a) the concept of immaterial labour, (b) the critique of the notion of immateriality, (c) questions concerning the relationship of technology and human practice in society, (d) elite and immiserated workers, and (e) the law of value. I will in this section explore connections of this discussion to the political economy of digital labour.

Immaterial Labour

Antonio Negri (1991) did not discuss the notion of the general intellect in his book on the *Grundrisse*, but did so in a number of other publications. He defines it as "modes of productive expression that are increasingly immaterial and intellectual" (Negri 2008, 116). Hardt and Negri (2000, 29–30, 364–367) associate with Marx's concept of general intellect the rise of informational capitalism and connect it to the rise of what they term "immaterial labour", a term introduced by Maurizio Lazzarato (1996, 132), who defines it as "labor that produces the informational and cultural content of the commodity". "General intellect is a collective, social intelligence created by accumulated knowledges, techniques, and know-how. The value of labor is thus realized by a new universal and concrete labor force through the appropriation and free usage of the new productive forces" (Hardt and Negri 2000, 364).

Paolo Virno (1996a, 21) argues that the general intellect extends from science and technology to communication, language, and the media (see also Virno 2007). It would be the foundation of "social cooperation" (Virno 1996b, 194) and in contemporary capitalism result in "all wage labor" having "something of the 'performing artist' about it" (195). "The general intellect manifests itself today, above all, as the communication, abstraction, self-reflection of living subjects" (Virno 2004, 65) and is for Virno not congealed in fixed capital. Christian Marazzi (2008, 44) makes the same point: "In post-Fordism the general intellect is not fixed in machines, but in the bodies of workers. The body has become, if you will, the tool box of mental work".

(A) The Concept of Immaterial Labour and Its Implications

A *first* important dimension of the concept of the general intellect as immaterial labour is that because of this type of labour's networked and cooperative organisation and knowledge's peculiar characteristics that support convergences, exploitation, value generation, and productive labour are not limited to wage-labour. This analysis resembles the arguments made by Marxist feminism and the theory of the new international division of labour that already in the 1970s and 1980s argued that labour in the Global South and housework are crucial for global value generation. It allows a connection to the theory of audience and digital labour.

Audiences of advertising-financed broadcast media and users of corporate social media such as Facebook, YouTube, Twitter, Weibo, Pinterest, Blogspot, and Instagram are nonpaid audiences and digital workers who create attention and data that is sold as commodity. They are productive workers in the sense of the understanding Marx grounded in the *Grundrisse* and *Capital Volume 1*, chapter 16: Their labour creates its own opposite—namely, commercial media companies' capital. They together with paid employees form commercial media's collective labourer, who is exploited in order to generate these companies' value and profits. Facebook and its likes are social factories, in which social workers perform unremunerated information labour. Social and mobile media advance contemporary capitalism's tendency towards creating boundaries between production/consumption, labour-time/leisure time, labour/play, office and factory/home, private/public, production/reproduction that blur and converge under the rule of capital so that we perform value-generating labour in many spaces outside of offices and factories at irregular times under conditions that foster precarious, informal, unrecognised, unremunerated, and casual labour.

Audience and digital labour stand in an antagonism to each other: Companies' advertising expenditures grew in the period of 2009 to 2013 by 25.8%: Online advertising's annual compound growth rate was 18.9%, whereas the one of newspaper advertising was 1.35% (data source: Ofcom 2014). In times of crisis, companies seem to consider targeted online advertising a more secure investment than traditional advertising, which results in the tendency that exploitation of audience labour turns into digital labour. But whereas Facebook and Google are highly profitable companies, other platforms such as Twitter and Weibo have thus far only made losses. The exploitation of digital labour creates value, but this value can only be turned into profit if users give attention to and click on online ads, which is not automatically to a sufficient degree the case. Companies' marketing departments are at the moment optimistic about investing in targeted online ads, but this confidence could quickly change in case that the one or the other social media company folds because its profits do not live up to stock market valuations.

(B) The Critique of the Notion of Immateriality: Materialism and Idealism

A *second* important question about the general intellect concerns philosophical materialism and idealism: In a materialist philosophy, matter is the process-substance of the world (Fuchs 2003): Systems are constituted by permanent reproduction and the creation of novelty that emerges out of existing structures. Production guarantees human existence and reproduction. The world is material because it has the capacity to produce itself and new forms of organisation. Society is material because in it humans produce structures, their own sociality, and ever-newer human practices so that society can reproduce itself and exist over time. To speak of immaterial labour introduces a dualist ontology that separates the world into a material and an immaterial substance.

If there are two substances, then the ground of the world can no longer be adequately specified, which, however, is according to the law of ground needed for any consistent philosophy. If there are two substances, then it cannot be explained what the unity, foundation, and ground of the world are in the last instance. One must then either leave the world unexplained or assume that an external force such as God created it. Avoiding such dualism and idealism requires a materialist concept of the world that sees the whole world and all of its systems as material and matter as a self-referential and self-producing substance. Matter is a causa sui: It is its own cause and enables the self-organisation of the world. The very notion of immaterial labour is philosophically idealist. Ideas are nonphysical, but material. They are generated by the brain, which is a physical system, and in the social relations of humans, who as species-beings create the social world by work and communication.

George Caffentzis (2013, 176–200) argues in this context that no labour is immaterial because all labour requires a physical foundation. Hardt and Negri would therefore "spiritualize the machine" (Caffentzis 2013, 200). Digital labour on social media is not immaterial labour, but rather information labour that as a form of materiality creates information as a non-physical good that can only be produced, disseminated, and consumed with the help of physical technologies such as computers, mobile phones, and fibreoptic cables, which are powered by energy consumption.

(C) Technology and Human Practice

Third, the concept of the general intellect as immaterial labour faces the danger of a technologically deterministic concept of history and revolution that sees communism as the automatic result of the development of the technological productive forces. Sylvia Federici (2012, 95) argues that the "Fragment" bears the threat of a "technologistic concept of revolution, where freedom comes through the machine" and that comes along with a focus on wage-labour as a revolutionary subject that neglects the "importance of reproductive work". Also Pier Aldo Rovatti warns against interpreting the "Fragment" in a techno-deterministic and fetishist manner, which reduces the relations of production to "moments within the dynamic of the productive forces" (Rovatti 1973, 60; for a recent formulation of this criticism, see Tomba and Bellofiore 2014). The collective worker constituted by the general intellect would not automatically become a "collective subject" (62). One must in this context see that Marx writes: "With that, production based on exchange value breaks down" (Marx 1857/1858 [English], 705).

This formulation has again and again resulted in controversies. Michael Heinrich (2014) interprets it as meaning that Marx in the *Grundrisse* had a "one-sided conception of crisis" (197) and predicted that the employment of machinery in capitalism "should have the consequence that capitalist production [. . .] collapses" (207). But one must see that with the formulation "with that" Marx means in reference back to the preceding sentence a condition where the "surplus labour of the mass has ceased to be the condition for the development of general wealth" (705). So when he speaks of a breakdown in the "Fragment" he does not mean an automatic collapse of capitalism, but rather that exchange value collapses within communism. The establishment of communism, however, presupposes a conscious revolutionary sublation of capitalism. The "Fragment" does not formulate an automatic breakdown of capitalism.

It is true that when Marx wrote the *Grundrisse*, he was optimistic that capitalism could in the course of the crisis that started in 1857 come to an end, which is evident from a letter to Engels from December 8, 1857: "I am working like mad all night and every night collating my economic studies so that I at least get the outlines ["Grundrisse" in the German original; MEW 29, 225] clear before the deluge" (MECW 40, 217). He did, however, not assume that a breakdown of capitalism is the effect of structural contradictions, but that it can only, but does not automatically and with necessity have to, break down in the course of class struggles that respond to crises. Consciousness and activity are crucial. Marx therefore not just speaks of the productive forces, but of both "forces of production and social relations" as the "material conditions to blow this foundation [capitalism] sky-high" (Marx 1857/1858, 706). Note that an objective material condition is a precondition, but not an automatism. Consciousness and praxis are decisive. Therefore Marx stresses that the "recognition [*Erkennung*] of the products as its own, and the judgement that its separation from the conditions of its realization is improper—forcibly imposed—is an enormous [advance in] awareness [*Bewusstsein*]" and is "itself the product of the mode of production resting on capital, and as much the knell to its doom" (463). Marx here connects the metaphor of the death bell with subjectivity (recognition, awareness, consciousness), which shows that he saw conscious political action based on material foundations as interacting aspects of revolution.

Moishe Postone (2008) stresses correctly that Marx is neither romantically affirming nor rejecting modern technology, but rather assumes that "the potential of the system of production developed under capitalism could be used to transform that system itself" (134). The deepening gap between material potentials and reality that expresses itself in crises can only be overcome through social struggles. Digital labour on social media is indicative of a high socialisation of the means of communicative production that within capitalist class relations furthers human exploitation and deepens class society, but that at the same time promises and creates potentials for a digital communist society that can only be created in and through political praxis, which is again no automatism and can be forestalled by ideology, violence, and repression.

(D) Elite and Immiserated Workers

Fourth, there have been discussions about privileged and immiserated labour of the general intellect. Autonomist Marxists such as George Caffentzis (2013) and the Midnight Notes Collective criticise Negri and his comrades' version of the general intellect as immaterial labour by arguing that it tends to focus on privileged Western high-tech workers and ignores the exploitation of the labour of house workers and slaves and other super-exploited workers in the global sweatshop economy. Caffentzis (2013, 79) says that computerisation and robotisation require the enclosure of "factories, lands, and brothels in the Third World" in order to "increase the total pool of surplus labor" and counteract the tendency of the profit rate to fall. The "computer requires the sweatshop, and the cyborg's existence is premised on the slave" (79).

Nick Dyer-Witheford (2005) suggests based on a reading of Negri and Caffentzis a "Cyber-Negri beyond Negri" perspective that conceives "'immaterial', 'material'[1] and 'immiserated' work as sectors of a broader class composition of 'universal labor'" (Dyer-Witheford 2005, 157) that forms a global worker who has the potential to act as a digital front against capital (Dyer-Witheford 2014). Building on Caffentzis and Negri allows a materialist concept of cultural and digital labour that avoids idealism and Western-centric narrowness. Such an approach can also build on Raymond Williams's approach of Cultural Materialism, which argues that "[c]ultural work and activity are not [. . .] a superstructure" (1977, 111) and that cultural and mental labour are "social and material" (1989, 206) (see Fuchs 2015).

Culture requires the production, circulation, and consumption of meaning as well as institutions and technologies that enable these processes. Cultural labour as materialist concept therefore covers both labour that produces culture's infrastructures and content.

"Cultural work" is a term that encompasses organisational levels of work that are at the same time distinct and dialectically connected (see Figure A2.2): Cultural work has an emergent quality—namely, information work—that creates content that is based on and grounded in physical cultural work, which creates information technologies through agricultural and industrial work processes. Physical

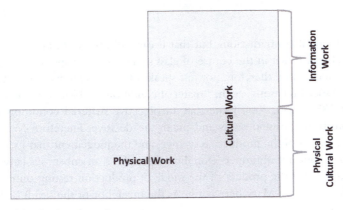

FIGURE A2.2 A model of cultural work

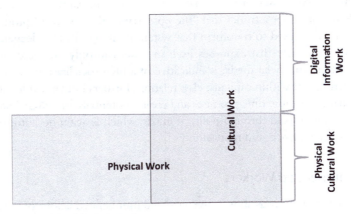

FIGURE A2.3 A stage model of digital work

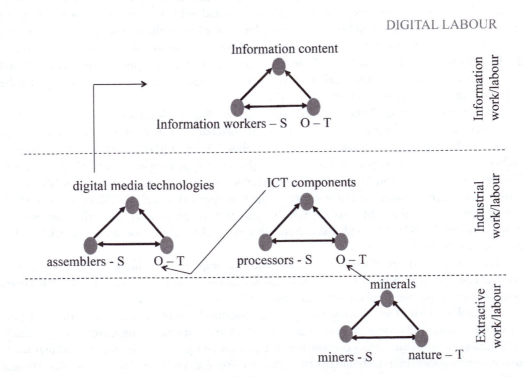

FIGURE A2.4 The network of cycles of digital labour

work takes place inside and outside of culture: It creates information technologies and its components (cultural physical work) as well as other products (noncultural physical work) that do not primarily have symbolic functions in society (such as cars, toothbrushes, or cups).

Digital work is a specific form of cultural work that creates and uses digital media. Digital labour is an alienated form of digital work. Just like cultural work, digital work encompasses both physical and information work (Figure A2.3).

Each work process consists of subjects that with the help of objects of work and technologies create products. Digital labour is organised in the form of an international division of digital labour (IDDL), which encompasses a complex network of interlinked cycles of production (see Figure A2.4) in which miners who are partly slaves in Congolese mines extract minerals that in a second step are by industrial assemblage workers, such as the highly exploited workers in the Chinese Foxconn and Pegatron factories, assembled into components and digital media technologies that information workers, such as Google's labour aristocracy, low-paid software engineers in India, precarious freelancers, and unpaid social media users, use for creating content and data (for details, see Fuchs 2014a, 2015). Digital labour is organised in an IDDL, which encompasses different modes of production (such as wage-labour, unpaid labour, precarious labour, slave-work, etc.) and different modes of organisation of the productive forces (agricultural/industrial/informational work). The general intellect that circulates on the Internet and via digital media requires a collective digital worker that is also a global worker. Digital capital exploits manifold forms of digital labourers, and they have the potential to resist their own exploitation if digital workers of the world manage to unite (Mosco and McKercher 2009).

(E) The Law of Value

Fifth, there have been discussions about the applicability of the law of value to the general intellect. Negri (1991, 172) argues that in the *Grundrisse* the "Law of Value dies". Virno (2004, 100) says that the law of value is "shattered and refuted by capitalist development itself". Hardt and Negri (2004, 145) argue that the "temporal unity of labor as the basic measure of value today makes no sense". Vercellone (2010, 90) writes that "cognitive capitalism" has resulted in the "crisis of the law of value" and "a crisis of measurement that destabilizes the very sense of the fundamental categories of the political economy; labor, capital and obviously, value" (90). He ascertains that the general intellect has brought about "the possibility of a direct transition to communism" (Vercellone 2007, 15) and the need for a "passage from a theory of time-value of labour to a theory of knowledge-value" (31). Arvidsson and Colleoni say that the law of value does not apply to "immaterial/intangible wealth" because this form of wealth would be produced in cooperation and its value would be determined by affects and intersubjective judgments so that an "affect-based law of value" (Arvidsson and Colleoni 2012, 142) would emerge.

Rosdolsky (1977, 428) in contrast to these authors writes in his book about the *Grundrisse* that in the "Fragment" Marx had the "withering away of the law of value under socialism" in mind, but not under capitalism. Moishe Postone (2008, 126) stresses the crisis of value in capitalism is "not simply superseded by a new form of wealth", but rather value "remains the necessary structural precondition of capitalist society". "Capitalism *does* give rise to the possibility of its own negation, but it *does not* automatically evolve into something else" (Postone 2008, 127). Massimo De Angelis (2007, 167) argues against Hardt and Negri that assuming that the law of value no longer applies today overlooks that capital as such "is constituted through a particular mode of *measuring* life activity". This is also the reason why the process of commodification has resulted in the emergence of "an immense battery of tests and examinations" (Harvie 2005, 149). So, for example, the prevalence of "task-specific contracts with temporal deadlines" in the information industries shows that information labour is "a process in time that can be (*and is*) measured" (Caffentzis 2013, 111; see also Caffentzis 2005 for a critique of Hardt and Negri's assumption that value has become immeasurable). Tony Smith (2014b) argues in a discussion of Vercellone's and Virno's approach that although there are nonprofit digital media projects operating outside the law of value, the world of digital media features a lot of exploited labour. He writes that also in an age of "mass intellectuality", "Marx's value-theory will retain descriptive accuracy and explanatory power" as long as there are features such as that the mediation of social reproduction by "the sale of commodities for money" (222).

The assumption that the law of value no longer applies today is not feasible because this law is a foundation for the existence of capitalism. Claims about the law's withering-away are based on a specific interpretation of a passage from Marx's *Grundrisse* in which Marx says that "labour time ceases and must cease to be" the measure of wealth (Marx 1857/1858, 705). He in the same passage makes clear that he is talking about a situation in which the "mass of workers" has appropriated "their own surplus labour" (Marx 1857/1858, 708)—that is, about a communist society. The prophets of the end of law of value in contrast interpret this passage in the "Fragment" as meaning that the law of value has come to an end within capitalism and that technology has created a communism of capital (Virno 2004, 110–111; Boutang 2011, 7) so that it merely needs to cast its capitalist skin in order to enable a fully communist society. Marx talks about a society, in which "production based on exchange value breaks down" (Marx 1857/1858, 705)—a communist society. He describes how the rise of technology and knowledge in capitalism advances the antagonism between necessary and surplus labour time and the productive forces and relations of production and that this antagonism creates the foundations of a communist society, in which free time is the measure of wealth and available to a maximum degree for all.

Morini and Fumagalli (2010) argue that the blurring of working time/life time, work place/life place, production/reproduction, and production/consumption necessitates a life theory of value because contemporary capitalism puts life to work. They do, however, leave open the question if average life value depends on measurable time or not. Given that all human activities and the number of humans in the world are always finite and that work takes place in space-time, one can argue that even a blurring of boundaries between dualities still requires a labour theory of value (Fuchs 2014a, 2015).

On Facebook and other commercial social media, the law of value means that the more time a certain group spends on the platform, the more valuable the corresponding data commodity gets on average. A group that on average spends a lot of minutes per day on Facebook (e.g., the group of those aged 15–25) compared to another group (e.g., the group of those aged 75–85) constitutes a more valuable data commodity because (a) it has a higher average labour/online time per day, which generates more data that can be sold, and (b) it spends more time online, during which targeted ads are presented to this group.

6. Conclusion

The *Grundrisse* is of high importance as a theoretical foundation for understanding digital labour and digital capitalism. Marx's concepts of productive and transport labour in the *Grundrisse* help us come to grips with the political economy of targeted online advertising. The *Grundrisse*'s "Fragment on Machines" should best not be read in isolation, but as a complement to a reading of *Capital* and the *Grundrisse*'s other notebooks.

The *Grundrisse* help us especially in respect to five dimensions of digital labour:

1. Digital labour on social media is a manifestation the general intellect that expresses the existence of a social factory in contemporary capitalism.
2. Digital labour is not an immaterial but a material aspect of production.
3. Digital labour is a manifestation of the general intellect's antagonism that creates foundations of communism and deepens exploitation, but does not automatically sublate capitalism, which points towards the need for conscious political praxis.
4. Digital labour is organised in the form of an international division of labour.
5. The law of value has not ceased to exist on social media, but rather expresses its antagonistic character in the online world.

Understanding digital labour requires what Karl Heinz Roth and Marcel van der Linden (2014) call a dynamic labour theory of value, in which all "persons who find themselves within the embattled process of expropriation, disciplining and employment/valorisation of their labour-capacity, constitute the global proletariat, the multiverse of the exploited" (478). Online media results in capitalism both in new forms of commodification and potentials for the "counter-usage of information technology" (Dyer-Witheford 1999, 228). Digital media change the human species-being towards the general intellect and point "unprecedented intensification of Empire, but also possibly to exodus from it" (Dyer-Witheford and de Peuter 2009, 229). The *Grundrisse* in combination with *Capital* can help us to come to grips with digital capitalism's contradictions and are excellent intellectual tools in the struggle for the transition from digital capitalism to digital communism.

Digital labourers are a "collective labourer" (Marx 1867, 644) conducting "communal or combined labour" (Marx 1857/1858, 470). They are by capital's rule confined to the status of "isolated worker[s]" and "alien objectivity". They are dominated by capital and machinery that form an "*animated monster*" (470). But due to capital's immanent barriers digital labour also contributes to the strengthening of the potentials for the "antithesis to political economy—namely socialism and communism" (884). Digital capitalism's negativity can only be negated into a new form of existence in and through class struggles.

Exercises for Appendix 2

Group exercise (G)
Project exercise (P)

Key Categories: General Intellect, Machinery

Exercise Appendix 2.1 (G)

Read the following and discuss the questions below.
   Marx, Karl. 1857/1858. Fragment on machines. In *Grundrisse*, 690–714. London: Penguin.

- How exactly does Marx define the general intellect?
- Discuss how the category of the general intellect matters in contemporary society, where digital media, the computer, the Internet, and knowledge work have come to play an important role.
- What are the antagonisms of labour time that Marx describes in the "Fragment"? What role do technology and the general intellect play in this context?
- What kind of antagonisms of labour time can we observe in contemporary informational capitalism? How do they express themselves? How can they be overcome politically?

Exercise Appendix 2.2 (P)

Work in groups: Conduct a literature search for articles about Marx's concept of the general intellect that have been published in the past 10 years.

Compare how the authors of these articles argue that this concept matters or does not matter today. Make a list of commonalities and differences of the arguments they employ. Assess the different opinions and views.

Note

1   In my view it is best to distinguish between physical and nonphysical work instead of material and immaterial labour if one wants to characterise human activity according to its product.

REFERENCES AND FURTHER READINGS

Adorno, Theodor W. 1968/2003. Late capitalism or industrial society? The fundamental question of the present structure of society. In *Can one live after Auschwitz?*, ed. Rolf Tiedemann, 111–125. Stanford, CA: Stanford University Press.

Adorno, Theodor W. 1973. *Negative dialectics*. London: Routledge.

Althusser, Louis. 1969. *For Marx*. London: Verso.

Althusser, Louis. 1993. *The future lasts forever: A memoir*. New York: The New Press.

Althusser, Louis and Étienne Balibar. 1970. *Reading Capital*. London: NLB.

Amin, Samir. 1974. Accumulation and development: A theoretical model. *Review of African Political Economy* 1 (1): 9–26.

Amin, Samir. 1976. *Unequal development: An essay on the social formations of peripheral capitalism*. New York: Monthly Review Press.

Amin, Samir. 1997. *Capitalism in the age of globalization: The management of contemporary society*. London: Zed Books.

Amin, Samir. 2010. *The law of worldwide value*. New York: Monthly Review Press.

Andersen, Esben Sloth. 2009. *Schumpeter's evolutionary economics: A theoretical, historical and statistical analysis of the engine of capitalism*. London: Anthem Press.

Anderson, Kevin B. 2010. *Marx at the margins: On nationalism, ethnicity, and non-Western societies*. Chicago: University of Chicago Press.

Aneesh, A. 2006. *Virtual migration: The programming of globalization*. Durham: Duke University Press.

Arendt, Hannah. 1958. *The human condition*, 2nd edition. Chicago: University of Chicago Press.

Arthur, Christopher J. 2004. *The new dialectic and Marx's Capital*. Leiden: Brill.

Árvay, János. 1994. *The Material Product System (MPS): A retrospective*. In *The accounts of nations*, ed. Z. Kenessey, 218–236. Amsterdam: IOS Press.

Arvidsson, Adam and Eleanor Colleoni. 2012. Value in informational capitalism and on the Internet. *The Information Society* 28 (3): 135–150.

Banaji, Jairus. 2011. *Theory as history: Essays on modes of production and exploitation*. Chicago: Haymarket Books.

Baran, Paul A. and Paul M. Sweezy. 1966. *Monopoly capital: An essay on the American economic and social order*. New York: Monthly Review Press.

Baudrillard, Jean. 1981. *For a critique of the political economy of the sign*. St. Louis, MO: Telos Press.

Bell, Daniel. 1974. *The coming of post-industrial society*. London: Heinemann.

Bellofiore, Ricardo, Guido Starosta, and Peter D. Thomas, eds. 2014a. *In Marx's laboratory: Critical interpretations of the Grundrisse*. Chicago: Haymarket Books.

Bellofiore, Ricardo, Guido Starosta, and Peter D. Thomas. 2014b. Introduction: In Marx's laboratory. In *In Marx's laboratory: Critical interpretations of the Grundrisse*, ed. Ricardo Bellofiore, Guido Starosta, and Peter D. Thomas, 1–14. Chicago: Haymarket Books.

Bentham, Jeremy. 1781. *An introduction to the principles of morals and legislation*. Kitchener: Batoche.

Bidet, Jacques. 2005. The dialectician's interpretation of Capital. *Historical Materialism* 13 (2): 121–146.

Bidet, Jacques. 2007. *A reconstruction project of the Marxian theory: From Exploring Marx's Capital (1985) to Alter-marxisme (2007), via Théorie Générale (1999) and Explication et reconstruction du Capital (2004)*. http://jacques.bidet.pagesperso-orange.fr/londongla.htm (accessed July 28, 2015).

Bidet, Jacques. 2009. *Exploring Marx's Capital: Philosophical, economic, and political dimensions*. Chicago: Haymarket Books.

Bourdieu, Pierre. 1977. *Outline of a theory of practice*. Cambridge: Cambridge University Press.

Bourdieu, Pierre. 1986a. *Distinction: A social critique of the judgement of taste*. New York: Routledge.

Bourdieu, Pierre. 1986b. The (three) forms of capital. In *Handbook of theory and research in the sociology of education*, ed. John G. Richardson, 241–258. New York: Greenwood Press.

Boutang, Yann Moulier. 2011. *Cognitive capitalism*. Cambridge: Polity.

Boyer, Robert. 1988. Technical change and the theory of "regulation". In *Technical change and economic theory*, ed. Giovanni Dosi, Christopher Freeman, Richard Nelson, Gerald Silverberg, and Luc L. Soete, 67–94. London: Pinter.

Braverman, Harry. 1974/1998. *Labor and monopoly capital*. New York: Monthly Review Press.

Briggs, Asa and John Callow. 2008. *Marx in London*. London: Lawrence and Wishart.

Caffentzis, George. 2005. Immeasurable value? An essay on Marx's legacy. *The Commoner* 5: 87–114.

Caffentzis, George. 2013. *In letters of blood and fire: Work, machines, and the crisis of capitalism*. Oakland, CA: PM Press.

Callinicos, Alex. 2014. *Deciphering capital. Marx's Capital and its destiny*. London: Bookmarks.

Carchedi, Guglielmo and Michael Roberts. 2013. A critique of Heinrich's "Crisis theory, the law of the tendency of the profit rate to fall, and Marx's studies in the 1870s". Monthly Review Online. http://monthlyreview.org/commentary/critique-heinrichs-crisis-theory-law-tendency-profit-rate-fall-marxs-studies-1870s#en1 (accessed on July 28, 2015).

Carstensen, Peter H. and Kjeld Schmidt. 1999. *Computer supported cooperative work: New challenges to systems design*. http://www.cscw.dk/schmidt/papers/cscw_intro.pdf (accessed on August 7, 2014).

Chotiner, Isaac. 2014. "Marx? I never really managed to read it"—an interview with Thomas Piketty. New Statesman Online, May 6. http://www.newstatesman.com/politics/2014/05/marx-i-never-really-managed-read-it-interview-thomas-piketty (accessed on July 28, 2015).

Cleaver, Harry. 2000. *Reading Capital politically*. Leeds: Anti/Theses.

Collins, Sean. 2014. Pricking the Piketty bubble. Spiked, May 9. http://www.spiked-online.com/review_of_books/article/pricking-the-Piketty-bubble/14997#.U4KWPy8UYWE (accessed on July 28, 2015).

Dalla Costa, Mariarosa and Selma James. 1972. *The power of women and the subversion of community*. Bristol: Falling Wall Press.

De Angelis, Massimo. 2007. *The beginning of history: Value struggles and global capital*. London: Pluto.

Demie, Feyisa. 2014. *The educational attainment of white working class pupils*. London: Lambeth Research and Statistics Unit.

Despain, Hans G. 2014. Review of Thomas Piketty's "Capital in the twenty-first century". *Marx & Philosophy Review of Books*. http://marxandphilosophy.org.uk/reviewofbooks/reviews/2014/1005 (accessed on July 28, 2015).

Douthat, Rose. 2014. *Marx rises again*. New York Times Online, April 19. http://www.nytimes.com/2014/04/20/opinion/sunday/douthat-marx-rises-again.html?_r=0 (accessed on July 28, 2015).

Dussel, Enrique. 2008. The discovery of the category of surplus value. In *Karl Marx's Grundrisse: Foundations of the critique of the political economy 150 years later*, ed. Marcello Musto, 67–78. New York: Routledge.

Dyer-Witheford, Nick. 1999. *Cyber-Marx*. Urbana: University of Illinois Press.

Dyer-Witheford, Nick. 2005. Cyber-Negri: General intellect and immaterial labor. In *The philosophy of Antonio Negri*, ed. Timothy S. Murphy and Abdul-Karim Mustapha, 136–162. London: Pluto.

Dyer-Witheford, Nick. 2014. The global worker and the digital front. In *Critique, social media and the information society*, ed. Christian Fuchs and Marisol Sandoval, 165–178. New York: Routledge.

Dyer-Witheford, Nick and Greig de Peuter. 2009. *Games of empire*. Minneapolis: University of Minnesota Press.

Ebermann, Thomas, Michael Heinrich, Robert Kurz, and Joseph Vogl. 2011. No way out? Kapital kaputt? Krisengipfel-Gespräch. *Konkret* 12: 12–16.

Dyson, Esther, George Gilder, George Keyworth, and Alvin Toffler. 1996/2004. Cyberspace and the American dream. In *The information society reader*, ed. Frank Webster, 31–41. Oxon: Routledge.

Eagleton, Terry. 1991. *Ideology: An introduction*. London: Verso.

Eagleton, Terry. 2011. *Why Marx was right*. New Haven, CT: Yale University Press.

Eisenstein, Zillah, ed. 1979. *Capitalist patriarchy and the case for socialist feminism*. New York: Monthly Review Press.

Engels, Friedrich. 1845. Speeches in Elberfeld. http://marxists.anu.edu.au/archive/marx/works/1845/02/15.htm (accessed on July 28, 2015).

Engels, Friedrich. 1847. Principles of communism. In *MECW*, Volume 6, 341–357. New York: International Publishers.

Engels, Friedrich. 1878. Anti-Dühring. Herr Eugen Dühring's revolution in science. In *MECW*, Volume 25, 1–311. New York: International Publishers.

Engels, Friedrich. 1891. A critique of the draft Social-Democratic Programme of 1891. http://marxists.anu.edu.au/archive/marx/works/1891/06/29.htm (accessed on July 28, 2015).

Erlanger, Steven. 2014. Taking on Adam Smith (and Karl Marx). New York Times Online, April 19. http://www.nytimes.com/2014/04/20/business/international/taking-on-adam-smith-and-karl-marx.html (accessed on July 28, 2015).

Federici, Sylvia. 2012. *Revolution at point zero: Housework, reproduction, and feminist struggle*. Oakland, CA: PM Press.

Feenberg, Andrew. 1995a. *Alternative modernity*. Berkeley: University of California Press.

Feenberg, Andrew. 1995b. Subversive rationalization: Technology, power, and democracy. In *Technology and the politics of knowledge*, ed. Andrew Feenberg and Alastair Hannay, 3–22. Bloomington: Indiana University Press.

Feenberg, Andrew. 1999. *Questioning technology*. London: Routledge.

Feenberg, Andrew. 2002. *Transforming technology: A critical theory revisited*. Oxford: Oxford University Press.

Feenberg, Andrew. 2010. *Between reason and experience*. Cambridge, MA: The MIT Press.

Feenberg, Andrew. 2012. Introduction: Toward a critical theory of the Internet. In *(Re)Inventing the Internet*, ed. Andrew Feenberg and Norm Friesen, 3–17. Rotterdam: Sense Publishers.

Fisher, Eran. 2010. *Media and new capitalism in the digital age: The spirit of networks*. New York: Palgrave Macmillan.

Fortunati, Leopoldina. 1995. *The arcane of reproduction: Housework, prostitution, labor and capital*. New York: Autonomedia.

Foucault, Michel. 1977. *Discipline & punish*. New York: Vintage.

Freeman, Alan. 2010. Trends in value theory since 1881. *World Review of Political Economy* 1 (4): 567–606.

Freeman, Alan, Andrew Kliman, and Julian Wells, eds. 2004. *The new value controversy and the foundation of economics*. Cheltenham: Edward Elgar.

Fröbel, Folker, Jürgen Heinrichs, and Otto Kreye. 1981. *The new international division of labour*. Cambridge: Cambridge University Press.

Fuchs, Christian. 2002. *Krise und Kritik in der Informationsgesellschaft*. Norderstedt: Libri BOD.

Fuchs, Christian. 2003. The self-organization of matter. *Nature, Society, and Thought* 16 (3): 281–313.

Fuchs, Christian. 2004. The antagonistic self-organization of modern society. *Studies in Political Economy* 73: 183–209.

Fuchs, Christian. 2008. *Internet and society: Social theory in the information age*. New York: Routledge.

Fuchs, Christian. 2009a. Information and communication technologies and society: A contribution to the critique of the political economy of the Internet. *European Journal of Communication* 24 (1): 69–87.

Fuchs, Christian. 2009b. Some theoretical foundations of critical media studies: Reflections on Karl Marx and the media. *International Journal of Communication* 3: 369–402.

Fuchs, Christian. 2010a. Alternative media as critical media. *European Journal of Social Theory* 13 (2): 173–192.

Fuchs, Christian. 2010b. Labor in informational capitalism and on the Internet. *The Information Society* 26 (3): 179–196.

Fuchs, Christian. 2011. How to define surveillance? *MATRIZes* 5 (1): 109–133.

Fuchs, Christian. 2012a. Dallas Smythe today—The audience commodity, the digital labour debate, Marxist political economy and critical theory: Prolegomena to a digital labour theory of value. *tripleC: Communication, Capitalism & Critique* 10 (2): 692–740.

Fuchs, Christian. 2012b. Political economy and surveillance theory. *Critical Sociology* 39 (5): 671–687.

Fuchs, Christian. 2014a. *Digital labour and Karl Marx*. New York: Routledge.

Fuchs, Christian. 2014b. *OccupyMedia! The Occupy movement and social media in crisis capitalism*. Winchester: Zero Books.

Fuchs, Christian. 2014c. *Social media: A critical introduction*. London: Sage.

Fuchs, Christian. 2014d. Social media and the public sphere. Inaugural lecture. *tripleC: Communication, Capitalism & Critique* 12 (1): 57–101.

Fuchs, Christian. 2015. *Culture and economy in the age of social media*. New York: Routledge.

Fuchs, Christian, Kees Boersma, Anders Albrechtslund, and Marisol Sandoval, eds. 2012. *Internet and surveillance: The challenges of web 2.0 and social media*. New York: Routledge.

Fuchs, Christian and Vincent Mosco, eds. 2012. Marx is back: The importance of Marxist theory and research for critical communication studies today. *tripleC: Communication, Capitalism & Critique* 10 (2): 127–632.

Fuchs, Christian and Vincent Mosco, eds. 2015a. *Marx and the political economy of the media*. Leiden: Brill.

Fuchs, Christian and Vincent Mosco, eds. 2015b. *Marx in the age of digital capitalism*. Leiden: Brill.

Fuchs, Christian and Marisol Sandoval, eds. 2014a. *Critique, social media and the information society*. New York: Routledge.

Fuchs, Christian and Marisol Sandoval. 2014b. Introduction: Critique, social media and the information society in the age of capitalist crisis. In *Critique, social media and the information society*, ed. Christian Fuchs and Marisol Sandoval, 1–47. New York: Routledge.

Fuchs, Christian and Marisol Sandoval. 2015. The political economy of capitalist and alternative social media. In *The Routledge companion to alternative and community media*, ed. Chris Atton, 165–175. London: Routledge.

Fuchs-Kittowski, Klaus. 2014. The influence of philosophy on the understanding of computing and information. In *Philosophy, computing and information* science, ed. Ruth Hagengruber and Uwe V. Riss, 45–56. London: Pickering & Chatto.

Furhoff, Lars. 1973. Some reflections on newspaper concentration. *Scandinavian Economic History Review* 21 (1): 1–27.

Galbraith, James K. 2014. Kapital for the twenty-first century? Dissent Magazine Online, Spring. http://www.dissentmagazine.org/article/kapital-for-the-twenty-first-century (accessed on July 28, 2015).

Gandy, Oscar. H. 1993. *The panoptic sort: A political economy of personal information*. Boulder, CO: Westview Press.

Garnham, Nicholas. 1990. *Capitalism and communication*. London: Sage.

Garnham, Nicholas. 2000. *Emancipation, the media, and modernity*. Oxford: Oxford University Press.

Garnham, Nicholas. 2004. Class analysis and the information society as mode of production. *Javnost* 11 (3): 93–104.

Giles, Chris and Ferdinando Giugliano. 2014. Flawed data on rich weaken Piketty's main argument. *Financial Times*, May 24/25: 5.

Golding, Peter and Graham Murdock, eds. 1997. *The political economy of the media: 2 volumes*. Cheltenham: Edward Elgar.

Habermas, Jürgen. 2008. *Ach, Europa*. Frankfurt am Main: Suhrkamp.

Habermas, Jürgen. 2011. *Zur Verfassung Europas. Ein Essay*. Frankfurt am Main: Suhrkamp.

Haggerty, Kevin. 2006. The new politics of surveillance and visibility. In *Surveillance and visibility*, ed. Kevin Haggerty and Richard Ericson, 3–33. Toronto: University of Toronto Press.

Hardt, Michael and Antonio Negri. 2000. *Empire*. Cambridge, MA: Harvard University Press.

Hardt, Michael and Antonio Negri. 2004. *Multitude*. New York: Penguin.

Hardy, Jonathan. 2014. *Critical political economy of the media: An introduction*. London: Routledge.

Harvey, David. 2003. *The new imperialism*. Oxford: Oxford University Press.

Harvey, David. 2005. *A brief history of neoliberalism*. Oxford: Oxford University Press.

Harvey, David. 2006. *Spaces of global capitalism. Towards a theory of uneven geographical development*. London: Verso.

Harvey, David. 2010. *A companion to Marx's Capital*. London: Verso.

Harvey, David. 2014. Afterthoughts on Piketty's Capital. http://davidharvey.org/2014/05/afterthoughts-pikettys-capital (accessed on July 28, 2015).

Harvie, David. 2005. All labour produces value for capital and we struggle against value. *The Commoner* 10: 132–171.

Haug, Wolfgang Fritz. 1986. *Critique of commodity aesthetics*. Cambridge: Polity Press.

Haug, Wolfgang Fritz. 2010. Historical-critical dictionary of Marxism: General intellect. *Historical Materialism* 18 (2): 209–216.

Haug, Wolfgang Fritz. 2013. *Das „Kapital" lesen—aber wie? Materialien*. Hamburg: Argument.

Hegel, Georg Wilhelm Friedrich. 1812/1833. *The science of logic*. Ed. and trans. George di Giovanni. Cambridge: Cambridge University Press.

Hegel, Georg Willhelm Friedrich. 1830a. *Encyclopaedia of the philosophical sciences, part 1: The encyclopaedia logic*. Indianapolis, IN: Hackett.

Hegel, Georg Wilhelm Friedrich. 1830b. *Encyclopaedia of the philosophical sciences, part 3: Philosophy of mind.* http://www.hegel.net/en/pdf/Hegel-Enc3.pdf (accessed on July 28, 2015).

Heinrich, Michael. 2013a. Crisis theory, the law of the tendency of the profit rate to fall, and Marx's studies in the 1870s. *Monthly Review* 64 (11): 15–31.

Heinrich, Michael. 2013b. Heinrich answers critics. Monthly Review Online. http://monthlyreview.org/commentary/heinrich-answers-critics%20%20/ (accessed on July 28, 2015).

Heinrich, Michael. 2014. The "fragment on machines": A Marxian misconception in the *Grundrisse* and its overcoming in *Capital*. In *In Marx's laboratory: Critical interpretations of the Grundrisse*, ed. Ricardo Bellofiore, Guido Starosta, and Peter D. Thomas, 197–212. Chicago: Haymarket Books.

Herman, Edward and Noam Chomsky. 1994. *Manufacturing consent: The political economy of the mass media.* London: Vintage Books.

Herodotus. 1920. *In four volumes: Books I and II.* Trans. A. D. Godley. Cambridge, MA: Harvard University Press.

Hess, Charlotte and Elinor Ostrom. 2007. Introduction: An overview of the knowledge commons. In *Understanding knowledge as a commons: From theory to practice*, ed. Charlotte Hess and Elinor Ostrom, 3–26. Cambridge, MA: The MIT Press.

Hobsbawm, Eric J. 1952. The machine breakers. *Past and Present* 1 (1): 57–70.

Hofkirchner, Wolfgang. 2013. *Emergent information: A unified theory of information framework.* Singapore: World Scientific.

Holman, David, Rosemary Batt and Ursula Holtgrewe. 2007. *The global call centre report: International perspectives on management and employment.* http://www.ilr.cornell.edu/globalcallcenter/upload/GCC-Intl-Rept-UK-Version.pdf (accessed on September 23, 2015).

Holman, David, David Wood, and Chris Stride. 2005. *Human resource management in call centres.* http://www.ilr.cornell.edu/globalcallcenter/research/upload/UK-CC-report.pdf (accessed on July 28, 2015).

House of Commons Committee of Public Accounts. 2013. *Tax avoidance—Google: Ninth report of session 2013–2014.* London: The Stationery Office Limited.

International Labour Organization (ILO). 2013. *Making progress against child labour: Global estimates and trends 2000–2012.* Geneva: International Labour Office.

International Labour Organization (ILO). 2014. *Global employment trends 2014.* Geneva: International Labour Office.

International Trade Union Confederation (ITUC). 2010. *On the job for a better future: A best practice on organising young people.* Brussels: ITUC.

International Working Men's Association. 1868. *Resolutions of the Congress of Geneva, 1866, and the Congress of Brussels, 1868.* London: Westminster Printing Company.

Jessop, Bob and Ngai-Ling Sum. 2006. *Beyond the regulation approach.* Cheltenham: Edward Elgar.

Jhally, Sut. 1987. *The codes of advertising.* New York: Routledge.

Jhally, Sut and Bill Livant. 1986/2006. Watching as working: The valorization of audience consciousness. In *The spectacle of accumulation. Essays in culture, media, & politics*, ed. Sut Jhally, 24–43. New York: Peter Lang.

Jin, Dal Yong and Andrew Feenberg. 2015. Commodity and community in social networking: Marx and the monetization of user-generated content. *The Information Society* 31 (1): 52–60.

Jones, Steven E. 2006. *Against technology: From the Luddites to Neo-Luddism.* New York: Routledge.

Kant, Immanuel. 1785. *Groundworks of the metaphysics of morals: A German-English edition.* Cambridge: Cambridge University Press.

Katz, Elihu, Jay G. Blumler, and Michael Gurevitch. 1973. Uses and gratifications research. *Public Opinion Quarterly* 73 (4): 509–523.

Katz, Elihu, Michael Gurevitch, and Hadassah Haas. 1973 On the use of the mass media for important things. *American Sociological Review* 38 (2): 164–181.

Katz, Katarina. 1997. Gender, wages and discrimination in the USSR: A study of a Russian industrial town. *Cambridge Journal of Economics* 21 (1): 431–452.

Kitching, John and David Smallbone. 2012. *UK freelance workforce, 2011.* Kingston upon Thames: Kingston University.

Kliman, Andrew. 2007. *Reclaiming Marx's "Capital": A refutation of the myth of inconsistency.* Lanham, MD: Lexington Books.

Kliman, Andrew. 2012. *The failure of capitalist production: Underlying causes of the great recession.* New York: Pluto.

Kliman, Andrew. 2014. "The 99%" and "the 1%" . . . of what? http://www.marxisthumanistinitiative.org/economic-crisis/%E2%80%9Cthe-99%E2%80%9D-and-%E2%80%9Cthe-1%E2%80%9D-%E2%80%A6-of-what.html (accessed on July 28, 2015).

Kliman, Andrew, Alan Freeman, Nick Potts, Alexes Gusey, and Brendan Cooney. 2013. *The unmaking of Marx's Capital: Heinrich's attempt to eliminate Marx's crisis theory*. SSRN Working Papers Series (22 July 2013). http://mpra.ub.uni-muenchen.de/48535/1/MPRA_paper_48535.pdf (accessed on July 28, 2015).

Knoche, Manfred. 2005. Medienkonzentration als Macht- und Legitimationsproblem für Politik und Wissenschaft. Kritisch-empirische Konzentrationstheorie versus apologetisch-normative Wettbewerbstheorie. In *Internationale partizipatorische Kommunikationspolitik*, ed. Petra Ahrweiler and Barbara Thomaß, 117–140. Münster: LIT.

Knoche, Manfred. 2013. Medienkonzentration. In *Mediensysteme im internationalen Vergleich*, ed. Barbara Thomaß, 2nd edition, 135–160. Konstanz: UVK.

Kołakowski, Leszek. 2005. *Main currents of Marxism: The founders, the golden age, the breakdown*. New York: W. W. Norton.

Kondratieff, Nikolai D. 1925. *The long wave cycle*. New York: Richardson & Snyder.

Kondratieff, Nikolai D. 1926. Die langen Wellen der Konjunktur. *Archiv für Sozialwissenschaft und Sozialpolitik* 56: 573–609.

Krugman, Paul. 2014a. Is Piketty all wrong? New York Times Online, May 24. http://mpra.ub.uni-muenchen.de/48535/1/MPRA_paper_48535.pdf (accessed on September 23, 2015).

Krugman, Paul. 2014b. Why we're in a new gilded age. *The New York Review of Books*, May 8, http://mpra.ub.uni-muenchen.de/48535/1/MPRA_paper_48535.pdf (accessed on September 23, 2015).

Lazzarato, Maurizio. 1996. Immaterial labor. In *Radical thought in Italy*, ed. Paolo Virno and Michael Hardt, 132–146. Minneapolis: University of Minnesota Press.

Lebowitz, Michael A. 1986. Too many blindspots on the media. *Studies in Political Economy* 21: 165–173.

Lenin, Vladimir Ilyich. 1920. *Preface to the French and German editions of "Imperialism, the highest stage of capitalism"*. http://www.marxists.org/archive/lenin/works/1916/imp-hsc/pref02.htm#fwV22E081 (accessed on September 23, 2015).

Linebaugh, Peter. 2012. *Nedd Ludd & Queen Mab: Machine-breaking, romanticism, and the several commons of 1811–12*. Oakland: PM Press.

Livant, Bill. 1979. The audience commodity: on the "blindspot" debate. *Canadian Journal of Political and Social Theory* 3 (1): 91–106.

Lukács, Georg. 1986. *Werke. Band 14: Zur Ontologie des gesellschaftlichen Seins. 2. Halbband.* Darmstadt: Luchterhand.

Luxemburg, Rosa. 1899. Reform or revolution. In *The essential Rosa Luxemburg*, ed. Helen Scot, 41–104. Chicago: Haymarket Books.

Luxemburg, Rosa. 1913/2003. *The accumulation of capital*. New York: Routledge.

Lyon, David. 1994. *The electronic eye: The rise of surveillance society*. Minneapolis: University of Minnesota Press.

Lyon, David. 2007. *Surveillance studies: An overview*. Cambridge: Polity Press.

Mage, Shane. 2013. Response to Heinrich—in defense of Marx's law. Monthly Review Online. http://monthlyreview.org/commentary/response-heinrich-defense-marxs-law/ (accessed on July 28, 2015).

Mandel, Ernest. 1978. *Late capitalism*. London: Verso.

Marazzi, Christian. 2008. *Capital and language*. Los Angeles: Semiotext(e).

Marcuse, Herbert. 1936/1988. The concept of essence. In *Negations*, 43–87. London: Free Association Books.

Marcuse, Herbert. 1941. *Reason and revolution: Hegel and the rise of social theory*. London: Routledge.

Marcuse, Herbert. 1972. *Counterrevolution and revolt*. Boston: Beacon Press.

Marx, Karl. 1843a. On the Jewish question. In *Writings of the young Marx on philosophy and society*, ed. Loyd D. Easton and Kurt H. Guddat, 216–248. Indianapolis, IN: Hackett.

Marx, Karl. 1843b. Toward the critique of Hegel's philosophy of law: Introduction. In *Writings of the young Marx on philosophy and society*, ed. Loyd D. Easton and Kurt H. Guddat, 249–265. Indianapolis, IN: Hackett.

Marx, Karl. 1844 [English]. *Economic and philosophic manuscripts of 1844 and* The Communist Manifesto. Amherst, NY: Prometheus.

Marx, Karl. 1844 [German]. Ökonomisch-philosophische Manuskripte. In *MEW*, Band 40, 465–588. Berlin: Dietz.

Marx, Karl. 1849. *Wage labour and capital*. https://www.marxists.org/archive/marx/works/1847/wage-labour/ch02.htm (accessed on July 28, 2015).

Marx, Karl. 1857. Condition of factory laborers. In *MECW*, Volume 15, 251–255. New York: International Publishers.

Marx, Karl. 1857/1858 [English]. *Grundrisse: Foundations of the Critique of Political Economy (Rough Draft)*. London: Penguin.

Marx, Karl. 1857/1858 [German]. *Grundrisse der Kritik der politischen Ökonomie*. MEW, Band 42. Berlin: Dietz.

Marx, Karl. 1859. A contribution to the critique of political economy. In *MECW*, Volume 29, 257–417. New York: International Publishers.

Marx, Karl. 1861–1863. *Economic manuscript of 1861–63: MECW*, Volume 30. New York: International Publishers.

Marx, Karl. 1862/1863. *Theories of surplus value: Parts 1, 2, 3*. London: Lawrence & Wishart.

Marx, Karl. 1863/1864. *Resultate des unmittelbaren Produktionsprozesses. Sechstes Kapitel des ersten Bandes des „Kapitals": Entwurf von 1863/1864*. Berlin: Dietz.

Marx, Karl. 1863–1865. Results of the immediate process of production. In *Capital Volume I*, 941–1084. London: Penguin.

Marx, Karl. 1865. *Value, price and profit*. http://www.marxists.org/archive/marx/works/1865/value-price-profit/ (accessed on July 28, 2015).

Marx, Karl. 1867/1976. *Capital: A critique of political economy*, Volume 1. Trans. by Ben Fowkes. London: Penguin.

Marx, Karl. 1875. Critique of the Gotha Programme. In *MECW*, Volume 24, 80–99. New York: International Publishers.

Marx, Karl. 1885. *Capital: A critique of political economy*, Volume 2. London: Penguin.

Marx, Karl. 1894. *Capital: A critique of political economy*, Volume 3. London: Penguin.

Marx, Karl. 1964. *Frammento sulle macchine*. Trans. Renato Solmi. *Quaderni Rossi* 4: 289–300.

Marx, Karl and Friedrich Engels. 1845. *The German ideology*. Amherst, NY: Prometheus.

Marx, Karl and Friedrich Engels. 1848a. *Demands of the Communist Party in Germany*. http://marxists.org/archive/marx/works/1848/03/24.htm (accessed on July 28, 2015).

Marx, Karl and Friedrich Engels. 1848b. Manifest der Kommunistischen Partei. In *MEW, Band 3*, 459–493. Berlin: Dietz.

Marx, Karl and Friedrich Engels. 1850. Addresses of the Central Committee to the Communist League. http://www.marxists.org/archive/marx/works/1847/communist-league/1850-ad1.htm (accessed on July 28, 2015).

Marx, Karl and Friedrich Engels. 1956–1990. *Marx Engels Werke (MEW)*. Berlin: Dietz.

Marx, Karl and Friedrich Engels. 1968. *Selected works in one volume*. London: Lawrence & Wishart.

Marx, Karl and Friedrich Engels. 1975–2005. *Marx Engels Collected Works (MECW)*. New York: International Publishers.

Mason, Paul. 2014. Thomas Piketty's *Capital*: Everything you need to know about the surprise bestseller. *The Guardian Online*, April 28. http://www.theguardian.com/books/2014/apr/28/thomas-piketty-capital-surprise-bestseller (accessed on July 28, 2015).

Mathiesen, Thomas. 2013. *Towards a surveillant society: The rise of surveillance systems in Europe*. Sherfield on London: Waterside Press.

Mattelart, Armand and Seth Siegelaub, eds. 1979. *Communication and class struggle, volume 1: Capitalism, imperialism*. New York: International Mass Media Research Center.

Mattelart, Armand and Seth Siegelaub, eds. 1983. *Communication and class struggle, volume 2: Liberation, socialism*. New York: International Mass Media Research Center.

McChesney, Robert W. 2004. *The problem of the media*. New York: Monthly Review Press.

McGuigan, Lee and Vince Manzerolle, eds. 2014. *The audience commodity in a digital age: Revisiting a critical theory of commercial media*. New York: Peter Lang.

McKercher, Catherine. 2014. Precarious times, precarious work: A feminist political economy of freelance journalists in Canada and the United States. In *Critique, social media and the information society*, ed. Christian Fuchs and Marisol Sandoval, 219–230. New York: Routledge.

McLellan, David. 2006. *Karl Marx: A biography*. Basingstoke: Palgrave Macmillan.

McLuhan, Marshall. 1964/2001. *Understanding media: The extensions of man*. New York: Routledge.

McQuail, Denis. 2010. *McQuail's mass communication theory*, 6th edition. Los Angeles: Sage.

Meehan, Eileen. 1984. Ratings and the institutional approach: A third answer to the commodity question. *Critical Studies in Mass Communication* 1 (2): 216–225.

Merton, Robert K. 1988. The Matthew effect in science, II: Cumulative advantage and the symbolism of intellectual property. *ISIS* 79 (4): 606–623.

Mies, Maria. 1986. *Patriarchy & accumulation on a world scale: Women in the international division of labour*. London: Zed Books.

Mies, Maria, Veronika Bennholdt-Thomsen, and Claudia von Werlhof. 1988. *Women: The last colony*. London: Zed Books.

Miliband, Ralph. 1969. *The state in capitalist society*. New York: Basic Books.

Mill, John Stuart. 1859. On liberty. In *On liberty and other essays*, ed. John Gray, 5–128. Oxford: Oxford University Press.

Mill, John Stuart. 1884. *Principles of political economy*. New York: D. Appleton & Company.

Miller, Toby, Nitin Govil, John McMurria, Richard Maxwell, and Ting Wang. 2004. *Global Hollywood 2*. London: British Film Institute.

Morini, Cristina and Andrea Fumagalli. 2010. Life put to work: Towards a life theory of value. *Ephemera* 10 (3/4): 234–252.

Morris, William. 1884. Useful work versus useless toil. In *The collected works of William Morris, volume 23: Signs of changes: Lectures on socialism*, 98–120. Cambridge: Cambridge University Press.

Morris, William. 1885. How we live and how we might live. In *The collected works of William Morris, volume 23: Signs of changes: Lectures on socialism*, 3–26. Cambridge: Cambridge University Press.

Morris, William. 1893. Communism. In *The collected works of William Morris, volume 23: Signs of changes: Lectures on socialism*, 264–276. Cambridge: Cambridge University Press.

Mosco, Vincent. 2009. *The political economy of communication*, 2nd edition. London: Sage.

Mosco, Vincent and Catherine McKercher. 2009. *The laboring of communication: Will knowledge workers of the world unite?* Lanham, MD: Lexington.

Moseley, Fred. 2013. Critique of Heinrich: Marx did not abandon the logical structure. Monthly Review Online. http://monthlyreview.org/commentary/critique-heinrich-marx-abandon-logical-structure/ (accessed on July 28, 2015).

Mount, Ferdinand. 2014. Piketty's decaff Marxism would be just oppressive and intrusive as the old variety. The Spectator Online, May 24. http://www.spectator.co.uk/books/9210671/capital-in-the-twenty-first-century-by-thomas-piketty-review/ (accessed on July 28, 2015).

Murdock, Graham. 1978. Blindspots about Western Marxism: A reply to Dallas Smythe. *Canadian Journal of Political and Social Theory* 2 (2): 109–119.

Murdock, Graham. 2006. Marx on commodities, contradictions and globalisations: Resources for a critique of marketised culture. *ecompós* 7: 1–23.

Murdock, Graham. 2011. Political economies as moral economies: Commodities, gifts, and public goods. In *The handbook of political economy of communications*, ed. Janet Wasko, Graham Murdock, and Helena Sousa, 13–40. Malden, MA: Wiley-Blackwell.

Murdock, Graham. 2014a. Commodities and commons. In *The audience commodity in a digital age: Revisiting a critical theory of commercial media*, ed. Lee McGuigan and Vincent Manzerolle, 229–244. New York: Peter Lang.

Murdock, Graham. 2014b. Producing consumerism: Commodities, ideologies, practices. In *Critique, social media, and the information society*, ed. Christian Fuchs and Marisol Sandoval, 125–143. New York: Routledge.

Murdock, Graham and Peter Golding. 1973. For a political economy of mass communications. *Socialist Register* 1973: 205–234.

Murdock, Graham and Peter Golding. 2005. Culture, communications and political economy. In *Mass media and society*, ed. James Curran and Michael Gurevitch, 60–83. London: Hodder Arnold.

Musto, Marcello, ed. 2008. *Karl Marx's Grundrisse: Foundations of the critique of political economy 150 years later*. London: Routledge.

Negri, Antonio. 1971/1988. Crisis of the planner-state: Communism and revolutionary organisation. In *Revolution retrieved: Selected writings on Marx, Keynes, capitalist crisis, & new social subjects 1967–83*, 91–148. London: Red Notes.

Negri, Antonio. 1982/1988. Archaeology and project: The mass worker and the social worker. In *Revolution retrieved: Selected writings on Marx, Keynes, capitalist crisis, & new social subjects 1967–83*, 199–228. London: Red Notes.

Negri, Antonio. 1988. *Revolution retrieved*. London: Red Notes.

Negri, Antonio. 1991. *Marx beyond Marx: Lessons on the* Grundrisse. New York: Autonomedia.

Negri, Antonio. 2008. *Reflections on Empire*. Cambridge: Polity.

New York Times. 2014. Was Marx right? New York Times Online, March 30. http://www.nytimes.com/roomfordebate/2014/03/30/was-marx-right (accessed on July 28, 2015).

Noah, Harold J. 1965. The "unproductive" labour of Soviet teachers. *Soviet Studies* 17 (2): 238–244.

Noam, Eli. 2009. *Media ownership and concentration in America*. Oxford: Oxford University Press.

Noble, David F. 1995. *Progress without people: New technology, unemployment, and the message of resistance*. Toronto: Between the Lines.

Ofcom. 2014. *International Communications Market Report 2014*. London: Ofcom.

Ogura, Toshimaru. 2006. Electronic government and surveillance-oriented society. In *Theorizing surveillance*, ed. David Lyon, 270–295. Portland, OR: Willan.

Owen, Robert. 1991. *A new view of society and other writings*. London: Penguin.

Perez, Carolta. 2010. Technological revolutions and techno-economic paradigms. *Cambridge Journal of Economics* 34 (1): 185–202.

Pethokoukis, James. 2014. The new Marxism. National Review Online, March 24. http://www.nationalreview.com/article/374009/new-marxism-james-pethokoukis (accessed on July 28, 2015).

Piketty, Thomas. 2014. *Capital in the twenty-first century.* Cambridge, MA: Belknap Press.

Popper, Karl. 1945. *The open society and its enemies.* London: Routledge.

Postone, Moishe. 1980. Anti-semitism and National Socialism: Notes on the German reaction to "Holocaust". *New German Critique* 19: 97–115.

Postone, Moishe. 1993. *Time, labor, and social domination: A reinterpretation of Marx's critical theory.* Cambridge: Cambridge University Press.

Postone, Moishe. 2008. Rethinking *Capital* in the light of the *Grundrisse.* In *Karl Marx's* Grundrisse, ed. Marcello Musto, 120–137. London: Routledge.

Poulantzas, Nicos. 1980. *State, power, socialism.* London: Verso.

Poulantazs, Nicos. 2008. *The Poulantzas reader.* London: Verso.

Rankin, Jennifer. 2014. Thomas Piketty accuses *Financial Times* of dishonest criticism. The Guardian Online, May 26. http://www.theguardian.com/business/2014/may/26/thomas-piketty-financial-times-dishonest-criticism-economics-book-inequality (accessed on July 28, 2015).

Ricardo, David. 1819. *On the principles of political economy and taxation.* Indianapolis, IN: Liberty Fund.

Richta, Radovan. 1969. *Civilization at the crossroads: Social and human implications of the scientific and technological revolution.* White Plains, NY: International Arts and Sciences Press.

Rosdolsky, Roman. 1977. *The making of Marx's "Capital".* London: Pluto.

Rossi-Landi, Ferruccio. 1983. *Language as work & trade: A semiotic homology for linguistics & economics.* South Hadley, MA: Bergin & Garvey.

Roth, Karl Heinz and Marcel van der Linden. 2014. Results and prospects. In *Beyond Marx,* ed. Marcel van der Linden and Karl Heinz Roth, 445–487. Leiden: Brill.

Rovatti, Pier Aldo. 1973. The critique of fetishism in Marx's *Grundrisse. Telos* 17: 56–69.

Said, Edward. 1978. *Orientalism: Western conceptions of the Orient.* New Delhi: Penguin.

Sánchez-Tabernero, Alfonso. 1993. *Media concentration in Europe.* London: John Libbey.

Sandoval, Marisol. 2013. Foxconned labour as the dark side of the information age: Working conditions at Apple's contract manufacturers in China. *tripleC: Communication, Capitalism & Critique* 11 (2): 318–347.

Sandoval, Marisol. 2014. *From corporate to social media: Critical perspectives on corporate social responsibility in media and communication industries.* Abingdon: Routledge.

Sandoval, Marisol and Christian Fuchs. 2010. Towards a critical theory of alternative media. *Telematics and Informatics* 27 (2): 141–150.

Sandoval, Marisol and Kristina Areskog Bjurling. 2013. Challenging labor: Working conditions in the electronics industry. In *Lessons for social change in the global economy: Voices from the field,* ed. Shae Garwood, Sky Croeser, and Christalla Yakinthou, 99–124. Lanham, MD: Lexington Books.

Say, Jean-Baptiste. 1803. *A treatise on political economy: Or the production, distribution and consumption of wealth.* New York: Augustus M. Kelley.

Schmidt, Kjeld and Liam Bannon. 1992. Taking CSCW seriously: Supporting articulation work. *Computer Supported Cooperative Work (CSCW)* 1 (1): 7–40.

Scholz, Trebor, ed. 2013. *Digital labor: The Internet as playground and factory.* New York: Routledge.

Schumpeter, Joseph A. 1939. *Business cycles: A theoretical, historical and statistical analysis of the capitalist process.* New York: McGraw-Hill.

Schumpeter, Joseph A. 1943. *Capitalism, socialism & democracy.* London: Routledge.

Sekine, Thomas T. 1998. The dialectic of capital: An Unoist interpretation. *Science & Society* 62 (3): 434–445.

Shenk, Timothy. 2014. Thomas Piketty and millennial Marxists on the scourge of inequality. The Nation Online, April 14. http://www.thenation.com/article/179337/thomas-piketty-and-millennial-marxists-scourge-inequality (accessed on July 28, 2015).

Shuchman, Daniel. 2014. Thomas Piketty revives Marx for the 21st century. The Wall Street Journal Online, April 21. http://online.wsj.com/news/articles/SB10001424052702303825604579515452952131592. (accessed on July 28, 2015).

Shuster, Sam. 2008. The nature and consequence of Karl Marx's skin disease. *British Journal of Dermatology* 158 (1): 1–3.

Smith, Adam. 1776. *An inquiry into the nature and causes of the wealth of nations.* Ware: Wordsworth.

Smith, Adam. 1790. *The theory of moral sentiments.* London: Penguin.

Smith, Tony. 1990. *The logic of Marx's Capital. Replies to Hegelian criticisms.* Albany: State University of New York Press.

Smith, Tony. 2004. Technology and history in capitalism: Marxian and neo-Schumpeterian perspectives. In *The constitution of capital: Essays on Volume 1 of Marx's Capital*, ed. Riccardo Bellofiore and Nicola Taylor, 217–242. Basingstoke: Palgrave Macmillan.

Smith, Tony. 2014a. Hegel, Marx, and the comprehension of capitalism. In *Marx's Capital and Hegel's Logic*, ed. Fred Moseley and Tony Smith, 17–40. Leiden: Brill.

Smith, Tony. 2014b. The "general intellect" in the *Grundrisse* and beyond. In *In Marx's laboratory: Critical interpretations of the Grundrisse*, ed. Ricardo Bellofiore, Guido Starosta, and Peter D. Thomas, 213–231. Chicago: Haymarket Books.

Smythe, Dallas W. 1954. Reality as presented by television. In *Counterclockwise. Perspectives on communication*, ed. Thomas Guback, 61–74. Boulder, CO: Westview Press.

Smythe, Dallas W. 1977. Communications: Blindspot of Western Marxism. *Canadian Journal of Political and Social Theory* 1 (3): 1–27.

Smythe, Dallas W. 1978. Rejoinder to Graham Murdock. *Canadian Journal of Political and Social Theory* 2 (2): 120–129.

Smythe, Dallas W. 1981. The audience commodity and its work. In *Dependency road: Communications, capitalism, consciousness, and Canada*, 22–51. Norwood, NJ: Ablex.

Smythe, Dallas W. 1994. *Counterclockwise.* Boulder, CO: Westview Press.

Students & Scholars against Corporate Misbehaviour (SACOM). 2013. *Widespread labour abuses at Disney and Mattel Factories: ICTI doesn't care about labour rights standards.* Hong Kong: SACOM.

Subcomandante Insurgente Marcos. 2001. *Our word is our weapon.* New York: Seven Stories Press.

Terranova, Tiziana. 2000. Free labor: Producing culture for the digital economy. *Social Text* 18 (2): 33–58.

The Economist. 2014. Piketty fever: Bigger than Marx. The Economist Online, May 3. http://www.economist.com/news/finance-and-economics/21601567-wonky-book-inequality-becomes-blockbuster-bigger-marx (accessed on July 28, 2015).

Thompson, Edward P. 1966. *The making of the English working class.* New York: Vintage Books.

Thompson, Edward P. 1978. The poverty of theory, or An orrery of errors. In *The poverty of theory and other essays*, 1–210. New York: Monthly Review Press.

Toffler, Alvin. 1980. *The third wave.* New York: Bantam.

Tomba, Massimiliano and Riccardo Bellofiore. 2014. The "Fragment on machines" and the *Grundrisse*: The workerist reading in question. In *Beyond Marx*, ed. Marcel van der Linden and Karl Heinz Roth, 345–368. Leiden: Brill.

Tronti, Mario. 1962. Fabrik und Gesellschaft. In *Arbeiter und Kapital*, 16–29. Frankfurt: Verlag Neue Kritik.

United Nations Development Programme (UNDP). 2013. *China Human Development Report 2013: Sustainable and liveable cities: Toward ecological urbanization.* Beijing: China Translation and Publishing Corporation.

Vercellone, Carlo. 2007. From formal subsumption to general intellect: Elements for a Marxist reading of the thesis of cognitive capitalism. *Historical Materialism* 15 (1): 13–36.

Vercellone, Carlo. 2010. The crisis of the law of value and the becoming-rent of profit. In *Crisis in the global economy*, ed. Andrea Fumagalli and Sandro Mezzadra, 85–118. Los Angeles: Semiotext(e).

Virno, Paolo. 1996a. The ambivalence of disenchantment. In *Radical thought in Italy*, ed. Paolo Virno and Michael Hardt, 13–33. Minneapolis: University of Minnesota Press.

Virno, Paolo. 1996b. Virtuosity and revolution: The political theory of exodus. In *Radical thought in Italy*, ed. Paolo Virno and Michael Hardt, 189–212. Minneapolis: University of Minnesota Press.

Virno, Paolo. 2004. *A grammar of the multitude.* New York: Semiotext(e).

Virno, Paolo. 2007. General intellect. *Historical Materialism* 15 (3): 3–8.

Wallraff, Günter. 2007. Undercover. *Die Zeit* 22. http://www.zeit.de/2007/22/Guenter-Wallraff (accessed on July 28, 2015).

Wallerstein, Immanuel. 2004. *World-systems analysis: An introduction.* Durham: Duke University Press.

Wasko, Janet. 2011. The study of the political economy of the media in the twenty-first century. *International Journal of Media & Cultural Politics* 10 (3): 259–271.

Wasko, Janet. 2014. The study of political economy of the media in the twenty-first century. *International Journal of Media & Cultural Politics* 10 (3): 259–271.

Wasko, Janet, Graham Murdock, and Helena Sousa, eds. 2011. *The handbook of political economy of communications.* Malden, MA: Wiley-Blackwell.

Weingart, Brigitte. 1997. *Arbeit—ein Wort mit langer Geschichte*. http://www.ethikprojekte.ch/texte/arbeit.htm (accessed on July 6, 2014).

Weinmann, Martin, Ursula Krause-Schmitt, and Anne Kaiser. 2001. *Das nationalsozialistische Lagersystem*, 4th edition. Frankfurt am Main: Zweitausendeins.

Wheen, Francis. 1999. *Karl Marx*. London: Fourth Estate.

Wheen, Francis. 2006. *Marx's Das Kapital: A Biography*. London: Atlantic.

Williams, Raymond. 1960/1969. Advertising: The magic system. In *Culture and materialism*, 170–195. London: Verso.

Williams, Raymond. 1974/1990. *Television*. New York: Routledge.

Williams, Raymond. 1977. *Marxism and literature*. Oxford: Oxford University Press.

Williams, Raymond. 1979. *Politics and letters. Interviews with* New Left Review. London: Verso.

Williams, Raymond. 1983. *Keywords*. New York: Oxford University Press.

Williams, Raymond. 1989. *What I came to say*. London: Hutchinson Radius.

Zasulich, Vera. 1881. *Letter to Marx*. http://www.marxists.org/archive/marx/works/1881/zasulich/zasulich.htm (accessed on July 28, 2015).

Žižek, Slavoj. 2001. Have Michael Hardt and Antonio Negri rewritten the *Communist Manifesto* for the twenty-first century?" *Rethinking Marxism* 13 (3/4): 190–198.

Žižek, Slavoj. 2014. *Towards a materialist theory of subjectivity: Talk at the Birkbeck Institute of Humanities*. May 22. http://simongros.com/audio/recordings/slavoj-zizek/towards-materialist-theory-subjectivity/ (accessed on July 28, 2015).

INDEX

Figures and tables are indicated by page numbers in italic type.